Encyclopedia of Minorities in American Politics

Titles in the American Political Landscape Series

Encyclopedia of Minorities in American Politics (2 volumes)
Encyclopedia of Religion in American Politics
Encyclopedia of Women in American Politics

Encyclopedia of Minorities in American Politics

Volume 2
Hispanic Americans and Native Americans

Edited by
Jeffrey D. Schultz, Kerry L. Haynie,
Anne M. McCulloch, and Andrew L. Aoki

Foreword by
Helen Thomas

Oryx Press
2000

The rare Arabian Oryx is believed to have inspired the myth of the unicorn. This desert antelope became virtually extinct in the early 1960s. At that time, several groups of international conservationists arranged to have nine animals sent to the Phoenix Zoo to be the nucleus of a captive breeding herd. Today, the Oryx population is over 1,000, and over 500 have been returned to the Middle East.

© 2000 by Jeffrey D. Schultz
Published by The Oryx Press
4041 North Central at Indian School Road
Phoenix, Arizona 85012-3397
http://www.oryxpress.com

Published simultaneously in Canada
Printed and bound in the United States of America

∞ The paper used in this publication meets the minimum requirements of American National Standard for Information Science—Permanence of Paper for Printed Library Materials, ANSI Z39.48, 1984.

Library of Congress Cataloging-in-Publication Data

Encyclopedia of minorities in American politics / edited by Jeffrey D. Schultz... [et al.].
    p. cm. — (The American political landscape series)
Includes bibliographical references and indexes.
ISBN 1-57356-129-0 (alk. paper)—ISBN 1-57356-148-7 (v. 1: alk. paper)—
ISBN 1-57356-149-5 (v. 2: alk. paper)
1. Minorities—United States—Political activity—Encyclopedias. 2. Afro-Americans—Politics and government—Encyclopedias. 3. Asian Americans—Politics and government—Encyclopedias. 4. Hispanic Americans—Politics and government—Encyclopedias. 5. Indians of North America—Politics and government—Encyclopedias. 6. United States—Politics and government—Encyclopedias. 7. United States—Ethnic relations—Encyclopedias. 8. United States—Race relations—Encyclopedias. I. Series. II. Schultz, Jeffrey D.
E184.A1 E574   2000
305.8'00973'03 21—dc21   99-043451
                                                                              CIP

Contents

Contents

Contributors for Volume 2

Academic Advisory Board

Peter P. d'Errico
University of Massachusetts, Amherst

John A. Garcia
University of Arizona

Don Toshiaki Nakanishi
UCLA Asian American Studies Center

Raymond Winbush
Fisk University

Editors

Andrew L. Aoki
Augsburg College

Kerry L. Haynie
Rutgers University

Anne M. McCulloch
Columbia College

Contributors— Hispanic Section

[AAB] Amilar A. Barreto
Northeastern University

[ASR] Adaljiza Sosa-Riddell
University of California, Davis

[CEM] Charles E. Menifield
Mississippi State University

[JRB] Jeff R. Bremer
California State University, Bakersfield

[JSR] John S. Robey
The University of Texas, Brownsville

[LAP] Luis A. Posas
Kansas State University

[MKT] Meta K. Townsend
Wagner College

[MP] Margaret Power

[NM] Nasser Momayezi
Texas A&M International University

[RLP] Richard L. Pacelle, Jr.
University of Missouri, St. Louis

[SCV] Santos C. Vega
Arizona State University

[SG] Sonia Garcia
St. Mary's University

[TIR] Tom I. Romero II

[VDD] Veronica D. DiConti

[YFN] Yolanda Flores Niemann
Washington State University

Contributors— Native American Section

[AHF] Andrew H. Fisher
Arizona State University

[AMM] Anne M. McCulloch
Columbia College

[BB] Bryan Brayboy
University of Pennsylvania

[CKR] Christopher K. Riggs

[DAN] David A. Nichols
University of Arizona

[DEW] David E. Wilkins
University of Arizona

[EFM] E. Fletcher McClellan
Elizabethtown College

[EW] Emilyann White
Columbia College

[GAM] Gerald A. McBeath
University of Alaska, Fairbanks

[GO] Greg O'Brien
University of Kentucky

[GTH] Gwen Torges-Hoffman
Indiana University of Pennsylvania

Contributors for Volume 2

[HHB] Heather Howard-Bobiwash
University of Toronto

[JN] Jon Norstog

[JP] Jaakko Puisto

[KJB] Kay J. Blalock
University of Toledo

[LCJ] Lilias C. Jones
University of South Dakota

[LL] Lin Lake
Columbia College

[MKJ] Meredith K. James

[MM] Melanie McCoy
Texas A&M University

[MR] Mara Rutten
Arizona State University

[MRC] Mary R. Cross
Columbia College

[MS] Michaly Segal
University of Pennsylvania

[MW] Margaret Warner
Columbia College

[PAP] Patricia Aqiimuk Paul

[PPE] Peter P. d'Errico
University of Massachusetts, Amherst

[RAC] Renee Ann Cramer

[RS] Ronald Steiner
Chapman University

[SR] Stephen Russell
University of Texas at San Antonio

[SRC] Samuel R. Cook

[TJH] Thomas J. Hoffman
St. Mary's University

[TMK] Todd M. Kerstetter
Texas Christian University

Foreword

by Helen Thomas

I have always felt greatly privileged to have a ringside seat to instant history at the White House. But I realized after a preview of the Oryx Press encyclopedias on women, religion, and minorities that there are big gaps in my education regarding the role these humanistic trends have played in American politics.

I believe the essays in these volumes are informative, objective, and in-depth, with a wealth of material for scholars, students, and researchers of all kinds. Of course, I was first drawn to the *Encyclopedia of Women in American Politics* for both personal and professional reasons. I am still outraged that women did not get the vote until 1920. Often when I am walking into the White House I look at the big black fence on Pennsylvania Avenue and I think of the suffragettes who chained themselves to it to gain the right to vote.

The strides women have made in the last half of this century are awesome, but not enough. World War II was the defining moment, but it has been a long struggle and women have miles to go to achieve true equality in the workplace.

I have often heard quoted the letter from that remarkable woman, Abigail Adams, who wrote to her husband, John Adams, on March 31, 1776, while he was attending the Continental Congress.

> I desire you would remember the ladies and be more generous and favorable to them than your ancestors. Do not put such unlimited power in the hands of the husbands.

I was covering the White House in 1961 when John F. Kennedy created the President's Commission on the Status of Women by executive order. It was considered a great leap forward in those days and the panel included the most prominent women leaders of the times, those who had reached the top in their fields. Eleanor Roosevelt, who had worked for so many years on behalf of women, was chosen as the chair.

Two years later, the Commission wrote a report that documented "pervasive discrimination against women in state and national laws in work and at schools." State commissions later pursued the goals of equal opportunity for women and followed up on complaints of sex-based employment discrimination.

Women then began to focus their efforts on ratification of the Equal Rights Amendment, but they failed to achieve the necessary two-thirds of the states. I thought it was a very sad day for the Republic. Women began to venture forth afterward more strongly into the path of political acceptance, and, by the 1970s, the women's movement to empower females had gained great momentum. But the movement hit a plateau when President Ronald Reagan moved into the White House in 1981 and the country became more conservative.

So women have had their hills and valleys, which are vividly illustrated in the biographies and the other entries in the *Encyclopedia of Women in American Politics*.

Every student of American history has some insight into the role that religion has played in the founding of the United States and into the profound impact of religious groups on the politics of different eras, dating back to colonial times. School children learn of the flight of the Pilgrims from religious persecution in England. The *Encyclopedia of Religion in American Politics* is a gold mine of information. As its introductory essay explains,

> The story of religion in American politics is largely an account of the quest to harness the moral idealism of religion for political purposes while attempting to restrain the potential of religion for bigotry. The overwhelming success of that quest for a civic-minded religion can be seen in the thriving diversity of religious groups in the United States today.

Fortunately, the *Encyclopedia* shows that religions fostered in the United States have not been all-consuming, domineering, or fanatical, so as to nurture the kind of age-old religious-cultural hatreds that have torn apart Northern Ireland, Bosnia, and the Middle East. Every day, the United States is involved in seeking to bring peace to these lands, where religion is a tinder box.

Ministers in the colonial era used their tracts and sermons to lay the groundwork for the American Revolution. The founding fathers were mostly religious, but they also devoutly believed in religious freedom.

Almost from its beginning, the United States has had a multiplicity of religions and therefore an admirable tolerance. The First Amendment stipulated that "Congress shall make no law respecting an establishment of religion or prohibiting the free exercise thereof." The founding fathers, while trying to reconcile the influences of reason and revelation on moral law, believed strongly in the separation of church and state.

Politics in the new Republic depended on a shared morality rather than on a shared theology. The ministers of the post-colonial era fought the removal of the Cherokees from Georgia to the West, an infamous episode in American history known as the "Trail of Tears." The churches in the North were also leaders in the movement to abolish slavery, while religious institutions in the South played an equally important role on the other side of the controversy.

In this century, the best known minister in the struggle for civil rights was Martin Luther King, Jr., who first came to national attention when he spearheaded the boycott of segregated buses in Montgomery, Alabama, in 1955–56. Later, many religions banded together in support of the civil rights movement and it took a southern president, Lyndon B. Johnson, to push through Congress the Civil Rights Act of 1964 and the Voting Rights Act of 1965.

But the influence of religion in American politics during the twentieth century has swung from left to right. During the late 1970s and 1980s, the Moral Majority gained a foothold and, after its demise, was replaced by the Christian Coalition. The domestic agenda of the political conservatives includes restoring prayer in public schools and promoting family and pro-life values. Despite the strict wall that the Supreme Court has interposed between church and state in the past, recent years have seen a chipping away at that barrier with rulings permitting religious groups to gather and use schoolrooms and public facilities for their meetings.

Equally fascinating is the documentation in the *Encyclopedia of Minorities in American Politics* of the struggle for political rights of minorities, who have been historically un-der-represented in the American political system and who have had to fight to attain their rightful place as citizens. The discrimination against racial and ethnic groups is vividly chronicled in the *Encyclopedia's* biographies and historical references to past eras that were dominated by white males. Included among those discriminated against were blacks, Latinos, Asian Americans, and Native Americans. I can remember how often President John F. Kennedy was appalled to see signs at Boston job sites that read, "No Irish allowed." A sea change is occurring in the nation, and once-deprived groups are becoming increasingly involved in shaping the political dialogue in this country and in winning public office. Witness the number of big city black mayors currently holding office in the United States. Furthermore, no politician would dare to ignore the Cubans in Florida or the Hispanics in the Southwest and expect to get elected.

All this is to the good. It makes real the unity and validity of the melting pot and there is no question that these groups will have an even bigger voice in the future. My only hope and prayer is that they do not divide along ethnic and racial lines and forget that we are one people.

The three volumes in Oryx's American Political Landscape Series are a treasure trove for scholars and students, and provide the key to the significant historic trends that have made the United States great.

Helen Thomas is White House Bureau Chief for United Press International.

Preface

The last 30 years of American political history have seen dramatic strides in the impact that minorities play in U.S. politics. This two-volume set, *The Encyclopedia of Minorities in American Politics*, addresses the historical and contemporary impact of four of the largest minority groups in the United States. Divided into four sections, the *Encyclopedia* addresses the political struggles of African Americans, Asian Americans, Hispanic Americans, and Native Americans. The work draws attention to those events, people, and ideas that have shaped and will continue to shape the political dialogue of a diverse America. The last 30 years have seen civil rights movements for all four of these groups, as well as an increase in both political participation and political officeholding. These trends are likely to continue as the number of minorities continues to grow.

In selecting entries for the volume, the emphasis was placed upon being as comprehensive as limitations would allow. The work consists of nearly 2,000 alphabetically arranged entries divided into four sections. The work is the collaborative effort of more than 100 scholars. Compound surnames have been alphabetized according to the best available information concerning the biographee's apparent preference. The entries cover people, events, court cases, movements, and organizations that have shaped the political struggles of African Americans, Asian Americans, Latinos, and Native Americans. Longer entries address some of the key issues that face minorities in American politics today. These "issue entries," such as those on affirmative action, immigration, bilingual education, and political participation (to name just a few), were written to give context to current politics and to show how these issues might be resolved.

Being a reference work, the *Encyclopedia* gives accurate information in manageable doses. And because a good reference work must be able to lead the reader to more information, *every entry* in the *Encyclopedia* has a bibliography that can serve as the next step for further research by the user of the volumes. In addition to bibliographies, entries are cross-referenced in two ways to aid the reader in successfully using the resources of the work. First, the work is internally cross-referenced through the use of **bold-faced** type. Bold-faced word(s) indicate to the reader that there is a separate entry on that person, event, concept, or issue. Second, many articles have **See also** listings at the end of the entry to offer other areas the reader may want to investigate. These two features, in addition to the index, will facilitate the user's ability to navigate the volumes.

The *Encyclopedia* also has appendixes. Each section offers reprints of selected important documents and speeches. Also, a directory of organizations that are directly or indirectly involved in politics is provided for each minority group. Each directory contains brief descriptions of the organization as well as contact information including Web sites (wherever possible). In addition, the one general appendix for the entire *Encyclopedia* is a four-column timeline of minorities in American politics. It appears at the ends of both volumes of this *Encyclopedia*. Starting with the adoption of the Constitution and running to the present day, the timeline draws attention to the diverse history of the United States in a comparative context.

A comprehensive index covering both volumes is included in each volume. *The Encyclopedia of Minorities in American Politics* is the most comprehensive single source of its kind. It will prove an invaluable information resource for college and secondary students in political science, social science, and minority studies programs and classes, and it will answer the questions of public library patrons interested in American history or politics or in minority issues.

Acknowledgments

Every encyclopedia is the work of many people who share in the volume's success, and *The Encyclopedia of Minorities in American Politics* is no different. Kerry Haynie of Rutgers University, Anne McCulloch of Columbia College, and Andrew Aoki of Augsburg College, my coeditors, have contributed to the volume in numerous ways including editing entries, writing last-minute additions or supplying entries that were no-shows, shaping the table of contents, suggesting documents, and simply lending an ear to a swamped series editor.

The volumes' contributors also share in any praise that this work may find. All of them should take heart to know that they have helped to write a worthwhile and timely reference work. A few deserve special mention. Peter D'Errico has contributed so much to the success of this work. At the last minute, he helped fill in some holes in the text that could only be filled by a scholar of Peter's quality, graciousness, and perseverance. The same can be said of Christopher Malone, who wrote the introductory essay for the African-American section with little advance warning. It is an excellent piece and deserves the reader's attention.

Barry Katzen, a freelance editor based in White Plains, New York, deserves mention for the yeoman work he has done to clean up the text and generally improve the quality of the volume. It is undoubtedly a much better work because of his skill as an editor. George and Annie Kurian have encouraged me throughout the time it has taken to produce these volumes. They are both dear friends and constant supporters.

Jessamyn West, Bill Baron, Jeff Coburn, Sarah Hadley, Nancy Schultz, and Anne DeStefano all contributed in many ways to the successful completion of this two-volume set. Without all of these people, the work would still be sitting on my desk, far from ready to go out the door. All of them stepped up when I needed them, and they should be recognized for their efforts.

At Oryx Press, I would like to thank Martha Wilke, the person charged with author relations in the home office. Martha has always been honest and helpful to me, even when I was a difficult author. I am thankful for her help and apologize for all the trouble I have caused her along the way.

And finally, to my wife Elena and our son Sasha who are always there for me.

Part 3
Hispanic Americans

Introduction
A Topography of Latinos in the United States
Politics, Policy, and Political Involvement

by John A. Garcia

The compilation of a body of information, perspectives, historical events, and data on Latinos in the United States is a formidable challenge. Similarly, an introductory overview of Latino politics represents an attempt to portray and analytically discuss a heterogeneous and dynamic set of cultural, social, and politically evolving communities. This overview will use the topography metaphor as a vehicle to develop an informed panorama of the composition, sociocultural milieu, political infrastructure, and policy preferences/activities of the aggregation of persons identified as Latinos. (The use of the term "Latino" refers to persons who come from—or whose ancestors are from—Latin America, the Spanish Caribbean, or the Iberian Peninsula. The use is a descriptive one and, in this text, the term "Hispanic" will be used in the same manner.) While this essay does not provide totally comprehensive coverage of all aspects of Latino community life, it will be sufficiently detailed to inform the reader and establish a foundation for further discussion and analysis.

In the 1990s, Latinos in the United States have received considerable attention from the mass media, business enterprises, and political leaders and parties. Part of this "heightened" attention is attributed to substantial population growth since the mid-1960s. The sheer growth in numbers of Latinos in the United States has brought not only greater attention, but also concerns among the majority public, **political leadership**, and social commentators. Some concerns have centered around political loyalty among Latinos, cultural "resistance" and balkanization, and the group's general integration into the U.S. mainstream. Within the Latino community, hopes and concerns center around greater political and economic empowerment, and fuller participation in agenda setting and policy implementation that positively incorporates the Latino community and its interests.

A fuller understanding of the Latino community in the United States entails the acceptance of distinctive histories, regional concentrations, and cultural manifestations among persons from the more than 20 countries or ancestries connected to Spanish origin. At the same times, experiences within the United States sociopolitical system have served to provide some commonalities among the various Latino subcommunities. In a real sense, Latino politics is formed by the "coexistence" of many Latino communities and the joint ventures by organizations and leaders to promote and advocate for all Latinos. This duality of distinctiveness and expanding common grounds is a perspective embraced within this discussion of Latino politics.

Consistent with the metaphor of a topography of Latino politics in the United States, an important starting point is a demographic profile of Latinos. This can help to establish the areas of distinction and patterns of common characteristics and circumstances. Once the demographic profile is created, then our discussion will be directed toward orientations, actions, and concerns of the Latino communities and their advocates.

Diversity and Latinos in the United States

The nomenclature of *Latinos* may require a brief clarification. That is, who are these people that are grouped together as Latinos? Ancestral origin has most commonly been used to identify Latinos, especially as governmental agencies and the mass media began to acknowledge the presence of Latinos with greater frequency. At the same time, resurgence of ethnic and racial identity has been more evident from the 1960s forward. Yet a variety of different terms, such as *Chicanos*, *raza*, *boricua*, *Cubanos*, *Mexican Americans*, and *Hispanos*, was used for national origin groups from Latin America. In 1973, the U.S. Department of Health, Education and Welfare adopted the term Hispanic as part of the recommendations of the Task Force on Race/Ethnic categories (del Pinal and Singer, 1997). The operationalization of the term Hispanic was to be applied to persons whose descent is tied to Spain or Spanish-speaking Latin American countries, including the Caribbean. Similarly, federal legislative action required all federal agencies to collect and report data on Spanish-origin populations. Again, ancestry or descent were the primary basis for distinguishing Latinos.

To some degree, the specification of the "Latino community" is part of the political realm of these communities. That is, self-definition and establishing communities' delimiters are part of the political empowerment process. The advent of the term Latino was primarily a counterresponse to the growing prevalence of the use of the term Hispanic. Some members of the Latino community challenged the reality of a Latino sub-community composed of persons of Spanish origin. The existence of national origin groups more closely approximates dynamic communities, and the development of a larger Latino community was embryonic, at best. The introduction of the term Latino represented the use of a more "internally" generated label with which to identify persons of Spanish origin. As long as governmental agencies, political leaders, and the mass media perpetuated the idea of a Latino community, Latino was introduced to designate a more "indigenous" label.

Finally, this brief discussion of establishing some definitional anchors for Latinos in the United States needs to include a dimension beyond ancestral origins. The role of culture, language, and historical events and experiences in the United States serves as the possible building blocks for a more integrated Latino community. In this sense, the use of Latino or Hispanic takes on meaning that centers around empowerment, access, influence, and representation for Latinos in general, as well as specific national origin groups under the Latino "umbrella." Whether the terms Latino and Hispanic represent artificial social constructions, there are efforts within the Latino communities to develop a more viable and dynamic relationship among persons of Mexican, Puerto Rican, Cuban, and Central/South American origin. Latino takes on dimensions of cultural/ethnic and racial identity in cultural, social, political, and administrative contexts.

Another perspective for the concept of Latinos is that of a social identity or grouping that is situationally constructed. That is, similarities based on cultural practices and beliefs and common interests help to establish a sense of group affiliation or community. Thus, being Latino gets defined as being a person of Spanish origin, whose cultural ties are connected to Spanish language, or Spanish and indigenous origins and influences (i.e., Spain and its colonization of the "New World"; Mayan, Incan, Aztec, etc. influences on food, cultural practices, beliefs, etc.). In addition, being Latino can apply to people concentrated in similar occupations or industries, similar economic statuses, etc., that create common issues and concerns. In this sense, Latino means a situational identity or ethnicity that is more constructed by leadership and organizations. Obviously, any discussion of Latino as a descriptor of the "Spanish origin" population involves a complex set of meanings.

Having noted the variety of national origin groups that fall under the Latino designation, a demographic profile of these groups would prove useful. The largest group is people of Mexican origin, who constitute 64 percent of U.S. Latinos (Current Population Reports, 1996). The second largest national group is Puerto Ricans (11 percent), followed by Cubans at 4 percent. The combined totals of Central/South American groups represent 14 percent of all Latinos (although they also represent more than 15 countries). As a matter of fact, the Central/South American groups are among the fastest growing elements of Latinos.

Table 1 portrays the size of the Latino population and its internal makeup. The significant growth rate of the Latino community has been documented by the U.S. Census Bureau, the mass media, political parties, and Latino organizations. The format of Table 1 highlights the extent of foreign-born among the aggregations we call Latinos. For the Cubans and Central/South Americans, more than two-thirds are foreign born. In the case of Mexican origin, almost two-fifths are foreign born. This raises issues of **citizenship** status and **political participation**. Since 1990, naturalization rates among Latinos have been increasing, especially for Cubans and Central/South Americans. At the same time, Latinos as a group have lower rates of naturalization than Asians, some Europeans, and other immigrants. (It is important to remember that all Puerto Ricans are U.S. citizens irrespective of birth on the mainland United States or Puerto Rico.) Another consequence of a significant proportion of foreign-born peoples among Latinos is the group's age structure. Overall, the median age for all Latinos is approximately 10 years younger than the non-Hispanic population. Yet, both Cubans and Central/South Americans (highest in foreign-born percentage) are also the oldest among Latinos.

Table 2 offers more information on all Latinos, including Puerto Ricans, over the past three censuses. In 1970, there were 4.5 million persons of Mexican origin, and in 1996 that category increased to more than 18 million. This represents a 300 percent increase over a 26-year period. Similarly, the Central/South American population almost doubled during this same time period. Over each of the last three decennial censuses, the Hispanic/Latino growth rate has been consistently four to six times higher than the total U.S. population growth rate.

Some of the implications of such dramatic growth rates for a sustained period would include the following: (1) greater national awareness of Latinos; (2) rising political concerns outside the Latino community regarding political power, immigration, **assimilation** (or lack of it), and an evolving policy agenda; (3) growing expectations among Latinos of greater

Table 1. Latino Population by U.S. Residence for Hispanics and Selected Racial/Ethnic Groups, 1996

Race/Ethnicity and Age	Total Pop. (In thousands)	First Generation (percent)	Second Generation (percent)	Third Generation (percent)
Non-Hispanics	235,876	6	9	86
Whites	191,221	3	9	88
Blacks	33,073	5	3	92
Other non-Hispanics	11,532	50	24	26
Hispanics	25,315	38	30	32
Mexicans	18,039	37	24	29
Puerto Ricans	3,123			
Cubans	1,127	69	29	2
Central/South American	4,060	68	30	3
Other Hispanic	2,089	27	28	45
Hispanics under 18	9,111	13	52	35
Mexicans	6,963	13	55	31
Cubans	213	15	80	5
Central/South Americans	1,270	26	71	4
Other Hispanics	664	8	47	45
Hispanics 18 and over	16,204	52	18	31
Mexicans	11,076	52	21	28
Cubans	914	81	17	31
Central/South Americans	2,790	87	11	2
Other Hispanics	1,425	36	19	45

Source: Jorge del Pinal and Audrey Singer. Generations of Diversity: Latinos in the United States. *Population Bulletin*, Vol. 52, No. 3 (October 1997).

Table 2. Population Growth of the U.S. Population by Hispanic Origin, 1970–1996

Race/ethnic Group	1970 Number (1,000s)	1980 Number (1,000s)	1980 Percent increase (1970–1980)	1990 Number (1,000s)	1990 Percent increase (1980–1990)	1996 Number (1,000s)	1996 Percent increase (1990–1996)
Total U.S.	203,212	226,546	11.5	248,710	9.8	264,314	6.3
Total Non-Hispanic	194,139	211,937	9.2	226,536	6.8	235,876	4.2
Hispanic	9,073	14,609	61.0	22,534	53.0	28,438	27.2
Mexicans	4,532	8,740	92.9	13,496	54.4	18,039	33.7
Puerto Ricans	1,429	2,014	40.9	2,728	35.5	3,123	14.5
Cubans	545	803	47.3	1,044	30.0	1,127	8.0
Others	2,566	3,051	18.9	5,086	66.7	6,149	20.9

political and economic power in the United States; and (4) the rise of Latino organizations and leaders in the national arena. In essence, the dramatic population growth has generated both positive and negative dimensions. That is, the image or perception of a growing force is certainly derivable from the demographic profile. At the same time, "counterpolitical" responses have resulted from different interest groups and political leaders. For example, the **English Only** and **English First** organizations have been successful with initiatives in more than 25 states. The state initiatives would require all public interactions and documents to be only in English as the official language of state and local governments.

A significant part of this effort has been in response to increased immigration, especially from Latin America. Latinos are often accused of staying detached from the U.S. mainstream, and charges of balkanization, of creating isolated cultural and linguistic enclaves, and of encouraging (perceived) a weak political identification with the United States are leveled at Latinos. Similarly, state initiatives, such as **California Proposition 187** and **California Proposition 209** (dealing with immigration and **affirmative action**, respectively) represent a political offensive directed toward Latinos.

Table 3. Educational Attainment by Race and Spanish Origin: United States, 1996

Race/ethnic Group	Number (1,000s)	Highest Level of Education (percent)			
		Less than 5th grade	Less than 9th Grade	H.S. graduate or higher	B.A./B.S. or higher
Total Population, age 25+	168,233	2	8	82	24
Non-Hispanic	153,782	1	6	85	25
Whites	128,810	1	5	86	26
Blacks	18,317	2	9	75	14
Other non-Hispanic	6,655	5	10	82	37
Hispanic	14,451	10	30	53	9
Age Group:					
Age 25–34	5,355	5	20	61	10
Age 35 and over	9,186	13	36	49	9
Origin:					
Mexicans	8,691	13	36	47	7
Puerto Ricans	1,592	5	19	60	11
Cubans	821	6	23	64	19
Central/South Americans	2,272	7	25	66	13
Place of birth:					
U.S.	5,672	4	13	70	12
Outside U.S.	8,869	15	41	42	8

Source: Jorge del Pinal and Audrey Singer. "Generations of Diversity: Latinos in the United States." *Population Bulletin*, vol. 52, no. 3 (October 1997), p. 32.

Another important dimension of Latino impact on the political arena is level of education. Education is viewed as a political resource: People with a greater number of years of schooling tend to be more knowledgeable, interested, and organizationally involved in public and political arenas. In addition, a higher level of education is associated with higher levels of political efficacy, trust, communication skills, and self-confidence. Substantial research by political scientists makes a direct connection between educational attainment and political participation, especially electoral involvement. The information in Table 3 indicates a significant difference in educational levels between Latinos and non-Hispanics. Overall, 85 percent of non-Hispanics are high school graduates, compared to 53 percent of Hispanic adults. However, among young Hispanics (25–34 years), 61 percent are at least high school graduates. Given the relative youthfulness of Hispanics, a gradual improvement in educational attainment will occur over time. At the same time, it is not as clear whether the gap between non-Hispanics and Hispanics will be reduced.

A closer examination of educational attainment by specific Hispanic subgroups does show some variation. As a group, the Mexican origin population has a lower rate of high school or higher completion than all Hispanics (47 percent). On the other hand, Cubans and Central/South Americans have higher rates, 64 and 66 percent, respectively. Given their relatively high percentage of foreign-born individuals, it would indicate a more educated immigrant pool than Mexican immigrants. Finally, educational attainment disparity is also evident by place of birth. U.S.-born Hispanics are 66.7 percent greater than foreign-born Hispanics to be high school graduates or higher. If one looks at educational attainment as a human capital resource for political participation, then Latinos have a more limited capital than non-Hispanics. This is compounded by the significant foreign-born element of this community.

An additional element of the human resource capital that Latinos can use in politics is their labor force participation and occupational status. The unemployment rate for non-Hispanic males and females in 1996 was 6 percent and 5 percent, respectively. For Hispanic males and females, unemployment rates were 10 percent for each. The nation's unemployment rate has been declining for the last two years. At the same time, there exists a 40 to 50 percent difference in unemployment rates between non-Hispanics and Latinos. There is some variation among Latinos, with Cubans experiencing an unemployment rate comparable to non-Hispanics. Obviously, the unemployment rates are influenced by an individual's human capital investments, local labor markets, the national economy, and treatment by employers. For example, social science research indicates that the unemployment rates among Latinos is much more sensitive to fluctuations with the national and regional economies than it is among non-Latinos. Part of the explanation lies with the industry location of Latino workers in manufacturing, agriculture, and construction.

Table 4. Labor Force Characteristics by Race and Spanish Origin: Some Selected Information, 1996						
	Percent Unemployed		**Occupation of Employed Workers**			
			Men		**Women**	
Race/ethnic group	Men	Women	Prof./Admin., Sales (percent)	Service, skilled/ unskilled labor (percent)	Prof./Admin., Sales (percent)	Service, skilled/ unskilled labor (percent)
Total	7	5	48	52	72	28
Non-Hispanic	6	5	50	50	74	26
Whites	5	4	51	49	76	24
Blacks	14	9	34	66	61	39
Other Non-Hispanics	7	5	58	42	67	33
Hispanic	10	10	27	73	56	44
Mexicans	10	10	23	77	55	45
Puerto Ricans	10	11	37	63	64	36
Cubans	6	6	44	56	72	28
Central/South Americans	8	10	29	71	48	52
OtherHispanics	16	7	45	55	60	40
Born in U.S.	10	9	41	59	72	28
Born outside U.S.	9	11	18	82	40	60

In Table 4, we can see the occupational distribution of non-Hispanics and Hispanics in service, skilled, and unskilled occupations and professional/administrative jobs. Again there is a significant disparity between the two populations. Overall, the percentage of non-Hispanic males and females in the service, skilled, and unskilled occupations is 50 percent and 26 percent, respectively. The percentages for Hispanic males and females are 73 percent and 44 percent, respectively. In a similar fashion, lower percentages of Latinos (males and females) are found in professional and administrative jobs. This deviation is more pronounced for Mexican, Puerto Rican, and Central/South American workers. In addition, foreign-born Latinos are disproportionately found in the lower occupational categories and are noticeably less active in professional/administrative positions. The themes of lower occupational status, worse case scenarios for the foreign-born, and slightly better situations for Cubans are recurring patterns on socioeconomic indicators.

The additional piece of the socioeconomic profile is that of income and the levels of poverty among Latinos. Table 5 shows information on family income levels, as well as percent of each population below poverty level. Again the gap between non-Latinos and Latinos is noticeable. Overall, 74 percent of all non-Latino families have income exceeding $25,000, whereas 49 percent of Latino families fall into this category. On the other hand, twice as many Latino families (16 percent vs. 7 percent) fall in the under $10,000 category. There is some variation among the Latino subgroups, with Cubans having the higher percentage of families over $25,000 (62 percent) and Puerto Ricans and Mexican origin families the lower percentages (i.e. 45 percent and 47 percent, respectively).

Not unexpectedly, the pattern persists when examining poverty levels. Latino families are three times more likely to be living below poverty levels than non-Hispanics (27 percent versus 9 percent, respectively). Similarly, the likelihood of female-headed households is about 150 percent greater for Hispanics than non-Hispanics (49 percent vs. 32 percent, respectively). Among the Latino subgroups, there are significant variations in the percentage of families below the poverty level. For Puerto Rican families, the gap is four times greater than compared to non-Latinos; and among female-headed households, it is twice as great (i.e., 64 percent vs. 30 percent). Lower rates of poverty are found among Cubans (16 percent for families), although their rate is still above the non-Hispanic level. Additionally, the income and poverty status of foreign-born Latinos is high. Thus the economic capital for Latinos is notably less than for non-Hispanics, this fact has implications for political participation.

It should be clear that a key distinction for Latinos is that a significant portion of the population is foreign born. While all Puerto Ricans are U.S. citizens, many Puerto Ricans are born in Puerto Rico and migrate to the mainland. Studies show that Puerto Ricans' political involvement, especially electoral participation, is significantly lower in the United States than in Puerto Rico. The drop in levels of participation may suggest some structural factors in the mainland U.S. political system that depresses Puerto Rican political involvement. The figures in Table 6 display citizenship levels among Latinos. Whereas 94 percent of non-Hispanics are citizens, only seven-tenths of Hispanics are. This includes 7 percent of Hispanics who are naturalized citizens. The percentages within Latino subgroups do vary; lower percentages of Cubans and Central/South Americans are citizens. At the same time, naturalization rates for these two groups have been rising dramatically

Table 5. Poverty Rates and Family Income by Race and Spanish Origin: United States, 1995

Race/ethnic group	Number of families (1,000s)	Family Income in 1995 (percent)			Percent below Poverty		
		Under $10,000	$10,000-24,999	$25,000 or more	All Families	Female-Headed	Elderly
Total	69,597	7	21	72	11	32	6
Non-Hispanic	63,311	7	20	74	9	30	5
Whites	52,861	5	18	77	6	22	4
Blacks	7,871	19	29	51	26	45	17
Other non-Hispanics	2,529	10	20	70	15	33	10
Hispanic	6,287	16	35	49	27	49	18
Mexicans	3,815	15	37	47	28	50	18
Puerto Ricans	742	26	29	45	36	64	19
Cubans	312	10	28	62	16	29	12
Central/South Americans	929	35	35	54	22	35	19
Other Hispanics	489	26	26	54	25	50	20
Born in U.S.	2,466	29	29	56	22	47	16
Born Outside U.S.	3,821	38	38	45	30	51	20

Table 6. Citizenship Status by Latino Origin Group, 1996 (from del Pinal and Singer, 1997)

Latino Ethnic Group	Not a U.S. Naturalized Citizen	U.S. Citizen	Citizen by birth
Non-Hispanic	3	3	94
Hispanic	31	7	62
Mexicans	32	5	63
Puerto Ricans	100		
Cubans	37	32	31
Central/South Americans	54	13	32
Other Hispanics	19	9	73

Source: Jorge del Pinal and Audrey Singer. "Generations of Diversity: Latinos in the United States." *Population Bulletin*, vol. 52, no. 3 (October 1997).

since 1990. As a matter of fact, the 1990s saw the greatest number of Latino immigrants becoming naturalized citizens. There is ample room for more Latinos to pursue citizenship, and Latino organizations and leaders are actively mobilizing Latino immigrants to do so. The current immigration debates and policy initiatives have also served to stimulate naturalization.

Table 7 presents information on the voting and registration history of Latinos since 1972. The **Voting Rights Act of 1965** included provisions for the collection of voting and registration data by race and ethnicity. The previous tables accented the significant foreign-born elements among the Latino subgroups and lower levels of socioeconomic status. In general, these factors also contribute to lower rates of voter registration and voting. The long-standing patterns shown in Table 7 reflect this situation for Latinos. Consistently, Latinos are 40 to 50 percent less likely to be registered and voting. These figures are "artificially" high, because they count all people of voting age, including noncitizens. If noncitizens are "removed" from these figures, the disparity remains, but it is not as dramatic (i.e., the figure improves by 15 or 20 percent).

The voting participation disparity between white and minority persons is also present for blacks, but the gap is narrower. Ironically, the percentages of Latinos who are registered has declined in both presidential election years, and, to a lesser degree, in off-year election periods. Latino voting percentages peaked with the 1984 presidential election at 40.1 percent, and the figure dipped to 31.3 percent in 1994. While the figures do not present an overly optimistic picture, a couple of positive factors can be significant. The Latino population overall is much younger than the general population; thus, over time, a greater percentage will be of voting age. In addition, the 1990s have seen a major increase in naturalization for all Latino subgroups. Similarly, exit polls from the 1996 presidential election show modest increases of Latino voters in California, Texas, and Florida. The electoral arena has been a challenge for Latinos to convert its population growth into a greater electoral force. We will discuss the participation patterns for Latinos, as well as Latino organizations and leadership, in the following sections.

Latinos, Politics, and Critical Dimensions

By presenting a demographic profile of Latinos, this discussion also touches upon a variety of political issues and

Table 7. Persons Reported Voting and Registering by Race, Hispanic Origin and Gender in November Elections: 1972–1994

Election	Total	White	Black	Hispanic Origin	Male	Female
Voting						
1994	45.0	47.3	37.1	20.2	44.7	45.3
1992	61.3	63.6	54.0	28.9	60.2	62.3
1990	45.0	46.7	39.2	21.0	44.6	45.4
1988	57.2	59.1	51.5	28.8	56.4	58.3
1986	46.0	47.0	43.2	24.2	45.8	46.1
1984	59.9	61.4	55.8	32.6	59.0	60.8
1982	48.5	49.9	43.0	25.3	48.7	48.4
1980	59.2	60.9	50.5	29.9	59.1	59.4
1978	45.9	47.3	37.2	23.5	46.6	45.3
1976	59.2	60.9	48.7	31.8	59.6	58.8
1974	44.7	46.3	33.8	22.9	46.2	43.4
1972	63.0	64.5	52.1	37.5	64.1	62.0
Registering						
1994	62.5	64.6	58.5	31.3	61.2	63.7
1992	68.2	70.1	63.9	35.0	66.9	69.3
1990	62.2	63.8	58.8	32.3	61.2	63.1
1988	66.6	67.9	64.5	35.5	65.2	67.8
1986	64.3	65.3	64.0	35.9	63.4	65.0
1984	68.3	69.6	66.3	40.1	67.3	69.3
1982	64.1	65.6	59.1	35.3	63.7	64.4
1980	66.9	68.4	60.0	36.3	66.6	67.1
1978	62.6	63.8	57.1	32.9	62.6	62.5
1976	66.7	68.3	58.5	37.8	67.1	66.4
1974	62.2	63.5	54.9	34.9	62.8	61.7

situations. For the balance of this introductory chapter, we will identify and elaborate on some of the major dimensions of Latinos and the political system. Certainly the issue of empowerment can capture the core of Latino politics. Part of the difficulty of unifying all segments of the Latino communities is both the diversity of national origin and the different historical–political experiences in the United States. For example, the Mexican-origin population inhabited and controlled much of the American Southwest prior to the **Mexican War** (1846–1848). So, on the one hand, they are part of the "indigenous" populations of the United States; at the same time, they represent some of the country's more recent immigrants.

Cubans, on the other hand, are more recent arrivals to the United States, mostly as political refugees. Puerto Ricans are United States citizens due to commonwealth status, yet culturally and linguistically they maintain their heritage with less "hostile" policy directed toward U.S. homogenization. The other Latino category is generally referred to as persons from Central and South America or the Dominican Republic. From a historical and political–economic perspective, they can be either "economic" migrants or political refugees. In any event, the diversity within the Latino umbrella serves as a basis for some commonalities, as well as more distinctive historical and structural relations with the U.S. political system.

One Latino Community or Numerous Communities?

Thus, a central dimension of the Latino community is precisely the nature of community among this aggregation of more than 20 national origin groups. Two general bases for a Latino community can be organized with the concepts of commonality of culture and commonality of interests (Garcia and Pedraza-Bailey, 1990). A community of culture exists when individuals are linked closely together by their participation in a common system of meaning with concomitant patterns of customary interactions and behaviors grounded in a common tradition (Cornell, 1985). Some examples of a common system could include national ancestry, language, religion, observance of holidays and celebrations, and familial networks. The work of Keefe and Padilla (1988) identifies these patterns of interactions as familial and primary. In addition, social contacts within a cultural milieu serve as vehicles for the transmission of customs, folklore, language, and the accumulation of common experiences (Yancey et al., 1976), but it is not clear whether common culture alone leads to organized community actions.

The idea of commonality of interests exists when persons are united by a common set of economic and political interests due, in part, to their concentration in certain industrial or occupational sectors, to residential segregation (Denton and Massey, 1988), or to political disenfranchisement (Smith, 1990). The result of such common interests would lead to the development of a shared sense of group identity, perceived common conditions, and structural relations with mainstream social and political institutions and public policies. If Latinos hold these common perspectives and experiences, it is assumed that this would encourage communitywide mobilization.

If the Latino community shares both a commonality of culture and interests, then the cultural symbols and cues would promote the cohesion of groups across national origin boundaries. In addition, common interests serve as the core for group goals and objectives. The significance of such a united community, in terms of culture and interests, can be substantial human and economic resources for effective mobilization. Other writers (i.e., Evangalista, 1994; Hayes-Bautista, 1993) speak of these dynamics as elements of pan-ethnicity in which a collection of several national origin groups coalesces under a broader identity and community reference.

On the other hand, if each national origin group is more distinctive than its sharing of commonalities of culture, language, and traditions, then the question of community may be more symbolic than organic or dynamic. In addition, this scenario would suggest than Latino subcommunities will remain singular ones, confined to the boundaries of being Mexican, Puerto Rican, Guatemalan, etc. On the other hand, groups that share interests and mutual identification can act as a community, reasonably in unison. As initially pointed out, the existence of a Latino community network and common bonds is a critical dimension of Latinos and politics.

Issues and Policy Agenda

In addition to the dynamic (or non-dynamic) nature of Latinos as a relatively cohesive community, the intersection of issues and concerns is another critical dimension. Can we say that there are specific common issues or concerns among Latinos? From this perspective, there are both broad or general issues and more specific policy concerns. The general issues would include expanding political empowerment, dispelling questions of loyalty, maintaining multiculturalism and Americanization, and promoting educational and economic mobility. The objective of greater political empowerment can produce some indicators, including political representation, visible and effective political leaders, major influential interest groups, and pivotal voting blocs for all levels of elections.

At the national level, in 1997, a total of 19 Latinos served in the U.S. House of Representatives. This number represents an increase of some 280 percent from 1962. At the same time, the Latino population has expanded by more than 600 percent. While impressive gains in formal political representation occurred through the last quarter of the twentieth century, the overall percentage of Latinos is still less than 3 percent of all elected officials. The larger gains have been at the local level,

especially school boards and city councils. In addition, the number of Latina elected officials has been dramatic. Credit for these gains can be attributed to organizational efforts by such organizations as the **Mexican American Legal Defense and Educational Fund (MALDEF)**, the **Southwest Voter Registration Education Project,** the **National Association of Latino Elected and Appointed Officials**, and the **Puerto Rican Legal Defense and Education Fund**. The organizational efforts have been focused on litigation that has challenged election systems (i.e., at-large elections, multimember districts, majority runoff requirements, etc.), voter mobilization with registration and education projects, and active promotion of naturalization among Latino immigrants. Thus, empowerment expansion has been directed, for the most part, to increasing the active Latino participatory base and defining critical issues areas and concerns for political institutions and leaders.

As we noted earlier, a significant portion of the Latino population is foreign born and has lower rates of naturalization than other "immigrant" groups. The combined pattern of cultural maintenance, especially linguistic, with a growing immigrant segment has raised the issue of political loyalty for Latinos. Nativists, political officials, and organizations such as English First and English Only have questioned the willingness of Latinos to blend within the U.S. melting pot. Public policies, particularly immigration and social welfare reform, have created major changes in legal and structural relations. For example, permanent resident aliens' access to social welfare programs such as Social Security have been eliminated. It has been suggested that stricter immigration controls and tighter border enforcement are in response to concerns about the extent of political loyalty of Latino immigrants, their willingness to be Americanized, and their negative impact on the economy and social services.

In some regard, anti-immigrant sentiments place the Latino community under siege and in a defensive posture. For example, several statewide initiatives in California in the late 1990s illustrate the schisms between segments of the U.S. populace and some leaders within the Latino community. **California Propositions 187, 209**, and 227 have focused on, respectively, policies regarding undocumented persons' access to educational and health "services," elimination of state affirmative action policies, and the time limit for children in **bilingual education** programs. Poll results in 1998 indicate that Proposition 227 had majority support across all segments of the electorate, and it was expected to pass. California is not only the most populous Latino state, but it is also the major port of entry for immigrants. As a result, Latino gains in population and political empowerment have stimulated a heightened state of competition and negative political initiatives.

Concomitant with a hostile climate directed toward undocumented (and legal) immigrants, as well as Latinos in general, are difficulties in the areas of multiculturalism and Americanization. Latinos have maintained their language, perpetuated their cultural traditions and practices, developed and expanded various ethnically based organizations, created ethnic enclaves, and continued a sense of community. At the same time, the Americanization process has affected the Latino community, especially the younger segments, in terms of popular culture, English-language use, lifestyles, and making socioeconomic progress. Yet the popular perception among many non-Latinos is that Latinos are culturally resistant to the Americanization process and prefer to live in isolated communities. Ironically, the results from the Latino National Political Survey (de la Garza et al., 1995) indicate a high degree of patriotism for the United States among Latinos and support for the widespread enhancement of English-language skills. For Latinos, the Americanization process includes the richness of cultural diversity.

The last general area of public policy concerns the socioeconomic mobility of Latinos. As stated earlier, the socioeconomic status of Latinos is generally lower than that of the general population, and of other minorities. Consistent with the theme of diversity and commonality, educational status varies within the Latino community. For the Mexican-origin and Central American populations, educational attainment is low. Slightly more than 50 percent of the Latino adults over 25 years have a high school education (the national average is over 75 percent). The years of schooling for Cubans and South Americans are closer to the national averages. At the same time, individual and household incomes are lower than national averages, and the percentage of families living below the poverty level is higher than other groups.

Some writers (i.e., Chavez, 1991) suggest that the continuous flow of Latino migration keeps the aggregate socioeconomic levels low. That is, less-educated and lower-waged immigrants depressed the gains made by native-born Latinos. In addition, conservative critics would point to Latino cultural values and beliefs (fatalism, nonscientific orientations, less entrepreneurial spirit, older forms of family socialization, etc.) as contributing factors for the slow degree of their socioeconomic mobility. Finally, these analysts predict that future gains in human capital skills over time will combine with greater degrees of assimilation to close the socioeconomic gap considerably.

On the other hand, other leaders and social scientists point to other circumstances that can slow down the upward mobility of Latinos, including structural factors (i.e., the global economy, restructuring of industries and jobs, fluctuations in the economy, bifurcation of the job market into lower-wage versus higher-wage jobs, etc.), **discrimination** in the labor market (hiring, promotion, and treatment), poor quality and limited resource allocations in the educational system for Latinos, besieged public policies (i.e., redistricting guidelines, restrictive immigration legislation, etc.), and the dismantling of affirmative action. While this conversation focuses upon the causes and the strategies to improve mobility for Latinos, the primary point is the significance of these areas for Latinos.

Specific Public Policies and Latinos

This essay has emphasized some major general policy concerns for Latinos. More specific public issues include (1) official English laws and initiatives; (2) the economic embargo with sanctions for Cuba; (3) a plebiscite on the political status of Puerto Rico; (4) political representation, redistricting legislation, and court decisions; (5) economic development and entrepreneurship; (6) bilingual education, school financing, and curriculum reform; (7) crime and public safety; (8) immigration policies—rights, social welfare access, quotas and admission categories, border enforcement; (9) environmental racism—such as toxic waste dumps, landfills, and lead poisoning; and (10) housing and home ownership.

Space considerations mean that all these specific policy issues cannot be discussed thoroughly, but it is useful to illustrate the concrete policy concerns and involvement within the Latino community. The continuous ties among Latinos with their countries of origin are reflected with two of the specific issues just identified. For Cubans, the exodus from Cuba began with the start of the Castro regime in 1959 and its communist political system. Their political refugee status became the basis both for the growth of the Cuban community in the United States (primarily in southern Florida) and for formal recognition by the U.S. government. The latter point illustrates the involvement of federal programs in assisting Cuban refugees to settle in the United States. The Cuban political agenda includes the demise of the Castro regime and restoration of a noncommunist political system. As a result, much of the Cuban-American community's political activities have focused on economic isolation via trade embargoes, Radio Marti, "liberation brigades," and strong anticommunist initiatives for the Caribbean and other parts of the Western Hemisphere. A tough stance against Castro's Cuba would be a central issue.

The ties to country of origin are also reflected within the Puerto Rican community. Movement from the island to the mainland United States has been an established pattern of migration since World War II. To some extent, circular migration is evident, because many Puerto Ricans have spells of residence in both the United States and Puerto Rico. Among Puerto Ricans, regular contact and visits to "the island" are not uncommon. The issue of the political status of Puerto Rico (i.e., commonwealth, statehood, or independence) has been the basis for political parties and movements. Currently, the U.S. Congress is deciding how and when to hold a plebiscite regarding Puerto Rico's future. One of the issues lies with the voting participation of Puerto Rican residents living on the mainland.

Similarly, the Mexican-origin community in the United States has developed more formal ties with Mexican political parties and governmental officials. For example, during the policy deliberations of the North American Free Trade Act (NAFTA), the Mexican government employed Mexican-

American leaders as lobbyists; in addition, the Mexican government lobbied the Congressional Hispanic Caucus and other national Latino organizations for support. The Mexican government passed a law that enables Mexican nationals living in the United States to keep their Mexican citizenship rights even if they choose to become naturalized U.S. citizens. There are other "foreign relations" concerns and connections with Central Americans in the United States regarding political stability, economic development, and human rights violations. Obtaining political refugee status among Central Americans has been a long-standing issue; the United States has been reluctant to recognize Salvadorans, Guatemalans, Hondurans, etc., as political refugees. In part, the significant immigrant segments within the Latino communities, the recent nature of the immigration experience, and continued strong cultural and familial ties are all salient factors that make homeland issues/conditions and United States foreign policy part of the Latino political agenda.

The remaining specific policy concerns center around domestic issues that affect socioeconomic mobility for Latinos. In the area of education, the issue of school financing and resources affect many Latinos who live in central cities and in poorer school districts. As a result, concerns for the quality of education (i.e., school expenditures, facilities, bilingual curriculum, quality of teachers, responsive administrators) represent a central core of educational issues.

More recently, bilingual education has come under strong opposition from the general public. In California, Proposition 227 requires a language immersion curriculum for limited or non-English-speaking students, rather than bilingual transitional or maintenance programs. A specified time period for language immersion is permitted before the student is mainstreamed into the regular classroom setting. Some of the underlying issues for supporters of Proposition 227 include (1) cost of bilingual programs; (2) lack of educational effectiveness; (3) cultural and linguistic isolation and resulting slow rate of Americanization; and (4) limited educational program options for non- or limited-English-speaking students.

On the other hand, when public opinion polls have been conducted in the 1970s, 1980s, and 1990s, the highest ranked public policy issue for Latinos has been education. In addition, support for bilingual education has consistently been over 70 percent of the survey respondents. Interestingly, public opinion polls in California indicate a good likelihood of passage of Proposition 227, with a significant portion of Latinos polled. The interpretation of such results would suggest that bilingual education is a multidimensional issue, and that factors other than educational pedagogies are involved. For example, a variety of language-based programs are designed to assist limited-English-speaking students improve their English communication skills. Thus, the enrollment of limited-English-speaking students is distributed across a variety of language-based programs. The actual numbers of students enrolled in these language-based programs does not represent Latino students only. Yet the aggregation of diverse programs are placed under the bilingual education umbrella and the public assumes that an overwhelming number of Latino students participates. Even the distinction of what is bilingual education or who is affected is not clearly known or understood. As a result, the reasons that individuals support Proposition 227 are not restricted to just pedagogy or program characteristics.

The primary importance of education to Latinos represents an understanding of this institution as a critical vehicle for socioeconomic mobility. Empirical and public policy research has dispelled the myth that Latino parents are unconcerned about their children's schooling and hold low expectations for their children's achievements. One result of the *Latino National Political Survey* indicates that the level of Latinos' participation in school-related matters—especially Mexican-origin Latinos and Puerto Ricans—is higher than the Anglos interviewed. Another indicator of policy salience is the gains among Latino officeholders at the school district level. Almost one-half of all positions held by Latino officeholders are on school boards. The concern about educational policies will continue well beyond the next millennium. Enduring patterns of high school dropout rates, disparaging low percentages of high school graduates, improving but still low numbers of Latinos in higher education, school financing disparities, "second-generation discrimination school practices" (Meier and Stewart, 1991), the need for greater representation on decision-making bodies, and anti-bilingual initiatives will keep the educational arena a focal point.

Latinos and U.S. Society

This introductory essay was designed to serve two purposes. The first is to present an interpretative demographic profile of the dynamic Latino community. While much has been made about the community's significant growth, our profile also illustrates the diversity within the Latino community. That diversity extends beyond the numbers of different countries of origin and relative size of the Latino subgroups to socioeconomic status, citizenship, and electoral participation. The "immigrant" segment of the Latino communities is noteworthy both for its size and for its policy/political implications. The latter implications refer to the preeminence of immigration as a national focus and the public's association of Latinos as an immigrant community. In addition, the conversion from immigrant status to being a U.S. citizen has become more prevalent among Latinos since the early 1990s. As a result, the electoral base is expanding, as is the Latino proportion of the voting population.

The second purpose of this essay is to explore the major concerns and issues that confront Latino communities. The development of an integrated community for each of the Latino subgroups is an evolving process. That is, political empowerment for Salvadorans, Puerto Ricans, Dominicans, etc., still requires leadership, organizational development and resources, an active membership base, and an identifiable policy agenda. This empowerment process can be focused at the local level and have nationally directed efforts as well. There is substantial evidence that Latinos are actively engaged in local arenas, concerned with service delivery and access, with protecting and further developing their neighborhoods, with economic opportunities (i.e., job creation, access to housing markets, entrepreneurship, etc.), with police services and **civil rights**, and with environmental protection. The process of political involvement by both the Latino constituencies and Latino leadership, irrespective of political arena, entails identification and use of resources (i.e., money, expertise, networks, awareness, information, commitment, social status, etc.) and the mobilization of such resources toward a common end and policy preference(s). Thus, Latinos and the U.S. system will include the expansion of national origin political development of Cubans, Mexican Americans, Salvadorans, Colombians, and the like to pursue their own particular interests and concerns. The evidence indicates that these Latino subgroups will not continue to be involved in politics that is not related to their own circumstances and conditions.

At the same time, commonalities of cultural origins and current linkages, as well as common interests, have forged some pan-ethnic community of Latinos. This broader community is more evident in the mass media treatment of persons of Spanish origin and public policies that aggregate Latinos as one group. In addition, the rise of (and in some cases the transformation of) Latino organizations to represent all Latinos is more evident. Even Latino organizations that are primarily concerned with a particular Latino subgroup have established working relationships with various other Latino subgroups. At times, this working arrangement can be effective (such as the efforts of the Congressional Hispanic Caucus on immigration reform legislation), or at times less cohesive (e.g., the extension of the economic embargo of Cuba or the approval of the North American Free Trade Act). Nevertheless, the growing pains of coalescing as a pan-ethnic community will continue to evolve. The utility of combined population bases, existing organizational infrastructures, and societal recognition and behavior toward Latinos as a national minority group serve to advance an operating Latino national community. Within the Latino communities, the contribution of leaders' mobilization and organizations' sustained efforts to promote Latino interests could well determine the extent of socioeconomic and political progress in the future. The further empowerment of the pan-ethnic community will manifest itself both in the electoral arena (i.e., increased levels of registered voters and higher turnout rates, more Latino candidates, etc.) and in pressure group activities at the national and state/local levels. For several decades, an ever-present theme for Latino subgroups (especially Mexican Americans) and the broader Latino community has been images of potential—a sleeping giant, a forthcoming day in the sun, and the like. In the latter half of the 1990s, there was clearer evidence of expanded and more effective political involvement, both collectively and individually. In addition, in the late 1990s the wave of anti-immigrant sentiment, anti-minority views, and anti-multiculturalism served as external catalysts for political mobilization and accumulation of political skills and resources.

References

Caspar, Lynn and Loretta Bass. "Voting and Registration in the Election of 1996." Current Population Reports. Washington, DC: U.S. Government Printing Office, 1996.

Chavez, Linda. *Out of the Barrio: Toward a New Politics of Hispanic Assimilation.* New York: Basic Books, 1991.

Cornell, Stephen. *Return of the Native: American Indian Political Resurgence.* New York: Oxford University Press, 1988.

del Pinal, Jorge and Audrey Singer. "Generations of Diversity: Latinos in the United States." *Population Bulletin* 53, no. 3 (October 1997).

Denton, N., and D. Massey. *American Apartheid: Segregation and the Making of the Underclass.* Cambridge, MA: Harvard University Press, 1993.

Evangalista, Yu. *Asian American Pan-Ethnicity: Bridging Institutions and Identities.* Philadelphia: Temple University Press, 1994.

Garcia, John A. and Sylvia Pedraza-Bailey. "Hispanicity and the Phenomenon of Community of Culture and Interests among Latinos in the U.S." Presented at the American Political Science Association meeting, Washington, DC, 1990.

Hayes-Bautista, David, E.R. Burciega Valdez, and Anthony Hernandez. *Redefining California: Latino Social Engagement in a Multicultural Society.* Los Angeles: Chicano Studies Research Center, UCLA, 1992.

Keefe, Susan and Amado Padilla. *Chicano Ethnicity.* Albuquerque: University of New Mexico Press, 1987.

Meier, Kenneth, and Joseph Stewart, Jr. *The Politics of Hispanic Education: Un Paso pa'lante y dos pa'tras.* Albany, NY: SUNY Press, 1991.

Smith, Tom. "Ethnic Survey." GSS Topical Report #19. Chicago: National Opinion Research Center, University of Chicago, 1990.

Yancey, William P. Ericksen, and Richard Juliani. "Emergent Ethnicity: A Review and Reformulation." *American Sociological Review* 41 (1976): 391–403.

Acculturation

Hispanic people comprise the second largest minority in the United States. The majority of Hispanics are Mexican Americans, many of whom call themselves Chicanos. Mexican Americans have begun in recent years to participate more fully in the political process. Other Hispanic groups include Puerto Ricans, Cubans, and immigrants from Central/South America. Each group's culture, proximity to its homeland, and time of arrival in the United States have influenced its respective acculturation.

Spanish-speaking citizens with a long history in the United States (such as descendants of the original Mexican settlers in the U.S. Southwest, whose ancestors lived in the area before it became part of the United States in 1848) are almost completely acculturated to Anglo-American society. Conversely, recently arriving immigrants remain unfamiliar with the English language and with U.S. culture, values, customs, and traditions.

Facilitators of effective acculturation include public educational systems and new employment opportunities created by industrial development since World War II. Barriers to acculturation include institutional racism, educational problems, and lack of political power. **See also** Assimilation; Citizenship; Community Organizations; Economic Equality; Educational Opportunity; Immigration Policy and Hispanics; Political Participation. **See** Treaty of Guadalupe Hidalgo (1848) in Appendix 1.

BIBLIOGRAPHY

Garcia, F. Chris and Randolph O. de la Garza. *The Chicano Political Experience: Three Perspectives*. North Scituate, MA: Duxbury Press, 1977.

Raymond L. Acosta (1925–)

During World War II, Raymond Acosta served with the U.S. Navy and participated in the landing at Normandy Beach in 1944. After the war, he earned a law degree and worked for the Federal Bureau of Investigation from 1954 to 1958. In 1959 he became assistant U.S. attorney for Puerto Rico, a post he held until he entered private practice in 1962. From 1980 to 1982, he served as U.S. attorney for Puerto Rico. In 1988 President Ronald Reagan appointed Acosta a judge on the U.S. District Court of Puerto Rico.

BIBLIOGRAPHY

"Suits are Settled in San Juan Fire." *The New York Times* (May 13, 1989): 8.

Maria Acosta-Colon (1949–)

Maria Acosta-Colon has been the director of the Mexican Museum, San Francisco, since 1989, and is a lifelong arts advocate and activist. She helped to establish the Arts Economic Development Consortium, assisted on several California Arts Council panels, and served as a member of the board of the San Francisco People's Coalition and as a site evaluator for the National Endowment for the Arts. In 1989 she organized the San Francisco Arts Democratic Club.

BIBLIOGRAPHY

Gaura, Maria Alicia. "Turmoil as Mexican Museum Turns 20." *The San Francisco Chronicle* (November 20, 1995): A1.

Affirmative Action

Affirmative action is a policy inspired by the **civil rights** movement to improve the chances of minority applicants to attain jobs, housing, employment, government contracts, or graduate admission by giving them a "boost" relative to white applicants with roughly the same qualifications. Proponents argue that this policy is appropriate because past **discrimination** has rendered it impossible for members of minority groups to achieve equality without some such boost.

Affirmative action applies most extensively to employment. It requires positive steps on the part of the employer to ensure that qualified minorities and women receive a fair share of jobs at all levels. Exactly what the positive steps and the fair share should be are the subject of much controversy.

Affirmative action programs were inaugurated in 1965 when President Lyndon B. Johnson issued an executive order requiring that federal contractors give a slight edge to minority applicants in bidding procedures. Between 1968 and 1971, the newly created Office of Federal Contract Compliance (OFCC) issued guidelines for federal contractors; these guidelines established certain goals and timetables for a contractor to follow if the percentage of African Americans and women employed by the contractor was lower than the percentage of those groups in the workforce more generally. Although the OFCC's requirements dealt only with federal contractors,

Congress in 1972 passed the Equal Employment Opportunity Act, which gave the Equal Employment Opportunity Commission (EEOC) broader power to litigate against employers if such employers did not eliminate discrimination in their hiring practices.

Supporters hailed affirmative action as necessary to remedy current discrimination and undo the effects of past discrimination. Opponents of affirmative action have often argued that the policy favors minorities over "qualified" whites. One argument is that affirmative action promotes "reverse discrimination," meaning that white males are victims of discrimination as a result of affirmative action on behalf of women, blacks, Hispanics, and other underrepresented groups. Opponents further argue that affirmative action amounts to harmful quotas that result in lower standards. But affirmative action usually does not require quotas per se. Admittedly, the terms blur; if employers are pressured to meet "goals," they interpret them to be quotas. But only occasionally, and only after finding deliberate and systematic discrimination, does affirmative action require setting actual quotas.

The U.S. Supreme Court has been willing to scrutinize affirmative action programs to ensure that they do not directly discriminate against whites. In *University of California Regents v. Bakke* (1978), the Court upheld the policy of the University of California at Davis Medical School to consider race as a factor in admissions, but it struck down the school's policy of establishing a quota of 16 spaces for minorities for every 100 spaces in the class. The Court ordered the university to admit Bakke to its medical school and to eliminate the special admissions program. It recommended that California consider an admissions program developed at Harvard University, which considers disadvantaged racial and ethnic background as a "plus" in an overall evaluation of an application, but does not set numerical quotas or exclude any person from competing for all positions.

However, the Supreme Court has approved affirmative action programs where there is evidence of past discriminatory practices. In *United Steelworkers of America v. Weber* (1979), the Court approved a plan developed by a private employer and a union to reserve half of higher-paying, skilled jobs for minorities. The primary factor in determining the legality of quotas is whether the employer or union has practiced discrimination in the past. While the University of California at Davis had no history of discrimination, other employers did.

Throughout the 1980s, the Reagan and Bush administrations intensified the attack on affirmative action and engaged in a systematic dismantling of its programs. In reexamining affirmative action, the Reagan administration took the position that the various Civil Rights Acts prohibited all racial and sexual discrimination, including discrimination against white males. The administration further argued that the Constitution does not permit the federal government to adopt remedies involving racial quotas to benefit persons who may have been victims of discrimination. The major impetus for changes in civil rights policy, especially affirmative action, came from the Department of Justice. The Justice Department under the Reagan administration argued that numerical hiring and promotion goals were unacceptable remedies for employment discrimination. The Justice Department took primary aim at the goals and timetable strategy that courts and executive agencies, such as the EEOC and OFCC, had used for over a decade to monitor compliance with affirmative action plans. In briefs before the Supreme Court, the Justice Department urged the elimination of all such goals and timetables. In 1984, the Reagan administration persuaded the Supreme Court to overturn a ruling by a federal district court requiring a fire department to suspend seniority rules when laying off employees.

The Rehnquist Court has also reduced the scope of affirmative action programs. In *City of Richmond v. Croson* (1989), the Court struck down an ordinance that set aside 30 percent of construction contracts in Richmond Virginia, for minority businesses. Although the Court did not bar affirmative action programs, a slim majority has made it more difficult for governments to adopt some programs. Governments must demonstrate a "compelling" reason (which apparently means they must have clear evidence of a pattern of specific and intentional discrimination), rather than cite the general pattern of historical discrimination, and they must further describe exactly how particular programs must ameliorate the problems. In a key 1995 decision, *Adarand Constructors v. Pena,* involving a Small Business Administration program giving a Hispanic-owned company an affirmative action advantage in bidding for a highway contract, the Supreme Court for the first time refused to uphold a federal program. Instead, the Court ruled that federal programs, like state and local affirmative action programs, must serve compelling governmental interests and must be designed to remedy specific instances of past discrimination, rather than remedy overall societal discrimination.

The Court also ruled by a 5-4 majority that the federal government must abide by the strict standards for affirmative action programs imposed on states in the *Richmond* case and could not award contracts using race as the main criterion. The Court expressed skepticism about governmental racial classifications, saying that "There is simply no way of determining what classifications are 'benign' and 'remedial' and what classifications are in fact motivated by illegitimate notions of racial inferiority or simple racial politics." In March 1996, the United States Court of Appeals for the 5th Circuit ruled in *Hopwood v. University of Texas* that admissions programs used by the University of Texas Law school that took race into account were unconstitutional. This ruling appeared to negate the *Bakke* decision and, if upheld on appeal, would have ended affirmative action programs altogether. In June 1996, however, the Supreme Court declined to hear the appeal. The *Hopwood* ruling, therefore, only applies to a few states in the South, although it has set a de facto precedent.

The Supreme Court's position is that various programs whose sole aim is to increase racial diversity are no longer acceptable. Programs must be designed to redress past discrimination in a particular occupation, business sector, or institution, and must not serve vaguely defined societal goals for increased minority representation. Such programs must also be only temporary efforts to transcend past practices, and not permanent features of hiring, contracting, or admissions.

The Court's direction on affirmative action has seemed to mirror the mood of the country, evident in California's passage of an anti-affirmative action proposition in 1996 (**California Proposition 209**), President Bill Clinton's suspension of minority "set asides" in federal contracts, various state anti-affirmative action initiatives, and attempts by a Republican-dominated Congress to end federal affirmative action programs. There appears to be a belief in The United States that minorities no longer need affirmative action. Efforts to eliminate or modify affirmative action draw support from public-opinion polls, which show that about two out of three people in the United States have serious doubts about affirmative action, especially when it involves hiring quotas and contract set-asides. They disapprove of making race or ethnicity a legitimate or predominant ground for awarding jobs, social benefits, or opportunities. Even some long-time supporters of affirmative action have come to view race-conscious programs as no longer necessary; they argue that current societal disadvantages are more class-based than race-based. If preferences are to be granted at all, they should be based on economic disadvantage rather than race.

Affirmative action programs have demonstrably helped some minorities and women. Companies that do business with the federal government, and who therefore are subject to affirmative action, have hired more minorities and women than other companies. Affirmative action has been most successful in increasing the number of minorities in government agencies, police departments, and various construction trades. Affirmative action has also made it more difficult for employers and educators to discriminate against minorities. And affirmative action certainly helped bring to the mainstream individuals who are genuinely disadvantaged. Similarly, the rapid growth in the enrollment and completion rates of minority students in colleges and universities in the 1970s can in part be attributed to affirmative action policies that encouraged higher education institutions to seek out minorities, as well as to the improved preparation of minority students resulting from school desegregation and improved educational opportunities. Affirmative action has been less successful in pulling minorities out of the "underclass." Many, from families with long-term poverty, experience unemployment because they lack the education and skills necessary to compete for available jobs.

At the same time, some minorities contend that affirmative action has actually hindered them, by encouraging them to rely on government programs, rather than on their own efforts, and by stigmatizing them. They say affirmative action casts doubt on minorities' credentials, in the minds of whites and minorities alike. Race-conscious government policies, they argue, have been more hurtful than helpful.

The debate over affirmative action remains heated, and will no doubt occupy a prominent place in future political campaigns. **See also** Civil Rights Act of 1964; Economic Equality; Educational Opportunity. (NM)

BIBLIOGRAPHY

Brown, W. Taylor. "Equal Protection and Isolation of the Poor." *Yale Law Journal* 95 (1986): 1709–10.

Carter, L. Steven. *Reflections of an Affirmative Action Baby*. New York: Basic Books, 1991.

Ezorsky, Gertrude. *Racism and Justice: The Case for Affirmative Action*. Ithaca, NY: Cornell University Press, 1991.

Hochschild, Jennifer. *Facing Up to the American Dream*. Princeton, NJ: Princeton University Press, 1995.

Konrad, M. Alison and Frank Linnehan. "Formalized HRM Structures: Coordinating Equal Employment Opportunity or Concealing Organizational Practices." *Academy of Management Journal* 38 (June 1995): 787.

Nelson, C. Dometrius and Lee Sigelman. "Assessing Progress Toward Affirmative Action Goals in State and Local Governments." *Public Administration Review* 44 (May/June 1984): 241–7.

Samuelson, J. Robert. "End Affirmative Action." *Washington Post National Weekly Edition* (March 6–12, 1995): 5.

Sowell, Thomas. *Preferential Treatment: An International Perspective*. New York: William Morrow, 1990.

Agrarian Reform

Many developing countries have attempted agrarian reform programs that seek a more equitable distribution of land among people. In Mexico, for example, the land that peasants' had lost over time to the aristocracy was returned to them following the 1910 revolution; the land was returned as one of two categories, private or *ejidal* (communal). In 1996 the Mexican government announced a new reform package giving farmers greater freedom to own and work their own lands, anticipating better living standards and greater agricultural production. **See also** Land Rights. (VDD)

BIBLIOGRAPHY

Briggs, Charles C. and John R. Van Ness, eds. *Land, Wake and Culture: New Perspectives on Hispanic Land Grants*. Albuquerque: University of New Mexico Press, 1987.

Robert P. Aguilar (1931–)

A successful lawyer, Robert Aguilar was named a judge of the California Superior Court for Santa Clara County in 1979. The following year, President Jimmy Carter named him to the U.S. District Court for the Northern District of California. In 1990, Aguilar became the first U.S. district judge ever to be indicted under the federal racketeering statute. He was found guilty of divulging wiretap information and was barred from legal practice. However, in 1994, the U.S. Court of Appeals overturned his conviction.

BIBLIOGRAPHY

Morain, Dan. "Robert Aguilar; Controversy Has Dogged Judge Much of Career." *Los Angeles Times* (June 14, 1989): 20.

Slater, Eric. "U.S. Drops Case Against Judge, Who Resigns." *Los Angeles Times* (June 25, 1996): 3.

Alamo

Throughout the eighteenth century, Spain established Catholic missions in Texas, California, and areas of the Southwest. The most famous among these, the Alamo in Texas, was established as a Franciscan mission in 1718 and marked the founding of San Antonio. The Alamo gained fame in 1836 by serving as a fortress in the Texas Revolution, when colonists, including Texas Mexicans, sought independence from Mexico and its settlement policies. In March 1836, a 13-day battle for freedom ensued. Colonel William Barrett Travis and his men fought Mexican General Antonio Lopez de Santa Anna. On March 6, 4,000 Mexican soldiers stormed the Alamo. Inside were 189 patriots, including colonists, volunteers such as Davy Crockett and his "Tennessee Boys," and native Texans of both Spanish and Mexican descent, all fighting for Texas independence. Despite their efforts, there were few survivors.

The Alamo is best remembered for the 13-day siege that occurred there in 1836. A symbol of Texas pride for many Anglo-Americans, the Alamo is the symbol of a conquered people for many Mexican Americans. *Library of Congress.*

Eventually, an alliance between the colonists and the Texas Mexican elite helped Texas win independence from Mexico. An independent nation for nearly a decade, Texas was officially annexed to the United States on December 29, 1845, making it the 28th state.

Today, the Alamo holds a diverse symbolism. For example, generations of Anglo-Americans view the mission as a symbol of Texas pride. But Mexican Americans, who fought and died alongside Anglos, regard this landmark as a symbol of a conquered people. For a period in the 1960s and early 1970s, such sentiments led to separatist rhetoric by some Chicano activists. But by the 1980s, even the most extreme elements among Mexican Americans had abandoned such efforts. **See also** Mexican War; Texas Statehood; Treaty of Velasco (1836). **See** Texas Declaration of Independence (1836); A Mexican Account of the Attack on the Alamo (1849) in Appendix 1. (VDD)

BIBLIOGRAPHY

Nance, John M. *After San Jacinto.* Austin: University of Texas Press, 1963.

Nunn, W. C. *Texas Under Carpetbaggers.* Austin: University of Texas Press, 1962.

Arthur L. Alarcon (1925–)

Judge Arthur Alarcon received his law degree from the University of California; his first position was as a Los Angeles County deputy district attorney from 1952 to 1961. In 1962 he served as the executive assistant and legal adviser to the governor of California. He then became the chairman of the Parole Board for the California Adult Authority in 1964, and shortly thereafter became a Los Angeles Superior Court judge, a position he held until 1978, when he became an associate justice in the California Court of Appeals and then, in 1979, a judge for the 9th Circuit Court of Appeals.

BIBLIOGRAPHY

Weinstein, Henry. "Dissension Over Death Penalty Flares Again Among Judges." *Los Angeles Times* (July 5, 1993): 3.

Richard Alatorre (1943–)

Richard Alatorre served as a California state assemblyman from 1973 to 1985. Alatorre, a Mexican-American Democrat, was honored as an "Outstanding State Legislator" by the Eagleton Institute of Politics, Rutgers University. In 1985 he was elected to the Los Angeles City Council and was one of the city's busiest public servants. He served as a staff member of the Los Angeles Community Services Program. Alatorre gained recognition as a Democratic Party political activist; he had served on the Democratic National Credentials Committee in 1972. In keeping with his political interests and concerns with minority issues, and his role as a political activist, Alatorre was also a member of the **National Association of Latino Elected and Appointed Officials**. **See also** Community Organizations; Political Participation; Political Leadership. (SCV)

BIBLIOGRAPHY

Rosales, F. Arturo. *Chicano! The History of the Mexican American Civil Rights Movement.* Houston: Arte Publico Press, 1997.

Pedro Albizu Campos (1891–1965)

Pedro Albizu Campos was one of the leading figures in the Puerto Rican independence movement. While advocating separation from the United States, Albizu endorsed the development of closer ties with Latin America and Spain. His political activism began in the 1910s while attending Harvard University, where he became active in the Irish liberation movement. Upon returning to Puerto Rico, Albizu helped to organize the Partido Nacionalista (Nationalist Party) in 1922, becoming its vice president in 1924, its delegate to Latin America in 1925, and its president in 1930. Albizu popularized the annual celebration of the 1868 **Grito de Lares** (Lares

Uprising) among separatists. During the turbulent 1930s he used this and other public events to denounce American dominion over Puerto Rico and U.S. intervention in Latin America. In 1936 Albizu was convicted of inciting rebellion against the United States. After his release from prison, Albizu organized the 1950 Gesta de Jayuya (Jayuya Uprising), for which he was charged with sedition and sentenced to a half-century in prison. In 1965 Pedro Albizu Campos died while still incarcerated. Albizu is still revered by many separatists as one of the movement's greatest leaders and is venerated by Puerto Rican nationalists as a martyr. **See also** Puerto Rican Statehood. (AAB)

BIBLIOGRAPHY
Ferrao, Luis Angel. *Pedro Albizu Campos y el Nacionalismo Puertorriqueno.* Rio Piedras, PR: Editorial Cultural, 1980.
Ribes Tovar, Federico. *Albizu Campos: Puerto Rican Revolutionary.* New York: Plus Ultra, 1971.

Albuquerque Walkout

During the early months of 1966, 50 Chicano leaders walked out of the federally sponsored Equal Employment Conference in Albuquerque, New Mexico. These leaders justified their actions by explaining that the rights of U.S. citizens with Spanish heritage were not being met at this conference. Further, they demanded that the administration of President Lyndon B. Johnson hold a White House conference to review problems affecting Mexican Americans.

In May 1966, President Johnson met with some of the walkout's leaders, as well as with other prominent Hispanic figures. This group collectively planned for a conference to be set up in El Paso, Texas, to review Mexican-American issues. However, three of the planning committee's members, **Cesar Chavez**, **Rodolfo "Corky" Gonzales**, and **Bert Corona**, soon became upset over the format and particular guidelines of the El Paso conference. As a result, these three Chicano leaders announced a general boycott of the conference, and later decided to lead a rival conference elsewhere in El Paso. This "counterconference," called the La Raza Unida Conference, brought together Chicano youth organizations and student groups while also making strong demands for equal and civil rights.

BIBLIOGRAPHY
Castro, Tony. *Chicano Power.* New York: Dutton, 1974.

Alianza Federal de Pueblos Libres

In 1960 **Reies Lopez Tijerina**, a militant Mexican-American leader, investigated the land-grant issue in New Mexico; he discovered that village common lands had been taken by the United States government after the **Mexican War,** which ended in 1848. To help these villages regain their common lands, he organized the Alianza Federal de Mercedes (Federal Alliance of Grants) organization in 1963. In May 1967 the organization became the Alianza Federal de Pueblos Libres (Federal Alliance of Free Towns). Through legal appeals, the alliance attempted to convince the U.S. government to return common lands to the villages. The group also employed more confrontational tactics; it took over the Rio Arriba County courthouse in Tierra Amarilla, New Mexico in 1967. **See also** Land Rights; People's Constitutional Party; Political Participation. (SCV)

BIBLIOGRAPHY
Blawis, Patricia Bell. *Tijerina and the Land Grants: Mexican Americans in Struggle for Their Heritage.* New York: International Publishers, 1971.
Garcia, Chris F. and Rudolph O. de la Garza. *The Chicano Political Experience: Three Perspectives.* North Scituate, MA: Duxbury Press, 1977.
Trejo, Arnulfo D., ed. *The Chicanos as We See Ourselves.* Tucson: University of Arizona Press, 1993.

Alianza Hispano-Americana

The Alianza Hispano-Americana was founded in Tucson, Arizona, in 1894. Organized into regional lodges, the Alianza initially provided death benefits for its members. By the 1920s, the Alianza also sought to meet social needs and provide legal rights for its members. After World War II, the Alianza became involved in educational matters as well. Internal dissension in the 1960s caused a decline in membership and the Alianza went into receivership, from which it never recovered. It is now disbanded. **See also** Community Organizations; Mutual Aid Societies. (SCV)

BIBLIOGRAPHY
Zurano Muno, Emilio. *Aliqnza Hispano-Americana.* Madrid, Spain: Impr. cle J Pueyo, 1928.

Saul Alinsky (1910–1972)

Saul Alinsky, a labor and **civil rights** activist from the 1910s until his death in 1972, embraced the concept of community development in urban areas through organizing neighborhoods. Alinsky's goal—a society in which there is legal and economic justice—encouraged positive social change by "rubbing raw the sores of discontent." Alinsky's community organizing model centered on giving a voice and power to the disenfranchised and oppressed by building strong neighborhood organizations so that people could act collectively against injustice. In 1940, Alinsky founded what would become the largest and oldest institution for community organizing in the United States, the Industrial Areas Foundation, in East Brooklyn, New York. Alinsky also inspired labor organizers such as **Cesar Chavez**, who was general director for Alinsky's Community Service Organization from 1952 through 1962. **See also** Community Organization for Public Service (COPS); Community Organizations; Economic Equality; Political Participation: United Farm Workers. (VDD)

BIBLIOGRAPHY
Alinsky, Saul. *Rules for Radicals: A Practical Primer for Realistic Radicals,* New York: Vintage Books, 1971.
Horwitt, Stanford. *Let Them Call Me Rebel: The Life and Legacy of Saul Alinsky.* New York: Alfred A. Knopf, 1989.
Stone, Clarence N. *Regime Politics: Governing Atlanta 1946–1988.* Lawrence: University of Kansas Press, 1989.

Everett Alvarez, Jr. (1937–)

Everett Alvarez, Jr., is noted for having been a naval aviator in the Vietnam conflict, an attorney, and a public official. In 1981, Alvarez was appointed deputy director of the Peace Corps by President Ronald Reagan. In 1982, Alvarez became deputy administrator of the Veterans Administration (VA), where he was in charge of 700 VA facilities. (SCV)

BIBLIOGRAPHY

Martinez, Al. *Rising Voices: Profiles of Hispanic-American Lives.* New York: New American Library, 1994.

Salazer, Veronica. "Alvarez Survived to Help Others," *San Antonio Sunday Express News* (October 2, 1983).

Luz Alvarez-Martinez (1942–)

Luz Alvarez-Martinez is director of the National Latina Health Organization (NLHO), an organization that provides bilingual health information for Hispanic women. In 1981, Alvarez-Martinez realized that Hispanic women were often given different information at the hospital than their English-speaking counterparts. Five years later, she received a grant that helped her (together with three others) to create the NLHO, which gives Hispanic women free access to physical and mental health information. Martinez is also a member of the **Mexican American Political Association** and helped organize the Latin Political Action Committee.

BIBLIOGRAPHY

Telgen, Diane and Jim Kamp, eds. *Notable Hispanic American Women.* Detroit: Gale Research, 1993.

American Coordinating Council on Political Education

Now defunct, the American Coordinating Council on Political Education was established in Arizona in the 1960s as a nonpartisan organization. The organization emerged from an initial meeting held to create an Arizona chapter of the **Political Association of Spanish-Speaking Organizations**. More suited to Arizona's political needs, the Arizona Coordinating Council quickly spread throughout the state. Its members were successful in obtaining town council and school board positions. This success was not translated, however, to county, state, or federal levels. **See also** Political Participation. (SCV)

BIBLIOGRAPHY

Quinones, Juan Gomez. *Chicano Politics.* Albuquerque: University of New Mexico Press, 1990.

American Council of Spanish-Speaking People

Initially formed during the 1950s in the Southwest, the American Council of Spanish-Speaking People sought to eliminate **discrimination** in education, housing, and employment and to increase the amount of Hispanic involvement in politics. The council began as a response to the **civil rights** demands of Hispanic people and was particularly active during the school desegregation movement. **See also** Educational Opportunity; Political Participation.

BIBLIOGRAPHY

Garcia, Mario T. *Mexican Americans.* New Haven, CT: Yale University Press, 1989.

American G.I. Forum

The American G.I. Forum, an organization for Hispanic veterans, emerged from a 1948 incident in Three Rivers, Texas. **Feliz Longoria**, a World War II veteran killed on the Philippine Island of Luzon, was buried overseas. After the war, he was refused reburial by the local mortuary in his hometown of Three Rivers. A bitter public dispute developed and was publicized throughout the country. Mexican-American veterans met at Corpus Christi, Texas, to protest the racism inherent in denying Longoria reburial, and, under the leadership of Dr. **Hector Perez Garcia,** the attendees organized the American G.I. Forum.

After its establishment, the organization soon broadened its scope. It conducted voter registration drives during the 1950s; the forum's concern with education led it to file lawsuits over civil, social, and educational **discrimination**. The G.I. Forum informed Mexican-American veterans about their rights under the G.I. Bill and later also provided information to the nonmilitary community about available government services.

The G.I. Forum created councils throughout Texas and other states through which it defended Mexican Americans in **civil rights** trials and demanded reforms. This activity encouraged widespread Mexican-American political involvement during the 1960 presidential election through **Viva Kennedy** clubs.

The G.I. Forum continues to promote nonpartisan political participation. In the 1990s the G.I. Forum's membership exceeded 20,000 nationwide. Its membership, representing middle-class professionals and businesspeople, gave the American G.I. Forum a voice and influence with the conservative Republican administrations of the 1980s and early 1990s. **See also** Political Participation; Voting Rights. (SCV)

BIBLIOGRAPHY

Allsup, Carl. *The American G.I. Forum.* Austin: University of Texas Press, 1982.

Ramos, Henry. *The American G.I. Forum.* Houston: Arte Publico Press, 1998.

Tony Anaya (1941–)

Tony Anaya earned his law degree in 1967 at American University's Washington College of Law and gained experience by working in the office of U.S. Senator **Dennis Chavez** (New Mexico). Anaya then returned to New Mexico and became administrative assistant to Governor Bruce King. In 1974 Anaya, a Democrat, was elected New Mexico's attorney general. In November 1982, Anaya was elected governor of New Mexico; as governor, he took controversial stands by increasing state income taxes, promoting a strong **affirmative action** program, and proclaiming New Mexico a sanctuary state for Central American refugees. Prior to the 1986 election, which he lost, Anaya was spoken of as a potential vice-presidential candidate in 1988. **See also** Immigration Policy and Hispanics; Political Leadership. (SCV)

BIBLIOGRAPHY

Gillott, Roger. "Ousted Leader of Latino Group Protests Appointment of Anaya." *Los Angeles Times.* (January 20, 1987): 3.

Lupe Anguiano (1929–)

Lupe Anguiano is an activist and educator devoted to women's issues and welfare reform. Appointed by President Lyndon Johnson to the U.S. Office of Education in 1967, she assisted with the Bilingual Education Act. In the 1970s, she worked briefly for **Cesar Chavez** and the **United Farm Workers,** as well as for the National Association for the Advancement of Colored People, before returning to Washington, D.C., to work at the U.S. Department of Health, Education, and Welfare from 1990 to 1992. Anguiano founded the National Women's Employment and Education Project in 1979 and was appointed as a consultant to the U.S. Department of Personnel Management, Division of Affirmative Recruitment. **See also** Bilingual Education; Educational Opportunity; Political Participation.

BIBLIOGRAPHY

Hoffman, Marilyn. "Lupe Anguiano: Helping Women Help Themselves Off the Welfare Roles." *The Christian Science Monitor* (April 19, 1983): 14.

Jerry Apodaca (1934–)

Jerry Apodaca, a Democrat, started his political career when he was elected to the New Mexico State Senate in 1966. In 1975, after eight years in the state legislature, he became the twenty-second governor of the state and the first Hispanic governor in 50 years. In 1977, President Jimmy Carter appointed him to the President's Council on Physical Fitness and Sports. His interests in energy issues led him to serve the Four Corners Regional Commission. **See also** Political Leadership. (SCV)

BIBLIOGRAPHY

Goshko, John M. and Christopher Dickey. "Carter Eyes Apodaca for Mexico Post." *The Washington Post* (October 26, 1979): A2.

Manuel Aragon

Manuel Aragon has spent his life working for the economic improvement of Latinos. He served as the director of the Economic and Youth Opportunities Agency of Los Angeles, which was established after Congress enacted the Economic Opportunity Act. Aragon was responsible for the management of programs to improve the socio-economic conditions of Los Angeles minorities. In 1973, Tom Bradley, the first African-American mayor of Los Angeles, selected Aragon as his deputy mayor. Aragon used his new position to continue his work fighting poverty.

BIBLIOGRAPHY

Quinones, Juan Gomez. *Chicano Politics.* Albuquerque: University of New Mexico Press, 1990.
Who's Who in American Politics. Chicago: Marquis, 1977.

Diego Archuleta (1814–1884)

Diego Archuleta served the Mexican and United States governments in political matters. He served as a Nuevo Mexicano representative to the National Congress in Mexico from 1843 to 1845. During the 1850s, he was elected to the New Mexico legislative assembly. During and after the Civil War, he was elected to the Mexican Legislative Council for seven terms. (SCV)

BIBLIOGRAPHY

Twitchell, Ralph E. *The History of the Military Occupation of the Territory of New Mexico from 1846 to 1851.* Chicago: Rio Grande Press, 1963.
Vigil, Maurilio. *Los Patrones: Profiles of Hispanic Political Leaders in New Mexico History.* Washington DC: University Press of America, 1980.

John A. Arguelles (1927–)

After serving in the U.S. Navy from 1942 to 1945, John Arguelles received his undergraduate degree in economics and his law degree from UCLA. He worked as a lawyer until 1963 when he became a judge in the East Los Angeles Municipal Court. From 1969 until 1984, he served as presiding criminal court judge in the Los Angeles Superior Court. In 1984, he became a 2nd Circuit Court judge in the U.S. Court of Appeals and was appointed to the California Supreme Court. He retired in 1987.

BIBLIOGRAPHY

Hager, Philip. "Arguelles to Leave State's Supreme Court on March 1." *Los Angeles Times* (November 22, 1988): 1.
———. "Deukmejian's Supreme Court Nominees; John A. Arguelles." *Los Angeles Times* (February 19, 1987): 1.

Manuel Armijo (1792–1853)

As territorial governor of Nuevo Mexico (1827–1829, 1845–1846), Manuel Armijo authorized 15 million acres in land grants. Many grants were made to provide political protection for Nuevo Mexico as American settlers began to move into the region from Texas. Armijo repulsed the Texas Santa Fe expedition of 1841, but during the **Mexican War** he failed to engage the forces of American Colonel Stephen W. Kearny during the U.S. invasion of Nuevo Mexico in 1846. As a result, U.S. forces took Santa Fe and the region without a battle. **See also** Land Rights. (SCV)

BIBLIOGRAPHY

Carnes, Mary L. *The American Occupation of New Mexico 1821–1852.* New York: Arno Press, 1976.

ASPIRA

Founded in 1969, ASPIRA, the Spanish word for "hope," is a grassroots organization dedicated to offering Chicanos a variety of services, including leadership development, educational assistance, and other skills required in gaining self-reliance. The group currently offers educational counseling to students on the high school and college level, while also backing high school clubs and assisting Hispanic students with financial aid for college. Additionally, the organization provides group discussion forums, tutoring, and workshops on a number of topics. The group also publishes its own quarterly newspaper, *ASPIRA News,* and a variety of reports on topics significant to the Latino community. ASPIRA sponsors a number of related organizations, including the ASPIRA Public Policy Research Program, the Natural Health Careers Program, and the Institute for Policy Research. **See also** Alice Cardona; Community Organizations; Educational Opportunity.

BIBLIOGRAPHY

King, Ledyard. "Aspira Helps Students Make Grade; School Board to Vote on Plan for At-Risk Middle Schoolers." *Sun-Sentinel* (March 5, 1996): 1B.

Assimilation

The Mexican American in the United States has encountered both aids and barriers to assimilation. Aids have included the public school system, movie theaters, professional sports events, county health immunization programs, mixed housing projects, and wars and the armed forces. Especially significant was the 1964 Economic Opportunity Act, which helped integrate people and programs through community projects. Barriers to assimilation have included restricted housing, prejudice in the workplace, and restricted working opportunities. The 1970 research study by Grebler, Moore, and Guzman asserted that Mexican Americans did not usually enter densely populated urban areas rich with opportunities for employment, but instead settled in thinly populated desert and mountain areas that provided work in primary industries like mining, agriculture, and ranching. When Mexican Americans migrated to large cities, they lived in unrestricted housing in barrios with large concentrations of Mexican Americans —areas historically vulnerable to neighborhood elimination resulting from urban renewal.

In *The Changing Mexican-American* (1972), Rudolph Gomez suggested that there is no such thing as a Mexican-American culture because the Mexican-American population is characterized by differences in class status, housing and employment (especially the contrasts between rural and urban settings), education levels, and length of time living in the United States. Thus, assimilation may occur differently for different segments of the Mexican-American population. For example, marriage of second- and third-generation Mexican Americans could be an indicator of assimilation. **See also** Acculturation; Civil Rights; Discrimination; Economic Equality; Educational Opportunity. (SCV)

BIBLIOGRAPHY

Gomez, Rudolph, ed. *The Changing Mexican-American.* Boulder, CO: Pruett Publishing Company, 1972.

Grebler, Leo, Joan W. Moore, and Ralph C. Guzman. *The Mexican-American People.* New York: The Free Press, 1970.

Stenfield, Melvin. *Cracks in the Melting Pot: Racism and Discrimination in American History.* Beverly Hills, CA: Glencoe Press, 1970.

Joaquin Avila (1948–)

After Joaquin Avila graduated from Harvard Law School in 1973, he served as staff attorney to the **Mexican American Legal Defense and Educational Fund**. In 1982, he was elected president of the organization. During his term, he sought to improve the political position of Latinos; he also worked for passage of the **Voting Rights Act Amendments of 1982**. Avila has continued to fight for the political rights of Latinos in the 1990s. (SCV)

BIBLIOGRAPHY

Motrain, Dan. "Election: Watsonville." *Los Angeles Times* (Dec 5, 1989): A 31.

Turner, Wallace. "Coast Inquiry on Voter Registration Criticized." *New York Times* (May 12, 1982): D20.

B

Joseph Francis Baca (1936–)

From 1965 to 1966, Joseph Francis Baca acted as assistant district attorney of the Santa Fe, New Mexico. Baca worked as a special assistant to New Mexico's attorney general from 1966 to 1972. In 1972, he was appointed by New Mexico's governor, Bruce King, to fill a vacancy on the State District Court; Baca served three consecutive six-year terms there as a judge. During this time, he also served as a member of the Board Governing Recording of Judicial Proceedings, beginning in 1985. In 1988 Baca was elected to an eight-year term as justice of the Supreme Court of New Mexico. In 1995, he became a chief justice.

BIBLIOGRAPHY

Hetter, Katia. "Hispanic Bar Seeks to Increase Presence." *Wall Street Journal* (July 27, 1993): B6.

Polly Baca-Barragan (1941–)

In 1978 Polly Baca-Barragan became the first Mexican-American/Chicana to be elected to the Colorado State Senate. Previously, she had served in the Colorado House of Representatives. She was reelected to the state senate in 1982. A Democrat, Baca-Barragan served as vice-chair of the Democratic National Committee and as chairwoman of the Colorado Senate Caucus. **See also** Political Leadership. (SCV)

BIBLIOGRAPHY

Chavez, Lucy. "Colorado's Polly Baca-Barragan." *Nuestro* 4, no. 2 (April 1980).
"Polly Baca-Barragan: A Woman on the Move." *La Luz* 9, no. 6 (August–September 1981).

Herman Badillo (1929–)

In 1972 Herman Badillo became the first Puerto Rican United States congressman; he represented New York City. In 1974, he sponsored the **Bilingual Education** Act of 1974. He is a practicing attorney and on the Board of The City University of New York. **See also** Political Leadership. (VDD)

BIBLIOGRAPHY

"Courting Badillo: A Last Hurrah as Comptroller." *New York Times* (May 20, 1993): B1(L).
"Mr. Badillo's First Salvo." *New York Times* 144 (October 6, 1994): A28.

Joan Chandos Baez (1941–)

Joan Baez, a folk singer and songwriter of Mexican descent, has used the musical spotlight to publicize her views on equal rights and nonviolence. During the height of her popularity in the 1960s and 1970s, Baez participated in the **civil rights** movement and numerous antiwar protests. (VDD)

BIBLIOGRAPHY

Baez, Joan. *And a Voice to Sing With*. New York: Summit Books, 1987.
Baez, Joan and David Harris. *Coming Out*. New York: Pocket Books, 1971.

Romana Acosta Banuelos (1925–)

In 1971 President Richard M. Nixon appointed Romana Acosta Banuelos to serve as treasurer of the United States. Banuelos had already earned high visibility for her achievements as a businesswoman and a banker in Los Angeles. In 1949 Banuelos began a small tortilla factory that expanded into a $12 million-a-year business. In 1964 she helped establish the Pan American National Bank in East Los Angeles, serving as a director and as chairman of the board. Prior to her appointment she had been named Outstanding Businesswoman of the Year (1969) by the Chamber of Commerce in Los Angeles. Banuelos was the first Mexican American (and the sixth woman) to have been appointed treasurer; she carried out her duties from 1971 to 1974. Although she retained an interest in politics after her term as treasurer, Banuelos returned to Los Angeles to devote herself to her business interests. (SCV)

BIBLIOGRAPHY

Martinez, Al. *Rising Voices: Profiles of Hispanic-American Lives*. New York: New American Library, 1974.
Martinez, Diana. "The Strength Is in Money Says Romana Banuelos." *Nuestro* 3, no. 5 (June–July 1979): 34.

Casimiro Barela (1847–1920)

Casimiro Barela moved with his family from his native New Mexico to Las Animas County in southern Colorado, where he began his public life when he was elected justice of the peace in 1869. He later served as county assessor and was elected to the territorial legislature. In 1874 he was elected county sheriff. While serving as sheriff, Barela served as a delegate to the 1875 state constitutional convention, where he secured provisions in the Colorado state constitution that protected the civil rights of Spanish-speaking residents. He was elected to the first Colorado State Senate in 1876 and thereafter was continuously reelected until 1916. His 40 years of service earned him the title of "The Perpetual Senator." A strong Democratic leader in southern Colorado, Barela was twice elected president of the senate by his fellow legislators. He was also elected to and appointed to various national, state, and local offices of importance. (SCV)

BIBLIOGRAPHY

Burrola, Ray. *Casimiro Barela: A Case Study . . . Perspectives on Chicano Studies.* Los Angeles: National Association of Chicano Social Science, 1977.

Hunt, Inez. *The Barela Brand.* Colorado Springs: Colorado Springs Public Schools, 1971.

Xavier Becerra (1958–)

Xavier Becerra, a member of the Mexican-American and California Bar Associations, was deputy attorney general for the California State Department of Justice from 1987 to 1990. Becerra was then elected as a California state assemblyman, holding this post from 1990 to 1992. In 1992 he was elected to the United States House of Representatives as a Democrat. While in the House, Becerra functioned as a member of the Education and Labor Committee, the Judiciary and Science Committee, and the Space and Technology Committee. **See also** Political Leadership.

BIBLIOGRAPHY

Alvarez, Lizette. "For Hispanic Law Makers, Time to Take the Offensive." *The New York Times* (August 29, 1997): 14.

Meyerson, Harold. "Los Angeles Time Interview; Xavier Becerra; On Immigrant's Rights and the Emerging 'Latino-ism' in U.S. Politics." *Los Angeles Times* (June 29, 1997): 3.

Jaime Benítez (1908–)

Jaime Benítez, author, academic, politician, began a career in education at the University of Puerto Rico that spanned four decades: he was associate professor of social and political sciences (1931–1942), chancellor (1942–1966), and president of the University System of Puerto Rico (1966–1971). In addition to his academic career, Benítez also maintained an active role in numerous national and international organizations: he was a member of the United States National Commission for the United Nations Educational, Scientific, and Cultural Organization (UNESCO) from 1948 to 1954, and attended the UNESCO conventions in Paris, France (1950), and Havana, Cuba (1952); he was a member of the Constitutional Convention of Puerto Rico and the chairman of the Committee on the Bill of Rights from 1951 to 1952. He served as president of the National Association of State Universities from 1957 to 1958.

In 1972 Benítez was elected resident commissioner of Puerto Rico for a four-year term. In the U.S. House of Representatives he was assigned to the Committee on Education and Labor. After an unsuccessful reelection bid, Benítez returned to Puerto Rico where he taught at the Inter-American University of Puerto Rico from 1980 to 1986. Since then he has been a professor of government at the American College in Bayamón, Puerto Rico. **See** Constitution of Puerto Rico (1952) in Appendix 1.

BIBLIOGRAPHY

Hispanic Americans in Congress. Washington, D.C.: Government Printing Office, 1995.

Newlon, Clarke. *Famous Puerto Ricans.* New York: Dodd, Mead & Company, 1985.

Maria Antonietta Rodriguez Berriozabal (1941–)

Maria Antonietta Rodriguez Berriozabal served as an elected government official in San Antonio, Texas, for 10 years. Her tenure of service begin in 1980 when she ran for the San Antonio City Council. Her victory made her the first Hispanic to be elected to a citywide office in a major city. Berriozabal became noted for the political support she gave to unpopular issues such as affordable housing and the empowerment of community leaders. In 1991, she lost her bid to become mayor of San Antonio. Her concern for poor neighborhoods led her to champion neighborhood development. Berriozabal became concerned with the increase in juvenile crime and sought ways to stop it. She has been a fellow at Harvard's John F. Kennedy School of Government and continues to volunteer on social issues. (SCV)

BIBLIOGRAPHY

Telgen, Diane and Jim Kemp, eds. *Notable Hispanic American Women.* Detroit: Gale, 1993.

Biculturalism

Historically, biculturalism reflected efforts made by Mexican Americans and others to retain their own culture and language while learning the language and culture of the United States. In *Lau v. Nichols* **(1974),** the U.S. Supreme Court held that failure by the schools to meet the special language needs of minority children violated both the **Civil Rights Act of 1964** and the Fourteenth Amendment. This Court decision inspired a reaction against biculturalism and bilingualism, such as the "**English Only**" movement (starting in 1978). The national organization U.S. English, based in Washington, D.C., introduced "English-only" legislation to the U.S. Congress.

In *Introduction to Chicano Studies* (1977), Chris Garcia and Rudolf O. de la Garza describe U.S. culture as being one culture, with Hispanic culture being one component of the total American culture.

Where cultural differences in the Southwest have caused discriminatory practices against Hispanic minorities, these groups have sought help in the courts, in their own "mutualistas" (**mutual aid societies**), and in the **Treaty of Guadalupe Hidalgo** of 1848, which serves as the basis of all land claims. Today, many Mexican-American organizations address biculturalism in some capacity. George Isidore Sanchez (1906–1972), of the University of Texas, Austin, taught and wrote extensively about biculturalism; he lectured widely and directed many workshops, institutes, and programs on bicultural education. His pioneering philosophy and methods have served as the basis of most bicultural and **bilingual educational** programs. **See also** Acculturation; Assimilation; Discrimination; Educational Opportunity. **See** Treaty of Guadalupe Hidalgo (1848) in Appendix 1. (SCV)

BIBLIOGRAPHY

Duran, Livie Isauro and H. Russell Bernard. *Introduction to Chicano Studies.* New York: Macmillan, 1973.

Garcia, Chris F. and Rudolph O. de la Garza. *The Chicano Experience: Three Perspectives.* North Scituate, MA: Duxbury Press, 1977.

Sanchez, George I. *Forgotten People.* Albuquerque: University of New Mexico Press, 1940.

Bilingual Education

Congress passed the 1968 Bilingual Education Act in recognition of the growing number of linguistically and culturally diverse children enrolled in schools who, because of their limited English proficiency, were not receiving an education equal to their English-proficient peers. The legislation required that when the curriculum systematically "excludes minority group children from effective participation in the educational program offered by a school district," then "the district must take affirmative steps to rectify the language deficiency in order to open its instructional programs to these students."

During the 1970s, as a result of this legislation, many bilingual education programs were developed, designed to enable linguistically diverse children to achieve the same challenging academic standards required of all children enrolled in the nation's schools. Two methods of bilingual education emerged: classical and English as a second language (ESL). Classical programs have classes in the student's native language, whereas ESL features a combination of classes taught in English and the native language. In the beginning such programs addressed homogeneous students groups; for example, in California and the Southwest, Spanish students dominated the programs.

After the U.S. Supreme Court decision in *Lau v. Nichols* **(1974)**, help became available to all limited-English-proficient students. The Court decided that schools were responsible for helping "students who are certain to find their classroom experiences wholly incomprehensible because they do not understand English." Following that decision, the government mandated compliance through the **Equal Educational Opportunity Act (EEOA)** of 1974. Although neither the *Lau* decision nor the EEOA prescribed bilingual education, it evolved as the preferred method of compliance. To help school districts comply, the Office of Bilingual Education and Minority Language Affairs was established in 1974.

In the late 1970s and 1980s, students with a variety of backgrounds entered the school system in large numbers. Students came from such countries and regions as Vietnam, Laos, Cambodia, Haiti, Korea, China, and the Middle East. In Oc-

tober 1994, President Bill Clinton signed into law the Improving America's Schools Act (IASA), which reauthorized the Elementary and Secondary Education Act of 1965. The 1994 act mandated, for the first time, that state plans must include strategies for meeting the educational needs of limited-English-proficient (LEP) students. **See also** Acculturation; Assimilation; Biculturalism; Educational Opportunity. (VDD)

BIBLIOGRAPHY

Cornell, Charles. "Reducing Failure of LEP Students in the Mainstream Classroom and Why It Is Important." *The Journal of Educational Issues of Language Minority Students* (Boise State University), 15 (Winter 1995).

Black Berets

The Black Berets were founded in 1969 as a nationalistic paramilitary youth organization dedicated to issues pertaining especially to the Hispanic community. The group developed primarily in California and New Mexico, gaining the support of high-school-age students, dropouts, and other concerned youths. The group patterned itself deliberately after the Black Panthers, a militant African-American activist organization, in the hopes of being an equivalent proactive force in the **Chicano Power Movement**. Besides this vocal, proactive stance, the Black Berets involved themselves in community service activities and participated in peaceful high school demonstrations and walkouts. In spite of its high level of activism, the organization never gained widespread acceptance from the Mexican-American community because the group's radical actions and overly anticapitalistic stand turned some Hispanics away. **See also** Brown Berets.

BIBLIOGRAPHY

Castro, Tony. *Chicano Power.* New York: Dutton, 1974.

Ben Blaz Garrido (1928–)

Elected in 1984 to the U.S. House of Representatives as a Republican nonvoting member from Guam, Ben Blaz served until 1992 when he lost his reelection bid. During his stay in the House, he was the key player in drafting a bill that would have given Guam commonwealth status, allowed Guam to control immigration, exempted Guam from federal tax laws and regulation, and given Guam the right of approval over treaties concerning the commonwealth. Prior to his service in the House, Blaz was a brigadier general in the U.S. Marine Corps. He served in the military from 1951 to 1980. In his almost 30 years of military service, he received the Legion of Merit Medal and the Navy Commendation Medal. In addition, he received the Bronze Medal and the Vietnamese Cross of Gallantry. (CEM)

BIBLIOGRAPHY

Trainor, Bernard E. "Washington Talk: Congress; Lack of Vote Doesn't Deter Delegate from Guam." *The New York Times* (February 23, 1988): G.

Bloody Christmas Case

Seven Hispanic youths were arrested in Los Angeles on Christmas Eve, 1951, for battery and interfering with police officers. They were taken back to the police station where a holiday party was underway; the youths were then beaten by intoxicated police officers during the party. In 1952, the Los Angeles grand jury indicted the eight police officers who were involved. All of the indicted officers were disciplined and some were sentenced to prison time.

BIBLIOGRAPHY

Skerry, Peter. *Mexican Americans.* New York: Free Press, 1993.

Henry Bonilla (1954–)

Henry Bonilla's election to the U.S. House of Representatives as a Republican member in 1992 was a surprise because he defeated an incumbent from the 23rd District of Texas (which covers the San Antonio area). Bonilla's election was very important for Republicans because Latinos tend to vote for Democrat candidates. He was one of two freshmen selected to sit on the powerful House Appropriations Committee. He has used his position on this committee to drum up support for bills that would provide funding for wastewater treatment facilities and Earned Income Credit. Prior to his election, Bonilla worked at TV stations across the country and served as the press secretary for Pennsylvania governor Richard Thornburg. Bonilla's ties with television were key assets in his election. He is known in his district—which is 63 percent Hispanic and one of the poorest in the state—as someone close to the people. **See also** Political Leadership. (CEM)

BIBLIOGRAPHY

Duncan, Philip D. and Christine C. Lawrence. *Politics in America: 1996. The 104th Congress.* Washington, DC: Congressional Quarterly Press, 1995.

Kurtz, Howard. "Big Apple Gets Plum Spot; NY Times Reporter to Head Bureau Here." *The Washington Post* (October 9, 1997): B4.

Tony Bonilla (1936–)

Tony Bonilla, a noted Mexican-American **civil rights** activist and attorney, began his political and public service career when he was a member of the Texas State Legislature from 1964 to 1967. For many years Bonilla has worked to ensure that issues confronting the Latino community are included in public debate. By the end of the 1970s, Bonilla believed that progressive political expression had been effectively stifled in the United States. To advance his political objectives, therefore, Bonilla cofounded the **National Hispanic Leadership Conference (NHLC)** in 1983. The NHLC started work in prevention and support programs against drug abuse in Hispanic communities. Through the NHLC, in coordination with other civil rights organizations, Bonilla has promoted economic improvement for Hispanics and other minorities. **See also** Political Participation. (SCV)

BIBLIOGRAPHY

Coleman, Milton. "Hispanics' Issues: Cutbacks, Clout; In Detroit, Blaming Reagan and Envying Black Success." *The Washington Post* (July 1, 1983): A2.

Hoffman, David. "Bush Promises to Name Hispanic to His Cabinet; Pledge Comes amid Competition for Voting Bloc in Three Key States." *The Washington Post* (July 7, 1988): A6.

Box Bill

The Box Bill, named after Congressman John C. Box of Texas, was a proposed amendment to the Immigration Act of 1924 that would have limited Mexican immigration to the United States to 2,000 people a year. This limitation would have brought the number of Mexicans allowed to immigrate in line with the numbers from European countries. National hearings were held on the proposal to determine the impact of such a restriction. Farmers, ranchers, and railroad executives were concerned that the limitation would reduce the labor pools and drive up both costs and prices. Labor unions supported the restrictions hoping to benefit from increased wages and employment. In the end, the commercial interests won out and the amendment was defeated. **See also** Immigration Policy and Hispanics.

BIBLIOGRAPHY

Kansas, Sidney. *Immigration and Nationality Act Annotated.* New York: Immigration Publishers, 1953.

Brown Berets

The Brown Berets were founded in 1967 in Los Angeles, California, by David Sanchez, Carlos Montez, and Ralph Ramirez. The Brown Berets were originally dedicated to serving the Mexican-American community by easing tensions between Chicanos and the police, but the organization soon adopted physical, proactive measures similar to the Black Panthers, the militant African-American activist group. Membership eventually began to grow, as large numbers of young Hispanics, especially high school dropouts, flocked to the group. As membership peaked, the group began sporting military-style garb, a reflection of their aggressive stand.

In March 1968, the Brown Berets organized a series of high school protests and demonstrations to illustrate the condition of Latino education. However, accusations soon arose that the group was attempting to start riots, sell narcotics, and spread communist ideas. The police were called in to break up the protests. For the next few years, the group operated the East Los Angeles Free Clinic, gaining financial support for the endeavor from the Ford Foundation.

In August 1972, 26 members of the Brown Berets took over Santa Catalina Island, one of the Channel Islands located off the coast of California. The group claimed that their invasion was in response to illegal U.S. occupation of Mexican land. Spokesman David Sanchez stated that according to the **Treaty of Guadalupe Hidalgo**, the Channel Islands were never given to the United States after the **Mexican War**. The Brown Berets occupied the island—which the group renamed Aztlan Libre—for 24 hours, after which time deputy police drove the protesters back to the mainland. Later that year, Sanchez officially disbanded the Brown Berets; while the group symbolized the protests of many Mexican Americans, disorganization and an unclear political refinement were sighted as the group's downfall. **See also** Black Berets. **See** Treaty of Guadalupe Hidalgo (1848) in Appendix 1.

BIBLIOGRAPHY

Costello, Michael. "Don't Blame Sam Smith for Hispanic Decline." *Lewiston Morning Tribune* (October 25, 1997): 10A.

Shorris, Earl. *Latinos: A Biography of the People.* New York: Avon Books, 1992.

Georgia L. Brown (1948–)

Georgia Brown, a Democratic Party activist, worked on Jimmy Carter's successful 1976 presidential campaign, as well as his failed attempt at reelection in 1980. Brown's involvement with the Carter campaign led Brown to begin a political consulting firm in 1977 with her husband Chris Brown. In 1992 she worked on the reelection campaigns of Nevada Senator Harry Reid, Maryland Congressman Steny H. Hoyer, and New Mexico Congressman Bill Richardson. Brown and her husband also worked on Gary Hart and Richard Gephard's Democratic Party presidential nomination bids in 1984 and 1998, respectively.

BIBLIOGRAPHY

Telgen, Diane and Jim Kamp, eds. *Notable Hispanic American Women.* Detroit: Gale Research, 1993.

Juan C. Burciaga (1929–)

After graduating from the U.S. Military Academy at West Point in 1952, Juan Burciaga served as 1st Lieutenant in the U.S. Air Force until 1959, when he returned to school to obtain his law degree. After school, he clerked for a U.S. district judge before becoming an associate at the law firm of McRae, Vissery, Mims, Ortega and Kitts. In 1979 Burciaga was named a judge to the federal district courts and went on to serve as chief U.S. district judge in Albuquerque, New Mexico.

BIBLIOGRAPHY

Armijo, Patrick. "State Gives Up Annuity Fight." *Albuquerque Journal* (February 17, 1995): 1.

"Burciaga Championed Individual Rights." *Albuquerque Journal* (March 7, 1995): A6.

Busing

Busing has been an issue in the Hispanic community since the 1960s. In Los Angeles, Chicano activists sometimes advocated busing in response to parental concerns about improving **educational opportunity**. In general, however, community leaders did not embrace busing and desegregation. In New York City, for example, integrationists shifted their demands from busing to local control of schools. In turn, parents would have greater influence in the education of their children. **See also** Civil Rights. (VDD)

BIBLIOGRAPHY

DiConti, Veronica D. *Interest Groups and Education Reform. The Latest Crusade to Restructure the Schools.* Lanham, MD: University Press of America, 1996.

Albert Garza Bustamante (1935–)

Born and reared in Asherton, Texas, Albert Bustamante, a Democrat, was elected to the U.S. House of Representatives in 1984 from San Antonio, Texas; he served in the House until he lost a reelection bid in 1992 to the Republican candidate, Matthew Martinez. Bustamante was known for his efforts in defending military spending for the San Antonio area rather than supporting military activities outside his district. In addition, he sought aid to improve public education, expand food programs for the Hispanic community, and increase benefits to retired military personnel. His membership on the House Armed Services and Government Operations committees facilitated his activities in these areas. In the late 1980s, the FBI began an investigation on racketeering relating to Bustamante's activities, and it was also revealed that he had overdrawn 30 checks in the House bank; these were two factors that led to his eventual defeat. Prior to his congressional career, he served on the Bexar County Commission and as a county judge. (CEM)

BIBLIOGRAPHY

Cardwell, Cary. "Bustamante Gets 3-1/2 Year Term for Racketeering." *The Houston Chronicle* (October 2, 1993): 29.

Fernando E. Cabeza de Baca (1937–)

A businessman and public servant, Fernando Cabeza de Baca was appointed special assistant to the president by President Gerald Ford in 1974. Earlier in his career, he served as commissioner of the New Mexico Department of Transportation and western regional director for the U.S. Department of Health, Education, and Welfare. He has worked closely with veterans groups and **civil rights** organizations, including the American Legion and the **League of United Latin American Citizens**. In addition, he has aided minority businesses and has lectured at Harvard University on the free enterprise system. (SCV)

BIBLIOGRAPHY

"Presidential Assistant Fernando C. de Baca." *La Luz* 4, no. 5 (September–October 1975).

Cabinet Committee on Opportunities for Spanish-Speaking People

Founded in 1969, and headed by Henry Ramirez, the cabinet committee was charged with continuing the work begun by President Lyndon Johnson's Inter-Agency Committee on Mexican Americans. The goal of the committee was to ensure that Spanish-speaking people were aware of federal programs designed to help them, and to create new federal programs to meet the needs of the Hispanic community. The committee got little support from President Richard Nixon and was widely criticized from within the Hispanic community for not accomplishing many of its goals. The committee was disbanded in 1974.

BIBLIOGRAPHY

Hero, Rodney E. *Latinos and the U.S. Political System.* Philadelphia: Temple University Press, 1992.
Moore, Joan and Harry Packon. *Hispanics in the United States.* Englewood Cliffs, NJ: Prentice Hall, 1985.

Jose A. Cabranes (1940–)

After practicing law from 1967 to 1973, Jose Cabranes served as a special counsel to the governor of Puerto Rico, as well as an administrator in Washington, D.C., for the Office of the Commonwealth of Puerto Rico. From 1975 to 1979, he served as general counsel for Yale University. During the late 1970s, Cabranes began his service in the administration of President Jimmy Carter; Cabranes was a member of the President's Commission on Mental Health from 1977 to 1978, a United States delegate to the Belgrade Conference on Security and Cooperation in Europe from 1977 to 1978, and a consultant to the U.S. secretary of state in 1978. In 1979 Cabranes was appointed a judge in the U.S. District Court of Connecticut, and in December 1988 he became a member of the Federal Courts Study Committee. In 1994 Cabranes became the first native Puerto Rican to be appointed to a federal appeals court in the continental United States.

BIBLIOGRAPHY

Lightman, David. "Cabranes Lauded in Judiciary Session." *The Hartford* [Connecticut] *Courant* (July 22, 1994): A3.
Navarrette, Ruben, Jr. "Hispanics Have Eye on Judge; Lawyers Agree He's Tops to Ascend to Supreme Court." *The Arizona Republic* (October 18, 1997): B1.

Angelina Cabrera

An advocate for the Hispanic and Puerto Rican communities, Angelina Cabrera began working on Democratic Senator George McGovern's presidential campaign in 1972 and subsequently became deputy director in 1975 of the Women's Division at the Executive Chamber (the State Cabinet). She helped organize the National Women's Conference in Houston in 1978 and was vice president of Capital Formation, which assists women and minority owned businesses. Cabrera also directed the National Puerto Rican Forum and worked as the assistant deputy commissioner for the New York State Department of Economic Development's Minority and Women's Business Division.

BIBLIOGRAPHY

Telgen, Diane and Jim Kamp, eds. *Notable Hispanic American Women.* Detroit: Gale Research, 1993.

California Anti-Vagrancy Act (1855)

This anti-vagrancy ordinance was adopted by the California legislature in 1855. The measure was largely anti-Mexican American; Section Two of the act identifies the subject of the law to be those persons "commonly known as Greasers." The law required a special application and tax to fulfill California's migrant labor laws. In 1856, the "Greaser" clause was removed from the act, but it still continued to have an anti-Mexican American bias. **See also** Discrimination.

BIBLIOGRAPHY

Pitt, Leonard. *The Decline of the Californios*. Berkeley: University of California Press, 1968.

California Proposition 187

This controversial ballot initiative, approved by 59 percent of California voters in November 1994, regulated the amount of government services that undocumented residents of the state could receive. This proposition banned residents who were not citizens from receiving any education from the publicly supported elementary, secondary, and postsecondary schools in California; the measure also banned other social welfare, health, or law enforcement protection. The day after the election a California Superior Court judge ordered that the ban on providing education to undocumented workers be blocked. A week later, a U.S. District Court judge issued a temporary order that halted the implementation of most of the ballot"s remaining provisions. The legal obstruction to implementing Proposition 187 arose in response to constitutional questions raised in lawsuits by the Los Angeles Unified School District. The proposition potentially increased the risk to the larger society by not allowing undocumented citizens to receive free immunizations or other health care. Other parts of the ballot that were blocked included the requirement that educators and social and health workers report suspected undocumented workers. Furthermore, Proposition 187 did not allow the provision of federally funded services to nonresidents. Such programs are funded on the basis of the number of clients served, and the loss of federal support for health and welfare programs could have cost California $15 billion in federal funds.

Regardless of the effective legal blocks on implementing Proposition 187, the approval of the measure provoked a firestorm of protest, led by Hispanic organizations. In 1994, the vast majority of the approximately 1.5 million undocumented workers in California were Hispanic. **See also** Discrimination; Educational Opportunity; Illegal Aliens; Immigration; Immigration Policy and Hispanics. (JRB)

BIBLIOGRAPHY

Cowley, Geoffrey and Andrew Murr. "Good Politics, Bad Medicine." *Newsweek* 124 (December 5, 1994): 31–35.
Gwynne, S.C. "The Unwelcome Mat." *Time* 144, no. 22 (November 28, 1994): 35–36.
Zuckerman, Mortimer. "Beyond Proposition 187." *U.S. News & World Report* 124, no. 117 (December 5, 1994): 124.

California Proposition 209

This state ballot proposition, which would have eliminated **affirmative action** in state contracting, education, and employment, sparked great controversy after it qualified for the 1996 elections in California. Proposition 209 promised to make it illegal for any state institution to use race and gender as selection criteria in the distribution of any state benefit. The proposition pitted vocal supporters of affirmative action against conservative critics who argued that preferential policies benefiting minorities, including women, helped to aggravate ethnic tensions by discriminating against qualified candidates. The proposition gained national attention in the 1996 presidential campaign when Republican candidate Robert Dole endorsed it. This proposition never gained national prominence, in part because President Bill Clinton ignored it. The proposition was approved by 54 percent of California voters on election day, but its provisions have not gone into effect due to continuing legal challenges that argue that the measure is unconstitutional. **See also** Assimilation; Discrimination; Economic Equality. (JRB)

BIBLIOGRAPHY

Lemann, Nicholas. "California Here We Come . . . ?" *Time* 148, no. 15 (October 7, 1996): 44–46.
Rice, Connie. "Toward Affirmative Reaction." *The Nation* 264, no. 2 (January 13–20, 1997): 22–24.

California Proposition 63

California Proposition 631986—called Proposition 63 by most people—declared that "English is the Official Language of California." The measure received a stunning 73 percent of the popular vote in the elections of November 1986. The proposition was spearheaded by U.S. English, an organization formed in 1983 by former U.S. Senator S. I. Hayakawa and others. The measure was opposed by **civil rights** organizations like the American Civil Liberties Union and the **National Council of La Raza,** which saw the measure as anti-Hispanic.

The successful adoption of the measure has led to similar measures being adopted and put on ballots across the country. At the time of the proposition's adoption seven states besides California (Nebraska, Illinois, Virginia, Indiana, Kentucky, Georgia, and Tennessee) had similar measures and 25 more states were considering adoption of such a measure. However, no state with non-English speaking populations as large as California had adopted or even seemed likely to adopt the measure. **See also** Acculturation; Biculturalism; English First/English Only.

BIBLIOGRAPHY

Chavez, Linda. *Out of the Barrio*. New York: Basic Books, 1991.
Ingram, Carl and Douglas Shuit. "Lawmakers Return, Face Tough New Issues." *Los Angeles Times* (December 2, 1986): 3.
Okerblom, Jim. "Hysteria against Hispanics Decried." *San Diego Union-Tribune* (January 10, 1987): B3.

California Rural Legal Assistance (CRLA)

Begun in 1966, California Rural Legal Assistance (CRLA) began offering free legal assistance to rural Californians, many of whom were Mexican American. Funded by the State Office of Economic Opportunity, the CRLA was soon handling thousands of cases each year. But despite its success, by the late 1960s, conservative politicians in California, including Republican Governor Ronald Reagan, opposed the agency and tried unsuccessfully to cut its' funding. With the election of Democratic Governor Jerry Brown, the opposition to CRLA subsided, and by the 1980s the agency had grown to 12 offices throughout rural California and was handling more than 10,000 cases a year. The CRLA also reports on the status of education, housing, and employment in rural areas and publishes a bimonthly newsletter called *Noticero*.

BIBLIOGRAPHY

Alvarez, Fred. "Oxnard Is Sued for Withholding Housing Funds." *Los Angeles Times* (August 24, 1993): B1.

Breton, Marcos. "State Group Has Long Toiled in Behalf of Farm Workers." *Sacramento Bee* (March 26, 1995): A13.

California Statehood

In January 1850, representatives from California asked to join the United States. The state's population had grown so rapidly (due to the huge influx of people in search of gold) that Californians asked for admittance to the United States years earlier than expected. California became a state in the autumn of 1850, as part of the **Compromise of 1850**, with its state constitution prohibiting slavery. The state brought with it a large native Hispanic population and a rapidly growing Chinese population. (JRB)

BIBLIOGRAPHY

Ellison, William. *A Self-Governing Dominion: California, 1846–1850.* Berkeley and Los Angeles: University of California Press, 1950.

Santiago E. Campos (1926–)

Santiago E. Campos served in the U.S. Navy during World War II. From 1954 to 1957, Campos acted as assistant attorney general for the State of New Mexico. He also served from 1971 to 1978 as a district judge in New Mexico. In 1978 Campos was appointed by President Jimmy Carter to serve in the U.S. States District Court for the District of New Mexico.

BIBLIOGRAPHY

"Judge Removes a Defendant in Newspaper Battle." *The New York Times* (June 22, 1980): 16.

Jose T. Canales (1877–1976)

A state legislative representative serving in the 29th to 31st and 35th to 36th legislative sessions from Brownsville, Texas, Jose Canales is best known for the charges he brought against the Texas Rangers in 1918. He alleged that the rangers were mistreating Mexican Americans; as a result of the suit, the rangers were reduced to five companies totaling 75 men from the nearly 1,000 men who had been appointed during World War I. Canales also served as president of the **League of United Latin American Citizens (LULAC)** from 1932 to 1933. **See also** Civil Rights.

BIBLIOGRAPHY

Samora, Julian, et al. *Gunpowder Justice.* Notre Dame, IN: University of Notre Dame Press, 1979.

Judy Canales (1962–)

Judy Canales has worked for the Low Income Housing Information Service and coauthored *The Hispanic Housing Crisis.* After receiving her M.A. in urban studies, she began working for the city of San Antonio, Texas, in the Department of Economic and Employment Development; she then moved to Phoenix, Arizona, where she became the counselor for the City of Phoenix Equal Opportunity Department. In 1987 she took the position of housing and community development policy fellow for the **National Council of La Raza.** Since 1991 Canales has served as president of the **Mexican American Women's National Association** (MANA) and as a legislative representative for housing, community development, and economic development for New York City.

BIBLIOGRAPHY

Garcia, Mario T. *Mexican Americans.* New Haven, CT: Yale University Press, 1989.

Telgen, Diane and Jim Kamp, eds. *Notable Hispanic American Women.* Detroit: Gale Research, 1993.

Cannery and Agricultural Workers Industrial Union (CAWIU)

A short-lived but powerful union, the Cannery and Agricultural Workers Industrial Union (CAWIU) began in 1931 as an offspring of the Agricultural Workers Industrial League and was associated with the Trade Union Unity League, a communist organization. Between 1932 and 1934, the CAWIU led approximately 24 agricultural strikes, which involved approximately 38,400 workers. The strikes taught Mexican-American workers how to organize and had a positive impact on conditions and wages of agricultural workers. During the San Francisco General Strike of 1934, the Sacramento offices of the union were invaded and many of the leaders were arrested. This, along with improved conditions for the workers, led to declining membership and interest in the CAWIU, and in 1935, it, along with the Trade Union Unity League, ceased to exist.

BIBLIOGRAPHY

Jamieson, Stuart. *Labor Unionism in American Agriculture.* Washington, DC: U.S. Government Printing Office, 1945.

Luisa Capetilla (1879–1922)

Luisa Capetilla was a labor organizer and defender of women's rights in Puerto Rico. In the early 1900s, she struggled to improve worker's living conditions and to obtain suffrage for women. Defying popular social conventions, she is also remembered as the first Puerto Rican woman to wear pants. **See also** Civil Rights; Voting Rights. (MP)

BIBLIOGRAPHY

Lopez, Antonetty Evelina. *Luisa Capetillo.* New York: Centro de Estudios Puertorriquenos (Hunter College), 1986.

Wilfredo Caraballo (1947–)

Wilfredo Caraballo was born in Puerto Rico. While studying law at New York University, he interned for the **Puerto Rican Legal Defense Fund** and worked as an academic counselor and advisor for the New York University School of Higher Educational Opportunities Program. Since 1988 he has been a professor and associate dean at Seton Hall University School of Law in New Jersey. Caraballo has served on the board of directors of the Puerto Rican Legal Defense Fund, and in 1993 he became president of the **Hispanic National Bar Association.** In 1997 he was elected to the New Jersey State Assembly.

BIBLIOGRAPHY

Gray, Jerry. "Vowing a Fight, Florio Names Advocate." *New York Times* (July 24, 1992): B5.

King, Wayne. "Public Advocate Troubling to New Jersey's Privileged." *New York Times* (September 9, 1991): B1.

Alice Cardona

In 1985, Alice Cardona worked as a program associate for the New York State Division for Women. In 1986, she formed the Hispanic AIDS Forum, an education group dedicated to informing Latinos about the disease. Cardona began two other advocacy groups: the Women and AIDS Project of the New York State Division for Women (which served as a support group for women affected by AIDS) and the Women and AIDS Research Network (which provided information and referrals to women). From 1970 to 1978, Cardona worked as an educational counselor, eventually becoming project coordinator of **ASPIRA**, a Puerto Rican educational service group. She also acted as the ASPIRA Parent/Student Guidance Program director from 1971 to 1973 and as ASPIRA's assistant executive director of community relations from 1973 to 1974. From 1973 to 1974, Cardona was an advisor to New York's Commission of Education, as well as a charter member of the National Conference of Puerto Rican Women.

BIBLIOGRAPHY

Bertrand, Donald. "Queens People in Profile." *New York Daily News* (November 18, 1996): 4.

McKenna, Sheila. "Alice Cardona." *Newsday* (May 26, 1994): 4.

Lourdes Casal (1938–1981)

Lourdes Casal was born in Havana, Cuba, and, as a student, sided with Castro. However, four years later, opposing the communist regime, she sought asylum in the United States. While earning a Ph.D. in 1975 from The New School for Social Research, she published a compilation of essays on the situation in Cuba and helped create the *Revista Areito*, a magazine devoted to Cuban issues. She organized two symposia on Cuban studies, and created the Instituto de Estudios Cubanos in New York. In 1973 she returned to Cuba and thereafter resumed being a devoted follower of the Castro regime believing that the communist regime was good for her country. She helped found the Antonio Maceo Brigade and continued to write and publish articles on Cuba.

BIBLIOGRAPHY

Casal, Lourdes. "Cubans in the United States: Their Impact on U.S.–Cuban Relations." In Martin Weinstein, ed. *Revolutionary Cuba in the World Arena.* Philadelphia: Institute for the Study of Human Issues, 1979.

Rivero, Eliana. "From Immigrants to Ethnics: Cuban Women Writers in the U.S." In Eliana Orrega et al., eds. *Breaking Boundaries: Latina Writing and Critical Readings.* Amherst: University of Massachusetts Press, 1989.

Leonel Castillo (1939–)

During the 1960s Leonel Castillo worked as a Peace Corps supervisor in the Philippines. In 1970 he was elected city comptroller for Houston, Texas; he continued in this position until becoming treasurer of the Texas Democratic Party in 1974. In 1977 he became the first Mexican American to be appointed commissioner of the United States **Immigration and Naturalization Service** (INS). He remained with the INS until resigning in 1979.

BIBLIOGRAPHY

Hispanic Border Leadership Institute Web site <http://www.nmsu.edu>.

Raul Castro (1920–)

Raul Castro, former governor of the state of Arizona, served in various political positions with the state Democratic Party. Castro was born in Mexico, but his family moved to Arizona when he was a youth. In 1955 he was elected Pima County attorney; he was elected judge in 1964 and became ambassador to Bolivia in 1968. In 1974 Castro became governor of Arizona. In 1977, during the Carter administration, he stepped down as governor to accept the post of ambassador to Argentina, a post he held until the Reagan administration took office in 1981. (SCV)

BIBLIOGRAPHY

Chanin, Abe and Mildred Chanin. *This Land, These Voices.* Flagstaff, AZ: Northland Press, 1977.

"La Luz Interview: Governor of Arizona." *La Luz* 4, no. 5 (October 1975).

Salvador B. Castro (1933–)

Salvador Castro became active in the **Mexican American Political Association** and the Democratic Party while in college in Los Angeles during the late 1950 and early 1960s. He began teaching in the Los Angeles city schools and is best remembered for his involvement in the 1968 BLOW-OUT, in which about 5,000 mostly Hispanic students staged walkouts, sit-ins, and demonstrations for two weeks. Castro, along with 12 others, was charged with having conspired to organize the demonstrations. All were released and later cleared of any charges, but Castro remained barred from teaching for five years. **See also** Educational Opportunity; Political Participation.

BIBLIOGRAPHY

Fineman, Mark. "Group's Anti-Corruption Crusade in Mexican Town Mirrors a Movement." *Los Angeles Times* (June 7, 1997): 5.

Lauro F. Cavazos (1927–)

Lauro Cavazos began his career as an educator, eventually becoming dean of Tufts University School of Medicine and president of Texas Tech University in Lubbock, Texas. Because of this experience, Cavazos was appointed secretary of education in 1988, where he served in President Ronald Reagan's cabinet. This role gained Cavazos the distinction of being the first Hispanic named to a cabinet-level position. In 1989 Cavazos was reappointed as secretary of education by President George Bush, whom he worked with in establishing the executive order that created the President's Council on Educational Excellence for Hispanic Americans. In December 1990, Cavazos resigned from his cabinet position.

BIBLIOGRAPHY

"The Amazing Cavazos Family." *Texas* (February 5, 1989): 5–7.

Hernandez, Antonia. "La Educacion: El Secretario Cavazos esta equivocado." *Replica* 21 (July 1990): 14–15.

Carmen Consuelo Cerezo (1940–)

Judge Carmen Cerezo was educated at the University of Puerto Rico. In 1967 he became a law clerk at the U.S. District Court in San Juan, and in 1972 he became a judge in the Superior Court of Puerto Rico. He later served as judge on the Puerto Rican Court of Intermediate Appeals; in 1980 he was appointed by President Jimmy Carter to be judge of the U.S. District Court in Hato Rey, Puerto Rico.

BIBLIOGRAPHY

"$32 Million Fire in Pollution Case." *The New York Times* (May 6, 1987): 22.

Maggie Cervantes (1958–)

Maggie Cervantes has been both a city official and a longtime grassroots activist in her native Los Angeles. While studying Chicano studies in college, she founded and served as president of the Loyola student chapter of **Comision Femenil Mexicana Nacional (CFMN),** an organization to empower and aid Hispanic women. She began her government career in the Human Resources Division of the Los Angeles Department of Water and Power, and was a member of the Hispanic Consumer Advisory Board of the Southern California Gas Company. She remained active in the community, aiding voter registration drives; in 1990, was named president of CFMN. The same year she was named secretary of the board of Professional Hispanics in Energy. In 1992 Cervantes became executive director for the New Economics for Women, an organization dedicated to housing and economic issues facing Hispanic women. After the riots in Los Angeles in 1992, she was instrumental in garnering financial support from outside sources to rebuild the community.

BIBLIOGRAPHY

Telgen, Diane and Jim Kamp, eds. *Notable Hispanic American Women.* Detroit: Gale Research, 1993.

Jose Francisco Chaves (1833–1904)

Jose Francisco Chaves was a member of the Union Army during the Civil War, eventually rising to the rank of lieutenant colonel. Chaves also served as a Republican in the U.S. Congress from March 4, 1865, to March 3, 1867, and again from February 20, 1869, to March 3, 1871, acting both times as delegate from the Territory of New Mexico. Chaves was a district attorney in New Mexico from 1875 to 1877, as well as a member and president of the 1889 State Constitutional Convention. In 1903, Chaves was made state superintendent of public instruction and state historian of New Mexico, a post he held until his assassination a year later.

BIBLIOGRAPHY

Vigil, Maurilio E. *Hispanics in Congress.* Lanham, MD: University Press of America, 1996.

Cesar Chavez (1927–1993)

Cesar Chavez was one of the most important Chicano leaders of the late twentieth century. As the grandchild of Mexican immigrants to the United States, he was born into poverty. His family moved to California in 1938 during the Great Depression, and Chavez worked as a migrant laborer in the agricultural fields of California for 14 years. In 1952 he joined the Community Service Organization, which had been created to help Hispanics in the West. Chavez worked with this group for 10 years, becoming increasingly occupied with the organization of migrant, mostly Mexican, farm laborers in the region and with the improvement of their working conditions. He left the Community Service Organization in 1962 to form a union for migrant workers in California.

In 1965 grape pickers began a strike in Southern California against an employer who cut their wages. Chavez persuaded the union, later to be known as the **United Farm Workers**, to join the strike. Inspired by the ideals of nonviolence articulated by Martin Luther King Jr., Chavez and the union organized a popular boycott of vineyard products beginning in October 1965. The strike lasted five years. Chavez gained powerful supporters for his cause, including Senator Robert F. Kennedy. In 1968 Chavez served as a delegate to the Democratic National Convention.

In 1970, 23 California growers signed a contract with Chavez's union, and the strike was lifted. The growers agreed to provide better wages and better working conditions. Chavez effectively used his personal charisma and communication skills to bring about important gains in the organization of farm workers and in the struggle for their rights. In 1975 the California legislature passed the Agricultural Labor Relations Act, the first act in the continental United States that allowed collective bargaining for agricultural workers. Chavez continued and broadened this struggle for equality until his death in 1993, after more than 40 years of fighting for the recognition of **civil rights** for farm workers and Hispanics. **See also** Saul Alinsky; Grape Boycott; Dolores Fernandez Huerta; Lettuce Strikes (Salinas); United Farmer Workers Organizing Committee. (JRB)

BIBLIOGRAPHY

Castillo, Richard. *Cesar Chavez: A Triumph of Spirit.* Norman: University of Oklahoma Press, 1995.

Rodriguez, Consuelo. *Cesar Chavez.* New York: Chelsea House, 1991.

Taylor, Ronald. *Chavez and the Farmworkers.* Boston: Beacon Press, 1975.

Dennis Chavez (1888–1962)

Dennis Chavez was the first Hispanic American Democrat ever elected to the United States Senate from New Mexico; he served from 1935 to 1962. Prior to his election, he was a member of the U.S. House of Representatives, where he had spent four years. Chavez began his political career with the help of Senator Andrieus A. Jones from New Mexico. Chavez served as a clerk in the office of the secretary of the Senate. Concurrently, he pursued a law degree at Georgetown University. After receiving the degree and passing the bar, he went back to New Mexico and began practicing law. His first stop on the way to becoming a U.S. senator was the New Mexico House of Representatives where he served for one term. **See also** Political Leadership. (CEM)

Dennis Chavez (D-NM) served in both the House of Representatives and the U.S. Senate. *Library of Congress.*

BIBLIOGRAPHY

Keleher, William A. *Memoirs: 1892–1969, A New Mexico Item.* Santa Fe, NM: Rydal Press, 1969.

Perrigo, Lynn I. *Hispanos: Historic Leaders in New Mexico.* Santa Fe, NM: Sunstone Press, 1985.

Linda Chavez (1947–)

During the 1970s, Linda Chavez worked with the Democratic National Committee, the National Education Association, and the Department of Health, Education, and Welfare. She also worked with the American Federation of Teachers (AFT), where she was editor of the AFT's quarterly magazine *American Educator.* In 1981 Chavez began serving as a consultant for President Ronald Reagan's administration, going on to serve Reagan in a number of capacities during the 1980s.

In 1983 Chavez held several posts in the U.S. States Commission on Civil Rights, eventually being appointed staff director. In this role, she helped monitor the enforcement of **civil rights** laws and sought reversal of racial hiring quotas. In 1985 Chavez was made director of the White House Office of Public Liaison, a position that made her the highest rank-ing woman in the Reagan administration. She left this position in 1986, focusing instead on an unsuccessful run for the U.S. Senate seat from Maryland. From 1986 to 1988, Chavez served as president of **U.S. English**, a group lobbying to make English the official (and only) national language. After this, she worked with the Manhattan Institute for Policy Research, where she published *Out of the Barrio: Toward a New Politics of Hispanic Assimilation* (1991). She currently is head of The Center for Equal Opportunity. **See also** Acculturation; Assimilation.

BIBLIOGRAPHY

Barrett, Paul M. "Linda Chavez and the Exploitation of Ethnic Identity." *Washington Monthly* 17 (June 1985): 25–29.

Chavez, Linda. *Out of the Barrio.* New York: Basic Books, 1991.

Chicago Riots of 1966

In 1966 hundreds of Chicago Puerto Rican youths went on a rampage, breaking windows and burning down many of the businesses in their neighborhoods. The riots were ostensibly in response to an incident of police brutality. The underlying causes, however, were much broader. The participants linked the causes to the urban blight that characterized their life in Chicago. This time also saw the rise of militant organizations that rejected the orientation of earlier groups. As the Chicano and black pride movements pervaded the consciousness of their respective communities, a similar voice was heard in the Puerto Rican barrios throughout the country. Foremost among the new militants were the **Young Lords**, a grass-roots youth group that was similar to the Black Panthers in the black community and the **Brown Berets** in the Chicano. They promoted Puerto Rican pride and put forth an agenda to change poverty-stricken neighborhoods. In both New York and Chicago, the Young Lords promoted neighborhood improvements using tactics such as sit-ins at inservice agencies and in churches.

BIBLIOGRAPHY

Miyares, Marcelino. *Models of Political Participation of Hispanic-Americans.* New York: Arno Press, 1980.

Young Lords Party and Michael Abramson. *Palante: Young Lords Party.* New York: McGraw-Hill, 1971.

Chicano Moratorium to the War in Vietnam (1970)

The Chicano Moratorium was planned as a Los Angeles rally against the Vietnam War by Chicano activist groups. Various student organizations, created through the **Chicano Power Movement**, decided to join together to protest the war and voice concern over its relatively high percentage of Mexican-American casualties. The **Brown Berets**, a leftist radical group, joined with the **Movimiento Estudiantil Chicano de Aztlan (MEChA)** and other groups to form the National Chicano Moratorium Committee, which planned the rally and demonstration. A march was planned to start the activities, followed by a rally, and finally a picnic with speeches at a park in East Los Angeles.

This was not the first protest rally of its kind in Los Angeles. An earlier rally occurred on December 19, 1969, at Obregon Park and was attended by approximately 2,000 people, and a second rally was held at Salazar Park on February 28, 1970. After these two successful experiences, the Chicano Moratorium Committee decided to carry out a national Chicano protest day.

This national event was staged on August 29, 1970, as a culmination of other demonstrations that had been held throughout the West and Southwest. The moratorium rally was attended by 30,000 participants, representing most states. On their way to Laguna Park in the heart of the East Los Angeles business district, the marchers saw their ranks increase with additional enthusiasts, as riot control officers and armed Los Angeles police and county sheriff deputies monitored the march.

This Chicano Moratorium ended in tragedy. Peace turned into turmoil as some people allegedly stole items from a store. Police were called and the problem was resolved, but riot-equipped police who were present decided to put a stop to the rally by forcing participants to leave the park. A line of uniformed officers moved into the crowd, meeting resistance from some demonstrators. The struggle escalated into a riot and three people were killed, among them **Ruben Salazar**, a Los Angeles *Times* columnist. A deputy sheriff had fired a tear-gas projectile into the Silver Dollar Cafe, where the projectile struck Salazar and killed him. (SCV)

BIBLIOGRAPHY

Rosales, F. Arturo. *Chicano! The History of the Mexican American Civil Rights Movement.* Houston: Arte Publico Press, 1996.

Chicano Power Movement

In the 1960s the Chicano Power Movement began as a response to Anglo-American racism, demanding **civil rights** and equal opportunity in a pluralistic society. The movement included student activists, adult groups, and those who promoted cultural nationalism, separation, and independence.

Other participants in the movement began to promote militant activism. There was a precedent for this. In 1931, during the **Lemon Grove incident** in California, Mexican-American parents called a boycott to fight school segregation. Their lawsuit alleging inferiority in their school was the first successful legal challenge to school segregation. Thirty years later, the Chicano Power Movement addressed cultural content, curriculum, and methodology in teaching. Students used school walkouts to negotiate their cases.

Cultural identity became important to the people involved in the Chicano Power Movement. The movement found its roots in Aztlan, the mythical home of the Aztec in Southwest America. **La Raza Unida Party** gave Chicanos a political voice and the concept of Chicano Power came into being. The movement's better known national leaders included **Reies Lopez Tijerina** of New Mexico, **Rodolfo (Corky) Gonzales** of Denver, **Jose Angel Gutierrez** of Texas, and **Cesar Chavez** of the **United Farm Workers** in California. Local and regional leaders in each state, and student participants in schools and colleges, were active as well.

The movement formulated an ideology and philosophy called Chicanismo, which is credited with being the spirit of the Chicano Power Movement. Chicanismo was indifferent to **acculturation** and **assimilation** and intent instead on cultural autonomy and self-determination. Chicanos turned to their Indian roots to find a true Chicano identity, culture, and history to form this ideology.

Many middle-class Mexican Americans did not support the Chicano Movement because they considered it to have a polarizing effect. Some people found the movement too strident, racist, and aggressive; they described it as "reverse-racist," "un-American," "naive," "counterproductive," and "unsophisticated." As the radical approach of the late 1960s and early 1970s waned so did the cohesive idea of Chicano Power. It was replaced by a more broad-based cultural pride movement. **See also** Community Organizations; El Movimiento; National Chicano Youth Liberation Conference. **See** Letter from the Santa Fe Jail by Reies Lopez Tijerina (1969) in Appendix 1. (SCV)

BIBLIOGRAPHY

Rosales, F. Arturo. *Chicano! The History of the Mexican American Civil Rights Movement.* Houston: Arte Publico Press, 1966.

Henry G. Cisneros (1947–)

Henry Cisneros showed political promise early on when, in 1971, as a graduate student at George Washington University in Washington, D.C., he became the youngest White House fellow in U.S. history. He earned a master's degree from Harvard University and a Ph.D. from George Washington University before returning to his hometown of San Antonio, Texas, to teach at the University of Texas. He was elected to the city council in 1975 and in 1981 he ran a successful campaign for mayor of San Antonio. He was reelected mayor three times and left that office in 1989 to start his own business, Cisneros Asset Management. In 1992 President Bill Clinton appointed him to head the Department of Housing and Urban Development. Cisneros resigned in 1996 and was ultimately indicted for lying to federal investigators during his background check. **See also** Political Leadership. (SCV)

BIBLIOGRAPHY

Gillies, John. *Senor Alcalde: A Biography of Henry Cisneros.* Minneapolis, MN: Dillon Press, 1988.

Lehman, Nicolas. "First Hispanic." *Esquire* 102, no. 6 (December 1984): 480–6.

Schultz, Jeffrey D. *Presidential Scandals.* Washington, DC: Congressional Quarterly, 1999.

Cisneros v. Corpus Christi Independent School District (1982)

In 1972, the Mexican-American pupils in the Corpus Christi, Texas, School District filed a class action suit against the school district claiming that the district was engaging in practices that resulted in segregation and won in U.S. District Court.

The court found the school district in violation of *Brown v. Board of Education* (1954) and stated that segregating the Mexican-American students was constitutionally unacceptable because segregating a race of students was in fact proof of intent to discriminate. The school district appealed without success, although the appellate court slightly changed the original ruling. In *Cisneros v. Corpus Christi Independent School District* (1982), Circuit Court Judge Dyer found the school district was in violation of the Fourteenth Amendment, and he ordered **busing** and clustered school zones in an attempt to end the segregation of Mexican-American pupils. **See also** Discrimination; Educational Equality.

BIBLIOGRAPHY

Garcia, Mario T. *Mexican Americans.* New Haven, CT: Yale University Press, 1989.

Citizenship

The **Treaty of Guadalupe Hidalgo** (1848) conferred United States citizenship on the nonimmigrant Mexican populations residing in the southwestern territories wrested by the United States from Mexico after the **Mexican War**. Many Mexicans who crossed the border after 1848 were either immigrant workers or refugees from the Mexican Revolution of 1910. Because most had the intention of returning home after the revolution, they did not initiate the naturalization process that usually took about 15 years. Even if they had, the naturalization process also was politically disrupted in the 1930s by the Mexican Repatriation. However, many Mexicans who later returned to the United States as immigrant workers decided to stay within Mexican-American communities where they more easily retained their culture and language and could feel comfortable with their noncitizen status. Nevertheless, Mexicans who served in the armed forces during World War II were granted United States citizenship. Also, the U.S. **Voting Rights Act of 1965** motivated voter-registration and citizenship efforts, and the Simpson–Rodino **Immigration Reform and Control Act (IRCA) of 1986** provided for an amnesty process that culminated in citizenship. The program was extended to aid those who had failed to meet the original deadline. The issue of immigration and the need for migrant workers continues to be a volatile topic in the 1990s. **See also** Acculturation; Assimilation; Illegal Aliens; Immigration Policy and Hispanics. **See** Treaty of Guadalupe Hidalgo (1848) in Appendix 1. (SCV)

BIBLIOGRAPHY

Rosales, F. Arturo. *Chicano! The History of the Mexican American Civil Rights Movement.* Houston: Arte Publico Press, 1997.

Civil Rights

Many Mexican-American leaders came of age politically during the 1960s civil rights movement, when African Americans were relying on protest politics to stir the conscience of the nation. Unlike African Americans, however, Hispanics comprised a much smaller minority. In 1960 there were only about seven million Hispanics in the United States, forming only 4 percent of the population. Most of these were either Mexican Americans who had lived in the Southwest for generations, many of whom were poor and uneducated, or Puerto Ricans who had migrated from the island and settled in New York City after World War II.

In the 1960s however, Hispanic immigration grew. One million Cuban refugees fleeing Fidel Castro's communist revolution added to the Hispanic population, settling mostly in southern Florida. These groups were diverse and shared no history or agenda. Within three decades, however, Hispanics became an important and powerful interest group, using many of the strategies employed by African Americans during their call for equality and opportunity.

For many Mexican-American leaders, their initiation into politics started with the **United Farm Workers (UFW)**. The union's leader, **Cesar Chavez**, relied heavily on nonviolent acts and acts of moral witness, such as fasts, religious services, and marches that reflected lessons learned from African Americans such as Martin Luther King. But the UFW was not the only vehicle for Chicano activism. In Texas, an array of marches, high school boycotts, and other protests inspired the founding of **La Raza Unida Party** by Chicano graduate students at St. Mary's University in San Antonio.

The **Civil Rights Act of 1964** also marked an important moment in the Hispanic civil rights movement. The act prohibited any program that received federal funds from discriminating on the basis of race or national origin. This act was followed by the Bilingual Education Act of 1968. By 1970 the Office of Civil Rights (OCR) issued guidelines for school districts whose enrollment exceeded 5 percent Hispanic or other national-origin minority groups; the act required such school districts to take "affirmative steps" to help non-English speaking children participate effectively in the educational program offered by the school district.

Finally, litigation helped secure greater rights for Hispanics. The **League of United Latin American Citizens (LULAC),** started in 1929, is the oldest Hispanic-American organization. To address the courts, LULAC created the **Mexican American Legal Defense and Educational Fund (MALDEF)** in 1968 to become its legal arm. MALDEF and the **Puerto Rican Legal Defense and Educational Fund (PRLDEF)** worked together on using the legal system to uphold and expand civil rights. Among other achievements, MALDEF forced school districts to allocate more funds to schools with predominantly low-income minority populations, compelled school districts to implement **bilingual education** programs, required employers to hire Chicanos, and challenged election rules and apportionment plans that undercounted or diluted the Hispanic vote. **See also** Acculturation; Assimilation; Joan Chandos Baez; Discrimination; Immigration Policy and Hispanics; Voting Rights. (VDD)

BIBLIOGRAPHY

Chavez, Linda. *Out of the Barrio: Toward a New Politics of Hispanic Assimilation.* New York: Basic Books, 1991.

Garcia, Chris F. *Latinos and the Political System.* Notre Dame, IN: University of Notre Dame Press, 1988.

Hero, Rodney E. *Latinos and the U.S. Political System: Two-Tiered Pluralism.* Philadelphia: Temple University Press, 1992.

Skerry, Peter. *Mexican Americans: The Ambivalent Minority.* Cambridge, MA: Harvard University Press, 1993.

Civil Rights Act of 1964

Among the most important legislation enacted since the Reconstruction period to end **discrimination** against all minorities was the **Civil Rights Act of 1964**. The **civil rights** movement had made significant progress toward equality in the early 1960s but there was still a long way to go. When the civil rights movement turned to private discrimination—discrimination practiced by owners of restaurants, hotels, and motels, private employers, and others who were not government officials—it had to take its fight to the Congress. The U.S. Constitution does not govern the activities of private individuals; only Congress at the national level could outlaw discrimination in the private sector.

In 1963 President Lyndon Johnson, invoking the memory of assassinated President John F. Kennedy, urged Congress to enact a civil rights law so that the country could move toward eliminating discrimination and oppression based upon race or color. After a 57-day filibuster led by southern senators (broken by Johnson's forceful persuasion), Congress passed the Civil Rights Act of 1964 by better than a two-thirds vote in both houses; it won the overwhelming support of both Republicans and Democrats.

The act was extremely comprehensive and greatly increased the federal government's ability to fight discrimination. Title II of the act prohibits discrimination and segregation on the grounds of race, color, religion, or national origin in any public accommodation, including hotels, motels, restaurants, movie theaters, other theaters, sports arenas, entertainment houses, and other places that serve the public. Title VII of the act is the most important statute addressing employment discrimination. It prohibits employment discrimination on the basis of race, color, religion, national origin, or sex. The act also protects against employment discrimination because of physical handicap, age, or Vietnam-era veteran status. The act covers employers with 15 or more employees; it also covers unions. Title VII also established the Equal Employment Opportunity Commission (EEOC) as a monitoring device to prevent job discrimination.

The statute was designed to protect Hispanic Americans and other minorities. It is still used to challenge unlawful denial of jobs to Hispanic Americans. (NM)

BIBLIOGRAPHY

Abraham, Henry J. and Barbara A. Perry. *Freedom and the Court: Civil Rights and Liberties in the United States.* New York: Oxford University Press, 1994.

Whalen, Charles and Barbara Whalen. *The Longest Debate: A Legislative History of the 1964 Civil Rights Act.* New York: Mentor Books, 1985.

Anthony Lee Coelho (1942–)

From 1965 to 1978 Anthony Coelho, a Democrat of Portuguese descent, was a staff member for California Representative B.F. Sisk; by 1970 he had become administrative assistant, and later served as staff director. In addition Coelho was a delegate to the Democratic National Conventions in 1976, 1980, 1984, and 1988. In 1978, with Sisk's support, Coelho was elected to the U.S. House of Representatives from California's 15th District. In his first general election he received 60 percent of the vote and was subsequently reelected five times. He served on the House Administration, Interior and Insular Affairs, and Agriculture committees. In 1981 Coelho chaired the Democratic Congressional Campaign Committee. Under his leadership, the committee was transformed into an effective organization, dramatically increasing contributions from political action committees. In 1985 Coelho became the first elected Democratic party whip. In May 1989 Coelho announced his resignation as majority whip after questions arose about his personal finances, and one month later he resigned his seat in the U.S. House of Representatives. He moved to New York where he is an investment banker. A strong advocate for people with epilepsy, he is the chairman of the President's Commission to Employ People with Disabilities. He is also an advisor to the Democratic Party.

BIBLIOGRAPHY

Hispanic Americans in Congress. Washington, DC: Government Printing Office, 1995.

Ana Colomar O'Brien (1938–)

Ana Colomar O'Brien taught English at the Vedada Institute in Havana, Cuba, from 1964 to 1969, after which she worked as a public relations assistant while continuing her education. From 1974 to 1982 she continued working in the field of public relations while acting as a vice president of Mackenzie McCheyne; in this role, she worked with Latin American heads of state and other governmental officials, arranged meetings with the State Department, and represented foreign-born U.S. clients before Congress and other organizations. In 1982 O'Brien began working with the Department of the Interior as an assistant to the assistant secretary of territorial and international affairs. While there, she functioned with governmental officials in advising on policy and providing programs in the Caribbean, American Samoa, the Virgin Islands, and other U.S. territories. In April 1986, O'Brien became chief of protocol for the Organization of American States, where she acted as liaison with the U.S. Department of State, organized international visits and treaty-signing ceremonies, and oversaw social functions for the Democratic Council, secretary general, and other high-ranking officers.

BIBLIOGRAPHY

Delsohn, Gary. "Mario Obledo, A Quiet Man Whose Rights Push Still Ripples." *Sacramento Bee* (February 16, 1998): 1.

Reyes, David. "California and the West: Seasoned Activists Passions Burn Bright Again." *Los Angeles Times* (August 7, 1998): 3.

Telgen, Diane and Jim Kamp, eds. *Notable Hispanic American Women*. Detroit: Gale Research, 1993.

Comision Femenil Mexicana Nacional (CFMN)

The Comision Femenil Mexicana Nacional (CFMN), or Comision Femenil as it is commonly known, is the oldest Mexican, Mexican-American, and Chicana organization functioning in the 1990s. Despite its national title, the CFMN was established in 1970 in Sacramento, California, and continues primarily as a California-based organization with a few chapters in other states. The CFMN directs its efforts to empowering Latino women and their families, ensuring they achieve leadership positions, and acknowledging their accomplishments. For the past 25 years, Comision Femenil has functioned as an advocacy and direct service organization; it has established the Chicana Service Action Center, Centro de Ninos, and Casa Victoria; contributed to the policy-making process by sponsoring task forces, conferences, and public forums; and served as a training ground for Latinas aspiring to political office. California's leading Chicana/Latina elected officials have been Comision Femenil members, including **Gloria Molina** (California State Assembly, Los Angeles City Council, and Los Angeles County Board of Supervisors), Hilda Solis (California State Senate), and **Lucille Roybal-Allard** (U.S. House of Representatives). **See also** Maggie Cervantes; Community Organizations; Political Leadership; Political Participation. (ASR)

BIBLIOGRAPHY

Boyer, Edward. "Que Pasa? People and Events." *Los Angeles Times* (November 8, 1990): 1.

Ruiz, Vicki L. *From Out of the Shadows*. New York: Oxford University Press, 1998.

Community Organization for Public Service (COPS)

Founded in San Antonio, Texas, in 1974, the Community Organization for Public Services (COPS) works for social change in the Mexican-American community. Originally a confrontational organization, COPS trained its leaders at **Saul Alinsky's** Industrial Areas Foundation in Chicago, Illinois. The focus of the group has been to increase the impact of Mexican Americans in the electoral process.

BIBLIOGRAPHY

Skerry, Peter. *Mexican Americans*. New York: Free Press, 1993.

Community Organizations

Historically, Mexican-Americans have protected their social and political rights from the disregard of the majority Anglo-American population by forming community organizations to aid in their struggles. Such organizations could address specific objectives toward achieving political equality on the local, regional, and national levels.

Early Mexican-American organizations reflected the needs of particular times, places, and challenges. In the 1800s Mexican-American groups reflected altruistic concerns as well.

For example, "mutualistas" (**mutual aid societies**) were created for mutual support and burial insurance. The **Alianza Hispanic-Americana** (now defunct) was founded in Tucson, Arizona, in 1894; in the 1920s it sought to provide legal rights for its members. Still later it became involved in political affairs. J. Carlos McCormick, the Alianza's supreme president, became national organizer for the **Viva Kennedy** Clubs.

In the 1960s and 1970s, the Chicano movement called for relevant organizations to meet new challenges and opportunities. These included the **La Raza Unida Party** (now defunct), which sought elected offices for Chicanos throughout the Southwest, and the **Southwest Voters Registration Education Project** (still active), which carried out voter registration and voting drives in hundreds of communities. Other organizations with a political agenda and purpose included the **Political Association of Spanish-Speaking Organizations** (started in Texas and now defunct) and the **American Coordinating Council of Political Education** of Arizona (also now defunct).

National organizations that address community political issues of Hispanic populations include the **Mexican American Legal Defense and Education Fund (MALDEF)** and the **National Council of La Raza**, both founded in 1968 and still active. **See also** Chicano Power Movement. (SCV)

BIBLIOGRAPHY

Acuna, Rodolfo. *Occupied America: The Chicano's Struggle Toward Liberation*. San Francisco: Canfield Press, 1972.

Gonzales, Sylvia Alicia. *Hispano American Voluntary Organizations*. Westport, CT: Greenwood Press, 1985.

Samora, Julian, ed. *La Raza: Forgotten Americans*. Notre Dame, IN: University of Notre Dame Press, 1966.

Mario Compean

Politically active as a student at St. Mary's University in San Antonio, Texas, Mario Compean, along with **Jose Angel Gutierrez**, **Willie Velasquez**, and others, founded the **Mexican American Youth Organization (MAYO)** in 1967. Compean became chairman of MAYO in 1969. In 1972, he was elected state chairman of the **La Raza Unida Party.** Compean sought elected political office only once: in 1978 he headed an unsuccessful bid for governor of Texas.

BIBLIOGRAPHY

Quinones, Juan Gomez. *Chicano Politics*. Albuquerque: University of New Mexico Press, 1990.

Compromise of 1850

The end of the **Mexican War** left the United States with the difficult problem of how to organize the newly acquired western territories. The northern and southern states were politically divided over the question of allowing slavery in the West. When California applied for statehood in January 1850, this debate became a crisis that threatened to divide the nation. The Compromise of 1850, which gave both North and South some of what they wanted, passed in the autumn. Under the terms of the compromise, California was admitted without slavery as a free state, the slave trade was banned in Washington, D.C., and southern slave interests received a more stringent fugitive slave law. New Mexico and Utah were organized as territories where settlers could vote on whether or not to allow slavery in those areas. Finally, a definite border was drawn between Texas and Arizona Territory and the Texan debt was paid off by the United States government. The compromise delayed the Civil War for a decade, and it also served to bring tens of thousands of native Mexicans into the United States. **See also** California Statehood; Texas Statehood; Treaty of Guadalupe Hidalgo; Treaty of Velasco. **See** Gadsden Treaty (1853), Texas Annexation Treaty (1844), Treaty of Guadalupe Hidalgo (1848) in Appendix 1. (JRB)

BIBLIOGRAPHY

Hamilton, Holman. *Prologue to Conflict: The Crisis and Compromise of 1850*. New York: W. W. Norton, 1966.

Congreso de Pueblos de Habla Espanola

The Congreso de Pueblos de Habla Española was founded in 1938 in Los Angeles by **Bert Corona** and **Luisa Moreno,** as an organization to advance the **civil rights** of Latinos. Its members came from all walks of life. Because it was one of the first national Hispanic civil rights organizations, it attracted the attention of the FBI, which often investigated its members. This scrutiny and World War II caused a decline in membership, and the organization ceased to exist by the mid-1940s.

BIBLIOGRAPHY

Mirande, Alfredo and Evangelina Enriquez. "Chicanas in the Struggle for Unions." *Introduction to Chicano Studies*. New York: Macmillan, 1982, pp. 325–37.

Congressional Hispanic Caucus (CHC)

Founded in 1977, the Congressional Hispanic Caucus (CHC) has worked to support the efforts of Hispanic members of Congress and to educate non-Hispanic members on issues that are of particular importance to the Latino community. **Edward Roybal** (D-CA) was the driving force in the founding of the CHC which added its first Republican member, **Manuel Lujan** (R-NM), in 1982 and its first woman, **Ileana Ros-Lehtinen** (R-FL), that same year. The group was a key leader in the passage of the **Immigration Reform and Control Act of 1986.** The group continues to grow in power and stature as Latinos continue to grow in importance as a political minority. **See also** Margarita Roque; Political Leadership.

BIBLIOGRAPHY

Breiter, T., A.J. Guernica, and P. Saavedra-Vela. "Hispanic Voices on Capitol Hill." *Agenda* 7, no. 4 (1977): 11–14.

Vigil, Maurillo. *Hispanics in Congress*. Lanham, MD: University Press of America, 1996.

Conservatism

A political ideology is a set of fundamental beliefs or principles about politics and government: What the scope of government should be, how decisions should be made, and what values should be pursued. In the United States, the most prominent ideologies are represented by the terms "liberalism" and "conservatism." Although these words are used in many ways, liberalism generally can be said to endorse the idea of social change and advocate the involvement of government in effecting such change, whereas conservatism seeks to defend the status quo and prescribes a relatively limited role for governmental activity.

A common theme of political conservatism is the acceptance of certain types of inequality. What characterizes conservatives of all kinds is a belief that the differences between people are more important than their similarities. Whereas classical liberals thought that people should be regarded for all civic purposes as equals, conservatives were more impressed with the need to treat individuals differently, depending on a variety of moral and economic criteria.

The political intent of conservatism involves a resistance to the use of government to further the cause of equality. This resistance is predicated in the writings of Edmund Burke (1729–1797), the premier articulator of traditional conservatism as a philosophy. Burke's historical emphasis was itself the outcome of deep currents in European thought, currents that rejected abstract reasoning as a method for understanding the human world. The flamboyance of Burke's rhetoric was instrumental in bringing conservatism as a philosophical position into the world. The defining criterion had to do with how best to maintain differentiation of status, authority, and rank that fit with the conservative conception of human nature. Traditionally, Hispanics in the U.S. have subscribed more to liberal than to conservative political ideals.

In the United States, ideological terms such as liberalism and conservatism connote reasonably integrated sets of values and beliefs. Moreover, when ideological labels are attached to people one might reasonably assume that these people are fairly consistent in applying their values and beliefs to public affairs. In reality, however, neither political leaders nor citizens always display integrated or consistent opinions; many hold conservative views on some issues and liberal views on others. Moreover, most people in the United States avoid ideological labeling, either by describing themselves as "moderate" or "middle-of-the-road" or by simply declining to place their views on an ideological scale.

Despite such inconsistencies and a widespread disdain for ideological labels, ideology continues to play an important role in U.S. politics. People do have beliefs about such matters as who should get what in society, even when they do not use ideological terms to describe those beliefs. To complicate matters further, public opinion data suggest that a large segment of the U.S. electorate uses the terms liberal and conservative more frequently to describe a set of social attitudes or lifestyles than to describe political beliefs.

Still, when people in the United States are asked to identify themselves as liberal or conservative, most are indeed able to do so. A consistently larger proportion of respondents call themselves conservative than liberal. At the same time, about a quarter of the population regards itself as ideologically middle-of-the-road. Conservatives are twice as likely to be Republicans as Democrats, and liberals are much more likely to be Democrats than Republicans. Also, the electorate tends to perceive the Democratic Party as liberal and the Republican Party as conservative.

Hispanics are traditionally far more numerous in Democratic than Republican organizations. The term Hispanic, however, has serious limitations in this context because it lumps together a variety of different people. It includes Mexicans, Cubans, Puerto Ricans, and a number of other minority groups from a variety of nations who often have little in common, except that they speak Spanish. In the 1990 U.S. Census, Hispanics were asked to categorize themselves as either Mexican, Mexican American or Chicano, Puerto Rican, Cuban, or other. Cubans, however, are distinct in a number of significant respects and are more conservative in their political outlook than other Hispanics in the United States. Politics, after all, prompted Cuban immigration in the first place, and participation in American politics was a way for Cuban Americans to advance their own political agenda, which was often the tightening of American anti-Castro policies.

The party affiliation of Mexican Americans is heavily Democratic. In Arizona, 77 percent of Mexican Americans are registered Democrats, while only about 15 percent are Republicans. This compares with a general U.S. population of 45 percent Republicans and 43 percent Democrats among all registered voters. In California, Texas, and New Mexico, Mexican-American affiliation with the Democratic Party ranges from 75 to 80 percent. These high levels are reflected, and sometimes magnified, in voting totals for Democratic candidates for national, state, and local offices. In New York City, about 80 percent of Puerto Ricans were registered as Democrats in 1982 and 1984, a pattern that still holds. This level of Democratic Party affiliation is commensurate with that of African Americans in New York City and somewhat higher than that of whites (about 65 percent). Little if any of this, however, pertains to Cubans. Hispanic party registration in Dade County, Florida, which includes heavily Cuban-American Miami, is heavily Republican, at 68 percent, while only 24 percent are registered Democrats. This strong Republican leaning is clear in Cuban voting patterns. The 1988 Democratic presidential candidate, Michael Dukakis, received only 15 percent of the vote in Dade County's heavily Hispanic precincts, while he received 45 percent in the country as a whole.

After the 1959 Cuban Revolution, the first waves of Cuban immigrants included not the dispossessed poor of that country, but accomplished professionals who, through a combination of personal initiative and an "open-armed" U.S. immigration policy and economic assistance, succeeded in establishing themselves in Miami. Subsequent waves of immigrants throughout the 1960s brought a large portion of the Cuban middle class, as well as the upwardly mobile working class, to the area. Although popular notions of Cuban wealth are often more allegory than fact, Cuban immigration has been accompanied by rapid economic advancement and a number of dramatic success stories. Overall, median income for Cubans is far higher nationally than median income for Mexican Americans and Puerto Ricans. The 1980 Mariel refugees, and many Cuban entrants since, have brought far larger numbers of refugees who were poor, nonwhite, unskilled, and without family ties in the United States. (The Mariel boat people were a small exodus of Cubans who fled Cuba on makeshift rafts and small fishing boats. Castro took the opportunity of the boat refugees to empty jails and asylums.) Thus, in recent years, class and racial differences have sometimes strained a sense of shared nationalistic ties among Cuban immigrants to the United States. However, such divisions have yet to manifest themselves in politically significant ways. Cubans as a group remain more likely to be conservative than other Hispanics.

Ultimately, economic status seems to have the single greatest impact on shaping political ideology. For more than 30 years, the Cuban exile community has been overwhelmingly Republican, largely because of its strongly held anti-communist views. The Republican Party, with its reliance on hard-line foreign policy rhetoric, became the natural home of Cuban exiles. However, Cuban American politics can no longer be understood solely in terms of militant exile politics. While the significance and force of anti-Castro symbolism is still alive, it is combined today with more mundane concerns for jobs, domestic social services, and other substantive policy issues. In recent years, there has been a drastic drop in support of Republicans among Florida's politically powerful Cuban Americans. In 1984, Ronald Reagan received 90 percent of the Cuban-American vote, and in 1992, George Bush received 80 percent. The traditionally Republican Hispanics in Florida gave Bob Dole, the 1996 Republican presidential candidate, only a 2 percent margin over Democrat Bill Clinton, rather than the 70 percent and 80 percent margins Reagan and Bush reached. In 1996, Bill Clinton was the first Democrat in 20 years to win Florida's 25 electoral votes. Moreover, Bob Dole won only 22 percent of the Hispanic vote nationally, the lowest percentage for a Republican presidential candidate since such figures have been tallied. Nationally, more than 70 percent of Hispanics voted for Clinton in 1996, 10 percent more than he received in 1992. During the 1996 presidential election, Republicans, whether fairly or unfairly, became known as the anti-immigrant party, thus driving away even conservative Hispanics, who usually find common ground with the Republicans but who were offended by what they saw as the xenophobic tone of much Republican discourse. Republicans also alienated middle-class Hispanics, who are ordinarily not far from mainstream Republicans, with similar views on taxes, crime, family values, and welfare reform. Several polls have indicated that Hispanics are in favor of tougher restrictions on welfare as well, including lifetime limits on benefits. But there is widespread anger among Hispanics that welfare reform bars most government aid to legal immigrants. President Clinton changed this section of the Welfare Reform Bill, as promised. Still, Cubans remain the principal foundation of Hispanic support for the Republicans, though this support shows signs of eroding.

Hispanics in the United States are less liberal overall than their heavily Democratic affiliation might imply. For example, Hispanics in New York City divide about equally into thirds in identifying themselves as liberals, moderates, and conservatives. In California, only a quarter of the Hispanic population identify themselves as liberals; almost equal numbers identify themselves as moderates (35 percent) or conservatives (34 percent). In Texas, 44 percent of Hispanics proclaim a moderate philosophy, and about 25 percent each fall into liberal and conservative camps. These figures may surprise observers who perceive Hispanics as generally liberal. They suggest instead fairly high numbers of conservatives and moderates among Hispanic voters. Overall, Hispanics tend to be liberal on economic issues and favorable to the idea of a larger public sector. But they are more likely to be conservative on social issues such as abortion, the death penalty, prayer in public schools, and handgun control. Other issues, such as increasing federal spending on **bilingual education** and making English the official language of the state and the nation, heavily influence Hispanics as well. **See also** English First/ English Only; Liberalism; Political Participation; Voting Patterns; Welfare Reform. (NM)

BIBLIOGRAPHY

Bennett, Stephen E. "Americans' Knowledge of Ideology, 1980–1992." *American Politics Quarterly* 23 (July 1995): 259–78.
Chavez, Linda. *Out of the Barrio: Toward a New Politics of Hispanic Assimilation.* New York: Basic Books, 1991.
Edwards, Carmine G. and James A. Stimson. *Issue Evolution: Race and the Transformation of American Politics.* Princeton, NJ: Princeton University Press, 1989.
Flanigan, William H. and Nancy H. Zingale. *Political Behavior of the American Electorate.* Washington, DC: Congressional Quarterly, 1994.
Hero, Rodney E. *Latinos and the U.S. Political System: Two-Tiered Pluralism.* Philadelphia: Temple University Press, 1992.
Jacoby, William G. "Ideological Identification and Issue Attitude." *American Journal of Political Science* 35 (February 1991): 178–205.
Vigil, Maurilio E. *Hispanics in American Politics: The Search for Political Power.* Lanham, MD: University Press of America, 1987.

Co-optation

Political co-optation occurs when a minority political activist or officeholder (for example a Chicano activist) becomes so successful over time that the minority agenda—comprised of issues, concerns, goals, and activities important to the Chicano community—eventually blends into the majority political agenda; the minority agenda ceases to be distinguished, supported, or advanced by the Chicano politician. The co-opted Chicano politician fails to work for the results necessary and expected by the minority political constituency. Once co-opted, the minority politician becomes unacceptable to the minority community, even though that same politician had previously been trusted to be the intermediary between the minority community and the majority power structure. The minority political leader must find ways and means to remain acceptable to both minority and majority populations.

The co-opted minority political leader may be called an "Uncle Tom," a "Tio Taco," or a "Coconut" (white inside and brown outside) and may be considered a "sell-out" or "Vendido." The co-opted political activist is perceived to be providing a greater service to the Anglo society, someone who has lost touch with the minority constituency. The ego gratification of successful experiences, the perceived improvements to the politician's economic and social status, or a gain in political power may motivate the minority politician to move out of the inner city and to larger housing and surroundings in the suburbs. The minority constituency may consider this move away from the community as a co-optation through a loss of "roots" to the old neighborhood or a denial of ethnic origins.

In other types of co-optation, groups in political control have redesigned political boundaries to favor their own demographic distributions to ensure election of their candidates in at-large elections, thereby co-opting minority political representation. **See also** Political Leadership; Political Participation. (SCV)

BIBLIOGRAPHY

Garcia, Chris F. and Rudolph O. de la Garza. *The Chicano Political Experience: Three Perspectives.* North Scituate, MA: Duxbury Press, 1977.
Gomez, Rudolph, ed. *The Changing Mexican-American.* El Paso: University of Texas, El Paso, 1972.

Jorge Luis Córdova Díaz (1907–1994)

Jorge Luis Córdova Díaz served as judge to the Superior Court of San Juan, Puerto Rico, from 1940 to 1945, followed by a two-year term on the Supreme Court of Puerto Rico. In 1967 Córdova Díaz, a lifelong supporter of **Puerto Rican statehood**, helped establish the **Nuevo Progresista Party** (New Progressive Party), and was elected resident commissioner the following year. He was elected to the Agriculture, Armed Services, and Interior and Insular Affairs committees. In conjunction with the delegates from the Virgin Islands and Guam, Córdova Díaz worked to extend certain United States laws to these islands, including social security benefits and the Automobile Information Disclosure Act. After an unsuccessful campaign for reelection in 1972, Córdova Díaz resumed a law practice in San Juan until 1984.

BIBLIOGRAPHY

Hispanic Americans in Congress. Washington, D.C.: Government Printing Office, 1995.

Felix Cordova Davila (1878–1938)

Felix Cordova Davila was judge of the municipal court of Caguas, Puerto Rico, in 1904, as well as judge of the municipal court of Manati from 1904 to 1908. In 1908 Davila served as district attorney for Aquadilla. He then served as a judge in various courts in Puerto Rico, including the district court of

Guayama from 1908 to 1910, the district court of Arecibo from 1910 to 1911, and the district court of San Juan from 1911 to 1917. Davila next served as resident commissioner to the United States from July 16, 1917, until his resignation on April 11, 1932. In 1932 Davila was appointed as an associated justice of the Puerto Rico Supreme Court, where he remained until his death.

BIBLIOGRAPHY

Biographical Directory of the United States Congress, 1774–1989. Washington, DC: United States Government Printing Office, 1989.

Bert Corona (1918–)

An activist and union organizer, Bert Corona became national Director of Hermandad Mexicana Nacional when he was only 19. He went on to found several Mexican-American organizations including the Mexican Youth Conference and the Community Service Organization of the National Conference of Spanish Speaking People. From 1960 to 1970, he was an organizer for the **Mexican American Political Association** and from 1964 to 1968, he served as regional organizer of the National Association of Mexican Americans for the Democratic Presidential Campaign Committee in California. In addition, Corona was professor at California State University at Northridge and has served as a consultant for the U.S. Labor Department. **See also** Congresso de Pueblos de Habla Espanola.

BIBLIOGRAPHY

Corona, Bert. *Bert Corona Speaks*. New York: Pathfinder Press, 1972.
Munoz, Sergio. "Guided by a Vision; How Bert Corona Met the Challenges of Latino Leadership; Memories of Chicano History: The Life and Narrative of Bert Corona." *Los Angeles Times* (October 9, 1994): 4.

Elaine Coronado (1959–)

Elaine Coronado worked as executive director of the National Hispanic Quincentennial Commission from 1989 to 1991. She left the commission to create and head the Hispanic Alliance for Free Trade. The organization informed Hispanic businesses about the benefits of the North American Free Trade Agreement (NAFTA) and worked to support its passage.

BIBLIOGRAPHY

Telgen, Diane and Jim Kamp, eds. *Notable Hispanic American Women*. Detroit: Gale Research, 1993.

Antonio Coronel (1817–1894)

A resident of Alta, California, Antonio Coronel served the Mexican government in a variety of roles including as a school teacher, territorial deputy, street commissioner, electoral commission member, and Los Angeles Irrigation Board member. In 1848, Coronel amassed some funds as a gold miner, but then he returned to his duties as Los Angeles city councilman and soon gained appointment as superintendent of schools. After California became part of the United States in 1850, Coronel continued his work with the irrigation board while also serving on the city council. During the 1850s and 1860s, Coronel continued to be active in local politics, eventually becoming mayor of Los Angeles. In 1867 he became state treasurer, holding this position until being elected to the state senate in the mid-1870s.

BIBLIOGRAPHY

Barrows, H.D. "Antonio F. Coronel." *Historical Society of Southern California Quarterly* 5, no. 1 (1900).
Sanchez, Federico A. "Antonio F. Coronel, a Californian and a Ranchero." Ph.D. dissertation, University of Southern California: 1983.

Baltasar Corrada del Río (1935–)

Baltasar Corrada del Río was appointed to the Civil Rights Commission of Puerto Rico in 1969, serving as chair from 1970 to 1971. During 1971–1972, he was a newspaper columnist for *El Mundo* and served as president and editor of the *Puerto Rico Human Rights Review*. He also founded and was the director of the Puerto Rico Teleradial Institute of Ethics. In 1976 Corrada del Río was elected resident commissioner to the U.S. House of Representatives and was reelected four years later. During both terms he served on the Interior and Insular Affairs Committee and the Education and Labor Committee. On the Education Committee, Corrada del Río worked to improve educational opportunities for Hispanics, including the Head Start program. In 1984 he did not seek reelection as resident commissioner. In 1985 Corrada del Río returned to Puerto Rico and was elected mayor of San Juan; from 1986 to 1989 he served as the president of the pro-statehood **Nuevo Progresista Party** (New Progressive Party) of Puerto Rico. In 1988 he challenged incumbent governor Rafael Hernández Colón for the governorship of Puerto Rico but was defeated.

BIBLIOGRAPHY

Hispanic Americans in Congress. Washington, DC: Government Printing Office, 1995.

Martha P. Cotera (1938–)

Martha Cotera, a librarian, historian, and bilingual educator, is nationally known as one of the first Chicana feminists because of her activities, articulation of a feminist consciousness, and important writings. She has been a leader and integral part of most major activities connected to the **Chicano Power Movement**, in particular the **Crystal City, Texas,** school walkouts, the Chicano political takeover of Crystal City politics, and the founding of the **La Raza Unida Party** and the Chicana feminist movement. Cotera set Chicana feminists apart from "Anglo feminists" by focusing on the struggle by women of color for liberation rather than on equal rights. Her major feminist writings and collected speeches, *Chicanas in Politics and Public Life* (1975), *Diosa y Hembra* (1976) and *Chicana Feminist: Essays* (1977), were directed at middle-class and college-educated Hispanic women to politicize them and help them reject stereotypes; her writings continue to be used by feminists everywhere. (ASR)

BIBLIOGRAPHY

Cotera, Martha P. *Chicana Feminist: Essays.* Austin, TX: Information Systems Development, 1977.
———. *Chicanas in Politics and Public Life.* Austin, TX: Information Systems Development, 1975.
———. *Diosa y Hembra.* Austin, TX: Information Systems Development, 1977.

Crusade for Justice

The Crusade for Justice was founded in Denver, Colorado, in 1966 under the leadership of **Rodolfo Gonzalez**. The group originally made demands for better housing, increased and improved educational services, and increased employment opportunities for Mexican-American and other Spanish-speaking people, as well as other Hispanic **civil rights** legislation. The organization also began publishing its own newspaper, *El Gallo: La Voz de la Justicia*, to cover Latino rights events, issues, and activities.

In 1968, the Crusade for Justice purchased extended facilities, which it called El Centro de la Cruzada para la Justicia, or the Center for the Crusade for Justice. This new building included administrative offices, a 500-seat auditorium, and a 3,000-square-foot ballroom. Because of these extensive facilities, the group was able to provide social events, cultural activities, educational classes, and other events for the benefit of the Chicano community. In 1968 and 1969, the group participated in protest marches and organized student walkouts against the Denver school system to combat **discrimination** against students, teachers, and administrators. Riots ensued and police arrested Gonzalez and 24 other Latinos. In late March 1969, the organization sponsored the first Chicano Youth Liberation Conference in Denver, Colorado, gathering together about 15,000 students to provide cultural and educational activities. Members of this conference also produced El Plan Espiritual de Aztlan, which focused on ethnic nationalism and cultural independence. In the 1970s, the Crusade for Justice's activities dwindled as Hispanics became less confrontational in their tactics. **See also** Community Organization; Economic Equality; Educational Opportunity.

BIBLIOGRAPHY

Castro, Tony. *Chicano Power, The Emergence of Mexican America.* New York: Saturday Review Press, 1974.
Hammerback, John C. et al., *A War of Words: Chicano Protest in the 1960s and 1970s.* Westport, CT: Greenwood Press, 1985.

Crystal City, Texas

Political movements frequently lead to the establishment of political organizations designed to represent and shape the broadly held preferences of social movements. Mexican Americans established a number of such political organizations. Like other minorities in the United States, Mexican Americans have realized that political power proceeds from organization. Power is created because large numbers of individuals pool their energies to accomplish political work. Mexican-American political activities in Texas during the presidential election of 1960 led to the creation of a statewide organization called the **Political Association of Spanish-Speaking Organization (PASSO)**, which worked on the local level with some success. In a dramatic and hostile contest in south Texas in 1963, Mexican-American activists (mostly PASSO leaders) won political control of Crystal City, in what eventually became known as the "first uprising." Located in Zavala County (on the Rio Grande plain in the "Winter Garden"), Crystal City is approximately 50 miles from the Mexican border. The population of the community was approximately 10,000, with an estimated 80 percent having a Spanish surname. Although Mexican Americans outnumbered Anglos four to one, the Anglos had usually controlled the city. Members of PASSO, in cooperation with members of the Teamsters and other unions, began actively campaigning for five Mexican-American candidates to the city council. The enthusiasm of the Mexican-American residents was soon aroused, resulting in the election of all five Mexican-American candidates. To a large degree this success lay in the local economy, which meant corporate agribusiness such as Del Monte. Local management attempted to intimidate Del Monte workers who were active in the campaign, but these attempts were blocked by the local union with the help of Teamster officials. However, Crystal City became a symbol of the potential political power of the Mexican Americans in the Southwest and encouraged similar efforts elsewhere. This was especially so in those communities where a large segment or majority of the population consisted of Mexican Americans. **See also** Chicano Power Movement; La Raza Unida Party; Voting Patterns; Voting Rights. (NM)

BIBLIOGRAPHY

Chandler, Charles R. "The Mexican American Protest Movement in Texas." Ph.D. dissertation, Tulane University, 1968.
Miller, Michael V. and James D. Preston. "Vertical Ties and the Redistribution of Power in Crystal City." *Social Science Quarterly* 53 (1973): 772–84.
Montejano, David. *Anglos and Mexicans: In the Making of Texas.* Austin: University of Texas Press, 1987.
Shockley, John S. *Chicano Revolt in a Texas Town.* Notre Dame, IN: University of Notre Dame Press, 1974.

Cuban American Legal Defense and Education Fund (CALDEF)

Established in 1980 and based in Fort Wayne, Indiana, the Cuban American Legal Defense and Education Fund (CALDEF) is a national nonprofit organization that serves Cuban-American and Latin American communities. Specifically, the organization supports equal treatment and opportunities that enhance the lives of Cuban Americans and other Latin Americans in the areas of employment, education, housing, and politics. It also serves to educate the general public about the plight of the Cuban American. CALDEF has initiated and won several class action suits to combat racism, sexism, and unfair treatment of Cuban Americans. In 1980 CALDEF forced the Wisconsin state government to investigate and ultimately to shut down refugee camps in Fort McCoy, Wisconsin, where Cuban minors were regularly being mis-

Cuban refugees thank President John F. Kennedy and the United States for their freedom during a rally in Miami, Florida. *National Archives.*

treated. CALDEF supports **bilingual education** and women's rights and has aided Hispanic women who have lost their jobs due to racism and sexism. **See also** Civil Rights; Discrimination; Mexican American Legal Defense and Educational Fund (MALDEF).

BIBLIOGRAPHY
Kneeland, Douglas E. "U.S. Admits Problems on Refugees." *New York Times* (August 30, 1980): 1.

Cultural Nationalism

Through much of the twentieth century, the image of the melting pot implied that immigrant cultures in the United States would mix with one another to create a new "American" population. The melting pot theory defined ethnic group politics as well. For example, many Latino organizations sought to assert their rights through assimilation and inclusion in a national American community, rather than asserting ethnic difference. Following World War II, Mexican-American organizations and leaders, drawn largely from the ranks of returning war veterans, turned to the courts to end legal segregation and discriminatory practices in schools and at the workplace. New reformist organizations, such as the **American G.I. Forum**, the **Mexican American Political Association (MAPA)**, and the Community Service Organization, joined with older groups, such as the **League of Latin American Citizens (LULAC)**, to work for equal **citizenship** rights in California, Texas, and other southwestern states. In demanding rights to assure their communities' survival, these groups found that **assimilation** became a by-product of their strategy.

Cultural nationalists, however, rejected assimilation, and by the 1960s the idea of cultural nationalism began to take root in the Latino community. Cultural nationalism gained prominence by challenging the image of the American melting pot. Instead, scholars emphasized ethnicity, to suggest that the United States should be perceived as a plurality of ethnic groups with competing interests.

The fundamental premise of cultural nationalism is that nations are rooted in cultural and ethnic differences. During the **civil rights** movement in the 1960s, Puerto Ricans and Mexican Americans joined other racial minority groups in the struggle to affirm their presence as citizens and to expand the boundaries of political inclusion in the national community. Like earlier generations of Latino leaders, their efforts sought to redress political and cultural exclusion, but with a new emphasis on their respective communities' histories in the United States.

For example, when working-class Puerto Rican youth and students in the 1960s became aware of the colonial status of the island, they renamed it Borinquen and began to identify themselves as Boricuas in an effort to return to the island's pre-Columbian, indigenous Taino roots. The new name and identity were their expression of political nationalism and part of a quest for independence from the United States. Although Puerto Rican independence quickly appeared an impossible goal for the near future, the independence movement continued through the 1960s and 1970s as an important nationalist symbol in the United States. As time progressed, there was a sharp decline in the independence movement. Despite this decline, identification among Puerto Ricans as Boricuas was still common in New York's Puerto Rican community even in the 1990s.

The continued colonial ties between Puerto Ricans and the United States differentiate their legacy from that of other people of Latin American descent. Other Latin groups have historically sought a cultural rather than separatist approach to differentiating their communities. For example, like Puerto Ricans, Mexican Americans in the civil rights movement reaffirmed national heritage and cultural roots through the pursuit of rights. In the Mexican-American community, cultural nationalism was addressed by at least two forms of political mobilization: the **Chicano Power Movement**, led by **Rodolfo "Corky" Gonzales**, and the **La Raza Unida Party**, founded by **Jose A. Gutierrez**.

Emphasizing Mexican-American empowerment, Chicano students and youth drew inspiration from national liberation struggles in third world countries. The call for Chicano power, like the rise of Chicano studies in many universities across the United States, became a significant goal of the movement. Movement participation was spread through new umbrella organizations, such as **Movimiento Estudiantil Chicano de Aztlan (MEChA)**. Students adopted the term "Chicano" to identify themselves, signifying an affirmation of their Latin American heritage. Chicano students' demands led to the creation of the La Raza Unida Party, by Jose Gutierrez, a Chicano nationalist from Texas, and his wife Luz, in 1970.

Like political mobilization, **bilingual education** became an important element in the Latino community's effort for cultural nationalism. Through bilingual education, Latinos affirmed their presence as citizens and ensured the survival of their cultural and linguistic traditions. Bilingual education began in the United States when Congress passed the Bilingual Education Act in 1968 in recognition of the growing number of linguistically and culturally diverse children enrolled in schools who, because of their limited English proficiency, were not receiving an education equal to their English-proficient peers. The legislation required that when the curriculum systematically "excludes minority group children from effective participation in the educational program offered by a school district," then "the district must take affirmative steps to rectify the language deficiency in order to open its instructional programs to these students."

Following the legislation, many 1970s bilingual education programs sought to help linguistically diverse children meet the same challenging academic standards required of all children enrolled in the nation's schools. Two program approaches to bilingual education gained popularity: classical and ESL. Classical programs taught classes in the student's native language, whereas ESL featured a combination of classes taught in English and the native language. In the beginning, the programs served homogeneous target groups. For example, in California and the Southwest, Spanish groups dominated the programs.

But in 1974, help was available to all limited-English students following the *Lau v. Nicols* decision. In that case, the U.S. Supreme Court decided to hold schools responsible for helping "students who are certain to find their classroom experiences wholly incomprehensible because they do no understand English." Following the decision, the government mandated compliance through the **Equal Educational Opportunity Act (EEOA)** of 1974. Although neither the *Lau* decision nor the EEOA prescribed bilingual education, it evolved as the preferred method of compliance. To help school districts comply, the federal Office of Bilingual Education and Minority Language Affairs was established in 1974.

Like bilingual education, multiculturalism also emerged as an important expression of cultural nationalism in the Latino community. Proponents of multiculturalism sought to preserve immigrant cultures and languages rather than see them absorbed by a host culture. In the public schools, a multicultural education has been advocated with various justifications. One approach to multiculturalism in education is through **cultural pluralism**, a solution proposed as a way to resolve conflict by recognizing that each race has its own culture and that different races can live peacefully in one nation. In the public school curriculum, cultural pluralism has been widely adopted as a way to teach tolerance and promote understanding between different cultures.

The movement from assimilation to cultural nationalism has been subject to a certain amount of backlash from the non-Latino community in the United States. By the late 1990s, disputes over bilingual education and multiculturalism dominated the national political agenda and educational debates. It was against this background that the movement to make English the official language of the U.S. arose. In 1981, Senator S. I. Hayakawa (R-CA), a leading critic of bilingual education and bilingual ballots, introduced in the U.S. Senate a constitutional amendment that would have made English the official language and would have prohibited federal and state laws that required the use of other languages. Hayakawa managed to gain some support, mostly from conservative members of the Senate, but was not ultimately able to gather enough votes from his Senate colleagues. As a result, the English Language Amendment died in the 97th Congress. For several years, however, similar bills awaited consideration in the U.S. House of Representatives. The Emerson Bill (H.R. 123) passed the House in 1996 and specified English as the official language of the government, requiring that the government "preserve and enhance" the official status of English.

Despite these efforts, by the 1990s discussions of ethnicity shifted from talk of assimilation to calls for cultural nationalism and ethnic pride. Moreover, it appears that calls for cultural nationalism are now firmly rooted in the U.S. political landscape and fully institutionalized. An action by the Clinton administration provides a good example. In October 1994, President Bill Clinton signed into law the Improving America's Schools Act (IASA), which reauthorized the Elementary and Secondary Education Act of 1965. The act mandated, for the first time, that state plans must include strategies for meeting the educational needs of limited-English-proficient students. **See also** Acculturation; Cultural Pluralism; English First/English Only.

BIBLIOGRAPHY

Chavez, Linda. *Out of the Barrio: Toward a New Politics of Hispanic Assimilation.* New York: Basic Books, 1991.

Hero, Rodney E. *Latinos and the Political System: Two-Tiered Pluralism.* Philadelphia: Temple University Press, 1992.

Oboler, Suzanne. *Ethnic Labels, Latino Lives: Identity and the Politics of (RE)Presentation in the United States.* Minneapolis: University of Minnesota Press, 1995.

Skerry, Peter. *Mexican Americans: The Ambivalent Minority.* Cambridge, MA: Harvard University Press, 1993.

Cultural Pluralism

Cultural pluralism is a solution proposed by scholars to resolve conflict when addressing the complex problems presented by race. Cultural pluralism achieves this resolution by recognizing that each race has its own culture and that different races can live peacefully in one nation. The idea of cultural pluralism frequently comes under attack. For example, many people perceive efforts to legislate English as the official language as a disregard for the Latin community's cultural identity. **See also** Assimilation; Biculturalism; Bilingual Education; Cultural Nationalism; English First/English Only. (VDD)

BIBLIOGRAPHY

Hackey, Sheldon. "Ever Think of What Makes You a Good Citizen of America?" *The Houston Post* (August 25, 1994): A21.

Eligio "Kika" de la Garza (1927–)

Although he was elected to the U.S. House of Representatives in 1964, Eligio "Kika" de la Garza began his political career in the late 1950s when he served in the Texas General Assembly. His district, which was the largest Democratic Hispanic stronghold in the state, comprised Bee, Brooks, Hidalgo, and San Patricio counties. Since the area was mostly agricultural, de la Garza was active on the House Agriculture Committee, where he was the ranking minority member. De la Garza was known as a master strategist and had an active role in passage of the North American Free Trade Agreement. He is also an active member of the **Congressional Hispanic Caucus**, has a law degree from St. Mary's University in San Antonio, and served in the U.S. Army and Navy. He did not seek reelection in 1996 and retired in 1997. **See also** Political Leadership. (CEM)

Kika de la Garza (D-TX), a longtime member of the U.S. House of Representatives, was considered a master political strategist. *Courtesy of U.S. House of Representatives.*

BIBLIOGRAPHY

de la Garza, E. "Kika." "Ceiling on Aid Would Hurt Farm Program." *USA Today* (May 18, 1990): 12A.

Duncan, Philip D. and Christine C. Lawrence. *Politics in America: 1996. The 104th Congress*. Washington, DC: Congressional Quarterly Press, 1995.

Lee, Steven H. "Economy to Dictate Agriculture's Future." *The Dallas Morning News* (November 15, 1992): 1H.

Ron de Lugo (1930–)

Congressman Ron de Lugo began his political career in 1956 as an at-large senator for the Virgin Islands legislature. In 1968 he was elected as a representative to Congress from the Virgin Islands. He has the distinction of being the first such delegate to Congress. He has served on the **Congressional Hispanic Caucus**, Congressional Human Rights Caucus, Committee of the Interior and Insular Affairs, and the Committee on Education. **See also** Political Leadership.

Democrat Ron de Lugo was the first delegate elected to represent the Virgin Islands in the U.S. Congress. *Courtesy of U.S. House of Representatives.*

BIBLIOGRAPHY

de Lugo, Ron. "Territories Deserve a Say." *USA Today* (January 4, 1993): 12A.

McAllister, Bill. "House Panel Backs Puerto Rican Vote on Statehood." *The Washington Post* (September 20, 1990): A7.

Federico Degetau (1862–1914)

Federico Degetau was Puerto Rico's first resident commissioner. He received his early education in Ponce, Spain, and continued his education in Barcelona. After graduating from the law school of the Central University of Madrid in 1887, he was admitted to the Spanish bar and practiced law. He also was active in the Liberal Reformist Party in Spain and in 1887 he established a newspaper, *La Isla de Puerto Rico*, which sought to make Spaniards aware of Puerto Rico's plight. After returning to Puerto Rico, Degetau became active in the Autonomist Party, under the leadership of Luis Muñoz Rivera. Degetau was among the party's four commissioners who journeyed to Spain in 1895 to petition for political autonomy for their island. The Spanish government denied the petition, but three years later Puerto Rico was granted an autonomic charter.

Degetau was in Spain in 1898 when the **Spanish-American War** broke out and U.S. troops invaded Puerto Rico. He quickly returned to Puerto Rico and was appointed secretary of the interior of the first governing cabinet formed under U.S. rule. The next year he was appointed member of the Insular Board of Charities. Both appointments were made by the commanding general of U.S. forces on the island. Degetau became a member of the Puerto Rican Insular Republican Party, which was established in 1899. From 1900 to 1901 he was the president of the Board of Education of San Juan.

Degetau was elected resident commissioner to the U.S. House of Representatives in 1900 and reelected in 1902. As a member of the Committee on Insular Affairs, he submitted a bill to grant U.S. **citizenship** to the people of Puerto Rico, but it was denied. He also worked toward providing Puerto Rico with sufficient revenues for a civil government and the construction of public buildings. He did not run for reelection in 1904.

BIBLIOGRAPHY

Hispanic Americans in Congress. Washington, DC: Government Printing Office, 1995.

Jane L. Delgado (1953–)

In 1986, Jane Delgado became president and chief executive officer of the National Coalition of Hispanic Heath and Human Services; since the mid-1960s, Delgado had worked in Washington, D.C., ensuring that Hispanic health issues were receiving national funding and federal attention. In addition to being the first Hispanic woman to serve in this position with the council, she also sits on a number of health advisory boards including the United Way of America. Delgado joined the U.S. Department of Health and Human Services in 1979 and worked in several departments before being named president and CEO of the Coalition of Spanish Speaking Mental Health Organizations, later called the National Coalition of Hispanic Health and Human Services.

BIBLIOGRAPHY

Garza, Melita Marie. "Latino Leader Hits Health Plan; Reforms Are Said to Shortchange Illegal Immigrants." *Chicago Tribune* (March 23, 1994): 8.

Sowers, Leslie. "A So Salad! Latino Health Guide Considers Care, Culture." *The Houston Chronicle* (October 16, 1997): 1.

Democratic National Committee Hispanic Caucus

Founded in 1977, the Democratic National Committee Hispanic Caucus is composed of Hispanic and Anglo politicians. It serves to bring national attention to Hispanic achievements and to address Hispanic concerns. It also concerns itself with executive and judicial issues affecting Spanish-speaking people. The caucus is privately funded and has a newsletter called *Avance.* **See also** Political Participation.

BIBLIOGRAPHY

Moore, Joan and Harry Packon. *Hispanics in the United States.* Englewood Cliffs, NJ: Prentice Hall, 1985.

Weyr, Thomas. *Hispanic USA.* New York: Harper and Row, 1988.

Lincoln Diaz-Balart (1954–)

After earning his law degree, Lincoln Diaz-Balart served as assistant state attorney in Miami for Janet Reno, who was then state attorney for Florida. He was elected to the Florida State House and State Senate before winning a seat in the U.S. House of Representatives as a Republican in 1992. As a U.S. representative, he has served on the Foreign Affairs Committee and as chairman of the Housing Task Force of the **Congressional Hispanic Caucus. See also** Political Leadership.

BIBLIOGRAPHY

Boswell, Thomas D. "The Cuban-American Homeland in Miami." *Journal of Cultural Geography* 13, no. 2 (Spring 1993): 133–47.

Clymer, Adam. "Minority Candidates See Congress as a Useful Tool." *New York Times* 142 (September 20, 1992): 15N, 26L.

Patricia Diaz Dennis (1946–)

Patricia Diaz Dennis worked as a lawyer in Los Angeles for many years, representing management in labor disputes; in 1983 she was nominated to the National Labor Relations Board by President Ronald Reagan. At the end of her tenure there in 1986, President Reagan appointed her commissioner of the Federal Communications Commission, where she implemented minority preferences in broadcasting licenses. After returning to the private sector briefly, she returned to public service in 1991 to become assistant secretary of state, overseeing the Department of Human Rights and Humanitarian Affairs in the administration of President George Bush. In 1993, she returned to the private sector in telecommunications.

BIBLIOGRAPHY

Keller, Bill. "Infighting at Labor Board Is Reported." *The New York Times* (July 11, 1984): 21.

Oberdorfer, Dan. "Hispanic Democrat Named to Head State Department's Human Rights Office." *The Washington Post* (May 9, 1992): A11.

Discrimination

Mexican Americans have suffered discrimination since the United States acquired the American Southwest in the **Treaty of Guadalupe Hidalgo** (1848) at the end of the **Mexican War**. In *The Chicano Political Experience* (1977), Chris Garcia explains that the majority of Americans, who consider themselves first-class citizens, see the conquered Mexican Americans, Chicanos, and Mexican immigrants as inferior. This negative, stereotypical assessment has caused most Mexican Americans to experience discrimination in employment, public places, and institutions, and to encounter barriers to successful participation in political, social, and economic endeavors. Many among the majority group, who control the country's political, social, and economic policy, have used differences between themselves and members of minority groups to discriminate.

Mexican Americans have created organizations to challenge all forms of **discrimination**, including the **American**

G.I. Forum, the **League of United Latin American Citizens (LULAC)**, and the politically oriented **Mexican American Political Association (MAPA)**. Economic changes have brought considerable discrimination as have changes in basic industry types, such as the shift from mining, ranching, and agriculture to manufacturing, service industries, and government installations.

Mexican Americans who left rural work for urban employment had to develop new skills and move to urban areas. By 1990 close to 94 percent of Mexican Americans were urban dwellers. Concern about discrimination shifted to issues more related to life in the cities, such as housing, education, health care, job training, and urban renewal projects in barrios.

Urban organizations were formed to face the new challenges of discrimination. These included the **Mexican American Legal Defense and Education Fund (MALDEF)**, the **National Council of La Raza**, and local **community organizations** that confronted urban discrimination issues. These organizations worked in cooperation with private corporations, local and federal agencies, and state and federal courts. The Mexican American depended on lawsuits in the courts, support from organizations formed to fight discrimination, government agencies, **affirmative action**, **bilingual education**, and voter registration drives. **See also** Acculturation; Civil Rights; Economic Equality of Latin Americans; Educational Opportunity; Immigration Policy and Hispanics; Political Participation. **See** Treaty of Guadalupe Hidalgo (1848) in Appendix 1. (SCV)

BIBLIOGRAPHY

Barrera, Mario. *Race and Class in the Southwest: A Theory of Racial Inequality.* Notre Dame, IN: University of Notre Dame Press, 1979.

Garcia, Christi. *The Chicano Political Experience.* North Scituate, MA: Duxbury Press, 1977.

Domestic Violence

Domestic violence is a problem for all cultures, but it was not until the 1980s and 1990s that domestic violence came under public scrutiny and became open to public policy debate. Brought to Congress's attention in 1978 by women's movement activists, the term was intended to defuse the focus on women as sole victims of violence. Congress could deal with the problems of violence against women if they were not viewed as a "women's problem." Latina feminist activists and scholars began to air the problem within the Latino community, not content to keep maintaining community silence or family secrets. Latina community activists began to mobilize on the problems of alcohol abuse, poverty, lack of adequate health care, workplace health problems, and lack of educational programs on these issues as a means to improving the status of the family. These Latina activists continue to move the issue out of the private sphere and into the public arena, thus challenging patriarchal structures within the family. There is a need for increased research and public awareness of domestic violence to ensure that public policy addresses related problems, and that the general public does not develop additional negative stereotypes about the Latino family. (ASR)

BIBLIOGRAPHY

Sanchez, Rosaura and Rosa Martinez Cruz, eds. *Essays on La Mujer.* Los Angeles: Chicano Studies Center Publications, 1977.

Economic Equality

The Latino community is not a cohesive ethnic subpopulation. Three major groups form the Latino community: Mexicans, Puerto Ricans, and Cubans. People of Mexican origin comprise 64 percent of all Latinos; Puerto Ricans and Cubans together constitute 16 percent. While immigrants from Central and South America have increased since 1978, they do not comprise a significant number. Concentration is therefore on the three major subpopulations that constitute 85 percent of Latinos residing in the United States. In terms of economic equality as measured by income, occupational status, and educational achievement, Cubans represent the most economically successful ethnic group among the three, followed by Puerto Ricans and Mexicans. Economic **discrimination** resulting from uneven resource distribution and stratification has been most severe for Mexicans and less severe for Puerto Ricans, but virtually nonexistent for the early anti-Castro Cuban refugees.

Since the end of the **Mexican War in 1848,** Mexican Americans have been the target of discrimination because they tend to retain their cultural traditions, including their language. As a result, negative stereotypes portraying them as lazy, prone to criminal acts, and violent have had an adverse impact on their economic success in employment, income, and occupational status. In contrast, economic inequality for Puerto Ricans (who became U.S. citizens through the annexation of Puerto Rico and the **Jones Act of 1917,** which allowed them to immigrate to the United States) took a different path. Similar to Mexicans, Puerto Ricans are identifiable because of their culture and language, and many are highly visible because of their dark skin color. Puerto Ricans have also been the target of negative stereotypes portraying them as lazy, sneaky, prone to crime and violence, and welfare dependent. These negative images have fueled economic discrimination in employment, income, and occupational status against Puerto Ricans. The anti-communist Cuban refugees have been the most successful among the three Latino groups in achieving economic equality in the United States. Initially, the Cubans came to the United States as political refugees. This group consisted of upper- and middle-class professionals and businesspeople with technical skills. However, the more recent waves in the 1980s of poor and often criminal Cubans, many of whom are black,

have increased the level of economic discrimination, and this may change the perception of Cubans in the future. With the assistance of the U.S. government, Cubans have been able to achieve economic success through federally supported programs. Their economic success coupled with their refugee status has cushioned them from discriminatory practices.

Overall, Latinos are viewed as a threat to mainstream society because of their increasing population. This perceived threat tends to reinforce negative stereotypes and anti-Latino sentiment and has established new patterns of economic inequality for this ethnic subpopulation. The best way to measure the economic equality and success of all three ethnic groups is through poverty rate, occupational status, employment, and income and educational level. The poverty rate for Mexican Americans and Puerto Ricans is more than twice that of non-Latinos, while the poverty rate for Cuban Americans is slightly higher than the rate for non-Latinos. Approximately 46 percent of Mexican Americans and 60 percent of Puerto Rican families living below the poverty level are headed by females, and about 37 percent of Mexican-American families and 48 percent of Puerto Rican families in poverty are headed by someone who did not graduate from high school. In terms of occupational status, 22 percent of the Cuban population holds managerial and professional positions, compared to 11 percent of Mexicans and 19 percent of Puerto Ricans. In contrast, approximately 33 percent of the Mexican population had positions in farming and laborer occupations, compared with 19 percent of Puerto Ricans and 20 percent of Cubans. Consequently, the higher percentage of Mexican Americans and Puerto Ricans in service, production, and laborer occupations accounts for income disparities among the three ethnic populations. The higher occupational status translates into increased job security, better benefits, and higher income.

Overall, the median income of all Latino families is below that of white, non-Latino families. Mexican-American families currently earn about 61 percent of the median income of white families, Puerto Rican families about 57 percent, and Cuban-American families about 87 percent. The income gap between Cuban-American and white, non-Latino families is smaller than for either Mexican-American or Puerto Rican families. Interestingly, Mexican-American families earned 70 percent and Puerto Rican families earned 66 percent of the Cuban-American median family income in 1994. The earnings of both Latino males and females are below those of white non-Latinos.

Equally important is the success of Latino businesses. While some sectors of the U.S. economy were decreasing in the early 1990s, the growth of Latino-owned businesses was increasing. For instance, between 1987 and 1992 the number of Latino-owned businesses increased 76 percent, from 489,973 in 1987 to 862,605 in 1992. During the same period, U.S. firms increased only 26 percent, from 13.7 to 17.3 million. Receipts for Latino-owned businesses increased by 134 percent between 1987 and 1992, from $32.8 to $76.8 billion. In 1995 Latino purchasing power stood at about $220 billion. Los Angeles had the largest number of Latino-owned businesses in the United States and the highest index of Latino purchasing power. However, Miami accounted for a larger share of the 1995 revenue for Latino-based businesses.

Economic success can also be measured by educational achievement. In this arena, Latinos are below the national average attained by all non-Latinos, which places them at a significant disadvantage in a society that equates economic success with higher educational achievement. In general, the educational level of Mexican Americans and Puerto Ricans is lower than that of Cubans. The majority of Mexican Americans have not completed four years of high school. In addition, there are fewer Mexican-American college graduates than Puerto Rican college graduates and slightly less than one-third the number of Cuban-American college graduates. Although there was an increase in the educational achievement of Cuban Americans and Puerto Ricans over Mexican Americans between 1970 and 1994, all three Latino populations fall significantly behind non-Latinos in terms of education.

Economic equality can be negatively affected by housing segregation. Not being able to live among the dominant groups in society reduces access to resources. Mexican Americans are highly concentrated in the West, while Puerto Ricans tend to live more in the East. In Los Angeles, where a significant number of Mexican Americans reside, they are less segregated than their Puerto Rican counterparts, who are highly concentrated in segregated communities in New York City. For Puerto Ricans, residential segregation is based largely on racism, because the majority of this ethnic group's members come from African origins. Consequently, they are more likely to be relegated to African-American communities that tend to be segregated. In contrast, Cuban Americans tend to be highly concentrated in Miami and experience much lower levels of residential segregation; this allows them a higher degree of access to mainstream society.

In sum, Latino ethnic populations vary in their access to such valued resources as education, occupation, income, and housing—which are all indicators of economic success. Of the three groups, Cubans enjoy more access to these resources than Puerto Ricans and Mexicans. Mexicans have the least access even though they are less residentially segregated than Puerto Ricans.

During the first half of the twentieth century, Mexican immigration into the United States was fueled by two factors. The first was that U.S. employers were seeking inexpensive labor to replace the American workers who were fighting in World War I. The second factor was the Mexican Revolution of 1910, which forced many Mexicans to seek political refuge and employment opportunities. Highly concentrated in the southwestern portion of the United States, the Mexican subpopulation was relegated to lower level occupations and low wages. The economic fluctuations in the southwestern economy led to a reduction in the demand for cheap laborers. For example, prior to the Great Depression, Mexicans enjoyed free access to the U.S. mainland to fill the demand for cheap labor by labor-intensive industries. This access changed with the onset of the Depression. Unemployed white males lost their jobs and began to compete with Mexicans for low-paying jobs and wages; this increased anti-Mexican sentiment. As a consequence, between 1929 and 1935 the U.S. government sent approximately half a million Mexican immigrants back to Mexico. While such government programs as Operation Wetback prohibited illegal immigration, these programs did not reduce the demand for cheap labor.

Although anti-Mexican sentiment fueled the repatriation movement, by the 1940s the federal government continued to fill low-level agricultural positions with Mexicans because of the growing labor shortage of white males, who were fighting in World War II. In an effort to stem illegal immigration and as a way to fill the demand for labor-intensive positions, the U.S. government (under **Public Law 45**) entered into a labor contract agreement with Mexico, thus establishing the Bracero Program (hired hands program) which operated from 1942 through 1964. Under this agreement Mexican workers were granted temporary work visas. Approximately 5 million Mexican workers were granted access to the United States labor force as seasonal workers.

The creation of the Bracero Program did not stem the wave of economic discrimination targeting the Mexican subpopulation in the second half of the twentieth century. Also, the identification of Mexicans as a colonized people who have retained their cultural traditions and language has continued to fuel economic discrimination. There are at least three contributing factors for economic discriminatory practices against Mexican Americans. First, they have been locked out of higher wage skilled positions as a result of active discriminatory practices by labor unions. This limits their economic mobility by forcing them into lower-level positions. Second, the large size of the unemployed Mexican-American labor force has reduced wages by increasing competition for jobs. Third, Mexican aliens do not protest unfair working conditions and low wages because of an increased fear of deportation. However, some Mexican Americans have gained success through legalized protest. During the 1960s **Cesar Chavez** used organized boycotts and strikes to unionize Mexican farm workers as part of the **United Farm Workers** of America. His efforts improved Mexican-American working conditions and wages. Today, the organization is still active in its mission of improving wages and working conditions. The organization's efforts have included the fight over barring chemical pesticides that affect workers. Given this limited success, Mexican Americans remain targets for cheap labor-intensive industries.

If education is the key to economic success in the United States, then Mexican Americans have not fared well. Mexican Americans are caught between dual cultures. They retain their own cultural traditions and language while attempting to assimilate into the mainstream society. Also, residential segregation and gerrymandering of local school districts has led to an underrepresentation of Latino administrators, teachers, and staff in the U.S. school system. This scenario creates a sense of alienation among Mexican-American students, leading them to have higher dropout rates in high school—which translates to lower occupational positions. Without an education in a society that values educational achievement, economic equality and success for Mexican Americans is dim. As a result of a long history of economic and educational discrimination against the Mexican subpopulation, Mexican Americans are clustered in lower occupational positions that disproportionately lock them into agricultural labor, urban barrios with high crime, and little hope for improved opportunities.

Unlike Mexican Americans, the Puerto Rican subpopulation has a different pattern of economic history in the United States. With the annexation of Puerto Rico in 1898 by the United States and the implementation of the Jones Act of 1917, Puerto Ricans were given free access to the United States and became U.S. citizens. They too came in search of an improved standard of living and in response to the U.S. economy's demand for cheap labor. Consequently, by the 1940s, approximately 70,000 Puerto Ricans had immigrated to the United States. Unlike Mexican Americans, Puerto Ricans tend to be more bilingual and are identified by their language and skin color. However, like Mexican Americans, Puerto Ricans have been targets of negative stereotypes that have fueled economic discrimination. The Puerto Rican subpopulation is concentrated in a few cities, and most Puerto Ricans reside in New York City. Puerto Ricans continued to migrate to the mainland U.S. At times migration patterns fluctuated between the two countries, with Puerto Ricans returning back to their country in light of increased unemployment on the mainland. Similar to the situations experienced by African Americans and Mexican Americans, Puerto Ricans have been exposed to economic discriminatory practices. They have been denied higher occupational positions due to language barriers, because of their skin color, and because they live in urban centers that no longer have a vibrant industrial base economy. Consequently, they have been forced to take temporary positions and low-wage jobs.

Similar to the educational experience of Mexican-American children, Puerto Ricans are caught in a dual cultural dilemma as they struggle to adapt to the U.S. educational system. Because of language barriers, movement to and from the island, and the need to support the family, there is a high dropout rate among Puerto Rican children, resulting in marginal career opportunities. The challenge for the Puerto Rican population is to assimilate economically into mainstream society. They continue to experience difficulty in moving into middle management positions, their population is too large to fully assimilate into key urban cities, and they lack adequate professional skills. Although an increasing number of Puerto Ricans have been elevated to the middle and upper classes, without a strong presence in the economy and the educational system, the majority of Puerto Ricans in the United States remain relegated to the lower stratum of American society.

Unlike other Latino groups, Cuban immigrants came to the United States as political refugees, after Fidel Castro overthrew Fulgencio Batista in 1959. At that time Cuban immigrants numbered fewer than 50,000 in the United States. By 1970, over half a million Cubans resided in the United States and by the end of the 1970s Cuban-American communities were firmly established in south Florida. The Cuban population grew to slightly more than 1 million by 1993, making it the smallest of the Latino ethnic groups.

In contrast to the immigration of Mexicans and Puerto Ricans, Cuban entry into the United States is distinguished by two main factors. First, they arrived in the United States as political refugees. As a result, the U.S. government responded by implementing a resettlement program for Cubans that provided financial, employment, business, and education assistance. Second, because the majority of Cuban refugees possessed professional, technical, and entrepreneurial skills and resources, they were able to avoid the low-status occupations that the other Latino groups had to accept. Cuban refugees were able to use their skills in the United States and thus gain upward mobility.

Cuban-owned enterprises in Miami increased from 919 in 1967 to more than 8,000 in 1980; close to one-third of all businesses in Miami are Cuban owned. In addition, 75 percent of the construction workforce in Miami is Cuban, and 40 percent of the industry is Cuban owned. Cubans control 20 percent of the banks in Miami, accounting for 16 out of 62 bank presidents and 250 bank vice presidents. In 1988 5 of the 10 largest Latino businesses were located in Dade County, Florida.

Because they received such assistance from the federal government, Cuban immigrants were not perceived as foreigners, and therefore they were not confronted with the same amount of socio-economic and cultural discrimination encountered by other Latino groups. Given their small numbers and the fact that they come from the upper and middle classes, Cuban immigrants were successfully assimilated into the mainstream American economy. Consequently, they have been overrepresented in white-collar professions and business while being underrepresented in agricultural and blue-collar occupations. Cuban refugees' entrepreneurial skills have led to the creation of their own "Little Havana" in Florida, which has facilitated the emergence of Cuban-owned business. These businesses have given newly arrived Cuban refugees economic opportunities that have made it possible to stratify Cuban refugees as employers or low-wage earners.

In contrast to the educational discrimination experienced by other Latino groups (which resulted in a lack of upward mobility), Cubans were given educational programs that facilitated their participation in mainstream society. Consequently, they have not experienced the same economic inequality as Mexicans and Puerto Ricans. While Cuban Americans (that is, those who were in the first wave of refugees from Cuba) can be considered the most successful Latino ethnic group, more recent Cuban immigrants—who are more likely to be dark complexioned, less skilled, and poor—will be exposed to the same economic discrimination as Mexicans, Puerto Ricans, and African Americans. Therefore, while Cubans as an aggregate are highly successful, considerable economic inequality and stratification do exist within the Cuban population.

However, all Latinos continue to be viewed as an economic threat by the Anglo workforce. This has reinforced economic discrimination, targeting Latinos in the areas of employment, occupational status, and income. As the United States moves into the twenty-first century, the increasing size of the Latino populations will only further exacerbate economic discriminatory practices but will also provide a window of opportunity for economic empowerment. **See also** Acculturation; Assimilation; Immigration Policy and Hispanics; Office of Economic Opportunity. (MKT)

BIBLIOGRAPHY

Aguirre, Adalberto, Jr. and Jonathan H. Turner. *American Ethnicity: The Dynamics and Consequences of Discrimination.* 2nd ed. New York: McGraw-Hill, 1995.

Bean, Frank and Marta Tienda. *The Hispanic Population of the United States.* New York: Russell Sage Foundation, 1987.

Hoffman, Abraham. *Unwanted Mexican Americans in the Great Depression: Repatriation Pressures, 1929–1939.* Tucson: University of Arizona Press, 1974.

Jaffe-Correa, Michael and David Leal. "Becoming Hispanic: Secondary Panethnic Identification among Latin American Origin Populations in the United States." *Hispanic Journal of Behavioral Sciences* 18 (1996): 214–54.

Massey, Douglas. *The Demographic and Economic Position of Hispanics in the United States: The Decade of the 1970s.* Washington, DC: National Commission for Employment Policy, 1983.

Munzo, Carlos, Jr. *Youth, Identity, Power: The Chicano Movement.* New York: Verso, 1989.

Shorris, Earl. *Latinos: A Biography of the People.* New York: Avon Books, 1992.

Wilson, Kenneth and Alejandro Portes. "Immigrant Enclaves: An Analysis of the Labor Market Experience of Cubans in Miami." *American Journal of Sociology* 86 (1980): 295–319.

Educational Opportunity

In the United States, there is a strong belief that education is vital to the proper functioning of democracy, economic development, and social stability. In an effort to further these interests, schools play an important role as egalitarian institutions that open opportunities to all social classes. Schools are thus expected to elevate the status of poor people and give them access to the mainstream economy. For many Americans, schools have come to be viewed largely as a mechanism of social mobility.

Despite this unifying belief across the nation, for many years children of different ethnic and racial backgrounds were segregated into schools that did not offer the same educational opportunities to all students. As a way to increase educational opportunity, efforts to end school segregation began in the wake of several U.S. Supreme Court decisions in the 1950s. At that time, African-American leaders had made great strides toward integrating the nation's schools. For example, suits such as *Sweatt v. Painter* and *McLaurin v. Oklahoma State Regents for Higher Education* effectively abolished segregation in colleges and universities. Later, the legalized color line was broken for the vast majority of American public elementary and secondary schools when the Supreme Court ruled that "separate was not equal" in the landmark 1954 *Brown v. Board of Education* case.

In the Latino community, groups such as the **League of United Latin American Citizens (LULAC)**, the oldest Hispanic organization in the United States, also sought to end segregation as a way to increase educational opportunity for their children. For example, in Santa Ana, California, representatives from a local LULAC council successfully sued to end the practice of segregating the state's public schools when it filed the **Menendez v. Westminister School District (1945)** lawsuit. The *Menendez* decision ended a century of segregation and forced the Orange County school system to integrate at a time when the public schools justified segregation on the grounds that Mexican children were "more poorly clothed and mentally inferior to white children."

Despite this victory, Latinos did not push for desegregation to the same extent that African Americans did. Instead, Latinos emphasized school reforms that addressed school finance issues and promoted bilingual education programs. In this effort, Latino community leaders pursued lawsuits that focused on educational disadvantages and sought to raise substandard educational opportunities.

In battles over school finance, LULAC struggled to remedy disparities between rich and poor school districts. Lawsuits over school finance concentrated on the educational disadvantages of Hispanic children by addressing inequalities in spending among school districts. To further protect Hispanic Americans through the court system, LULAC created the **Mexican American Legal Defense and Education Fund (MALDEF)** in 1968 as the legal arm of the Latino community, after securing a $2.2 million grant from the Ford Foundation.

MALDEF immediately litigated one of the earliest challenges to state school-spending inequities. The suit began in 1968 on behalf of parents of Mexican-American school children in various San Antonio (Texas) school districts. Like most states, Texas relies on a combination of state funding and local property taxes. In 1973, MALDEF challenged Texas's school finance formula in *San Antonio Independent School District v. Rodriquez*. The suit charged that the state's program discriminated against minority children in property-poor school districts throughout the state and violated a fundamental, constitutionally protected right to education. The U.S. Supreme Court, however, rejected MALDEF's argument. In its decision, the Supreme Court overturned a lower court ruling that found the Texas plan discriminatory. Instead, the divided Court refused to find that the Texas school-funding law—under which the state appropriated a set dollar amount to each school district per pupil but also allowed wealthier districts to enrich educational programs from other funds—violated the equal protection clause of the Fourteenth Amendment. The Court concluded that education was not a fundamental right and, therefore, the charge of **discrimination** based on wealth could be examined only under a minimal standard of review.

Despite MALDEF's defeat in the *Rodriquez* decision, school finance reform lawsuits were largely successful in state courts. For example, in *Serrano v. Priest* (1971), the California State Supreme Court ruled that California's constitution did not permit the quality of a child's education to be determined by the wealth of his or her parents and neighbors. Ultimately, some 28 states passed school finance reform laws. But it was not until 1982 that educational opportunity for disadvantaged children increased significantly, when the Texas State Supreme Court found in *Plyler v. Doe* that Texas public schools were constitutionally required to educate the foreign-born children of illegal immigrants.

Litigation as a means of expanding educational opportunities was not limited to the Mexican-American community or to school finance lawsuits. For example, in 1974 Puerto Rican plaintiffs won a consent decree that guaranteed bilingual instruction for New York City's 150,000 Hispanic students. In another case, a federal district court in Patchogue-Medford, New York, struck down a program for Hispanic youngsters that provided only special English as a Second Language (ESL) instruction and failed to teach students about their native culture.

Bilingual education became central to the quest for educational opportunity for Hispanic children, and congressional legislation was one way to achieve desired outcomes. For example, Congress passed the Bilingual Education Act of 1968 in recognition of the growing number of linguistically and culturally diverse students who, because of their limited English proficiency, were not receiving an education equal to their English-proficient peers. This legislation required that when a curriculum systematically "excludes minority group children from effective participation in the educational program offered by a school district," then "the district must take affirmative steps to rectify the language deficiency in order to open its instructional programs to these students."

As efforts proceeded, the federal role in bilingual education increased. By 1970 the Office of Civil Rights (OCR)

issued guidelines for school districts whose enrollment exceeded 5 percent Hispanic or other national-origin minority groups, The guidelines said that such school districts should take "affirmative steps" to help non-English speaking children participate effectively in the educational program offered by the school district. In fact, the 1970s saw many bilingual education programs that sought to make it possible for linguistically diverse children to attain the challenging academic standards required of all children enrolled in the nation's schools. In California and the Southwest, Spanish groups dominated such programs.

In 1974, the **Equal Educational Opportunity Act** (EEOA) also granted greater rights to bilingual education. The act was in response to a U.S. Supreme Court decision handed down in *Lau v. Nichols* (1974). The act states, in part, that "no state shall deny equal educational opportunity to an individual on account of his race, color, sex or national origin, or the failure by an educational agency to take appropriate action to overcome language barriers that impede equal participation by its students in its instructional program." To help school districts comply with the Court order, Congress established the Office of Bilingual Education and Minority Language Affairs in 1974. Although neither the *Lau* decision nor the EEOA mentioned or prescribed bilingual education as a remedy, such education evolved as the preferred method of adherence.

As the need for bilingual education increased, two programs gained popularity: classical bilingual education and ESL. Classical bilingual programs conduct classes in the student's native language, whereas ESL combines English and the native language. But classical programs in the public school curriculum proved more popular than ESL programs, as school boards, educators, and parents in the 1980s embraced the notion of a multicultural society. Ethnicity in this period became widely recognized as a permanent feature of American life, and emphasis moved from **assimilation**, or the "melting pot" theory, to **cultural pluralism**, with a consequent concern about maintaining ethnic pride.

Thus, these two forms of bilingual education came to serve two essential functions in the Latino community. First, they increased educational opportunities for disadvantaged students by allowing them to participate fully in school programs. Second, bilingual education contributed to multiculturalism by allowing Latinos to maintain their native language and ethnic identity.

Educational opportunities for Latinos expanded further in October 1994, when President Bill Clinton signed into law the Improving America's Schools Act (IASA), which reauthorized the Elementary and Secondary Education Act of 1965. The 1994 act mandated, for the first time, that state plans must include strategies for meeting the educational needs of limited-English-proficient students.

By the 1990s, Latinos had become an important and powerful education constituency that could effectively direct and change school policy at the elementary and secondary school levels. This was also true in higher education, where Chicano studies programs have been offered in colleges and universities. In the Latino community, both school finance reform and bilingual education have remained central to securing educational opportunity for all Latino children. **See also** Acculturation; Biculturalism. (VDD)

BIBLIOGRAPHY

Chavez, Linda. *Out of the Barrio: Toward a New Politics of Hispanic Assimilation.* New York: Basic Books, 1991.

Cornell, Charles. "Reducing Failure of LEP Students in the Mainstream Classroom and Why It Is Important." *The Journal of Educational Issue of Language Minority Students* 15 (Winter 1995): 1–16.

DiConti, Veronica. *Interest Groups and Education Reform: The Latest Crusade to Restructure the Schools.* Lanham, MD: University Press of America, 1996.

Garcia, Chris F. *Latinos and the Political System.* Notre Dame, IN: University of Notre Dame Press, 1988.

Gitlin, Todd. *The Sixties: Years of Hope, Days of Rage.* New York: Bantam Books, 1987.

Haveman, Robert H. *A Decade of Federal Antipoverty Programs.* New York: Academic Press, 1977.

Hero, Rodney. *Latinos and the U.S. Political System: A Two-Tiered Pluralism.* Philadelphia: Temple University Press, 1992.

Pitsch, Mark. "The Letter of the Law." *Education Week* 14, no. 39 (March 1995).

Williams, Juan. *Eyes on the Prize: America's Civil Rights Years 1954–1965.* New York: Penguin Books, 1998.

El Grito de Lares (1868)

The Grito de Lares was a Puerto Rican insurrection against the Spanish Crown. It is named after the town of Lares where the ultimately unsuccessful rebellion began on September 23, 1868. Most of the participants in the uprising were from the western municipalities of Puerto Rico. This insurrection was organized by Ramon Emeterio Betances, who had been exiled to the Dominican Republic. The president of the short-lived provisional government of the Republic of Puerto Rico was Francisco Ramirez Medina. The Grito de Lares was planned to coincide with the Cuban rebellion against Spain— the Grito de Yara. Many present supporters of Puerto Rican independence revere it as a major milestone in the development of Puerto Rican identity and the debut of the independence movement. The annual celebration of the Grito de Lares was popularized among separatists by **Pedro Albizu Campos** and the Nationalist Party in the 1930s. (AAB)

BIBLIOGRAPHY

Jimenez de Wagenheim, Olga. *Puerto Rico's Revolt for Independence: El Grito de Lares.* Princeton, NJ: Markus Wiener Publishing, 1993.

El Grito del Norte

In the Southwest, the practice of publishing Spanish-language newspapers that provided political news, community interest articles, information, and *corridos* (ballads) on social issues antedated the **Mexican War** with the United States from 1846 to 1848. In this long Southwest tradition, *El Grito del Norte (The Northern Call)* was published in the 1960s and 1970s in Albuquerque, New Mexico, as an independent newspaper to cover the **Chicano Power Movement**. Elizabeth "Betita" Martinez, an out-of-state activist and writer, published and edited the newspaper. *El Grito del Norte* provided political coverage for Chicano movement events, activists, and experiences during the 1960s and 1970s. The paper was not associated with **La Alianza de los Pueblos Libres** in New Mexico. (SCV)

BIBLIOGRAPHY

Gomez, Rudolph, ed. *The Changing Mexican-American.* El Paso: University of Texas, El Paso, 1972.

Martinez, Elizabeth, ed. *500 Years of Chicano History in Pictures.* Albuquerque: Southwest Community Resources, 1991.

Rosales, F. Arturo. *Chicano! The History of the Mexican American Civil Rights Movement.* Houston: Arte Publico Press, 1997.

El Movimiento

During the 1960s and 1970s, politically active Mexican Americans asserted their identities as Chicanos based on a perceived Aztec heritage rooted in the mythical homeland of Aztlan, located in the southwestern United States, and participated in a social process called El Movimiento.

Among the leaders of El Movimiento were **Rodolfo "Corky" Gonzales**, who organized the **Crusade for Justice** in Denver to confront urban inequalities for Chicanos; **Jose Angel Gutierrez**, who sought political change through **La Raza Unida Party**; **Reies Lopez Tijerina**, who organized **La Alianza Federal de Pueblos Libres** and led efforts to regain land grants from the U.S. government and common lands for northern New Mexico villages; and **Cesar Chavez**, who spearheaded the efforts of the **United Farm Workers** for recognition and rights to negotiate labor contracts with agribusiness.

During 1967 and 1968, great numbers of high school and college youths staged school walkouts and boycotts to gain educational equality. El Movimiento deteriorated in the mid-1970s and thereafter ended. **See also** Chicano Power Movement; Educational Opportunity. **See** Letter from the Santa Fe Jail by Reies Lopez Tijerina (1969) in Appendix 1. (SCV)

BIBLIOGRAPHY

Rosales, F. Arturo. *Chicano! The History of the Mexican American Civil Rights Movement.* Houston: Arte Publico Press, 1997.

Weber, David F. *Foreigners in the Native Land: Historical Roots of the Mexican Americans.* Albuquerque: University of New Mexico Press, 1973.

El Partido del Pueblo Unido (United People's Party)

El Partido del Pueblo Unido was founded in 1890 in San Miguel County, New Mexico, by Mexican Americans who were dissatisfied with the two major political parties in the United States. The party was associated locally with the Caballeros de Labor and nationally allied itself with the Populist Party and had some success in local elections in 1890 and 1892. The party managed to secure candidates for county offices in these two elections, but party support declined after 1892 and no party candidates were put forth in the 1894 elections.

BIBLIOGRAPHY

Beck, Warren A. *New Mexico*. Norman: University of Oklahoma Press, 1962.

El Partido Liberal Mexicano (PLM)

In the late nineteenth century, many Mexicans, because of lack of work, scarcity of land, and poverty, had migrated to the United States and had worked for U.S. railroads and mining companies. They returned to Mexico with new political and social ideas and with labor union experience. Mexican citizens who wanted economic and social improvements in Mexico inspired the creation of Partido Liberal Mexicano (PLM), a radical liberal political party. The more militant organizers, such as the brothers **Ricardo Flores Magon** and **Enrique Flores Magon**, who had a violent philosophy and radical tactics, were exiled from Mexico to the United States in 1904. They helped to organize the party from their exile. Fund-raising activities for the PLM were organized in the barrios of Los Angeles and throughout the Southwest. The Mexican Revolution of 1910, promoted by the Partido Liberal Mexicana, terminated the political rule of President Porfirio Diaz. **Chicano Power Movement** activists and scholars consider the PLM an example of revolutionary politics supported by Chicanos/Latinos in the United States. (SCV)

BIBLIOGRAPHY

Garcia, Mario T. *Mexican Americans*. New Haven, CT: Yale University Press, 1989.
Ruiz, Ramon Eduardo. *Triumphs and Tragedy: A History of the Mexican People*. New York: W.W. Norton, 1992.

Rita Elizondo (1953–)

Rita Elizondo began her political career working for Democratic vice-presidential candidate Walter Mondale in 1976 and quickly moved up the ranks to the national level. Elizonda has spent her life trying to increase the number and visibility of Hispanic political leaders. She began as a voter registration coordinator in San Antonio, Texas, and subsequently moved to Washington where she worked on the Mondale-Ferraro campaign in 1984. After working briefly for the director of the **National Association of Latino Elected and Appointed Officials,** she became the executive director of the **Congressional Hispanic Caucus** Institute, which informs the public about current and future Hispanic leaders. **See also** Political Participation; Voting Rights.

BIBLIOGRAPHY

Vaughan, Vicki. "Hispanic Chamber Picks New President." *San Antonio Express-News* (July 7, 1998): 2.

Emigrant Agency Law

The Emigrant Agency Law was created in 1929 by the state of Texas in response to the hiring of Mexican and Chicano workers by the area's sugar beet companies. The legislation required out-of-state labor recruiters to pay a $1,000 occupational tax for foreign workers. It also called for a $10 employment license fee as outlined by employment agency law and a $5,000 bond charge. This money was then given to the county in which the paying employer worked. While this law was meant to help local Texans gain work and to control sugar beet prices by discouraging cheap labor, it did little to discourage hiring practices of Mexican Americans and native Mexican labor. **See also** Illegal Aliens; Immigration Policy and Hispanics.

BIBLIOGRAPHY

Garcia, Mario T. *Mexican Americans*. New Haven, CT: Yale University Press, 1989.

English Only/English First

Latinos are the second largest ethnic minority group in the United States. Sometime within the next several decades, Latinos will surpass African Americans as the nation's largest minority group. Consequently, scholars, journalists, and policy makers are increasingly focusing attention on the Latino population to understand more about this group and its impact on U.S. society.

Although categorized as one ethnic group, Latinos or "Hispanics" are actually many groups. The category of Latinos is made up of Puerto Ricans, Mexican Americans, Cubans, Central and South Americans, and other "Spanish Americans." Each of these groups has a distinct experience in the United States and their histories are therefore as varied as their experiences.

The largest Latino group is of Mexican origin, making up about 60 percent of the Latino population. Puerto Ricans make up about 15 percent, Cubans 5 percent, and Central and South Americans, and other "Spanish Americans" make up about 20 percent of the Spanish-origin population.

The history of Latinos, particularly Mexican Americans, reflects indigenous and immigrant origins, and their experiences are distinct as well as similar to other U.S. ethnic groups. These experiences have continued to affect their interaction with U.S. public policies. For example, in the United States there is currently a debate between proponents of English as the official language of the United States and immigrants and non-English speakers.

At the time of the nation's founding, it was commonplace to hear as many as 20 languages spoken in daily life, including Dutch, French, German, and numerous Native American languages. Even the Articles of Confederation were printed in German as well as English. During the nineteenth and early twentieth centuries, the nation's linguistic diversity grew as successive waves of Europeans immigrated to these shores and U.S. territory expanded to include Puerto Rico, Hawaii, and the Philippines.

Just as languages other than English have always been a part of our history and culture, the debate over establishing a national language dates back to the country's beginnings. John Adams proposed to the Continental Congress in 1780 that an official academy be created to "purify, develop, and dictate usage of" English. His proposal was rejected as undemocratic and a threat to individual liberty.

Nonetheless, restrictive language laws have been enacted periodically since the late nineteenth century, usually in response to new waves of immigration. These laws, in practice if not in intent, have punished immigrants for their foreignness and violated their **civil rights.**

In the early 1980s—again during a period of concern about new immigration—a movement arose seeking to establish English as the nation's official language. The English Only movement promoted the enactment of legislation that restricts or prohibits the use of languages other than English by government agencies and, in some cases, by private businesses. The movement has met with some success; English Only laws have been passed in several states. An English Language Amendment to the Constitution has also been proposed.

These English Only laws can abridge the rights of individuals who are not proficient in English; among other effects, the laws perpetuate false stereotypes of immigrants and non-English speakers. Such laws are contrary to the spirit of tolerance and diversity embodied in the Constitution of the United States. To the millions of Latinos in the United States, an English Language Amendment to the Constitution poses one more barrier to proving their "loyalty" to the United States. To the millions whose families have been in the United States since the creation of the country, such an amendment would continue to depict them as foreigners. To the millions who emigrate to the United States legally, and who are fully prepared to learn English, such laws disenfranchise them by criminalizing their lack of proficiency in English.

English Only laws vary from state to state. Some state statutes simply declare English as the "official" language of the state. Other state and local edicts limit or bar how much the government can provide non-English language assistance and services. For example, some local laws restrict **bilingual education** programs, prohibit multilingual ballots, or forbid non-English government services in general—including such services as courtroom translation or multilingual emergency police lines. Sixteen states have English Only laws, and many others are considering such laws. In some states these laws were passed decades ago during upsurges of nativism—most however have been passed since the 1980s. Among the English Only states are Arizona, Arkansas, California, Colorado, Florida, Georgia, Illinois, Indiana, Kentucky, Mississippi, Nebraska, North Carolina, North Dakota, South Carolina, Tennessee, and Virginia.

The consequences of these laws vary from state to state. Some versions of the proposed English Language Amendment would void almost all state and federal laws that require the government to provide services in languages other than English. The services affected would include health, education, and social welfare services; job training; translation assistance to crime victims and witnesses in court and administrative proceedings; voting assistance and ballots; drivers licensing exams; and AIDS-prevention education.

Passage of an English Only ordinance by Florida's Dade County in 1980, barring public funding of activities that involved the use of languages other than English, resulted in the cancellation of all multicultural events and bilingual services, ranging from directional signs in the public transit system to medical services at the county hospital.

Where basic human needs are met by bilingual and multilingual services, the consequences of their elimination could be dire. For example, the *Washington Times* reported in 1987 that a 911 emergency dispatcher who spoke Spanish was able to save the life of a Salvadoran woman's baby son, who had stopped breathing, by instructing the woman in performing cardiopulmonary resuscitation until paramedics arrived.

English Only laws are primarily aimed at government services and programs. However, such laws can also affect private businesses. For example, several southern California cities have passed ordinances that forbid or restrict the use of foreign languages on private business signs.

Some English Only advocates have opposed a telephone company's use of multilingual operators and multilingual directories, the Federal Communications Commission's licensing of Spanish-language radio stations, and bilingual menus at fast-food restaurants.

These English Only laws target primarily Latinos and Asians, who make up the majority of recent immigrants. Most language minority residents are Spanish-speaking, a result of the sharp rise in immigration from Latin America during the mid-1960s. These laws deprive people of their rights under the Equal Protection Clause of the Fourteenth Amendment. For example, laws that have the effect of eliminating courtroom translation severely jeopardize the ability of people on trial to follow and comprehend the proceedings. English Only laws interfere with the right to vote by banning bilingual ballots, or with a child's right to education by restricting bilingual instruction. Such laws also interfere with the right of workers to be free of discrimination in workplaces where employers have imposed "speak English only" rules.

Restrictions of immigrants and their language is nothing new, however. Our nation was tolerant of linguistic diversity up until the late 1800s, when an influx of Eastern and Southern Europeans, as well as Asians, aroused nativist sentiments and prompted the enactment of restrictive language laws. A 1911 Federal Immigration Commission report falsely argued that the "old" Scandinavian and German immigrants had assimilated quickly, while the "new" Italian and Eastern European immigrants were inferior to their predecessors, less willing to learn English, and more prone to political subversion.

To "Americanize" the immigrants and exclude people who were perceived to be of the lower classes and undesirable, English literacy requirements were established for public employment, naturalization, immigration, and suffrage. The New York State constitution was amended to disenfranchise over one million Yiddish-speaking citizens. The California constitution was similarly amended to disenfranchise Chinese, who were seen as a threat to the "purity of the ballot box."

During the same period, the government sought to "Americanize" Native American Indian children by taking them from their families and forcing them to attend English-language boarding schools, where they were punished for speaking their indigenous languages.

The intense anti-German sentiment that accompanied the outbreak of World War I prompted several states, where bilingual schools had been commonplace, to enact extreme language laws. For example, Nebraska passed a law in 1919 prohibiting the use of any other language than English through the eighth grade. The U.S. Supreme Court subsequently declared the law an unconstitutional violation of due process.

The late-twentieth-century English Only laws are founded on false stereotypes of immigrant groups. Such laws do not simply disparage the immigrants' native languages but assault the rights of the people who speak the languages.

Elections within the United States have for over 30 years required bilingual ballots. Many question why bilingual ballots are needed because **citizenship** is required to vote, English literacy is required for citizenship, and political campaigns are largely conducted in English. In fact, these are necessary because naturalization for U.S. citizenship does not require English literacy for people over 50 or who have been in the United States for 20 years or more. Thus, there are many elderly immigrant citizens whose ability to read English is limited, and who cannot exercise their right to vote without bilingual ballots and other voter materials. Moreover, bilingual campaign materials and ballots foster a better informed electorate by increasing the information available to people who lack English proficiency. Finally, even if people acquire English language skills, they may still understand issues better in their native language.

Others believe that bilingual education delays immigrant children's learning of English, in contrast to the "sink or swim" method that was used in the past. In fact, the primary purpose of bilingual programs in elementary and secondary schools—which use both English and a child's native language to teach all subjects—is to develop proficiency in English and thus facilitate the child's transition to all-English instruction. Although debate about this approach continues, the latest studies show that the more extensive the native language instruction, the better students perform all around, and that the bilingual method engenders a positive self-image and self-respect by validating the child's native language and culture. Further, while many think that the "sink or swim" experiences of past immigrants served them well and should not be altered for recent immigrant waves, research has show that this older experience left more of them "underwater" than not. In 1911, the U.S. Immigration Service found that 77 percent of Italian, 60 percent of Russian, and 51 percent of German immigrant children were one or more grade levels behind in school, compared with 28 percent of U.S.-born English-only children. Moreover, those immigrants who did manage to "swim" unaided in the past, when agricultural and factory jobs were plentiful, might not do so well in today's "high-tech" economy, with its more rigorous educational requirements.

Finally, English Only laws are believed to speed up the assimilation of recent immigrants by diminishing the isolation of their own language. In fact, recent immigrants are acquiring English proficiency and assimilating as quickly as did earlier generations of Italian, Russian, and German immigrants. For example, research studies show that over 95 percent of first-generation Mexican Americans are English proficient, and that more than 50 percent of second-generation Mexican Americans have lost their native tongue entirely. The issue is really one of literacy for recent immigrants, and since the majority of them emigrate to the United States to work, their literacy skills are their first priority as well. Latinos are affected differentially depending on where they reside within the United States. These laws, many based on misunderstanding and stereotyping of the Latino cultures, only serve to exacerbate already tense situations in many major U.S. cities. **See also** Biculturalism; Discrimination; Economic Equality; Educational Opportunity; Voting Rights.

BIBLIOGRAPHY

Adams, Karen L. and Daniel T. Brink, eds. *Perspectives on Official English: The Campaign for English as the Official Language of the USA.* New York: Mouton de Gruyter, 1990.

De la Peña, Fernando. *Democracy or Babel? The Case for Official English in the United States.* Washington, DC: U.S. English, 1991.

Lang, Paul C. *The English Language Debate: One Nation, One Language?* Springfield, NJ: Enslow Publishers, 1995.

Tatalovich, Raymond. *Nativism Reborn? The Official English Language Movement and the American States.* Lexington: University Press of Kentucky, 1995.

Equal Educational Opportunity Act of 1974

The Equal Educational Opportunity Act (EEOA) of 1974 mandated compliance with a U.S. Supreme Court decision handed down in *Lau v. Nichols* **(1974).** In the *Lau* decision, the Supreme Court held schools responsible for helping students who might find their "classroom experiences wholly incomprehensible because they do not understand English." At that time, the education of limited-English-proficient students became a public school concern, particularly for Hispanics. The act states, in part, that "no state shall deny equal educational opportunity to an individual on account of his race, color, sex or national origin, or the failure by an educational agency to take appropriate action to overcome language barriers that impede equal participation by its students in its instructional program." Although neither the *Lau* decision nor the EEOA mentioned or prescribed **bilingual education** as a remedy, such a method evolved as the preferred means of adherence. **See also** Educational Opportunity. (VDD)

BIBLIOGRAPHY

Cornell, Charles. "Reducing Failure of LEP Students in the Mainstream Classroom and Why It Is Important." *The Journal of Educational Issue of Language Minority Students.* 15 (Winter 1995): 1–16.

Espinoza v. Farah Manufacturing (1973)

A massive strike began in 1972 at the Farah manufacturing plant in El Paso, Texas, after the company refused to allow plant workers to join the Amalgamated Clothing Workers of America. During the **Farah strike**, Celia Espinoza, who had been denied employment by Farah, brought suit against the company; she alleged that Farah had discriminated against her on the basis of her Mexican citizenship. In *Espinoza v. Farah Manufacturing*, the U.S. Supreme Court ruled against Espinoza and asserted that **discrimination** on the basis of alienage was permissible under the **Civil Rights Act of 1964.**

BIBLIOGRAPHY

Berlin, Philip. "Crackdown on Bias toward Immigrants." *Legal Times* (September 30, 1991): 29.

Ernestine D. Evans (1917–)

In 1941, Ernestine Evans ran for the state legislature of New Mexico at the urging of the state's Democratic Party to fill the candidacy of her deceased husband, Alcadio Griego. After her successful election bid, Evans served in the legislature from 1941 to 1943. In 1945, she went on to become an administrator in the New Mexico Land Office. Evans later functioned as manager of finance for the State Board of Education beginning in 1953, after which she went on to work as a member of the legislative council and as the administrative secretary to the governor. In 1967, Evans was elected secretary of state, being reelected in 1978. After retiring from active politics, she wrote *Turquoise and Coral* (1986), which contains stories about the people of northern New Mexico.

BIBLIOGRAPHY

Soto, Monica. "A New Mexico Original Has Her 80th Birthday." *The Santa Fe New Mexican* (September 8, 1997): A2.

Fair Employment Practices Committee

The Fair Employment Practices Committee was established in 1941 by executive order of President Franklin D. Roosevelt. The committee was a division of the Office of Production Management and was dedicated to dealing with employment-related complaints from Mexican Americans in the Southwest. The committee investigated **discrimination** charges issued against private companies working under federal contracts and held the power to eliminate any wrongful employment practices. The organization also helped maintain fair hiring and promotion practices for Mexican Americans while broadening existing employment opportunities.

After World War II, President Harry Truman proposed a continuation of the committee, but the request was overturned by the U.S. Senate. However, the discontinuation of the Fair Employment Practices Committee caused similar organizations to form, including a New Mexico group that maintained legislative powers under the state's fair employment practices act. Another group formed was the federal Equal Employment Opportunity Commission, a group created by Congress to accomplish many of the tasks of the defunct Fair Employment Practices Committee.

BIBLIOGRAPHY

Garcia, Mario T. *Mexican Americans.* New Haven, CT: Yale University Press, 1989.

Farah Strike (1972–1974)

In 1972 employees of Farah Manufacturing, a maker of men's slacks at plants in El Paso, Texas, expressed interest in joining the Amalgamated Clothing Workers of America. The company was determined to defeat unionization, and a massive strike ensued. Thousands of employees, most of whom were Mexican Americans, were arrested, but Farah's operations were crippled. The strike gained media attention when Farah resorted to using dogs against the strikers. As a result, Catholic leaders spoke out in support of the strikers and people began boycotting Farah clothing on a national scale. In 1974 after tremendous financial loss and adverse rulings by the National Labor Relations Board, Farah conceded defeat. **See also** *Espinoza v. Farah Manufacturing* (1973).

BIBLIOGRAPHY

Coyle, Laurie, Gail Hershatter, and Emily Honig. "Women at Farah." In Magdalena Mora and Adelaida DelCastillo, eds. *Mexican Women in the United States.* Los Angeles: University of California Chicano Studies Resource Center, 1980.

Finger, Bill. "Victoria Sobre Farah." *Southern Exposure* 4 (1976): 45–49.

Federation for American Immigration Reform (FAIR)

With its headquarters in Washington, D.C., the Federation for American Immigration Reform (FAIR) works to reform the nation's immigration policies. With more than 70,000 members nationwide, FAIR maintains that large-scale immigration does not serve the national interest. FAIR argues for a temporary moratorium on all immigration except spouses and minor children of U.S. citizens and a limited number of refugees. Such a moratorium, they argue, would allow time to regain control of U.S. borders and reduce overall levels of immigration to 300,000 a year.

FAIR began in 1978 as an outgrowth of the population environment movement, because the focus for groups such as Zero Population Growth (ZPG) was strictly on the impact of unchecked population growth generally, and not on politically sensitive immigration issues. Since its founding, FAIR has been among the most outspoken organizations in the call for immigration reform. **See also** Immigration and Naturalization Service; Immigration Policy and Hispanics. (VDD)

BIBLIOGRAPHY

Telephone interview with Jack Martin, press officer for the Federation for American Immigration Reform, September 2, 1997, Washington, D.C.

Antonio Manuel Fernandez (1902–1956)

Antonio Fernandez was elected to the U.S. House of Representatives as a Democrat from New Mexico in 1943 and served until his death. Prior to his election, he received formal training at Highlands University in Las Vegas, New Mexico, and a law degree from Cumberland University in Lebanon, Tennessee. Before his election to Congress, Fernandez served in the New Mexico House of Representatives (1935) and as the first assistant attorney general for New Mexico from 1937 to 1941. (CEM)

Antonio Fernandez (D-NM) served more than a dozen years in the U.S. House of Representatives. *Library of Congress.*

and served for 10 years. Before Fernandez was in Congress, he served in the Louisiana General Assembly as a representative and senator. He was called to active duty as a lieutenant commander in the U.S. Navy Reserve in 1941.

BIBLIOGRAPHY
Vigil, Maurilio E. *Hispanics in Congress.* Lanham, MD: University Press of America, 1996.

Antonio Fernós-Isern (1885–1974)

Antonio Fernós-Isern, a physician and politician, served as resident commissioner to the U.S. House of Representatives for 19 years, becoming the longest serving commissioner from Puerto Rico. From 1919 to 1933 he held various administrative positions in the health services: health officer of the city of San Juan (1919), assistant commissioner of health of Puerto Rico (1920–1931), and commissioner of health of Puerto Rico (1931–1933 and 1942–1946). In 1933, due to ideological differences with the Coalitionist government, he resigned from his position as commissioner. In 1937 Fernós-Isern, along with Luis Muñoz Marín, organized the Liberal Party of Puerto Rico, which later became the **Popular Democratic Party**. In 1940 he was an unsuccessful candidate for resident commissioner.

During his 19 years as resident commissioner, Antonio Fernós-Isern played an important part in giving Puerto Ricans a greater role in governing their island. *Library of Congress.*

BIBLIOGRAPHY
Biographical Directory of the United States Congress, 1774–1989. Washington, DC: United States Government Printing Office, 1989.

Joachim Octave Fernandez (1896–1978)

Joachim Fernandez, a Democrat, was the second Hispanic elected to the U.S. House of Representatives from Louisiana, a state that does not have a large Hispanic community. He was elected in 1931

In 1945 the newly appointed governor of Puerto Rico, Jesús T. Piñero, selected Fernós-Isern as his replacement for resident commissioner to the U.S. Congress. Subsequently Fernós-Isern was reelected four times. During his tenure as commissioner, Fernós-Isern played an important part in giving Puerto Ricans a greater role in governing the island. On August 5, 1947, the Crawford project, allowing Puerto Ricans to elect their governor, was approved by Congress and signed into law by President Harry Truman.

On June 8, 1950, the Senate approved **Public Law 600**, allowing Puerto Rico to establish its own constitutional government. Fernós-Isern served as president of the constitutional convention, which formulated the status of Commonwealth or Estado Libre Asociado. The constitution was approved and ratified by the convention, and on July 25, 1952, the Commonwealth relationship between the United States and Puerto Rico was established.

Fernós-Isern did not seek reelection in 1964; he returned to Puerto Rico the following year, where he was elected to the Senate, serving from 1965 to 1969. **See** Constitution of Puerto Rico (1952) in Appendix 1.

BIBLIOGRAPHY
Hispanic Americans in Congress. Washington, DC: Government Printing Office, 1995.

Maurice Ferre (1935–)

Maurice Ferre began his political career in 1966 when he was elected to the Florida House of Representatives as a Democrat. In 1967, he became city commissioner of Miami, serving until 1970. He was elected mayor of Miami in 1973 for the first of three terms. Serving from 1973 until 1985, Ferre was mayor during Miami's rapid growth, including large influxes of immigrants from Cuba. As the city struggled in the late 1990s to find a mayor who could return integrity to the office after a wave of scandals, Ferre was considered for the post by the city council but not nominated.

BIBLIOGRAPHY
"Acquittals Fueled Fire in Miami." *Chicago Tribune* (December 5, 1990): 5.
Weaver, Jay. "Miami in State of Major Limbo." *Sun-Sentinel* (March 7, 1998): A1.

Francisca Flores (1913–1996)

Francisca Flores worked for the rights of Chicanos and Latinos well before the advent of the **Chicano Power Movement**. She helped organize the defense committee for the young Chicano defendants of the **Sleepy Lagoon** murder case, cofounded the **Mexican American Political Association (MAPA)** that helped get **Edward R. Roybal** elected to Congress in 1960 and cofounded **Commission Femenil Mexicana Nacional** in 1970. **See also** Civil Rights; Community Organizations. (ASR)

BIBLIOGRAPHY
Ruiz, Vicki L. *From Out of the Shadows.* New York: Oxford University Press, 1998.

Patricio Fernandez Flores (1929–)

Patricio Flores, as archbishop of the San Antonio archdiocese, supported the **civil rights** of Mexican Americans. He served as chairman of the Texas Advisory Committee of the U.S. Civil Rights Commission. In 1972 he inaugurated the Mexican American Cultural Center in San Antonio. In 1974 he helped establish the **Communities Organization for Public Service (COPS)**. (SCV)

BIBLIOGRAPHY

McMurtrey, Martin. *Mariachi Bishop: The Life Story of Patricio Flores*. San Antonio, TX: Corona Publishing, 1985.

Enrique Flores Magon (1887–1954)

Enrique Flores Magon was a Mexican liberal; in August 1900 he and his brother **Ricardo Flores Magon** published *Regeneracion*, a Mexico City weekly newspaper that spoke out against the presidency of Porfirio Diaz and supported an anti-Diaz group. Both brothers were arrested in 1901 and were imprisoned for a year. Subsequently, they renewed their anti-Diaz activities and promoted a free and liberal press in Mexico. After two more arrests and imprisonments, they fled to San Antonio, Texas, and later to St. Louis, Missouri, where they continued their activities. They solicited funds from U.S. supporters and from liberal clubs organized throughout Mexico in opposition to the Diaz government. Enrique urged his fellow Mexicans to prepare for the day of liberation. In St. Louis, they helped to organize **El Partido Liberal Mexicano** (Mexican Liberal Party), and they also organized a junta. The Flores Magon brothers were arrested and charged with violating U.S. neutrality laws; they were convicted and imprisoned in Leavenworth Penitentiary. Released from jail in 1923, Enrique moved to Mexico where he died in 1954. The brothers' writings have served as a model for writers in the **Chicano Power Movement**. (SCV)

BIBLIOGRAPHY

Leon-Portilla, Miguel, ed. *Diccionario Porrua.* 5th ed. Mexico, D.F.: Editorial Porrua, 1964.

Meyer, Michael C. and William L. Sherman. *The Course of Mexican History.* Oxford: Oxford University Press, 1995.

Ricardo Flores Magon (1873–1922)

Ricardo Flores Magon gained recognition as a journalist and as a political leader. Both Ricardo and his brother **Enrique Flores Magon** were liberal ideologues of the Mexican Revolution of 1910. The brothers published *Regeneracion*, a Mexico City weekly newspaper that spoke out against the dictatorial regime of Mexican president Porfirio Diaz. Ricardo's antigovernment actions led to his arrest and imprisonment. After his release, he continued his attacks on Diaz's government, this time through the periodical, *El Hijo del Ahuizote*. Again he was imprisoned. To escape Diaz's oppression, Ricardo fled to San Antonio, Texas, and subsequently to St. Louis, Missouri, where, in 1906, he and his brother created **El Partido**

Liberal Mexicano (Mexican Liberal Party). In 1907 he published a paper in Los Angeles titled *Revolucion*. He influenced Chicano and Mexican workers of the southwestern United States. In time, Ricardo preached anarchism. He was convicted of violating U.S. neutrality laws and was imprisoned at Leavenworth Penitentiary, where he died in 1922. (SCV)

BIBLIOGRAPHY

Cockcroft, James. *Intellectual Precursors of the Mexican Revolution.* Austin: University of Texas, 1968.

Leon-Portilla, Miguel, ed. *Diccionario Porrua.* 5th ed. Mexico, D.F.: Editorial Porrua, 1964.

Foraker Act of 1900

The Foraker Act was a federal law that ended military rule in Puerto Rico following the **Spanish-American War** and became Puerto Rico's constitution until passage of the **Jones Act of 1917**. Under the Foraker Act, Puerto Ricans, who were formerly Spanish citizens, became U.S. nationals but not United States citizens. Goods exchanged between Puerto Rico and the United States were charged tariffs. This act also authorized the president of the United States to appoint Puerto Rico's governor and supreme court justices. The governor appointed some legislators, others were elected. (AAB)

BIBLIOGRAPHY

Gould, Lyman J. *La ley Foraker: Raices de la politica colonial de los Estados Unidos.* 2nd ed. Rio Piedras, PR: Editorial Universitaria, 1975.

Jose Antonio Fuste (1943–)

After obtaining a law degree from the University of Puerto Rico, Jose Antonio Fuste worked on the island as a lawyer from 1968 to 1985. In 1985, President Ronald Reagan appointed Fuste as a judge on the U.S. District Court for the District of Puerto Rico.

BIBLIOGRAPHY

American Bar Association. *Directory of Minority Judges in the United States.* Chicago: The Association, 1994.

Brownson, Charles B. *Judicial Staff Directory.* Mt. Vernon, VA: Congressional Staff Directory, 1997.

Jamie B. Fuster (1941–)

Jamie Fuster, a native Puerto Rican, has divided his career between Washington, D.C., and Puerto Rico. He served as U.S. deputy assistant attorney general in the 1980s and then returned to Puerto Rico where he was president of Catholic University. From 1984 to 1992, Fuster served as the resident commissioner of Puerto Rico to the U.S. Congress, being elected as a Democrat.

BIBLIOGRAPHY

Barone, Michael. *Politics in America.* Washington, DC: National Journal, 1984.

Biographical Dictionary of the United States Congress, 1774–1989. Washington, DC: U.S. Government Printing Office, 1989.

Gadsden Treaty (1853)

The Gadsden Treaty involved the last major addition of land to the United States in continental North America. Congressmen from the American Southwest supported a transcontinental railroad that followed a southern route, and the best route passed through territory owned by Mexico. In 1853 Congress sent James B. Gadsden to negotiate with Mexican President Santa Anna, who desperately needed the $10 million the United States was offering for the land. The territory secured now forms the southern boundary of New Mexico and Arizona, and the international border with Mexico. **See** Gadsden Treaty (1853) in Appendix 1. (JRB)

BIBLIOGRAPHY

Garber, Paul Neff. *The Gadsden Treaty.* Philadelphia: Morris Press, 1923.

Ernesto Galarza (1905–1984)

Ernesto Galarza was a scholar, an activist, and an organizer in California. His dedication to projects in education, agricultural labor, and research demonstrated his conviction to both principal and action. His political and academic contributions included work in education, literature, urban sociology, and Chicano studies. He wrote about these issues in more than 100 publications. His research and creative works are frequently cited in Chicano writings and are included in major Chicano bibliographies.

Together with his wife, Galarza was owner of the private Gardner School–San Jose, which was dedicated to progressive education. Through the operation of the Gardner School, Galarza challenged educational philosophy, curriculum, and methodology. He similarly contributed to agricultural labor issues through his work with labor unions. Galarza was recognized for his contributions to the U.S. Chicano community and was nominated by his international supporters for the Nobel Peace Prize. (SCV)

BIBLIOGRAPHY

Webster, Staten W. "An Interview with Ernesto Galarza." In Staten W. Webster, ed. *Ethnic Minority Groups.* Scranton, PA: International Textbook Company, 1972.

Jose Manuel Gallegos (1815–1875)

Born in New Mexico, Jose Gallegos was elected to the provincial legislature in 1843, just prior to the U.S. conquest. After New Mexico became a part of the United States, he was elected to the first territorial council, and in 1853 he became the territorial delegate to the U.S. Congress. After losing his bid at reelection, he was reinstated to the provincial legislature in 1860 and was appointed speaker of the house. During the Civil War, he was jailed briefly by Texan Confederate forces for siding with the Union, but in 1865 he was named territorial treasurer. In 1870 he was elected to his last term as territorial delegate to the U.S. Congress.

BIBLIOGRAPHY

Horgan, Paul. *Lamy of Santa Fe.* New York: Farrar, Straus and Giroux, 1975.
Twitchell, Ralph E. *The History of the Military Occupation of New Mexico from 1846 to 1851.* New York: Arno Press, 1976.

Gangs

Gangs and gang activity in the United States date back to the 1920s and prohibition, when gangs became associated with the bootlegging of liquor, drug trafficking, and other forms of crime. Until the 1950s, street gangs were predominantly white; however, as of the 1990s, gang members are primarily African Americans, Latinos, and Asian Americans. Racism, as exemplified in the 1943 **zoot suit riots**, was influential in the development of Latino gangs, as was the poor schooling system, low socio-economic status, and general feelings of disenfranchisement among Latino youth. Today, gang activity is primarily concentrated in California, Florida, and New York, and the most notorious gangs are TMC, the Bloods, the Crips, Al Capone, and Clarence Street. In addition, there are exclusively Latino gangs such as the Mexican Mafia, La Familia, and the 1 Paso, who speak Spanish and Calo. Gang members are usually in their teens and early twenties, and gang activity typically involves graffiti (called tagging), crime, drugs, and guns. However, despite their negative stereotyping, gangs often pride themselves on the benefits they offer their members; and are often the subject of police brutality and discriminatiion. Since the 1980s Latino girls have increasingly been drawn to gangs and gang activity.

BIBLIOGRAPHY

Knox, George W. *An Introduction to Gangs*. Barrien Springs, MI: Vande Vere Publishing, 1991.

Vigil, James Diego. *Barrio Gangs: Street Life and Identity in Southern California*. Austin: University of Texas Press, 1988.

Hector Garcia (1914–1996)

Hector Garcia was born in Mexico on January 17, 1914. His family moved to Mercedes, Texas, in 1918 to escape the Mexican Revolution. One of seven children, Garcia attended the University of Texas at Austin and received his bachelor's degree in zoology in 1936. He received his medical degree in 1940 from the University of Texas Medical Branch at Galveston and completed his surgical internship in 1942 at St. Joseph's Hospital, Creighton University, in Omaha, Nebraska. Garcia joined the army upon completing his medical training, and was awarded the Bronze Star with six battle stars for service during World War II. He eventually rose to the rank of major in the Medical Corps.

In 1946, Garcia started his medical practice in Corpus Christi, Texas. He contracted with the Veterans Administration (VA) to treat World War II veterans with service-connected disabilities, and often provided free medical care to people who could not afford to pay him. Many veterans told Garcia that the VA was not complying with the GI Bill of Rights, which entitled them to financial assistance for educational training and health benefits. In March 1948, Garcia called a meeting at a Corpus Christi elementary school to address the veterans' concerns. The meeting led to the founding of the **American G.I. Forum**, of which Garcia was elected chairman.

The organization captured national attention in 1949 when a Texas funeral home refused the use of a chapel to bury army private **Felix Longoria**, a veteran killed during World War II. The director of the funeral home said Longoria could be buried in the town's segregated "Mexican" cemetery, but that the chapel could not be used because the local "whites would not like it." When the owner of the funeral home refused Garcia's request to reconsider, Garcia wrote letters to members of the state legislature and to the Texas congressional delegation. Through Garcia's efforts, Longoria was eventually buried at Arlington National Cemetery.

In 1954, Garcia was a member of the Advisory Council of the Democratic National Committee. In 1960, he was chairman of the Mexican-Spanish section of the Nationalities Division of the Democratic National Committee, and helped organize **Viva Kennedy** clubs in support of Democratic presidential candidate John F. Kennedy, who appointed Garcia to the American delegation that signed a treaty between the United States and the Federation of the West Indies in 1961. President Lyndon B. Johnson appointed Garcia to the National Advisory Council on Economic Opportunity and later as U.S. ambassador to the United Nations. Garcia was also a commissioner of the U.S. Commission on Civil Rights in 1968. In 1972, Garcia was appointed to the Texas Advisory Committee on Civil Rights, and, in 1978, was a member of the White House Conference on Balanced National Growth and Economic Development. In 1979, he was a member of the U.S. attorney general's Hispanic Advisory Committee on Civil Rights.

In the 1960s, Garcia fought for repeal of the Texas poll tax, and, in 1987, he spoke out against a bill in the Texas legislature to make English the official language of the state. In 1984, President Ronald Reagan awarded Garcia the Presidential Medal of Freedom, the highest honor given a civilian by the president. In Corpus Christi, a city park and post office are named after Garcia, and a bronze sculpture of him was placed on the campus of Texas A&M University—Corpus Christi. Garcia died in 1996 at the age of 82. **See also** Felix Longoria.

BIBLIOGRAPHY

Shorris, Earl. *Latinos, a Biography of the People*. New York: W.W. Norton Co., 1992.

Hippolito Frank Garcia (1925–)

Hippolito Garcia served in the U.S. Army from 1943 to 1945 and was awarded the certificate of merit by the American Legion for his service. After receiving his law degree from St. Mary's University 1951, he worked in the San Antonio District Attorney's Office, becoming judge of the Texas County Court in 1964 and a U.S. district court judge in 1980.

BIBLIOGRAPHY

Plume, Janet. "Colonel Not at Fault in Civilian Fight." *United Press International* (August 11, 1986): Section: Regional News.

Jesus G. Garcia (1956–)

From 1980 to 1984, Jesus Garcia worked as assistant director of the Little Village Neighborhood Housing service in Chicago, Illinois. Garcia continued to serve the public as deputy commissioner of water for the city of Chicago from 1984 to 1986. He then served as Chicago city alderman from 1986 until 1992, and in 1992 he was elected to the Illinois State Senate. While in the state senate, Garcia chaired the Aviation Committee, and was also a member of the Budget and Government Operations Committee, the Education Committee, and the Finance Committee.

BIBLIOGRAPHY

Coffey, Raymond R. "UIC Job Accord Falls Flat; Key Latinos' Rivalry Helped Fuel Criticism." *Chicago Sun-Times* (December 5, 1997): 8.

Garza, Melita Marie. "Hispanic Candidates Going on the Attack." *Chicago Tribune* (March 5, 1996): 1.

Robert Garcia (1933–)

As a result of the **Voting Rights Act Amendments of 1975**, new congressional districts were created in New York, and, in 1978, Robert Garcia was elected from one of these districts as a representative to the U.S. Congress. Prior to this, Garcia had served 12 years in the New York State Senate and one year in the New York State Assembly. He was forced to resign in 1990 after he was convicted of extortion. The verdict was later overturned by the U.S. Court of Appeals. **See also** Political Participation; José E. Serrano.

BIBLIOGRAPHY

Vigil, Maurilo E. *Hispanics in Congress.* Lanham, MD: University Press of America, 1996.

Ben Garza, Jr.

Ben Garza was a pioneering civil rights leader for Mexican Americans. Based in Corpus Christi, Texas, he was to play a prominent role in the shaping of several Mexican-American civil rights organizations. In 1926, Garza called upon other Mexican-American leaders in south Texas to form a social/political organization to empower Mexican Americans. The resulting group, the **League of United Latin American Citizens (LULAC)** was formalized at Obreros Hall on February 17, 1929. LULAC has today become one of the most influential Latino organizations in the United States. Garza was LULAC's first president, serving for 1929–1930.

BIBLIOGRAPHY

Marquez, Benjamin. *LULAC.* Austin: University of Texas Press, 1993.

Emilio M. Garza (1947–)

After attending the University of Notre Dame and the University of Texas, Emilio Garza began working as a private practice lawyer in 1976. Garza then served as a judge in the U.S. District Court of the Western District of Texas, starting in 1988. In 1991, President George Bush elevated Garza to the United States Court of Appeals.

BIBLIOGRAPHY

"Hispanic Heads Bush Candidates for High Court." *The San Diego Union-Tribune* (July 1, 1991): Al.

Kurkjian, Stephen. "Bush Reported to Consider Three for High Court." *The Boston Globe* (July 1, 1991): 1.

Reynaldo Garza (1915–)

Reynaldo Garza became a U.S. district court judge in 1961, after serving in the U.S. Air Force and establishing his own law practice in Texas. In 1979 President Jimmy Carter appointed Garza to the U.S. Court of Appeals, Fifth District. In 1987 Garza was appointed to the Emergency Court of Appeals of the United States and later served as the chief judge of that court. While serving on the Emergency Court, he turned down the cabinet position of attorney general, choosing instead his lifetime appointment as a federal judge.

BIBLIOGRAPHY

"Carter Says Hispanic American was First Choice for Cabinet Job." *The New York Times* (November 3, 1980): 13.

DeLeon, Jessica. "Federal Judge Sets Benchmark for Success in South Texas." *The Houston Chronicle* (December 29, 1996):4.

Gilberto Gierbolini (1926–)

From 1951 to 1957, Gilberto Gierbolini served as a captain in the U.S. Army, seeing action in the Korean War. After his military service, Gierbolini earned a law degree in 1961 from the University of Puerto Rico, and then served as a superior court judge in Puero Rico from 1966 to 1969. Gierbolini was assistant secretary of justice for Puerto Rico from 1969 to 1972 and solicitor general from 1970 to 1972. He then became a private practice lawyer from 1972 until 1980. In 1980, President Jimmy Carter appointed Gierbolini to the U.S. District Court, where the judge served the District of Puerto Rico.

BIBLIOGRAPHY

Schanberg, Sydney H. "A Judge's Shift in D'Amato-Linked Cases." *Newsday* (December 15, 1992): 22.

Arlene F. Gillespie (1936–)

Born in Puerto Rico, Arlene Gillespie has dedicated herself to improving the economic situation of the poor and disadvantaged in Puerto Rico and the United States. She was special assistant to the secretary of labor in Puerto Rico, before moving to Washington, D.C., to serve under President John F. Kennedy in the Alliance for Progress. In 1979 she began working at the Washington, D.C., Mayor's Office on Latino Affairs, and, from 1984 to 1991, she served as director of the office. In 1991 she was appointed vice president of the National Puerto Rican Coalition, Inc.

BIBLIOGRAPHY

Sanchez, Carlos. "Emerging Leadership Challenges Hispanic Community Old Guard." *The Washington Post* (December 6, 1989): B1.

Sargent, Edward D. "Economist Named to Latino Post; Gillespie Needs Conformation of City Council." *The Washington Post* (April 12, 1984): C1.

Rodolfo "Corky" Gonzales (1928–)

Of all the leaders that emerged during the **Chicano Power Movement**, no one was more closely identified with urban youth than Rodolfo "Corky" Gonzales. As a popular boxer in Denver, Colorado, Gonzales became an active member of the city's local Democratic political machinery during the 1950s. Known as being brash and fiery, Gonzales' ability as a community organizer garnered him positions as codirector of Colorado's **Viva Kennedy** campaign in 1960 and as director of Denver's Neighborhood Youth Corps (1964) and the city's' War on Poverty program (1965). By 1966 Gonzales founded the **Crusade for Justice** after becoming disillusioned with party politics. In works such as *Yo Soy Joaquin*, Gonzales called for a cultural and political revolution among Chicano youth to establish **bilingual education**, independent Chicano schools, and economic and political separation from Anglo society.

While Gonzales earned the adoration of thousands of students, he alienated a significant portion of the Mexican-American community with his controversial separatist rhetoric. Many criticized Gonzales as self-promoting for not only the absolute control he maintained over the Crusade for Justice, but for his negative critiques of popular leaders such as **Jose Angel Gutierrez** and **Cesar Chavez**. Moreover, many Mexican-American women and men rejected the **machismo** boxing chauvinism that Gonzales' militant rhetoric embodied. Despite these criticisms, Gonzales helped inspire a new generation of Chicano youth to articulate forcefully the demands of an increasingly urban Mexican-American community. **See also** Albuquerque Walkout; Cultural Nationalism; El Movimiento; La Raza Unida Party; National Chicano Youth Liberation Conference. (TIR)

BIBLIOGRAPHY

Gonzales, Rodolfo "Corky." "Chicano Nationalism: The Key to Unity for La Raza." In Wayne Moquin, ed. *A Documentary History of the Mexican American.* New York: Bantam Books, 1972.

Marin, Christine. *A Spokesman of the Mexican American Movement: Rodolfo "Corky" Gonzales and the Fight for Chicano Liberation, 1966–1972.* San Francisco: R & E Research Associates, 1977.

Stephanie Gonzales (1950–)

In 1987, Stephanie Gonzales became deputy secretary of state for the state of New Mexico, a position she held for three years before becoming the New Mexico secretary of state in 1991. In 1994, she was reelected to the post of secretary of state. In 1993 she was appointed by President Bill Clinton to the Commission of White House Fellowships. An active member of both the **League of United Latin American Citizens (LULAC)** and the **National Association of Latino Elected and Appointed Officials**, Gonzales ran a failed attempt in 1998 for the post of lieutenant governor of New Mexico.

BIBLIOGRAPHY

Domrzalsk, Dennis. "Gonzales's Money-Saving Goal Is Costly." *Albuquerque Tribune* (April 9, 1998): C1.

"For Lieutenant Governor, Stephanie Gonzales." *Santa Fe New Mexican* (May 18, 1998): A9.

Henry Babosa Gonzalez (1916–)

Henry Babosa Gonzalez was chief probation officer of Bexar County, Texas, from 1945 to 1947, as well as a member of the San Antonio, Texas, City Council from 1953 to 1956. Gonzalez served in the Texas state senate, where he remained from 1956 to 1961 and was elected to the United States Congress in 1961. In more than 30 years of service with Congress, Gonzalez was chairman of the Select Committee on Assassinations and the Subcommittee on Housing and Community Development, as well as a member of the Banking, Finance, and Urban Affairs committees, the National Commission on Con-

Henry Babosa Gonzalez (D-TX) has served over 30 years in the U.S. House of Representatives. *Courtesy of U.S. House of Representatives.*

sumer Finance, and the U.S.-Mexico Interparliamentary Conference. He retired in 1998. His son, Charles A. Gonzales, was elected to his father's position. **See also** Political Leadership.

BIBLIOGRAPHY

Burka, Paul. "Henry B. and Henry C." *Texas Monthly* 14, no. 1 (January 1986): 182, 218–30.

Rodriguez, Eugene. *Henry B. Gonzalez: A Political Profile.* New York: Arno Press, 1976.

Graham v. Richardson (1971)

Carmen Richardson and Elise Mary Jane Leger moved to the United States and became naturalized citizens. Later, health complications caused each woman to seek federal assistance, yet their respective states denied this help due to the fact that they had not been born in the United States. In a joint case, Richardson argued against Arizona statutes and Leger against Pennsylvania laws; their attorneys argued that exclusion of welfare benefits to aliens violated the Equal Protection Clause of the Fourteenth Amendment. After the lower courts found for the women, the case was appealed to the U.S. Supreme Court.

In *Graham v. Richardson,* 403 U.S. 365 (1971), the Court found that the state laws, by placing conditions on constitutional benefits, were indeed illegal. Besides commenting on the infringement of constitutional rights, the Court also pointed out that restrictive alien welfare statutes overstepped state legislative powers; the Court maintained that only the federal government has jurisdiction over such citizenship issues.

BIBLIOGRAPHY

Garcia, Mario T. *Mexican Americans.* New Haven, CT: Yale University Press, 1989.

Grape Boycott

In 1965 the **United Farm Workers** of America (UFWA) began a strike against grape growers in Delano, California. Labor organizer **Cesar Chavez** led the strike. The UFWA's goal was to improve living and working conditions for migrant farm laborers in the San Joaquin Valley. The strikers tried to convince consumers not to purchase grapes produced by workers who were not part of the UFWA. Such boycotts attempted to pressure growers to allow collective bargaining by grape workers and to end health risks posed to farm workers by agricultural pesticides. Workers boycotted markets, picketed grape growers, and marched to publicize their campaigns. The boycott eventually spread throughout the United States. The movement eventually received the support of the American Federation of Labor–Congress of Industrial Workers, the most important union organization in the United States, as well as the support of Senator Robert F. Kennedy. The Delano strike ended in 1970, when 23 growers signed a contract with the UFWA. However, the harsh working conditions and difficulties faced by farm workers, most of whom are Hispanic immigrants, still continue. **See also** Lettuce Strikes (Salinas); March to Sacramento. (JRB)

BIBLIOGRAPHY

Dunne, John. *Delano: The Story of the California Grape Strike.* New York: Farrar, Straus & Giroux, 1967.

Steinbacher, John. *Bitter Harvest.* Whittier, CA: Orange Tree Press, 1970.

Linda Griego (1935–)

Linda Griego successfully opened and ran several restaurants in Los Angeles before being asked to serve as deputy mayor. While still in college in Washington, D.C., she worked for U.S. Representative Tom Morris and then for California Senator Alan Cranston in Washington, D.C., and Los Angeles, before deciding to open her first restaurant. She has also been on the boards of the Constitutional Rights Foundation, the Los Angeles Cultural Affairs Commission, and the Community Redevelopment Agency. Griego is now president of Rebuild LA, the recovery program created following the 1992 Los Angeles riots, which still works to improve small- and medium-sized businesses in Los Angeles and economically impoverished areas of the city.

BIBLIOGRAPHY

Feldman, Paul. "Griego and Cook Take RLA Helm; Riot Recovery: Their Election is Part of an Effort to Streamline the Agency's Operation." *Los Angeles Times* (February 16, 1994): B.

———. "The Sunday Profile; Great Expectations; As Head of RLA, Linda Griego has Definite Ideas About Getting Things Done." *Los Angeles Times* (June 5, 1994): E1.

Stella G. Guerra

Stella Guerra became assistant secretary of the interior for territorial and international affairs in 1989. She began her political career in 1980, as a staff assistant to the White House chief of protocol. From there she moved to the Department of Education in 1981, where she worked as a special assistant for international affairs. In 1983 she became the deputy for equal opportunity and director of Equal Employment Opportunity for the Air Force. She has also served on the Presidential Task Force for Women, Minorities, and the Handicapped in Science and Technology.

BIBLIOGRAPHY

Schwartz, Maralee and Frank Swoboda. "Around the Departments." *The Washington Post* (June 21, 1989): A21.

Jimmy Gurule (1951–)

Jimmy Gurule began his career in law as a professor at the University of Notre Dame Law School and as president of the **Hispanic National Bar Association**. On August 3, 1990, Gurule was sworn in as assistant attorney general, having been nominated by President George Bush; his position made him the highest ranking Hispanic ever to serve in the Department of Justice. In his role as assistant attorney general, Gurule coordinated policy making and management for the Washington, D.C., based Office of Justice Programs. He also connected federal, state, and local governmental officials to provide a united stand against violence, substance abuse, and other crimes.

BIBLIOGRAPHY

LaFraniere, Sharon. "No Justice for a Boss in Justice; Hill Law Gives Power to Subordinates in Grant-Dispensing Bureaus." *The Washington Post* (February 13, 1991): A17.

Mauro, Tony. "Women, Minorities "'Disappointed' at Bush's Choice." *USA Today* (July 25, 1990).

Alfredo Gutierrez (1945–)

Alfredo Gutierrez, noted for his student activist participation in the 1960s on the Arizona State University campus, won election as a Democrat to the Arizona state legislature in 1972. Now retired from the state senate, Gutierrez devotes his time to public affairs with the political consulting firm of Jamieson and Gutierrez in Phoenix. (SCV)

BIBLIOGRAPHY

Luckingham, Bradford. *Minorities in Phoenix.* Tucson: The University of Arizona Press, 1994.

Ana Sol Gutierrez (1942–)

Born in El Salvador, Ana Sol Gutierrez grew up in the United States and studied aeronautical engineering. She divides her time and energy between her career and being an activist for Hispanic education issues. Since 1992 she has worked for the Federal Aviation Administration and has been involved with programs for the National Aeronautics and Space Administration and the Goddard Space Flight Center in Greenbelt, Maryland. She was elected to the board of education in Montgomery County, Maryland, after many years of being an active member of the Montgomery County PTA and a member of the education committee of the **League of United Latin American Citizens (LULAC)**. **See also** Educational Opportunity.

BIBLIOGRAPHY

Beyers, Dan. "School Board Wants to Restore Programs Lost to Recession." *The Washington Post* (December 1, 1994): M1.

Hill, Beth. "A Minority Voice in a Majority of Causes; School Board's Ana Guitierrez, Last Hispanic Elected Official in Maryland, Seems to Be Everywhere at Once." *The Washington Post* (May 9, 1991): M1.

Jose Angel Gutierrez (1944–)

Jose Angel Gutierrez was one of the **civil rights** leaders who helped stage the Chicano student walkout in **Crystal City, Texas,** in 1968. As a result of that protest, he was elected to the city council and also served on the city's school board where he was a strong advocate for **bilingual education.** In 1970 he founded the Mexican-American political party, **La Raza Unida**, to work for political participation and empowerment of Mexican Americans. In 1986 he became the executive director of the Greater Texas Legal Foundation and was appointed an administrative law judge in Dallas in 1990. In 1993, he ran an unsuccessful U.S. Senate campaign for the seat of Lloyd Bentsen. **See also** Mexican American Youth Organization (MAYO).

BIBLIOGRAPHY

Garcia, Ignacio. *United We Win.* Washington, DC: University Press of America, 1989.

Shockley, John S. *Chicano Revolt in Texas*. Notre Dame, IN: University of Notre Dame Press, 1974.

Luis Gutierrez (1953–)

Born in Chicago, Luis Gutierrez is the first Hispanic congressman elected from Illinois. He was elected as a Democrat in 1992. He worked as a teacher and social worker before entering the political arena in 1986, when he was elected to the Chicago City Council. In Washington, D.C., he has served on the House Banking, Finance and Urban Affairs Committee and on the Veterans Affairs Committee. **See also** Political Leadership.

BIBLIOGRAPHY

Kass, John. "Gutierrez's Tax Bill Proves That Miracles Still Do Happen." *Chicago Tribune* (August 2, 1998): 3.
Obejas, Achy. "Luis Gutierrez Wants to Be Known As the Arts Congressman . . . , So He Had a Few Creative Types Over to Rap." *Chicago Tribune* (October 6, 1997): 1.

Nancy C. Gutierrez

In 1991 Nancy Gutierrez became the director of the California Department of Consumer Affairs' Fair Employment and Housing Department. A long-standing member of the National Women's Employment and Education Foundation and the National Network of Hispanic Women, she was well versed in work and recruitment problems in the Hispanic community, and she was able to tackle such problems as family leave policy, and the aftermath of the 1992 Los Angeles riots. **See also** Civil Rights; Economic Equality.

BIBLIOGRAPHY

"California in Brief; Sacramento; Gutierrez Named to Civil Rights Post." *Los Angeles Times* (July 27, 1991): 25.

Harris Bill (1930)

The Mexican Revolution of 1910 forced thousands of immigrants to seek security and employment in the United States, whose vast industrial, agricultural, and mining enterprises absorbed Mexican immigrant labor. The large emigration from Mexico engendered opposition such as the Harris Bill. Sponsored by Senator William J. Harris, the bill was just one congressional attempt to limit Mexican immigration by including Mexico in the quota system of immigration. However, the House and Senate could not agree on the same version of the measure and the Harris bill did not become law. In 1926, the **Box Bill**, another restrictive quota bill relating to Mexico, was proposed but also failed to become law. **See also** Immigration and Naturalization Service (INS); Immigration Policy and Hispanics. (SCV)

BIBLIOGRAPHY

Divine, Robert A. *American Immigration Policy, 1924–1952.* New Haven, CT: Yale University Press, 1957.

Antonia Hernandez (1948–)

Antonia Hernandez is president and general counsel for the **Mexican American Legal Defense and Education Fund (MALDEF)**, the major Latino rights advocacy organization in the United States. Born in Mexico and an immigrant to the United States, she obtained her law degree from UCLA. Hernandez came to MALDEF after working with advocacy groups, holding a position with the United States Senate Judiciary Committee, and acquiring some political campaign experience. **See also** Civil Rights; Community Organizations. (ASR)

BIBLIOGRAPHY

"Hernandez Leads Huge Legal Staff." *Rocky Mountain News* (September 27, 1997): 54A.

Jackson, Robert. "A. Hernandez a Pioneer Lawyer." *Rocky Mountain News* (May 10, 1994): 62A.

Benigno Cardenas Hernandez (1862–1954)

Benigno Cardenas Hernandez began his political career as a probate clerk and recorder of deeds for Rio Arriba County, New Mexico, from 1900 until 1904. Hernandez then became the sheriff of the county, a position he held from 1904 to 1906. In 1908 Hernandez was elected county treasurer and collector of taxes. From 1912 to 1913, Hernandez held the post of receiver for the land office in Santa Fe. He served as a delegate to the 1912 and 1916 Republican National Conventions. During World War I, Hernandez was a member of the state exemption board. On March 4, 1915, Hernandez was elected as a Republican to the U.S. House of Representatives, where he represented New Mexico for two terms. In 1921, President Warren G. Harding appointed Hernandez collector of internal revenue for the district of New Mexico, a position he held until 1933. He later became a member of the Selective Service Board, where he served from 1940 to 1947.

BIBLIOGRAPHY

Vigil, Maurilio. *Los Patrones: Profiles of Hispanic Political Leaders in New Mexico History.* Washington, DC: University Press of America.

Christine Hernandez (1951–)

Christine Hernandez was the first Hispanic woman to be elected to the Texas Association of School Boards, to sit on the Board of Directors of the Star Bar of Texas, and to be elected to the Texas House of Representatives (representing San Antonio). She was also a delegate to the 1988 Democratic National Convention and a member of the Mexican American Legislators Policy Issues Committee.

BIBLIOGRAPHY

Walt, Kathy. "Legislator Seeks Big Pay Raises for Teachers." *The Houston Chronicle* (January 31, 1995): 11.

Hernandez v. New York (1991)

Hernandez v. New York, 111 S. Ct. 1859 (1991), raised the issue of jury selection in a trial that involved a Hispanic American. The defendant claimed that Hernandez's rights under the Equal Protection Clause of the Fourteenth Amendment had been violated because Spanish-speaking jurors were excluded using preemptory challenges, which are challenges to jurors for which neither the prosecution nor the defense need show cause. However, the issue exclusion was addressed by the trial court and the prosecution showed cause for exclusion. Once convicted, Hernandez carried his appeal to the U.S. Supreme Court, which ruled that the exclusion of Spanish-speaking jurors was not discriminatory. For a violation of the Equal Protection Clause to have occurred, there had to be proof of racial **discrimination**.

BIBLIOGRAPHY
Fukurai, Hiroshi. *Race and the Jury.* New York: Plenum, 1993.

Hernandez v. Texas (1954)

Hernandez v. Texas, 374 US 475 (1954), was a landmark U.S. Supreme Court case in which Chief Justice Earl Warren overturned the murder conviction of Pete Hernandez on the grounds that no person of Mexican descent had served as jury commissioners, grand jurors, or petit jurors at his trial, or any other trial in Jackson County, Texas, in 25 years and that this pattern of **discrimination** constituted a violation of the Fourteenth Amendment. This trial was the first Supreme Court case briefed and argued by Mexican-American lawyers. Hernandez's attorneys showed statistics that proved that at each stage of Hernandez's court procedures, including his trial, persons of Mexican-American descent who lived in Jackson County were systematically excluded from serving on juries. At his trial, Hernandez was convicted of murdering Joe Espinoza and was sentenced to life imprisonment, but Chief Justice Warren overturned the conviction. (SG)

BIBLIOGRAPHY
Garcia, Mario T. *Mexican Americans.* New Haven, CT: Yale University Press, 1989.

Joseph Marion Hernández (1793–1857)

Joseph Marion Hernández was the first Hispanic to serve in Congress and the first delegate from the territory of Florida. In 1822, Hernández was elected delegate to the U.S. House of Representatives, where he served until March 3, 1823. Hernández later became a member and the presiding officer of the Territorial House of Representatives. He was appointed brigadier general of volunteers in the war against the Florida Indians. From 1835 to 1838 he served in the U.S. Army. In 1837 he commanded the expedition that captured the Indian Chief Oceola and was appointed brigadier general of the Mounted Volunteers. In 1845 Hernández ran for the

Serving from 1822 to 1823 as a Whig, Joseph Marion Hernández was the first Hispanic to serve in Congress and the first delegate from the territory of Florida. *Library of Congress.*

United States Senate as a Whig candidate but was defeated. He then moved to Cuba where he managed his family's sugar estate in the district of Coliseo, near Matanzas.

BIBLIOGRAPHY
Hispanic Americans in Congress. Washington, DC: U.S. Government Printing Office, 1995.

Maria Latigo Hernandez (1893–1986)

In 1929, Maria Latigo Hernandez and her husband, Pedro, helped found the Orden Caballeros de America, a **civil rights** group. Through this organization (and through La Liga Por Defensa Escolar en San Antonio, which the Hernandezes created in 1934), Maria fought against the problems of Hispanic students in education. In the 1930s Hernandez began hosting "La Voz de las Americas," a daily radio show that was one of the first Spanish-speaking programs in San Antonio. In the 1960s she hosted a weekly television program, "La Hora de la Mujer." In 1939 Hernandez was appointed goodwill ambassador to Mexico, where she represented several San Antonio groups. Hernandez also had a writing career, expressing her political and social views in the 1945 book, *Mexico y los cuatro poderes que dirigen al pueblo.* In the 1970s Hernandez worked with **La Raza Unida Party,** a political party focusing on issues and offices for Mexican Americans. **See also** Educational Equality; Political Participation.

BIBLIOGRAPHY
Cotera, Martha. *Profile of the American Woman.* Austin, TX: National Educational Laboratory Publishers, 1976.

Sally B. Hernandez-Pinero (1952–)

After receiving her law degree at New York University, Sally Hernandez-Pinero delved straight into city politics. During her career, Hernandez-Pinero worked as the deputy president of the Borough of Manhattan, commissioner of the City of New York's Financial Services Corporation, and Commissioner of Financial Services in 1989. In 1992 she became chairperson of the New York City Housing Authority.

BIBLIOGRAPHY
Marinaccio, Paul and Harry Berkowitz. "An Appointment Based on Trust; Potential Pick Has Experience, Loyalty." *Newsday* (December 7, 1989): 25.
Polner, Rob. "City Houses Are Pinero's Project." *Newsday* (February 22, 1993): 6.

Edward Hidalgo (1912–1995)

Born in Mexico City, Edward Hidalgo earned law degrees in both the United States and Mexico. During World War II, he served in the United States Navy and became special assistant to the secretary of the navy from 1945 to 1946. After World War II, he went into private practice. In 1977 he was appointed assistant secretary of the navy and in 1979, President Jimmy Carter appointed him secretary of the navy. He returned to private law practice in 1981.

BIBLIOGRAPHY
"Edward Hidalgo: Former Secretary of the Navy." *Obituary. Los Angeles Times* (January 23, 1995): 22.
"Edward Hidalgo, 82, Lawyer, Former U.S. Navy Secretary." *Obituary. The Atlantic Journal and Constitution* (January 23, 1995): 8.

Hilda Hidalgo (1928–)

Born in Puerto Rico, Hilda Hidalgo has been an activist in the Hispanic community since 1975, when she helped found and became the first president of the Puerto Rican Congress of New Jersey, a statewide agency aimed at helping Hispanic communities. From 1977 to 1992, Hidalgo taught social work at Rutgers University in New Jersey, where she helped to develop a master's program in social work for Hispanics. Hidalgo has also been involved with a number of regional and national organizations aimed at increasing the number of Latinos who are pursuing higher education. **See also** Civil Rights; Educational Opportunity.

BIBLIOGRAPHY

Nieves, Evelyn. "Official and Three Journalists Arrested in Newark." *The New York Times* (October 21, 1993): 6.

Higher Education

Access to higher education for women and minorities of color has been a motivating force for most socio-political movements. Higher education is viewed not only as having intrinsic value but also as a path to self-actualization, economic equity, political awareness, community advocacy, and a generally better quality of life. Conversely, it is also viewed as the path to proper socialization, assimilation, and abandonment of a parochial world view common to those who reside in racially or ethnically segregated communities. The struggle for higher educational access for people of color takes many forms, ranging from student recruitment programs in the middle schools and high schools, to the establishment of ethnic-based schools such as Boricua College in New York, National Hispanic University, and historically black colleges. The last decade of the twentieth century is marked by battles over affirmative action, primarily in California, but also in Texas. These battles over student admissions are intense because admission is the entry point to higher education. (ASR)

BIBLIOGRAPHY

Meier, Kenneth and Joseph Stewart, Jr. *The Politics of Hispanic Education*. New York: State University of New York Press, 1991.
———. *Race, Class, and Education*. Madison: University of Wisconsin Press, 1989.

Ricardo H. Hinojosa (1950–)

After achieving degrees at the University of Texas in 1972 and Harvard University Law School in 1975, Ricardo Hinojosa became a private practice lawyer in Texas from 1976 to 1983. In 1983, President Ronald Reagan appointed Hinojosa to the U.S. District Court, where he served the Southern District of Texas. Because Hinojosa was politically conservative and tough on crime, many considered him to be a leading candidate for the Supreme Court if President George Bush had been reelected in 1992.

BIBLIOGRAPHY

Geyer, Georgie Ann. "Hispanics Who Inspire Pride in America." *The Denver Post* (June 18, 1995): E4.
Johnston, Oswald. "A Look at Possible Supreme Court Candidates; Richardo H. Hinojosa." *Los Angeles Times* (June 29, 1991): 18.

Hispanic Elected Local Officials Caucus (HELO)

Located in Washington, D.C., the Hispanic Elected Local Officials Caucus (HELO) is the Latino wing of the National League of Cities. Founded in 1976, the caucus started as the National League of Spanish-Speaking Elected Officials. In 1980 it changed its name to the Elected Spanish-Speaking Officials. In 1984, the organization adopted its current name. However, its focus has remained the same—to share information and experiences about local government with its Hispanic membership. (VDD)

BIBLIOGRAPHY

Schorr, Alan E. *Hispanic Resource Directory*. Juneau, AK: Denali Press, 1996.

Hispanic National Bar Association

The Hispanic National Bar Association was created in 1972 as La Raza National Lawyers Association, a group dedicated to helping Hispanic Americans seek rights through the U.S. legal system. Membership of the association consists of Latino attorneys and law professors. The group provides testimony to congressional and other government committees, while also working on litigation relevant to issues concerning the Chicano community and providing support to legislative and other political candidates with Hispanic rights in mind.

The Hispanic National Bar Association strives for the overall goal of insuring that future generations of Hispanic lawmakers have continued or improved opportunities in the years to come. In doing so, it established a Law Student Division to unite Hispanic law school students to work on their own success and that of their community. The division currently has more than 300 members and working relationships with about 85 law schools. The association holds an annual convention for both the student division and the main membership assembly. This convention covers pressing legal issues and difficulties within the law profession while brainstorming and discussing possible resolutions. **See also** Civil Rights; Jimmy Gurule; La Raza Unida Party.

BIBLIOGRAPHY

Alvord, Valerie. "Vega Heads Hispanic Bar Group." *The San Diego Union-Tribune* (August 24, 1997): B8.
Miller, William F. "Hispanic Lawyers to Convene in Cleveland." *The Plain Dealer* (April 17, 1998): 21.

Hispanic Political Action Committee

The Hispanic Political Action Committee is a relatively small PAC whose aim is to help Democratic candidates of Hispanic origin. The committee is associated with Representative **Esteban E. Torres** (D-CA). From 1993 through 1997, the Hispanic PAC contributed more than $50,000 to 26 candidates.

BIBLIOGRAPHY

Congressional Quarterly. *Federal PACs Directory*. Washington, DC: Congressional Quarterly Press, 1998.

Dolores Fernandez Huerta (1930–)

Cofounder, vice president, principal negotiator, lobbyist, legislative advocate, and speaker for the **United Farm Workers,** Dolores Huerta is a leader in labor organizing, higher education advocacy, humanitarianism, political activism, and articulation of women's issues. Huerta gave up a professional career and middle-class lifestyle for a life of struggle for justice, dignity, and a decent life on behalf of American farm workers. Huerta was born in Dawson, New Mexico, and grew up in Stockton, California. She has been the subject of countless books, articles, *corridos* (ballads), murals, and poems. She has had 11 children, has been arrested numerous times, has led countless demonstrations, and has suffered injuries.

Although she never took center stage from **Cesar Chavez,** also a cofounder of the UFW, she nevertheless has an enormous following. Huerta created the slogan "*Si se puede*" (yes, it can be done), a slogan as applicable to higher education as to farm labor organizing. Huerta continues to reside at UFW headquarters in Keene, California, living as humbly as those she organizes, and participating in labor and radical politics. (ASR)

BIBLIOGRAPHY

Garcia, Richard A. "Dolores Huerta: Woman, Organizer, and Symbol." *California History* (Spring 1993): 57–71.

Jensen, Joan M., ed. *With These Hands: Women Working on the Land.* New York: McGraw-Hill, 1981.

I

Santiago Iglesias Pantín (1872–1939)

Labor leader and organizer of Puerto Rico's first major socialist party, Santiago Iglesias Pantín participated in union organizing activities and served as secretary to the Workingmen Trades Circle from 1889 to 1896. In May 1897 he established *Ensayo Obrero*, a newspaper advocating the unionization of the working class in Puerto Rico. After spending seven months in prison, Iglesias and other political prisoners were released at the request of the U.S. government. Immediately after his release, Iglesias resumed his labor organizing activities, which brought him to the attention of the military governor of the island, General John R. Brooke, who interceded on his behalf when the Spanish Government requested his extradition. On October 23, 1898, Iglesias helped found the Regional Federation of Workers and *Porvenir Social*, a newspaper he published until 1900.

In 1900 Iglesias traveled to the United States, where he established a relationship with the president of the American Federation of Labor (AFL), Samuel Gompers, who appointed him general organizer of the AFL for Puerto Rico and Cuba. Iglesias returned to Puerto Rico, where he organized unions throughout the island, and in 1903 he established the newspaper, *Unión Obrera*. Three years later he became one of the founders of the Free Federation of Puerto Rican Workers, which was affiliated with the American Federation of Labor. In 1908 he was the Free Federation of Puerto Rican Workers candidate for resident commissioner but he was defeated by **Tulio Larrinaga.**

Iglesias believed that **Puerto Rican statehood** was necessary to improve conditions for workers in Puerto Rico. In 1915 he organized the Socialist Party, which campaigned for statehood. Under Iglesias' leadership, the Socialist Party grew rapidly. In 1916, under the banner of the Socialist Party, he was elected to the Insular Senate and was subsequently reelected, serving until 1932. During this time he also participated in the international labor movement; he served as secretary to the Pan American Federation of Labor from 1925 to 1933.

On November 8, 1932, Iglesias was elected to a four-year term as resident commissioner to the U.S. House of Representatives. His victory was a result of a coalition between the Republican Union Party and the Socialist Party; four years later this same coalition reelected Iglesias. While in Congress Iglesias served on the Committee on Insular Affairs, the Agriculture and Labor Committee, and the Committee on Territories.

BIBLIOGRAPHY

Córdova, Gonzalo F. *Santiago Iglesias Pantín, Creator of the Labor Movement in Puerto Rico*. Rio Piedras, Puerto Rico: Editorial Universitaria, 1980.
Hispanic Americans in Congress. Washington, DC: U.S. Government Printing Office, 1995.

Illegal Aliens

The terms "illegal" and "undocumented" alien designate people who have crossed United States borders without meeting legal requirements specified by the U.S. **Immigration and Naturalization Service**. Theses terms were unknown until the 1970s, when the U.S. government increased efforts to apprehend such immigrants.

Whether or not crossing into the United States is illegal has depended on acts of Congress and how laws have been enforced. In 1917 the U.S. Selective Service Act discouraged immigration because it exposed immigrants to the draft. However, railroad and agricultural economic interests pressured the government to permit the active recruitment of workers in Mexico. Congress therefore waived immigration requirements that might have called for them to serve in the armed forces.

During World War II, the United States and Mexico created a labor agreement (under **Public Law 45**) called the "Bracero Program," which recruited and hired Mexicans as temporary contract workers in the United States. The program existed from August 1942 to December 1964, although the need for Mexican workers, undocumented or otherwise, continued after that period. **See also** Educational Opportunity; Immigration Policy and Hispanics; *Plyler v. Doe* (1982); Public Law 78. (SCV)

BIBLIOGRAPHY

Rosales, F. Arturo. *Chicano! The History of the Mexican American Civil Rights Movement*. Houston: Arte Publico Press, 1996.

Immigration Act of 1990

In 1990 President George Bush signed the Immigration Act (IMMAC90) into law. The act constituted a major revision of the **McCarran–Walter Immigration and Nationality Act**

Mexicans wait at the U.S. immigration station in El Paso, Texas. *Library of Congress.*

of 1952. The McCarran–Walter Act combined multiple immigration and naturalization laws into one comprehensive statute, and for decades the act remained the basic immigration law of the land. By the 1980s, however, concern increased over the 1952 act's preference system, which mandated a national origins quota system, limited immigration from the Far East, established preferences for the immigration of skilled workers, and provided for the admission of immediate relatives of U.S. citizens above the numerical limit.

The 1990 act changed the national origins quota system, which had favored northern and western Europe. Its changes included an increase in total immigration, an increase in annual employment-based immigration from 54,000 to 140,000 people, and a permanent provision for the admission of "diversity immigrants" from "underrepresented" countries. This new system provided for a permanent annual level of approximately 700,000 immigrants from 1992 through 1994. The preference system also underwent major revisions. The 1990 act established a three-track preference system for family-sponsored, employment-based, and diversity immigrants. Additionally, the work-related non-immigrant categories for temporary admissions changed significantly.

Refugees were the only major group not included in the new legislation. Later revisions to the 1990 act provided undocumented Salvadorans with temporary protected status and amended the 1952 act to authorize the U.S. attorney general to grant temporary protected status to nationals of designated countries in the event of armed conflict or natural disaster. **See also** Illegal Aliens; Immigration and Nationality Act of 1965; Immigration and Naturalization Service (INS); Immigration Policy and Hispanics; Immigration Reform and Control Act of 1986. (VDD)

BIBLIOGRAPHY

Skerry, Peter. "Many Borders to Cross: Is Immigration the Exclusive Responsibility of the Federal Government?" *Publius* 25, no. 3 (Summer 1995): 71–85.

Immigration and Nationality Act of 1965

The 1965 amendments to the **McCarran–Walter Immigration and Nationality Act of 1952** reflected complex changes in public perceptions, values, and politics. The legislation was a product of the mid-1960s and the heavily Democratic 89th Congress, which also produced major **civil rights** legislation.

As a result of the 1965 amendments, the major source of immigration to the United States shifted from Western Europe to Latin America and Asia, reversing a trend that began with the founding of the nation. To accomplish this change, the amendments permitted an annual ceiling on immigration from the Far East of 170,000 people with a limit of 20,000 people per country. Within these restrictions, immigrant visas were distributed according to a seven-category preference system, placing priority on reuniting families, attracting needed skills, and admitting refugees. By 1968 the new law would cap immigration from Western Europe at 120,000 people annually, without per-country limits or a preference system. **See also** Illegal Aliens; Immigration Act of 1990; Immigration and Naturalization Service (INS); Immigration Policy and Hispanics; Immigration Reform and Control Act of 1986. (VDD)

BIBLIOGRAPHY

Skerry, Peter. "Many Borders to Cross: Is Immigration the Exclusive Responsibility of the Federal Government?" *Publius* 25, no. 3 (Summer 1995): 71–85.

Immigration and Naturalization Service (INS)

The Immigration and Naturalization Service (INS), created in 1891 to process the waves of immigrants entering the United States from Europe, is today a division of the Department of Justice. A commissioner heads the agency and reports to the U.S. attorney general. In its dual capacity as both an administrative and enforcement agency, the INS provides the public with information and service on matters of **citizenship** and resident status, while also exercising its enforcement responsibilities. Policy and executive direction flows from the INS headquarters in Washington, D.C., to 33 districts and 21 border patrol sectors throughout the United States. These offices help the INS grant benefits under the immigration laws and prevent unlawful entry, employment, or benefits to those who are not entitled; INS also removes aliens who enter or remain illegally in the United States. **See also** Illegal Aliens; Immigration Act of 1990; Immigration and Nationality Act of 1965; Immigration Policy and Hispanics; Immigration Reform and Control Act of 1986. (VDD)

BIBLIOGRAPHY

Shorris, Earl. *Latinos; A Biography of the People.* New York: Avon Books, 1992.

Immigration Policy and Hispanics

One of the most persistent problems facing U.S. policy makers has been how to develop and implement an **immigration** policy that is equitable, does not abuse human rights, and maintains border security. For decades, individuals who needed work and employers who needed labor have had a symbiotic relationship. During World War II, the need for labor was so acute that the U.S. government assisted immigrants who wished to come to the Southwest on a temporary basis. This assistance eventually led to official recognition (through **Public Law 45** and extended by **Public Law 78**), inaugurating the "Bracero" Program by the Mexican and U.S. governments to help both employers and immigrants.

Under this program, farm workers were provided legal temporary entry into the United States, but the program did not comprehensively address many other problems. What rights did the children of immigrants have to publicly funded education? What should become of the millions of immigrants who came to the United States illegally? Should immigrants be entitled to the social and welfare programs that are available to citizens? What border-control policies might bring about maximum social gain? These and other complex issues were left unaddressed.

In 1986 Congress passed the Simpson–Rodino **Immigration Reform and Control Act.** A major effort to address problems involving Hispanics, immigration, and border control, the Simpson–Rodino Bill provided for enhanced legal sanctions against employers who knowingly hired an employee who was not authorized to work in the United States. Employers were required to verify and vouch for the papers of prospective employees prior to offering employment. The Office of Special Counsel was created in the Justice Department to prosecute individuals who engaged in unlawful immigration activities. The **Immigration and Naturalization Service (INS)** was provided with additional funding, and states were required to verify the legal status of people who applied for public assistance.

Perhaps most important for the immigrants who were illegally in the United States, the legislation provided for amnesty and an opportunity to obtain legal status by proving continuous residence in the country since 1982. Additional protections were provided for some agricultural workers, many of whom had been taken advantage of by unscrupulous employers. It was not uncommon for workers who were in the United States illegally to be denied the wage that they had been promised. The Simpson–Rodino Bill did provide some additional legal protection from exploitation by employers, but it also limited the social and welfare benefits to which immigrants might be entitled. Congress mandated that agencies responsible for implementing immigration policies must submit periodic reports to ensure that the will of the Congress was being carried out. Lastly, the law stated that Mexico was to be consulted before any of the provisions of Simpson–Rodino were to be implemented.

It is estimated that about half of the 700,000 to 1 million legal immigrants to the United States each year come from a Spanish-speaking country. The INS estimates an even higher percentage for the estimated 300,000 illegal immigrants that arrive annually. Mexico has for years looked upon the United States as a way of relieving pressure from high unemployment rates. In 1994 the peso was devalued and Mexico had to

rely on a loan guarantee from the United States to obtain adequate funding to meet its financial obligations. This devaluation led to one of the most severe economic recessions in Mexico's modern history, with both high rates of unemployment and illegal immigration to the United States.

This illegal immigration generated a conservative backlash in the normally progressive state of California. In 1996 voters overwhelmingly (59 percent to 41 percent) endorsed **California Proposition 187**. Campaigning for its passage, Republican Governor Pete Wilson estimated that about half of all illegal immigrants from Mexico were destined for California. At that time there were approximately 1.7 million illegal immigrants in California, out of a state population of 33 million. California was having its own economic problems and illegal immigrants were estimated to be costing California taxpayers about $3 billion annually in health, welfare, and education needs. Proposition 187 would deny illegal immigrants health care (except in emergency situations), welfare assistance, and the right to attend California's public schools.

Because of legal challenges, Proposition 187 has yet to be implemented. One such challenge stems from *Plyler v. Doe* **(1982).** In this case, the U.S. Supreme Court had previously maintained that even if a child was in the country illegally, no state could deny the child access to education. Nevertheless, many Hispanics interpreted Proposition 187 as a slap in the face. Governor Wilson had suggested that if a teacher thought a pupil might not be in the country legally, than INS should be asked to investigate. He also suggested the use of "tamper proof" identity cards to show **citizenship** and increased fines for employers who hire **illegal aliens**. These suggestions led to a protest march on the U.S. embassy in Mexico City. Teachers in Tijuana handed out leaflets denouncing the proposition as "racist," and Mexicans threatened to boycott U.S. stores along the border. The *New York Times* declared the proposition to be "mean-spirited, impractical, and probably unconstitutional."

In an effort to bring some physical control to the problem of illegal immigration, the U.S. Border Patrol in El Paso, Texas, under the command of Silvestre Reyes, stationed agents at intervals at the El Paso–Juarez border where they would be in sight of one another. In addition, a 1.3-mile-long fence was constructed at the Sunland Park area near El Paso. This was an area where illegal crossing was most frequent, and several crimes had been reported in the area. Reacting to criticism that raising the fence was "draconian," Reyes responded in a letter to the *El Paso Times* that the border patrol was "simply trying to do our job as professionally and effectively as possible to ensure a safer and better-managed international border."

Because of the high success rate of this strategy, it was again used in the Chula Vista–Imperial Beach–Tijuana area of California. This area was considered the most porous along the U.S.–Mexican border. President Bill Clinton authorized construction of a 15-mile-long, brightly lit fence. A total of $25 million was authorized for the effort, and 38 additional agents were added to a previously authorized force of more than 200 officers. The agents were equipped with infrared night-vision equipment, sophisticated communications devices, and special patrol vehicles. In Arizona, a seven-mile-long fence was constructed and the U.S. Department of Defense deployed a military effort, Joint Task Force Six (JTF-6), to control the border.

Supporters of the program estimated these efforts cut illegal immigration by 50 percent. Detractors claimed that the program was driving would-be immigrants further out into the desert and into other more dangerous areas. As a result, more deaths were occurring among potential immigrants. Research published in 1996 by the Center for Immigration Research at the University of Houston found that at least 190 people die each year on the Texas border with Mexico, and possibly as many as 330. In reaction to U.S. immigration policy, in 1996 Hispanic interest groups launched "Coordinadora 96," which brought tens of thousands of Latinos to Washington, D.C., to express concerns about xenophobia and amnesty for immigrants.

Nevertheless, U.S. lawmakers toughened immigration policies that same year. Many Central Americans who had been allowed into the United States as refugees during the civil wars in El Salvador, Guatemala, and Nicaragua were informed that they had never been "warranted permanent residents." With the temporary protected status of these refugees now revoked, the INS began conducting interviews to determine if residents would qualify for political asylum. Asylum could be granted only if immigrants could prove that returning to their respective homelands would subject them to persecution based on race, nationality, political opinion, or membership in a particular social group. Because these are difficult conditions to prove, U.S. Attorney General Janet Reno suspended deportations on humanitarian grounds until January 1998.

In 1997 the Border Patrol launched "Operation Rio Grande" in the Brownsville–Matamoros area of Texas. Again, massive numbers of border patrol agents were deployed, high-intensity lighting was used, and a paramilitary "low intensity" conflict posture was taken on the border. One teenager tending to his goats in West Texas was killed by soldiers participating in the operation and another man was wounded on the banks of the Rio Grande in Brownsville, Texas, when he unknowingly stumbled into a military unit hiding in the brush. Concerns have been raised about the proper role of the military in conducting what many critics think are police activities. The fences and night lights allegedly molest the habitats of endangered species such as the ocelot and jaguarundi. In addition, Mexican authorities have deployed consular officials to help Mexican citizens who may have had their basic human rights violated by U.S. efforts to control illegal immigration. **See also** Civil Rights; Immigration Act of 1990; Immigration and Nationality Act of 1965; McCarran–Walter Immigration and Nationality Act of 1952. (JSR)

BIBLIOGRAPHY

Guitierrez, David G., ed. *Between Two Worlds.* Wilmington, DE: SR Press, 1996.

Hart, Dianne W. *Undocumented in L.A.* Wilmington, DE: SR Press, 1997.

"Indecent Proposal in California." *New York Times* (October 25, 1997): A27.

"Operation Rio Grande Reroutes Illegal Immigrants." *The Brownsville Herald* (September 14, 1997): 7.

"Out of the Shadows." *Time* (May 4, 1987): 14–17.

"Passage of Proposition 187 Sets Up Bitter Social Battle." *The Wall Street Journal* (November 10, 1994): A7.

Immigration Reform and Control Act of 1986

The Immigration Reform and Control Act of 1986 was created with the intention of being an alien registration program. The act extended U.S. resident status to applicants previously held to be **illegal aliens** before January 1982. The **Immigration and Naturalization Service (INS)** was charged with reviewing all applications and accepting appropriate candidates for a period of one year, May 1987 to May 1988. Each case was examined to determine whether candidates could demonstrate continuous U.S. residency since 1982; if this was found, these undocumented immigrants were extended legal residency. More than 3 million people applied for U.S. residency through this act, and more than 90 percent of these applicants were given at least temporary lawful resident status.

Antidiscrimination hiring provisions were also included in the act, as well as sanctions against the employment of undocumented aliens. The legislation also offered legal citizen status to special agricultural workers who could prove that they had worked on specific crops or on related agriculture projects in the U.S. for at least 90 days; applicants from these candidates were reviewed and accepted or denied by the INS from June 1, 1987, to November 30, 1988.

Some problems with the act occurred, including a controversy over what documentation was needed to illustrate eligibility and prove that an individual had been in the United States since 1982. Many of these disputes went to court, where a number of immigrants were denied citizenship. Despite these problems, the act was seen as an overall success for U.S. minority groups. Not only did the act help clear up approximately 2 million incorrect Social Security accounts, it also increased the use of public health facilities and legal rights, because applicants no longer feared questions regarding their immigration status. The act also led to better-paying and higher-profile jobs because newly documented lawful citizens were better accepted. Out of all minority groups, Hispanics benefited the most from this act; out of all the applicants, 69 percent were from Mexico, while 11 percent came from Central America, 2 percent from countries in the Caribbean, about 1.5 percent from South America, and the remaining 16 percent to 17 percent from various other countries. **See also** Civil Rights; Citizenship; Discrimination; Economic Equality; Immigration Act of 1960; Immigration and Nationality Act of 1965; Immigration Policy and Hispanics.

BIBLIOGRAPHY

Berestein, Leslie. "Out of Hiding, Into Citizenship." *The Orange County Register* (May 6, 1997): A1.

Trejo, Frank. "Immigration Coalition to Celebrate 10 Years of Working for Rights." *The Dallas Morning News* (January 23, 1997): 31A.

Independence Party

The Independence Party (also known as the Puerto Rican Independence Party [PIP] or Partido Independentista Puertorriqueno) is the smallest of the island's three main political parties. It is affiliated with the International Socialist Party and is committed to achieving the island's separation from the United States through peaceful means. It was founded in 1946 by a group of Popular Democratic Party dissidents expelled by **Luis Muñoz Marin** for their separatist leanings. PIP's first president was Gilberto Concepcion de Garcia. (AAB)

BIBLIOGRAPHY

Berrios Martinez, Ruben. *La independencia de Puerto Rico: Razon y lucha.* Mexico, DF: Editorial Linea, 1983.

Intergroup Relations between Hispanics and Blacks

The color of the United States is rapidly changing, and racial minority issues are no longer simply a question of black and white. According to 1990 census figures, black and Hispanic population growth is projected at 24 percent and 45 percent, respectively. Because contact between these populations will inevitably increase, a new examination of attitudes and perceptions affecting black and Hispanic relations seems appropriate.

Although research directly examining such relations has been sparse, some literature from the 1990s indicates certain conclusions. For instance, 1,200 randomly selected blacks and Hispanics were interviewed in Houston, Texas, regarding the relationship between their groups; when asked for their perceptions of conflict, approximately 52 percent of Hispanic and 45 percent of black respondents indicated that there was "much" conflict between the two groups (Mindiola, Rodriguez, and Niemann, 1996). Both groups also indicated a belief that prejudice existed between the groups. A *Los Angeles Times* survey found intergroup antagonism as well (Oliver and Johnson, 1984). Significantly, black antagonism toward Hispanics seemed concentrated on one factor— blacks' belief that immigrants take away jobs. Another study found that Mexicans and Mexican Americans report that the primary thing they have in common with each other is conflict with blacks. Research on intergroup attitudes, therefore, generally indicates that relations between Hispanics and blacks are negative.

In addition to expressed attitudes, another indicator of intergroup dynamics is the social distance groups maintain from each other. In their examination of social distance, Mindiola et al. (1996) found that blacks and Hispanics generally maintain distance from each other, with a large percentage of foreign-born Hispanics indicating that they almost never interact with blacks, and indeed that more than 40 percent of

black and Hispanic respondents indicated they would not approve of their children dating members of the other group. Black males often mentioned fear of reprisal from Hispanic males, particularly if a date necessitated going into a Hispanic barrio. Other research has found that reluctance to date from within other groups can be ascribed to differences in language, religion, and values. The issue of language as a contributor to social distance has been pointed out in other research as well. For instance, researchers in the Changing Relations Project found that language is the most contested issue in relations among newcomers and established residents in a given community (Bach, 1993). They concluded that language acts to both bind individuals together and separate them into groups. Significantly, data also indicate that the social distance blacks and Hispanics keep from each other is greater than that each minority keeps from the majority Anglo group.

Intergroup relations may be affected by socio-demographic factors as well. For instance, younger Hispanics seem more accepting of blacks that do older Hispanics, and Hispanics with higher levels of education are evidently more positive toward blacks than are their less educated counterparts (Bach, 1993). Similarly, blacks with more education feel more positive about Hispanics than do less educated blacks, and non-Baptist Protestant blacks are more positive toward Hispanics than are Catholic and Baptist blacks.

Stereotypes clearly also affect intergroup relations. To assess current group stereotypes, Niemann et al. (1994) asked an ethnically diverse group of 259 urban college students to list the first words that came to mind in relation to Mexican Americans and blacks. Blacks provided the following terms in reference to Mexican American males: antagonistic, hard workers, pleasant, caring, lower class, intelligent, alcohol users, short, dark hair, attractive, speak loudly, speak softly, criminal, family oriented, and humorous. Terms blacks used most frequently to describe Mexican American females were: pleasant, attractive, caring, overweight, intelligent, baby makers, unmannerly, long hair, dark hair, bad tempered, passive, ambitionless, talkative, sociable, and sexy.

Terms Mexican Americans used most frequently to describe black males were: athletic, antagonistic, pleasant, speak loudly, muscular, criminal, tall, dark skin, unmannerly, sociable, good dancer, lower class, intelligent, achievement oriented, and egotistical. Terms Mexican Americans used most frequently to describe black females were: speak loudly, athletic, egotistical, unmannerly, sociable, dark skin, antagonistic, fashion conscious, lower class, ambitionless, pleasant, intelligent, complainer, tall, and good dancer.

In other recent stereotype research, Mindiola et al. (1996) asked 600 randomly selected U.S.-born and foreign-born Hispanic and 600 black respondents (all in Houston, Texas) to provide three words that in their opinion best described the other group and to indicate how positive that word was when used about that group. With that methodology, the favorability of the provided terms was determined by respondents, not by researchers. Their findings indicated that a significant percentage of both groups viewed the other negatively. Taken together, such data indicate that, while each group perceives some positive traits about the other, intergroup perceptions are largely negative.

The foregoing review leads to several conclusions. First, Hispanics and blacks perceive prejudice and conflict between their groups. In addition, they maintain social distance from each other, including an unwillingness for their children to date members of the other group. Also, intergroup stereotypes are largely negative.

What are the reasons for these negative perceptions and relations? Disparities in quality of life may underlie negative intergroup relations and attitudes. Research indicates that, in the case of blacks and Hispanics, the comparative states of employment, education, political power, housing, and health may be a source of conflict. Of these realms, political power may have the most far-reaching implications. For instance, many U.S. Hispanics are relatively recent immigrants with no **citizenship** rights. Even when Hispanics are citizens, stereotypes lead to perceptions of them as outsiders, which leads to **discrimination**, especially given the anti-immigrant climate that was present in the United States during the 1980s and 1990s. Hispanics may thus see themselves as powerless and subject to greater discrimination than blacks.

On the other hand, blacks may perceive that Hispanics have substantial power and are immune to the worst kinds of discrimination because historically discrimination against Hispanics has not been as widely spread as it has been against blacks. Blacks may not be aware of everyday discrimination against Hispanics. Therefore, blacks' perception may be that they, and not Hispanics, have been the targets of discrimination, while the reality may be that, due to the political attention conferred on blacks, discrimination is no longer the problem for blacks that it is for Hispanics. It may therefore be possible to alleviate negative attitudes by increasing intergroup awareness of different types of discrimination directed toward each group.

However, contact between persons of equal status has also been shown to reduce negative stereotypes and intergroup hostility, although most of the work on the effects of such contact has thus far focused on blacks and whites. More research is needed on the role of contact between blacks and Hispanics in changing intergroup relations. For instance, foreign-born Hispanics have significantly less contact with blacks than do U.S.-born Hispanics; the lower level of contact likely causes more negative stereotypes. It is possible, therefore, that increased contact between blacks and Hispanics may bring awareness to their mutual plight as members of oppressed groups, increasing perceptions of affinity between the groups and reducing prejudice. Without this awareness the inevitably increasing contact between blacks and Hispanics could well lead to increased intergroup tension and prejudice. **See also** Acculturation; Assimilation; Economic Equality. (YFN)

BIBLIOGRAPHY

Bach, R. *Changing Relations Project*. New York: Ford Foundation, 1993.

Brown, R. *Prejudice: Its Social Psychology*. Oxford: Blackwell, 1995.

Dyer, J., A. Vedlitz, and S. Worchel. "Social Distance among Racial and Ethnic Groups in Texas: Some Demographic Correlates." *Social Science Quarterly* 70, no. 3 (1989): 607–16.

Lampe, P.E. "Towards Amalgamation: Interethnic Dating among Blacks, Mexican Americans, and Anglos." *Ethnic Groups* 3 (1981): 97–109.

Mindiola, T., A. Rodriguez, and Y.F. Niemann. *Intergroup Relations between Hispanics and Blacks in Harris County*. Houston, TX: Center for Mexican American Studies, University of Houston, 1996.

Niemann, Y.F., L. Jennings, R.M. Rozell, J.D. Baxter, and E. Sullivan. "Use of Free Response and Cluster Analysis to Determine Stereotypes of Eight Groups." *Personality and Social Psychology Bulletin* 20, no. 4 (1994): 379–90.

Oliver, M.L. and J.H. Johnson. Inter-ethnic Conflict in an Urban Ghetto: The Case of Blacks and Hispanics in Los Angeles." *Research in Social Movements, Conflict, and Change* 6 (1984): 57–94.

Involuntary Sterilization

Involuntary sterilization is referred to as unconsenting sterilization in reference to Latinas and other women of color. It is an example of covert population control through seemingly neutral medical practices. In 1974, a class action law suit, *Madrigal v. Quilligan*, was filed by a group of Mexican women against the University of Southern California Hospital. Although the women lost the case, the practice of unconsenting sterilization as population control for Latinas came under public scrutiny and required changes in medical practices. **See also** Civil Rights; Discrimination. (ASR)

BIBLIOGRAPHY

Hernandez, Antonia. "Chicanas and the Issues of Involuntary Sterilization." *Chicano Law Review* 3, no. 3 (1976): 3–37.

Shapiro, Thomas M. *Population Control Politics: Women, Sterilization, and Reproductive Choice*. Philadelphia: Temple University Press, 1985.

Mari-Luci Jaramillo (1928–)

Mari-Luci Jaramillo, born in New Mexico, pursued higher education at a time when few Hispanic women did so. She progressed from teaching in a New Mexican town to teaching at the University of New Mexico (Albuquerque), and finally to statewide leadership roles in teaching language and cultural awareness. Through her involvement in the university's programs in Latin America, and her commitment to the Chicano **civil rights** movement, she gained national and international recognition. In 1976, President Jimmy Carter appointed Jaramillo as ambassador to Honduras. She currently holds several national advisory positions. (ASR)

BIBLIOGRAPHY

Perez, Theresa. *Portraits of Mexican Americans: Pathfinders in the Mexican American Communities.* Carthage, IL: Good Apple, 1991.

Rebolledo, Tey Diana, ed. *Nuestras Mujeses.* Albuquerque, NM: El Norte Publications, 1992.

Jones Act of 1917

The Jones Act of 1917, also known as the Jones-Shafroth Act, served for 35 years as Puerto Rico's "organic law," or territorial constitution. It was passed in response to local protests that the **Foraker Act of 1900,** Puerto Rico's initial organic law under U.S. rule, was undemocratic and largely responsible for the island's impoverishment. The Jones Act altered the status of the Puerto Rican people and changed the process by which their lawmakers were chosen, but the act did not grant the territorial government greater autonomy or otherwise improve the island's status as a possession of the U.S. government. The period during which the Jones Act of 1917 was in effect saw a heightening of tensions between Puerto Ricans and the U.S. government and a significant rise in both moderate and militant strains of Puerto Rican nationalism.

The Jones Act conferred U.S. citizenship on Puerto Ricans and allowed goods to pass to and from Puerto Rico and the U.S. without tariffs. The Jones Act, unlike its antecedent, allowed Puerto Ricans the right to elect their territorial legislators. However, the president still appointed Puerto Rico's governor, education commissioner, and supreme court justices. Under the act, several of these presidentially appointed governors and education commissioners vigorously promoted a federally backed policy of "Americanization," the aim of which was the cultural **assimilation** of Puerto Ricans, with a strong emphasis on making Puerto Ricans English-speakers. Congress amended the Jones Act in 1947 to allow Puerto Ricans to elect their own governor. The only chief executive elected in this way was **Luis Muñoz Marin,** the founder of Partido Popular Democratico (the Popular Democratic Party) and principal architect of Puerto Rico's Commonwealth Constitution of 1952. Like the 1900 Foraker Act and the 1952 constitution, the Jones Act allowed Puerto Ricans to elect a resident commissioner, or nonvoting delegate, to the U.S. House of Representatives. However, as U.S. citizens living in a territory (as opposed to a state), Puerto Ricans cannot vote for president, elect senators, or elect voting members to the House of Representatives. (AAB)

BIBLIOGRAPHY

Morales Carrion, Arturo. *Puerto Rico: A Political and Cultural History.* New York: W.W. Norton, 1983.

Trias Monge, Jose. *Historia Constitucional de Puerto Rico.* vol. 2. Rio Piedras, PR: Editorial Universitaria, 1981.

Know-Nothing Party

The Know-Nothing Party, a secret political organization that supported "nativism" and discriminated against immigrants, evolved in the early 1850s throughout the United States; it took its name from the fact that the party originally required members to answer all questions about the organization by saying that they knew nothing about it. Nativism—that is, hostility toward new immigrants—arose as the influx of new religious practices, languages, and cultural ideas seemed to threaten the homogeneity of the antebellum United States. The Know-Nothing Party avoided divisions over slavery by proposing to unite Americans against all foreigners, whether Catholics, Chinese, Hispanics, or any other non-Anglo group. Nativists were successful in such diverse states as Massachusetts, Pennsylvania, and California, and their gains reflected an American dissatisfaction with the political system of the early 1850s. Split over the issue of slavery, the Know-Nothing Party died out by the mid-1850s, when most of its members joined the new Republican Party. (JRB)

BIBLIOGRAPHY

Leonard, Ira M. and Carleton Beals. *American Nativism, 1830–1860.* New York: W.W. Norton, 1971.

George La Plata (1924–)

George La Plata served as a colonel in the U.S. Marine Corps from 1942 to 1945, and from 1952 to 1954. He received his law degree in 1955 from the Detroit College of Law and worked as a trial lawyer from 1956 to 1978. In 1979 he became a judge in the Michigan Circuit Court, and in 1985 he became a U.S. federal judge.

BIBLIOGRAPHY

Josar, David. "Midwest's First Hispanic Federal Judge to Retire." *The Detroit News* (July 30, 1996): C2.

La Raza Unida Party

During the **Chicano Power Movement** in the late 1960s, the La Raza Unida Party emphasized getting votes and influencing party politics in Texas. **Jose Angel Gutierrez** organized local Mexican Americans into the La Raza Unida Party in **Crystal City, Texas,** in 1969. In the April 1970 local elections, the party won three school board and two city council seats, and enjoyed similar success in several nearby towns.

Interest in the La Raza Unida Party spread throughout the Southwest, and to other areas where Mexican Americans comprised sufficient numbers to run for local and regional offices. Conventions were held throughout Colorado to raise the consciousness of voters, and party leader **Rodolfo "Corky" Gonzales** sought to form a national Chicano party, recommending that this party some day field a presidential candidate.

Over time, however, the party became fragmented and lacked grass-roots support. These failures, among others, eventually led to its demise in the 1970s. **See also** Richard Alatorre; Civil Rights; Community Organizations; Cultural Nationalism; El Movimiento; Hispanic National Bar Association; Liberalism; Mexican American Legal Defense and Educational Fund (MALDEF); Political Participation; Voting Patterns. (SCV)

BIBLIOGRAPHY

Castro, Tony. *Chicano Power: The Emergence of Mexican America.* New York: Saturday Review Press, 1974.

Hammerbach, John C., et al. *A War of Words: Chicano Protest in the 1960s and 1970s.* Westport, CT: Greenwood Press, 1985.

Carmela Gloria Lacayo (1949–)

In 1976, at the age of 27, Carmela Gloria Lacayo created the National Association for the Hispanic Elderly in Los Angeles. In that same year, President Jimmy Carter named her as one of the two vice-chairpeople of the Democratic National Committee. She also cofounded Hispanas Organized for Political Equality (HOPE) in 1989. She has since sat on the Supplemental Security Income Advisory Panel and on the Census Bureau Committee on Minority Populations. In 1991 she was appointed to the Los Angeles County Housing Commission.

BIBLIOGRAPHY

Bevette, Beverly. "Group Finds Jobs for Latino Seniors; Holiday Party Brings Spanish-Speaking Elderly Together." *Los Angeles Times* (December 25, 1985): 1.

Hector M. Laffitte (1934–)

After receiving a degree from Inter-American University in 1955, the University of Puerto Rico in 1958, and Georgetown University in 1960, Hector Laffitte served from 1969 to 1972 as the civil rights commissioner for the Commonwealth of Puerto Rico. After this, Laffitte worked as a lawyer in Puerto Rico from 1972 to 1983. In 1983, Laffitte was appointed to the U.S. District Court for the District of Puerto Rico by President Ronald Reagan.

BIBLIOGRAPHY

"Ex Customs Aides Guilty in Slaying." *The New York Times* (September 22, 1987): A25.

Walzer, Robert P. "Court Rules Puerto Rico Authority Can Be Sued." *Journal of Commerce* (February 12, 1992): 2B.

LaFollette Committee (1936–1940)

The LaFollette Committee was a U.S. Senate subcommittee headed by Senator Robert LaFollette, Jr. (R-WI) to investigate whether industries were impeding the civil liberties of workers, specifically the workers' right to organize. The committee studied the mining, steel, and auto industries, and committee members held public hearings in Los Angeles and San Francisco to investigate the agricultural industries. The committee's findings were issued in a report in 1942. They disclosed that the use of violence against workers was commonplace among the agricultural industries and charged the

Associated Farmers of espionage, blacklisting, and vigilantism. The committee recommended that laws be enacted to ensure fair wages and labor practices. However, because the report was issued at the start of World War II, none of these recommendations was adopted.

BIBLIOGRAPHY

Auerbach, Jerold S. *Labor and Liberty: The LaFollette Committee and the New Deal.* Indianapolis: Bobbs-Merrill, 1966.

Land Act of 1851

The Land Act of 1851 reviewed the land claims of all Mexican land owners in California in the mid-1850s by establishing a three-man board of U.S. commissioners to evaluate all titles to state property and judge the validity of each. Between one-quarter and one-half of all Mexican lands were lost in the process, totaling millions of acres. Any property without sufficient title reverted to the U.S. government or to Anglo settlers, who then took the lands for themselves. This act proved devastating to the economic and social status of Mexicans in California. (JRB)

BIBLIOGRAPHY

Gates, Paul W. "The California Land Act of 1851." *California Historical Quarterly* 50, no. 3 (December 1971): 395–430.

Robinson, W.W. *Land in California.* Berkeley and Los Angeles: University of California Press, 1948.

Land Rights

Mexican-American land rights after the 1848 **Mexican War** were based on the **Treaty of Guadalupe Hidalgo**. Article IX of the treaty provided for the protection of Mexican-American property. However, those rights were not honored. In *United States v. Sandoval* (1897), the U.S. Supreme Court decided that Spanish and Mexican community grants were U.S. public domain. The U.S. Forest Service then administered the newly owned government land. In 1963, **Reies Lopez Tijerina** created the Alianza Federal de Mercedes (Federal

Land rights have always been a concern for Spanish-Americans in the Southwest. Here ranchers meet with officials from the Department of Agriculture in Chamisal, New Mexico, in 1943. *Library of Congress.*

Alliance of Land Grants)—later called the **Alianza Federal de Pueblos Libres** (Federal Alliance of Free Towns)—with the objective of returning pueblo common lands to their rightful original owners.

Spanish and Mexican custom and law form the basis for land use in the Southwest. In Ebright's *Spanish and Mexican Land Grants and the Law*, it is stated that the Spanish King allowed pueblo governments municipal control over Crown lands. Both Spain and Mexico gave land grants to settlers to help colonize Mexico's northern frontiers. **See also** Agrarian Reform; Water Rights. **See** Letter from the Santa Fe Jail by Reies Lopez Tijerina (1969); Treaty of Guadalupe Hidalgo (1848) in Appendix 1. (SCV)

BIBLIOGRAPHY

Blawis, Patricia Bell. *Tijerina and the Land Grants: Mexican Americans in Struggle for Their Heritage.* New York: International Publishers, 1971.

Duran, Livie Isauro and H. Russell Bernard. *Introduction to Chicano Studies.* New York: Macmillan, 1973.

Ebright, Malcolm, ed. *Spanish and Mexican Land Grants and the Law.* Manhattan, KS: Sunflower University Press, 1989.

Octaviano A. Larrazola (1859–1930)

Octaviano Larrazola became the first Latino to serve in the United States Senate when he was appointed to the vacated seat of New Mexico Senator A.A. Jones in 1928. However, because of poor health, Larrazola chose not to seek a full term and retired from politics in 1929. Prior to his appointment to the Senate, Larrazola had a distinguished record of service to the territory and state of New Mexico. He failed three times to be elected as a delegate to the U.S. States Congress in 1900, 1906, and 1908. In 1911, he left the Democratic Party because of its opposition to the proposed New Mexico State Constitution. In 1918, as a

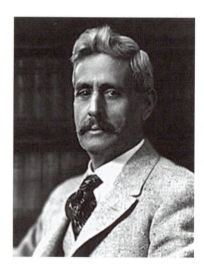

A controversial political figure in New Mexico, Republican Octaviano Lazzaro was the first Latino to serve in the U.S. Senate. *Library of Congress.*

Republican, he was elected as the fourth governor of New Mexico. His term was controversial because he supported the adoption of the first state income tax and the ratification of the Nineteenth Amendment (women's suffrage). He lost his reelection bid in the primary. From 1927 to 1928 he served in the State House of Representatives. **See also** Political Leadership.

BIBLIOGRAPHY

Virgil, Maurilio E. *Hispanics in Congress*. Lanham, MD: University Press of America, 1996.

Walter, Paul A. "Octaviano Ambrosio Larrazolo." *New Mexico Historical Review* (April 1932): 97–104.

Tulio Larrinaga (1847–1917)

Tulio Larrinaga was a skillful advocate of fair government for Puerto Rico under the civil administration of the United States. While he served as resident commissioner, he respected the American form of government and its institutions, but he also protested against the unkept promises of the United States. Larrinaga was appointed assistant secretary of the interior in a provisional Autonomist Cabinet, formed after the Spanish government granted Puerto Rico a Constitutional Charter on November 25, 1897, giving the island autonomy and guaranteeing individual rights. Larrinaga, at first a member of the Liberal Party, joined with Luis Muñoz Rivera to become one of the founders of the Federal Party in 1899. Most members of the Federal Party joined the Unionist Party when it was formed in 1904.

Larrinaga was elected resident commissioner in 1904 and was reelected in 1906 and 1908. Larrinaga's first act in Congress was the introduction of a bill to amend the **Foraker Act** and grant U.S. **citizenship** to Puerto Ricans. The bill was referred to the Committee on Insular Affairs, on which Larrinaga served, but it was never successfully reintroduced during Larrinaga's tenure.

In 1906, during his service as resident commissioner, Larrinaga was appointed delegate from the United States to the Third Pan American Congress at Rio de Janeiro. After serving as resident commissioner for three terms, he returned to San Juan, Puerto Rico, where he resumed his professional practice of civil engineering. From 1913 to 1917 he was a member of the executive council of Puerto Rico.

BIBLIOGRAPHY

Hispanic Americans in Congress. Washington, DC: U.S. Government Printing Office, 1995.

Lau v. Nichols (1974)

Kinney Lau, a non-English-speaking student in San Francisco, California, was denied appropriate assistance in overcoming her language difficulties when her school refused to create a program to deal with her language deficiency. Lau's attorneys argued that denying Spanish-speaking Mexican-American students equal opportunities for educational growth simply because of their language placed an unnecessary, harmful burden on the students. They argued such actions to be a violation of the **Civil Rights Act of 1964** and the Equal Protection Clause of the Fourteenth Amendment.

In *Lau v. Nichols*, 414 U.S. 563 (1974), the U.S. Supreme Court found that the failure of the San Francisco school system to provide English language instruction to Lau and the approximately 1,800 foreign-speaking students in its jurisdiction denied them the opportunity to advance their education.

The Court affirmed that such discriminatory practices violated Title VI of the Civil Rights Act of 1964, and the *Lau* decision helped establish more bilingual programs for Mexican-American students in primary schools. **See also** Assimilation; Bilingual Education; Educational Opportunity.

BIBLIOGRAPHY

Garcia, Mario T. *Mexican Americans*. New Haven, CT: Yale University Press, 1989.

Ladislas Lazaro (1872–1927)

Ladislas Lazaro, a Democrat, was the first Hispanic from Louisiana to serve in the U.S. House of Representatives. In 1894 he graduated from Louisville Medical College in Kentucky and practiced his profession in Washington, Louisiana.

In addition to his medical practice, he had an interest in farming; he also served as president of his parish school board for four years. He ran unopposed in his 1908 bid for a seat in the Louisiana State Senate, where he served until 1912.

Ladislas Lazaro (D-LA) served eight terms in the U.S. House of Representatives beginning in 1912. *Library of Congress.*

In 1912 Lazaro was elected to the U.S. House of Representatives and was subsequently reelected seven times. He ran unopposed in his first bid for Congress and in five of his seven subsequent elections. Lazaro took his seat on March 4, 1913, and served on the Committees on Enrolled Bills; Merchant Marine and Fisheries; and Coinage, Weights, and Measures. In 1919 he argued to amend and moderate the law on national prohibition, permitting the use of alcohol for medicinal purposes.

BIBLIOGRAPHY

Hispanic Americans in Congress. Washington, DC: U.S. Government Printing Office, 1995.

League of United Latin American Citizens (LULAC)

The League of United Latin American Citizens (LULAC) is the oldest and largest Hispanic organization in the United States. LULAC was founded in 1929 in Corpus Christi, Texas, as an amalgamation of groups representing Mexican-American interests under one set of objectives and one constitution. **Ben Garza**, the leader of Order of the Sons of America (Council Number Four), became the driving force behind such an amalgamation. LULAC began as a nonpartisan effort by middle-class Mexican Americans seeking to improve their status through **assimilation**. In its 65-year history, LULAC has worked to bring about many social and economic changes for Hispanic Americans. In *Menendez v. Westminister School District* (1945), a California LULAC council successfully sued to integrate the Orange County School System, which had been segregated on the grounds that Mexican children were "more poorly clothed and mentally inferior to white children." Additionally, LULAC won another landmark case, *Hernandez v. State of Texas* (1954) to protest the fact that not a single Mexican American in Texas had ever been called to jury duty. The U.S. Supreme Court ruled such exclusion unconstitutional.

To further its protection of Hispanic Americans through the court system, LULAC created the **Mexican American Legal Defense and Education Fund (MALDEF)** in 1968 as the legal arm of the Latino community, after securing a $2.2 million start-up grant from the Ford Foundation.

Working with MALDEF, LULAC has successfully challenged election plans that make it more difficult for Hispanics to win elective office. In 1990, for example, a U.S. Court of Appeals ruled that Los Angeles County's governing body intentionally diluted Hispanic voting strength when it redrew county election districts after the 1980 census. Nine candidates, eight of whom were Hispanic, ran in a new district the county was forced to create in the wake of this ruling.

Since that time, LULAC has fought for **voting rights**, access to the political process, and equal **educational opportunity** for Hispanic children. LULAC acts through councils set in communities across the nation, holding voter registration drives and **citizenship** awareness sessions, sponsoring fairs and tutorial programs, and raising scholarship money for the LULAC National Scholarship Fund. **See also** Community Organizations; *League of United Latin American Citizens v. Pasadena Independent School District* (1987); Political Leadership; Political Participation. (VDD)

BIBLIOGRAPHY

Chavez, Linda. *Out of the Barrio: Toward a New Politics of Hispanic Assimilation.* New York: Basic Books, 1991.

Rosen, Jeffrey. "Why the Courts Can't Save Us. The War on Immigrants." *The New Republic* (January 30, 1995).

League of United Latin American Citizens v. Pasadena Independent School District (1987)

In *League of United Latin American Citizens* [LULAC] *v. Pasadena Independent School District*, 622 F. Supp. 443 (S.D. 1987), LULAC brought suit against the school district on behalf of undocumented aliens who were terminated from their employment as school district custodial workers because they provided false Social Security numbers. The U.S. District Court for the Southern District of Texas found for LULAC, ruling that the plaintiffs should be reinstated to the positions they occupied prior to their dismissal because their termination violated the antidiscrimination provision of the **Immigration Reform and Control Act of 1986**. **See also** Discrimination; Illegal Aliens; League of United Latin American Citizens. (NM)

BIBLIOGRAPHY

Garcia, Mario T. *Mexican Americans.* New Haven, CT: Yale University Press, 1989.

Legal Services Corporation

The Legal Services Corporation was created in 1974 by the federal Legal Services Act to provide assistance to the Hispanic community. Besides funding 16 national support centers, the organization provides services to Chicanos and represents the poor in pertinent legal issues. The corporation also maintains relationships with thousands of legal offices across the nation to help all Latinos in the United States. By 1989 the group provided funding and representation for more than 232,000 cases involving Mexican Americans. **See also** Migrant Legal Action Program.

BIBLIOGRAPHY

Fried, Rinat. "Legal Services Corp. Has Urge to Merge." *The Recorder.* (San Francisco) (April 2, 1998): 1.

———. "LSC Cuts Off Alameda Legal Aid." *The Recorder.* (San Francisco) (June 29, 1998): 1.

Lemon Grove Incident

In July 1931, Mexican-American parents in Lemon Grove, California, near San Diego, challenged through the courts the local school board's decision to construct a separate school for Mexican-American children. This early political lawsuit against school segregation resulted in a court decision that Mexicans were considered white and therefore could not be segregated into separate schools. In the later 1930s the Bliss Bill, a legislative attempt at "separate-but-equal" school segregation, was defeated in the California legislature because lawmakers had problems placing Mexican-American children in separate school facilities after the precedent set by the Lemon Grove decision. (SCV)

BIBLIOGRAPHY

Rosales, F. Arturo. *Chicano! The History of the Mexican American Civil Rights Movement.* Houston: Arte Publico Press, 1997.

Lettuce Strikes (Salinas)

Organized by **Cesar Chavez** of the **United Farm Workers,** the lettuce strikes in Salinas, California, followed the successful settlement of the grape strike in July 1970. Fearing Chavez, lettuce growers in the region signed a multiyear deal with the Teamsters Union in fraudulent elections. In August, nearly 7,000 workers struck. When a quick settlement to the strike failed, Chavez called for a national boycott of lettuce. Chavez was jailed for his activities from December 4 until December 23, 1970. The general strike continued without resolution for several years. Conflict between the United Farm Workers and the Teamsters continued into 1977 until a major agreement to share the work ended the conflict. However, in February 1979, more than 3,000 United Farmer Worker union members struck over wages. By September the growers settled with the strikers, agreeing to provide better wages and benefits. **See also** Grape Boycott.

BIBLIOGRAPHY
Meister, Dick and Anne Loftis. *A Long Time Coming.* New York: Macmillan, 1977.

Liberalism

Liberalism in the United States has revolved around the right of individual liberty. This basic belief in the right of individual liberty influenced the efforts of Mexican-American/Spanish-speaking populations in the Southwest as they worked to redress wrongs through **civil rights** action.

Another source that influenced Southwest Mexican-American/Chicano organizations and the **Chicano Power Movement** was liberalism from Mexico. The Chicano civil rights movement of the 1960s and 1970s showed the influence of **Ricardo Flores Magon** and his brother **Enrique Flores Magon** and others who organized **El Partido Liberal Mexicano** (the Mexican Liberal Party) in exile in 1905. In 1906, the Flores Magon Junta in St. Louis, Missouri, published its liberal plan, listing objectives such as freedom of speech and of the press, educational reform in favor of the poor, prison reform emphasizing rehabilitation rather than punishment, and prohibition of child labor.

American and Mexican liberalism, as well as Mexican political exiles, served to define the politics of the Chicano civil rights movement. Through organization, marches, events, and the courts, the movement addressed many of the issues outlined in the Flores Magon Junta's liberal plan of 1906. Mexican political exiles in the Southwest organized workers and encouraged union leaders to promote political activism. Mexican/Chicano labor organizations included the National Farm Workers Union (NFWU), which under **Ernesto Galarza's** leadership led to a strike against the Digiogio Fruit company from 1947 to 1950. By the end of the decade, the AFL-CIO established the Agricultural Workers Organizing Committee. These efforts as well as those of the **United Farm Workers**, organized by **Cesar Chavez** and others, addressed the need for agricultural workers' civil rights, safe working conditions, better wages, and, most important, the recognition of the agricultural union's rights to negotiate work contracts.

Other influences emerging from American liberalism and Mexico's liberalism included community economic development, promoted through **Jose Angel Gutierrez's** Mexican American Unity Council (MAUC) to help small business owners provide job training. **Crusade for Justice**, in Denver, Colorado, worked to defend the civil rights of Chicanos. Later, El Plan Espiritual De Aztlan, created by the **National Chicano Youth Liberation Conference** in 1969, declared objectives for education reform. An attempt to achieve political freedom, freedom of speech, and freedom of expression could be seen through voter registration drives and **La Raza Unida** conferences.

The Chicano civil rights movement thus integrated its objectives with American and Mexican liberalism. From the political principles of American and Mexican liberalism emerged a number of federal programs. For example, the New Deal era under President Franklin D. Roosevelt orchestrated several public works programs that employed Mexican Americans. Under President John F. Kennedy, the Democratic Party agenda created such programs as Volunteers in Service to America (VISTA), which brought volunteers to Mexican-American barrios. In response, Mexican Americans created "**Viva Kennedy** Clubs," which motivated the formation of other regional or state level political organizations. Further, the liberal G.I. Bill provided opportunities for education and training for veterans, including many Mexican-American servicemen.

President Lyndon Johnson's "Great Society" gave minorities economic opportunity through the War on Poverty Act of 1964. It was during this decade that civil rights issues were initiated, such as **bilingual education**, **affirmative action,** community service, and small business administration programs.

The Chicano civil rights movement opposed poll taxes, gerrymandering, and Anglo political dominance. **Willie Velasquez** promoted the Raza Unida Conferences and conducted voter registration drives to address other political abuses. Jose Angel Gutierrez led the **Crystal City, Texas,** political takeover. **Reies Lopez Tijerina** struggled to obtain the return of community common lands in New Mexico to villagers whose families had received Spanish and Mexican land grants, based on the **Treaty of Guadalupe Hidalgo**. Cesar Chavez and the United Farm Workers sought contracts with growers to improve agricultural laborers' rights, working conditions, and wages.

American liberalism influenced the Chicano civil rights movement, influenced in turn by the national civil rights movement and Martin Luther King, Jr. Mexico's revolution, including the struggle by Emiliano Zapata for land reform and Mexico's subsequent return of common lands to Indian villages, greatly influenced the Chicano power movement as well. Chicanos, influenced by Mexico's reclamation of its Indian heritage and attempt to incorporate it into Mexico's nationhood, also turned their attention to their Indian heritage, extolling the Mechica (Aztec) and reevaluating the great Mayan and Aztec civilizations.

Liberalism sought liberty for the individual, and for civil rights, equality, and the rule of law, as well as capitalism's expansion through competition in work for grants and services. This can be seen in Ernesto Galarza's efforts to improve the lot of agricultural laborers through various strikes and contract negotiations.

Current liberalism is challenging new barriers to democracy, especially sweat shops and **maquiladoras**, assembly plant programs whereby Mexicans cross the border to work in the U.S. factories that underpay employees with unlivable wages. Also, children work or play around fields saturated with agricultural chemicals, and agricultural labor continues to struggle for recognition and fair wages.

Affirmative action opened doors for employment in public and private sector institutions. The Small Business Administration, private bank loan programs, and government loans stimulated the growth of Hispanic businesses and increased Hispanic employment in corporate America. Hispanic publications and Hispanic Chamber of Commerce organizations also increased in number.

However, by the 1980s, opposition to U.S. liberalism grew stronger. This opposition was aimed largely at the liberal programs of the past. The changes in U.S. society that were accomplished during the Chicano movement in the 1960s were challenged. Gains won by the national civil rights movement, such as an end to segregated schools and equal employment through affirmative action, were opposed at every turn.

The Chicano power movement had sought to realize liberalism's ideal that all individuals should have an opportunity for participation in government and in economic endeavors, and should benefit from government agencies. However, the 1980s and 1990s have brought political, economic, and social forces to bear against liberalism. Organized efforts against affirmative action, bilingual education, biculturalism, desegregation in public school systems, and the **English First/English Only** movement have unleashed powerful political powers toward ending the liberal programs of the 1960s. **See also** Acculturation; Alianza Federal de Pueblos Libres; Assimilation; Conservatism; El Movimiento; Economic Equality; Land Rights; Political Participation; Voting Rights; Welfare Reform. (SCV)

BIBLIOGRAPHY

Deutsch, Kenneth L., and Walter Soffer. *The Crisis of Liberal Democracy: A Straussian Perspective.* Albany: State University of New York Press, 1987.

Foster, James D., Mary C. Segers, with Mary C. Thornberry and Bette Novit Evans. *Elusive Equality: Liberalism, Affirmative Action, and Social Change in America.* Port Washington, NY: National University Publications/Associated Faculty Press, 1983.

Garcia, Chris F., and Rudolph O. de la Garza. *The Chicano Political Experience: Three Perspectives.* North Scituate, MA: Duxbury Press, 1977.

Garry, Patrick M. *Liberalism and American Identity.* Kent, OH: Kent State University Press, 1992.

Gerber, William. *American Liberalism: Laudable End, Controversial Means.* Boston: Twayne Publishers, 1975.

Hollinger, Robert. *The Dark Side of Liberalism: Elitism vs. Democracy.* Westport, CT: Praeger, 1996.

Leiss, William. *C.B. Macpherson: Dilemmas of Liberalism and Socialism.* New York: St. Martin's Press, 1988.

McAuliffe, Mary Sperling. *Crisis on the Left: Cold War Politics and American Liberals, 1947–1954.* Amherst: University of Massachusetts Press, 1978.

Meier, Matt S., and Feliciano Ribera. *Mexican Americans/American Mexicans: From Conquistadors to Chicanos.* New York: American Century Press, Hill and Wang, 1993.

Meyer, Michael C., and William L. Sherman. *The Course of Mexican History.* New York: Oxford University Press, 1995.

Watson, George. *The Idea of Liberalism: Studies for a New Map of Politics.* London: MacMillan, 1985.

Liga Protectiva Mexicana

Liga Protectiva Mexicana was created in 1921 in Kansas City, Missouri, to provide a united protective front for the area's Mexican Americans. At the time, rumors were spreading across the United States that all people of Mexican descent would be deported; the rumors said that the federal government sought to relieve the post-World War I recession by eliminating all of the country's Hispanic workers to provide more jobs for its Anglo citizens. Concerned about these rumors, the Liga Protectiva Mexicana quickly formed to prevent such deportation. The group readied itself for petitioning, lobbying, and any other legal and, if necessary, illegal acts needed to secure the continued **citizenship** rights of the Mexican-American community. The group never had to take any drastic steps, however, because the deportation rumors were eventually found to be false. As a result, Liga Protectiva Mexicana officially disbanded in 1923. **See also** Community Organizations.

BIBLIOGRAPHY

Ruiz, Vicki L. *From Out of the Shadows.* New York: Oxford University Press, 1998.

Felix Longoria

In 1944 Felix Longoria was drafted into the United States Army as a private, eventually serving in the Pacific in 1945. While in service, Longoria was killed and temporarily buried in the Philippines, as was the practice during the time. In 1948 his remains were transported to his birthplace of Three Rivers, Texas. However, the local funeral home refused to provide services because Longoria was a Mexican American. The situation made national headlines, and the Texas Good Neighbor Commission and a new organization that was founded because of the incident, the **American G.I. Forum,** began pressuring the government to address the problem. Senator Lyndon B. Johnson eventually intervened and Longoria was buried in Arlington National Cemetery. **See also** Civil Rights; Hector Garcia.

BIBLIOGRAPHY

Castro, Tony. *Chicano Power: The Emergence of Mexican America.* New York: Saturday Review Press, 1974.

Lino M. Lopez (1910–1978)

From the 1940s to the 1960s, Lino Lopez worked to forge positive relationships among students, schools, parents, community leaders, and political institutions in Illinois, Texas, Colorado, and California. As both a government administrator and prominent member of the **League of United Latin American Citizens** and the **American G.I. Forum**, Lopez earned a reputation for pioneering progressive antidiscrimination, cultural education, and student leadership programs in the communities that he served. Focusing on empowering Mexican-American youth, Lopez advocated **bilingual education** while urging parents and children to become more actively involved in **community organizations. See also** Political Leadership; Political Participation. (TIR)

BIBLIOGRAPHY

Marquez, Benjamin. *LULAC*. Austin: University of Texas Press, 1993.

Villarreal, Roberto E. and Norma G. Hernandez. *Latinos and Political Coalitions*. Westport, CT: Greenwood, 1991.

Rudy Lozano (1942–)

Born in Indiana, Rudy Lozano attended Indiana University and received his law degree in 1966. From 1966 to 1988, he worked as an attorney in the firm of Jennings, Spangler & Dougherty, and became a partner in the firm. In 1988 he became a judge in the U.S. District Court for the Northern District of Indiana. Lozano is a member of the Federal Judges Association, the **Hispanic National Bar Association**, and the Hispanic Bar Association of Northern Indiana.

BIBLIOGRAPHY

Boyd, John. "Judge Bars Independent Truckers from Uniting to Fight Steel Cutbacks." *Journal of Commerce* (October 21, 1991): 2B.

Thomas, Karen M. "First Hispanic Joins Indiana Federal Bench." *Chicago Tribune* (March 28, 1988): 1.

Manuel Lujan, Jr. (1928–)

Manuel Lujan (R-NM) served as secretary of interior from 1989 until 1993. *Library of Congress.*

Manuel Lujan, Jr., a Republican from New Mexico, was elected to the U.S. House of Representatives in 1968 and served until 1988. He spent most of his time working with environmental issues, trying to get laws passed to protect the wilderness. He was elected from the Albuquerque area, a district that is mostly white and Hispanic. His family was involved with politics and insurance. Lujan launched his career by running for the state senate in 1964. He was also secretary of the interior during the Bush administration. **See also** Congressional Hispanic Congress. (CEM)

BIBLIOGRAPHY

Kenworthy, Tom. "Lujan Likely to Approve North Carolina Jetties; Outer Banks Wall Project Faces Opposition." *The Washington Post* (October 6, 1992): A3.

Plevin, Nancy. "Ex-Interior Boss Lujan Defends His Stewardship of Public Lands." *Los Angeles Times* (May 9, 1993): 5.

LULAC. *See* League of United Latin American Citizens

Tranquilino Luna (1849–1892)

Tranquilino Luna, a delegate to the 1880 and 1888 Republican National Conventions, gained his first national political role when he was elected to the United States Congress for the Territory of New Mexico; he retained this seat from March 4, 1881, to March 3, 1883. Luna went on to present his credentials as a delegate-elect to Congress on March 4, 1883, serving until March 5, 1884. **Francisco Manzanares** defeated him for reelection in 1884. In 1888, Luna became sheriff of Valencia County, New Mexico, a role he filled until his death in 1892.

BIBLIOGRAPHY

Vigil, Maurilio E. *Hispanics in Congress*. Lanham, MD: University Press of America, 1996.

M

Machismo

"Machismo," usually defined as an exaggerated masculine superiority complex particularly attributed to Latin males, is controversial in theory and practice. Chicana feminists consider machismo as another manifestation of patriarchy. Nationalist Chicanas interpret machismo as a legacy of colonialsm. Chicano/Latino men often redefine machismo as a cultural trait meriting preservation. The implications of machismo for politics are that Latino men tend to take public leadership roles while Latina women tend to work behind the scenes. (ASR)

BIBLIOGRAPHY

Hardy-Fanta, Carol. *Latina Politics, Latino Politics*. Philadelphia: Temple University Press, 1993.

Francisco Antonio Manzanares (1843–1904)

Francisco Antonio Manzanares was a successful politician and businessman whose financial and commercial endeavors contributed to the economic development of New Mexico. He participated in the planning and founding of the Las Vegas Waterworks Association. He also played a major role in the development of the state's financial infrastructure. Because of his efforts, branches of the First National Bank were established in the cities of Santa Fe, Las Vegas, and Raton. In 1884 Manzanares was seated as a delegate to the U.S. House of Representatives after he contested the election of Republican **Tranquilino Luna**. After completing his term in Congress, Manzanares pursued his business affairs and served as county commissioner in San Miguel County in 1886 and 1897.

BIBLIOGRAPHY

Hispanic Americans in Congress. Washington, DC: U.S. Government Printing Office, 1995.

Maquiladoras

The Border Industrialization Program, established in 1963 by the U.S. and Mexican governments, authorized the assembling of parts produced outside of Mexico in plants (maquiladoras), located in Mexico's border zones. Maquiladoras are considered by some to be an economic necessity and by others to be a human nightmare wherever they exist in Mexico. Writers document both benefits and problems, including local eco-nomic development, high labor force participation rates, high wages, health problems caused by environmental degradation, non-unionized labor forces, mental and physical abuses on job sites, and disruptions to family life. (ASR)

BIBLIOGRAPHY

Kopinak, Kathryn. *Desert Capitalism*. Tucson: University of Arizona Press, 1996.

Sklair, Leslie. *Assembling for Development*. San Diego: Center of U.S.-Mexican Studies, University of California, San Diego, 1993.

March to Austin (1966)

On July 4, 1966, farm workers began marching from Rio Grande City, Texas, to Austin, the state capital. Their goal was to include farm workers in the Texas $1.25 per hour minimum wage. Led by Eugene Nelson, the workers marched from July 4 until Labor Day and listened to supportive speeches along the way given by Archbishop Robert E. Lucey and Texas Senator Ralph Yarborough. However, Texas Governor John Connally told the group he would not meet them in Austin, nor would he call the legislature into a special session on their behalf. In 1967 their demand for minimum wage was defeated, but the march brought attention to the concerns of the Texas farm workers and wages improved slightly.

BIBLIOGRAPHY

Garcia, Mario T. *Mexican Americans*. New Haven, CT: Yale University Press, 1989.

Majka, Linda C. "Labor Militancy among Farm Workers and the Strategy of Protest." *Social Problems* 28 (1981): 533–547.

March to Sacramento (1966)

The March to Sacramento, which began on March 17, 1966, was organized to help publicize the boycott of the National Farm Workers Association (the precursor to the **United Farm Workers**) against Schenley Industries, a major grape and fruit producer with noted discriminatory practices; the march was also designed to highlight other injustices against the Hispanic community. About 60 marchers began the 300-mile march from Delano, California, to the state capital of Sacramento, a trip that would take 25 days. In each town the group passed through, local supporters provided supplies and places to sleep, while the marchers held rallies, created local strike committees, and performed satirical skits. On the day before Easter, right before arriving in Sacramento, the marchers were informed that Schenley Industries had agreed to meet with members of the National Farm Workers Association. As a result, the group marched into Sacramento victorious, telling the gathered crowd of 8,000 people that they had triumphed over Schenley and would next turn their attention to another major fruit grower, the Di Giorgio Corporation. **See also** Cesar Chavez.

BIBLIOGRAPHY

Pulaski, Alex. "Farmworkers Begin Chavez March; Pilgrimage to Honor Pioneering Union Organizer Retraces Route He Led Them on in 1966 Action." *The San Francisco Examiner* (April 11, 1994): A4.

Alfredo Chavez Marquez (1922–)

After receiving his law degree from the University of Arizona in 1950, Alfredo Marquez worked as assistant attorney general for the state of Arizona from 1951 to 1952 and as deputy county attorney from 1953 to 1954. He then worked as administrative assistant to Democratic Congressman Morris Udall. In 1988 he became a U.S. district judge for the District of Arizona.

BIBLIOGRAPHY

"Judge Sides with HMO Patients; Ruling on Medicare Calls for Explanation If Service Is Denied." *Sun-Sentinel* (November 1, 1996): 1A.

Steward, Sally Ann. "New Page in English-Only Debate." *USA Today* (June 25, 1993): 8A.

Arabella Martinez (1937–)

In 1959 Arabella Martinez began working as a case worker for the Alameda County Welfare Department in Oakland, California. In 1963 she worked on the Aid to Families with Dependent Children Program for the Contra Costa Social Services Department. Martinez became a member of the Mexican-American Community Service Organization and served in 1964 as the first chairperson of the Spanish Speaking Unity Council (SSUC). In 1966 she became executive director of the Valley Communities Economic Opportunity Organization and then served as executive director of SSUC from 1969 to 1974.

In January 1977, Martinez was appointed by President Jimmy Carter to be assistant secretary of the Office of Human Development Services, a division of the U.S. Department of Health, Education, and Welfare. In this role, she helped maintain services relating to **civil rights**, health care, and welfare. Martinez also became involved in hostilities between Congress and the Department of Health, Education, and Welfare concerning the department's hiring practices, including those used in Martinez's own appointment. As a result, she left the federal government in 1979.

In 1980 Martinez founded and became the first president of the Center of Policy Development. Through this organization, Martinez helped in establishing fund-raising campaigns, in assisting community programs dealing with women and minority economic advancement, and with many other similar projects. In 1989 Martinez returned to the SSUC as the group's chief executive officer. **See also** Community Organizations; Economic Equality.

BIBLIOGRAPHY

"Key HEW Posts Expected to Go to Two Women." *The Washington Post* (January 19, 1977): A5.

Matthew G. Martinez (1929–)

After a brief stint in the California Assembly as a Republican, Matthew "Marty" Martinez was elected as a Democrat to the U.S. House of Representatives in 1982 from the Monterey Park area of California. In the 104th Congress, he was one of the ranking members on the Economic and Educational Opportunities Committee and one of the longest-serving Hispanic members in Congress. Prior to his election to Congress, Martinez served as mayor of Monterey Park from 1976 to 1980. In 1980, he was elected to the California State Assembly. **See also** Political Leadership.

BIBLIOGRAPHY

Ducan, Philip D. and Christine C. Lawrence. *Politics in America: 1996. The 104th Congress.* Washington, DC: Congressional Quarterly Press, 1995.

Vigil, Maurilio E. *Hispanics in Congress.* Lanham, MD: University Press of America, 1996.

Robert Martinez (1934–)

In 1979, Robert Martinez, a Republican, began his political career as mayor of Tampa, Florida, serving two terms. He was elected governor of Florida in 1988. In that same year, President Ronald Reagan named him to the White House Conference on a Drug-Free America, and in 1991 President George Bush appointed him to the Office of National Drug Control Policy, a position he held until 1993.

BIBLIOGRAPHY

Chavez, Linda. *Out of the Barrio.* New York: Basic Books, 1991.

Robert Martinez (1943–)

While working toward his M.A. in sociology in 1971 from the University of Colorado, Robert Martinez worked for the Educational Opportunity Program at the University of Colorado. After graduating he worked as program director of Special Services at the University of Southern Colorado from 1971 to 1974. He then took the position of director of the Academic Advising Center at the University of Colorado and later became director of the Migrant Action Program. In 1984 he became a Colorado State Representative, and in 1985 Martinez was elected to the state senate. He is an honorary lifetime member of the United States Hispanic Chamber of Commerce and in 1989 won *Freedom* magazine's Human Rights Advocate Award. **See also** Human Rights; Political Participation.

BIBLIOGRAPHY

McDonough, Beverly. *Who's Who in American Politics.* New Providence, NJ: R.R. Bowker, 1993.

Who's Who Among Hispanic Americans. Detroit: Gale, 1991.

Robert Lee Martinez (1944–)

After working briefly as dean of students for the University of Albuquerque, Robert Lee Martinez moved to Washington in 1981 to become the deputy director of Congressional Relations. He then was offered the position of director of the Affirmative Employment Programs and in 1986 he became the director of the Education Management Improvement Service. He has worked at the Department of Justice since 1987, first as the deputy associate attorney general and then as the assistant commissioner for the **Immigration and Naturalization Service**. Martinez has written numerous studies and reports and is the recipient of several awards, including the Department of Justice's Edmund J. Randolph Award in 1988.

BIBLIOGRAPHY

Ostrow, Ronald J. "US Creating Panels for Cuban's Appeals." *Los Angeles Times*. (December 12, 1987): 24.

Vilma Socorro Martinez (1944–)

Vilma Martinez, as general counsel and president of the **Mexican American Legal Defense and Education Fund (MALDEF)** from 1973 through 1982, worked to expand the **Voting Rights Act of 1965**; Congress complied and, in the **Voting Rights Act Amendments of 1975,** voting protection was extended to Mexican Americans. Martinez was instrumental in many cases, including *Plyler v. Doe* **(1982)** in which the U.S. Supreme Court ruled that the state of Texas was required to educate foreign-born children of illegal immigrants. (SCV)

BIBLIOGRAPHY

Rosales, F. Arturo. *Chicano! The History of the Mexican American Civil Rights Movement*. Houston: Arte Publico Press, 1997.

Mathews v. Diaz (1976)

Diaz, a Mexican American who was a resident alien in the United States, alleged that it was unconstitutional for the Social Security Administration to deny him Medicare benefits. Diaz, who was 65, also maintained that it was unconstitutional to require aliens to have resided in the United States for more than five years before they were eligible for Medicare. The U.S. District Court ruled that this practice was unconstitutional, but in *Mathews v. Diaz*, 426 U.S. 67 (1976), the U.S. Supreme Court reversed the decision, stating that the federal government could make an alien's eligibility for Medicare and any other federal program contingent on continuous residence in the United States. **See also** Citizenship; Immigration Policy and Hispanics.

BIBLIOGRAPHY

Hull, Elizabeth. "The Unkindest Cuts." *Gonzaga Law Review* (1997/1998): 471–500.

McCarran–Walter Immigration and Nationality Act of 1952

The McCarran–Walter Immigration and Nationality Act of 1952 embodied the concept of amnesty and defined the authorized importation of workers (designated as H-2 workers, from the section of the act that describes them). Government and economic interest groups used these two provisions to import labor and control the problem of undocumented workers. (Amnesty, spelled out subsequently in the Simpson–Rodino **Immigration Reform and Control Act of 1986**, authorized large groups of aliens to apply for continued residency and employment in the United States.)

In 1951, **Public Law 78** reauthorized the Bracero Program (originally authorized by **Public Law 45** in 1943), which allowed for the entry into the United States of agricultural workers from Mexico to help relieve the labor shortages caused by the Korean War. However, P.L. 78 was terminated in December 1964. At that time, William Wirtz, secretary of labor, approved the use of section H-2 of the McCarran–Walter Act to resume bringing in temporary Mexican workers. Section H-2 workers averaged 35,000 to 40,000 people per year within a decade.

The McCarran–Walter Act, which passed during the Cold War period, further authorized the U.S. attorney general to deport immigrants, even if they were naturalized citizens. **See also** Civil Rights; Illegal Aliens; Immigration Act of 1990; Immigration and Nationality Act of 1965; Immigration Policy and Hispanics. (SCV)

BIBLIOGRAPHY

McAuliffe, Mary Sperling. *Crisis on the Left: Cold War Politics and American Liberals, 1947–1954*. Amherst: University of Massachusetts Press, 1978.

McGovern Bill (1960)

The McGovern Bill, H.R. 11211 (1960), was proposed by Democratic Representative George McGovern of South Dakota; the bill proposed to reduce the number of braceros, or Mexican day-laborers, let into the United States by 20 percent each year until 1965, at which time the program would be abolished. McGovern argued that widespread hiring of bracero workers decreased job opportunities for Americans and caused product price deflation at the expense of low wages and poor working conditions. Members of the AFL-CIO supported the bill, as did representatives from the National Council of Churches. Even so, the bill was eventually rejected because it was found to be too discriminatory. **See also** Economic Equality; Illegal Aliens; Immigration Policy and Hispanics; Public Law 45 (1943); Public Law 78 (1951).

BIBLIOGRAPHY

Garcia, Mario T. *Mexican Americans*. New Haven, CT: Yale University Press, 1989.

Harold R. Medina, Sr. (1888–1991)

Born in Brooklyn, New York, Harold Medina graduated from Columbia Law School in 1912. He entered private practice and also lectured at Columbia Law School. In 1918, he formed his own firm that specialized in appellate work. His most famous case involved Anthony Cramer, who was accused of aiding Nazi spies during World War II. In 1951, President Harry Truman appointed Medina to the U.S. Court of Appeals for the 2nd District.

BIBLIOGRAPHY

American Bar Association. *Directory of Minority Judges in the United States.* Chicago: The Association, 1994.

Brownson, Charles B. *Judicial Staff Directory.* Mt. Vernon, VA: Congressional Staff Directory, 1986.

Margarita Melville (1929–)

Scholar and activist, Margarita Melville has devoted her life to social justice, humanitarian causes, and women's liberation. Born in Mexico and educated in Texas, she became a Catholic nun, worked in Guatemala, and then returned to the United States to join the movement against the Vietnam War. One of the Catsonville Nine, Melville was convicted of burning draft records and went to federal prison. After her release, she completed her Ph.D. and eventually joined the University of California at Berkeley faculty as an associate professor and then as associate dean. (ASR)

BIBLIOGRAPHY

Telgen, Diane and Jim Kamp, eds. *Notable Hispanic American Women.* Detroit: Gale Research, 1993.

Olga A. Mendez (1925–)

In 1978, Olga Mendez, a delegate to the 1980 Democratic National Convention, was first elected to the New York State Senate, a position she continues to hold. In the state senate, Mendez has served on a number of committees dedicated to women's issues, including the Minority Task Force on Women's Issues, the Women's Legislative Caucus, and the Task Force on Women in Courts, while also holding membership on the Minority Task Force on Housing. She also served as a member of state senate committees covering a variety of issues, such as finance, alcoholism and drug abuse, cities, elections, housing and community development, investigations, and tax and government operations.

BIBLIOGRAPHY

Carroll, Maurice. "Party Time for Mendez." *Newsday* (February 28, 1995): A24.

Lombardi, Frank. "Mendez Backing Outsider." *New York Daily News* (September 6, 1996): 12.

Robert Menendez (1954–)

Robert Menendez, a Cuban American, was elected to the U.S. House of Representatives from New Jersey in 1992. Being a Democrat and a social liberal (both rare for a Cuban American), Menendez advocates policies to stimulate economic growth. A member of the **Congressional Hispanic Caucus**, he also serves on the Economic and Educational Opportunities Committee.

Prior to his election to Congress, Menendez served as mayor of Union City, New Jersey, from 1986 until 1992. During this time he also served in the New Jersey State Assembly in 1987 and the State Senate in 1991. **See also** Political Leadership.

BIBLIOGRAPHY

Duncan, Philip D. and Christine C. Lawrence. *Politics in America: 1996. The 104th Congress.* Washington, DC: Congressional Quarterly Press, 1995.

Vigil, Maurilio E. *Hispanics in Congress.* Lanham, MD: University Press of America, 1996.

Menendez v. Westminister (1945)

In Santa Ana, California, representatives from a local council of the **League of United Latin American Citizens (LULAC)** ended a century of segregation in the state's public schools by filing the lawsuit *Menendez v. Westminister* (1945). LULAC attorneys successfully sued to integrate the Orange County school system at a time when public schools practiced segregation on the grounds that Mexican children were "more poorly clothed and mentally inferior to white children." **See also** Civil Rights; Discrimination; Educational Opportunity. (VDD)

BIBLIOGRAPHY

Wollenberg, Charles. "*Mendez vs. Westminister*: Race, Nationality, and Segregation in California Schools." *California Historical Quarterly* 53, no. 4 (Winter 1974): 317–32.

Mestizaje

Mestizaje is a blending process of racial types and cultures from which emerges a new type of race incorporating the characteristics of the others. Specifically applied to Mexican Americans and other minorities, *mestizaje* takes place over a long period of time. For example, after the conquest of the Aztecs by Spain, the influence of Spanish (and Moorish) culture blended with the indigenous people and cultures of Mexico. (SCV)

BIBLIOGRAPHY

Rodriguez, Roberto. "Latinos Coast to Coast Gear Up for Momentous March in Washington." *The Fresno Bee* (November 13, 1995): B7.

Rodriguez, Roberto and Patricia Gonzales. "What the Melting Pot Needs Now Is Some Mestizaje." *Sacramento Bee* (July 8, 1994): B7.

Mexican American Legal Defense and Education Fund (MALDEF)

The social and political protests that characterized much of the United States in the mid-1960s touched the Hispanic community as well. Hispanic radicalism, however, came to an end at the same time political protest in general subsided nationally. **La Raza Unida Party** was replaced with more moderate, middle-class oriented organizations such as the Mexican American Legal Defense and Education Fund (MALDEF), organized in 1968. The leadership of MALDEF accepted the premise that meaningful change could be achieved through the U.S. legal system. Leaders found that by moderating their strategy, they could achieve a portion of their earlier, radical objectives, and they could also play a greater role in the traditional political system.

MALDEF emerged as a potent force in protecting Hispanic constitutional rights. While not endorsing candidates, the group makes itself felt in the political arena much the same way as the NAACP does for African Americans. In terms of education, MALDEF addresses segregation, biased testing, inequities in school financing, and the failure to address bilingualism. MALDEF has been involved in litigation over employment practices and immigration reform as well, and it has emerged as the primary **civil rights** group on behalf of Hispanics. **See also** Joaquin Avila; Bilingual Education; Cuban American Legal Defense and Education Fund (CALDEF); Community Organization; Antonia Hernandez; Vilma Socorro Martinez; Gloria Molina; Political Leadership; Political Participation. (NM)

BIBLIOGRAPHY
Vigil, Maurilio. "The Ethnic Organization as an Instrument of Political and Social Change: MALDEF, a Case Study." *The Journal of Ethnic Studies* 18 (Spring 1990): 15–31.
Villarreal, Roberto E., Norma G. Hernandez, and Howard D. Neighbor. *Latino Empowerment: Progress, Problems, and Prospects.* New York: Greenwood Press, 1988.

Mexican American Political Association (MAPA)

The Mexican American Political Association was created in 1959 in Fresno, California, by Edwardo Quevedo, **Bert Corona**, **Francisca Flores**, and other Mexican Americans who felt the American two-party system did not accommodate Chicanos. The group established several goals for itself, including lobbying on issues relevant to Mexican Americans, backing Chicano candidates; supporting and encouraging Latino voting, political involvement, and **civil rights**; and striving for the overall betterment of Hispanics. Quevedo became the organization's first director; from this position he helped support **Edward Roybal's** run for Congress in 1962. Quevedo and MAPA also supported other campaigns of Hispanics in the California legislature and courts. Corona took over as director in 1966, after which he helped form a Texas branch of the association. Membership in the group dwindled in the 1970s when Edward Sandoval took over as the organization's president, then membership numbers later picked up. In 1979 some effort was made to establish chapters of the association in Chicago, Kansas City, and the Southwest, but the group has remained primarily California based.

BIBLIOGRAPHY
Briseno, Olsa. "Hispanics Unveil Drive for More Political Clout." *The San Diego Union-Tribune* (August 22, 1987): A3.
Ko, Mimi. "Orange County Focus: County Wide; Latino Group MAPA Forms New Chapter." *Los Angeles Times* (July 29, 1994): 2B.

Mexican American Study Project

In 1963, the University of California at Los Angeles began the Mexican American Study Project, which was the first major study of Mexican Americans. The Ford Foundation provided the funding for the project, which lasted for five years and included field research in 20 cities across the United States. The study produced a report that contained information on the history, demography, institutions, and political participation of Mexican Americans. It was published in 1970 under the name *The Mexican-American People: The Nation's Second Largest Minority,* by Leo Grebler, Joan Moore, and Ralph Guzman.

BIBLIOGRAPHY
Chavez, Linda. *Out of the Barrio.* New York: Basic Books, 1991.
Grebler, Leo, Joann Moore, and Ralph Guzman. *The Mexican-American People: The Nation's Second Largest Minority.* New York: Free Press, 1970.

Mexican American Women's National Association (MANA)

As one of the few Mexican-American organizations based in Washington, D.C., the Mexican American Women's National Association (MANA) continues to be an important advocate for Mexican-American women's concerns, policy issues, and advancements. Established in 1974 to deal specifically with women of color and Hispanic women when the National Organization for Women (NOW) seemed to ignore them, MANA currently has chapters in 15 states. MANA focuses on Hispanic women's leadership training, economic equity, voter education, increasing the visibility of women of color in the political process, and promoting their appointment to high-ranking positions in the federal government and political parties. The organization continues to fund scholarships and sustain a Hermanitas (Little Sisters) program to encourage young Mexican-American women to stay in school. Despite MANA's political orientation, leadership potential, and base in the nation's capital, few Latinas who have won elected statewide or national office have been MANA members or have used MANA as a pathway to political office. **See also** Economic Equality; Mujeres Activas en Letres y Cambio Social (MALCS); Political Participation; Blandina Cardenas Ramirez; Voting Patterns. (ASR)

BIBLIOGRAPHY
Vasquez, Sherri. "MANA Celebrates 11 Years in Denver." *Rocky Mountain News* (August 21, 1995): 4D.

Mexican American Youth Organization (MAYO)

Founded in 1968 in **Crystal City, Texas**, by **Jose Angel Gutierrez, Mario Compean, Willie Velasquez,** and others, the Mexican American Youth Organization focuses its activities on high-school-age students. Active throughout the Southwest, especially in Texas and California, the group encourages students to finish high school and continue on to college. The organization also offers youth a forum for political and social issues that affect them.

BIBLIOGRAPHY
Meier, Matt S. and Feliciano Rivera. *The Chicanos.* New York: Hill and Wang, 1972.
Shorris, Earl. *Latinos: A Biography of the People.* New York: W.W. Norton, 1992.

Mexican Protective Association

The Mexican Protective Association was founded in 1911 in Texas as one of the first Mexican-American labor organizations in the United States. The group was mutualist in nature, pooling all the members' resources to provide economic assistance for the entire group. The services to the association's members included providing money to cover the costs of funerals, insurance, and other necessities. The organization was composed mainly of tenant farmers, day laborers and braceros, and small-time farmers with Mexican backgrounds. While the group did have an immediate impact in its local area, it never gained as great an impact on Texas's overall Mexican-American labor policies as did other, more radical groups. **See also** United Farm Workers.

BIBLIOGRAPHY

Garcia, Mario T. *Mexican Americans*. New Haven, CT: Yale University Press, 1989.

Mexican War (1846–1848)

The annexation of Texas by the United States in 1845 caused Mexico to break diplomatic relations with its northern neighbor. President James K. Polk insisted on the Rio Grande as the international border between Mexico and Texas, even though both sides had previously recognized the Nueces River, 150 miles north of the Rio Grande, as the border. Polk sent American troops south toward the Rio Grande and dispatched Captain John C. Fremont to California. In April 1846, Mexico refused to meet with a U.S. negotiator to discuss selling additional territory to the United States. Polk decided on war, but the Mexican army struck first, attacking U.S. troops on the Rio Grande. The United States declared war in May 1846.

A U.S. army of 2,000 led by Stephen Kearny captured Sante Fe, New Mexico, without a fight in August 1846. In California, Fremont began the "Bear Flag Revolt" and secured that area until a revolt by Mexican "Californios" in Los Angeles defeated both a local garrison and part of Kearny's army. However, the Californios capitulated in January 1847. On the Texas border, U.S. forces won several battles and occupied northern Mexico, but Mexico did not surrender. A U.S. army, under the command of General Winfield Scott, landed at

General Zachary Taylor, a future president of the United States, sits astride his horse in this painting of a battle during the Mexican War. *Library of Congress.*

Veracruz, Mexico, and marched inland to capture Mexico City. By the autumn of 1847, the U.S. Army had conquered the Mexican capital; the **Treaty of Guadalupe Hidalgo**, which ended the war, was signed in February 1848.

The conclusion of the Mexican War virtually ended U.S. continental expansionism and left the United States as the dominant economic and military power in the hemisphere, with a severely weakened, politically divided Mexico to the south. The Mexican War added more than a million square miles of land to the United States, but it also placed the nation on a course toward civil war, as both North and South debated the future of slavery in the new territories. Tens of thousands of culturally and linguistically distinct new citizens had been added to the American population, and the war had created a long-lasting suspicion and mistrust between the United States and Mexico. **See also** Manuel Armijo; Gadsden Treaty (1853); Texas Statehood; Treaty of Velasco (1836). **See** Gadsden Treaty (1853); Texas Declaration of Independence (1836); Texas Annexation Treaty (1844); Treaty of Guadalupe Hidalgo (1848) in Appendix 1. (JRB)

BIBLIOGRAPHY

Bauer, Jack. *The Mexican War, 1846–1848*. New York: Macmillan, 1974.

Eisenhower, John S.D. *So Far from God: The United States War with Mexico, 1846–1848*. New York: Doubleday, 1989.

Singletary, Otis. *The Mexican War.* Chicago: University of Chicago Press, 1960.

Migrant Health Act of 1962

The Migrant Health Act of 1962 initiated programs (such as free vaccination distribution) to help migrant and seasonal farm workers and their families by extending project grants to government and private health providers who worked with underserved populations. The medical care of migrant workers, once under the domain of the U.S. Health Services Administration, was transferred to the Health Resources and Services Administration's Bureau of Health Care Delivery and Assistance. (VDD)

BIBLIOGRAPHY

Gutienez, Luz Bazan. "Chicano Health Care in the '80s." *La Chicana: Building for the Future, an Action Plan for the '80s.* Oakland, CA: National Hispanic University, 1981: 91–106.

Migrant Legal Action Program

The Migrant Legal Action Program was created in 1970 to protect and better the rights, interests, and needs of migrant and seasonal farm workers within the United States; many of these farm laborers made up the poorest group in the country. The program came under the funding of the **Legal Services Corporation** and worked closely with state and federal government offices. Besides providing legal assistance to people under the program's jurisdiction, the group now also works with about 70 migrant field attorney offices, as well as with numerous private groups and attorneys, to better provide services to eligible clients. Services provided by the group include policy development, public education and training, litigation support and backing, distribution of resource materials, labor conditions lobbying, and work toward laborer housing. **See also** Civil Rights; Economic Opportunity.

BIBLIOGRAPHY

"Allegations of Misused Funds May End a Migrant Legal Aid Project." *Los Angeles Times* (October 4, 1986): 20.

Loe, Victoria. "Study Suggests Explosion in Migrant Worker Ranks; Center Documents 3 Million Transitory Jobs in U.S." *The Dallas Morning News* (July 11, 1993): 39A.

Gloria Molina (1948–)

Best known for her articulation of community concerns and her many "firsts," Gloria Molina is California's most prominent elected official. Her firsts include being the first Chicana/Latina assemblywoman, the first Chicana/Latina Los Angeles city councilwoman, and the first Chicana/Latina on the Los Angeles County Board of Supervisors. Raised in Los Angeles, Molina completed college and became involved in community politics. From 1972 to 1982, she founded Comision Femenil de Los Angeles (a chapter of **Comision Femenil Mexicana Nacional**); worked in the office of Assemblyman Art Torres; become Comision national chair; and served in the Department of Intergovernmental and Congressional Affairs, Department of Health and Human Services, in Washington, D.C., before returning to California to work in the assembly speaker's office. In 1982 she ran for the state assembly as a Democrat despite opposition from local Chicano leaders. Molina's ability to run for city council and county board of supervisors depended on the success of lawsuits by the **Mexican American Legal Defense and Educational Fund (MALDEF)** challenging the gerrymandering of electoral districts. She was forced to challenge local Chicano leaders, including Torres, her former mentor. Her victories established her as the leading Chicana office holder in California and a strong force in the Democratic Party. **See also** Civil Rights; Community Organizations; Political Leadership. (ASR)

BIBLIOGRAPHY

Mills, Kay. "Gloria Molina." *Ms.* 13 (January 1985): 80–91.

Tobar, Hector. "Gloria Molina and the Politics of Anger." *Los Angeles Times Magazine* (January 3, 1993): 10–13, 24–32.

Joseph Manuel Montoya (1915–1978)

In 1936 at age 22, Joseph M. Montoya, who was still at Georgetown University, became the youngest person in the history of the state to be elected to the New Mexico House of Representatives. In 1938 Montoya graduated from law school and was reelected. The following year he was elected Democratic majority floor leader. In 1940, Montoya was elected to the state senate, once again becoming the youngest person to be elected to that body. By the time he left the senate in 1946, Montoya had been reelected twice and held the positions of majority whip as well as chairman of the Judiciary Committee. From 1947 to 1957 he was elected lieutenant governor three times and also served two additional terms in the state senate.

In 1957 Montoya was elected to the U.S. House of Representatives in a special election after the sudden death of the recently reelected New Mexican Congressman **Antonio Manuel Fernández.** In Congress Montoya gained recognition as a political moderate, a dedicated Democrat, and a diligent legislator. In 1963 he became a member of the House Appropriations Committee. A strong advocate of education measures, he authored the Vocational Education Act. In 1964 Montoya won the 1964 U.S. Senate election to complete the term of **Dennis Chávez,** beginning an 11-year career in the Senate, where he served on the Appropriations Committee; the Public Works Committee; the Joint Committee on Atomic Energy; and, most memorably, the Senate Select Committee on Presidential Campaign Activities, popularly known as the Watergate Committee. Montoya also worked on behalf of **civil rights**, education, health care, alien workers, and maintained a strong interest in the economic well-being of his constituents. In 1976 Montoya was defeated by Harrison Schmitt, a former astronaut.

Jospeh M. Montoya (D-NM) began his long career in elected office at the age of 22 while still in law school. *Library of Congress.*

BIBLIOGRAPHY

Hispanic Americans in Congress. Washington, DC: U.S. Government Printing Office, 1995.

Vigil, Maurilio and Luján, Roy. "Parallels in the Career of Two Hispanic U.S. Senators." *New Mexico Historical Review* 47 (October 1972): 362–81.

Nestor Montoya (1862–1923)

After working as a journalist and as the editor of the Spanish-language paper *La Bandera Americana*, Nestor Montoya became a member of New Mexico's Territorial House of Representatives from 1892 to 1903, during which time he eventually served as speaker. Montoya next became a member of the New Mexico Territorial Senate, where he served from 1905 to 1906. From 1908 to 1923, Montoya was president of the state press association, as well as a delegate to the 1910 Territorial Convention that created and adopted New Mexico's state constitution. Montoya was a regent of the University of New Mexico from 1916 to 1919 and a member of the Council of National Defense from 1917 to 1919. During World War I, Montoya was chairman of the Bernalillo County draft board, and from 1919 to 1920 he acted as county clerk. On March 4, 1921, Montoya was elected as a Republican to the U.S. Congress, where he served until his death. **See also** Political Leadership.

BIBLIOGRAPHY

Vigil, Maurilio. *Los Parrones: Profiles of Hispanic Political Leaders in New Mexico History.* Washington, DC: University Press of America, 1980.

Frederico A. Moreno, Sr. (1952–)

Born in Caracas, Venezuela, Frederico Moreno immigrated to the United States in 1963. He graduated from the University of Miami Law School in 1978, after which he held a number of public and private law positions. His public posts included serving as a judge in Dade County (1986–1987) and as a member of Florida's Circuit Court from 1987 to 1990. In 1990, he was appointed to the U.S. District Court for Southern Florida by President George Bush.

BIBLIOGRAPHY

American Bar Association. *Directory of Minority Judges in the United States.* Chicago: The Association, 1994.
Brownson, Charles B. *Judicial Staff Directory.* Mt. Vernon, VA: Congressional Staff Directory, 1997.

Luisa Moreno (1907–1990)

Born in Guatemala, Luisa Moreno was educated in the United States and began her labor organizing career in New York City. A leader in the United Cannery, Agricultural, Packing, and Allied Workers of America (UCAPAWA), Moreno, along with **Emma Tenayuca**, was investigated by the House Committee on Un-American Activities. Moreno was deported under the terms of the **McCarren–Walter Immigration and Nationality Act** because of her radical labor activities, but continued her support for workers' and human rights. **See also** Congresso de Pueblos de Habla Espanola.

BIBLIOGRAPHY

Acuna, Rodolfo. *Occupied America: A History of Chicanos.* New York: Harper and Row, 1981.
Camarillo, Albert. *Chicanos in California.* San Francisco: Boyd and Fraser, 1984.

Movimiento Estudiantil Chicano de Aztlan (MEChA)

Movimiento Estudiantil Chicano de Aztlan (MEChA) is the premier Chicano, Latino, Mexican American, and Hispanic college campus student organization in the United States. MEChA was officially formed in 1969 at a conference at the University of California, Santa Barbara, from several predecessor organizations, including United Mexican American Students (UMAS), Mexican American Student Confederation (MASC), **Mexican American Youth Organization (MAYO)**, and Mexican American Student Association (MASA). Dedicated to the principles expressed in El Plan de Santa Barbara, that of "demanding the university work for our people," MEChA functions as a direct link between college campuses and the Chicano community by pursuing voluntary teaching, tutoring, and mentoring programs in grades K-12 of public school systems. Because of its mission to pursue change, its extensive obligations to a large, complex community, and its intense internal struggles, MEChA often provides many college students with their first political experiences, thus serving as a training ground for many Chicano and Latino community activists and elected officials. (ASR)

BIBLIOGRAPHY

Gomez-Quinonez, Juan. *Mexican Students Por La Raza.* Santa Barbara: Editorial La Causa, 1978.
Munoz, Jr., Carlos. *Youth, Identity, and Power.* New York: Verso, 1989.
Navarro, Armando. *Mexican American Youth Organization.* Austin: University of Texas, 1995.

Mujeres Activas en Letres y Cambio Social (MALCS)

After 10 years of participating in the establishment of Chicano Studies programs, the **National Association for Chicana and Chicano Studies**, the National Women's Studies Association, and various caucuses within specialized academic organizations, Chicana and Latina scholars found themselves few in number, isolated, harassed, discriminated against, excluded, or subsumed. In 1982, a small group of women met at the Berkeley and Davis campuses of the University of California and formed an organization that would allow them to integrate their academic world with their community while pursuing social change on behalf of women of color. The founders of Mujeres Activas en Letres y Cambio Social (MALCS) advocated placing women's issues in the foreground; supported research, teaching, and publications specifically on women's issues; and encouraged the development of explanatory theories and critical analysis on the relationship of gender and sexuality to issues of race and class. MALCS also created a great deal of controversy within Chicano studies scholarly circles by its articulation of Chicana and Latina (women's) issues, issues pertinent to lesbians, and exposure of harassment within the Chicano and Latino community. **See also** Adaljiza Sosa-Riddell; Mexican American Women's National Association (MANA). (ASR)

BIBLIOGRAPHY

Yaqub, Reshma Memon. "Latinas Conference Seeks Unifying Goals Agenda." *Chicago Tribune* (July 11, 1993): 2.

Luis Muñoz Marin (1898-1980)

Luis Muñoz Marin was governor of Puerto Rico from 1949 to 1965. Muñoz Marin gave up a career as a journalist and poet in New York City to enter politics in Puerto Rico. In 1938, he organized and led the **Popular Democratic Party (PDP)** on a platform of economic and social reform. He also became editor of *La Democracia*, a San Juan newspaper founded by his father-in-law, **Luis Muñoz Rivera**, who was one of the most important political leaders of Puerto Rico in the early twentieth century. With the slogan "bread, land, and liberty," Muñoz Marin developed an enthusiastic following among the Puerto Rican lower classes, and won the island's first free popular election for governor in 1948. Re-elected in 1952 and 1956, Muñoz Marin supported commonwealth status for

Puerto Rico and was instrumental in bringing about the 1952 proclamation of the island as an Associated Free State. As governor, he promoted economic development and close cooperation with the United States. Although the Roman Catholic Church opposed his re-election in 1960 because of his support for birth control, Muñoz Marin won the election easily. In 1964, he chose not to seek another term and retired from politics. **See also** Puerto Rican Statehood.

BIBLIOGRAPHY

Aitken, Thomas, Jr. *Poet in the Fortress: The Story of Luis Muñoz Marin*. New York: New American Library, 1964.

Mathews, Thomas G. *Luis Muñoz Marin: A Concise Biography*. New York: American R.D.M. Corp., 1967.

Luis Muñoz Rivera (1859–1916)

One of the most famous men in the political history of Puerto Rico, Luis Muñoz Rivera devoted his life to the struggle for the political autonomy of Puerto Rico. In 1887 Muñoz Rivera became one of the founders of the Autonomist Party, which sought to establish an independent government for Puerto Rico under the Spanish colonial system. To provide a voice for the Autonomist Party, Muñoz Rivera founded the newspaper *La Democracia*. In March 1895 he was a delegate to Spain as part of a four-member commission that met with Praxedes Mateo Sagasta, the leader of Spain's Liberal Party. Sagasta signed a pact which stated that if he and the liberals assumed power in Spain, he would grant Puerto Rico autonomy. The Liberal Party of Puerto Rico endorsed the pact.

In November 1897 Sagasta granted the Autonomist Charter and Muñoz Rivera was appointed secretary of state and chief of the Cabinet of the newly independent government of Puerto Rico. He served in this position until the U.S. invasion of Puerto Rico and establishment of a military government in July 1898.

In 1899 Muñoz Rivera founded the newspaper *El Territorio*, which expressed the concerns of Puerto Rican landowners, who were unable to export their crops due to a U.S.-imposed trade blockade. In 1901, while living in New York, Muñoz Rivera established the *Puerto Rican Herald*, a bilingual newspaper. In the first issue Muñoz Rivera wrote an open letter to President William McKinley in which he lambasted the **Foraker Act** as a disgrace to both the United States and Puerto Rico.

Muñoz Rivera returned to Puerto Rico in 1904 and became one of the founders of the Unionist Party. In 1906 he was elected to the House of Delegates as a Unionist and was twice reelected, serving until 1910, when he was elected resident commissioner to the U.S. House of Representatives. The work of Muñoz Rivera led to the enactment of the **Jones Act** which granted United States **citizenship** to Puerto Ricans; it also gave the Puerto Rican government more autonomy by establishing a two-chamber legislative assembly, which included a 19-member Senate and a 39-member House of Delegates, elected by universal male suffrage. **See also** Independence Party; Popular Democratic Party; Puerto Rican Statehood; Spanish-American War.

BIBLIOGRAPHY

Hispanic Americans in Congress. Washington, DC: Government Printing Office, 1995.

Norris, Marianna. *Father and Son for Freedom*. New York: Dodd, Mead & Company. 1968.

Mutual Aid Societies

Mutual aid societies, also known as mutualistas, were joint resource organizations that pooled the resources of all their members to seek the betterment of the entire group. In doing so, these societies helped members with funeral costs, insurance benefits, low-interest loans, and other financial necessities. These groups often provided discussion forums, self-help instruction, and social events centered around the entire community, while also providing the foundation for a number of labor and civil rights groups. Examples of mutual aid societies include **Alianza Hispano-Americana**, Sociedad Espanola de Beneficiencia Mutua, Sociedad Ignacio Zaragoza, Sociedad Benito Juarez, and the Fraternal Aid Union. In many Hispanic communities, mutualistas became the most important institution after the church. **See also** Community Organizations.

BIBLIOGRAPHY

McCartney, Patrick. "A Revitalized Role for Latin Mutual-Aid Club." *Los Angeles Times* (July 2, 1993): 1.

National Association for Chicana and Chicano Studies (NACCS)

The National Association for Chicana and Chicano Studies (NACCS) was formed by young social scientists active within Chicano caucuses in their respective professional discipline-based organizations. These young scholar-activists believed a national academic interdisciplinary association was needed to nurture their research agendas, support Chicano studies programs, and connect to their community. Meeting for the first time on May 18–20, 1973, at New Mexico Highlands University, the National Caucus of Chicano Social Scientists organized its first conference in November 1973 at the University of California, Irvine. In 1976, the Caucus became the National Association for Chicano Studies, and then the National Association for Chicana and Chicano Studies, as women insisted on ending generic terminology that subsumed them. Still growing, changing, and extending its activities to Mexico, the NACCS has encouraged scholarly writing, research, and teaching on the Chicano and Latino experience in the United States. Now well established, the NACCS reflects the successes and struggles endemic to an emerging discipline, as Chicana and Chicano Studies programs remain precarious and controversial on college campuses. (ASR)

BIBLIOGRAPHY

Munoz, Carlos, Jr. *Youth, Identity, and Power*. New York: Verso, 1989.
Garcia, Ignacio M. "Juncture in the Road: Chicano Studies Since 'El Plan de Santa Barbara.'" Maciel, David, and Isidro Ortiz, eds. *Chicanas/Chicanos at the Crossroads*. Tucson: University of Arizona Press, 1996.

National Association of Cuban-American Women

The National Association of Cuban-American Women is an advocacy group that works on behalf of Hispanic and minority women. The group began in 1972 under the name Asociacion Nacional de Mujeres Cubanianoamericanas de los Estados Unidos de America. In 1986 the organization joined with the National Association of Cuban Women and Men of the United States. The mission of the group is to secure equal education, employment, and fair immigration policies for Hispanic women. The organization produces a biweekly bilingual radio program, which helps the group to distribute information on schooling, jobs, and financial assistance as well as programs offered by local, state, and federal agencies. In addition, the group maintains a library that includes books of Cuban history and human rights violations in Cuba, and the group encourages participation in task forces and on legislation having to do with Cuban-American issues. **See also** Educational Opportunity; Economic Equality; Immigration Policy and Hispanics.

BIBLIOGRAPHY

Alma-Bonilla, Yara I. "National Latina Groups Still Struggle to Surmount Obstacles." *Hispanic Link* (September 21, 1997): 1.

National Association of Latino Elected and Appointed Officials (NALEO)

Founded in 1975 as an organization for Spanish-surnamed politicians, the National Association of Latino Elected and Appointed Officials (NALEO) is committed to increasing Hispanic participation in voting. The non-partisan organization serves as a national lobby for Spanish-speaking Americans on a variety of issues, including **bilingual education.** The organization publishes a monthly newsletter, the *NALEO Washington Report*. **See also** Political Leadership; Voting Rights; Voting Patterns.

BIBLIOGRAPHY

Skerry, Peter. *Mexican Americans*. New York: Free Press, 1993.
Vigil, Maurillo. *Hispanics in Congress*. Lanham, MD: University Press of America, 1996.

National Chicano Youth Liberation Conference

The National Chicano Youth Liberation Conference, sponsored by the **Crusade for Justice** and held in Denver, Colorado, in March 1969, represented the first time that large numbers of Mexican Americans came together to discuss the strategies, goals, and ideology of a nationwide Chicano political mobilization. Attracting more than 2,000 delegates representing Mexican-American youth, students, political organizations, and community organizers, the conference attempted to unify Mexican Americans by defining and articulating a distinct Chicano racial and ethnic identity. Heavily influenced by the writings of Chicano poet Alurista, and Crusade chairman **Rodolfo "Corky" Gonzales**, the delegates drafted "El Plan Espiritual de Aztlan." In workshops addressing such disparate topics as economic investment, political organization, and dance, the delegates proposed to address the needs of Mexican Americans by demanding control over educational, political, economic, and cultural institutions. Although the conference had been criticized as embodying mostly symbolic rhetoric, it spurred the emergence of student-led Mexican-American organizations and helped place Chicano identity at the center of Mexican-American politics. **See also** Chicano Power Movement; Community Organization; Political Participation. (TIR)

BIBLIOGRAPHY

Gutierrez, David G. *Walls and Mirrors: Mexican Americans, Mexican Immigrants, and Politics of Ethnicity.* Berkeley: University of California Press, 1995.

Munoz, Carlos Jr. *Youth, Identity, Power: The Chicano Movement.* London: Verso, 1989.

National Council of La Raza

The National Council of La Raza began in 1968 as the Southwest Council of the **La Raza Unida Party**, a group dedicated to gaining social, economic, and political betterment for Chicanos. Early on, the council backed local community groups in gaining financial assistance for housing and economic development. It also undertook studies in Hispanic **voting patterns** and Los Angeles social service projects. The group also provided **bilingual education** and multicultural education programs for the community.

In 1970 the council lost its funding from the Ford Foundation and moved to Washington, D.C., where it gained federal support. The Southwest Council of La Raza renamed itself as the National Council of La Raza in 1973. From 1978 to 1979, the group conducted studies on employment difficulties and Mexican-American youth needs for the United States Department of Labor. It soon established offices in New Mexico, Texas, Arizona, and Illinois, while also working with more than 100 **community organizations.** Other services the group currently provides include training in resource development, proposal writing, and management, as well as publishing pamphlets, books, and the bimonthly *Agenda* magazine. The council has three main goals: advocating national Latino needs, conducting relevant research and analysis, and supporting local organizations through technical assistance funding. **See also** Assimilation; Economic Equality; Educational Opportunity; Political Participation; Marta Sotomayor; Voting Rights.

BIBLIOGRAPHY

Rodriguez, Cynde. "High on Hope for Hispanics; Conference Infuses Latino Leader with Optimism." *The Hartford Courant* (July 27, 1998): B1.

Weber, Brian. "DPS Tries to Throttle Group That Blasted Board Member." *The Rocky Mountain News* (May 15, 1998): 8A.

National Immigration Law Center

The National Immigration Law Center, formerly known as the National Center for Immigrants' Rights, was created to meet the legal need of the Hispanic community. The center provides support on immigration laws and alien rights to nonprofit groups, legal service programs, and other organizations needing assistance. Besides this, the group focuses on legalization, processing of visas, deportation, and alien rights, along with other beneficial programs. In addition, the center has participated in litigation against the **Immigration and Naturalization Service** on grounds of unlawful conduct and unconstitutional actions. **See also** Illegal Aliens; Immigration Policy and Hispanics

BIBLIOGRAPHY

Rojas, Aurelio. "Suit Filed Over INS Plan to Deport Residents' Spouses." *The San Francisco Chronicle* (November 29, 1993): 5A.

Tipton, Virgil. "McNary Criticizes Civil Rights Groups; Immigration Advocate Calls Remarks: 'Abhorrent.'" *St. Louis Post-Dispatch* (July 25, 1992): 3A.

National Puerto Rican Coalition

In 1977 a group of community leaders met in Washington, D.C., at the invitation of the Commission on Civil Rights to discuss the future of the Puerto Rican community in the United States. From those discussions, the idea for the National Puerto Rican Coalition emerged and was incorporated later that year. The coalition continues to work on furthering the social, economic, and political position of Puerto Ricans throughout the United States and in Puerto Rico by representing their interests before national policy makers.(VDD)

BIBLIOGRAPHY

National Puerto Rican Coalition Web site: <www.incacorp.com/nprc>

National Puerto Rican Forum

The National Puerto Rican Forum was founded in 1957 to help the overall improvement of the Puerto Rican and Hispanic community within the United States. The group provided programs in work counseling, job training and placement, and English-language courses. Besides publishing various reports pertaining to the Hispanic community, the New York-based group dedicated itself to offering nationwide job placement and career counseling services to Chicanos. **See also** Assimilation; Economic Opportunity; Educational Equality; National Puerto Rican Coalition.

BIBLIOGRAPHY

Kihss, Peter. "Study Finds Puerto Ricans in an Awesome Crisis." *The New York Times* (November 2, 1980): 53.

Woodward, Catherine. "Pulling the Welfare System in New Directions; Combining Classes with Child Care." *Newsday* (June 12, 1988): 75.

New Progressive Party (PNP)

The New Progressive Party (Partido Nuevo Progresista, or PNP), one of the two largest political parties in Puerto Rico, was founded in 1967 by Luis A. Ferre to promote the admission of Puerto Rico as the fifty-first U.S. state. Ferre, **Carlos Romero Barcelo**, and others organized the New Progressive Party when its predecessor, the Statehood Republic Party, refused to promote the **Puerto Rican statehood** option in the

1967 status plebiscite in Puerto Rico. Traditionally, most statehood parties in Puerto Rico have focused on forging strong ties with the Republican Party on the U.S. mainland. In contrast, the PNP has aggressively developed links to the mainland Democratic Party. The New Progressive Party, like its chief rival, the **Popular Democratic Party**, usually garners between 45 percent and 50 percent of the popular vote in Puerto Rican elections. The New Progressives have historically fared well in urban areas, while the Popular Democrats have usually mustered greater support in the rural areas. (AAB)

BIBLIOGRAPHY

Melendez, Edgardo. *Movimiento anexionista en Puerto Rico.* Rio Piedras, PR: Editorial de la Universidad de Puerto Rico, 1993.

Philip Newman (1916–)

Philip Newman, of German and Mexican descent, was the first Mexican-born American appointed as a U.S. judge. Newman's parents left Mexico for the United States during the Mexican Revolution of the 1910s. After graduating from law school in 1941, Newman championed individual rights, winning a number of important search and seizure cases that led to changes in immigration law. In 1964, Newman was appointed as a Los Angeles municipal judge by Governor Edmund Brown. Newman served on the court until 1982 when he retired.

BIBLIOGRAPHY

Mills, James R. *A Disorderly House.* Berkeley, CA: Heyday Books, 1987.

Skerry, Peter. *Mexican Americans.* New York: Free Press, 1993.

Antonia Novello (1944–)

Antonia Novello, a Puerto Rican, was the first woman to be awarded the University of Michigan's Pediatrician Intern of the Year Award in 1971. She would go on to have a distinguished medical and public service career, including serving as surgeon general of the United States under President George Bush from 1989 until 1993. During her tenure, she focused on the growing impact of AIDS and also coordinated an educational advertising campaign to inform minors about the impact of alcohol. Prior to her appointment as surgeon general, she was the deputy director of the National Institute of Child Health and Human Development.

BIBLIOGRAPHY

Hilts, Philip J. "President Picks Hispanic Woman to Become U.S. Surgeon General." *New York Times* (October 18, 1989): A20.

Telgen, Diane and Jim Kamp, eds. *Notable Hispanic American Women.* Detroit: Gale, 1993.

Mario Guerra Obledo (1932–)

With degrees in pharmacy and law, Mario Obledo is a leading political figure in California. Dedicated to enhancing political participation of minorities, he has served as California's secretary of health and welfare, chaired the National Rainbow Coalition, the California chapter of the **League of United Latin American Citizens**, and the California Coalition of Hispanic Organizations. **See also** Civil Rights; Political Participation. (ASR)

Office of Economic Opportunity (OEO)

Title VI of the Economic Opportunity Act of 1964 created the Office of Economic Opportunity (OEO). The office became the planning agency for President Lyndon Johnson's legislative "War on Poverty." The following decade brought a major expansion in federal responsibility for the disadvantaged, as OEO administered more than 150 federal programs, including Head Start and the Job Corps, designed to help the poor participate in the benefits of a growing and prosperous nation. **See also** Economic Equality. (VDD)

BIBLIOGRAPHY

Haveman, Robert H. *A Decade of Federal Antipoverty Programs.* New York: Academic Press, 1977.

Graciela Gil Olivarez (1928–1987)

In 1970 Graciela Olivarez became the first woman graduate of Notre Dame University School of Law. In 1977 President Jimmy Carter appointed her director of the Community Service Administration in Washington, D.C. A community activist, she served in public affairs in Arizona and New Mexico. **See also** Community Organizations; Political Leadership. (SCV)

BIBLIOGRAPHY

"Graciela Olivarez." *Phoenix Gazette* (September 23, 1987): C4.

Operation Bootstrap

In 1948 Puerto Rico's **Popular Democratic Party** (PPD) initiated a massive economic development program known as Operation Bootstrap, designed to modernize the island and lower unemployment. To attract investment, it offered U.S. businesses three incentives: freedom from taxes for a 17-year period; eased environmental laws; and an educated, cheap labor force. Operation Bootstrap appeared successful—hundreds of factories opened, 50,000 jobs were created, and Puerto Rico's infrastructure improved. However, the program also resulted in a net loss of jobs, high levels of pollution, the migration of Puerto Ricans to the U.S. mainland, and increased economic dependence on the United States. (MP)

BIBLIOGRAPHY

Lopez, Alfredo. *Dona Licha's Island. Modern Colonialism in Puerto Rico.* Boston: South End Press, 1987.
Silen, Juan Angel. *We, the Puerto Rican People. A Story of Oppression and Resistance.* New York: Monthly Review Press, 1971.

Operation WetBack

Following World War II, a growing number of undocumented aliens entered the United States to gain employment. Many of these immigrants and day laborers worked inexpensively for farms, factories, and agricultural businesses in the Southwest and along the U.S.–Mexico border. In June 1954, Operation WetBack was developed to allow for more effective enforcement of immigration legislation and deportation of undocumented immigrants. U.S. Attorney General Herbert Brownell, Jr. became a major proponent of this program and helped usher it into practice; as a result, Operation WetBack made public demands that undocumented aliens return voluntarily to Mexico or face deportation.

In the first year of the program's existence, more than a million **illegal aliens** were forced to leave the United States. While the program improved the economic conditions among the remaining (legal) Hispanic-American citizens, it also caused harsh criticism. Many Latinos argued that the process violated their **civil rights**, while others feared being intimidated. Families also suffered from Operation WetBack because children, spouses, or other family members were often separated. Despite the program's actions, the number of undocumented alien workers in the United States continued to grow. **See also** Immigration Policy and Hispanics.

BIBLIOGRAPHY

Dillin, John. "Clinton Promise to Curb Illegal Immigration Recalls Eisenhower's Border Crackdowns." *The Christian Science Monitor* (August 25, 1993): 6.

Katherine D. Ortega (1934–)

Katherine Ortega was active in Republican Party politics in New Mexico for a number of years, including serving as a link to both Hispanic and women voters and working on the senatorial campaigns of Pete Domenici (R-NM). In 1983, she began six years of public service when she was appointed by President Ronald Reagan as treasurer of the United States. In 1984, she gave the keynote address at the Republican National Convention. Retiring form public life in 1989, she was named alternative representative to the United Nations in 1990 by President George Bush.

BIBLIOGRAPHY

McFadden, Robert D. "Woman in the News, Choice for Treasurer." *New York Times* (September 13, 1983): B14.

Telgen, Diane and Jim Kamp, eds. *Notable Hispanic American Women*. Detroit: Gale, 1993.

Solomon P. Ortiz (1937–)

With no previous political experience, Solomon Ortiz, a Hispanic American, was first elected to the U.S. House of Representatives as a Democrat in 1982 from the Corpus Christi, Texas, area. He was instrumental in preventing the closure of two military installations in his district. He is the ranking Democrat on the Military Installations Committee. **See also** Congressional Hispanic Caucus; Political Leadership. (CEM)

BIBLIOGRAPHY

Cooper, Kenneth. "Congress's Hispanic Membership Likely to Grow 50% for Next Term; Caucus's Makeup to Better Reflect the Latino Community's Diversity." *The Washington Post* (October 3, 1992): A11.

Duncan, Philip D. and Christine C. Lawrence. *Politics in America: 1996. The 104th Congress.* Washington, DC: Congressional Quarterly Press, 1995.

Sallee, Rad. "Garcia Still Democrats' Top Choice, Ortiz Reassures Him on U.S. Attorney Job." *The Houston Chronicle* (November 27, 1997): 1.

Mariano Sabino Otero (1844–1904)

Mariano Sabino Otero began his political career as a probate judge of Bernalillo County, New Mexico. He served in this position from 1871 to 1879. On March 4, 1879, Otero became a Republican member of the U.S. Congress. He served the territory of New Mexico in this capacity until March 3, 1881, at which time he decided not to run for reelection. After this, Otero served from 1884 to 1886 as commissioner of Bernalillo County. He was later an unsuccessful congressional candidate in 1888 and 1890.

BIBLIOGRAPHY

Vigil, Maurilio E. *Hispanics in Congress*. Lanham, MD: University Press of America, 1996.

Miguel Antonio Otero (1829–1882)

A major contributor to the economic development of New Mexico, Miguel Antonio Otero was born in Valencia, Nuevo México (now New Mexico), on June 21, 1829. In 1852 Otero became the private secretary to the governor of New Mexico, William C. Lane, and was elected to the second legislative assembly of the territory of New Mexico. In 1854 he was appointed attorney general for the territory, and he served for two years. On March 4, 1856, he was seated as a delegate to the U.S. House of Representatives, after successfully contesting the election of José Manuel Gallegos. Otero, a Democrat, was reelected to the next two Congresses, but he did not run again in 1860. An outspoken congressman and a strong supporter of the railroad, Otero devoted many of his efforts to the construction of the transcontinental railroad through New Mexico. After Otero had completed his term in Congress, President Abraham Lincoln nominated him to be minister to Spain in 1861. Otero declined that office to accept an appointment as secretary of the territory, but the U.S. Senate did not confirm him because of his pro-Confederate inclinations. Otero failed in an 1880 bid for reelection to Congress. **See also** Miguel A. Otero, Jr.

BIBLIOGRAPHY

Vigil, Maurilio. *Los Patrones: Profile of Hispanic Political Leaders in New Mexico History*. Washington, DC: University Press of America, 1980.

Miguel A. Otero, Jr. (1859–1944)

From a prominent political family and the son of former Democratic Congressman **Miguel Antonio Otero**, Miguel A. Otero, Jr., began his political career as a member of the Republican Party. In 1894, he was a serious candidate for the vice presidency. However, he was not selected to run with William McKinley in 1896. Instead, McKinley appointed him governor of the New Mexico Territory. During the **Spanish-American War**, Otero raised four cavalry companies for the Rough Riders. In 1901, he convened the New Mexico statehood convention in which he sought to separate New Mexico and Arizona into separate states for admission. In 1907, he had a disagreement with President Teddy Roosevelt over national forest policy; Otero stepped down as governor and switched political parties. In 1909 he was appointed secretary of the territory and in 1917 served as U.S. marshal of the Panama Canal Zone. **See** Plea for New Mexican Statehood (1901) in Appendix 1.

BIBLIOGRAPHY

Otero, Miguel A., Jr. *My Life on the Frontier, 1864–1882*. New York: Press of the Pioneers, 1935.

——. *My Life on the Frontier, 1882–1897*. Albuquerque: University of New Mexico Press, 1939.

——. *My Nine Years as Governor of the Territory of New Mexico*. Albuquerque: University of New Mexico Press, 1940.

P

Romualdo Pacheco (1831–1899)

Romualdo Pacheco was the only Hispanic to serve as governor of California. He began his political career in 1853, when he was elected judge of the San Luis Obispo Superior Court. His fluency in English and Spanish, in addition to his ability to garner the support of both prominent California families and the newly arrived Anglos, contributed to his political success. He became active in the Democratic Party, and in 1857 he was elected to the state senate. Pacheco was one of the first Hispanics to denounce slavery and pledge allegiance to the Union, and in the early 1860s he changed party affiliation to the Union Party.

In 1861, he was elected as a Republican to the California State Senate. However, he did not spend much time in Sacramento because Governor Leland Stanford appointed Pacheco a brigadier general, with command of the First Brigade of California's "Native Cavalry." In September 1862, Pacheco was reelected to the state senate where he served until 1863. During the Republican State Convention of 1863, Governor Stanford nominated Pacheco for the position of state treasurer; he was elected and served in this position until 1866. In 1869 Pacheco was once again elected to the state senate. In June 1871 Pacheco received the Republican Party nomination for lieutenant governor, with Newton Booth receiving the nomination for governor. Both Pacheco and Booth were elected. During his service as lieutenant governor, Pacheco was warden of the San Quentin penitentiary, where he worked to improve conditions. In 1875, when Newton Booth was elected to the U.S. Senate, Pacheco became governor of California. As governor, he stressed the importance of higher education and worked for the development of the University of California and the State Normal School in San Francisco.

In November 1876 Pacheco was elected to the U.S. House of Representatives by a margin of one vote. His opponent, Peter D. Wigginton, contested the election and the case was referred to the House Committee on Elections. Pacheco was seated on October 17, 1877, and was appointed to the Committee on Public Lands. On February 7, 1878, the House Committee on Elections refused to accept Pacheco's certificate of election and voted in favor of Wigginton. In 1879 Pacheco was once again elected to the U.S. House of Representatives and was reelected two years later. In the 47th Congress Pacheco chaired the Committee on Private Land Claims, becoming the first Hispanic to chair a standing committee in Congress.

In December 1890, Pacheco was appointed U.S. Envoy Extraordinary and Minister Plenipotentiary to the Central American States. The duties involved in maintaining diplomatic relations with the entire region were more than one man could handle; therefore, in July 1891, Pacheco was named minister plenipotentiary to Honduras and Guatemala, a post he held until June 21, 1893.

BIBLIOGRAPHY

Genini, Ronald and Richard Hitchman. *Romualdo Pacheco: A Californio in Two Eras*. San Francisco: The Book Club of California, 1985.
Hispanic Americans in Congress. Washington, DC: U.S. Government Printing Office, 1995.

Bolívar Pagán (1897–1961)

Bolívar Pagán, a distinguished historian, journalist, and politician, became the vice president of the Socialist Party of Puerto Rico in 1919. In 1924, Pagán ran unsuccessfully as a Socialist Party candidate for election to the Puerto Rican Senate. The following year, he began a four-year tenure as city treasurer of San Juan. In 1928, he ran again for the Puerto Rican Senate but was not elected. He succeeded on his third try, and he served as a member of the Puerto Rican Senate from 1933 until 1939. In 1939 Pagán was appointed resident commissioner to the U.S. House of Representatives by the governor of Puerto Rico, William B. Leahy, to fill the vacancy caused by the death of Pagán's father-in-law, **Santiago Iglesias Pantín**. In 1940, he was elected resident commissioner by a coalition of the Socialist Party and the Republican Union Party. In Congress he continued the work of his father-in-law and successfully advocated the extension of social security benefits to Puerto Rico and the application of workers' compensation laws to the island. Pagán returned to Puerto Rico and was again elected to the Senate of Puerto Rico in 1944. He was reelected in 1948 and served until 1953.

BIBLIOGRAPHY

Hispanic Americans in Congress. Washington, DC: U.S. Government Printing Office, 1995.

Antonia Pantoja (1922–)

In 1961, Antonia Pantoja was responsible for the founding of **ASPIRA** (a group dedicated to empowering Latinos) in New York City. A consistent advocate for educational improvement and other social services, Pantoja was awarded the Presidential Medal of Freedom by President Bill Clinton in 1995.

BIBLIOGRAPHY

Peralta, Maria and Moe Foner. *Women of Hope.* Princeton, NJ: Films for the Humanities, 1996.
Torres, Andres and Jose E. Velasquez. *Puerto Rican Movement.* Philadelphia: Temple University Press, 1998.

Lucia Gonzalez Parsons (1852–1942)

Chicana/Chicano studies scholars rescued Lucia Gonzalez Parsons from a tangential role in U.S. labor history by focusing on her as a Chicana (of Spanish-Indian origins) activist. The wife of Albert Parsons, famed for his martyrdom in the Haymarket Square riot (1886), Gonzalez Parsons was herself a radical labor organizer, writer, community activist, orator, and intellectual leader for the working class. She helped found the Industrial Workers of the World. (ASR)

BIBLIOGRAPHY

Ashbaugh, Carolyn. *Lucy Parsons.* Chicago: Ken, 1976.

Partido Nuevo Progresista *See* New Progressive Party

Ed Pastor (1943–)

An Arizona native, Ed Pastor was born in the mining community of Claypool. He graduated from Arizona State University with a degree in chemistry in 1966 and earned his law degree from Arizona State in 1974. He also taught chemistry at North High School in Phoenix and served as deputy director of the Guadalupe Organization, Inc. Pastor served on the staff of Democratic Governor Raul Castro in 1975–76 and was elected to the Maricopa County Board of Supervisors in 1976. He served on the board until May 1991, when he resigned to run for Congress. He won election to fill the unexpired term of Congressman Morris Udall in September 1991, and has won reelection to the seat in all the congressional elections through 1998. In the 106th Congress, Pastor served as one of the chief Democratic whips and as a member of the House Appropriations Committee, the House Committee on Standards of Official Conduct, and the **Congressional Hispanic Caucus**. (CEM)

BIBLIOGRAPHY

Duncan, Philip D. and Christine C. Lawrence. *Politics in America: 1996. The 104th Congress.* Washington, DC: Congressional Quarterly Press, 1995.

Juan B. Patron (1855–1884)

In 1876 Juan Patron was elected to the New Mexico territorial legislature, an act that made him one of the highest elected Spanish-American citizens in the region. Patron's position led to a great deal of resentment among the local Anglo citizens. In fact, Patron was shot in the back during the mid-1870s while attempting to arrest some whites who were suspected of killing two Mexicans. Patron also became a leading figure in the Lincoln County War (1879–80)—a bloody, lawless conflict between rival cattlemen that resulted in President Rutherford B. Hayes eventually declaring a state of emergency. In 1884 Patron was murdered at a local saloon; charges were never brought against the assailant because of complications that arose relating to lingering hostilities from the Lincoln County War. **See also** Francisco Perea.

BIBLIOGRAPHY

Fulton, Maurice G. *History of the Lincoln County War.* Tucson: University of Arizona Press, 1968.

Pecan Shellers' Strike of 1938

Beginning in the late 1800s, numerous Mexican Americans were hired at low wages to gather, crack, and shell pecans for the Texas pecan industry. By the mid-1930s, an average pecan sheller in the San Antonio area made around two to three cents per pound of nuts, which earned them as little as two dollars a week. In 1937, approximately 10,000 to 12,000 workers organized several unions, including the Texas Pecan Shelling Workers Union, an affiliate of the United Cannery, Agriculture, Packing and Allied Workers of America.

After a January 1938 announcement was made stating pecan employers planned to lower wages by 15 percent, unions began an immediate strike. **Emma Tenayuca** became the leader of the women strikers, although her communist ties caused a number of problems for the union, as dissenters claimed the strike was a communist ploy. These accusations, as well as inaccurate allegations of rioting, caused more than 1,000 of the 6,000 strikers to be arrested, while tear gas, raids, vigilante acts, and other extreme measures were taken against the Hispanic organizers. In March 1938, the strike ended as a 7.5 percent decrease in wages was reluctantly agreed upon.

In October 1938, the strike settlement was voided by the Fair Labor Standards Act, which called for a 25-cent minimum wage. Because of this act, many employers in the Texas pecan industry turned to mechanized plants, replacing Hispanic laborers with easily maintained machines. By the end of World War II, only 2,000 workers were still employed by the pecan industry, and all pecan unions in the area were closed.

BIBLIOGRAPHY

Nelsen-Cisneros, Victor B. "The Working Class in Texas, 1920–1940." *Aztlan* 6, no. 2 (1976): 453–77.

Frederico F. Pena (1947–)

In 1993, Frederico Pena was selected as the twelfth secretary of transportation by President Bill Clinton. Previously, Pena was the service secretary for the United States Coast Guard. On his watch, the Coast Guard rescued 56,000 Haitian and Cuban boat people. From 1983 through 1991, Pena served as mayor of Denver and supported the building of one of the largest airports in the world. After Clinton's reelection in 1996,

Pena was appointed secretary of energy, a post he held until 1998.

BIBLIOGRAPHY

Devall, Cheryl. "Transportation Secretary Nominee Pena Profile." *NPR* (December 25, 1992).

Music, Kimberly. "Pena Likely to Face Barrage of Questions on Experience." *The Oil Daily* 47, no. 1 (January 2, 1997): 1.

People's Constitutional Party

The People's Constitutional Party gained notoriety in 1968 when ex-evangelist and native Texan **Reies Lopez Tijerina**, a leading land-grant activist, ran unsuccessfully for governor of New Mexico as a candidate on that party's ticket. Tijerina had become popular in 1963 when he founded the Alianza Federal de Mercedes (Federal Alliance of Land Grants)—later called the **Alianza Federal de Pueblos Libres** (Federal Alliance of Free Towns)—in New Mexico; the organization was dedicated to reclaiming historic land grants promised to Mexican Americans by the 1848 **Treaty of Guadalupe Hidalgo**. **See also** Land Rights; Political Participation. **See** Letter from the Santa Fe Jail by Reies Lopez Tijerina (1969); Treaty of Guadalupe Hidalgo (1848) in Appendix 1. (VDD)

BIBLIOGRAPHY

DeLeon, David. *Leaders from the 1960s.* Westport, CT: Greenwood Press, 1994.

Francisco Perea (1830–1913)

Born in New Mexico, Francisco Perea was a successful businessman before being elected to the New Mexico territorial legislature's upper house in 1858. He actively supported the North during the Civil War and was lieutenant colonel of a military group called "Perea's Battalion." Shortly after the war ended, he served two years as territorial delegate to the U.S. Congress. **See also** Juan B. Patron.

BIBLIOGRAPHY

Fulton, Maurice G. *New Mexico's Own Chronicle.* Dallas: B. Upshaw, 1937.

Twitchell, Ralph Emerson. *The Leading Facts of New Mexican History.* Albuquerque, NM: Horn and Wallace, 1963.

Pedro Perea (1852–1906)

Pedro Perea studied at Georgetown University, Washington, D.C., and St. Louis University, St. Louis, Missouri, before returning to New Mexico where he became a successful stock trader and banker. In 1889 Perea, a Republican, was elected to the New Mexico territorial legislature's upper house, where he served three terms before becoming a territorial delegate to the U.S. Congress in 1898. He chose not to run for reelection in 1900. **See also** Political Participation.

BIBLIOGRAPHY

Vigil, Maurilio E. *Hispanics in Congress.* Lanham, MD: University Press of America, 1996.

Juan M. Perez-Gimenez (1941–)

Juan Perez-Gimenez received degrees in law during the 1960s from the University of Puerto Rico and George Washington University, Washington, D.C. He served from 1971 to 1975 as assistant United States attorney for Puerto Rico. In 1979, President Jimmy Carter made Perez-Gimenez a judge in the U.S. District Court for the District of Puerto Rico.

BIBLIOGRAPHY

Ross, Karl. "Monitor Urges Takeover of Puerto Rican Prisons; Gangs Control Corrections System, Official Says." *The Washington Post* (September 7, 1997): A16.

José Lorenzo Pesquera (1882–1950)

In 1917 José Lorenzo Pesquera was elected by the 4th District to the Puerto Rico House of Representatives and served there until 1920. In 1932 Pesquera was appointed to be a nonpartisan resident commissioner to the U.S. House of Representatives after **Felix Cordova Davila's** resignation from the position. Pesquera spoke in the House in favor of a bill to change the name of the island back to the original Puerto Rico, instead of "Porto Rico," which the U.S. government had used as its official name since the **Foraker Act.** The bill encountered opposition from some representatives, particularly William Stafford of Wisconsin, who opposed it for various reasons including the expense in changing printed material from "Porto" to "Puerto." Pesquera argued that the bill was of no economic importance to the United States but would be of immense significance to the people of Puerto Rico. In May 1932 a joint resolution of the Senate changed the name back to the original spelling. Pesquera did not run for reelection in 1932. He returned to Puerto Rico, where he continued his law practice and agricultural pursuits.

BIBLIOGRAPHY

Hispanic Americans in Congress. Washington, DC: U.S. Government Printing Office, 1995.

Jesús T. Piñero (1897–1952)

In 1928 Jesús Piñero began his political career as a member of the municipal assembly of Carolina, Puerto Rico. He later became president of the assembly and served in this position until 1932. In 1935, he was appointed to the Puerto Rico Reconstruction Administration. In 1940 Piñero was one of the founders of the **Popular Democratic Party,** headed by **Luis Muñoz Marín.** The same year he was elected to the Puerto Rico House of Representatives and began a four-year term. In 1944 he was elected resident commissioner to the U.S. House of Representatives, where he served on the Committees of Agriculture, Insular and Interior Affairs, Labor, Military Affairs, Naval Affairs, and Territories. In September 1946 Piñero resigned as resident commissioner when President Harry Truman appointed him the first Puerto Rican governor of the island, a position he held until December 1948.

BIBLIOGRAPHY

Hispanic Americans in Congress. Washington, DC: U.S. Government Printing Office, 1995.

Plan de San Diego

The Plan de San Diego was created with the intention of encouraging uprisings along the U.S–Mexican border; these uprisings, instigated and perpetrated by Mexican Americans, were part of an attempt to create a separate republic, one that would possibly later be united with Mexico. In January 1915, the plan was discovered through documents captured from an arrested Latino who had been participating in border raids connected to the Mexican Revolution.

According to the captured documents, the plan was organized by a group called the Supreme Revolutionary Congress of San Diego, California. The uprisings were to occur in February 1915. The plan stated that all Anglo-Americans over the age of 16 were to be killed on sight, with exceptions made only for the elderly. After the Plan de San Diego came to the attention of the general public, many whites along the Texas border began to panic; concern grew after a few Hispanic riots and Mexican raids occurred, even though no conclusive connection to the plan could be made. Even so, a rise of white vigilante action against Mexican Americans occurred, and military and police officials began increased border patrols. By the autumn of 1915, most of the panic caused by the Plan de San Diego had passed.

BIBLIOGRAPHY

Sandos, James A. *Rebellion in the Borderlands.* Norman: University of Oklahoma Press, 1992.

Plyler v. Doe (1982)

Plyler v. Doe, 457 U.S. 202 (1982), was a landmark decision by the U.S. Supreme Court concerning education rights for undocumented aliens. In 1975, because of the drain on its budgetary resources, the state of Texas revised its education policies to withhold state funds from local school districts for the education of children who were not legal U.S. residents. Because Mexican children could not prove legal status, they were denied admission to the public schools. A lawsuit was filed on their behalf.

The Supreme Court affirmed the trial court's judgment that the Texas law violated the Equal Protection Clause of the Fourteenth Amendment. In his opinion for the narrowly divided Court, Justice William Brennan held that while education is not a fundamental right and undocumented aliens were not a suspect classification, the Texas law had overstepped its boundaries. Brennan argued that denying education would condemn undocumented aliens to a life of illiteracy, and that the policy was flawed because it was aimed at children, who were not responsible for their economic or political status. **See also** Educational Opportunity; Illegal Aliens; Vilma Socorro Martinez. (RLP)

BIBLIOGRAPHY

Epstein, Lee and Thomas G. Walker. *Constitutional Law for a Changing America: Rights, Liberties, and Justice.* 2nd ed. Washington, DC: CQ Press, 1995.

Santiago Polanco-Abreu (1920–1988)

Santiago Polanco-Abreu began his public service in 1943 when he served as legal advisor to the Tax Court of Puerto Rico; he was also one of the founders of the Institute for Democratic Studies in San José, Costa Rica. In 1949 he served on the House of Representatives of the Commonwealth of Puerto Rico, where he served until 1964. He was Speaker of the House from 1962 to 1964. During 1951 and 1952 he participated in the Constitutional Convention of Puerto Rico. In 1964 Polanco-Abreu was elected to a four-year term as Puerto Rico's resident commissioner to the U.S. House of Representatives. In the House, he served on the Committees on Agriculture, Armed Services, and Interior and Insular Affairs. A strong advocate of education, Polanco-Abreu introduced and supported numerous pieces of legislation on education, including bills aimed at strengthening educational quality and opportunities, including **bilingual education** programs. In 1968, Polanco-Abreu was unsuccessful in his bid for reelection. **See** Constitution of Puerto Rico (1952) in Appendix 1.

BIBLIOGRAPHY

Hispanic Americans in Congress. Washington, DC: U.S. Government Printing Office, 1995.

Political Association of Spanish-Speaking Organizations (PASSO)

The success and influence of the **Viva Kennedy** Club during the 1960 presidential election led to the formation of the first overtly political statewide Mexican-American organization in Texas. Originally called Mexican Americans for Political Action (MAPA), it changed its name in early 1961 to the Political Association of Spanish-Speaking Organizations (PASSO). PASSO leaders hoped to unite all people interested in the cause of Spanish-speaking people; such a united front could apply political pressure and be able to support Mexican-American candidates for elected office and governmental appointments.

PASSO's most significant role as a political action group occurred in 1962–1963, when it joined forces with the Teamsters Union to help Hispanics gain political control of **Crystal City,** a south Texas town of about 10,000 people, the overwhelming majority of whom were poor Mexican Americans. Anglos had dominated government, business, and agriculture for years. The efforts of the historic coalition between PASSO and the Teamsters resulted in the 1963 sweep of all five city council seats by Mexican Americans, achieving an unprecedented victory in south Texas, and creating a Hispanic-led city government for the next two years.

PASSO's success gave rise to the formation of other Hispanic organizations, such as the **Mexican American Legal Defense and Educational Fund (MALDEF)** and the **Southwest Voter Registration Education Program**, which fight for **civil rights** in rural areas. **See also** Community Organizations; Political Participation; Voting Rights. (NM)

BIBLIOGRAPHY

Montejano, David. *Anglos and Mexicans: In the Making of Texas, 1836–1986.* Austin: University of Texas Press, 1987.

Rosenbaum, Robert J. *The History of Mexican Americans in Texas.* Boston: American Press, 1980.

Political Leadership

Although this brief overview of Hispanic political leadership in the United States is limited to political leadership in the U.S. Congress, numerous state and local leaders and administrators at the national level (e.g., **Henry Cisneros** and **Frederico Pena**) are outstanding representatives of the Hispanic community. It is difficult to make generalizations about Hispanics and their leaders because they are such a diverse and complex people. The cosmopolitan resident from Buenos Aires, the indigenous people from Guatemala, and the African American from the Dominican Republic are very different and yet they can all legitimately be considered Hispanics. This diversity is reflected in their leaders and it has contributed to the richness of Hispanic culture in the United States.

Hispanics in the United States originated from three main geographical areas. The largest group is the Mexicans who constitute about 65 percent of the nation's Hispanic population. Most of the Mexican population is found in Texas, California, New Mexico, and Arizona. Puerto Ricans account for about 11 percent of the Hispanic population. They are concentrated in large numbers in New York City and Chicago. Cubans are found in large numbers in Florida and make up about 5 percent of the Hispanic population. Most of the remainder have come from other countries in Central or South America and the Caribbean.

The Mexican-American community has suffered from **discrimination** in much the same way as African Americans. In many cases Hispanics had the additional burdens of not speaking English or of being in the country illegally. Mexican Americans did not have government-funded educational institutions (e.g., the land-grant universities) to use as a base from which to organize interest groups and prepare leaders who would maintain and develop a sense of group identity and purpose. Despite these challenges, the Mexican-American community has produced a number of outstanding political leaders.

The first Hispanics to be U.S. senators were **Dennis Chavez** and **Joseph M. Montoya**, both Democrats who represented New Mexico. Chavez served from 1935 to 1962, and Montoya served from 1964 to 1977. Both were regarded as progressive liberals concerned about agriculture, water, immigration, and **civil rights**. Senator Chavez and Representative **Henry Barbosa Gonzalez** (D-TX), served as national co-chairmen of the Hispanic effort to elect John F. Kennedy president. Senator Montoya is perhaps best remembered for his service during the Watergate hearings.

Senators Chavez and Montoya were not the first Hispanics elected to Congress, however. That distinction goes to **Joseph Marion Hernandez**, who served in the House of Representatives from the territory of Florida in the 1820s. Another early leader was Representative **Romauldo Pacheco**, a California Republican who served in the 1870s and 1880s. New Mexico sent three Hispanics to Congress in the early and mid-twentieth century as well. **Benigno Cardenas Hernandez**, a Republican, served in the House from 1915 to 1917 and again from 1919 to 1921. **Nestor Montoya**, a Republican, served in the House from 1921 to 1923, and **Antonio Manuel Fernandez**, a Democrat, served there from 1943 until 1956. These early Hispanic political leaders came from an established population base in the southwestern states, and faced less discrimination at the polls than did Hispanics in Texas.

In 1961, Henry Gonzalez became the first Hispanic elected to congress from Texas and has served longer than any other Hispanic member of Congress. Gonzalez has served as chairman of the Banking, Finance, and Urban Affairs Committee, and as Chairman of the Subcommittee on Housing and Community Development. He has supported legislation designed to benefit Hispanics, although he has not run for office on an ethnic platform. He receives support not only from the Hispanic community, but from Anglos as well. He has supported civil rights and social welfare issues and is interested in Latin American affairs. He supported ending the Bracero program (started under **Public Law 78**) and was influential in reforming the savings and loan industry.

Representative **Eligio "Kika" de la Garza** (D-TX) has been another senior leader of the Hispanic community. When he retired in 1997, he had served in Congress more than 30 years. A Democrat from the Rio Grande Valley, Garza was influential in agricultural matters and assisted in the passage of three omnibus farm bills. He served as chairman of the Agriculture Committee for 13 years and strongly supported passage of the North American Free Trade Agreement (NAFTA).

Representative **Solomon P. Ortiz** (D-TX), in Congress since 1983, serves on the Armed Services Committee and favors a strong national defense. He supported deployment of the MX missile, opposed the 1983 resolution to ban nuclear weapons testing, and has tried to prevent the closure of military installations in south Texas. He has served on the Merchant Marine and Fisheries Committee as well. Viewed as a conservative, Ortiz has supported efforts to reduce the deficit and chaired the **Congressional Hispanic Caucus** during the 102nd Congress.

Henry Bonilla is the first Republican Hispanic elected from Texas. Elected in 1993 from San Antonio, he has supported term limits, private property rights, and efforts to reduce federal regulations.

William B. Richardson was elected to Congress from New Mexico in 1983. He served as one of the House Democrats' four chief deputy whips, which made him the highest-ranking Hispanic member of Congress. He attempted to balance the desires of environmentalists and the energy industry in his service on the Energy and Commerce Committee;

led the fight for the passage of NAFTA; and supported the balanced budget amendment, the 1993 Deficit Reduction package, and the 1994 Crime Bill. The Clinton administration sent him to North Korea to negotiate the release of two U.S. pilots. In 1994 he negotiated a settlement in Haiti that resulted in the peaceful departure of General Raoul Cedras. In 1996, President Clinton appointed him U.S. ambassador to the United Nations. Clinton appointed Richardson secretary of transportation in 1998 and secretary of energy in 1999.

In 1991, **Ed Pastor** became the first Hispanic elected to Congress from Arizona. He has served on the Appropriations Committee and the Steering and Policy Committee, as well as being chairman of the Congressional Hispanic Caucus. He has shown interest in policies relating to energy, agriculture, and education, as well as the activities of the Food and Drug Administration.

Representative **Jose E. Serrano**, born in Puerto Rico and raised in New York City, was elected to Congress in 1990 and served on the Education and Labor Committee. He was able to pass legislation intended to reduce school dropout rates and was a chief sponsor of the Voting Rights Assistance Act. In 1993, Serrano was appointed to a highly coveted seat on the Appropriations Committee. Serrano, a Democrat, supported Puerto Ricans having the 1988 plebiscite to decide what type of relationship the Commonwealth will have with the mainland.

Representative **Luis V. Gutierrez** is another Hispanic leader of Puerto Rican descent. The first Hispanic elected to Congress from Illinois, Gutierrez was a public school teacher in Chicago and Puerto Rico, and also served as an alderman in Chicago. Elected to Congress in 1992, Gutierrez has served on the Banking, Finance, and Urban Affairs Committee and the Veterans' Affairs Committee. He has worked on immigration reform, issues involving Puerto Rico, and the Minority Health Opportunity Enhancement Act.

Ileana Ros-Lehtinen, a Florida Republican of Cuban descent, is the first Hispanic woman to be elected to Congress. She has supported drug-free workplace regulations and tuition assistance legislation, sits on the House Foreign Affairs Committee, and was influential in passage of the Cuban Democracy Act, which prohibits subsidiaries of U.S. corporations from doing business with Cuba. She has also been appointed to two House committees dealing with African and Latin American affairs.

Representative **Lincoln Diaz-Balart** is another member of Congress of Cuban descent. He is the first Hispanic to win a seat on the House Rules Committee. Objecting to certain provisions of the "Contract with America," Diaz-Balart was one of only three Republicans to vote against it. He is a strong supporter of the embargo on Cuba and of social welfare legislation.

Robert Underwood is Guam's elected delegate to Congress. He has served in Congress since 1992 and has been appointed to the House Armed Services, Natural Resources, and Educational and Labor committees. He supports **bilin-gual education** programs and is chair of the Chamorro Language Commission.

These leaders serve as testimony to Hispanic diversity. As the number of Hispanics grows (by 2010, Hispanics will be the most numerous minority group in the United States), Hispanic political influence increases as well. Evidence of that trend may be seen in the rapid growth of the Congressional Hispanic Caucus. As of 1997, there were 19 Hispanics serving in Congress. Democrats, Republicans, conservatives, and liberals, they form a uniquely valuable component of the great American mosaic. **See also** Assimilation; Civil Rights; Economic Equality; Educational Opportunity; Illegal Aliens; Immigration Policy and Hispanics; Political Participation; Voting Rights. (JSR)

BIBLIOGRAPHY

Gutierrez, David G. ed. *Between Two Worlds.* Wilmington, DE: SR Press, 1996.

Handleman, Howard. *Mexican Politics.* New York: St. Martin's Press, 1997.

Hart, Dianne W. *Undocumented in L.A.* Wilmington, DE: SR Press, 1997.

Jeret, Charles. *Contemporary Racial and Ethnic Relations.* New York: Addison Wesley Longman, 1995.

Kromkowski, John A. *Race and Ethnic Relations: Annual Editions.* Guilford, CT: Dushkin/McGraw-Hill, 1997.

Schafer, Richard T. *Racial and Ethnic Groups.* New York: Addison Wesley Longman, 1996.

Winsberg, Morton and Patricia Braus. "Specific Hispanics." *American Demographics* (February 1994): 44–53.

Political Participation

The political participation of Latinos (persons residing in the United States whose own or parental origin is Mexican, Central American, South American, or Spanish colonized Caribbean), is as varied and complex as the people themselves. Variation in forms, goals, and styles of political participation reflect different historical experiences, country of origin, generational differences, spatial dispersion, socio-economic class, educational level, gender differences, legal status, and connection to a specific political movement. To speak of "Latino politics" as being as generic as "minority politics" is to deal only in generalities, negative stereotypes, and inaccurate information.

For each Latino sub-group, there is an extensive array of political activities. Latino politics thus mirrors national politics with additional dimensions of national origin and historical variance. Chicanos (Mexican-origin residents of the seven southwestern states of the United States) and Latinos currently and historically have participated in all types of activities defined as political, from simple protest to full-scale revolution. For Latinos, participation and experience in politics has not been commonly found in the electoral arena but rather in grassroots community organizations, labor organizing, legal protest, and resistance activities. Using the broadest historical and spatial context of Latino political activity, scholars argue for including the time period from 1600 to the present (Garcia, Falcon, and de la Garza 1977; Gomez-Quinones,

1990). Scholars have outlined four historical periods of Chicano politics: politics of resistance (1846–1915); politics of accommodation (1915–1945); politics of social change (1945–1965); and politics of protest (1965–1972). Some researchers have argued against a linear model, presenting evidence of a variety of political activity prior to the **Mexican War** and during each of these time periods.

The intricacies of Chicano/Latino politics are better understood as political activity trends. Three clear continuous trends are (1) politics of self-determination, defined as activities directed toward achieving autonomy from the existing political structures, (2) reformist politics, defined as activities seeking to work within or reform the existing political structure, and (3) activites blending both reformist and self-determination politics.

Hispanic political participation in the twenty-first century will see many new trends. Issue-based political alliances will allow ballot box victories rarely realized in the twentieth century. Successful coalition politics will no longer refer exclusively to interethnic or interracial collective actions, but will include coalitions among the different and various national origin groups. While the Chicano Movimiento oversaw the decline of the hyphenated American, the last decade of this century has seen the emergence of a sizable number of ampersand Latinos, in particular the Dominican & American and Mexican & American. Dual citizenship (ampersand citizenship) challenges traditional notions of citizenship and nationhood, ethnic identity, and assimilation. The United States is peculiarly open to dual citizenship since the 1967 U.S. Supreme Court decision allowing dual citizenship even for naturalized citizens.

Among Latinos, dual citizenship assumes greater importance as the Mexican government approves Mexican citizenship for Mexicans and for their descendants living in the United States. While dual citizenship conveys new opportunities and a greater sense of political efficacy to Latinos, other forces increase barriers to participation. Political analysts are already positing new uses of electronic technology in the political process, from registration to actual voting. Simultaneously, the Latino population is losing ground in educational attainment and access to electronic technology. As the twenty-first century dawns, Latinos find new opportunities in the political process, but also face new challenges and barriers. (ASR)

BIBLIOGRAPHY

De Sipio, Louis. *Counting on the Latino Vote: Latinos as a New Electorate*. Charlottesville: University of Virginia Press, 1996.

Garcia, F. Chris, Angelo Falcon, and Rodolfo O. de la Garza. "Ethnicity and Politics: Evidence from the Latino National Political Survey." *Hispanic Journal of Behavioral Sciences*, 1996.

Gomez-Quinones, Juan. *Chicano Politics: Reality and Promise* 1940-1990. Albuquerque: University of New Mexico Press, 1990.

———. *Roots of Chicano Politics*, 1600-1940. Albuquerque: University of New Mexico Press, 1989.

Hardy-Fanta, Carol. *Latina Politics, Latino Politics*. Philadelphia: Temple University Press, 1993.

Hero, Rodney. *Latinos and the U.S. Political System*. Philadelphia: Temple University Press, 1992.

Munoz, Carlos. *Youth, Identity, and Power: The Chicano Movement*. New York: Verso, 1989.

Sierra, Christine M. and Adaljiza Sosa-Riddell. "Chicana Political Actors." *National Political Science Review*, 1993.

Poor People's Campaign

The Poor People's Campaign, an event that occurred in May and June of 1968, was originally organized and planned by Ralph Abernathy and Martin Luther King, Jr., as a minority **civil rights** march in Washington, D.C. **Reies Lopez Tijerina** was brought in to head the Southwest delegation as well as other majority Chicano areas. Tijerina used the march to confront the State Department over the **Treaty of Guadalupe Hidalgo**, which ended the **Mexican War** and ceded more than 1 million acres of land to the United States. He argued that this action took unfair advantage of the Mexicans and that reparations should be made. Another Hispanic leader working with the Poor People's Campaign, **Rodolfo "Corky" Gonzales**, used the march on Washington to issue his Plan del Barrio, which called for greater **cultural nationalism**, improved education, better housing, and other reforms. Even though African American groups gained more attention, the campaign is still considered an important political step in the movement toward gaining Latino rights. **See also** Discrimination; Economic Equality; Political Participation. **See** Letter from the Santa Fe Jail by Reies Lopez Tijerina (1969); Treaty of Guadalupe Hidalgo (1848) in Appendix 1.

BIBLIOGRAPHY

Garrow, David J. "His Dream; Martin Luther King Jr.; Legacy of His Nonviolence Obscures Strength." *Newsday* (April 4, 1993): 10.

"Vital Signs: Taking the Pulse of Life on Long Island." *Newsday* (January 19, 1997): E2.

Popular Democratic Party (PDP)

The Popular Democratic Party (Partido Popular Democratico or PPD, one of the two largest parties in Puerto Rico, is the principal supporter of the island's commonwealth status. It was founded in 1938 by **Luis Muñoz Marin**, Puerto Rico's first elected governor. Early on, the party welcomed moderate separatists and those seeking Puerto Rican autonomy. However, Munoz expelled most of the party's independence supporters in 1946. Since its inception, the PPD has maintained strong ties to the Democratic Party on the U.S. mainland. **See also** Antonio Fernós-Isern; New Progressive Party; Operation Bootstrap; Puerto Rican Statehood. (AAB)

BIBLIOGRAPHY

Munoz Marin, Luis. *La Historia del Partido Popular Democratico*. San Juan, PR: Editorial El Batey, 1984.

Public Law 45 (1943)

Passed by Congress on April 29, 1943, Public Law 45 authorized the implementation of an international political agreement between the United States and Mexico that initi-

Originally passed in 1943, Public Law 45, which authorized Mexicans to come into the United States to work, was enacted to help cover labor shortages in the United States. These workers came into the U.S. during World War II to harvest crops. *National Archives.*

ated the Bracero Program (helping hands program), which allowed for contracting with Mexican workers for seasonal employment to fill the labor shortage created by the U.S. military draft during World War II. The Bracero Program was operational through World War II and continued until December 1947; it was revived for a second period from February 1948 to 1951. Under the agreement, agents from the U.S. Department of Agriculture determined prevailing wage rates and interpreted details or policy. After June 1943, direction of the Bracero Program was turned over to the War Food Administration.

The Bracero Program actually lasted 22 years, from 1942 to 1964. **Public Law 78** renewed the program for a third period in 1951, because of labor needs during the Korean War; the program continued until its repeal in 1964. The Bracero Program's four million Mexican workers helped sustain U.S. agriculture. **See also** Economic Equality; Illegal Aliens; Immigration Policy and Hispanics; McCarran–Walter Immigration and Nationality Act of 1952; McGovern Bill (1960). (SCV)

BIBLIOGRAPHY
Acuno, Rodolfo. *Occupied America: The Chicano's Struggle Toward Liberation.* San Francisco: Canfield Press, 1972.

Public Law 600 (1950)

Enacted by the U.S. Congress in 1950, Public Law 600 authorized a joint self-determination process for the Puerto Rican people to create and approve their own constitution in the form of a compact with the United States. In a referendum held on June 4, 1951, Puerto Ricans voted 76.5 percent in favor of P.L. 600. Pursuant to the new law, the Puerto Rican people continued the process, which culminated in the establishment of internal constitutional self-government for Puerto Rico. The constitution of Puerto Rico took effect on July 25, 1952.

In addition, P.L. 600 provided that the **Treaty of Paris** of 1898 (which ended the **Spanish-American War**), the **Foraker Act of 1900**, and the **Jones Act of 1917**, which together defined the political, economic, and fiscal relationship between Puerto Rico and the United States, should remain in full force. Thus P.L. 600 created the commonwealth relationship that Puerto Rico has with the United States. **See** Treaty of Paris (1898); Constitution of Puerto Rico (1952) in Appendix 1. (SCV)

BIBLIOGRAPHY
Bhana, Surendra. *The United States and the Development of the Puerto Rican Status Question 1936–1968.* Lawrence: University Press of Kansas, 1975.
Lewis, Gordon K. *Puerto Rico: Freedom and Power in the Caribbean.* New York: MR Press, 1963.
Lopez, Adalberto, ed. *The Puerto Ricans: Their History, Culture, and Society.* Cambridge, MA: Schenkman Publishing, 1980.

Public Law 78 (1951)

Public Law 78, introduced by Louisiana Senator Allen Ellender and Texas Representative William Poage, was passed on July 12, 1951. Also known as the Migratory Labor Agreement of 1951, Public Law 78 imported Spanish day-workers, or braceros, into the United States to provide more labor for U.S. needs during the Korean War. (The Bracero Program was actually created during World War II under the authority of **Public Law 45**.)

Public Law 78, which gained the favor of employer groups and southwestern agricultural industries, allowed the U.S. secretary of labor to declare a need for workers, recruit Mexican farm laborers, arrange transportation across the border, manage processing of labor contracts, and ensure good relations between employers and braceros. Other provisions were made to provide contracts to undocumented alien laborers who had resided within the United States for at least five years. A number of groups criticized the legislation, including labor organizations, church groups, social workers, and Mexican-American groups. Employers argued that the program contained too many safeguards, contract stipulations, and other red tape procedures that were overly favorable to braceros. The program continued until 1964, when pressures placed on the U.S. Congress by organized labor led to Public Law 78's repeal. **See also** Economic Equality; Illegal Aliens; Immigration Policy and Hispanics; McGovern Bill (1960).

BIBLIOGRAPHY
Meier, Matt S. and Feliciano Rivera. *The Chicanos.* New York: Hill and Wang, 1972.

Puerto Rican Legal Defense and Education Fund (PRLDEF)

Started in New York City in 1972 as a nonprofit organization, the Puerto Rican Legal Defense and Education Fund (PRLDEF) seeks to change discriminatory practices through advocacy and litigation. Through its efforts, PRLDEF has helped to secure **bilingual education** in the public schools

The debate over the status of Puerto Rico has sometimes turned violent. In this photo relatives of nationalists killed in the Ponce Massacre stand in front of the nationalist headquarters in Ponce, Puerto Rico, in December 1937. *Library of Congress.*

and made it mandatory for some federal and state forms to be available in Spanish as well as English. The organization has also expanded civil job opportunities and made low-income housing available for Latinos living in New York. The organization has also increased the number of Latino elected officials at all levels and has filed lawsuits against gerrymandering. In addition, they encourage Latinos to study and practice law by offering LSAT preparatory classes, internships, and mentoring programs. **See also** Civil Rights; Community Organizations;

Economic Equality; Educational Opportunity; English First/ English Only; Voting Rights.

BIBLIOGRAPHY

Rich, Eric and Colin Poitras. "Activists Denounce Ban on Spanish, Meriden Housing Director Not Willing to Back Down." *The Hartford Courant* (September 19, 1997): A1.

Rich, Eric and Brent Spodek. "Board Rescinds Rule on English." *The Hartford Courant* (September 30, 1997): A3.

Puerto Rican Statehood

The political movement that strives to make Puerto Rico a U.S. state emerged in 1899, a year after the island became a U.S. territory. The first pro-statehood party in Puerto Rico, the Partido Republicano (Republican Party), emerged that same year. Its most renowned leader was Jose Carlos Barbosa, who advocated the "Americanization" of Puerto Ricans. Less than a year later, **Luis Muñoz Rivera** (father of **Luis Muñoz Marin**) and Antonio R. Barcelo (grandfather of **Carlos Romero Barcelo**) organized a second pro-statehood party, the Partido Federal (Federal Party), which opposed cultural **assimilation**. These two parties epitomized the two tendencies within the Puerto Rican statehood movement. By the late 1990s, the movement's principal supporter was the **New Progressive Party**. This party's goal has been to petition Congress for statehood in the aftermath of a favorable show of support in a recent status plebiscite. **See** Constitution of Puerto Rico (1952) in Appendix 1. (AAB)

BIBLIOGRAPHY

Melendez, Edgardo. *Movimiento anexionista en Puerto Rico.* Rio Piedras, PR: Editorial de la Universidad de Puerto Rico, 1993.

R

Blandina Cardenas Ramirez (1944–)

Born and raised in southern Texas in a traditional Mexican household, Blandina Ramirez completed a doctorate by her late 20s. She quickly moved into leadership roles in Texas politics, community and **civil rights** advocacy, and higher education. She is a founding member of the **Mexican American Women's National Association (MANA)** and has served on the United States Commission on Civil Rights and the American Council on Education. **See also** Community Organizations; Educational Opportunity; Political Leadership; Political Participation. (ASR)

BIBLIOGRAPHY

Carrier, Lynne. "Rights Panel Convenes with Familiar Furor." *The San Diego Union-Tribune* (January 9, 1985): B3.

Pear, Robert. "Two Members of Rights Commission Sue to Bar Dismissal by President." *The New York Times* (October 27, 1983): 13.

Sara Estela Ramirez (1881–1916)

The life of Sara Ramirez represents the intersection of various political forces. Born in Coahuila, Mexico, she lived and worked in Laredo, Texas. A schoolteacher concerned for the rights of Mexican Americans in Texas, she joined the **Partido Liberal Mexicano** and made her contributions through her writings by communicating the party's policies and articulating a role for women. **See also** Civil Rights. (ASR)

BIBLIOGRAPHY

Zamora, Emilio. "Sara Estela Ramirez: Una Rosa Roja en el Movimiento." In Magdalena Mura and Adelaida R. del Castillo, eds. *Mexican Women in the United States: Struggles Past and Present.* Los Angeles: University of California, Chicano Studies Research Center, 1980.

Manuel Lawrence Real (1924–)

Manuel Lawrence Real began his career as an assistant attorney in the U.S. Department of Justice, a position he held from 1952 to 1955. He left to work in private practice, but in 1964 he returned to the Justice Department as a U.S. attorney. In 1966 he was named U.S. district judge, and from 1982 to 1994 he was chief judge of the U.S. District Court of Central California.

BIBLIOGRAPHY

Johnson, John. "Judge Indicated He May Void Plea Bargain for Hacker." *Los Angeles Times* (February 28, 1995): B1.

Pierce, Emmet. "Battle Heats Up Over News Racks Carrying Sex-Oriented Material." *The San Diego Union-Tribune* (April 21, 1995): 7–8.

Reclamation Act of 1902

The Reclamation Act of 1902 helped to create the modern American West by providing billions of dollars in federal money to build irrigation projects. The construction of dams and canals carried water to western cities and to millions of acres of agricultural lands. These projects in turn greatly increased the need for agricultural labor, which resulted in a tremendous increase of Mexican immigration. The supply of water helped such western cities as Los Angeles to grow rapidly, while newly created jobs helped spur immigration as well. **See also** Illegal Aliens; Immigration Policy and Hispanics. (JRB)

BIBLIOGRAPHY

Dowdy, Doris. *Congress in Its Wisdom: The Bureau of Reclamation and the Public Interest.* Boulder, CO: Westview Press, 1989.

Worster, Donald. *Rivers of Empire: Water, Aridity, and the Growth of the American West.* New York: Pantheon Books, 1985.

Redistricting

The racial and ethnic makeup of Congress and state legislatures is strongly affected by the demographics of the districts from which members are elected. States that gain or lose seats in the U.S. Congress and states with population shifts within the state must redraw their district boundaries in a process called "redistricting." The drawing of such boundaries is always a hot political issue because the precise boundaries of a particular district can influence the election prospects of candidates and parties.

Before 1962, many states drew districts in such a way that some legislators represented many more people than did other legislators. In part, this inequity was caused by a failure to change boundaries as populations shifted and grew. As a result, cities and minority groups were underrepresented in legislatures dominated by rural and small town interests. State senatorial districts in particular were malapportioned because of a tendency to give equal representation to geographical units, such as counties, rather than to population masses.

Population growths and shifts within each district can vary dramatically over time. To keep the numerical size of districts relatively equal, it becomes necessary from time to time to redraw district lines and even to adjust the number of representatives allotted to each state. This process is known as "reapportionment." Each reapportionment of federal House seats reflects the nation's population shifts since the last federal census. Consequently, reapportionment and redistricting occurs every 10 years in the United States, always producing winners and losers. Because of recent population growth in the South and Southwest, such states as California, Texas, and Florida gained seats after the 1990 census, while population losses in the industrial North and Northeast led to a reduction in the number of representatives from such states as New York, Pennsylvania, and Ohio.

Within these districts, one finds every imaginable variation. Each district has its own character; none is an exact replica of the larger society of which it is a component. An enormous political struggle ensues when a new census changes the number of seats a state will receive. State legislatures must redraw the boundaries of congressional districts and state legislative districts. This process is not a matter of simply counting voters and redrawing boundaries to make districts equal. There are many ways to carve out numerically equal congressional districts; some ways will help Democrats get elected, others will help Republicans. Boundary lines may be drawn to create a large ethnic or racial majority within a single district or, conversely, to dilute the political influence of an ethnic or racial voting bloc by dispersing the bloc's members into multiple white-majority districts. Therefore, redistricting is inherently political, and state legislators naturally seek to establish district boundaries that will favor candidates from their own party.

Majority parties in state legislatures continue to secure political advantages by "gerrymandering," a term used to describe the often bizarre district boundaries that are drawn to favor the party in power. This word was coined in the early nineteenth century after Republican governor Elbridge Gerry of Massachusetts signed a redistricting bill that created an oddly shaped district to encompass most of the voters who supported his party. The term is now used to describe any attempt to create a "safe" seat for one party, in which the number of registered voters of one party in a particular district is large enough to guarantee a victory for that party's candidate. State legislative majorities show remarkable ingenuity in laying out districts that will lead to partisan advantage in elections.

Even though apportionment discrepancies throughout the United States were great and growing by the middle of the twentieth century, it was unrealistic to expect elected officials to address the problem themselves. Yet most people in the United States seemed to assume that this problem, like many others, had a legal solution. Accordingly, voters from grossly underrepresented urban areas turned for relief to the federal courts, citing, among other things, the Equal Protection Clause of the Fourteenth Amendment. In *Colegrove v. Green* (1946), the U.S. Supreme Court considered redistricting to be a political question, not one that should be dealt with judicially. Writing for the Court, Justice Felix Frankfurter contended that the "Court ought not to enter this political thicket. The remedy for unfairness in districting is to secure state legislatures that will apportion properly, or to invoke the ample powers of Congress." The Court thus merely affirmed the status quo. In many states, legislatures were not constitutionally required to reapportion on a regular basis. Moreover, even when reapportionments did occur, legislative boundaries were often gerrymandered to give unfair advantage to the dominant political party.

Finally, the Supreme Court stepped in. In *Baker v. Carr* (1962), the Court held that voters indeed have standing to challenge legislative apportionment, and that such questions should be considered by the federal courts. Arbitrarily and capriciously drawn districts deprive people of their constitutional rights, and federal judges may take jurisdiction over such cases. The Court held in *Baker* that reapportionment was a legal question subject to judicial remedies.

The judicial remedy was that the "one man, one vote" formula was the constitutional rule to follow in reapportioning both houses of state legislatures. In the Court's view, this principle applied not only to the house of representative at the state level (where the districting was usually based on population anyway), but also to state senates, where representation was often based on counties or on some other geographical units.

Building on this critical decision, the Court refined the meaning of fair apportionment in the 1970s and 1980s. In subsequent decisions on congressional redistricting, the Court has made it clear that it would tolerate virtually no population variation among districts.

Regarding the struggle for fair apportionment, the Court has examined the use of "multimember" districts in state legislative elections. These districts have been challenged on the grounds that they diminish the possibility that minorities can gain representation in the legislature. In the first case of this type, decided in 1971, the Court held that a single multimember district in Hinds County, Mississippi, from which were elected 12 state representatives and 5 senators, had to be divided into single-member districts. The Court's order made it inevitable that several black candidates would be elected to the Mississippi legislature from Hinds County. Two years later, in *White v. Regester* (1973), the Court upheld a district court decision ordering the creation of single-member districts from two Texas multimember districts, one that discriminated against blacks and the other against Mexican Americans. In 1997, racial representation again came to the fore. In *United Jewish Organization v. Carey* (1977), the Court upheld a New York state apportionment act that used race as the primary consideration in drawing certain district lines. The use of racial criteria in this instance, the Court observed, did not violate either the Fourteenth or Fifteenth Amendments.

In 1982, Congress strengthened the **Voting Rights Act of 1965** by outlawing any electoral arrangement that had the effect of weakening minority voting power. This more stringent "effects test" replaced the earlier "intent test," under which redistricting was outlawed only if boundaries were intentionally drawn to dilute minority political influence. Since 1982, the U.S. Department of Justice has used the Voting Rights Act to prod states into creating districts designed to give minority voters representation in proportion to their population. The **Voting Right Act Amendments of 1982** also required that certain states (currently 16 states with histories of discriminatory voting practices and low voter turnout) must receive clearance from the U.S. attorney general or the U.S. district court for the District of Columbia for any proposed change to their election laws and practices, including redistricting plans. Clearance is required to prevent changes that would lead to losses in minority voting strength.

The first interpretation of the 1982 amendments by the Supreme Court occurred in *Thornburg v. Gingles* (1986). In this case, the Court established the following three tests for determining the existence of vote dilution and the need for a new district: (1) a minority group is sufficiently large and geographically compact to enable it to form a majority in a single-member district, (2) that minority group votes cohesively, and (3) the white majority ordinarily casts bloc votes sufficient to defeat the minority's preferred candidates. The effect of this ruling was the creation of predominantly minority (labeled "majority-minority") districts whenever possible.

The vigorous enforcement of the Voting Rights Act under the Bush administration led to dramatic gains in black and Hispanic legislative representation following the 1990 census. In 1992, in the first election held after the new district lines were drawn, 13 new African-American representatives and 6 new Hispanic members were elected to the House. All 19 were reelected in 1994. The constitutionality of majority-minority districts was quickly challenged in a spate of lawsuits. In *Shaw v. Reno* (1993), a case involving North Carolina's congressional districts, the Supreme Court ruled that a state's redistricting plan can be ruled as unconstitutional racial gerrymandering if it contains districts of "bizarre" or "irrational" configuration, even if the plan's central purpose was to increase the representation of blacks. Writing for the majority, Justice Sandra O'Connor observed that "reapportionment is one area in which appearances do matter. A reapportionment plan that includes in one district individuals who belong to the same race, but who are otherwise widely separated by geographical and political boundaries, and who may have little in common with one another but the color of their skin, bears an uncomfortable resemblance to political apartheid."

Race-conscious districting came to the fore again in a case involving one of Georgia's congressional districts. In *Miller v. Johnson* (1995), the Supreme Court struck down the "race-based" redistricting plan in Cynthia McKinney's 260-mile-long 11th District in Georgia, saying that race cannot be a "predominant factor" in drawing district lines. On the same day that the Court rendered its decision in *Miller*, however, it upheld a California redistricting plan that contained a number of majority black and Hispanic districts.

Substantial litigation will be required to spell out the significance of race in redistricting. It is not clear which race-based redistricting plan will be overturned and which will be upheld. Likely court challenges in Texas, Florida, Louisiana, and North Carolina may offer opportunities to develop consistent guidelines on the appropriate interplay between race, ethnicity, and geography in the ongoing processes of redistricting. **See also** Discrimination; Voting Patterns; Voting Rights. (NM)

BIBLIOGRAPHY

Basehart, Harry and John Commer. "Partisan and Incumbent Effects in State Legislative Redistricting." *Legislative Studies Quarterly* 16 (February 1991): 65–79.

Bullock, Charles III. "Redistricting and Congressional Stability, 1962–1972." *Journal of Politics* 37 (May 1975): 569–75.

Campagna, Janet and Bernard Grofman. "Party Control and Partisan Biases in 1980, Congressional Redistricting." *Journal of Politics* 52 (November 1990): 1242–57.

Dixon, Robert G. *Democratic Representation: Reapportionment in Law and Politics.* New York: Oxford University Press, 1968.

Gelman, Andrew and Gary King. "Enhancing Democracy through Legislative Redistricting." *American Political Science Review* 88 (September 1994): 541–59.

Jacobson, Garry C. *The Politics of Congressional Elections.* New York: HarperCollins, 1992.

Refugee Act of 1980

The Refugee Act of 1980 was designed to update the alien entry laws for the United States and make them more inclusive. Under previous entry legislation, provision allowed all people fleeing oppression in the Middle East or communist countries to be admitted into the United States despite any other contrary restrictions. It was the hope that such laws would help provide sanctuary to people from around the world. While such legislation helped Vietnamese escaping from a communist government and Cubans escaping from communist dictator Fidel Castro, it did little to help victims of violence in Central America. As a result, the Refugee Act was created to reach out to these and other persecuted people by redefining the term "refugee"; no longer were people only fleeing from communist regimes considered—all oppressed people now came under the refugee category. The Refugee Act of 1980 subsequently allowed large numbers of oppressed Central Americans into the United States. **See also** Immigration Policy and Hispanics.

BIBLIOGRAPHY

Lewin, Tamar. "Supreme Court Case May Determine Fate of Thousands Seeking Asylum." *The New York Times* (January 3, 1992): 28.

Peterson, Iver. "Haitians Provide a Test for Disputed Refugee Act." *The New York Times* (February 9, 1992): 12.

Regeneracion

Regeneracion was a Chicano magazine founded in 1970 that originally focused on the activities and goals of **La Raza Unida.** The journal was named after a publication founded by **Ricardo Flores Magon** at the beginning of the twentieth century. In 1971 the magazine expanded its focus to include the general themes of the **Chicano power movement;** by 1972, *Regeneracion* began to include literary contributions.

BIBLIOGRAPHY

Meier, Matt and Felicia Rivera. *The Chicanos.* New York: Hill & Wang, 1972.

Shirley Rodriguez Remenski (1938–)

From 1965 to 1971, Shirley Rodriguez Remenski headed the Department of Social Services for Bronx Borough President **Herman Badillo,** serving the community's health, employment, and educational needs. From 1971 to 1978, Remenski worked with Badillo, who was then a member of the U.S. House of Representatives, serving as his district manager for the Bronx, Queens, and Manhattan. In 1978 she became assistant deputy mayor of New York City, holding this post until 1979. Remenski next served as legislative coordinator for the South Bronx Development Organization and later as the district administrator for the New York State Department of Social Services. In 1986 she was appointed head of the Office of Hispanic Affairs by New York Governor Mario Cuomo. She held that post until 1993 when she became an executive at the New York State Urban Development Corporation.

BIBLIOGRAPHY

Telgen, Diane and Jim Kamp, eds. *Notable Hispanic American Women.* Detroit: Gale Research, 1993.

Republican National Hispanic Assembly of the United States (RNHA)

The Republican National Hispanic Assembly of the United States (RNHA) was founded in 1972 as a way to encourage Latinos to be active in Republican Party politics at all levels of government. The organization also offered support to Hispanic members of Congress. Today, the RNHA is an official auxiliary of the Republican National Committee; it is based in Washington, D.C., and has chapters in seven states. **See also** Political Participation.

BIBLIOGRAPHY

Vigil, Maurilio. *Hispanics in Congress.* Lanham, MD: University Press of America, 1996.

Silvestre Reyes

Silvestre Reyes was born in Canutillo, Texas, just outside El Paso. Reyes holds an associates degree from El Paso Community College and attended the University of Texas at Austin and El Paso. After serving in Vietnam, Reyes joined the U.S. Immigration and Naturalization Service (INS) in 1969. He served as assistant regional commissioner for the INS in Dallas in 1975 and became the head of the U.S. Border Patrol in 1984, a post he held until his retirement in 1995. In 1996, he was elected to Congress as a Democrat from the 16th Congressional District of Texas, which is located in El Paso County at the western tip of the state. Reyes was handily reelected in 1998. In Congress, he has focused on U.S.-Mexican border issues, such as drugs, immigration, and economic development. Reyes currently serves on the House Armed Services Committee and the Veterans Affairs Committee. He is a member of the **Congressional Hispanic Caucus** and a founding member of the Missing and Exploited Children Caucus. He was selected by the House Democratic leadership to serve on the Democratic Task Force on Drugs and the Congressional Interparlimentary Group.

BIBLIOGRAPHY

Congressman Silvestre Reyes' Web site <www.house.gov/reyes/>.

Cruz Reynoso

Cruz Reynoso, professor of law at the University of California, Los Angeles, and vice chair of the United States Commission on Civil Rights, is a leading advocate for **civil rights** for minority and disenfranchised communities. Reynoso attended Fullerton Community College, Pomona College, and Boalt School of Law, University of California, Berkeley. Reynoso's community service ranges from his private practice and his work as general counsel for several California state agencies, boards, and commissions, to his membership on various federal boards and commissions and his positions as professor of law and court judge. He is the only Hispanic who has ever sat on the California State Supreme Court. As vice chair of the United States Commission on Civil Rights, Reynoso is involved in the emergence of major civil rights issues, including **affirmative action,** economic justice, language rights, immigrant rights, and environmental justice. Reynoso has been the leading Latino spokesperson on behalf of affirmative action, which he argues is not about preference but about society's need to achieve racial and ethnic diversity. The ultimate goal for Reynoso is **economic equality** so that American minorities can have the resources to defend their own rights. **See also** Immigration Policy and Hispanics. (ASR)

BIBLIOGRAPHY

Castro, Mike. "Cruz Reynoso Is in the Political Limelight—Again." *Sacramento Bee* (November 7, 1993): D4.
"Ex-Justice Reynoso Still Active with Law." *Sacramento Bee* (March 16, 1977): A3.

Rita Ricardo-Campbell (1920–)

In 1940 Rita Ricardo-Campbell was the first woman and the first Hispanic to teach economics at Harvard; in 1968 she became the first woman appointed senior fellow at Stanford University's Hoover Institute. Several years later, she became the only woman to sit on the board of directors of two Fortune 500 companies, and in the 1980s she served as the only woman on the Presidential Economic Policy Board. **See also** Economic Equality.

BIBLIOGRAPHY
Sneed, Michael and Kathy O'Malley. "Big Stuffffffff . . ." *Chicago Tribune* (October 9, 1985): 16.

William Blain Richardson (1947–)

In 1982, Bill Richardson was first elected to Congress to represent a newly created district in New Mexico. As Congressman, he was a member of the House leadership and served as chief deputy majority whip. He sat on the Democratic Steering Committee, the House Energy and Commerce Committee, and the House Interior and Insular Affairs Committee. In 1996 President Bill Clinton appointed Richardson to the cabinet level post of United Nations Ambassador. Richardson had earlier established himself in international circles through his diplomatic trips to Central America. In 1998 Richardson was appointed

William "Bill" Richardson (D-NM) has served as a member of the House of Representatives, as U.S. ambassador to the UN, and as secretary of transportation and secretary of energy. *Courtesy of U.S. House of Representatives.*

secretary of transportation. He did not stay in that position long because he was appointed secretary of energy in 1999.

BIBLIOGRAPHY
Brooke, James. "Traveling Troubleshooter Is Ready to Settle Down." *New York Times* (December 14, 1996): 11.
Crow, Patrick. "The Nominee Speaks." *The Oil and Gas Journal* 96, no. 30 (July 27, 1998): 44.

Dorothy Comstock Riley (1924–)

After receiving her degrees in politics and law, Dorothy Comstock Riley went into private practice in 1950, serving in Detroit as a lawyer and eventually establishing the firm of Riley and Roumell in 1968. From 1976 to 1982, Riley sat on the Michigan Court of Appeals; in 1982 she was named an associate justice of the Michigan Supreme Court. In 1987, Riley was made chief justice of the Michigan Supreme Court, maintaining this role until 1991, at which time she returned to her role as an associate justice in the Michigan Supreme Court.

BIBLIOGRAPHY
Cain, Charlie. "Colleagues Portray Riley as a Stickler for Details." *The Detroit News* (August 31, 1997): A14.
Cole, Kenneth. "Budyn Gets New Trial; Never Stays in Prison; Court's Decision Pleases Few, Surprises Many." *The Detroit News* (August 1, 1997): A1.

Rodino Bill of 1973

The Rodino Bill of 1973, named after the man who introduced it, Congressman Peter Rodino (D-NJ), called for the House of Representatives to make it illegal for an employer to knowingly hire **illegal aliens** in the United States. The bill also provided guidelines where a $500 fine would be applied for each undocumented worker, while a $1,000 fine and/or a one-year prison sentence would be issued to people found guilty of a second conviction. While some Mexican-American leaders, such as **Cesar Chavez**, had previously called for such measures to be taken, most politicians opposed the bill. These individuals thought it discriminated unnecessarily against Mexican and Mexican-American workers by singling them out, requiring that they prove their legal citizenship, and assessing heavy fines based solely on a person's ethnic background. As a result of this dissent, the bill was not passed. **See also** Immigration Policy and Hispanics.

BIBLIOGRAPHY
Barr, Evan T. "Borderline" Hypocrisy: Congress and Immigration Reform." *New Republic* 195 (July 14, 1986): 12–14.
Engelberg, Stephen. "Rodino Plan Seen Aiding Chances of Bill on Aliens." *New York Times* (July 25, 1985): A21.

Ciro D. Rodriguez (1946–)

Ciro D. Rodriguez was elected to the House of Representatives from Texas in a special election in 1997 to fill the term of **Frank Tejeda,** who died of a brain tumor. A Democrat, Rodriguez won reelection in 1998. A liberal who served in the Texas House of Representatives from 1986 until 1997, Rodriguez serves on the National Security and Veterans' Affairs Committees.

BIBLIOGRAPHY
Barone, Michael. *The Almanac of American Politics*. Washington, DC: The National Journal, 1998.

Gloria Rodriguez (1948–)

Gloria Rodriguez is the executive director of AVANCE, an organization that was established to help minority mothers foster healthy relations with their preschool children, and which now offers literacy and job training to minority fathers and mothers. Rodriguez has been invited to the White House Conference on families, has testified in Congress on family issues, and has received grants from the Federal Head Start Bureau.

BIBLIOGRAPHY
Morales-Zamarripa, Linda. "Local Avance Founder Given Benitia Award." *San Antonio Express-News* (August 21, 1996): 3.
Ramos, Cindy. "AVANCE's Rodriguez Honored by Magazine." *San Antonio Express-News* (February 2, 1998): 1D.

Joseph H. Rodriguez (1930–)

Joseph Rodriguez was a lawyer in private practice from 1959 to 1982, as well as an instructor at Rutgers University School of Law from 1972 to 1982. From 1982 to 1985, Rodriguez was appointed as a New Jersey public advocate, a state cabinet position in which he worked on landmark education and housing cases. In 1985, President Ronald Reagan appointed Rodriguez to the U.S. District Court for the District of New Jersey.

BIBLIOGRAPHY

Sullivan, Joseph F. "Judicial Appointee Eager to Start Job." *The New York Times* (May 7, 1985): 2.

Rita Rodriguez (1942–)

Born in Cuba, Rita Rodriguez received her B.B.A. from the University of Puerto Rico and her M.B.A. from New York University. She began working as a research assistant for the National Bureau for Economic Research in 1965. From 1968 to 1969, she was a lecturer of economics at New York University. She then worked at the Harvard Business School, first as an assistant professor from 1969 to 1974, and then as an associate professor from 1974 to 1978. Rodriguez was professor of finance at the University of Illinois from 1978 to 1982. In 1982 she was appointed by President Ronald Reagan to be the director of the Export–Import Bank of the United States, a post she still holds.

BIBLIOGRAPHY

Telgen, Diane and Jim Kamp, eds. *Notable Hispanic American Women.* Detroit: Gale Research, 1993.

Trinidad Romero (1835–1918)

Trinidad Romero was a member of one of the oldest and most prominent Hispanic families of New Mexico. In 1863 he became a member of the Territorial House of Representatives, and was appointed probate judge in San Miguel County, New Mexico, in 1869 and 1870. In 1876 he was elected as a delegate to the U.S. Congress, but was not a candidate for reelection in 1878. President Benjamin Harrison appointed him United States marshal and he held that position from November 13, 1889, to May 30, 1893.

BIBLIOGRAPHY

Hispanic Americans in Congress. Washington, DC: U.S. Government Printing Office, 1995.

Carlos Antonio Romero-Barceló (1932–)

Carlos Romero-Barceló was the first former governor of Puerto Rico to serve in Congress as resident commissioner. In 1968 Romero-Barceló was elected mayor of San Juan and was reelected four years later. During his terms in office he modernized and improved local government. A strong supporter of **Puerto Rican statehood,** Romero-Barceló served as president of Citizens for State 51 from 1965 to 1967. He emerged as a leader among statehood advocates during his service as mayor, and in 1974 he was elected president of the pro-statehood **New Progressive Party**, serving in this position until 1986.

In 1976, Romero-Barceló became the first Hispanic American to be elected president of the National League of Cities. That same year he was elected governor of Puerto Rico, and he was reelected four years later, serving from 1977 to 1985, becoming the fifth elected governor of Puerto Rico. In 1992 Romero-Barceló was elected to a four-year term as resident commissioner to the U.S. House of Representatives. He was reelected to the post in 1996 for another four-year term.

BIBLIOGRAPHY

Hispanic Americans in Congress. Washington, DC: U.S. Government Printing Office, 1995.

Romero-Barceló, Carlos. "Puerto Rico, U.S.A.: The Case for Statehood." *Foreign Affairs* 59 (Fall 1980): 58–81.

Margarita Roque (1946–)

In 1983 Margarita Roque interned with Senator Paul Sarbanes (D-MD) in Washington, D.C.; she then worked with the Churches' Committee for Voter Registration and the Women's Vote Project. In 1987 Roque became executive director of the **Congressional Hispanic Caucus;** in this role, she coordinated about 13 members of the Congress and 84 associate members of the House and the Senate to provide policy agendas that are helpful to Hispanic Americans. Roque has strived throughout her career for a heightened role by Latinos in the governmental process and an improvement in educational opportunities for the Hispanic community.

BIBLIOGRAPHY

Harris, H.R. "Priests Battle on Streets for Calm; Churchmen Were on Front Line in Mt. Pleasant Disturbances." *The Washington Post* (May 22, 1991): D7.

Ileana Ros-Lehtinen (1952–)

As the first Cuban American, and the first Latina woman, ever elected to the U.S. House of Representatives (and the first Cuban-American woman elected to the Florida state legislature, first as a representative and then as a senator), Ileana Ros-Lehtinen continues to be a controversial figure. Ros-Lehtinen was born in Cuba and came to the United States with her family in 1960. Her parents were immediately involved in private and government efforts to overthrow the Castro government in Cuba. As she began to seek public office, Ros-Lehtinen's turbulent and ethnically divided campaigns reflected not only her ethnic al-

Ileana Ros-Lehtinen (R-FL), the first Cuban-American and first Latina elected to Congress, was born in Cuba and came to the United States with her family in 1960. *Courtesy of U.S. House of Representatives.*

legiance to Cuba, but also her ideology opposing the Cuban Revolution. A fervent anti-Castro Republican, she nevertheless supports some liberal causes, including **bilingual education**, some gun control legislation, improved veterans' benefits, and human rights concerns. Ros-Lehtinen has taken some difficult positions, such as opposing Nelson Mandela's visit to Florida in 1990 and opposing **Xavier Becerra's** 1996 visit to Cuba to meet with Fidel Castro. Ros-Lehtinen's political views demonstrate the ideological differences within Latinos as a group, differences based upon historical experience and national origin. **See also** Civil Rights; Congressional Hispanic Caucus; Political Leadership. (ASR)

BIBLIOGRAPHY
Bonillo-Sanhigo, Gloria. *Breaking Ground and Barriers: Hispanic Women Developing Effective Leadership.* San Diego, CA: Marin Publications, 1992.
Women in Congress, 1917–1990. Washington, DC: Government Printing Office, 1991.

Edward R. Roybal (1916–)

Prior to entering the House of Representatives as a Democrat in 1962, Edward Roybal served on the Los Angeles City Council from 1949 to 1962; he also served two years in the U.S. Army from 1944 to 1945. Roybal's district is 64 percent Spanish heritage; it includes Pasadena, Pomona, Ventura, Glendale, Santa Ana, and Boyle Heights. He took the spotlight in the early 1980s when a new immigration bill was brought to the floor. The bill required employers to pay fines if they employed **illegal aliens**. Roybal believed that this law would disproportionately affect

Edward R. Roybal (D-CA) was first elected to the U.S. House of Representatives in 1962. *Courtesy of U.S. House of Representatives.*

Hispanic citizens. As chairman of the **Congressional Hispanic Caucus**, he led the unsuccessful fight to defeat the bill. Roybal did not stand for reelection in 1992. **See also** Immigration Policy and Hispanics; Lucille Roybal-Allard. (CEM)

BIBLIOGRAPHY
Diaz, Katherine A. "Congressman Edward Roybal: Los Angeles before the 1960s." *Caminos* 4, no. 7 (July–August 1983).

Duncan, Philip D. and Christine C. Lawrence. *Politics in America: 1996. The 104th Congress.* Washington, DC: Congressional Quarterly Press, 1995.

Lucille Roybal-Allard (1941–)

Lucille Roybal-Allard's trajectory to political office has been through her involvement in **Comision Femenil Mexicana Nacional** and her relationship with **Gloria Molina**. Perhaps because she comes from a prominent Democratic political family—her father is the distinguished retired California Congressman **Edward Roybal**—and had experienced a lack of privacy and personal identity, Roybal-Allard had concluded that she did not want to enter the electoral political arena. Instead, after completing her college education, she choose community and advocacy work. But she quickly learned about barriers to resolution of community problems, barriers often imposed by elected officials themselves. Thus, when Molina's state assembly seat in the 56th Los Angeles district became available in 1986, Roybal-Allard was ready. Once elected, she set about a number of formidable tasks, including stopping the construction of a new prison in East Los Angeles. Other similar battles earned Roybal-Allard a solid reputation as an advocate for her constituency. Since her election to the United States Congress from the 33rd Congressional District in Los Angeles in 1992, she is emerging as a very effective legislator. As the first California Latina elected to Congress, Roybal-Allard's successes have opened the door for more Latinas to run for statewide and national elected office. (ASR)

BIBLIOGRAPHY
Bornemeier, James. "Marshaling California's Democratic Forces." *Los Angeles Times* (February 7, 1997): 3.
Renwick, Lucille. "They're Out in the Cold; The New Conservative Agenda in Washington Could Spell Trouble for Many Inner City Services and Funding." *Los Angeles Times* (January 1, 1995): 12.

Rumford Fair Housing Act of 1963

California's Rumford Fair Housing Act of 1963 prohibited **discrimination** in the sale or rental of housing in dwellings containing more than four units. Among other definitions, the law stipulated that discrimination occurred if a real estate agent provided information on the ethnic background of a potential buyer or renter. The law was replaced in 1980 by the state's Fair Employment and Housing Act, which prohibits discrimination on the basis of race, color, religion, sex, national origin, ancestry, age, marital status, and familial status. **See also** Economic Equality. (VDD)

BIBLIOGRAPHY
Garcia, Mario T. *Mexican Americans.* New Haven, CT: Yale University Press, 1989.

Louis E. Saavedra (1933–)

After serving as president of the Albuquerque (New Mexico) Technical Vocational Institute, Louis Saavedra served on the Albuquerque City Commission from 1967 to 1974, becoming chairman from 1973 to 1974. In 1989 Saavedra was elected mayor of Albuquerque, a post he maintained until 1994. During his career, Saavedra was also a member of the board of directors for the National League of Cities and vice president of the New Mexico Municipal League.

BIBLIOGRAPHY

"Former President of School Chosen Albuquerque Mayor." *The New York Times* (November 5, 1989): 24.

Ruben Salazar (1928–1970)

Ruben Salazar, a Mexican-American journalist, was killed in 1970 during a rally for the **Chicano Moratorium to the war in Vietnam** at Los Angeles; he was struck by a tear-gas projectile fired by police at short range. Salazar, a popular Los Angeles newspaper and television reporter, was covering the moratorium for the *Los Angeles Times* and the Spanish-language TV station KMEX at the time. Salazar is now remembered as a Chicano movement **civil rights** martyr.

The national Chicano Moratorium rally was staged to protest the high percentage of Chicano casualties in the Vietnam War. The August 29 rally, which began with a moratorium march, was a climax to demonstrations throughout the West and Southwest. The march attracted some 30,000 participants from all 50 states. In the course of monitoring the march, some 1,200 police and sheriff's deputies descended on the participants in Laguna Park, creating a chaotic scene of intimidation and mass arrests. Late in the afternoon, Salazar and two KMEX co-workers entered the Silver Dollar Cafe. Soon afterwards, deputies surrounded the bar and fired in a number of high-velocity tear-gas projectiles, one of which struck Salazar in the head. The police defended their actions as necessary to control the crowds and curtail riotous activity. Salazar, born in Ciudad Juarez, Mexico, served in the U.S. military and had attained U.S. citizenship. (SCV)

BIBLIOGRAPHY

Salazar, Ruben. *Border Correspondent: Selected Writings, 1955–1970.* Berkeley: University of California Press, 1995.
Weingarten, Steve. "The Life and Curious Death of Ruben Salazar." *Reader* 3, no. 44 (August 26, 1981).

Salt of the Earth

Salt of the Earth is a 1953 movie based on the struggle of Mexican-American miners and women. During a labor strike at a mine, when an injunction prevented the men from picketing, the miners' women continued the fight—braving their husbands' disapproval, violent assaults from the police, and imprisonment. The wives' participation encouraged the women to stand up for their own rights and challenge their husbands' assumptions about gender roles. Made by communists at the height of the McCarthy hearings, the film was banned and not shown publicly until 1975. (MP)

BIBLIOGRAPHY

Silverton Rosenfelt, Deborah. *Salt of the Earth.* Old Westbury, NY: Feminist Press, 1978.

Salt War (1866–1877)

The "Salt War" saw Mexican Americans and Anglos clash over a huge deposit of salt discovered in the 1860s near El Paso, Texas. Initially, access to the salt was free, but Anglo businessmen eventually bought and fenced off the lands. In late 1877, after the deposits were closed off, a series of riots broke out against the salt owners. Two Hispanics were killed, a leader of the salt owners was executed in revenge, and Mexicans were subsequently attacked on the streets of El Paso in return. The U.S. Army was brought in to restore order, but no white American was ever brought to justice for the outbreak of racial violence. (JRB)

BIBLIOGRAPHY

Romero, Mary. "El Paso Salt War: Mob Action or Political Struggle?" *Aztlaan* 10, nos. 1–2 (Spring 1985): 119–43.

San Antonio Independent School District v. Rodriquez (1968)

During the 1960s, *San Antonio Independent School District v. Rodriquez,* 411 U.S. 1 (1968), defined an early challenge to state school-spending inequities. The suit began in 1968 on behalf of Mexican-American parents in various San Antonio, Texas, school districts. As in most states, the Texas school-funding system relies on a combination of state funding and local property taxes. By 1973 the **Mexican American Legal Defense and Education Fund (MALDEF)** challenged the Texas school finance formula by filing the lawsuit *San Anto-*

nio v. Rodriquez. The suit charged that the state's program discriminated against minority children in property-poor school districts across the state and violated a fundamental, constitutionally protected right to education. The U.S. Supreme Court, however, rejected MALDEF's argument. Subsequently, the fight for school finance shifted to the Texas legislature, where Mexican Americans have since been at the center of efforts to overhaul the state's school finance system. **See also** Civil Rights; Educational Opportunity; *Serrano v. Priest* (1971). (VDD)

BIBLIOGRAPHY

DiConti, Veronica. *Interest Groups and Education Reform: The Latest Crusade to Restructure the Schools.* Lanham: University Press of America, 1996.
Skerry, Peter. *Mexican Americans: The Ambivalent Minority.* Cambridge, MA: Harvard University Press, 1993.

Loretta Sanchez (1960–)

Loretta Sanchez, a California Democrat, was elected to the U.S. House of Representatives in 1996, defeating the long-term and ultraconservative incumbent, Robert K. Dornan. Her election was close, with fewer than 1,000 votes separating the candidates. Her victory was marred somewhat by election irregularities, including more than 800 documented ineligible voters and an ongoing investigation that ended in February 1998. In November 1998, she again defeated Dornan to retain her seat in Congress. Prior to her election, she was a business consultant and community activist.

BIBLIOGRAPHY

Gugliotta, Guy. "Dornan Challenge to Sanchez Rejected." *Washington Post* (February 5, 1998): A4.
Yang, John E. "Democrat Sanchez Claims Victory Over Rep. Dornan." *Washington Post* (November 14, 1996): A4.

José E. Serrano (1943–)

In 1974, Puerto Rican-born Jose Serrano, a Democrat, was elected to the New York State Assembly, where he served for 15 years; he was chairman of the Education Committee from 1983 to 1990. During that time he sponsored several pieces of landmark legislation, including the reform of the election process for members of local school boards. He was a delegate to the Democratic National Convention in 1976, 1984, 1988, and 1992. Serrano was elected to the U.S. House of Representatives with 92 percent of the vote in a special election called in March 1990 to fill the unexpired term of **Robert Garcia**, who had resigned. Serrano won reelection in 1992, 1994, 1996, and 1998. In the 102nd Congress, he was the principal sponsor of the Voting Rights Language Assistance Act, which strengthened and expanded the **Voting Rights Act of 1965.** In the 103rd Congress, he was elected to a two-year term as chairman of the **Congressional Hispanic Caucus** and the Congressional Hispanic Caucus Institute. **See also** Political Participation.

BIBLIOGRAPHY

Hispanic Americans in Congress. Washington, DC: U.S. Government Printing Office, 1995.

Serrano v. Priest (1971)

The California Supreme Court ruled in *Serrano v. Priest,* 5 Cal. 3d 584; 487 P.2d 1241 (1971), that the state's school finance system, with its substantial reliance on local property taxes, created wide disparities in school revenue and thus violated the equal protection clause of the Fourteenth Amendment. The court ruled that education was a fundamental right that could not be dependent upon wealth. The court ruled that state funding discriminated against poor people because the quality of education was a function of the wealth of a child's parents and neighbors. This decision had effects well beyond California because similar constitutional challenges to school funding schemes were initiated in almost every state. **See also** Civil Rights; Educational Opportunity; *San Antonio Independent School District v. Rodriquez* (1968). (RLP)

BIBLIOGRAPHY

Crowley, Donald. "Implementing *Serrano*: A Study in Judicial Impact." *Law and Policy Quarterly* 4, no. 3 (July 1982): 299–326.
Fischel, William A. "How *Serrano* Caused Prop 13." *Journal of Law and Policy* 12, no. 4 (Fall 1996): 607–36.

Sinarquista Movement

Members of the Sinarquista movement, which had an extreme right-wing political philosophy, entered the Southwest from Mexico during World War II and approached Mexican Americans with ideas about the return of the Southwest to Mexico. No longer active, "Sinarquismo" promoted separation from the United States. Ultimately, Mexican Americans rejected these appeals. Increased involvement in wartime employment, service in the armed forces, growing national mobility, and active participation in labor unions largely nullified Sinarquista's appeal to Mexican Americans. **See also** Economic Opportunity. (SCV)

BIBLIOGRAPHY

Ruiz, Ramon Eduardo. *Triumphs and Tragedy: A History of the Mexican People.* New York: W. W. Norton, 1992.

Sleepy Lagoon Defense Committee

On August 2, 1942, Jose Diaz died after being beaten and having his skull fractured in an area near Los Angeles called Sleepy Lagoon. Investigations into the murder pointed to 23 Mexican Americans and one white male who were all members of the 38th Street youth gang, a group that had been involved in a fight near the Sleepy Lagoon swimming hole on the evening of Diaz' death. All 24 gang members were arrested and indicted by a grand jury. Out of this group, 22 were tried en masse on about 60 charges, which raged from criminal conspiracy to murder; the other two members were tried separately after asking for this right.

Throughout the trial, a number of questionable, discriminatory practices occurred. For example, the prosecution often pointed out the youths' Mexican ancestry. The gang members were also denied haircuts and changes of clothing, so that their appearance would continue to accent their "dangerous" background. On January 13, 1943, the jury found three of the youths guilty of first-degree murder, nine guilty of second-degree murder, five guilty of assault, and five free of all charges. That autumn, Carey McWilliams formed the Sleepy Lagoon Defense Committee, a group created to organize a national funding campaign that would finance an appeal of the verdicts. On October 4, 1944, the committee was successful in helping orchestrate the reversal of the lower court finding. **See also** Francisca Flores; Tenney Committee; Zoot Suit Riots of 1943.

BIBLIOGRAPHY

Rowe, Peter. "At 80, She's Still at Great Stage in Life." *The San Diego Union-Tribune* (October 23, 1997): E1.

Adaljiza Sosa-Riddell (1937–)

After receiving her Ph.D. at the University of California, Riverside, in 1974, Adaljiza Sosa-Riddell began teaching political science at the University of California, Davis. In 1985 she became a lecturer of Chicano Studies at the University of California, Berkeley. She is a founding member of the **National Association of Chicana and Chicano Studies** and the **Mujeres Activas en Letras y Cambio Social** and has received numerous awards, including the Outstanding Latina Leadership Award in 1992.

BIBLIOGRAPHY

Ruiz, Vicki L. *From Out of the Shadows.* New York: Oxford University Press, 1998.

Marta Sotomayor (1939–)

Marta Sotomayor has pursued a unique career in public policy by becoming president of the National Hispanic Council on Aging, a Washington, D.C., think tank. She also serves on the board for the **National Council of La Raza**, the oldest and most important Hispanic organization dedicated to political and social issues. (ASR)

BIBLIOGRAPHY

Perez, Felix. "Quality of Life Prospects Are Still Glum for Hispanic Elderly." *The San Diego Union-Tribune* (October 8, 1989): C8.

Southwest Voter Registration Education Project (SVREP)

William C. (Willie) Velasquez, a native of San Antonio and a veteran of Chicano activist politics in south Texas, founded the Southwest Voter Registration Education Project (SVREP) in 1974. Over the next decade, Velasquez visited Mexican-American communities throughout the Southwest to increase voter registration efforts. Today, SVREP is a national, nonprofit, nonpartisan organization committed to increasing the participation of Latinos and other minority groups in U.S elections. All operating funds are received from contributions by private foundations, corporations, and individuals.

Since its inception, SVREP has conducted more than 1,800 voter registration and voter education campaigns in approximately 200 communities in California, Arizona, New Mexico, Colorado, Texas, Oklahoma, Utah, Nevada, Idaho, Montana, Wyoming, and South Dakota. As a result of these efforts, more than 40,000 Latino community leaders have been trained in organization, registration, and get-out-the-vote techniques. The Southwest Voter Registration Project also works in communities to educate citizens about voting systems, as well as to muster support for the project's selected candidates. Through the efforts of SVREP, more than 2,000 Latinos have been elected to office and, since 1974, more than two million Latinos have been registered to vote.

At the state level, through citizenship campaigns and voter registration efforts, SVREP has helped raise the number of Hispanic members in legislatures. For example, California's 80-member assembly went from 4 Hispanic officeholders prior to the 1990 election to 10 in 1992 and 14 in 1996.

National leaders have recognized SVREP for several reasons. First, SVREP, through its Southwest Voter Research Institute (SVRI), has become a major source of political information on Latino political behavior and opinion. Second, with steady increases in turnout, Latinos are now considered the fastest growing electorate in the Southwest and the United States. This fact has not escaped the attention of the White House. On May 5, 1995, in front of 800 Latino leaders, President Bill Clinton and First Lady Hillary Rodham Clinton were honored guests at SVREP's first annual Cinco de Mayo reception in Washington, D.C.; the event recognized the importance of the Latino vote in 1996 and SVREP's contribution to expanding that vote. **See also** Assimilation; Political Participation; Voting Rights. (VDD)

BIBLIOGRAPHY

Alma-Bonilla, Yara I. and Joseph Torres. "Latinos Lead Way as Hispanics Gain 11 State Legislative Seats." *Hispanic Link News Service.* Washington, DC, November 1998.

Chavez, Linda. *Out of the Barrio: Toward a New Politics of Hispanic Assimilation.* New York: Basic Books, 1991.

Spanish-American War (1898)

The brief Spanish-American War erupted in reaction to Spain's attempt to crush a rebellion against its rule in Cuba; in the end, the war marked a vast expansion in the role of the United States in the world. The Cuban revolt had begun in 1895, and reports of vicious Spanish attacks on civilians—and fears about the stability of U.S. economic investments in Cuba—led to increased pressure by the American public on the U.S. government to intervene. American presidents Grover Cleveland and William McKinley tried to end the conflict through diplomacy, but Spanish reforms failed to gain the support of Cuban rebels. In February 1898, two events occurred that pushed the Untied States closer to war with Spain. First, the *New York Times* published a letter from Spain's ambassador to the United States criticizing President McKinley. Then, on February 15, the USS *Maine* exploded and sank in the harbor of Havana, Cuba. Last-minute U.S. efforts to negotiate a peace between Spain and the Cuban rebels failed. In April 1898, McKinley asked Congress to authorize sending U.S. troops to Cuba, while still asking that Spanish peace efforts be taken

Teddy Roosevelt poses with other Rough Riders on San Juan Hill in Cuba in 1898. *Library of Congress.*

into account. A joint resolution, passed by Congress, recognized Cuba's independence and demanded Spanish withdrawal. Spain refused, and by April 25 Spain and the United States had declared war on each other.

The war lasted less than four months, and Spain suffered total defeat. On May 1, 1898, the Spanish fleet, which was in the Philippines and anchored in Manila harbor, was destroyed. In Cuba, U.S. troops landed near Santiago to capture Spanish forts overlooking the harbor, where another U.S. fleet waited. In late June and early July, U.S. troops successfully took the forts and forced Spanish ships to attempt to break through a U.S. naval blockade. This Spanish fleet was also sunk. In mid-July, the Spanish army in Santiago surrendered. In addition, U.S. forces invaded and captured Puerto Rico, Guam, and Manila, the capital of the Philippines. When the **Treaty of Paris** was signed on December 10, 1898, the Spanish colonial empire had collapsed, to be replaced by a rising U.S. overseas empire that now controlled territory in the Philippines, Puerto Rico, and Guam.

The Spanish-American War marked the entrance of the United States onto the world stage and signaled increasing U.S. political and military strength. While Cuba gained its independence from Spain, the United States kept the other lands it had taken. The Philippines later gained independence following World War II, but Guam and Puerto Rico remain U.S. territories. **See also** U.S.–Latin American Relations. **See** Treaty of Paris (1898) and Cuba Agreement (1903) in Appendix 1. (JRB)

BIBLIOGRAPHY

Friedel, Frank. *The Splendid Little War.* Boston: Little, Brown, 1958.
Morgan, H. Wayne. *America's Road to Empire: The War with Spain and Overseas Expansion.* New York: Wiley, 1965.
Trask, David. *The War with Spain in 1898.* New York: Macmillan, 1981.

Xavier L. Suarez (1949–)

After earning degrees from Villanova University, Harvard Law School, and the John F. Kennedy School of Government at Harvard, Xavier Suarez went on to practice law in Miami, Florida, from 1975 to 1984. He was also a member of the board of directors for the Legal Services of Miami in 1979 and chairman of the Affirmative Action Commission for the City of Miami in 1981. In 1985 Suarez was elected mayor of Miami, gaining reelection in 1987 and 1989. In 1988 he was a member of the Nominating Committee of the United States Conference of Mayors and the Task Force on Urban Growth Patterns. In 1991, Suarez was appointed by President George Bush to the board of directors of the **Legal Services Corporation**. **See also** Political Leadership.

BIBLIOGRAPHY

Baker, Donald P. "New Mayoral Election Is Ordered for Miami; 'Fraud and Abuse' Prevalent, Judge Says." *The Washington Post* (March 5, 1998): A2.
Duryea, Bill. "The Mayor Who Can't Sit Still." *St. Petersburg Times* (January 13, 1998): 1D.

Frank M. Tejeda (1945–)

Frank Tejeda, a Democrat, served in the Texas House of Representatives from 1976 to 1987, and in the Texas Senate from 1987 to 1993. He continued his education while serving in the state legislature; he received an M.A. in public administration from the John F. Kennedy School of Government at Harvard University in 1980 and an LL.M. from Yale University School of Law in 1989. In 1992 Tejeda was elected to the U.S. House of Representatives from the 28th District in Texas with 87 percent of the vote. He was reelected in 1994, 1996, and 1998. In Congress he continued his support of issues affecting veterans; he serves on the Armed Services and Veterans' Affairs Committees. He helped organize and also led a National Veterans Task Force in support of Bill Clinton's candidacy for president in 1992. **See also** Political Participation.

BIBLIOGRAPHY

Hispanic Americans in Congress. Washington, DC: U.S. Government Printing Office, 1995.

Emma Tenayuca (1916–)

A school teacher born and raised in San Antonio, Texas, Emma Tenayuca is most often honored for work as a community labor organizer. From an early age, she championed worker's rights, Mexican rights, and the rights of immigrants. Joining the Communist Party in the 1930s, she and her husband published an analysis, "The Mexican Question in the Southwest," wherein they argued for educational and cultural equality and the right of the Mexican people to speak Spanish, and they opposed economic **discrimination**, social oppression, Jim Crowism, and political repression. Throughout the 1930s, she organized pecan-shellers in San Antonio until the United Cannery, Agricultural, Packing and Allied Workers of America (UCAPAWA) union leadership removed her as strike leader. The leadership of the UCAPAWA, part of the Congress of Industrial Organizations (CIO), needing to distance itself from communist affiliations to gain legitimacy, replaced Tenayuca with **Luisa Moreno**. Although Tenayuca eschewed her Communist Party affiliations in 1940, she was blacklisted by the House Committee on Un-American Activities. During the **Chicano Power Movement**, Chicano studies scholars "dis-

covered" Tenayuca, and, in 1984, she was honored by the **National Association for Chicana and Chicano Studies** for her contributions to the Chicano community. Tenayuca exemplifies Chicana political activism with her activities ranging from community organizing to participation in left-wing radical organizations. **See also** Civil Rights; Economic Equality; Pecan Shellers' Strike of 1938. (ASR)

BIBLIOGRAPHY

Croxdale, Richard and Melissa Hield, eds. *Women in the Texas Workforce: Yesterday and Today.* Austin: People's History in Texas, 1979.

Rips, Geoffrey and Emma Tenayuca. "Living History: Emma Tenayuca Tells Her Story." *Texas Observer* (October 28, 1983): 7–15.

Tenney Committee

The Tenney Committee was established in 1941 by the California legislature as a group dedicated to investigating "un-American" activities. This group, which was based on the federal Fact-Finding Committee on Un-American Activities, was headed by state assemblyman Jack Tenney. From 1943 to 1944, the committee subpoenaed and questioned members of the **Sleepy Lagoon Defense Committee** in an attempt to find communist ties. The Tenney Committee also questioned witnesses of the 1947 Di Giorgio farms strike that was coordinated by the National Farm Labor Union, including leaders H.L. Mitchell and Hank Hasiwar. In 1949, Tenney and other committee members helped spearhead the University of California loyalty oath controversy in which faculty and administrators were challenged about their political leanings. More questionable acts occurred as the committee began to accuse California legislators of being communist sympathizers. Jack Tenney was forced to resign his position in June 1949. Senator Hugh M. Burns replaced Tenney as chairman, and the commission lost most of its overly aggressive practices.

BIBLIOGRAPHY

Garcia, Mario T. *Mexican Americans.* New Haven, CT: Yale University Press, 1989.

Texas Statehood

Americans first entered Texas at the invitation of Spain in 1821, when Moses Austin led 300 families into the territory. Spain granted Mexico control of Texas in the same year and Mexico followed the Spanish lead, bringing Americans into the area as a barrier to Native Americans. Immigrants from the United States were guaranteed free land, but were asked to practice Catholicism. By 1830, when Mexico halted American immigration, there were twice as many Americans as native Mexicans. A fear of American revolts against Mexican rule, combined with an influx of slaves (brought by the immigrants) to Mexican territory, where slavery was prohibited, provoked the halt in immigration. But illegal immigration from the United States continued until there were more than 30,000 Americans (plus their slaves) in Texas in 1835.

Americans in Texas resented Mexican control and desired more open trade and the legal recognition of Texas slavery. Eventually, political and economic discontent led to a Texan attack on a Mexican garrison in 1835. Mexican dictator Santa Anna then sent thousands of troops to Texas. In March 1836, Americans in Texas declared independence from Mexico. The Americans lost battles at the **Alamo** and Goliad, but they finally defeated Santa Anna in the battle of San Jacinto River in April 1836. Santa Anna, who survived the Mexican defeat, was forced to grant independence to American Texas (under the **Treaty of Velasco** in 1836). Texas, however, did not immediately join the United States but remained an independent nation until 1845 because the United States did not wish to provoke further conflict with Mexico by annexing Texas too quickly. The eventual addition of Texas to the United States provoked the **Mexican War** in 1846. In this conflict, Mexico lost approximately half its territory. The American victory added not only huge tracts of territory to the United States, but also tens of thousands of Spanish-speaking peoples. **See also** Treaty of Guadalupe Hidalgo (1848). **See** A Mexican Account of the Attack on the Alamo (1849); Texas Declaration of Independence (1836); Texas Annexation Treaty (1844); Treaty of Guadalupe Hidalgo (1848) in Appendix 1. (JRB)

BIBLIOGRAPHY

Fehrenbach, T. R. *Lone Star: A History of Texas and the Texans.* New York: Colliers, 1968.

Merk, Frederick. *Slavery and the Annexation of Texas.* New York: Alfred A. Knopf, 1972.

Pletcher, David. *The Diplomacy of Annexation: Texas, Oregon, and the Mexican War.* Columbia: University of Missouri Press, 1973.

Reies Lopez Tijerina (1926–)

In the 1950s, Reies Lopez Tijerina researched and studied the history of Spanish and Mexican land grants in the U.S. Southwest. New Mexico village common lands were taken over by the U.S. government under the terms of the **Treaty of Guadalupe Hidalgo**, which ended the **Mexican War**. Starting in 1963, Tijerina used this treaty to promote the return of the village lands through the efforts of his Alianza Federal de Mercedes (Federal Alliance of Land Grants)—later called the **Alianza Federal de Pueblos Libres** (Federal Alliance of Free Towns). Tijerina, through the Alianza, intended that pueblo common lands be returned to the heirs of the original grantees.

A former Protestant minister and a forceful speaker with preaching experience, Tijerina recruited members for the alliance from the villages of northern New Mexico. Within three years, his land-grant organization grew in size to 20,000 followers. Activities included a 60-mile march from Albuquerque to Santa Fe, the state capital, to present the organization's demands to Governor Jack Campbell in 1966. Additionally, his organization occupied a parcel of land in the Kit Carson National Forest in October 1966. In 1967, his group gained world recognition when Tijerina led a raid on New Mexico's Tierra Amarilla County Courthouse to arrest authorities the alliance held responsible for withholding the disputed land. **See also** Land Rights. (SCV)

BIBLIOGRAPHY

Tijerina, Reies Lopez. *Mi lucha por la tierra.* Mexico, D.F.: Fondo De Cultura Economica, 1978.

Tolan Committee

On April 22, 1940, the U.S. House of Representatives empowered a Select Committee on the Interstate Migration of Destitute Citizens, which was chaired by John Tolan (D-CA). The committee was charged with investigating the conditions and economic impact of migrant families during the Great Depression. There was widespread concern that white workers were being displaced by Mexican migrant workers. Texas was serving as an entry point for thousands of workers who were then transported to western and northern states in fulfillment of labor contracts. The committee held hearings across the country to explore the impact of these practices. On April 3, 1941, the committee reported that new regulations were needed to protect not only white workers, but also migrant Mexicans who were recruited for labor contracts.

BIBLIOGRAPHY

Derber, Milton and Edwin Young, eds. *Labor and the New Deal.* Madison: University of Wisconsin Press, 1957.

Hoffman, Abraham. *Unwanted Mexican Americans in the Great Depression.* Tucson: University of Arizona Press, 1974.

Art Torres (1946–)

Art Torres, a Democrat, was first elected to the California State Assembly in 1974 where he served until 1983. Upon leaving the assembly, he began service in the state senate where he fought for Latinos on such issues as education. In addition to his position in California, Torres serves on the Council on Foreign Relations in New York where he is an expert on Latin America and federal policy toward that region. Since 1995, Torres has been practicing law. In 1997, he became chairman of the California State Democratic Party.

BIBLIOGRAPHY

Skerry, Peter. *Mexican Americans.* New York: Free Press, 1993.

Esteban Edward Torres (1930–)

Esteban Edward Torres served in the U.S. Army from 1949 to 1953, eventually gaining the rank of sergeant first class. He later went on to become a representative of the United Auto Workers (UAW) and an international labor consultant from 1954 to 1968, a community affairs organizer from 1968 to 1974, and a UAW official from 1975 to 1976. From 1976 to 1977, Torres acted as a consultant for the Office of Technology Assessment before serving from 1977 until 1979 as U.S. ambassador to the United Nations Educational, Scientific, and Cultural Organization in Paris, France.

Esteban Torres served as a special assistant to President Jimmy Carter from 1979 to 1981 before being elected to the U.S. House of Representatives as a Democrat from California. *Courtesy of U.S. House of Representatives.*

In 1979 Torres returned to the United States to serve under President Jimmy Carter as a special assistant to the White House; he remained in this position until 1981. Torres also acted as a delegate to a number of California state conventions from 1968 to 1983, as well as the Democratic National Conventions in 1984 and 1988. After being an unsuccessful congressional candidate in 1974, Torres was finally elected in 1982 to the U.S. House of Representatives as a Democrat. While in Congress, Torres participated with the House Appropriations Committee and subcommittees on Military Construction, Foreign Operations, Export Financing, and related programs. He was also an official observer of the Geneva Arms Reduction Talks from 1986 to 1990. He retired from office in 1998.

BIBLIOGRAPHY

Moran, Julio. "Esteban Torres: Our Hot Line to the President." *Nuestro* 4, no. 1 (March 1980).

Maria de Los Angeles Torres (1955–)

Maria Torres came to the United States from Cuba after the Cuban Revolution (1959). Although her parents supported the Revolution, the family emigrated to the United States. Torres abhors stereotypes of Cubans as politically conservative and is recognized for her radical ideas, support for Puerto Rican independence and advocacy for better immigration laws. (ASR)

BIBLIOGRAPHY

Garza, Melita Marie. "'60s Airlift Turned Kids to Victims; Cuban-Americans Seek Answers." *Chicago Tribune.* (January 13, 1998): 1.

Ojito, Mirta. "Cubans Face Past as Stranded Youths in US." *The New York Times.* (January 12, 1998): 7.

Juan R. Torruella (1933–)

Juan Torruella was named a judge in the U.S. District Court of Puerto Rico in 1974, a position he held until 1985, when he was named a judge in the U.S. Court of Appeals. He is a member of the Judicial Conference Committee on the Administration of the Federal Magistrate System and the Association of Labor Relations Practitioners in Puerto Rico and the Virgin Islands.

BIBLIOGRAPHY

"Around the Nation: Attempt to Send Haitians to Puerto Rico is Delayed." *The New York Times* (December 10, 1980): 14.
Neuffer, Elizabeth. "Torruella: A Judge of Law and the Island." *The Boston Globe* (March 4, 1989): 22.

Treaty of Guadalupe Hidalgo (1848)

The Treaty of Guadalupe Hidalgo ended the **Mexican War** on February 2, 1848, and granted the United States nearly half of Mexico's land area, including the territories of California and New Mexico and the independent Republic of Texas, a former Mexican state. The treaty ended a year and a half of warfare between the two countries and completed the westward expansion of the United States. However, the treaty embittered Mexico and harmed Mexican–U.S. relations for decades to come, because Mexico subsequently viewed the United States with suspicion and distrust.

The treaty resulted from the stubborn efforts of the American representative to Mexico, Nicholas Trist. After the United States declared war in May 1846, Mexican forces near the Texas border were quickly defeated and California and New Mexico were captured. However, Mexico refused to surrender the territory. American troops, having landed at Veracruz, began to march inland toward the capital, Mexico City, in early 1847. Trist accompanied this army, seeking to negotiate an end to the conflict and a cession of Mexican lands to the United States. With the U.S. army on the outskirts of Mexico City, the Mexican government agreed to surrender California, but not New Mexico. The U.S. occupied Mexico City, but Trist found no one to negotiate with because the Mexican president, Santa Anna, had fled the city with his army.

American President James K. Polk was forced by Congress to remove Trist as negotiator in October 1847, but Trist did not receive Polk's termination letter until after new negotiations had begun with an interim Mexican president. In January 1848, Trist threatened to end negotiations altogether and demanded a settlement from Mexico. In early February 1848, the treaty was signed and Mexico surrendered the desired territory for a payment of $15 million. The U.S. government also agreed to pay $3 million to U.S. citizens with financial claims against Mexico, relieving Mexico of that burden. On March 10, 1848, the U.S. Senate ratified the treaty. **See also** Acculturation; Biculturalism; Citizenship; Land Rights; Water Rights. **See** Texas Declaration of Independence

(1836); Texas Annexation Treaty (1844); Treaty of Guadalupe Hidalgo (1848) in Appendix 1. (JRB)

BIBLIOGRAPHY

Hammond, George P. *The Treaty of Guadalupe Hidalgo.* Berkeley and Los Angeles: University of California Press, 1949.

Treaty of Paris (1898)

The Treaty of Paris ended the **Spanish-American War.** Under its provisions Spain ceded Puerto Rico, Guam, and the Philippines to the United States and gave up all authority over Cuba. In return, the United States gave Spain $20 million for the nonmilitary public works Spain had built in the Philippine Islands. The U.S. treaty delegation was headed by the former secretary of state William R. Day. Signed on December 10, 1898, the treaty was not ratified by the United States Senate until February 6, 1899. Much of the criticism of the treaty revolved around the taking of the Philippines, because this action made the United States an imperialist power. **See** Treaty of Paris (1898) in Appendix 1.

BIBLIOGRAPHY

Trexel, David. *1898: The Birth of the American Century.* New York: Knopf, 1998.

Treaty of Velasco (1836)

On May 14, 1836, the Treaty of Velasco was signed by General Antonio Lopez de Santa Anna and Texas President David G. Burnet. The treaty occurred after Santa Anna's capture on April 21, 1836, at the Battle of San Jacinto, and it marked a temporary end to hostilities between Texas and Mexico. The treaty itself stated that Texas would thereafter be independent of Mexico and that all Mexican troops in the area would be withdrawn south of the Rio Grande. By doing so, it also made the Rio Grande the unofficial Texas boundary.

Santa Anna later denied certain agreements made in the treaty, and the Mexican government declared the document void because it was made while the general was imprisoned. The Rio Grande boundary mark also became disputed because there was no written qualification as to its official use as a separating line. In the early 1840s, the treaty became the basis for land claims in New Mexico, as well as the Santa Fe Expedition, an ill-fated invasion into the area. It also led the way for the Compromise of 1850, which gave Texas $10 million in exchange for the restructuring of territorial boundaries by the United States government. **See also** Treaty of Guadalupe Hidalgo (1848). **See** Texas Declaration of Independence (1836); Texas Annexation Treaty (1844); Treaty of Guadalupe Hidalgo (1848) in Appendix 1.

BIBLIOGRAPHY

Feherenbach, T.R. *Lone Star: A History of Texas and the Texans.* New York: Macmillan, 1987.

Robert A. Underwood (1948–)

Robert Underwood had a notable career at the University of Guam as instructor and director of the Bilingual Bicultural Training Program from 1976 to 1981, as assistant professor from 1981 to 1983, as dean of the College of Education from 1988 to 1990, and as academic vice president from 1990 to 1992. From 1983 to 1988, he was director of Bilingual Education Assistance for Micronesia. He also served as chair of the Chamorro Language Commission and was a member of the Guam Review Board for Historic Preservation. He was one of the founding members of the Guam Council for Humanities and also was active in the political status task force established by the government of Guam. In 1992 Underwood was elected delegate to the U.S. House of Representatives and was reelected in 1994, 1996, and 1998. In Congress, he serves on the Armed Services, Natural Resources, and Education and Labor Committees.

BIBLIOGRAPHY

Hispanic Americans in Congress. Washington, DC: U.S. Government Printing Office, 1995.

United Farm Workers (UFW)

The United Farm Workers (UFW), an affiliate union of the American Federation of Labor–Congress of Industrial Organizations (AFL-CIO) and founded by **Cesar Chavez** in 1971, continues to be an active organizing group. The union often uses direct-mail campaigns, and it initiated a third grape boycott in 1984 to protest excessive and negligent use of dangerous pesticides by growers.

The union initially started in California in 1962, when **Cesar Chavez**, **Dolores Fernandez Huerta**, and Gil Padilla organized the National Farm Workers Association (NFWA). In August 1966, NFWA merged with the Filipino-dominated Agricultural Workers Organizing Committee (AWOC) to become a new group called the **United Farm Workers Organizing Committee (UFWOC)**. In 1971, the UFWOC became the UFW.

In 1973, the UFW experienced a setback when most grape growers did not renew their contracts with the union but signed with the Teamsters Union instead. The UFW called for a boycott of grapes in response. In 1975 the California legislature enacted the Agricultural Labor Relation Act, which is among the UFW's most significant achievements. The UFW suffered a loss of political power as a result of declining membership and increased labor competition throughout the 1980s and early 1990s. The organization still exists, but does not have the political and economic clout it exercised in the 1960s and 1970s. **See also** Grape Boycott; Lettuce Strikes (Salinas). (SCV)

BIBLIOGRAPHY

London, Joan and Henry Anderson. *So Shall Ye Reap: The Story of Cesar Chavez and the Farmworkers Movement.* New York: Thomas Crowell, 1971.
Meister, Dick and Ann Loftis. *A Long Time Coming: The Struggle to Unionize America's Farm Workers.* New York: Macmillan, 1977.

United Farm Workers Organizing Committee (UFWOC)

The United Farm Workers Organizing Committee (UFWOC) was formed in 1966 through the merger of two labor groups: the Filipino-dominated Agricultural Workers Organizing Committee (AWOC), established in 1960 by the American Federation of Labor–Congress of Industrial Organizations (AFL-CIO), and **Cesar Chavez**'s National Farm Workers Association (NFWA), established in 1962. In 1971, UFWOC was renamed the **United Farm Workers (UFW)**. The process of organizing farm labor involved advocating for safe working conditions and better wages. In 1960 AWOC led a strike against the Di Giorgio and Schenley Liquors farms. Chavez's NFWA joined the struggle. Eventually, the necessity of winning the votes of workers forced Chavez to merge his union with the AWOC. (SCV)

BIBLIOGRAPHY

Meister, Dick and Ann Loftis. *A Long Time Coming: The Struggle to Unionize America's Farm Workers.* New York: Macmillan, 1977.

U.S.–Latin American Relations

Historically, the relationship between the United States and its Latin American neighbors to the south has been one of enforced dependency. In its endeavor to maintain advantage, the United States has shifted its policies over time to fulfill two objectives. The first has been to direct the attention of rival Western European powers away from Latin American countries. The second has been to defend U.S. political and economic interests and maintain dominance in the region. Still, this relationship has not been static, and Latin American countries have over time gained substantial bargaining power, particularly after World War II. Latin Americanist Howard Wiarda (1984) suggests that the relationship has changed from one of domination and unilateralism to one based on cooperation and multilateralism.

The main objective behind early U.S. policy toward Latin America was to minimize the involvement of European powers in the region, such as Great Britain, France, and Spain. The first formal U.S. policy toward Latin America can be found in the Monroe Doctrine, which acknowledged the intention of "a U.S. hemisphere." The doctrine was issued by President James Monroe on December 2, 1823, in response to a decision by the European Holy Alliance to recover Spain's American colonies. Scholar Charles Stansifer (1991) suggests that although the United States in fact lacked the ability to protect the entire hemisphere in the early 1800s, the policy served nonetheless to claim Latin America as its area of influence nonetheless.

The Monroe Doctrine served to legitimize U.S. expansion and control over the frail Latin American governments that had emerged in the wake of several independence movements. Expansion into Mexican territories in the 1840s demonstrated once and for all that rather than "protecting the hemisphere," the United States was pursuing its own interests. While the United States enforced the Monroe Doctrine in 1867 to pressure France to withdraw its forces from Mexico, which France had occupied since 1861, it consistently used the doctrine to promote imperialist expansion by creating a hemispheric organization to encourage close economic relations among countries in the region. This strategy led to the formation of the Pan American Union in October 1889, although this organization ultimately fell short of its proposed objectives. Additionally, the United States intervened where its economic interests were threatened. For example, Michael Kryzanek (1996) suggests that internal political upheavals in Cuba in 1895 threatened economic interests, which included more than $50 million in foreign investment and $100 million in trade. Consequently, President William McKinley ordered a military intervention (the **Spanish-American War**) and forced Spain, under the **Treaty of Paris of 1898**, to grant Cuba independence. In March 1901, however, the United States converted Cuba into its protectorate with the Platt Amendment.

The defeat of Spanish forces marked the emergence of the United States as a geopolitical power and permitted a reexamination of its Latin American policy. United States interventionism was formalized with the passage of the Roosevelt Corollary, which gave the United States broad power to intervene in the internal affairs of hemispheric nations. This policy was first applied in 1905 through military and administrative intervention in both the Dominican Republic and Cuba. However, growing discontent over the policy among Latin Americans had to be taken seriously because the United States used the region as its main supplier of raw material and agricultural products. Shortly after the start of the Great Depression in 1929, the United States overturned this policy and promoted instead a more cooperative arrangement as championed by Franklin D. Roosevelt and his 1933 Good Neighbor policy. The United States agreed to respect the sovereignty of Latin American nations and, as an example, annulled the Platt Amendment and granted Cuba independence in 1934.

After World War II, the United States began to identify Soviet expansion into the hemisphere as a threat and made "national security" the nation's primary policy objective. Similarly, Latin American countries were confronted with increasing discontent as a result of internal inequalities and inadequate access by the masses to social and economic resources. These conditions coincided in Guatemala in the early 1950s in a situation that would repeat itself in Chile in the early 1970s. In both cases, the U.S. government and domestic Latin American elites perceived that the internal reforms initiated by the governments of Jacobo Arbens in Guatemala and Salvador Allende in Chile threatened their economic interests. Consequently, the United States initiated covert operations through the Central Intelligence Agency (CIA) to destabilize these governments and support the rise of the military regimes of Carlos Castillo Arenas in Guatemala (1953) and Augusto Pinochet in Chile (1973).

Discontent in Latin America led the United States to strengthen existing institutions and create new institutions to promote stability in the hemisphere. In 1948 the Organization of American States (OAS) was organized in Bogota, Colombia, as a successor of the Pan American Union. Its main objective, as Federico Gil (1988) suggests, was to foster democratic governance and promote economic cooperation in the region. Eventually, this organization served as a conduit for Latin American countries to express dissatisfaction over U.S. interventionism, such as the failed attempt by the CIA to covertly overthrow the leftist regime of Cuban Fidel Castro in 1961. In addition, the United States began to recognize internal socio-economic and political conditions in Latin America and in 1960 created the Inter-American Development Bank (IDB) as a low-interest lending institution designed to promote development in the region. Subsequent programs were short-lived, such as President John F. Kennedy's Alliance for Progress, intended to aid socio-economic development. Finally, the Carter administration issued a policy against human rights abuses and reduced support for those military regimes with the worst records of abuse. Wiarda (1996) suggests that all these efforts were based on naive assumptions that Latin America could adopt Western-style development. Instead, Latin America experienced little economic growth and, for example, without the United States to support it, Nicaragua fell into the hands of the Sandinistas, who established a leftist regime.

During the 1980s, President Ronald Reagan sought to contain Soviet influence in Latin America, especially El Salvador, by linking internal social discontent with Nicaraguan and Cuban activities. His initial objectives were to destabilize the regimes in both nations, to reduce what he considered communist expansion in Latin America. In this pursuit, Reagan reestablished military and economic support for military regimes, maintained support for right-wing organizations in El Salvador, increased arms sales and military support to non-leftist governments in the region, and supported a covert CIA operation against the Sandinista regime in Nicaragua. Hartlyn et al. (1992) contend that these objectives, coupled with the U.S. invasion of Grenada and U.S. support for Great Britain in the Malvinas–Falkland War against Argentina in 1982, indicated that the United States no longer adhered to the rules of the very regional institutions it helped create. Such indifference on the part of the Reagan groups established a resistance to U.S. policies in Central America. This conflict began to wind down, however, when the five Central American countries signed a regional peace plan put together by Oscar Arias, the president of Costa Rica, in 1987. The plan called for, among other things, internal dialogue, guarantees of democratization, and an end to outside military intervention.

Furthermore, the Reagan administration's economic policies exacerbated the crises that Latin American countries experienced through the 1980s. Roett (1988) indicates that as a result of the liquidity of dollars from the petroleum economic boom of the 1970s and the push to promote U.S.-approved development strategies, Latin American countries accumulated an external debt of more than $200 billion by the early 1980s. In 1981, the Reagan administration defined its economic policies by maintaining high interest rates. This decreased the access of Latin American goods to markets in industrialized nations. Protectionist policies among Western nations created a shortage of exchange currency, which led to further borrowing by Latin American countries to fulfill debt service obligations from previous decades. Consequently, in 1982 Mexico announced that it could no longer honor repayment of its $19.5 billion debt. Mexican financial desperation was followed by economic defaults in most Latin American nations, triggering involvement by the International Monetary Fund (IMF). Currently, the IMF addresses debt renegotiation among Latin American countries on the merits of each country. These countries often have to accept the imposition of orthodox economic adjustment measures, including lowering the rate of inflation, cutting the public deficit, and reducing the money supply. These measures frequently have the effect of raising the cost of basic goods and services and exacerbating, at least in the short run, social inequalities.

The demise of the Soviet Union in 1989 reduced the danger of communist expansionism and later provided the Clinton administration with the opportunity to redefine the U.S. relationship with Latin America. In the process, illegal and legal immigration from Latin America was viewed as the new threat to U.S. national security, a perception encouraged by anti-immigration political environments in Texas, Florida, and California. In addition, the Clinton administration has continued support for democratizing efforts, as depicted by its involvement in Haiti in 1994.

Finally, the Clinton administration secured passage of the North American Free Trade Agreement (NAFTA), proposed by the Bush administration. Viewed as the beginning of a new era of cooperation between the United States and Latin America, Clinton pledged during the Summit of the Americas in December 1994 that the United States would work to expand the free trade zone to Latin America by the year 2005. These efforts, he suggested, would begin immediately with legislation to include Chile as the next participant, although Argentina and Colombia have also made efforts for early inclusion. Despite this assurance, the Clinton administration has been uneasy discussing furthering the expansion of the free trade zone, especially after the Mexican economic crisis of 1995. Certainly, Latin American countries are eager for inclusion in the free trade zone the Clinton administration has promised. Still, critics claim that NAFTA may have, at least in the short run, the same negative socio-economic effects on Latin American countries that earlier IMF-led structural adjustments had. **See also** Immigration Policies and Hispanics. (LAP)

BIBLIOGRAPHY

Gil, Federico G. "The Kennedy–Johnson Years." In John D. Martz, ed. *United States Policy in Latin America: A Quarter Century of Crisis and Change, 1961–1986.* Lincoln: University of Nebraska Press, 1988.

Hartlyn, Johnathan, Lars Shoultz, and Augusto Varas. "Introduction" to Johnathan Hartlyn, Lars Shoultz, and Augusto Varas, eds. *The United States and Latin America in the 1990s: Beyond the Cold War.* Chapel Hill: The University of North Carolina Press, 1992.

Kryzanek, Michael. *US–Latin American Relations.* Westport, CT: Praeger, 1996.

Roett, Riodan. "The Debt Crisis: Economics and Politics." In John D. Martz, ed. *United States Policy in Latin America: A Quarter Century of Crisis and Change, 1961–1986.* Lincoln: University of Nebraska Press, 1988.

Stansifer, Charles. "United States–Central American Relations, 1824–1850." In T. Ray Shurbutt, ed. *United States–Latin American Relations, 1800–1850.* Tuscaloosa: The University of Alabama Press, 1991.

Watson, Cynthia. "Latin America: The New Interdependence and Possibilities for Partnership." In Howard Wiarda, ed. *U.S. Foreign and Strategic Policy in the Post-Cold War Era: A Geopolitical Perspective.* Westport, CT: Greenwood Press, 1996.

Wiarda, Howard. *In Search of Policy: The United States and Latin America.* Washington, DC: American Enterprise Institute for Public Policy Research, 1984.

———. "Introduction. From Cold War to Post Cold War: Change and Continuity in U.S. Foreign and Strategic Policy." In Howard Wiarda, ed. *U.S. Foreign and Strategic Policy in the Post-Cold War Era: A Geopolitical Perspective.* Westport, CT: Greenwood Press, 1996.

Filemon P. Vela (1935–)

After graduating from law school at St. Mary's University in 1962, Filemon Vela entered private practice, also serving as an attorney for the **Mexican American Legal Defense and Educational Fund (MALDEF)**. In 1975, Vela left private practice to serve on the district court of Texas, a post he held until 1980. In that year, President Jimmy Carter appointed Vela to the U.S. District Court for the Southern District of Texas, where he currently still presides.

BIBLIOGRAPHY

American Bar Association. *Directory of Minority Judges in the United States*. Chicago: The Association, 1994.

Brownson, Charles B. *Judicial Staff Directory*. Mt. Vernon, VA: Congressional Staff Directory, 1997.

William C. (Willie) Velasquez (1944–1988)

William C. Velasquez was born May 9, 1944, in Orlando, Florida. He was raised in San Antonio, Texas, where he completed his education and in 1974 founded the **Southwest Voter Registration Education Project** and the Southwest Voter Research Institute in 1984, directing both until his death on June 15, 1988. Velasquez's principal concern was voter registration, voter education, and voting activity to increase Latino **political participation** and improve the political and social position of the Southwest's minority Mexican-American population. Through the project, Velasquez made a lasting contribution to political participation by Southwest Mexican-Americans. The project operated in five southwestern states and performed hundreds of voter registration education campaigns. In cooperation with the **Mexican American Legal Defense and Education Fund (MALDEF)**, the project won numerous voting rights lawsuits defending the political rights of minorities in the Southwest. Both of Velasquez's organizations engaged in litigation to assure that southwestern electoral systems complied with the **Voting Rights Act of 1965**. **See also** Mexican American Youth Organization (MAYO); Voting Rights. (SCV)

BIBLIOGRAPHY

Katz, Jesse. "Pomona Puts Up Tough Fight for Its Election System." *Los Angeles Times* (June 15, 1986): 1.

Rose, Andy. "Group Regards Latino Vote as Sleeping Giant to Be Awakened." *Los Angeles Times* (November 17, 1986): 1.

Nydia M. Velazquez (1953–)

Nydia Velazquez was the first Hispanic woman to serve on the New York City Council and the first Puerto Rican woman elected to Congress. In 1992 she was able to win the Democratic Party nomination from Stephen J. Solarz, a nine-term incumbent. She won the general election to New York's 12th District with more than 75 percent of the vote, and in 1994 and in 1998 she was reelected with by large majorities. Prior to entering Congress, she worked as a special assistant to Congressman Edolphus Towns in 1983. In 1984, she served on the New York City Council. From May 1986 to July 1989, she was the national director of the Migration Division Office in the Depart-

Nydia M. Valezquez (D-NY) is the first Puerto Rican woman to serve in Congress. *Courtesy of U.S. House of Representatives.*

ment of Labor and Human Resources of Puerto Rico. From 1989 to 1992 she was director of the Department of Puerto Rican Community Affairs in the United States for the Commonwealth of Puerto Rico. **See also** Political Leadership.

BIBLIOGRAPHY

Hispanic Americans in Congress. Washington, DC: U.S. Government Printing Office, 1995.

Telgen, Diane and Jim Kamp, eds. *Notable Hispanic American Women*. Detroit: Gale, 1993.

Catalina Vasquez Villapando (1940–)

In 1989 Catalina Vasquez Villapando was appointed the 39th treasurer of the United States. Prior to this, she had served as President Ronald Reagan's White House special assistant for public liaison from 1983 to 1985 and as the director of the Republican Party of Texas. Villapando stepped down as treasurer in January 1993 and pleaded guilty to tax fraud in February 1994.

BIBLIOGRAPHY

"Ex-US Treasurer Admits Tax Fraud." *Newsday* (February 18, 1994): 19.

Viva Kennedy Club

The Viva Kennedy Club movement was established during the 1960 presidential elections to support Democratic candidate John F. Kennedy. Kennedy was seen as being sympathetic, understanding, and supportive of Latino political, economic, and social needs. The group was lead by **Hector Garcia**, one of the country's leading Mexican-American **civil rights** leaders, and Carlos McCormick, who, like Garcia, was a member of the **American G.I. Forum**. Numerous Viva Kennedy Clubs originated from Garcia and McCormick's efforts, and soon many Mexican Americans began to involve themselves enthusiastically in the electoral process for the first time. The movement not only contributed to Kennedy's presidential victory, but it also provided confidence and support to Hispanic leaders across the nation. After the election, members of the Viva Kennedy campaign helped organize the Texas-based Mexican Americans for Political Action and also established the **Political Association of Spanish-Speaking Organizations**. **See also** Acculturation; Assimilation; Political Participation.

BIBLIOGRAPHY

Navarrette, Ruben, Jr. "Latinos: The Forgotten Democratic Constituency." *Los Angeles Times,* (November 10, 1992): 3.

Voting Patterns

Voting patterns are discovered by gathering information about how many voters vote for or against a particular issue or candidate in a specific location. For example, the data may show distinct voting patterns in precincts where minority residents prevail. In political campaigns involving minority groups, researchers may give attention to patterns of interaction between the individual and his or her social group. For example, during the **La Raza Unida Party** campaigns in **Crystal City, Texas**, in the early 1970s, Latino candidates were threatened by the majority Anglo-American population who controlled the town's economy and institutions. The impact of the elections on the community political structure in south Texas towns and in state regions with majority Mexican-American populations was another factor influencing the vote.

On one occasion, county officials disqualified a Latino candidate because he did not own property, but with the help of the **Mexican American Legal Defense and Education Fund (MALDEF)**, his candidacy was reinstated. Such a political situation affected both minority and majority voting patterns. The La Raza Unida Party campaign in Crystal City and other nearby towns threatened also to undermine total control by Anglo-Americans of the school boards and town councils, further motivating disparate voting patterns.

The study of elections and voting decisions is one way to examine political behavior. It is well documented that except in New Mexico, Mexican Americans vote less than Anglo-Americans and often less than African Americans as well.

Political behavior is especially important to the electoral process. **William C. "Willie" Velasquez,** founder and director of the **Southwest Voter Registration Education Project,** worked to promote voter education. The project conducted registration education campaigns in more than 1,000 southwestern cities and Native American Reservations. This initiative resulted in thousands of new voters and heightened **political participation**, successfully changing Mexican-American voter patterns. For example, voter registration among Hispanics in Arizona rose 65 percent between 1976 and 1988, from 92,500 to 141,900.

Increasing participation in the electoral process of Mexican Americans, however, may require more than registration. Education in voting procedures, understanding of issues, investigating the candidates, and learning how to hold officials accountable are all important as well. In addition, for generations the majority of Mexican Americans from California, Texas, and other southwestern areas suffered social, psychological, and cultural barriers to participation in the electoral process. Where Mexican Americans were in the minority, aspirants would not run for office because of the unlikelihood of winning an election when the majority Anglo-Americans would vote only for their own candidates. Occasionally, however, white voters did cross racial lines, especially when a candidate ran as a member of one of the two major political parties. In Arizona, **Raul Castro** was elected governor in 1974 with the support of the Democratic Party, which included voters from diverse ethnic groups.

During the **Chicano Power Movement**, however, the La Raza Unida Party and other organizations were confronting decades of discrimination that limited their ability to participate. Historically, such barriers have included the poll tax, literacy tests, and annual registration requirements. Indeed, literacy tests as a requirement for voting have only recently been abolished. For years, gerrymandering denied representation to minority voters as well, through various procedures, including "at-large" voting districts, in which the majority won all the elected positions because the majority in the district as a whole could outvote the minority. Similarly, through "cracking," districts were fragmented throughout two or more voting boundaries. In "stacking," a minority population was placed within larger Anglo-American majority districts. Finally, in "packing," the minority-elected official was outnumbered by other district representatives. Such political strategies on the part of those in control were employed throughout the Southwest to disenfranchise the Mexican-American voter, systematically affecting voting patterns.

Chicano political organizations in the Southwest confronted these barriers. The results were significant gains in La Raza voter registration—and subsequently greater voter turnout, thus changing voter patterns in the Southwest significantly.

The **Voting Rights Act of 1965** (extended by the **Voting Rights Act of 1970** and the **Voting Rights Act Amendments of 1975**), further promoted political participation and affected voting patterns.

Voting patterns may further be influenced by socio-economic characteristics associated with low levels of political activity, such as low formal education (about 50 percent of Chicanos currently do not complete high school, and in the 1950s and 1960s this percentage was still higher), low income and occupational level, and rural background. United States census statistics place relatively large percentages of Hispanics within these disadvantageous categories. When such socio-economic factors are combined with systemic factors such as gerrymandering and social threats, results can be extremely negative for minority populations. For example, in California, where Latinos make up more than 25 percent of the population, they hold only 7 percent of elected positions Exacerbating this situation, poverty and low-paying jobs generally correlate with low levels of both naturalization and political participation. The 1990 U.S. census showed that while family income had improved overall, 25 percent of Mexican-origin families were still below the poverty level.

Another personal statistic that influences voter patterns is the age level of the voters. The median age of Mexican Americans in 1990 was 24.3 years, but for the non-Hispanic population it was 33.8 years. The fact that Mexican Americans have a proportionately much larger population under the voting age than non-Hispanics helps explain why Mexican Americans, despite their numbers, have not achieved greater political participation.

Another factor in voting patterns is the discrepancy between potential voters and those registered. This discrepancy may involve the aforementioned systemic and socio-economic barriers to political participation by Mexican Americans, but there is undoubtedly a psychological barrier as well. There is widely held cynicism among Mexican Americans about the political processes, politicians, and local governments that affect their lives. In part, the causes of this cynicism may be historical in nature, stemming from a long negative experience both in Mexico and in the southwestern states, regions, and localities, where governments and groups with political power have failed to promote justice and have used politics to institutionalize racism. As a result, many Mexican Americans have been estranged from the political process. A smaller percentage of Mexican Americans follow political affairs, discuss politics with friends, and can identify members of the city council more readily than Anglo-Americans or African Americans can.

At the same time, when a well-liked Mexican-American candidate ran for office, the Southwest Voter Registration Education Project and other organizations made it easy for Mexican Americans to register. Mexican Americans in great numbers registered as a show of support. The **Viva Kennedy** Clubs had just such an effect on Mexican Americans and other minorities in the 1960s. These clubs believed that positive change could be made through the electoral process, and members were motivated to register and vote in great numbers. Registration became easy because a registrar would go directly to the home of a potential voter. But while the potential to vote existed, voting required time, transportation, knowledge, discussion (elections are many times filled with referendums, funding issues, bond elections, and other concerns that can be difficult to understand) as well as an inner motivation to act. Many people are unwilling or unable to make the commitment to vote on election day.

There remains a need to study the relationship between low socio-economic status and voting. Characteristics such as low wages, low educational attainment, inadequate housing, transportation problems, and the requirements of manual labor may act as barriers to voting. Therefore, it became necessary in the 1960s during the Chicano Movement to found the MALDEF, the **Southwest Voter Registration Education Project**, and other organizations to challenge barriers to electoral participation.

In addition to individual, ethnic group, and political process voting patterns, the institutional voting patterns of governing bodies and courts are apt subjects for study. Groups representing special interests attempt to affect the way votes are cast, creating powerful and well-financed groups that often spend millions of dollars to influence voting. Voting tendencies on issues such as immigration, abortion, English-language use, welfare programs, health programs, and education can all be tracked to discern meaningful patterns. **See also** Economic Equality; Voting Rights; Voting Rights Act Amendments of 1982. (SCV)

BIBLIOGRAPHY

Boskoff, Alvin and Harmon Zeigler. *Voting Patterns in a Local Election.* New York: J.B. Lippincott, 1964.

Heer, David M. *Undocumented Mexicans in the United States.* Cambridge: Cambridge University Press, 1990.

Roberts, Sam. *Who We Are: A Portrait of America Based on the Latest U.S. Census.* New York: Times Books, 1995.

Voting Rights

The right to vote lies at the core of democratic political systems. It is the basic feature of a democratic polity that makes all other political rights significant.

In the early United States, the franchise (the legal right to vote) was quite restricted. Among the most important developments in the political history of the United States has been the expansion of the franchise. The struggle for the right to vote has been a lengthy process, lasting more than 200 years. It has not been smooth or simple; surges of democratization have sometimes been followed by setbacks, and victories have been achieved only through vigorous political activism. The right to vote has been expanded mostly through constitutional amendments, acts of Congress, and Supreme Court decisions.

Although the Declaration of Independence declares that "all men are created equal," the right to vote initially was denied most Americans. The authors of the Constitution allowed the states to decide who should vote, and in some states as few as 10 percent of white males could vote, where in other states as many as 80 percent could.

Controversial property qualifications existed in many states. Some argued that only those with an economic stake in society should have a say in political life. Because the Constitution gave states the power to regulate suffrage, the elimination of property requirements came only gradually. By the 1820s, most property requirements were gone, although some lingered to mid-century.

By the time of the Civil War, state action had significantly expanded the rights of white men. Nevertheless, slaves, Native Americans, and free southern blacks could not vote, although northern blacks could vote in a few states. Women's voting rights were confined to local elections in a few states.

The **American Civil War** began the long, slow, and often violent process of extending full citizenship to blacks. Between 1865 and 1870, the Thirteenth, Fourteenth, and Fifteenth Amendments were passed to give political rights to former slaves and to protect voting rights. For a short time after the ratification of these amendments, blacks voted and were even elected to office in the South, where 90 percent of African Americans lived. They could exercise these rights in part because of a federal military presence, and because the federal government monitored southern politics closely during Reconstruction.

The brief enfranchisement of African Americans ended, however, after 1877, when southern Democrats regained control of state governments after federal troops were withdrawn after Reconstruction. The removal of black and minority voting rights was then systematically legitimized in southern constitutions and laws through a series of changes to the electoral system that obstructed many from voting. By the 1920s, voting in the South among blacks, other minorities, and poor whites had been virtually eliminated.

The southern states attached conditions to the right to vote that did not violate the Fifteenth Amendment as such, but which minorities could nevertheless not meet. These disenfranchising devices were created gradually. For example, Georgia retained as law a poll tax from the time when the payment of taxes was a common requirement for voting. In 1877, Georgia moved to make this poll tax permanent and added a literacy test during its constitutional convention in 1890. Florida and Tennessee followed suit quickly thereafter, followed by Arkansas in 1894.

After 1896, the remaining southern states acted similarly by introducing poll tax laws where none had existed, making the amount of the poll tax higher, even charging would-be voters retroactively. In Texas, a poll tax had first been proposed in 1875, on the ostensible grounds that it would eliminate "irresponsible voters." But Texas was the birthplace and organizing center of the Farmers' Alliance, and it was not until 1902 that a state constitutional amendment establishing the poll tax was approved, this time as a white-supremacy measure. Actually, poll taxes had reduced voting participation among both whites and nonwhites in five southern states, but it brought greater hardship on minorities, a higher proportion of whom were poor. Furthermore, the poll tax was unequally enforced among whites and nonwhites. The result was that poll tax states had voter turnout in national elections equal to only about 50 percent of those in states without poll taxes.

Southern states added literacy tests to poll tax barriers. The political purpose behind the literacy test was to disenfranchise Native Americans, blacks, Mexican Americans, and Asians. To overcome the opposition of poor and illiterate whites, who would also be disenfranchised by these measures, grandfather clauses and "fighting grandfather" (pertaining to those whose grandfathers had served in the Confederate army) clauses were introduced to exempt illiterate whites threatened with disenfranchisement. The grandfather clause assured the franchise for those who could prove their grandfathers had voted prior to 1867. Meanwhile, southern states granted local election officers latitude to enforce these new procedures unevenly and selectively. Literacy tests, for example, could be administered differently at different sites and for various groups of people.

Finally, the "white" primary was adopted by conservative Democrats to exclude minorities from participating in the selection of nominees for the general election. Because Democrats always won general elections in the South, the most important contests were the Democratic primaries. The U.S. Supreme Court, in *Grovey v. Townsend* (1935), upheld such exclusion.

Less formal means were also used to exclude minorities from voting. Registrars often closed their offices when blacks or other minorities tried to register, or whites threatened minorities with the loss of their jobs or housing if they tried to vote. Polling places were sometimes moved at the last minute without notifying potential voters. If these means failed, whites threatened violence.

Over time, the Supreme Court and Congress outlawed these barriers to minority voting in the South. In *Guinn v. United States* (1915), the Court invalidated the grandfather clause, and in *Smith v. Allwright* (1944), the Court invalidated the white primary. The poll tax was eliminated next. In 1962, Congress proposed a constitutional amendment to prohibit poll taxes in presidential or congressional elections. According to the Twenty-fourth Amendment in 1964, the poll tax could be collected only for state and local elections. The Supreme Court, however, disallowed even these non-federal poll taxes, when in *Harper v. Virginia State Board of Elections* (1966) it nullified a Virginia law requiring voters to pay a poll tax to vote in non-federal elections.

As soon as the federal courts invalidated one set of barriers to voter participation, the southern states quickly established other discriminatory techniques to perpetuate conservative white dominance at state and local levels. Even after the demise of the white primary and poll taxes, opponents of minority voting rights continued to devise methods to reduce the political influence of ethnic minorities in the South. The conservative-dominated state legislatures established a registration law that was almost as restrictive as the poll tax had been. Annual registration was required almost a year in advance of the general election. Other practices included the gerrymandering of districts, the use of at-large elections, the selective annexation of Anglo suburbs to dilute minority voting strength, voter intimidation, and selective enforcement of electoral laws. These obstacles, coupled with elections fraught with corruption, resulted in the weakening of minority voting strength.

The major legal weapons against such discriminatory practices turned out to be reapportionment lawsuits and the resulting **Voting Rights Act of 1965**, which was extended to the Southwest by the **Voting Rights Act Amendments of 1975**. The reapportionment battles began with *Reynolds v. Sims* (1964), in which the Supreme Court ruled that each legislator in a state's legislative body should represent an equal number of people.

One of the most significant pieces of federal legislation since Reconstruction, the 1965 Voting Rights Act, made it illegal to interfere with anyone's right to vote. A major success of the **civil rights** movement, this act suspended the use of literacy tests and, most important, sent federal voter registrars into counties where less than 50 percent of the voting age population was registered—under the premise that if so few potential voters had registered, there must have existed serious barriers to registration. Those who sought through intimidation to deter minorities from voting now had to face the federal government. The Voting Rights Act was renewed and expanded in 1970, 1975, and 1982. It now covers more states and other minorities, such as Hispanics, Asians, Native Americans, and Eskimos, and thus serves as a basic protection for minority voting rights. For example, states must provide bilingual ballots in counties in which 5 percent or more of the local population does not speak English. In most instances, this has alleviated the language barrier for Hispanics unable to read English.

The 1982 amendments of the Voting Rights Act and the act's subsequent judicial interpretation expanded the applicability of the act. In addition to protecting minorities' voting rights, the act now requires states with large minority populations to draw boundaries that will increase the probability that minorities will win seats. After the 1990 census, 11 new congressional districts were created for African Americans, and 6 for Hispanics. All but one district were then won by blacks and Hispanics in the 1992 elections. Partly as result of this **redistricting**, blacks were elected to Congress for the first time since Reconstruction in states such as Alabama, Florida, North Carolina, South Carolina, and Virginia. Hispanics were elected for the first time in Illinois and New Jersey. In all, 39 blacks and 19 Hispanics were elected to Congress, a dramatic increase from the 25 African Americans and 10 Hispanics serving before the 1992 election. Hispanics have thus dramatically improved their representation in national political office, from a little more than 3,000 Hispanic public officials in 1985 to nearly 5,200 in 1998.

In sum, although progress seems slow, Hispanics, like other ethnic groups, are beginning to achieve political clout through elections. **See also** Discrimination; Political Participation; Voting Rights Act of 1970; Voting Rights Act Amendments of 1982. (NM)

BIBLIOGRAPHY

Bensel, Richard F. *Sectionalism and American Political Development.* Madison: University of Wisconsin Press, 1984.

Garcia, John A. "The Voting Rights Act and Hispanic Political Representation in the Southwest." *Publius: The Journal of Federalism* 16 (1986): 49–66.

Harris, Joseph P. *Registration of Voters in the United States.* Washington, DC: Brookings Institution, 1929.

Klepner, Paul et al. *The Evolution of American Electoral Systems.* Westport, CT: Greenwood Press, 1981.

Phillips, Kevin P., and Paul H. Blackman. *Electoral Reform and Voter Participation.* Stanford, CA: American Enterprise Institute and the Hoover Institute of War, Revolution, and Peace, 1975.

Villarreal, Roberto E., Norma G. Hernandez, and Howard D. Neighbor. *Latino Empowerment: Progress, Problems, and Prospects.* New York: Greenwood Press, 1988.

Viteritti, Joseph P. "Unapportioned Justice: Local Elections, Social Science and the Evolution of the Voting Right Act." *Cornell Journal of Law and Public Policy* (Fall 1994): 210–70.

Williamson, Chilton. *American Suffrage from Property to Democracy.* Princeton, NJ: Princeton University Press, 1960.

Voting Rights Act of 1965

One of the most significant pieces of federal legislation since Reconstruction, the 1965 Voting Rights Act held out greater promise for minorities than mere reapportionment. In direct response to marches and demonstrations throughout the South (particularly in Selma, Alabama), the act sought to eliminate restrictions on voting that had been used to discriminate against blacks and other minority groups. The act was structured to severely limit the power of states to control registration and voting, and to allow federal supervision of the voting process. In any state or political subdivision where less than 50 percent of persons of voting age had been registered to vote in the November 1964 election, the act specified that the following legal devices would be suspended: literacy and "constitutional understanding" tests, requirements of educational achievement or knowledge in a particular subject, and "good moral character" requirements. In addition, the act gave the U.S. attorney general the power to appoint federal "voting examiners" to oversee voter registration in counties with a particularly bad record of **discrimination**.

As did African Americans, Hispanic Americans benefited from the Supreme Court's rulings on the Voting Rights Act of 1965. In *Katzenbach v. Morgan* (1966), for example, the Court upheld a portion of the act that outlawed the use of an English literacy test in New York. However, the act's potential for Hispanic Americans was not fully realized until it was extended and amended in 1970. When the act came up for renewal in 1970, Congress made permanent the national ban on literacy tests; in subsequent years, Congress has extended and toughened the act's requirements even further, most notably requiring that bilingual voting information be provided to citizens. **See also** Political Participation; Voting Patterns; Voting Rights; Voting Rights Act of 1970; Voting Rights Act Amendments of 1975; Voting Rights Act Amendments of 1982. (NM)

BIBLIOGRAPHY

Bell, Derrick A., Jr. *Race, Racism, and American Law.* Boston: Little, Brown, 1980.

Phillips, Kevin P. and Paul H. Blackman. *Electoral Reform and Voter Participation.* Stanford, CA: American Enterprise Institute and the Hoover Institution of War and Peace, 1975.

Voting Rights Act of 1970

The 1970 Voting Rights Act lowered the voting age so that qualified citizens who were 18 years old could vote. Previous attempts to enfranchise people at this age occurred during World War II, and pressure to lower the voting age continued to build during the Vietnam War, when people who were 18 to 20 years old were once again asked to risk their lives for their country but were then denied the right to vote. In 1970 the Supreme Court reviewed *Oregon v. Mitchell*, which dealt with the constitutionality of this statutory approach (making the changes by making a law to that effect). The Court found that Congress had the authority to extend the vote to people who were 18 years old; at the same time, however, the Court stated that Congress did not have the authority to establish similar voter qualifications for state and local elections. The Court's decision raised the prospect of dual voting systems, one for federal elections and another for state and local elections. In an effort to standardize the law, Congress moved rapidly to pass the Twenty-sixth Amendment in 1971, which extended voting rights to people 18 years old and older. **See also** Political Participation; Voting Patterns; Voting Rights; Voting Rights Act of 1965; Voting Rights Act Amendments of 1975; Voting Rights Act Amendments of 1982. (VDD)

BIBLIOGRAPHY

Garcia, John A. "The Voting Rights Act and Hispanic Political Representation in the Southwest." *Publius* 16 (1986): 49–66.

Villarreal, Roberto E., Norma G. Hernandez and Howard D. Neighbor. *Latino Empowerment: Progress, Problems and Prospects.* New York: Greenwood Press, 1988.

Voting Rights Act Amendments of 1975

The **Voting Rights Act of 1965** sought to guarantee the right of African Americans to vote, particularly in southern states. The most important features of the 1965 law were the suspension of literacy tests and the assignment of federal voting registrars to those states and counties that had seen fewer than half the eligible African-American population vote in the 1964 election. The Voting Rights Act Amendments of 1975, however, changed the focus of the legislation when the **civil rights** movement succeeded in supplanting the notion of equal opportunity with the notion of equal results. Thus, the right to vote was equated with the right of minorities to elect minority candidates. To accomplish this outcome, the 1975 amendments entitled Hispanic, Asian, Native American, and Alaskan native voters to ballots in their own languages. Additionally, the jurisdiction in which members of these groups lived became subject to extensive monitoring of their electoral process. **See also** Political Participation; Voting Patterns; Voting Rights; Voting Rights Act of 1970; Voting Rights Act Amendments of 1982.

BIBLIOGRAPHY

Thernstrom, Abigail. *Whose Votes Count? Affirmative-Action and Minority Voting Rights.* Cambridge, MA: Harvard University Press, 1987.

Voting Rights Act Amendments of 1982

The Voting Rights Act Amendments of 1982 extended the original **Voting Rights Act of 1965** to include the process of redistricting. Redistricting occurs each decade as the U.S. Census Bureau counts the nation's population; the 435 seats of the House of Representatives are reapportioned to reflect significant changes in each state's population. Based on the 1982 amendments, and following the 1990 census, state legislatures designated "minority" districts in which minorities became the majority of these districts' voting populations. Not all states, however, were in compliance with the 1982 law. In 1988 the U.S. Department of Justice charged the Los Angeles County Board of Supervisors with discriminating against Hispanics in its 1981 redistricting plan. As a result, *Garza v. County of Los Angeles*, a Voting Rights Act lawsuit, resulted in the creation of a Hispanic majority district, which elected assemblywoman **Gloria Molina** to the County Board of Supervisors. **See also** Political Participation; Voting Patterns; Voting Rights; Voting Rights Act of 1970; Voting Rights Act Amendments of 1975. (VDD)

BIBLIOGRAPHY

Wasserman, Gary. *The Basics of American Politics.* New York: Harper Collins, 1994.

Welfare Reform

In August 1996, President Bill Clinton signed HR 3734, the Personal Responsibility and Work Opportunity Reconciliation Act of 1996, into law. He claimed the new law would end "welfare as we know it." The U.S. welfare system had long been criticized for contributing to chronic dependency, and HR 3734 was intended to reform the national welfare system in a way that promoted work, marriage, and personal responsibility.

The welfare system in place before 1996 had operated for six decades. There are 77 major federal welfare programs, most of which are "means-tested," which means they provide aid directly to people in the form of cash, food, housing, and medical care on the basis of the recipient's income. Of these programs, Aid to Families with Dependent Children (AFDC) has come to be regarded as the cornerstone of the U.S. welfare system. AFDC has been the primary cash benefit program targeted to the poor, and it was premised on the idea of entitlement. Entitlement meant two things in the AFDC program: first, a federally defined guarantee of assistance to families with children who met the statutory definition of need and complied with other conditions of the law, and second, a similar guarantee to the states that the federal government would provide a matching share of money to help those who qualified for help. AFDC provided cash payments to children of families whose fathers or mothers were absent, incapacitated, deceased, or unemployed, and to certain others in the household of those children. All 50 states, the District of Columbia, Puerto Rico, and Guam operated AFDC programs, each of which determined its own benefits levels and, within certain federal restrictions, eligibility requirements. Funding thus came from both the federal and state governments, with the federal portion varying from 50 to 80 percent. On average, the federal government provided 55 percent of such AFDC funding.

The 1996 law replaced the AFDC program with Temporary Assistance for Needy Families (TANF). Under AFDC, every dollar that a state appropriated was matched by $1 to $4 of federal money, with a more generous matching formula for poorer states. Under TANF, states get a federal block grant with an essentially fixed dollar amount. If a state wants to spend more than it has in the past, either because the cost of living has risen, the number of single mothers who need help has increased, or mothers who have hit their time limit still cannot find work, that state will have to pay the remainder of the cost from its own funds. Conversely, if a state limits eligibility for TANF or cuts benefits, it can, within very broad limits, keep every dollar that it saves.

The 1996 plan also set a five-year maximum lifetime limit on benefits and prescribed stringent work requirements for recipients. States are required to have 25 percent of their recipients working by 1998, and 50 percent by 2002. This provision, reformers argued, would end chronic welfare dependency permanently.

Immigrant benefit reform was a significant part of the 1996 legislation as well. In fact, the new welfare bill had its greatest effect on immigrants. Legal immigrants who are not citizens are barred from receiving food stamps, federal disability, and virtually all other means-tested federal assistance, even though they pay taxes. Under the new provisions, most immigrants currently in the country and nearly all future legal immigrants will be denied Supplemental Security Income (SSI) and food stamps. The SSI cuts are the most extensive. In 1997, almost 800,000 legal immigrants received SSI, and most of these people would be removed from the rolls. New immigrants would be excluded from most federal means-tested programs, including Medicaid, for the first five years they are in the country. Such a cut was projected to save $22 billion over next six years, accounting for about 40 percent of the savings in the bill.

The extensive cuts were made despite the lack of evidence that immigrants contribute significantly to the welfare rolls. In fact, legal immigrants use welfare at approximately the same rate as native-born Americans. Still, even those figures may overstate welfare use by immigrants, because most immigrant welfare use is either by refugees who of necessity come to the United States with few assets or by elderly immigrants who frequently use SSI as a substitute for Social Security, to which they are not entitled. Those two groups represent only 21 percent of the immigrant population, but they account for 40 percent of immigrant welfare use. With the exception of those groups, immigrants use welfare slightly less than native-born Americans. Moreover, immigrants as a group pay more in taxes that they consume in government services.

Illegal immigrants, on the other hand, use less welfare than legal immigrants, both because they are ineligible for many programs and because they fear that applying for services means they will be detected and deported. Illegal immigrants from Mexico, for example, are often portrayed as a drain on welfare, even though only 2 percent use AFDC or Medicaid. Use of food stamps is only slightly higher, while use of most other welfare programs is lower.

Despite this evidence, welfare reform was politically attractive for lawmakers as well as the president. Since the explosion of the welfare rolls in the 1960s, more people began to assert their right to welfare, while every president has attempted to reform the system. Until the 1960s, a relatively small portion of eligible people received benefits. The welfare rights movement and subsequent court decisions encouraged women to claim assistance for which they were eligible and made it difficult for authorities to deny assistance. As a result, the number of women claiming benefits went from less than one-third to fully nine-tenths.

But subsequent demographic changes in the welfare program would spur calls for reform. The original welfare provisions were designed to help widows with children, the "deserving" poor. The provisions began in the 1920s and were the outgrowth of mothers' pensions. With small pensions from the state, these women would not have to leave home to go to work. In 1935, the Economic Security Act, or Social Security Act, as it is more popularly called, replaced state provisions. Included in the 1935 act was the Aid to Dependent Children program, later renamed Aid to Families with Dependent Children. Following the welfare rights movement, the number of widows on the rolls decreased while the number of unwed mothers increased, as did the proportion of women of color. By the 1960s, widows made up only about half of the recipients.

In addition to the increase in welfare rolls, demographic changes in the 1970s placed the system under close scrutiny, especially by conservatives. At the start of the 1970s, the number of women working outside the home increased, making it difficult to argue that women should be paid to stay out of the workforce to take care of their children. Welfare, reformers argued, was now going to those less deserving of it.

Since the 1970s, welfare reform has been part of every president's domestic agenda. President Richard Nixon proposed a "Family Assistance Plan" as his domestic policy centerpiece, a proposal that sought to eliminate welfare and provide direct cash assistance to all families instead. President Gerald Ford's 1974 Income Supplementation Plan was an enlarged version of Nixon's Family Assistance Plan. When President Jimmy Carter took office in 1977, he made welfare reform an early priority by unveiling the Program for Better Jobs and Income. All these programs, however, failed to receive enough support from Congress to become law.

It was not until 1988 that Congress would pass a major piece of welfare-reform legislation. Called the Family Support Act, this bill was based on extensive state experimentation in the 1980s with new welfare-to-work initiatives. Still, the Family Support Act was never fully implemented, largely because of a general recession that rendered the states unable to provide the matching funds necessary to receive their share of job-related federal money.

Welfare reform in the 1990s succeeded largely because of calls for budget cuts to control the national budget deficit. But welfare reform also reflected a shift toward conservative thinking across the nation. For example, voters in California took welfare reform one step further by voting **California Proposition 187** into law in 1994. This law made **illegal aliens** ineligible for public social services, public health care services (unless for an emergency, as required under federal law), and public school education at elementary, secondary, and postsecondary levels. Falling benefits and tighter eligibility standards, policy makers in California and Washington, D.C., argued, would force more people into work, remove the "undeserving" poor from the public rolls, and in the process produce savings for taxpayers. **See also** Conservatism; Economic Equality; Liberalism.

BIBLIOGRAPHY

Anderson, Martin. *Welfare: The Political Economy of Welfare Reform in the United States*. Stanford, CA: Hoover Institution Press, 1978.

Edelman, Peter. "The Worst Thing Bill Clinton Has Done." *The Atlantic Monthly* (March 1997): 43–58.

Galambos, Louis, ed. *The New American State: Bureaucracies and Policies since World War II*. Baltimore: Johns Hopkins University Press, 1987.

Haveman, Robert H., ed. *A Decade of Federal Antipoverty Programs: Achievements, Failures, and Lessons*. New York: Academic Press, 1977.

Hero, Rodney E. *Latinos and the U.S. Political System: Two-Tiered Pluralism*. Philadelphia: Temple University Press, 1992.

Jencks, Christopher. "The Hidden Paradox of Welfare Reform." *The American Prospect* (May–June 1997): 33–40.

Skolnick, Arlene. "Family Values: The Sequel." *The American Prospect* (May–June 1997): 86–94.

Tanner, Michael. *The End of Welfare: Fighting Poverty in the Civil Society*. Washington, DC: Cato Institute, 1996.

Young Lords

In the late 1960s, Puerto Rican youths in Chicago began a street gang called the Young Lords, whose primary motivation was to address community concerns and to stop police harassment. In New York City, several already existing Puerto Rican groups merged to form the Young Lords Party. The New York chapter started a radio program and a biweekly newspaper. In addition, the New York Young Lords held several events to bring attention to Puerto Rican community problems. The first such event was held in 1969 and involved building road blockades and piling up garbage to point out poor sanitation conditions. The second event involved occupying a church for 11 days in 1970 and organizing food programs, collecting clothing, and offering classes. It was estimated that 3,000 people participated in this event. Also in that year, the Young Lords occupied an abandoned building in the Bronx and offered tests for lead poisoning and tuberculosis and day care for children. One of their members was arrested for burning garbage and died of strangulation in jail, which the police called a suicide. The funeral had a march that attracted 8,000 people, and the organization announced its intent to change its no arms policy. In 1973 the organization changed its name to the Puerto Rican Revolutionary Workers Organization. The prominence of the group waned as its more radical tactics were no longer considered appropriate. **See also** Chicago Riots of 1966; Community Organizations; Political Participation.

BIBLIOGRAPHY

Gonzales, David. "About New York; Young Lords: Vital in 60's, A Model Now." *The New York Times* (October 16, 1996): 1.

Raul Yzaguirre (1939–)

Since 1974, Raul Yzaguirre has served as president of the **National Council of La Raza,** which advances the social and economic well-being of Hispanic Americans. From the 1960s on, he has been one of the leading activists seeking to improve the lives of Hispanic Americans. His organization has sponsored programs to increase voter participation, improve the level of economic resources, and fight **discrimination** against Hispanics throughout the nation. Yzaguirre was appointed in 1994 as a member of President Bill Clinton's "Initiative on Race" but resigned from the panel in 1996 over differences of opinion as to the group's mission.

BIBLIOGRAPHY

Christie, Rick. "Q&A with Raul Yzaguirre." *The Atlanta Journal and Constitution* (December 12, 1997): 17A.

Holmes, Steven A. "Hispanic Rights Chief Quits Clinton Panel." *New York Times* (April 14, 1996): 20.

Z

Judith Zaffirini (1946–)

Judith Zaffirini, a Democrat, represents the 21st Senatorial District of Texas. Elected in 1986 to the state senate from a field of four Democrats and two Republicans, she was reelected in 1996 with a 2-to-1 margin districtwide and a 3-to-1 margin in her hometown. This was her third landslide victory in which she carried all counties in the large and diverse district, something no one else has ever accomplished. Zaffirini is the first Hispanic woman senator in Texas to serve as president pro tempore of the Texas Senate.

BIBLIOGRAPHY

Telgen, Diane and Jim Kemp, eds. *Notable Hispanic American Women.* Detroit: Gale, 1993.

Zimmerman Telegram

The Zimmerman telegram was a 1917 proposal to Mexican President Venustiano Carranza by the German government. The message asked that Mexico form an alliance with Germany during World War I; in return, Germany, if victorious, offered to return to the Mexican government the southwestern part of the United States that was lost in the **Mexican War.** On January 16, 1917, the telegram was intercepted and the plot was revealed to the U.S. government. Recognizing the dangers of a potential Mexican–German alliance, the U.S. government was furious over the proposed seizure of its land. Even though the Mexican government stated that no agreements or communication with Germany had ever been made, a feeling of mistrust of Mexicans and other Latinos grew in the U.S. during World War I.

BIBLIOGRAPHY

Tuchman, Barbara W. *The Zimmerman Telegram.* New York: Bantam Books, 1921.

Zoot Suit Riots of 1943

The Zoot Suit Riots occurred in Los Angeles in June 1943 in the wake of several minor incidents between "zoot suiters" (Hispanic youths in distinctively tailored suits and long hair) and Anglo military personnel. What had started as street brawls quickly turned into a full-fledged, week-long race riot incited by the press and largely ignored by major law enforcement agencies. Military personnel, as well as hundreds of restless Anglo sailors and soldiers, attacked zoot suiters by stopping buses and yanking them off to beat them and cut their hair. There were strong reactions to these outrages throughout the country, and *Time* magazine later called the Los Angeles violence an ugly brand of mob action. Meanwhile, the Los Angeles English-language press fomented trouble by printing sensational headlines and strident editorials directed against the servicemen's victims. The public mostly blamed the zoot suiters for the trouble, more because of the zoot suiters' long hair and cut of trousers than for any proof of wrongdoing—and largely because the press exploited the term "zoot-suit."

Luis Valdez's 1978 play (and later film) *Zoot Suit* was based on the "Sleepy Lagoon" murder case, so titled by the Los Angeles press. The case began in August 1942, predating the Zoot Suit Riots. In January 1943, a jury found 22 youths (possibly gang members) guilty of varying degrees of murder and assault; there was evidence of racist and discriminatory conduct at the trial. The verdict led to the creation of the **Sleepy Lagoon Defense Committee**, chaired by Carey McWilliams. Based on the efforts of the committee, the California District Court of Appeals reversed the lower court's convictions and dismissed all charges in October 1944, citing lack of evidence.

In similar fashion, the Zoot Suit Riots underwent official inquiry. On June 11, 1943, a formal inquiry was begun by the U.S. State Department at the request of the Mexican ambassador in Washington, D.C. Later, the Department of the Navy declared downtown Los Angeles "out of bounds" for all Navy personnel. Thus, the disastrous international effects of the riots were made evident to Los Angeles city officials and the Los Angeles press.

A citizen's committee appointed by California Governor Earl Warren and headed by Los Angeles Catholic Bishop Joseph McGucken found that, while the causes were complex, the riots had been principally the result of racial antagonism provoked by inflammatory news reporting and prejudicial police practices. **See also** Hector Garcia. (SCV)

BIBLIOGRAPHY

Garcia, Chris F., and Rudolph O. de la Garza. *The Chicano Political Experience: Three Perspectives.* North Scituate, MA: Duxbury Press, 1977.

Grebler, Leo, Joan W. Moore, and Ralph C. Guzman. *The Mexican-American People: The Nation's Second Largest Minority*. New York: The Free Press, 1970.

Meier, Matt S., and Feliciano Ribera. *Mexican Americans/American Mexicans from Conquistadors to Chicanos*. New York: American Century Press, Hill and Wang, 1993.

Appendixes

1 Documents

1. Texas Declaration of Independence (1836)

The Unanimous Declaration of Independence made by the Delegates of the People of Texas in General Convention at the town of Washington on the 2nd day of March 1836.

When a government has ceased to protect the lives, liberty and property of the people, from whom its legitimate powers are derived, and for the advancement of whose happiness it was instituted, and so far from being a guarantee for the enjoyment of those inestimable and inalienable rights, becomes an instrument in the hands of evil rulers for their oppression.

When the Federal Republican Constitution of their country, which they have sworn to support, no longer has a substantial existence, and the whole nature of their government has been forcibly changed, without their consent, from a restricted federative republic, composed of sovereign states, to a consolidated central military despotism, in which every interest is disregarded but that of the army and the priesthood, both the eternal enemies of civil liberty, the everready minions of power, and the usual instruments of tyrants.

When, long after the spirit of the constitution has departed, moderation is at length so far lost by those in power, that even the semblance of freedom is removed, and the forms themselves of the constitution discontinued, and so far from their petitions and remonstrances being regarded, the agents who bear them are thrown into dungeons, and mercenary armies sent forth to force a new government upon them at the point of the bayonet.

When, in consequence of such acts of malfeasance and abdication on the part of the government, anarchy prevails, and civil society is dissolved into its original elements. In such a crisis, the first law of nature, the right of self-preservation, the inherent and inalienable rights of the people to appeal to first principles, and take their political affairs into their own hands in extreme cases, enjoins it as a right towards themselves, and a sacred obligation to their posterity, to abolish such government, and create another in its stead, calculated to rescue them from impending dangers, and to secure their future welfare and happiness.

Nations, as well as individuals, are amenable for their acts to the public opinion of mankind. A statement of a part of our grievances is therefore submitted to an impartial world, in justification of the hazardous but unavoidable step now taken, of severing our political connection with the Mexican people, and assuming an independent attitude among the nations of the earth.

The Mexican government, by its colonization laws, invited and induced the Anglo-American population of Texas to colonize its wilderness under the pledged faith of a written constitution, that they should continue to enjoy that constitutional liberty and repub-

lican government to which they had been habituated in the land of their birth, the United States of America.

In this expectation they have been cruelly disappointed, inasmuch as the Mexican nation has acquiesced in the late changes made in the government by General Antonio Lopez de Santa Anna, who having overturned the constitution of his country, now offers us the cruel alternative, either to abandon our homes, acquired by so many privations, or submit to the most intolerable of all tyranny, the combined despotism of the sword and the priesthood.

It has sacrificed our welfare to the state of Coahuila, by which our interests have been continually depressed through a jealous and partial course of legislation, carried on at a far distant seat of government, by a hostile majority, in an unknown tongue, and this too, notwithstanding we have petitioned in the humblest terms for the establishment of a separate state government, and have, in accordance with the provisions of the national constitution, presented to the general Congress a republican constitution, which was, without just cause, contemptuously rejected.

It incarcerated in a dungeon, for a long time, one of our citizens, for no other cause but a zealous endeavor to procure the acceptance of our constitution, and the establishment of a state government.

It has failed and refused to secure, on a firm basis, the right of trial by jury, that palladium of civil liberty, and only safe guarantee for the life, liberty, and property of the citizen.

It has failed to establish any public system of education, although possessed of almost boundless resources, (the public domain,) and although it is an axiom in political science, that unless a people are educated and enlightened, it is idle to expect the continuance of civil liberty, or the capacity for self government.

It has suffered the military commandants, stationed among us, to exercise arbitrary acts of oppression and tyranny, thus trampling upon the most sacred rights of the citizens, and rendering the military superior to the civil power.

It has dissolved, by force of arms, the state Congress of Coahuila and Texas, and obliged our representatives to fly for their lives from the seat of government, thus depriving us of the fundamental political right of representation.

It has demanded the surrender of a number of our citizens, and ordered military detachments to seize and carry them into the Interior for trial, in contempt of the civil authorities, and in defiance of the laws and the constitution.

It has made piratical attacks upon our commerce, by commissioning foreign desperadoes, and authorizing them to seize our vessels, and convey the property of our citizens to far distant ports for confiscation.

It denies us the right of worshipping the Almighty according to the dictates of our own conscience, by the support of a national religion, calculated to promote the temporal interest of its human functionaries, rather than the glory of the true and living God.

It has demanded us to deliver up our arms, which are essential to our defense, the rightful property of freemen, and formidable only to tyrannical governments.

It has invaded our country both by sea and by land, with intent to lay waste our territory, and drive us from our homes; and has now a large mercenary army advancing, to carry on against us a war of extermination.

It has, through its emissaries, incited the merciless savage, with the tomahawk and scalping knife, to massacre the inhabitants of our defenseless frontiers.

It hath been, during the whole time of our connection with it, the contemptible sport and victim of successive military revolutions, and hath continually exhibited every characteristic of a weak, corrupt, and tyrannical government.

These, and other grievances, were patiently borne by the people of Texas, until they reached that point at which forbearance ceases to be a virtue. We then took up arms in defense of the national constitution. We appealed to our Mexican brethren for assistance. Our appeal has been made in vain. Though months have elapsed, no sympathetic response has yet been heard from the Interior. We are, therefore, forced to the melancholy conclusion, that the Mexican people have acquiesced in the destruction of their liberty, and the substitution therfor of a military government; that they are unfit to be free, and incapable of self government.

The necessity of self-preservation, therefore, now decrees our eternal political separation.

We, therefore, the delegates with plenary powers of the people of Texas, in solemn convention assembled, appealing to a candid world for the necessities of our condition, do hereby resolve and declare, that our political connection with the Mexican nation has forever ended, and that the people of Texas do now constitute a free, sovereign, and independent republic, and are fully invested with all the rights and attributes which properly belong to independent nations; and, conscious of the rectitude of our intentions, we fearlessly and confidently commit the issue to the decision of the Supreme arbiter of the destinies of nations.

Richard Ellis, President of the Convention and Delegate from Red River.

Charles B. Stewart	Thos. J. Gazley	Martin Palmer
Tho. Barnett	R. M. Coleman	Edwin O. Legrand
John S. D. Byrom	Sterling C. Robertson	Stephen W. Blount
Francis Ruis	James Collinsworth	Jms. Gaines
J. Antonio Navarro	Edwin Waller	Wm. Clark, Jr.
Jesse B. Badgett	Asa Brigham	Sydney O. Pennington
Wm D. Lacy	Geo. C. Childress	Wm. Carrol Crawford
William Menifee	Bailey Hardeman	Jno. Turner
Jn. Fisher	Rob. Potter	Benj. Briggs Goodrich
Matthew Caldwell	Thomas Jefferson Rusk	G. W. Barnett
William Motley	Chas. S. Taylor	James G. Swisher
Lorenzo de Zavala	John S. Roberts	Jesse Grimes
Stephen H. Everett	Robert Hamilton	S. Rhoads Fisher
George W. Smyth	Collin McKinney	John W. Moore
Elijah Stapp	Albert H. Latimer	John W. Bower
Claiborne West	James Power	Saml. A. Maverick (from Bejar)
Wm. B. Scates	Sam Houston	Sam P. Carson
M. B. Menard	David Thomas	A. Briscoe
A. B. Hardin	Edwd. Conrad	J. B. Woods
J. W. Burton		H. S. Kimble, Secretary

2. Texas Annexation Treaty (1844)

A TREATY OF ANNEXATION, CONCLUDED BETWEEN THE UNITED STATES OF AMERICA AND THE REPUBLIC OF TEXAS.

The people of Texas having, at the time of adopting their constitution, expressed by an almost unanimous vote, their desire to be incorporated into the Union of the United States, and being still desirous of the same with equal unanimity, in order to provide more effectually for their security and prosperity; and the United States, actuated solely by the desire to add to their own security and prosperity, and to meet the wishes of the Government and people of Texas, have determined to accomplish, by treaty, objects so important to their mutual and permanent welfare:

For that purpose, the President of the United States has given full Powers to John C. Calhoun, Secretary of State of the said United States, and the President of the Republic of Texas has appointed, with like powers, Isaac Van Zandt and J. Pinckney Henderson, citizens of the said Republic: and the said plenipotentiaries, after exchanging their full powers, have agreed on and concluded the following articles:

ARTICLE I.

The Republic of Texas, acting in conformity with the wishes of the people and every department of its government, cedes to the United States all its territories, to be held by them in full property and sovereignty, and to be annexed to the said United States as one of their

Territories, subject to the same constitutional provisions with their other Territories. This cession includes all public lots and squares, vacant lands, mines, minerals, salt lakes and springs, public edifices, fortifications, barracks, ports and harbours, navy and navy-yards, docks, magazines, arms, armaments and accoutrements, archives and public documents, public funds debts, taxes and dues unpaid at the time of the exchange of the ratifications of this treaty.

ARTICLE II.

The citizens of Texas shall be incorporated into the Union of the United States, maintained and protected in the free enjoyment of their liberty and property and admitted, as soon as may be consistent with the principles of the federal constitution, to the enjoyment of all the rights, privileges and immunities of citizens of the United States.

ARTICLE III.

All titles and claims to real estate, which are valid under the laws of Texas, shall be held to be so by the United States; and measures shall be adopted for the speedy adjudication of all unsettled claims to land, and patents shall be granted to those found to be valid.

ARTICLE IV.

The public lands hereby ceded shall be subject to the laws regulating the public lands in the other Territories of the United States, as far as they may be applicable; subject, however, to such alterations and changes as Congress may from time to time think proper to make. It is understood between the parties that if, in consequence of the mode in which lands have been surveyed in Texas, or from previous grants or locations, the sixteenth section cannot be applied to the purpose of education, Congress shall make equal provision by grant of land elsewhere. And it is also further understood, that, hereafter, the books, papers and documents of the General Land Office of Texas shall be deposited and kept at such place in Texas as the Congress of the United States shall direct.

ARTICLE V.

The United States assume and agree to pay the public debts and liabilities of Texas, however created, for which the faith or credit of her government may be bound at the time of the exchange of the ratifications of this treaty; which debts and liabilities are estimated not to exceed, in the whole, ten millions of dollars, to be ascertained and paid in the manner hereinafter stated.

The payment of the sum of three hundred and fifty thousand dollars shall be made at the Treasury of the United States within ninety days after the exchange of the ratifications of this treaty, as follows: Two hundred and fifty thousand dollars to Frederick Dawson, of Baltimore, or his Executors, on the delivery of that amount of ten per cent bonds of Texas: One hundred thousand dollars, if so much be required, in the redemption of the Exchequer bills which may be in circulation at the time of the exchange of the ratifications of this treaty. For the payment of the remainder of the debts and liabilities of Texas, which, together with the amount already specified, shall not exceed ten millions of dollars, the public lands herein ceded and the net revenue from the same are hereby pledged.

ARTICLE VI.

In order to ascertain the fun amount of the debts and liabilities herein assumed, and the legality and validity thereof, four commissioners shall be appointed by the President of the United States, by and

with the advice and consent of the Senate, who shall meet at Washington, Texas, within the period of six months after the exchange of the ratifications of this treaty, and may continue in session not exceeding twelve months, unless the Congress of the United States should prolong the time. They shall take an oath for the faithful discharge of their duties, and that they are not directly or indirectly interested in said claims at the time, and will not be during their continuance in office; and the said oath shall be recorded with their proceedings. In case of the death, sickness, or resignation of any of the commissioners, his or their place or places may be supplied by the appointment as aforesaid or by the President of the United States during the recess of the Senate. They, or a majority of them, shall be authorized, under such regulations as the Congress of the United States may prescribe, to hear, examine and decide on all questions touching the legality and validity of said claims, and shall, when a claim is allowed, issue a certificate to the claimant, stating the amount, distinguishing principal from interest. The certificates so issued shall be numbered, and entry made of the number, the name of the person to whom issued, and the amount, in a book to be kept for that purpose. They shall transmit the records of their proceedings and the book in which the certificates are entered, with the vouchers and documents produced before them, relative to the claims allowed or rejected, to the Treasury Department of the United States, to be deposited therein, and the Secretary of the Treasury shall, as soon as practicable after the receipt of the same, ascertain the aggregate amount of the debts and liabilities allowed; and if the same, when added to the amount to be paid to Frederick Dawson and the sum which may be paid in the redemption of the Exchequer bills, shall not exceed the estimated sum of ten millions of dollars, he shall, on the presentation of a certificate of the commissioners, issue, at the option of the holder, a new certificate for the amount, distinguishing principal from interest, and payable to him or order, out of the net proceeds of the public lands, hereby ceded, or stock, of the United States, for the amount allowed, including principal and interest, and bearing an interest of three per cent. per annum from the date thereof; which stock, in addition to being made payable out of the net proceeds of the public lands hereby ceded shall also be receivable in payment for the same. In case the amount of the debts end liabilities allowed, with the sums aforesaid to be paid to Frederick Dawson and which may be paid in the redemption of the Exchequer bills, shall exceed the said sum of ten millions of dollars, the said Secretary, before issuing a new certificate, or stock, as the case may be, shall make in each case such proportionable and rateable reduction on its amount as to reduce the aggregate to the said sum of ten millions of dollars, and he shall have power to make an needful rules and regulations necessary to carry into effect the powers hereby vested in him.

ARTICLE VII.

Until further provision shall be made, the laws of Texas as now existing shall remain in force, and all executive and judicial officers of Texas, except the President, Vice-President, and Heads of Departments, shall retain their offices, with any power and authority appertaining thereto, and the Courts of justice shall remain in all respects as now established and organized.

ARTICLE VIII.

Immediately after the exchange of the ratifications of this treaty, the President of the United States, by and with the advice and consent of the Senate, shall appoint a commissioner; who shall proceed to Texas, and receive the transfer of the territory thereof, and all the archives and public property and other things herein conveyed, in the name of the United States. He shall exercise all executive authority in said territory necessary to the proper execution of the laws, until otherwise provided.

ARTICLE IX.

The present treaty shall be ratified by the contracting parties and the ratifications exchanged at the City of Washington, in six months from the date hereof, or sooner if possible.

In witness whereof, we, the undersigned plenipotentiaries of the United States of America and of the Republic of Texas, have signed, by virtue of our powers the present treaty of Annexation, and have hereunto affixed our seals respectively

Done at Washington, the twelfth day of April, eighteen hundred and forty-four

[Seal] J C. CALHOUN
[Seal] ISAAC VAN ZANDT
[Seal] J. PINCKNEY HENDERSON

3. Treaty of Guadalupe Hidalgo (1848)

TREATY OF PEACE, FRIENDSHIP, LIMITS, AND SETTLEMENT BETWEEN THE UNITED STATES OF AMERICA AND THE UNITED MEXICAN STATES CONCLUDED AT GUADALUPE HIDALGO, FEBRUARY 2, 1848; RATIFICATION ADVISED BY SENATE, WITH AMENDMENTS, MARCH 10, 1848; RATIFIED BY PRESIDENT, MARCH 16, 1848; RATIFICATIONS EXCHANGED AT QUERETARO, MAY 30, 1848; PROCLAIMED, JULY 4, 1848.

IN THE NAME OF ALMIGHTY GOD

The United States of America and the United Mexican States animated by a sincere desire to put an end to the calamities of the war which unhappily exists between the two Republics and to establish upon a solid basis relations of peace and friendship, which shall confer reciprocal benefits upon the citizens of both, and assure the concord, harmony, and mutual confidence wherein the two people should live, as good neighbors have for that purpose appointed their respective plenipotentiaries, that is to say: The President of the United States has appointed Nicholas P. Trist, a citizen of the United States, and the President of the Mexican Republic has appointed Don Luis Gonzaga Cuevas, Don Bernardo Couto, and Don Miguel Atristain, citizens of the said Republic; Who, after a reciprocal communication of their respective full powers, have, under the protection of Almighty God, the author of peace, arranged, agreed upon, and signed the following: Treaty of Peace, Friendship, Limits, and Settlement between the United States of America and the Mexican Republic.

ARTICLE I.

There shall be firm and universal peace between the United States of America and the Mexican Republic, and between their respective countries, territories, cities, towns, and people, without exception of places or persons.

ARTICLE II.

Immediately upon the signature of this treaty, a convention shall be entered into between a commissioner or commissioners appointed by the General-in-chief of the forces of the United States, and such as may be appointed by the Mexican Government, to the end that a provisional suspension of hostilities shall take place, and that, in the places occupied by the said forces, constitutional order may be reestablished, as regards the political, administrative, and judicial branches, so far as this shall be permitted by the circumstances of military occupation.

ARTICLE III.

Immediately upon the ratification of the present treaty by the Government of the United States, orders shall be transmitted to the commanders of their land and naval forces, requiring the latter (pro-

vided this treaty shall then have been ratified by the Government of the Mexican Republic, and the ratifications exchanged) immediately to desist from blockading any Mexican ports and requiring the former (under the same condition) to commence, at the earliest moment practicable, withdrawing all troops of the United States then in the interior of the Mexican Republic, to points that shall be selected by common agreement, at a distance from the seaports not exceeding thirty leagues; and such evacuation of the interior of the Republic shall be completed with the least possible delay; the Mexican Government hereby binding itself to afford every facility in its power for rendering the same convenient to the troops, on their march and in their new positions, and for promoting a good understanding between them and the inhabitants. In like manner orders shall be despatched to the persons in charge of the custom houses at all ports occupied by the forces of the United States, requiring them (under the same condition) immediately to deliver possession of the same to the persons authorized by the Mexican Government to receive it, together with all bonds and evidences of debt for duties on importations and on exportations, not yet fallen due. Moreover, a faithful and exact account shall be made out, showing the entire amount of all duties on imports and on exports, collected at such custom-houses, or elsewhere in Mexico, by authority of the United States, from and after the day of ratification of this treaty by the Government of the Mexican Republic; and also an account of the cost of collection; and such entire amount, deducting only the cost of collection, shall be delivered to the Mexican Government, at the city of Mexico, within three months after the exchange of ratifications.

The evacuation of the capital of the Mexican Republic by the troops of the United States, in virtue of the above stipulation, shall be completed in one month after the orders there stipulated for shall have been received by the commander of said troops, or sooner if possible.

ARTICLE IV.

Immediately after the exchange of ratifications of the present treaty all castles, forts, territories, places, and possessions, which have been taken or occupied by the forces of the United States during the present war, within the limits of the Mexican Republic, as about to be established by the following article, shall be definitely restored to the said Republic, together with all the artillery, arms, apparatus of war, munitions, and other public property, which were in the said castles and forts when captured, and which shall remain there at the time when this treaty shall be duly ratified by the Government of the Mexican Republic. To this end, immediately upon the signature of this treaty, orders shall be despatched to the American officers commanding such castles and forts, securing against the removal or destruction of any such artillery, arms, apparatus of war, munitions, or other public property. The city of Mexico, within the inner line of intrenchments surrounding the said city, is comprehended in the above stipulation, as regards the restoration of artillery, apparatus of war, etc.

The final evacuation of the territory of the Mexican Republic, by the forces of the United States, shall be completed in three months from the said exchange of ratifications, or sooner if possible; the Mexican Government hereby engaging, as in the foregoing article to use all means in its power for facilitating such evacuation, and rendering it convenient to the troops, and for promoting a good understanding between them and the inhabitants.

If, however, the ratification of this treaty by both parties should not take place in time to allow the embarkation of the troops of the United States to be completed before the commencement of the sickly season, at the Mexican ports on the Gulf of Mexico, in such case a friendly arrangement shall be entered into between the General-in-Chief of the said troops and the Mexican Government, whereby healthy and otherwise suitable places, at a distance from the ports not exceeding thirty leagues, shall be designated for the residence of such troops as may not yet have embarked, until the return of the healthy season. And the space of time here referred to as, comprehending the sickly season shall be understood to extend from the first day of May to the first day of November.

All prisoners of war taken on either side, on land or on sea, shall be restored as soon as practicable after the exchange of ratifications of this treaty. It is also agreed that if any Mexicans should now be held as captives by any savage tribe within the limits of the United States, as about to be established by the following article, the Government of the said United States will exact the release of such captives and cause them to be restored to their country.

ARTICLE V.

The boundary line between the two Republics shall commence in the Gulf of Mexico, three leagues from land, opposite the mouth of the Rio Grande, otherwise called Rio Bravo del Norte, or opposite the mouth of its deepest branch, if it should have more than one branch emptying directly into the sea; from thence up the middle of that river, following the deepest channel, where it has more than one, to the point where it strikes the southern boundary of New Mexico; thence, westwardly, along the whole southern boundary of New Mexico (which runs north of the town called Paso) to its western termination; thence, northward, along the western line of New Mexico, until it intersects the first branch of the river Gila; (or if it should not intersect any branch of that river, then to the point on the said line nearest to such branch, and thence in a direct line to the same); thence down the middle of the said branch and of the said river, until it empties into the Rio Colorado; thence across the Rio Colorado, following the division line between Upper and Lower California, to the Pacific Ocean.

The southern and western limits of New Mexico, mentioned in the article, are those laid down in the map entitled "Map of the United Mexican States, as organized and defined by various acts of the Congress of said republic, and constructed according to the best authorities. Revised edition. Published at New York, in 1847, by J. Disturnell," of which map a copy is added to this treaty, bearing the signatures and seals of the undersigned Plenipotentiaries. And, in order to preclude all difficulty in tracing upon the ground the limit separating Upper from Lower California, it is agreed that the said limit shall consist of a straight line drawn from the middle of the Rio Gila, where it unites with the Colorado, to a point on the coast of the Pacific Ocean, distant one marine league due south of the southernmost point of the port of San Diego, according to the plan of said port made in the year 1782 by Don Juan Pantoja, second sailing-master of the Spanish fleet, and published at Madrid in the year 1802, in the atlas to the voyage of the schooners Sutil and Mexicana; of which plan a copy is hereunto added, signed and sealed by the respective Plenipotentiaries.

In order to designate the boundary line with due precision, upon authoritative maps, and to establish upon the ground land-marks which shall show the limits of both republics, as described in the present article, the two Governments shall each appoint a commissioner and a surveyor, who, before the expiration of one year from the date of the exchange of ratifications of this treaty, shall meet at the port of San Diego, and proceed to run and mark the said boundary in its whole course to the mouth of the Rio Bravo del Norte. They shall keep journals and make out plans of their operations; and the result agreed upon by them shall be deemed a part of this treaty, and shall have the same force as if it were inserted therein. The two Governments will amicably agree regarding what may be necessary to these persons, and also as to their respective escorts, should such be necessary.

The boundary line established by this article shall be religiously respected by each of the two republics, and no change shall ever be made therein, except by the express and free consent of both nations, lawfully given by the General Government of each, in conformity with its own constitution.

ARTICLE VI.

The vessels and citizens of the United States shall, in all time, have a free and uninterrupted passage by the Gulf of California, and by the river Colorado below its confluence with the Gila, to and from their possessions situated north of the boundary line defined in the preceding article; it being understood that this passage is to be by navigating the Gulf of California and the river Colorado, and not by land, without the express consent of the Mexican Government.

If, by the examinations which may be made, it should be ascertained to be practicable and advantageous to construct a road, canal, or railway, which should in whole or in part run upon the river Gila, or upon its right or its left bank, within the space of one marine league from either margin of the river, the Governments of both republics will form an agreement regarding its construction, in order that it may serve equally for the use and advantage of both countries.

ARTICLE VII.

The river Gila, and the part of the Rio Bravo del Norte lying below the southern boundary of New Mexico, being, agreeably to the fifth article, divided in the middle between the two republics, the navigation of the Gila and of the Bravo below said boundary shall be free and common to the vessels and citizens of both countries; and neither shall, without the consent of the other, construct any work that may impede or interrupt, in whole or in part, the exercise of this right; not even for the purpose of favoring new methods of navigation. Nor shall any tax or contribution, under any denomination or title, be levied upon vessels or persons navigating the same or upon merchandise or effects transported thereon, except in the case of landing upon one of their shores. If, for the purpose of making the said rivers navigable, or for maintaining them in such state, it should be necessary or advantageous to establish any tax or contribution, this shall not be done without the consent of both Governments.

The stipulations contained in the present article shall not impair the territorial rights of either republic within its established limits.

ARTICLE VIII.

Mexicans now established in territories previously belonging to Mexico, and which remain for the future within the limits of the United States, as defined by the present treaty, shall be free to continue where they now reside, or to remove at any time to the Mexican Republic, retaining the property which they possess in the said territories, or disposing thereof, and removing the proceeds wherever they please, without their being subjected, on this account, to any contribution, tax, or charge whatever.

Those who shall prefer to remain in the said territories may either retain the title and rights of Mexican citizens, or acquire those of citizens of the United States. But they shall be under the obligation to make their election within one year from the date of the exchange of ratifications of this treaty; and those who shall remain in the said territories after the expiration of that year, without having declared their intention to retain the character of Mexicans, shall be considered to have elected to become citizens of the United States.

In the said territories, property of every kind, now belonging to Mexicans not established there, shall be inviolably respected. The present owners, the heirs of these, and all Mexicans who may hereafter acquire said property by contract, shall enjoy with respect to it guarantees equally ample as if the same belonged to citizens of the United States.

ARTICLE IX.

The Mexicans who, in the territories aforesaid, shall not preserve the character of citizens of the Mexican Republic, conformably with what is stipulated in the preceding article, shall be incorporated into the Union of the United States, and be admitted at the proper time (to be judged of by the Congress of the United States) to the enjoyment of all the rights of citizens of the United States, according to the principles of the Constitution; and in the mean time, shall be maintained and protected in the free enjoyment of their liberty and property, and secured in the free exercise of their religion without restriction.

ARTICLE X.

[Stricken out]

ARTICLE XI.

Considering that a great part of the territories, which, by the present treaty, are to be comprehended for the future within the limits of the United States, is now occupied by savage tribes, who will hereafter be under the exclusive control of the Government of the United States, and whose incursions within the territory of Mexico would be prejudicial in the extreme, it is solemnly agreed that all such incursions shall be forcibly restrained by the Government of the United States whensoever this may be necessary; and that when they cannot be prevented, they shall be punished by the said Government, and satisfaction for the same shall be exacted all in the same way, and with equal diligence and energy, as if the same incursions were meditated or committed within its own territory, against its own citizens.

It shall not be lawful, under any pretext whatever, for any inhabitant of the United States to purchase or acquire any Mexican, or any foreigner residing in Mexico, who may have been captured by Indians inhabiting the territory of either of the two republics; nor to purchase or acquire horses, mules, cattle, or property of any kind, stolen within Mexican territory by such Indians.

And in the event of any person or persons, captured within Mexican territory by Indians, being carried into the territory of the United States, the Government of the latter engages and binds itself, in the most solemn manner, so soon as it shall know of such captives being within its territory, and shall be able so to do, through the faithful exercise of its influence and power, to rescue them and return them to their country, or deliver them to the agent or representative of the Mexican Government. The Mexican authorities will, as far as practicable, give to the Government of the United States notice of such captures; and its agents shall pay the expenses incurred in the maintenance and transmission of the rescued captives; who, in the mean time, shall be treated with the utmost hospitality by the American authorities at the place where they may be. But if the Government of the United States, before receiving such notice from Mexico, should obtain intelligence, through any other channel, of the existence of Mexican captives within its territory, it will proceed forthwith to effect their release and delivery to the Mexican agent, as above stipulated.

For the purpose of giving to these stipulations the fullest possible efficacy, thereby affording the security and redress demanded by their true spirit and intent, the Government of the United States will now and hereafter pass, without unnecessary delay, and always vigilantly enforce, such laws as the nature of the subject may require. And, finally, the sacredness of this obligation shall never be lost sight of by the said Government, when providing for the removal of the Indians from any portion of the said territories, or for its being settled by citizens of the United States; but, on the contrary, special care shall then be taken not to place its Indian occupants under the necessity of seeking new homes, by committing those invasions which the United States have solemnly obliged themselves to restrain.

ARTICLE XII.

In consideration of the extension acquired by the boundaries of the United States, as defined in the fifth article of the present treaty, the Government of the United States engages to pay to that of the Mexican Republic the sum of fifteen millions of dollars.

Immediately after the treaty shall have been duly ratified by the Government of the Mexican Republic, the sum of three millions of dollars shall be paid to the said Government by that of the United States, at the city of Mexico, in the gold or silver coin of Mexico. The remaining twelve millions of dollars shall be paid at the same place, and in the same coin, in annual installments of three millions of dollars each, together with interest on the same at the rate of six per centum per annum. This interest shall begin to run upon the whole sum of twelve millions from the day of the ratification of the present treaty by the Mexican Government, and the first of the installments shall be paid at the expiration of one year from the same day. Together with each annual installment, as it falls due, the whole interest accruing on such installment from the beginning shall also be paid.

ARTICLE XIII.

The United States engage, moreover, to assume and pay to the claimants all the amounts now due them, and those hereafter to become due, by reason of the claims already liquidated and decided against the Mexican Republic, under the conventions between the two republics severally concluded on the eleventh day of April, eighteen hundred and thirty-nine, and on the thirtieth day of January, eighteen hundred and forty-three; so that the Mexican Republic shall be absolutely exempt, for the future, from all expense whatever on account of the said claims.

ARTICLE XIV.

The United States do furthermore discharge the Mexican Republic from all claims of citizens of the United States, not heretofore decided against the Mexican Government, which may have arisen previously to the date of the signature of this treaty; which discharge shall be final and perpetual, whether the said claims be rejected or be allowed by the board of commissioners provided for in the following article, and whatever shall be the total amount of those allowed.

ARTICLE XV.

The United States, exonerating Mexico from all demands on account of the claims of their citizens mentioned in the preceding article, and considering them entirely and forever canceled, whatever their amount may be, undertake to make satisfaction for the same, to an amount not exceeding three and one-quarter millions of dollars. To ascertain the validity and amount of those claims, a board of commissioners shall be established by the Government of the United States, whose awards shall be final and conclusive; provided that, in deciding upon the validity of each claim, the board shall be guided and governed by the principles and rules of decision prescribed by the first and fifth articles of the unratified convention, concluded at the city of Mexico on the twentieth day of November, one thousand eight hundred and forty-three; and in no case shall an award be made in favor of any claim not embraced by these principles and rules.

If, in the opinion of the said board of commissioners or of the claimants, any books, records, or documents, in the possession or power of the Government of the Mexican Republic, shall be deemed necessary to the just decision of any claim, the commissioners, or the claimants through them, shall, within such period as Congress may designate, make an application in writing for the same, addressed to the Mexican Minister of Foreign Affairs, to be transmitted by the Secretary of State of the United States; and the Mexican Government engages, at the earliest possible moment after the receipt of such demand, to cause any of the books, records, or documents so specified, which shall be in their possession or power (or authenticated copies or extracts of the same), to be transmitted to the said Secretary of State, who shall immediately deliver them over to the said board of commissioners; provided that no such application shall be made by or at the instance of any claimant, until the facts which it is expected to prove by such books, records, or documents, shall have been stated under oath or affirmation.

ARTICLE XVI.

Each of the contracting parties reserves to itself the entire right to fortify whatever point within its territory it may judge proper so to fortify for its security.

ARTICLE XVII.

The treaty of amity, commerce, and navigation, concluded at the city of Mexico, on the fifth day of April, A.D. 1831, between the United States of America and the United Mexican States, except the additional article, and except so far as the stipulations of the said treaty may be incompatible with any stipulation contained in the present treaty, is hereby revived for the period of eight years from the day of the exchange of ratifications of this treaty, with the same force and virtue as if incorporated therein; it being understood that each of the contracting parties reserves to itself the right, at any time after the said period of eight years shall have expired, to terminate the same by giving one year's notice of such intention to the other party.

ARTICLE XVIII.

All supplies whatever for troops of the United States in Mexico, arriving at ports in the occupation of such troops previous to the final evacuation thereof, although subsequently to the restoration of the custom-houses at such ports, shall be entirely exempt from duties and charges of any kind; the Government of the United States hereby engaging and pledging its faith to establish and vigilantly to enforce, all possible guards for securing the revenue of Mexico, by preventing the importation, under cover of this stipulation, of any articles other than such, both in kind and in quantity, as shall really be wanted for the use and consumption of the forces of the United States during the time they may remain in Mexico. To this end it shall be the duty of all officers and agents of the United States to denounce to the Mexican authorities at the respective ports any attempts at a fraudulent abuse of this stipulation, which they may know of, or may have reason to suspect, and to give to such authorities all the aid in their power with regard thereto; and every such attempt, when duly proved and established by sentence of a competent tribunal, they shall be punished by the confiscation of the property so attempted to be fraudulently introduced.

ARTICLE XIX.

With respect to all merchandise, effects, and property whatsoever, imported into ports of Mexico, whilst in the occupation of the forces of the United States, whether by citizens of either republic, or by citizens or subjects of any neutral nation, the following rules shall be observed:

1. All such merchandise, effects, and property, if imported previously to the restoration of the custom-houses to the Mexican authorities, as stipulated for in the third article of this treaty, shall be exempt from confiscation, although the importation of the same be prohibited by the Mexican tariff.

2. The same perfect exemption shall be enjoyed by all such merchandise, effects, and property, imported subsequently to the restoration of the custom-houses, and previously to the sixty days fixed in the following article for the coming into force of the Mexican tariff at such ports respectively; the said merchandise, effects, and property being, however, at the time of their importation, subject to the payment of duties, as provided for in the said following article.

3. All merchandise, effects, and property described in the two rules foregoing shall, during their continuance at the place of importation, and upon their leaving such place for the interior, be exempt from all duty, tax, or imposts of every kind, under whatsoever title or denomination. Nor shall they be there subject to any charge whatsoever upon the sale thereof.

4. All merchandise, effects, and property, described in the first and second rules, which shall have been removed to any place in the interior, whilst such place was in the occupation of the forces of the United States, shall, during their continuance therein, be exempt from all tax upon the sale or consumption thereof, and from every kind of impost or contribution, under whatsoever title or denomination.

5. But if any merchandise, effects, or property, described in the first and second rules, shall be removed to any place not occupied at

the time by the forces of the United States, they shall, upon their introduction into such place, or upon their sale or consumption there, be subject to the same duties which, under the Mexican laws, they would be required to pay in such cases if they had been imported in time of peace, through the maritime custom-houses, and had there paid the duties conformably with the Mexican tariff.

6. The owners of all merchandise, effects, or property, described in the first and second rules, and existing in any port of Mexico, shall have the right to reship the same, exempt from all tax, impost, or contribution whatever.

With respect to the metals, or other property, exported from any Mexican port whilst in the occupation of the forces of the United States, and previously to the restoration of the custom-house at such port, no person shall be required by the Mexican authorities, whether general or state, to pay any tax, duty, or contribution upon any such exportation, or in any manner to account for the same to the said authorities.

ARTICLE XX.

Through consideration for the interests of commerce generally, it is agreed, that if less than sixty days should elapse between the date of the signature of this treaty and the restoration of the custom houses, conformably with the stipulation in the third article, in such case all merchandise, effects and property whatsoever, arriving at the Mexican ports after the restoration of the said custom-houses, and previously to the expiration of sixty days after the day of signature of this treaty, shall be admitted to entry; and no other duties shall be levied thereon than the duties established by the tariff found in force at such custom-houses at the time of the restoration of the same. And to all such merchandise, effects, and property, the rules established by the preceding article shall apply.

ARTICLE XXI.

If unhappily any disagreement should hereafter arise between the Governments of the two republics, whether with respect to the interpretation of any stipulation in this treaty, or with respect to any other particular concerning the political or commercial relations of the two nations, the said Governments, in the name of those nations, do promise to each other that they will endeavor, in the most sincere and earnest manner, to settle the differences so arising, and to preserve the state of peace and friendship in which the two countries are now placing themselves, using, for this end, mutual representations and pacific negotiations. And if, by these means, they should not be enabled to come to an agreement, a resort shall not, on this account, be had to reprisals, aggression, or hostility of any kind, by the one republic against the other, until the Government of that which deems itself aggrieved shall have maturely considered, in the spirit of peace and good neighborship, whether it would not be better that such difference should be settled by the arbitration of commissioners appointed on each side, or by that of a friendly nation. And should such course be proposed by either party, it shall be acceded to by the other, unless deemed by it altogether incompatible with the nature of the difference, or the circumstances of the case.

ARTICLE XXII.

If (which is not to be expected, and which God forbid) war should unhappily break out between the two republics, they do now, with a view to such calamity, solemnly pledge themselves to each other and to the world to observe the following rules; absolutely where the nature of the subject permits, and as closely as possible in all cases where such absolute observance shall be impossible:

1. The merchants of either republic then residing in the other shall be allowed to remain twelve months (for those dwelling in the interior), and six months (for those dwelling at the seaports) to collect their debts and settle their affairs; during which periods they shall enjoy the same protection, and be on the same footing, in all respects, as the citizens or subjects of the most friendly nations; and, at the expiration thereof, or at any time before, they shall have full liberty to depart, carrying off all their effects without molestation or hindrance, conforming therein to the same laws which the citizens or subjects of the most friendly nations are required to conform to. Upon the entrance of the armies of either nation into the territories of the other, women and children, ecclesiastics, scholars of every faculty, cultivators of the earth, merchants, artisans, manufacturers, and fishermen, unarmed and inhabiting unfortified towns, villages, or places, and in general all persons whose occupations are for the common subsistence and benefit of mankind, shall be allowed to continue their respective employments, unmolested in their persons. Nor shall their houses or goods be burnt or otherwise destroyed, nor their cattle taken, nor their fields wasted, by the armed force into whose power, by the events of war, they may happen to fall; but if the necessity arise to take anything from them for the use of such armed force, the same shall be paid for at an equitable price. All churches, hospitals, schools, colleges, libraries, and other establishments for charitable and beneficent purposes, shall be respected, and all persons connected with the same protected in the discharge of their duties, and the pursuit of their vocations.

2. In order that the fate of prisoners of war may be alleviated all such practices as those of sending them into distant, inclement, or unwholesome districts, or crowding them into close and noxious places, shall be studiously avoided. They shall not be confined in dungeons, prison ships, or prisons; nor be put in irons, or bound or otherwise restrained in the use of their limbs. The officers shall enjoy liberty on their paroles, within convenient districts, and have comfortable quarters; and the common soldiers shall be disposed in cantonments, open and extensive enough for air and exercise and lodged in barracks as roomy and good as are provided by the party in whose power they are for its own troops. But if any office shall break his parole by leaving the district so assigned him, or any other prisoner shall escape from the limits of his cantonment after they shall have been designated to him, such individual, officer, or other prisoner, shall forfeit so much of the benefit of this article as provides for his liberty on parole or in cantonment. And if any officer so breaking his parole or any common soldier so escaping from the limits assigned him, shall afterwards be found in arms previously to his being regularly exchanged, the person so offending shall be dealt with according to the established laws of war. The officers shall be daily furnished, by the party in whose power they are, with as many rations, and of the same articles, as are allowed either in kind or by commutation, to officers of equal rank in its own army; and all others shall be daily furnished with such ration as is allowed to a common soldier in its own service; the value of all which supplies shall, at the close of the war, or at periods to be agreed upon between the respective commanders, be paid by the other party, on a mutual adjustment of accounts for the subsistence of prisoners; and such accounts shall not be mingled with or set off against any others, nor the balance due on them withheld, as a compensation or reprisal for any cause whatever, real or pretended. Each party shall be allowed to keep a commissary of prisoners, appointed by itself, with every cantonment of prisoners, in possession of the other; which commissary shall see the prisoners as often as he pleases; shall be allowed to receive, exempt from all duties and taxes, and to distrib-

ute, whatever comforts may be sent to them by their friends; and shall be free to transmit his reports in open letters to the party by whom he is employed. And it is declared that neither the pretense that war dissolves all treaties, nor any other whatever, shall be considered as annulling or suspending the solemn covenant contained in this article. On the contrary, the state of war is precisely that for which it is provided; and, during which, its stipulations are to be as sacredly observed as the most acknowledged obligations under the law of nature or nations.

ARTICLE XXIII.

This treaty shall be ratified by the President of the United States of America, by and with the advice and consent of the Senate thereof; and by the President of the Mexican Republic, with the previous

approbation of its general Congress; and the ratifications shall be exchanged in the City of Washington, or at the seat of Government of Mexico, in four months from the date of the signature hereof, or sooner if practicable. In faith whereof we, the respective Plenipotentiaries, have signed this treaty of peace, friendship, limits, and settlement, and have hereunto affixed our seals respectively. Done in quintuplicate, at the city of Guadalupe Hidalgo, on the second day of February, in the year of our Lord one thousand eight hundred and forty-eight.

N.P. TRIST
LUIS P. CUEVAS
BERNARDO COUTO
MIGL. ATRISTAIN

4. A Mexican Account of the Attack on the Alamo (1849)

On this same evening, a little before nightfall, it is said that Barrett Travis, commander of the enemy, had offered to the general-in-chief, by a woman messenger, to surrender his arms and the fort with all the materials upon the sole condition that his own life and the lives of his men be spared. But the answer was that they must surrender at discretion, without any guarantee, even after such an answer, they all prepared to sell their lives as dearly as possible. Consequently, they exercised the greatest vigilance day and night to avoid surprise.

On the morning of March 6, the Mexican troops were stationed at 4 o'clock, A.M., in accord with Santa Anna's instructions. The artillery, as appears from these same instructions, was to remain inactive, as it received no order; and furthermore, darkness and the disposition made of the troops which were to attack the four fronts at the same time, prevented its firing without mowing down our own ranks. Thus the enemy was not to suffer from our artillery during the attack. Their own artillery was in readiness. At the sound of the bugle they could no longer doubt that the time had come for them to conquer or to die. Had they still doubted, the imprudent shouts for Santa Anna given by our columns of attack must have opened their eyes. As soon as our troops were in sight, a shower of grape and musket balls was poured upon them from the fort, the garrison of which at the sound of the bugle, had rushed to arms and to their posts. The three columns that attacked the west, the north, and the east fronts, fell back, or rather, wavered at the first discharge from the enemy, but the example and the efforts of the officers soon caused them to return to the attack. The columns of the western and eastern attacks, meeting with some difficulties in reaching the tops of the small houses which formed the walls of the fort, did, by a simultaneous movement to the right and to left, swing northward until the three columns formed one dense mass, which under the guidance of their officers, endeavored to climb the parapet on that side.

This obstacle was at length overcome, the gallant General Juan V. Amador being among the foremost. Meantime the column attacking the southern front under Colonels Jose Vicente Minon and Jose Morales, availing themselves of a shelter, formed by some stone houses near the western salient of that front, boldly took the guns defending it, and penetrated through the embrasures into the square formed by the barracks. There they assisted General Amador, who having captured the enemy's pieces turned them against the doors of the interior houses where the rebels had sought shelter, and from

which they fired upon our men in the act of jumping down onto the square or court of the fort. At last they were all destroyed by grape, musket shot, and the bayonet.

Our loss was very heavy. Colonel Francisco Duque was mortally wounded at the very beginning, as he lay dying on the ground where he was being trampled by his own men, he still ordered them on to the slaughter. This attack was extremely injudicious and in opposition to military rules, for our own men were exposed not only to the fire of the enemy but also to that of our own columns attacking the other fronts; and our soldiers being formed in close columns, all shots that were aimed too low, struck the backs of our foremost men. The greatest number of our casualties took place in that manner; it may even be affirmed that not one-fourth of our wounded were struck by the enemy's fire, because their cannon, owing to their elevated position, could not be sufficiently lowered to injure our troops after they had reached the foot of the walls. Nor could the defenders use their muskets with accuracy, because the wall having no inner banquette, they had, in order to deliver their fire, to stand on top where they could not live one second.

The official list of casualties, made by General Juan de Andrade, shows: officers 8 killed, 18 wounded; enlisted men 52 killed, 233 wounded. Total 311 killed and wounded. A great many of the wounded died for want of medical attention, beds, shelter, and surgical instruments.

The whole garrison were killed except an old woman and a negro slave for whom the soldiers felt compassion, knowing that they had remained from compulsion alone. There were 150 volunteers, 32 citizens of Gonzales who had introduced themselves into the fort the night previous to the storming, and about 20 citizens or merchants of Bexar.

Considering the disposition made for attack, our loss should have been still greater if all the cannon in the fort could have been placed on the walls, but the houses inside prevented it, and from their situation they could only fire in front. Furthermore, they had not a sufficient number of gunners. Indeed, artillery cannot be improvised as readily as rebellions. Also our movement from the right and the left upon the north front, and the movement executed by Minon and Morales with their column on the western salient, changing the direction from the southern front as instructed, rendered unavailable the pieces of artillery which the enemy had established on the three other fronts.

Finally, the place remained in the power of the Mexicans, and all the defenders were killed. It is a source of deep regret, that after the excitement of the combat, many acts of atrocity were allowed which are unworthy of the gallantry and resolution with which this operation had been executed, and stamp it with an indelible stain in the annals of history. These acts were reproved at the time by those who had the sorrow to witness them, and subsequently by the whole army, who certainly were not habitually animated by such feelings, and who heard with disgust the horror, as becomes brave and generous Mexicans who feel none but noble and lofty sentiments, of certain facts which I forebear to mention, and wish for the honor of the Mexican Republic had never taken place.

In our opinion the blood of our soldiers as well as that of the enemy was shed in vain, for the mere gratification of the inconsiderate, purile, and guilty vanity of reconquering Bexar by force of arms, and through a bloody contest. As we have said, the defenders of the Alamo, were disposed to surrender, upon the sole condition that their lives should be spared. Let us even grant that they were not so disposed—what could the wretches do, being surrounded by 5,000 men, without proper means of resistance, no possibility of retreating, nor any hope of receiving proper and sufficient reinforcements to compel the Mexicans to raise the siege? Had they been supplied with all the resources needed, that weak enclosure could not have withstood for one hour the fire of our 20 pieces of artillery which if properly directed would have crushed it to atoms and leveled down the inner buildings. . . . The massacres of the Alamo, of Goliad, of Refugio, convinced the rebels that no peaceable settlement could be expected, and that they must conquer, or die, or abandon the fruits of ten years of sweat and labor, together with their fondest hopes for the future.

5. Gadsden Treaty (1853)

By The President of the United States of America

A Proclamation

WHEREAS a treaty between the United States of America and the Mexican Republic was concluded and signed at the City of Mexico on the thirtieth day of December, one thousand eight hundred and fifty-three; which treaty, as amended by the Senate of the United States, and being in the English and Spanish languages, is word for word as follows:

IN THE NAME OF ALMIGHTY GOD:

The Republic of Mexico and the United States of America desiring to remove every cause of disagreement which might interfere in any manner with the better friendship and intercourse between the two countries, and especially in respect to the true limits which should be established, when, notwithstanding what was covenanted in the treaty of Guadalupe Hidalgo in the year 1848, opposite interpretations have been urged, which might give occasion to questions of serious moment: to avoid these, and to strengthen and more firmly maintain the peace which happily prevails between the two republics, the President of the United States has, for this purpose, appointed James Gadsden, Envoy Extraordinary and Minister Plenipotentiary of the same, near the Mexican government, and the President of Mexico has appointed as Plenipotentiary "ad hoc" his excellency Don Manuel Diaz de Bonilla, cavalier grand cross of the national and distinguished order of Guadalupe, and Secretary of State, and of the office of Foreign Relations, and Don Jose Salazar Ylarregui and General Mariano Monterde as scientific commissioners, invested with full powers for this negotiation, who, having communicated their respective full powers, and finding them in due and proper form, have agreed upon the articles following:

ARTICLE I.

The Mexican Republic agrees to designate the following as her true limits with the United States for the future: retaining the same dividing line between the two Californias as already defined and established, according to the 5th article of the treaty of Guadalupe Hidalgo, the limits between the two republics shall be as follows: Beginning in the Gulf of Mexico, three leagues from land, opposite the mouth of the Rio Grande, as provided in the 5th article of the treaty of Guadalupe Hidalgo; thence, as defined in the said article, up the middle of that river to the point where the parallel of 31° 47' north latitude crosses the same; thence due west one hundred miles; thence south to the parallel of 31° 20' north latitude; thence along the said parallel of 31° 20' to the 111th meridian of longitude west of Greenwich; thence in a straight line to a point on the Colorado River twenty English miles below the junction of the Gila and Colorado rivers; thence up the middle of the said river Colorado until it intersects the present line between the United States and Mexico.

For the performance of this portion of the treaty, each of the two governments shall nominate one commissioner, to the end that, by common consent the two thus nominated, having met in the city of Paso del Norte, three months after the exchange of the ratifications of this treaty, may proceed to survey and mark out upon the land the dividing line stipulated by this article, where it shall not have already been surveyed and established by the mixed commission, according to the treaty of Guadalupe, keeping a journal and making proper plans of their operations. For this purpose, if they should judge it necessary, the contracting parties shall be at liberty each to unite to its respective commissioner, scientific or other assistants, such as astronomers and surveyors, whose concurrence shall not be considered necessary for the settlement and of a true line of division between the two Republics; that line shall be alone established upon which the commissioners may fix, their consent in this particular being considered decisive and an integral part of this treaty, without necessity of ulterior ratification or approval, and without room for interpretation of any kind by either of the parties contracting.

The dividing line thus established shall, in all time, be faithfully respected by the two governments, without any variation therein, unless of the express and free consent of the two, given in conformity to the principles of the law of nations, and in accordance with the constitution of each country respectively.

In consequence, the stipulation in the fifth article of the treaty of Guadalupe upon the boundary line therein described is no longer of any force, wherein it may conflict with that here established, the said line being considered annulled and abolished wherever it may not coincide with the present, and in the same manner remaining in full force where in accordance with the same.

ARTICLE II.

The government of Mexico hereby releases the United States from all liability on account of the obligations contained in the eleventh article of the treaty of Guadalupe Hidalgo; and the said article and the thirty-third article of the treaty of amity, commerce, and navigation between the United States of America and the United Mexican States concluded at Mexico, on the fifth day of April, 1831, are hereby abrogated.

ARTICLE III.

In consideration of the foregoing stipulations, the Government of the United States agrees to pay to the government of Mexico, in the city of New York, the sum of ten millions of dollars, of which seven millions shall be paid immediately upon the exchange of the ratifications of this treaty, and the remaining three millions as soon as the boundary line shall be surveyed, marked, and established.

ARTICLE IV.

The provisions of the sixth and seventh articles of the treaty of Guadalupe Hidalgo having been rendered nugatory, for the most part, by the cession of territory granted in the first article of this treaty, the said articles are hereby abrogated and annulled, and the provisions as herein expressed substituted therefor. The vessels, and citizens of the United States shall, in all time, have free and uninterrupted passage through the Gulf of California, to and from their possessions situated north of the boundary line of the two countries. It being understood that this passage is to be by navigating the Gulf of California and the river Colorado, and not by land, without the express consent of the Mexican government; and precisely the same provisions, stipulations, and restrictions, in all respects, are hereby agreed upon and adopted, and shall be scrupulously observed and enforced by the two contracting governments in reference to the Rio Colorado, so far and for such distance as the middle of that river is made their common boundary line by the first article of this treaty.

The several provisions, stipulations, and restrictions contained in the 7th article of the treaty of Guadalupe Hidalgo shall remain in force only so far as regards the Rio Bravo del Forte, below the initial of the said boundary provided in the first article of this treaty; that is to say, below the intersection of the 31° 47' 30" parallel of latitude, with the boundary line established by the late treaty dividing said river from its mouth upwards, according to the fifth article of the treaty of Guadalupe.

ARTICLE V.

All the provisions of the eighth and ninth, sixteenth and seventeenth articles of the treaty of Guadalupe Hidalgo, shall apply to the territory ceded by the Mexican Republic in the first article of the present treaty, and to all the rights of persons and property, both civil and ecclesiastical, within the same, as fully and as effectually as if the said articles were herein again recited and set forth.

ARTICLE VI.

No grants of land within the territory ceded by the first article of this treaty bearing date subsequent to the day—twenty-fifth of September—when the minister and subscriber to this treaty on the part of the United States, proposed to the Government of Mexico to terminate the question of boundary, will be considered valid or be recognized by the United States, or will any grants made previously be respected or be considered as obligatory which have not been located and duly recorded in the archives of Mexico.

ARTICLE VII.

Should there at any future period (which God forbid) occur any disagreement between the two nations which might lead to a rupture of their relations and reciprocal peace, they bind themselves in like manner to procure by every possible method the adjustment of every difference; and should they still in this manner not succeed, never will they proceed to a declaration of war, without having previously paid attention to what has been set forth in article twenty-one of the treaty of Guadalupe for similar cases; which article, as well as the twenty-second is here reaffirmed.

ARTICLE VIII.

The Mexican Government having on the 5th of February, 1853, authorized the early construction of a plank and railroad across the Isthmus of Tehuantepec, and, to secure the stable benefits of said transit way to the persons and merchandise of the citizens of Mexico and the United States, it is stipulated that neither government will interpose any obstacle to the transit of persons and merchandise of both nations; and at no time shall higher charges be made on the transit of persons and property of citizens of the United States, than may be made on the persons and property of other foreign nations, nor shall any interest in said transit way, nor in the proceeds thereof, be transferred to any foreign government.

The United States, by its agents, shall have the right to transport across the isthmus, in closed bags, the mails of the United States not intended for distribution along the line of communication; also the effects of the United States government and its citizens, which may be intended for transit, and not for distribution on the isthmus, free of custom-house or other charges by the Mexican government. Neither passports nor letters of security will be required of persons crossing the isthmus and not remaining in the country.

When the construction of the railroad shall be completed, the Mexican government agrees to open a port of entry in addition to the port of Vera Cruz, at or near the terminus of said road on the Gulf of Mexico.

The two governments will enter into arrangements for the prompt transit of troops and munitions of the United States, which that government may have occasion to send from one part of its territory to another, lying on opposite sides of the continent.

The Mexican government having agreed to protect with its whole power the prosecution, preservation, and security of the work, the United States may extend its protection as it shall judge wise to it when it may feel sanctioned and warranted by the public or international law.

ARTICLE IX.

This treaty shall be ratified, and the respective ratifications shall be exchanged at the city of Washington within the exact period of six months from the date of its signature, or sooner, if possible.

In testimony whereof, we, the plenipotentiaries of the contracting parties, have hereunto affixed our hands and seals at Mexico, the thirtieth (30th) day of December, in the year of our Lord one thousand eight hundred and fifty-three, in the thirty-third year of the independence of the Mexican republic, and the seventy-eighth of that of the United States.

JAMES GADSDEN,
MANUEL DIEZ DE BONILLA
JOSE SALAZAR YLARBEGUI
J. MARIANO MONTERDE,

And whereas the said treaty, as amended, has been duly ratified on both parts, and the respective ratifications of the same have this day been exchanged at Washington, by WILLIAM L. MARCY, Secretary of State of the United States, and SENOR GENERAL DON JUAN N. ALMONTE, Envoy Extraordinary and Minister Plenipotentiary of the Mexican Republic, on the part of their respective Governments:

Now, therefore, be it known that I, FRANKLIN PIERCE, President of the United States of America, have caused the said treaty to be made public, to the end that the same, and every clause and ar-

ticle thereof, may be observed and fulfilled with good faith by the United States and the citizens thereof.

In witness whereof I have hereunto set my hand and caused the seal of the United States to be affixed.

Done at the city of Washington, this thirtieth day of June, in the year of our Lord one thousand eight hundred and fifty-four, and of the Independence of the United States the seventy-eighth.
BY THE PRESIDENT:
FRANKLIN PIERCE,
W. L. MARCY, Secretary of State.

6. Treaty of Paris between the United States and Spain (1898)

The United States of America and Her Majesty the Queen Regent of Spain, in the name of her august son Don Alfonso XIII, desiring to end the state of war now existing between the two countries, have for that purpose appointed as plenipotentiaries:

The President of the United States, William R. Day, Cushman K. Davis, William P. Frye, George Gray, and Whitelaw Reid, citizens of the United States;

And Her Majesty the Queen Regent of Spain,

Don Eugenio Montero Rios, president of the senate, Don Buenaventura de Abarzuza, senator of the Kingdom and ex-minister of the Crown; Don Jose de Garnica, deputy of the Cortes and associate justice of the supreme court; Don Wenceslao Ramirez de Villa-Urrutia, envoy extraordinary and minister plenipotentiary at Brussels, and Don Rafael Cerero, general of division;

Who, having assembled in Paris, and having exchanged their full powers, which were found to be in due and proper form, have, after discussion of the matters before them, agreed upon the following articles:

ARTICLE I.

Spain relinquishes all claim of sovereignty over and title to Cuba. And as the island is, upon its evacuation by Spain, to be occupied by the United States, the United States will, so long as such occupation shall last, assume and discharge the obligations that may under international law result from the fact of its occupation, for the protection of life and property.

ARTICLE II.

Spain cedes to the United States the island of Porto Rico and other islands now under Spanish sovereignty in the West Indies, and the island of Guam in the Marianas or Ladrones.

ARTICLE III.

Spain cedes to the United States the archipelago known as the Philippine Islands, and comprehending the islands lying within the following line:

A line running from west to east along or near the twentieth parallel of north latitude, and through the middle of the navigable channel of Bachi, from the one hundred and eighteenth (118th) to the one hundred and twenty-seventh (127th) degree meridian of longitude east of Greenwich, thence along the one hundred and twenty-seventh (127th) degree meridian of longitude east of Greenwich to the parallel of four degrees and forty-five minutes (4 ° 45') north latitude, thence along the parallel of four degrees and forty-five minutes (4° 45') north latitude to its intersection with meridian of longitude one hundred and nineteen degrees and thirty-

five minutes (119° 35') east of Greenwich, thence along the meridian of longitude one hundred and nineteen degrees and thirty-five minutes (119° 35') east of Greenwich to the parallel of latitude seven degrees and forty minutes (7° 40') north, thence along the parallel of latitude of seven degrees and forty minutes (7° 40') north to its intersection with the one hundred and sixteenth (116th) degree meridian of longitude east of Greenwich, thence by a direct line to the intersection of the tenth (10th) degree parallel of north latitude with the one hundred and eighteenth (118th) degree meridian of longitude east of Greenwich, and thence along the one hundred and eighteenth (118th) degree meridian of longitude east of Greenwich to the point of beginning. The United States will pay to Spain the sum of twenty million dollars ($20,000,000) within three months after the exchange of the ratifications of the present treaty.

ARTICLE IV.

The United States will, for the term of ten years from the date of the exchange of the ratifications of the present treaty, admit Spanish ships and merchandise to the ports of the Philippine Islands on the same terms as ships and merchandise of the United States.

ARTICLE V.

The United States will, upon the signature of the present treaty, send back to Spain, at its own cost, the Spanish soldiers taken as prisoners of war on the capture of Manila by the American forces. The arms of the soldiers in question shall be restored to them.

Spain will, upon the exchange of the ratifications of the present treaty, proceed to evacuate the Philippines, as well as the island of Guam, on terms similar to those agreed upon by the Commissioners appointed to arrange for the evacuation of Porto Rico and other islands in the West Indies, under the Protocol of August 12, 1898, which is to continue in force till its provisions are completely executed.

The time within which the evacuation of the Philippine Islands and Guam shall be completed shall be fixed by the two Governments. Stands of colors, uncaptured war vessels, small arms, guns of all calibres, with their carriages and accessories, powder, ammunition, livestock, and materials and supplies of all kinds, belonging to the land and naval forces of Spain in the Philippines and Guam, remain the property of Spain. Pieces of heavy ordnance, exclusive of field artillery, in the fortifications and coast defenses, shall remain in their emplacements for the term of six months, to be reckoned from the exchange of ratifications of the treaty; and the United States may, in the meantime, purchase such material from Spain, if a satisfactory agreement between the two Governments on the subject shall be reached.

ARTICLE VI.

Spain will, upon the signature of the present treaty, release all prisoners of war, and all persons detained or imprisoned for political offenses, in connection with the insurrections in Cuba and the Philippines and the war with the United States.

Reciprocally, the United States will release all persons made prisoners of war by the American forces, and will undertake to obtain the release of all Spanish prisoners in the hands of the insurgents in Cuba and the Philippines.

The Government of the United States will at its own cost return to Spain and the Government of Spain will at its own cost return to the United States, Cuba, Porto Rico, and the Philippines, according to the situation of their respective homes, prisoners released or caused to be released by them, respectively, under this article.

ARTICLE VII.

The United States and Spain mutually relinquish all claims for indemnity, national and individual, of every kind, of either Government, or of its citizens or subjects, against the other Government, that may have arisen since the beginning of the late insurrection in Cuba and prior to the exchange of ratifications of the present treaty, including all claims for indemnity for the cost of the war.

The United States will adjudicate and settle the claims of its citizens against Spain relinquished in this article.

ARTICLE VIII.

In conformity with the provisions of Articles I, II, and III of this treaty, Spain relinquishes in Cuba, and cedes in Porto Rico and other islands in the West Indies, in the island of Guam, and in the Philippine Archipelago, all the buildings, wharves, barracks, forts, structures, public highways and other immovable property which, in conformity with law, belong to the public domain, and as such belong to the Crown of Spain.

And it is hereby declared that the relinquishment or cession, as the case may be, to which the preceding paragraph refers, can not in any respect impair the property or rights which by law belong to the peaceful possession of property of all kinds, of provinces, municipalities, public or private establishments, ecclesiastical or civic bodies, or any other associations having legal capacity to acquire and possess property in the aforesaid territories renounced or ceded, or of private individuals, of whatsoever nationality such individuals may be.

The aforesaid relinquishment or cession, as the case may be, includes all documents exclusively referring to the sovereignty relinquished or ceded that may exist in the archives of the Peninsula. Where any document in such archives only in part relates to said sovereignty, a copy of such part will be furnished whenever it shall be requested. Like rules shall be reciprocally observed in favor of Spain in respect of documents in the archives of the islands above referred to.

In the aforesaid relinquishment or cession, as the case may be, are also included such rights as the Crown of Spain and its authorities possess in respect of the official archives and records, executive as well as judicial, in the islands above referred to, which relate to said islands or the rights and property of their inhabitants. Such archives and records shall be carefully preserved, and private persons shall without distinction have the right to require, in accordance with law, authenticated copies of the contracts, wills, and other instruments forming part of notorial protocols or files, or which may be contained in the executive or judicial archives, be the latter in Spain or in the islands aforesaid.

ARTICLE IX.

Spanish subjects, natives of the Peninsula, residing in the territory over which Spain by the present treaty relinquishes or cedes her sovereignty, may remain in such territory or may remove therefrom, retaining in either event all their rights of property, including the right to sell or dispose of such property or of its proceeds; and they shall also have the right to carry on their industry, commerce and professions, being subject in respect thereof to such laws as are applicable to other foreigners. In case they remain in the territory they may preserve their allegiance to the Crown of Spain by making, before a court of record, within a year from the date of the exchange of ratifications of this treaty, a declaration of their decision to preserve such allegiance; in default of which declaration they shall be held to have renounced it and to have adopted the nationality of the territory in which they may reside.

The civil rights and political status of the native inhabitants of the territories hereby ceded to the United States shall be determined by the Congress.

ARTICLE X.

The inhabitants of the territories over which Spain relinquishes or cedes her sovereignty shall be secured in the free exercise of their religion.

ARTICLE XI.

The Spaniards residing in the territories over which Spain by this treaty cedes or relinquishes her sovereignty shall be subject in matters civil as well as criminal to the jurisdiction of the courts of the country wherein they reside, pursuant to the ordinary laws governing the same; and they shall have the right to appear before such courts, and to pursue the same course as citizens of the country to which the courts belong.

ARTICLE XII.

Judicial proceedings pending at the time of the exchange of ratifications of this treaty in the territories over which Spain relinquishes or cedes her sovereignty shall be determined according to the following rules:

1. Judgments rendered either in civil suits between private individuals, or in criminal matters, before the date mentioned, and with respect to which there is no recourse or right of review under the Spanish law, shall be deemed to be final, and shall be executed in due form by competent authority in the territory within which such judgments should be carried out.

2. Civil suits between private individuals which may on the date mentioned be undetermined shall be prosecuted to judgment before the court in which they may then be pending or in the court that may be substituted therefor.

3. Criminal actions pending on the date mentioned before the Supreme Court of Spain against citizens of the territory which by this treaty ceases to be Spanish shall continue under its jurisdiction until final judgment; but, such judgment having been rendered, the execution thereof shall be committed to the competent authority of the place in which the case arose.

ARTICLE XIII.

The rights of property secured by copyrights and patents acquired by Spaniards in the Island of Cuba and in Porto Rico, the Philippines and other ceded territories, at the time of the exchange of the ratifications of this treaty, shall continue to be respected. Spanish scientific, literary and artistic works, not subversive of public order in the territories in question, shall continue to be admitted free of duty into such territories, for the period of ten years, to be reckoned from the date of the exchange of the ratifications of this treaty.

ARTICLE XIV.

Spain will have the power to establish consular officers in the ports and places of the territories, the sovereignty over which has been either relinquished or ceded by the present treaty.

ARTICLE XV.

The Government of each country will, for the term of ten years, accord to the merchant vessels of the other country the same treatment in respect of all port charges, including entrance and clearance dues, light dues, and tonnage duties, as it accords to its own merchant vessels, not engaged in the coastwise trade.

ARTICLE XVI.

It is understood that any obligations assumed in this treaty by the United States with respect to Cuba are limited to the time of its occupancy thereof; but it will upon termination of such occupancy, advise any Government established in the island to assume the same obligations.

ARTICLE XVII.

The present treaty shall be ratified by the President of the United States, by and with the advice and consent of the Senate thereof, and by Her Majesty the Queen Regent of Spain; and the ratifications shall be exchanged at Washington within six months from the date hereof, or earlier if possible. In faith whereof, we, the respective Plenipotentiaries, have signed this treaty and have hereunto affixed our seals. Done in duplicate at Paris, the tenth day of December, in the year of Our Lord one thousand eight hundred and ninety-eight.

[Seal] William R. Day
[Seal] Cushman K. Davis
[Seal] William P. Frye
[Seal] Geo. Gray
[Seal] Whitelaw Reid
[Seal] Eugenio Montero Rios
[Seal] B. de Abarzuza
[Seal] J. de Garnica
[Seal] W. R. de Villa Urrutia
[Seal] Rafael Cerero

7. Plea for New Mexican Statehood by Governor Miguel A. Otero (1901)

Fellow citizens: It is with pride and pleasure that I greet you on this occasion when for the 21st year the metropolis of New Mexico celebrates her territorial fair.

This occasion is one of unusual significance and importance to you and the whole territory, as upon your action today will largely depend the action of Congress in regard to that question of supreme importance to our future, our admission as a state of the Union.

My own views upon this subject are too well known to need repetition here; in each message to the legislature, and in every report to the secretary of the interior, I have urged the passage of an enabling act and set out in full the reasons and arguments for it. I have issued the proclamation calling this meeting of the people that they might express themselves directly instead of through their legislature or governors.

For more than half a century we have been of, yet not one of, the United States; during all that period we have been true and loyal to the laws and flag of that glorious Union of which we hope to become a part, and have freely given of our blood and treasure to maintain its supremacy and glory. During that time we have seen fifteen states admitted, one of them taken largely from within our borders, and a territory created out of one of our counties; each of these states save one, when admitted had less population and taxable property than we now possess, and none was in any respect better equipped for self government than we.

As early as June 1850, a constitution was adopted by our people for the formation of a state which prohibited slavery in New Mexico, showing at that early day that our people were fully alive to the dangers that threatened the republic, and the only course if could pursue to carry out the great future which these United States have wrought in proclaiming liberty throughout the world and to the peoples thereof. Under this constitution, two United States senators and a member of congress were elected, who were not recognized by Congress. But it did in September of that year create us into a territory by the organic act which is still our fundamental law.

Nothing further was done of a public nature towards our admission until 1874, when a bill for the purpose was introduced by Honorable S.B. Elkins, our delegate. This was defeated but the effort was renewed at the next and each succeeding Congress. With every renewed effort and additional reasons for our admission the opposition has grown the stronger, until the conclusion is irresistible that some strong personal and financial interests are arrayed against us for selfish aggrandizement. One evidence of this is the Elephant Butte dam; and another the segregation of large areas of public domain for so-called forest reserves, and the effort being made for a government lease law. As a territory, we cannot combat these schemes; we have no voice in the disposition of that land that we have struggled so long to maintain as a part of our territory, while, as a state, we would be able to assert and retain our rights.

In 1889, as distinguished a body of men assembled for the purpose of framing a constitution for the new state of New Mexico as had ever gathered for a similar purpose, and after deliberating for nearly a month, formulated a constitution which is the peer of any similar document in the Union. It is so fair, so liberal, and so comprehensive that I caused it to be published in my last report as the strongest showing that could be made upon our capacity for self government. Owing to an unfortunate combination of circumstances, this most admirable constitution was rejected by the people at the election held in 1890, but it will stand as a monument to the wisdom and statesmanship of its framers.

I believe that the time is now ripe for the fruition of our hopes; that Congress knows the merit of our claims and will no longer deny us the privilege we have sought so long, and that the action of this assemblage of representative citizens of the territory will prove a potent help toward that end.

I do not, on an occasion like this, wish to speak of disagreeable facts, but it is well that we should realize and face them and then apply the remedy.

Our ridiculously low assessment for taxation is constantly spoken of and reflected upon. The present assessed value of the territory is less than forty millions, while it is a notorious fact recognized by all who know anything about the subject that it ought to at least be three times that amount. The figures show that we have dropped from forty-five millions, in 1890, to less than thirty-eight million, in 1901, and the reduction still goes on, until, as a means of self preservation, in order to protect our credit and pay the actual expense of the government, the territory board of equalization last month made a raise on the returned value of all the property it could reach. This, my fellow citizens, is a lamentable state of affairs and one that must be remedied by you. You must see to it that proper men are elected to assess the property and equalize its value, so that we may appear to the world that we are in fact, as to our wealth and ability, able to pay our obligations.

This I believe to be the principal objection to our immediate admission, and if at this meeting you will adopt suitable resolutions upon this most important and vital subject and determine to see them carried out, you will have taken a long step toward the object for which we are here assembled.

I understand that some timorous people are afraid of the expense and responsibility attached to our becoming a state, but such fears are unworthy of American manhood; if they were to prevail in the ordinary affairs of life no one would exercise his rights of citizenship, or incur the duties and responsibilities of family life. The history of every newly admitted state is one of growth, advance, and prosperity, and we would be no exception to this rule, but, on the contrary, by our location midway of the oceans which bound the nation, with our natural wealth of mineral, timber, and lands, and the railroad connections we already have, New Mexico will at once assume a commanding position in the sisterhood of states, and the present motto, "Cresit Eundo" on our seal will assume added meaning and significance from the date of our admission.

8. Cuba Agreement (1903)

Whereas the Congress of the United States of America, by an Act approved March 2, 1901, provided as follows:

Provided further, That in fulfillment of the declaration contained in the joint resolution approved April twentieth, eighteen hundred and ninety-eight, entitled, "For the recognition of the independence of the people of Cuba, demanding that the Government of Spain relinquish its authority and government in the island of Cuba, and to withdraw its land and naval forces from Cuba and Cuban waters, and directing the President of the United States to use the land and naval forces of the United States to carry resolutions into effect," the President is hereby authorized to "leave the government and control of the island of Cuba to its people" so soon as a government shall have been established in said island under a constitution either as a part thereof or in an ordinance appended thereto, shall define the future relations of the United States with Cuba, substantially as follows:

"I.—That the government of Cuba shall never enter into any treaty or other compact with any foreign power or powers which will impair or tend to impair the independence of Cuba, nor in any manner authorize or permit any foreign power or powers to obtain by colonization or for military or naval purposes or otherwise, lodgement in or control over any portion of said island."

"II.—That said government shall not assume or contract any public debt, to pay the interest upon which, and to make reasonable sinking fund provision for the ultimate discharge of which, the ordinary revenues of the island, after defraying the current expenses of government shall be inadequate."

"III.—That the government of Cuba consents that the United States may exercise the right to intervene for the preservation of Cuban independence, the maintenance of a government adequate for the protection of life, property, and individual liberty, and for discharging the obligations with respect to Cuba imposed by the Treaty of Paris on the United States, now to be assumed and undertaken by the government of Cuba."

"IV.—That all Acts of the United States in Cuba during its military occupancy thereof are ratified and validated, and all lawful rights acquired thereunder shall be maintained and protected."

"V.—That the government of Cuba will execute, and as far as necessary extend, the plans already devised or other plans to be mutually agreed upon, for the sanitation of the cites of the island, to the end that a recurrence of epidemic and infectious diseases may be prevented thereby assuring protection to the people and commerce of Cuba, as well as to the commerce of the southern ports of the United States and the people residing therein."

"VI.—That the Isle of Pines shall be omitted from the proposed constitutional boundaries of Cuba, the title thereto being left to future adjustment by treaty."

"VII.—That to enable the United States to maintain the independence of Cuba, and to protect the people thereof, as well as for its own defense, the government of Cuba will sell or lease to the United States lands necessary for coaling or naval stations at certain specified points to be agreed upon with the President of the United States."

"VIII.—That by way of further assurance the Government of Cuba will embody the foregoing provisions in a permanent treaty with the United States.."

Whereas the Constitutional Convention of Cuba, on June twelfth, 1901, adopted a Resolution adding to the Constitution of the Republic of Cuba which was adopted on the twenty-first of February 1901, an appendix in the words and letters of the eight enumerated articles of the above cited act of the Congress of the United States;

And whereas, by the establishment of the independent and sovereign government of the Republic of Cuba, under the constitution promulgated on the 20th of May, 1902, which embraced the foregoing conditions, and by the withdrawal of the Government of the United States as an intervening power, on the same date, it becomes necessary to embody the above cited provisions in a permanent treaty between the United States of America and the Republic of Cuba;

The United States of America and the Republic of Cuba, being desirous to carry out the foregoing conditions, have for the purpose appointed as their plenipotentiaries to conclude a treaty to that end,

The President of the United States of America, Herbert G. Squiers, Envoy Extraordinary and Minister Plenipotentiary at Havana,

And the President of the Republic of Cuba, Carlos de Zaldo y Beurmann, Secretary of State and Justice,—who after communicating to each other their full powers found in good and due form, have agreed upon the following articles:

Article I.

The Government of Cuba shall never enter into any treaty or other compact with any foreign power or powers which will impair or tend to impair the independence of Cuba, nor in any manner authorize or permit any foreign power or powers to obtain by colonization or for military or naval purposes, or otherwise, lodgement in or control over any portion of said island.

Article II.

The Government of Cuba shall not assume or contract any public debt to pay the interest upon which, and to make reasonable sinking-fund provision for the ultimate discharge of which, the ordinary revenues of the Island of Cuba, after defraying the current expenses of the Government, shall be inadequate.

Article III.

The Government of Cuba consents that the United State may exercise the right to intervene for the preservation of Cuban independence, the maintenance of a government adequate for the protection of life, property, and individual liberty, and for discharging the obligations with respect to Cuba imposed by the Treaty of Paris on the United States, now to be assumed and undertaken by the Government of Cuba.

Article IV.

All acts of the United States in Cuba during its military occupancy thereof are ratified and validated, and all lawful rights acquired thereunder shall be maintained and protected.

Article V.

The Government of Cuba will execute, and, as far as necessary, extend the plans already devised, or other plans to be mutually agreed upon, for the sanitation of the cities of the island, to the end that a recurrence of epidemic and infectious diseases may be prevented, thereby assuring protection to the people and commerce of Cuba, as well as to the commerce of the Southern ports of the United States and the people residing therein.

Article VI.

The Island of Pines shall be omitted from the boundaries of Cuba specified in the Constitution, the title thereof being left to future adjustment by treaty.

Article VII.

To enable the United States to maintain the independence of Cuba, and to protect the people thereof, as well as for its own defense, the Government of Cuba will sell or lease to the United States lands necessary for coaling or naval stations, at certain specified points, to be agreed upon with the President of the United States.

Article VIII.

The present Convention shall be ratified by each party in conformity with the respective Constitutions of the two countries, and the ratifications shall be exchanged in the City of Washington within eight months form this date.

In witness whereof, we the respective Plenipotentiaries, have signed the same in duplicate in English and Spanish, and have affixed our respective seals, Havana, Cuba, this twenty-second day of May, year nineteen hundred and three.

H.G. Squiers
Carlos De Zaldo

9. Constitution of Puerto Rico (1952)

We, the people of Puerto Rico, in order to organize ourselves politically on a fully democratic basis, to promote the general welfare, and to secure for ourselves and our posterity the complete enjoyment of human rights, placing our trust in Almighty God, do ordain and establish this Constitution for the commonwealth which, in the exercise of our natural rights, we now create within our union with the United States of America.

In so doing, we declare:

The democratic system is fundamental to the life of the Puerto Rican community;

We understand that the democratic system of government is one in which the will of the people is the source of public power, the political order is subordinate to the rights of man, the free participation of the citizen in collective decisions is assured;

We consider as determining factors in our life our citizenship of the United States of America and our aspiration continually to enrich our democratic heritage in the individual and collective enjoyment of is rights and privileges; our loyalty to the principles of the Federal Constitution; the coexistence in Puerto Rico of the two great cultures of the American Hemisphere; our fervor for education; our faith in justice; our devotion to the courageous, industrious, and peaceful way of life; our fidelity to individual human values above and beyond social position, racial differences, and economic interests; and our hope for a better world based on these principles.

Article I

The Commonwealth

Section 1.—The Commonwealth of Puerto Rico is hereby constituted. Its political power emanates from the people and shall be exercised in accordance with their will, within the terms of the compact agreed upon between the people of Puerto Rico and the United States of America.

Section 2.—The government of the Commonwealth of Puerto Rico shall be republican in form and its legislative, judicial and executive branches as established by this Constitution shall be equally subordinate to the sovereignty of the people of Puerto Rico.

Section 3.—The political authority of the Commonwealth of Puerto Rico shall extend to the Island of Puerto Rico and to the adjacent islands within is jurisdiction.

Section 4.—The seat of the government shall be the city of San Juan.

Article II

Bill of Rights

Section 1.—The dignity of the human being is inviolable. All men are equal before the law. No discrimination shall be made on account of race, color, sex, birth, social origin or condition, or political or religious ideas. Both the laws and the system of public education shall embody these principles of essential human equality.

Section 2.—The laws shall guarantee the expression of the will of the people by means of equal, direct, and secret universal suffrage and shall protect the citizen against any coercion in the exercise of the electoral franchise.

Section 3.—No law shall be made respecting an establishment of religion or prohibiting the free exercise thereof. There shall be complete separation of church and state.

Section 4.—No law shall be made abridging the freedom of speech or of the press, or the right of the people peaceably to assemble and to petition the government for a redress of grievances.

Section 5.—Every person has the right to an education which shall be directed to the full development of the human personality and to the strengthening of respect for human rights and fundamental freedoms. There shall be a system of free and wholly non-sectarian public education. Instruction in the elementary and secondary schools shall be free and shall be compulsory in the elementary schools to the extent permitted by the facilities of the state. No public property or public funds shall be used for the support of schools or educational institutions other than those of the state. Nothing contained in this provision shall prevent the state from furnishing to any child non-educational services established by law for the protection or welfare of children.

Section 6.—Persons may join with each other and organize freely for any lawful purpose, except in military or quasi-military organizations.

Section 7.—The right to life, liberty and the enjoyment of property is recognized as a fundamental right of man. The death penalty shall not exist. No person shall be deprived of his liberty or property without due process of law. No person in Puerto Rico shall be denied the equal protection of the laws. No laws impairing the obligation of contracts shall be enacted. A minimum amount of property and possessions shall be exempt from attachment as provided by law.

Section 8.—Every person has the right to the protection of law against abusive attacks on his honor, reputation, and private or family life.

Section 9.—Private property shall not be taken or damaged for public use except upon payment of just compensation and in the manner provided by law. No law shall be enacted authorizing condemnation of printing presses, machinery, or material devoted to publications of any kind. The buildings in which these objects are located may be condemned only after a judicial funding of public convenience and necessity pursuant to procedure that shall be provided by law, and may be taken before such a judicial finding only when there is placed at the disposition of the publication an adequate site in which it can be installed and continue to operate for a reasonable time.

Section 10.—The right of the people to be secure in their persons, houses, papers, and effects against unreasonable searches and seizures shall not be violated.

Wire-tapping is prohibited.

No warrant for arrest or search and seizure shall issue except by judicial authority and only upon probable cause supported by oath or affirmation, and particularly describing the place to be searched and the persons to be arrested or the things to be seized.

Evidence obtained in violation of this section shall be inadmissible in the courts.

Section 11.—In all criminal prosecution, the accused shall enjoy the right to have a speedy and public trial, to be informed of the nature and cause of the accusation and to have a copy thereof, to be confronted with the witnesses against him, to have compulsory process for obtaining witnesses in his favor, to have assistance of counsel, and to be presumed innocent.

In all prosecutions for a felony the accused shall have the right of trial by an impartial jury composed of twelve residents of the district, who may render their verdict by a majority vote which in no case may be less than nine.

No person shall be compelled in any criminal case to be a witness against himself and the failure of the accused to testify may be neither taken into consideration nor commented upon against him.

No person shall be twice put in jeopardy of punishment for the same offense.

Before conviction every accused shall be entitled to be admitted to bail.

Incarceration prior to trial shall not exceed six months nor shall bail or fines be excessive. No person shall be imprisoned for debt.

Section 12.—Neither slavery nor involuntary servitude shall exist except in the latter case as a punishment for crime after the accused has been duly convicted. Cruel and unusual punishments shall not be inflicted. Suspension of civil rights including the right to vote shall cease upon service of the term of imprisonment imposed.

No ex post facto law or bill of attainder shall be passed.

Section 13.—The writ of habeas corpus shall be granted without delay and free of costs. The privilege of the writ of habeas corpus shall not be suspended, unless the public safety requires it in case of rebellion, insurrection or invasion. Only the Legislative Assembly shall have the power to suspend the privilege of the writ of habeas corpus and the laws regulating is issuance.

The military authority shall always be subordinate to civil authority.

Section 14.—No titles of nobility or other hereditary honors shall be granted. No officer or employee of the Commonwealth shall accept gifts, donations, decorations or offices from any foreign country or officer without prior authorization by the Legislative Assembly.

Section 15.—The employment of children less than fourteen years of age in any occupation which is prejudicial to their health or morals or which places them in jeopardy of life or limb is prohibited.

No child less than sixteen years of age shall be kept in custody in a jail or penitentiary.

Section 16.—The right of every employee to choose his occupation freely and to resign therefrom is recognized, as is his right to equal pay for equal work, to a reasonable minimum salary, to protection against risks to his health or person in his work or employment, and to an ordinary workday which shall not exceed eight hours. An employee may work in excess of this daily limit only if he is paid extra compensation as provided by law, at a rate never less than one and one-half times the regular rate at which he is employed.

Section 17.—Persons employed by private businesses, enterprises, and individual employers and by agencies or instrumentalities of the government operating as private businesses or enterprises, shall have the right to organize and to bargain collectively with their employers through representatives of their own free choosing in order to promote their welfare.

Section 18.—In order to assure their right to organize and to bargain collectively, persons employed by private businesses, enterprises, and individual employers and by agencies or instrumentalities of the government operating as private businesses or enterprises, in their direct relations with their own employers shall have the right to strike, to picket, and to engage in other legal concerted activities.

Nothing herein contained shall impair the authority of the Legislative Assembly to enact laws to deal with grave emergencies that clearly imperil the public health or safety or essential public services.

Section 19.—The foregoing enumeration of rights shall not be construed restrictively nor does it contemplate the exclusion of other rights not specifically mentioned which belong to the people in a democracy. The power of the Legislative Assembly to enact laws for the protection of the life, health, and general welfare of the people shall likewise not be construed restrictively.

Section 20.—The Commonwealth also recognizes the existence of the following human rights:

The right of every person to receive free elementary and secondary education.

The right of every person to obtain work.

The right of every person to a standard of living adequate for the health and well-being of himself and of his family, and especially to food, clothing, housing and medical care and necessary social services.

The right of every person to social protection in the event of unemployment, sickness, old age, or disability.

The right of motherhood and childhood to special care and assistance.

The rights set forth in this section are closely connected with the progressive development of the economy of the Commonwealth and require, for their full effectiveness, sufficient resources and an agricultural and industrial development not yet attained by the Puerto Rican community.

In the light of their duty to achieve the full liberty of the citizen, the people and the government of Puerto Rico shall do everything in their power to promote the greatest possible expansion of the system of production, to assure the fairest distribution of economic output, and to obtain the maximum understanding between individual initiative and collective cooperation. The executive and judicial branches shall bear in mind this duty and shall construe the laws that tend to fulfill it in the most favorable manner possible.

Letter from the Santa Fe Jail by Reies Lopez Tijerina (1969)

From my cell block in this jail I am writing these reflections. I write them to my people, the Indo-Hispanos, to my friends among the Anglos, to the agents of the federal government, the state of New Mexico, the Southwest, and the entire Indo-Hispano world—"Latin America."

I write to you as one of the clearest victims of the madness and racism in the hearts of our present-day politicians and rulers.

At this time, August 17, I have been in jail for 65 days—since June 11, 1969, when my appeal bond from another case was revoked by a federal judge. I am here today because I resisted an assassination attempt led by an agent of the federal government—an agent of all those who do not want anybody to speak out for the poor, all those who do not want Reies Lopez Tijerina to stand in their way as they continue to rob the poor people, all those many rich people from outside the state with their summer homes and ranches here whose pursuit of happiness depends on thievery, all those who have robbed the people of their land and culture for 120 years. . . .

What is my real crime? As I and the poor people see it, especially the Indo-Hispanos, my only crime is UPHOLDING OUR RIGHTS AS PROTECTED BY THE TREATY OF GUADALUPE HIDALGO which ended the so-called Mexican-American War of 1846–48. My only crime is demanding the respect and protection of our property, which has been confiscated illegally by the federal government. Ever since the treaty was signed in 1848, our people have been asking every elected president of the United States for a redress of grievances. Like the Black people, we too have been criminally ignored. Our right to the Spanish land grant pueblos in the real reason why I am in prison at this moment.

Our cause and our claim and our methods are legitimate. Yet even after a jury in a court of law acquitted me last December, they still call me a violent man. But the right to make a citizen's arrest, as I attempted to make that day on Evans, is not a violent right. On the contrary, it is law and order—unless the arrested person resists or flees to avoid prosecution. No honest citizen should avoid a citizen's arrest.

This truth is denied by the conspirators against the poor and by the press which they control There are also the Silent Contributors. The Jewish people accused the Pope of Rome for keeping silent while Hitler and his machine persecuted the Jews in Germany and other countries. I support the Jews in the right to accuse those who contributed to Hitler's acts by their SILENCE. By the same token, I denounce those in New Mexico who have never opened their mouths at any time to defend or support the thousands who have been killed, robbed, raped of their culture. I don't know of any church or Establishment organization or group of elite intellectuals that has stood up for the Treaty of Guadalupe-Hidalgo. We condemn the silence of these groups and individuals and I am sure that, like the Jewish people, the poor of New Mexico are keeping a record of the Silence which contributes to the criminal conspiracy against the Indo-Hispano in New Mexico.

As I sit in my jail cell in Santa Fe, capital of New Mexico, I pray that all the poor people will unite to bring justice to New Mexico. My cell block has no day light, no ventilation of any kind, no light of any kind. After 9 P.M., we are left in a dungeon of total darkness. Visiting rules allow only 15 minutes per week on Thursdays from 1 to 4 P.M. so that parents who work cannot visit their sons in jail. Yesterday a 22-year-old boy cut his throat. Today, Aug. 17, two young boys cut their wrists with razor blades and were taken unconscious to the hospital. My cell is dirty and there is nothing to clean it with. The whole cell block is hot and suffocating. All my prison mates complain and show a daily state of anger. But these uncomfortable conditions do not bother me, for I have a driving dream to give me strength: the happiness of my people.

I pray to God that all the Indo-Hispano people will awake to the need for unity, and to our heavenly and constitutional responsibility for fighting peacefully to win our rights. Already the rest of the Indo-Hispano world—Latin America—knows of our struggle. It is too late to keep the story of our land struggle from reaching the ears of the Indo-Hispano world. All the universities of Latin America know about our problems when Rockefeller went there last summer. Will Latin America ignore our cry from here in New Mexico and the Southwest? Times have changed and the spirit of the blood is no longer limited by national or continental boundaries.

The Indo-Hispano world will never trust the United States as long as this government occupies our land illegally. The honest policy of the United States will have to begin at home, before Rockefeller can go to Latin America again to sell good relations and friendship. Our property, freedom, and culture must be respected in New Mexico, in the whole Southwest, before the Anglo can expect to be trusted in South America, Mexico, and Canada.

This government must show its good faith to the Indo-Hispano in respect to the Treaty of Guadalupe-Hidalgo and the land question by forming a presidential committee to investigate and hold open hearings on the land question in the northern part of New Mexico. We challenge our own government to bring forth and put all the facts on the conference table. We have the evidence to prove our claims to property as well as to the cultural rights of which we have been deprived. WE ARE RIGHT—and therefore ready and willing to discuss our problems and rights under the Treaty with the Anglo federal government in New Mexico or Washington, D.C., directly or through agents.

This government must also reform the whole educational structure in the Southwest before it is too late. It should begin in the northern part of New Mexico, where 80 percent of the population are Indo-Hispanos, as a pilot center. If it works here, then a plan can be developed based on that experience in the rest of the state and wherever the Indo-Hispano population requires it.

Because I know WE ARE RIGHT, I have no regrets as I sit in my jail cell. I feel very, very proud and happy to be in jail for the reason that I am. June 8 in Coyote could have been my last day on earth. My life was spared by God, and to be honored by that miracle at Coyote will keep me happy for many years to come. I am sure that not one of my prison days is lost. Not one day has been in vain. While others are free, building their personal empires, I am in jail for defending and fighting for the rights of my people. Only my Indo-Hispano people have influenced me to be what I am. I am what I am, for my brothers.

Hispanic American Organizations

American G.I. Forum of the United States
1315 Bright Street
Corpus Christi, TX 78405
(512) 883-7602
(512) 882-2123 Fax
Website: www.incacorp.com/agif
Founder: Dr. Hector P. Garcia

Formed in 1948. Membership includes veterans of the U.S. Armed Forces, especially those of Mexican descent, and their families. Seeks to promote democracy, religious and political freedom, and equal opportunity. Provides business development assistance, scholarship and educational programs focused on Hispanics, and outreach activities. Also focuses on civil rights, housing, former prisoners of war, and political representation.

American G.I. Forum Women
c/o Marianne Martinez
4817 South 131st Street, Apt. 10
Omaha, NE 68137-1848
(402) 593-1248
Chairperson: Marianne Martinez

Founded in 1948 as the American G.I. Forum Auxiliary. Membership consists of female U.S. citizens that are married to or otherwise related to members of the American G.I. Forum of the United States. Seeks to support democracy, the U.S. Constitution, and religious and political freedom for the benefit of Hispanics and other Americans. Also supports educational issues. Publishes *The Forumeer*, a monthly newsletter.

Aspira Association
1112 16th Street NW, Ste. 340
Washington, D.C. 20036
(202) 835-3600
(202) 223-1253 Fax
Website: www.aspira.org
Executive Director: Ronald Blackburn-Moreno

Founded in 1969. Works to provide leadership training and educational assistance to the Hispanic community. Provides educational counseling, workshops, tutoring, discussion forums, and scholarship, loan, and college application assistance. Supports the National Health Careers Program, which strives to improve the level of health care provided to the Latino community, as well as to increase the number of Hispanic doctors and health care providers available. Also offers the Aspira Public Policy Leadership Program, which provides leadership training to high school students and has them analyze social, economic, and political issues. Provides a number of publications.

Asociacion Nacional Pro Personas Mayores
3325 Wilshire Blvd., Ste. 800
Los Angeles, CA 90010
(213) 487-1922
(213) 385-3014 Fax
President: Carmela G. Lacayo

Founded in 1975, the Asociacion Nacional Pro Personas Mayores is also known as the National Association for Hispanic Elderly. The group seeks to provide better health care services for Hispanics and low income elderly individuals. Administers the Senior Community Service Employment Program, which, under funding provided by the U.S. Department of Labor, helps gain employment for more than 1,900 low-income people over the age of 55. Also offers publications, social research, social services programs, and training opportunities.

Association of Hispanic Arts
173 East 116th Street, 2nd floor
New York, NY 10029
(212) 860-5445
(212) 427-2787 Fax
Executive Officer: Jane Arce Bello

Founded in 1975 in order to support the Hispanic arts. Promotes individuals and nonprofit organizations that exhibit art, dance, theater, and music reflective of Hispanic history, culture, social conditions, beliefs, and attitudes. Also provides technical assistance and referral services on administrative matters, financial management, and fund raising, as well as offering information relating to art organizations artists, and the media.

Black, Indian, Hispanic, and Asian Women in Action
122 West Franklin Avenue, Ste. 306
Minneapolis, MN 55404
(612) 870-1193
(612) 870-0855 Fax
Executive Director: Alice O. Lynch

Founded in 1983. Advocates educational programs for Black, Indian, Hispanic, and Asian women. Also focuses on issues concerning family violence, chemical dependency, social change, and physical, mental, and emotional health. Manages library holdings and publishes a quarterly newsletter called *Unison*.

Center for U.S.-Mexican Studies
c/o University of California
9500 Gilman Drive, Dept. 0510
La Jolla, CA 92093
(619) 534-4503
(619) 534-6447 Fax

E-mail: usmex@weber.edu

Website: http://weber.ucsd.edu/Depts/UsMex

The Center for U.S.-Mexican Studies was founded in 1979. Conducts research on the relationship between Mexico and the United States, as well as related topics. Offers library holdings and a number of publications, including reports and a newsletter.

Centro Gerontologico Latino

305 7th Avenue, 11th Floor

New York, NY 10001

(212) 633-0435

(212) 633-0645 Fax

President: Mario E. Tapia

Founded in 1991, Centro Gerontologico Latino seeks to improve the quality of life for Hispanic senior citizens. Operates a cable television show in Manhattan, NY, and provides a question and answer column in an area newspaper, for the purpose of providing information on and assisting Latino seniors. Also provides Thanksgiving meals to needy families.

Chicana Research and Learning Center

1502 Norris Drive

Austin, TX 78704

(512) 444-7595

Executive Officer: Martha P. Cotera

Formed in 1974 in order to provide educational and research services focused on Hispanic women. Provides assertiveness training, a speakers' bureau, library holdings, research programs, charity activities, and other functions dedicated to the advancement of Chicana women. Publishes *Mujeres Celebres: A Biographical Encyclopedia of Hispanic Women*.

Chicano Family Center

7524 Avenue E

Houston, TX 77012

(713) 923-2316

(713) 923-4243 Fax

Executive Director: Elena R. Vergana

Founded in 1971. Works to improve the Chicano community through mental health support, social work services, and cultural awareness programs. Also focuses on nutrition, citizenship, interpersonal skills, English language skills, AIDS education, teen pregnancy, emergency food assistance, and family and individual counseling. Provides the Huellas program for sixth-grade students in order to build assertiveness, self-esteem, and other skills.

Comision Femenil Mexicana Nacional

379 South Loma Drive

Los Angeles, CA 90017

(213) 484-1515

(212) 484-0880 Fax

President: Nina Aguayo Socin

Formed in 1970. Strives to support and better Latino women's rights and to advance Hispanic women socially, economically, politically, and educationally. Operates a number of special programs, such as the Chicana Service Action Center, which offers job training; Casa Victoria, a group home for troubled Hispanic teens; and Centro de Ninos, which is designed to provide bilingual development for children. Also focuses on issues such as development, education, legislation, health and welfare, teen pregnancy, and reproductive rights.

Committee for Hispanic Arts and Research

P.O. Box 12865

Austin, TX 78711

(512) 479-6397

Director: Romeo Rodriguez

The Committee for Hispanic Arts and Research was founded in 1980. The group promotes Hispanic art and artists, as well as supporting and encouraging their work. Offers scholarships, seminars, and charity programs. Publishes *La Gente*, a monthly newsletter.

Congressional Hispanic Caucus

244 Ford House Office Building

Washington, D.C. 20515

Website: www.house.gov/roybal-allard/CHC.htm

Executive Director: Richard Lopez

Founded in 1976 with membership consisting of Congress members of Hispanic origin and descent. Works toward advancing, supporting, and voicing the needs of Hispanic Americans through the legislative process.

Feministas Unidas

Department of Languages and Literatures

Arizona State University

P.O. Box 870202

Tempe, AZ 85287-0202

(480) 965-6446

(480) 965-0135 Fax

Website: www.asu.edu/clas/dll/femunida

President: Elizabeth Horan

Secretary: Cynthia Tomkins

Founded in 1979, Feministas Unidas includes feminist scholars in Hispanic, Chicano, Puerto Rican, and Luso-Brazilian studies. Provides forum discussions, workshops, and other services involving women's issues in Hispanic culture. Also provides panel discussions and *The Feministas Unidas Newsletter*.

Grand Council of Hispanic Societies in Public Service

P.O. Box 636, Stuyvesant Sta.

New York, NY 10009

(212) 460-4883

President: Luis Gonzalez

Founded in 1966, the Grand Council of Hispanic Societies in Public Service combines the efforts of 32 Hispanic groups. This larger organization supports equal employment, affirmative action, and economic opportunities for Hispanics.

Hispanic American Geriatrics Society

1 Cutts Road

Durham, NH 03824-3102

(603) 868-5757

President: Dr. Eugene E. Tillock

Founded in 1980, the Hispanic American Geriatrics Society advocates the needs of older Hispanic Americans. Provides health care services, advice, and health education programs. Publishes a newsletter called *Hispanic Aging and Health*.

Hispanic Elected Local Officials

National League of Cities

1301 Pennsylvania Avenue NW

Washington, D.C. 20004

(202) 626-3000

(202) 626-3169

(202) 626-3043 Fax

Contact: Mary France Gordon

Founded in 1976, the Hispanic Elected Local Officials has also been known as the National League of Spanish Speaking Elected Officials and as Elected Spanish Speaking Officials. The group works on local government issues, as well as on allowing and assisting elected officials in sharing information and experiences surrounding their political involvement. Publishes the quarterly *Constituency and Member Group Newsletter*.

Hispanic National Bar Association

Website: http://www.incacorp.com/hnba

Founded in 1972. Previously known as La Raza National Lawyers Association and La Raza National Bar Association. Goals include promoting jurisprudence, seeking law reform, and striving for justice and advancement in the legal profession. Also works to instill integrity, honor, and professional courtesy among Hispanic lawyers. Offers legal counseling, financial assistance, placement services, and professional training seminars. Has committees in civil rights, health care, immigration, legislation and public affairs, and similar areas.

Hispanic Policy Development Project

36 East 22nd Street, 9th Floor

New York, NY 10010

(212) 529-9323

(202) 822-8414

(212) 477-5395 Fax

Founded in 1982, the Hispanic Policy Development Project focuses on improving employment and secondary education for Hispanics. Also seeks to raise public interest in issues plaguing Latinos, as well as foster communication among all people. Strives to gain Hispanic participation in policy debates. Sponsors the National Commission on Secondary Schooling for Hispanics. Publications include books, reports, and other resources.

Instituto De Liturgia Hispana

P.O. Box 29387

Washington, D.C. 20017-0387

(202) 319-5481

(202) 526-1995

(202) 319-5875 Fax

Founded in 1970, the Instituto De Liturgia Hispana strives to produce liturgical spirituality to U.S. Hispanics. Also focuses on issues such as art and the environment. Provides lectures, workshops, and publications.

Labor Council for Latin American Advancement

815 16th Street NW, Ste. 310

Washington, D.C. 20006

(202) 347-4223

(202) 347-5095 Fax

Executive Director: Alfredo C. Montoya

Founded in 1973 as a Hispanic organization representing 43 American and international trade unions. Strives to unite the American Hispanic labor community, as well as provide them with social dignity, political and economic justice, and a better standard of living. Also strives for increased voter education, registration, and political participation among Latin workers.

Las Hermanas—United States of America

P.O. Box 15792

San Antonio, TX 78212

(210) 434-0947

Coordinator: Dolores Florez

Founded in 1971 by Roman Catholic Women of Hispanic origin. Las Hermanas—United States of America seeks to engage Hispanic women in active ministry pursuits, support cultural awareness, and overcome injustice. Sponsors workshops and offers *Informer*, a quarterly newsletter.

League of United Latin American Citizens (LULAC)

221 North Kansas, Ste. 1200

El Paso, TX 79901

(915) 577-0726

(915) 577-0914 Fax

Website: http://www.incacorp.com/lulac

President: Belen Robles

Founded in 1929, the League of United Latin American Citizens strives for gaining better social, political, economic, and educational rights for Hispanics in America. Also supports Hispanics Organized for Political Education, which encourages Latino political awareness and voter registration, and LULAC National Education Centers. Offers training programs, employment assistance, and research information on post secondary schooling for Hispanics.

LULAC National Educational Service Centers

Founded in 1973 as a part of the League of United Latin American Citizens. Strives to provide educational opportunities for Hispanic students, especially in the area of access to higher education services and institutions. Provides assistance in career planning, financial aid, and educational counseling, as well as offering the LULAC National Scholarship Fund to qualified students. Operates a three-day leadership development conference, the Washington Week Seminar, for high school students.

Medical Society of the United States and Mexico

634 South Spring Street, 11th Floor

Los Angeles, CA 90014

(213) 489-3365

(213) 629-8016 Fax

Contact: Abelardo de la Pena, Jr.

Founded in 1968 in order to promote, protect, and foster civil rights for American Latinos. Offers leadership development programs, parent organizations, and educational services. Also provides litigation services for Hispanics. Publications include two biannual newsletters, *Leading Hispanics* and *Mallef*.

Mexican American Legal Defense and Educational Fund (MALDEF)

634 South Spring Street, 11th Floor

Los Angeles, CA 90014

(213) 629-2512

(213) 629-1916 Fax

Website: http://www.maldef.org

President: Antonia Hernandez

Founded in 1968 with the main goal of protecting Hispanic civil rights. Offers civil rights class-action litigation and other legal services in areas such as education, employment, voting rights, and immigration. Offers library holdings, leadership training, and publications.

Mexican-American Opportunity Foundation

401 North Garfield Avenue
Montebello, CA 90640
(213) 890-9600
(213) 890-9616
(213) 890-9637 Fax
President: Dionicio Morales

The Mexican-American Opportunity Foundation was founded in 1962. Works to overcome problems facing Hispanics and other minorities. Programs include child care services, bilingual and bicultural development, senior citizen training and assistance, employment services, home repair assistance, educational and vocational opportunities, and counseling services. Publishes the quarterly *Information and Referral Newsletter*.

Mexican American Unity Council

2300 West Commerce
San Antonio, TX 78207
(210) 978-0500
(210) 978-0540 Fax
Contact: Sylvia Serrata

Founded in 1967 to improve living conditions in inner-city San Antonio, as well as to strive for the betterment of the Mexican-American community in the area. The Mexican American Unity Council offers educational programs and other services to help further its goals.

Movimiento Familiar Cristiano

3727 View Ct.
Santa Rosa, CA 95403
(707) 526-4892
Presidents: Rodrigo and Stella Aguadelo

Founded in 1969, membership in Movimiento Familiar Cristiano consists of husbands and wives working in unison in order to improve living conditions for Hispanic communities. Focuses studies on relations between spouses, relations between parents and children, and family relationships with society. Also sponsors retreats and offers publications.

Mujeres Activas en Letras y Cambio Social

c/o Ethnic Studies Program
Santa Clara University
Santa Clara, CA 95053
(408) 554-4511
(408) 554-4189 Fax
Website: http://h-net2.msu.edu/~ethniclann/cfp/cfp-chicana.html
Chairperson: Dr. Alma Garcia

Founded in 1982 with membership consisting of Hispanic women in higher education. Fights to overcome race, class, and gender oppression in universities, as well as strive for social change. Provides research, educational materials, and teaching items on the Chicana experience. Also focuses on women's conditions at home and in the workplace, as well as economic and social justice. Offers a speakers' bureau, placement services, and informative publications.

National Alliance of Spanish-Speaking People for Equality

16th Street NW, Ste. 601
P.O. Box 2385
Washington, D.C. 20013
(202) 234-8198
(202) 234-8198 Fax
President: Dr. Miguel Sandoval

Founded in 1970. Membership in the group consists of journalists and other Hispanics working within the media. Collects and distributes information of value to the Hispanic community, such as on topics such as education, health, housing, foreign policy, and immigration. Works to provide a public voice for Latinos on issues that affect them, as well as initiate communication among Hispanic organizations and government agencies. Works in conjunction with the Congressional Hispanic Caucus, the National Council of La Raza, and the Consortium of National Hispanic Organizations.

National Association for Chicana and Chicano Studies

c/o Dr. Carlos S. Maldonado
Eastern Washington University
Chicano Education Program
Monroe Hall 202, MS-170
Cheney, WA 99004
(509) 359-2404
(509) 359-2310 Fax
Director: Carlos S. Maldonado

Founded in 1971 as a gathering of university professors, researchers, and students interested in Chicano studies. Works to build Chicano political, educational, and cultural awareness, as well as to increase their political involvement. Also supports the study of Chicano history and achievements. Publications include *Community Empowerment and Chicano Scholarship*, *Chicano Discourse*, and other related resources.

National Association of Hispanic Federal Executives

P.O. Box 469
Herndon, VA 22070
(703) 787-0291
(703) 787-4675 Fax
Website: http://www.nahfe.org
President: Manuel Oliverez

The National Association of Hispanic Federal Executives was formed in 1984 as the Association of Hispanic Federation Executives. The organization promotes federal government employment practices and opportunities, as well as offering productivity training to current federal employees. Also provides a speakers' bureau, placement services, educational programs, statistics and research information, and a quarterly newsletter, *The Hispanic Executive*.

National Association of Latino Elected and Appointed Officials

NALEO Education Fund
5800 S. Eastern Avenue, Suite 365
Los Angeles. CA 90040
(323) 720-1932
(323) 720-9519 Fax
Website: www.naleo.org
Executive Director: Dr. Aturo Vagas

Founded in 1975 as the National Association of Latino Appointed Democratic Officials. Focuses on issues such as economic development, U.S. citizenship, legalization, and child poverty in order to assist the Hispanic community. Provides citizenship information and Latino voting statistics. Works to voice Hispanic needs and concerns in Washington, D.C., and other areas, such as the southwestern United States. Membership includes government officials and corporate leaders, which provides a strong basis on which the group can operate.

National Association of Puerto Rican Hispanic Social Workers

P.O. Box 651
Brentwood, NY 11717
(516) 864-1536
(516) 231-9751
(516) 864-1536 Fax
E-mail: sonia1536@aol.com
President: Eva Figueroa

Founded in 1955 in order to promote the needs and professional development of Hispanic social workers. Provides a *Code of Ethics and Standards* for the social work profession. Also provides informative publications, conducts educational and credential programs, and lobbies on legislation related to social work.

National Concilio of America

41 Sutter, Ste. 1067
San Francisco, CA 94104
(415) 550-0785
(415) 550-0437 Fax
President: Edward Vargas

Founded in 1977 as a collective of 100 community-based Hispanic organizations in order to produce Latino leaders. Also provides other training, public relations work, and fund raising. Publications include the quarterly *Executive Brief* and *Horizon Tes*.

National Council of Hispanic Women

P.O. Box 23266, L'Enfant Plaza Station
Washington, D.C. 20026
(301) 588-5152
(202) 401-1971 Fax
President: Yolanda Ruiz

Membership includes Hispanic women, universities, corporations, and government representatives striving to strengthen the role of Latino women within society. Goals include gaining more influence by Hispanic women in decision-making processes, promoting American ideals, and improving social and economic conditions within the Hispanic community. Also voices Latino issues in interviews, at conferences, and during public policy debates.

National Council of La Raza

810 1st Street NE, 3rd Floor
Washington, D.C. 2002
(202) 289-1380
(202) 289-8173 Fax
Website: http://www.nclr.org
President: Raul Yzaguirre

Known previously as the Southwest Council of La Raza, the National Council of La Raza was formed in 1968 in order to provide civil rights and economic opportunities for Hispanics. Focuses on economic development, community development, housing, employment, health, business assistance, and related topics. Also offers policy analysis, research programs, and committees on legislation, advocacy, and public information. Offers numerous publications, including *Education Network News*, *State of Hispanic America*, and other reports, newsletters, manuals, and handbooks.

National Hispana Leadership Institute

1901 North Moore Street, Ste. 206
Arlington, VA 22209
(703) 527-6007
(703) 527-6009 Fax
Website: www.incacorp.com/nhli

President: Nancy Leon

The National Hispana Leadership Institute was founded in 1987 in order to promote leadership, education, and social potential in regards to Hispanic women. Offers various programs and publications.

National Hispanic Council on Aging

2713 Ontario Road NW
Washington, D.C. 20009
(202) 265-1288
(202) 754-2522 Fax
Website: www.incacorp.com/nhcoa
President: Marta Sotomayor

Formed in 1980 in order to assist the Hispanic American elderly. Focuses its efforts toward research, policy analysis, training, demonstration projects, and educational resources development. Also provides networking to groups with similar goals, as well as a speakers' bureau. Publications include a quarterly newsletter called *Noticias on Hispanic Elderly Issues* and various book offerings, such as *Hispanic Elderly: Issues and Solutions for the 21st Century*, *Triple Jeopardy: Hispanic Older Women*, and *The Hispanic Elderly: A Cultural Signature*.

National Hispanic Leadership Agenda

1730 Rhode Island Avenue NW, No. 708
Washington, D.C. 20036
(202) 785-3314
(202) 785-3318 Fax
Executive Director: Frank N. Newton

The National Hispanic Leadership Agenda was formed in 1991. It strives to overcome issues plaguing Hispanic Americans. Also offers policy recommendations and a number of publications, such as books and reports.

National Hispanic Scholarship Fund

P.O. Box 728
Novato, CA 94948
(415) 892-9971
(415) 898-6673 Fax
Website: http://www.nhsf.org
Executive Director: Ernest Z. Robles

The National Hispanic Scholarship Fund was founded in 1975. It provides educational funding for undergraduate and graduate Hispanic American students, as well as providing information on similar services. Also strives for access to government education grant money.

National Institute for Resources in Science and Engineering

4302 Star Lane
Rockville, MD 20852
(301) 770-1437
Executive Director: Alvin D. Rivera

Founded in 1980. Seeks to increase the number of Hispanic and minority engineers, as well as striving for the needs of those currently in the workplace. Offers assistance and information on government and private sector science and engineering opportunities. Also assists professionals and students in accessing government resources, conducts workshops, and provides technical assistance to relevant parties. Gathers information on minority engineers and science professionals from universities and other organizations in order to help government offices in bettering education standards and availability.

National League of Cuban-American Community-Based Centers

2119 Webster Street
Fort Wayne, IN 46802
(219) 745-5421
(219) 744-1363 Fax
Executive Director: Graciela Beecher

Founded in 1980 to form links among Cuban-American community centers and assist in creating new centers. Analyzes education, training, manpower development, and health care needs of minority communities in order to gain assistance for them. Assists Hispanics in understanding employment opportunities within local, state, and federal agencies.

National Puerto Rican Forum

31 East 32nd Street, 4th floor
New York, NY 10016
(212) 685-2311
(212) 689-5034 Fax
Website: www.incacorp.com/nprt
Contact: Coni Batlle

Founded in 1957. Seeks to help Hispanic communities by identifying problems that face them and then formulating preventive strategies. Provides programs in job counseling, training, and placement, as well as in English language skills and family services. Publications include *The First Step Toward Equality: Hispanic Population Statistics for New York State and New York City*, *The Next Step Toward Equality: A Comprehensive Study of Puerto Ricans in the U.S. Mainland*, and other reports and resources.

People for a New System

P.O. Box 533
White Plains, NY 10603-1596
(908) 758-0449
(908) 933-9833 Fax
Contact: Murray Block

Founded in 1980 out of a merger by the League for Social Reconstruction and the New Union Party, the People for a New System was originally known as the Industrial Union Party. The group currently seeks to bring the economy under the control of a government consisting of industrial unions. Goals include supporting all workers under one union, meeting human needs, and spreading the concept of social ownership. Offers the quarterly *People for a New System* and other resources.

Puerto Rican Association for Community Affairs

853 Broadway, 5th floor
New York, NY 10003
(212) 673-7320
(212) 529-8917 Fax
Administrative Director: Yolanda Sanchez

Founded in 1953 the Puerto Rican Association for Community Affairs was previously known as the Hispanic Young Adults Association. Goals of the group include preserving Puerto Rican culture and heritage, developing a positive self-image among Hispanics, providing leadership skills to the Hispanic community, and supporting human rights and civil liberties. Also seeks to share resources with other groups with similar goals and interests. Provides day care, adoption, and foster care services for needy Hispanic children, as well as after-school programs and emergency protection boarding houses.

Puerto Rican Family Institute

145 West 15th Street
New York, NY 10011
(212) 924-6320
(212) 924-6330
(212) 691-5635 Fax

The Puerto Rican Family Institute was founded in 1960 to meet the health needs of Puerto Rican and Hispanic families within the United States, as well as strive for their general well-being. Operates mental health clinics, community residences for severely mentally retarded young adults, and migrant family assistance facilities. Special activities include the Program to Preserve the Integration of Puerto Rican Migrant Family, which provides social work, educational, psychiatric, and psychological services for immigrants, and the Placement Prevention Program for Juveniles on Probation.

Republican National Hispanic Assembly of the United States

440 1st Street NW, Ste. 414
Washington, D.C. 20001
(202) 662-1355
(202) 662-1408 Fax
Chairperson: Antonia Monroig

The Republican National Hispanic Assembly of the United States was founded in 1974. It seeks to educate Hispanics about the American political system, as well as recruit more registered Latino voters and gain Hispanics for the Republican Party. Offers a speakers' bureau, leadership training programs, and support to Hispanic political candidates. Publications include the annual *RNHA Leadership Directory* and *The American Hispanic*, a quarterly newsletter.

Secretariat for Hispanic Affairs (National Conference of Catholic Bishops)

3211 4th Street NE
Washington, D.C. 20017
(202) 541-3150
(202) 541-3322 Fax
Director: Ronaldo Guz

Founded in 1945, the Secretariat for Hispanic Affairs has been known as the Bishops' Committee for the Spanish Speaking, the Division for the Spanish Speaking, and the Secretariat for the Spanish Speaking. Works to meet the pastoral and spiritual needs of Hispanics in the United States. Works with other churches, institutions, and government agencies in order to meet the needs of the Latino community.

Society of Mexican American Engineers and Scientists

23 Los Arboles Drive
Secretary: Robert Van Pattern
(714) 964-3683
Website: http://www.tamu.edu/maes/

Founded in 1974 as the Mexican-American Engineering society. Goals include supporting Hispanics in entering and prospering in the fields of science and engineering; seeking to improve employment and educational opportunities for Latino scientists and engineers; and fostering cooperation among industry, government, and the academic community for the betterment of Mexican Americans. Also focuses on education, government communication and issues, professional development, and scholarship. Offers a speakers' bureau, placement services, retreats, junior and high school programs, and various publications.

Southwest Voter Registration Education Project
403 East Commerce, Ste. 220
San Antonio, TX 78205
(210) 222-0224
(800) 404-VOTE
(210) 222-8474 Fax

Founded in 1975 as a collection of church, civic, labor, and fraternal groups seeking to increase minority voting awareness, registration, and participation in the west and southwest United States. Conducts nonpartisan voter education projects, as well as compiles information on area Hispanic and Native American political organization participation. Also trains regional voter registration coordinators. Publications include *National Hispanic Voter Registration Campaign* and other reports, newsletters, and research studies.

U.S. Hispanic Chamber of Commerce
1030 15th Street NW, Ste. 206
Washington, D.C. 20005
(202) 842-1212
(202) 842-3221 Fax
Website: www.ushcc.com
President: Jose Nino

Founded in 1979. Seeks to develop Hispanic businesses, promote leadership, and support economic interests for the Latino community. Also works to provide a positive Hispanic image. Provides workshops, conferences, management training, and various publications.

3

Tables

Hispanic Members of the U.S. House of Representatives

Name	State or Territory	Party	Dates
Joseph Marion Hernandez	Florida	Whig	1822–1823
Jose Manuel Gallegos	New Mexico	Republican	1853–1857; 1871–1873
Miguel Antonio Otero	New Mexico	Democrat	1856–1861
Francisco Perea	New Mexico	Republican	1863–1865
Jose Francisco Chaves	New Meixco	Republican	1865–1867
Romualdo Pacheco	California	Republican	1877–1878; 1879–1883
Trinidad Romero	New Mexico	Republican	1877–1879
Mariano Sabino Otero	New Mexico	Republican	1879–1881
Tranquilino Luna	New Mexico	Republican	1881–1884
Francisco Antonio Manzanares	New Mexico	Democrat	1884–1885
Pedro Perea	New Meixco	Republican	1899–1901
Frederico Degetau	Puerto Rico	Liberal Reformist	1901–1905
Tulio Larrinaga	Puerto Rico	Unionist	1905–1911
Luis Munoz Rivera	Puerto Rico	Unionist	1911–1916
Ladislas Lazaro	Louisiana	Democrat	1912–1927
Benigno Cardenas Hernandez	New Mexico	Republican	1915–1917; 1919–1921
Felix Cordova Davila	Puerto Rico	Unionist	1917–1932
Nestor Montoya	New Mexico	Republican	1921–1923
Dennis Chavez	New Mexico	Democrat	1931–1935
Joachim Octave Fernandez	Louisiana	Democrat	1931–1941
Jose Lorenzo Pesquera	Puerto Rico	Nonpartisan	1932–1933
Santiago Iglesias	Puerto Rico	Coalitionist	1932–1939
Bolivar Pagan	Puerto Rico	Coalitionist	1939–1945
Antonio Manuel Fernandez	New Mexico	Democrat	1943–1956
Jesus T. Pinero	Puerto Rico	Popular Democrat	1945–1946
Antonio Fernos-Isern	Puerto Rico	Popular Democrat	1946–1965
Joseph Manuel Montoya	New Mexico	Democrat	1957–1964
Henry B. Gonzalez	Texas	Democrat	1961–1998
Edward R. Roybal	California	Democrat	1963–1993
Santiago Polanco-Abreu	Puerto Rico	Popular Democrat	1965–1969
Eligio "Kika" de la Garza II	Texas	Democrat	1965–1997
Jorge Luis Cordova Diaz	Puerto Rico	New Progressive	1969–1973
Manuel Lujan, Jr.	New Mexico	Republican	1969–1989
Herman Badillo	New York	Democrat	1971–1977
Jaime Benitez	Puerto Rico	Popular Democrat	1973–1979
Ron de Lugo	Virgin Islands	Democrat	1973–1979; 1981–1995
Baltasar Corrada del Rio	Puerto Rico	New Progressive	1977–1985
Robert Garcia	New York	Democrat	1978–1990
Anthony Lee Coelho	California	Democrat	1979–1989
Matthew G. Martinez	California	Democrat	1982–
William B. Richardson	New Mexico	Democrat	1983–1997

Hispanic Members of the U.S. House of Representatives (continued)

Name	State or Territory	Party	Dates
Solomon P. Ortiz	Texas	Democrat	1983–
Estaban Torres	California	Democrat	1983–1998
Jaime B. Fuster	Puerto Rico	Democrat	1985–1992
Ben Blaz Garrido	Guam	Republican	1985–1993
Albert G. Bustamante	Texas	Democrat	1985–1993
Ileana Ros-Lehtinen	Florida	Republican	1989–
Jose E. Serrano	New York	Democrat	1990–
Ed Lopez Pastor	Arizona	Democrat	1991–
Antonio J. Colorado	Puerto Rico	Democrat	1992–1993
Frank M. Tejeda	Texas	Democrat	1993–1997
Xavier Becerra	California	Democrat	1993–
Henry Bonilla	Texas	Democrat	1993–
Lincoln Diaz-Balart	Florida	Republican	1993–
Luis Gutierrez	Illinois	Democrat	1993–
Robert Menendez	New Jersey	Democrat	1993–
Carlos Antonio Romero-Barcelo	Puerto Rico	New Progressive	1993–
Lucille Roybal-Allard	California	Democrat	1993–
Robert A. Underwood	Guam	Democrat	1993–
Nydia M. Velazquez	New York	Democrat	1993–
Ruben Hinojosa	Texas	Democrat	1997–
Silvestre Reyes	Texas	Democrat	1997–
Ciro D. Rodriguez	Texas	Democrat	1997–
Loretta Sanchez	California	Democrat	1997–
Charles A. Gonzalez	Texas	Democrat	1999–
Grace Napolitano	California	Democrat	1999–

Hispanic Members of the U.S. Senate

Name	State	Party	Dates
Octaviano Larrazo	New Mexico	Republican	1928–1929
Dennis Chavez	New Mexico	Democrat	1935–1962
Joseph Manuel Montoya	New Mexico	Democrat	1964–1977

Part 4
Native Americans

Introduction
Native Americans in American Politics

by Peter P. d'Errico

Native American issues in late twentieth-century American politics present the same basic conflicts as in the late eighteenth century: land and water rights, hunting and fishing, religious freedom, criminal and civil jurisdiction. That this continuity of issues may be surprising is itself evidence of suppression of an accurate history of the United States.

> Neither the indigenous histories and concerns of native peoples nor the complex relations between them and the Euro-Americans can be comprehended by the providential history that has generally passed for the actual history of the United States. To include these would undermine the construction of the particular ideological history that has shaped "America" as a virgin land settled by God's chosen people. . . . (O'Connell, 1992, xvii)

America was not a virgin land when the United States was formed, nor previously in the colonial era. From the earliest days to the present, Native Americans have been a factor in American politics. In an even wider perspective, current Native American issues reflect the scope and content of relations between indigenous peoples and colonizers on the continent as a whole beginning over five centuries ago: Wampanoag and Narraganset fishermen charged with violations of Massachusetts and Rhode Island regulations for fishing in ocean bays where their peoples have fished since time immemorial; United States antagonism toward traditional leadership of Hopi and Western Shoshone peoples; Alaska native land titles ignored or denied; native spirituality interfered with or destroyed by government action; heated controversy surrounds the issue of civil and criminal jurisdiction over Native Americans on their own lands. These issues are only a small sample of twentieth-century conflicts that can also be dated in the seventeenth, eighteenth, and nineteenth centuries.

Nationally and internationally visible hot spots emerge from time to time—Ojibwa fishing in Wisconsin and Puyallup fishing in Washington, Black Hills in the Dakotas and Big Mountain in Navajo and Hopi territory, Venetie Village in Alaska and Mohawk communities on the New York-Cana-

dian border, and Pequot gaming in Connecticut and Seminole gaming in Florida. These are only heightened examples of continual and widespread political conflict involving Native Americans in the United States.

At any given time, at least one region of the country is facing at least one Native American issue in at least one venue, including subsistence rights, grave desecration and repatriation, child and family custody matters, and sports mascot and other commercial use of native names and images. The latter issue may appear wholly "modern," with no precedent in colonial or early U.S. history, but sports mascots are contemporary manifestations of what appeared in colonial fundraising: the Puritans of the Massachusetts Bay Company circulated in English churches cartoon images of a Native American holding out his hands and saying, "Come over and help us" (Jennings, 1976, 229). This image was the official seal of the Company between 1629 and 1684. Native Americans have had no end of "help" and no end of exploitation for the financial benefit of others.

The persistence of basic issues is an important characteristic of Native Americans in American politics. It can truly be said in this context, "the more things change, the more they remain the same." This persistence demonstrates the continuing presence of Native Americans as distinct peoples, despite repeated attempts to make them disappear. The existence of Native Americans as peoples—as self-governing groups, rather than simply individuals sharing personal and cultural traits—is what sets Native Americans apart from other "minorities" in American politics. This feature warrants a theoretical and historical overview, so that the variety of particular issues and controversies alive at any given time or place can be understood in an overall perspective.

Civil Rights and Sovereignty

A "minority" is conventionally defined as a group of persons whose shared cultural and personal characteristics distinguish them from the rest of the population, by whom they are outnumbered. A corollary implication of minority status is that the distinguishing characteristics are a basis for discrimination against members of the minority group. An ameliorative response to this kind of discrimination in American politics is "civil rights"—legal measures designed to ensure toleration of, if not actual advancement for, individuals oppressed by discrimination on account of their status as minorities.

Civil rights struggles have been a more or less constant feature of American politics over many decades, perhaps since adoption of the Constitution, when a "Bill of Rights" was politically necessary for ratification. The focal point of civil rights politics has varied over time, but its basic concerns have remained relatively constant. These concerns include the idea that the state should propound limits to its own power; that state power should weigh or benefit all persons equally, regardless of their majority or minority status; and that a proper focus of American politics is the use of state power to address, if not redress, social inequality due to invidious discrimination.

Native American political struggles differ markedly from civil rights, although the surface aspects of particular conflicts may not reveal this difference. Controversies about the use of Native American images for sports mascots, for example, appear as a conventional dispute about equality and respect for ethnic difference. But the deeper issues of Native Americans in American politics go beyond a concern for equal treatment and respect for difference. The deepest, most pervasive, and clearly persistent issues involve land and group rights—territorial integrity and self-determination of and by Native American societies. Native Americans are present in American politics not only as individuals but more profoundly as independent societies.

Native American issues involve the assertion of sovereignty—a challenge to the jurisdiction of state and federal governments, intended to preserve or extend an arena of self-determination as separate peoples. Native Americans asserting sovereignty are not seeking a "fair share" in American society, but are declaring the existence of a separate domain. The sovereignty demands of the American Indian Movement (AIM) in the 1970s departed radically from the concerns of the Black civil rights movement, which was sometimes cited as an inspiration for AIM. The only other group in American politics to come close to raising a sovereignty issue is the separatist wing of Black politics, which has from time to time called for the creation of a separate Black homeland in North America. In that context, the demand is clearly revolutionary, whereas in Native American terms, sovereignty is not revolutionary but traditional.

Self-government is thus the primary factor that distinguishes Native Americans from other minorities and, indeed, from all other persons in American politics. This crucial difference has generated envy from some twentieth-century "militia" groups seeking independence from state and federal controls, and hostility from some "white supremacist" and other groups who see the special position of Native Americans in American politics as a form of inequality that violates

everyone else's rights. The use of Native American independence as a model to emulate or criticize is itself a recurring phenomenon in American politics. Benjamin Franklin's observation is one of the most oft-quoted early examples:

> It would be a very strange Thing, if six Nations of ignorant Savages should be capable of forming a Scheme for such a Union, and be able to execute it in such a Manner, as that it has subsisted Ages, and appears indissoluble, and yet that a like Union should be impracticable for ten or a Dozen English Colonies. . . . (Washburn, 1995, 49)

Native Americans—because of sovereignty issues—do not fit neatly within a multi-cultural perspective of American society. Multi-culturalism is a view of American society as a conglomerate of people belonging to different ethnic groups. Ethnic difference in multi-cultural America is a matter for pride and not discrimination, but ethnicity is not a basis for political independence. The uniqueness of Native Americans, even in a multi-cultural perspective, is that Native American ethnicity may be expressed through independent political structures. This situation is defined in the phrase "government-to-government relationship," which is used to explain that the United States relates to Native Americans as sovereign groups, rather than as individuals.

Self-Government under Federal Law

One must immediately add qualifiers to the assertion that self-government and institutionalized political independence form the fulcrum of Native Americans in American politics. Native American sovereignty is not as complete as the government-to-government relationship suggests. Indeed, the first time the United States dealt with Native Americans through the State Department—the normal vehicle for government-to-government relationships—was in May 1996. This "consultation" meeting was held preparatory to the United States taking a position in the United Nations with regard to a Draft Declaration of the Rights of Indigenous Peoples under consideration in the international arena. Prior to that meeting, and continuing since, the government-to-government relationship consists of Native American governments dealing with the United States through various domestic agencies, primarily the Department of the Interior. From an historical perspective, more government-to-government dealing occurred when the United States acted towards Native Americans through the War Department, where the first Bureau of Indian Affairs was created in 1824, than in the subsequent years when "Indian affairs" became institutionalized as a "domestic" concern.

A straightforward legal explanation of the special position of Native Americans in American politics was provided in 1973 by the Federal District Court for the District of Montana, in the case of *United States v. Blackfeet Tribe,* 364 F. Supp. 192 (1973). The facts of the case were simple: The Blackfeet Business Council had passed a resolution authorizing gambling on the reservation and licensing slot machines.

An FBI agent seized four machines. The Blackfeet Tribal Court issued an order restraining all persons from removing the seized articles from the reservation. The FBI agent, after consultation with the United States Attorney, removed the machines from the reservation. A tribal judge then ordered the U.S. Attorney to show cause why he should not be cited for contempt of the tribal court. The U.S. Attorney applied to federal court for an injunction to block the contempt citations. The Blackfeet Tribe argued that it was sovereign and that the jurisdiction of the tribal court flows directly from this sovereignty. The federal court said:

> No doubt the Indian tribes were at one time sovereign and even now the tribes are sometimes described as being sovereign. The blunt fact, however, is that an Indian tribe is sovereign to the extent that the United States permits it to be sovereign—neither more nor less. . . . While for many years the United States recognized some elements of sovereignty in the Indian tribes and dealt with them by treaty, Congress by Act of March 3, 1871 . . ., prohibited the further recognition of Indian tribes as independent nations. Thereafter the Indians and the Indian tribes were regulated by acts of Congress. The power of Congress to govern by statute rather than treaty has been sustained. *United States v. Kagama*, 118 U.S. 375, 6 S.Ct. 1109, 30 L.Ed. 228 (1886). That power is a plenary power . . . and in its exercise Congress is supreme. . . . It follows that any tribal ordinance permitting or purporting to permit what Congress forbids is void. . . . It is beyond the power of the tribe to in any way regulate, limit, or restrict a federal law officer in the performance of his duties, and the tribe having no such power the tribal court can have none. (*United States v. Blackfeet Tribe*, 364 F. Supp. 194 [1973])

The fundamental definition of "American Indian sovereignty" in United States law, as the District Court made clear, is that it is not really sovereignty. According to the fundamental jurisprudence of federal Indian law—a vast, complex body of United States statutes and court decisions designed to govern Native Americans—"tribal" peoples have a diminutive form of sovereignty, which turns out to be not self-determination, but dependence. This theory was articulated by Supreme Court Chief Justice John Marshall in *Cherokee Nation v. Georgia,* 5 Pet. 1 (1831). Marshall wrote that Native American societies, though they are "nations" in the general sense of the word, are not fully sovereign; he suggested that they are "domestic, dependent nations," a phrase suggesting that native peoples are wards of the United States, a concept that almost immediately passed from dictum to dogma. Native American sovereignty has been the object of a kind of legal shell game—"now you see it, now you don't"—since the beginning of federal Indian law.

Over the years since Marshall coined the phrase "domestic, dependent nations," federal power has truncated and parceled tribal sovereignty in myriad ways, developing a system of overlapping and contradictory rules premised on a notion that the United States has plenary power to act as trustee for tribal wards. That the words plenary power, trustee, and ward are nowhere in the United States Constitution is no more than a small nuisance to the judges who have declared its existence. In fact, the Constitution mentions "Indians" only twice:

once to exclude "Indians not taxed" from calculations to apportion representatives and direct taxes, and again to centralize regulation of "commerce . . . with the Indian tribes" in congressional power (U.S. Constitution, Art. 1, Sections 2, 8).

American Indian sovereignty under federal plenary power is a legal scheme especially useful to the United States because it denies indigenous power in the name of indigenous sovereignty, while at the same time justifying federal control over lands and economic resources that might otherwise be viewed as subject to state and local jurisdictions. On the basis of this judicially created non-sovereign tribal sovereignty, the United States has built an entire apparatus for dispossessing indigenous peoples of their lands, social organizations, and original powers of self-determination.

One of the most visible issues of Native Americans in American politics at the close of the twentieth century is gaming—high-stakes casino gambling operations on Indian reservations, out of reach of state tax and regulatory powers. Tax and regulatory issues are also present in controversies over smoke-shop and other business operations that take place on reservations legally separate from state authority. Some states—New York in the case of Mohawk businesses—have fought for control over revenue streams developed from such Native American economic ventures; other states—Connecticut in the case of the monumentally profitable Pequot casino—have accommodated themselves to a negotiated share of the proceeds. Still other states—Maine in the case of Penobscott-Passamaquoddy investments—have simply accepted benefits that overflow from businesses based outside their powers but inside their borders.

Economic success has not immunized Native Americans from discrimination. Before the era of reservation casinos, Native Americans were accused of welfare dependency, as if the federal services provided to them were largesse and not the result of treaty agreements in which land sufficient for self-subsistence was exchanged for promises of government economic support. After the success of high-stakes gaming, Native Americans were criticized as recipients of undeserved wealth, protected by an inequality of rights in their favor.

Not all casinos are productive, let alone of great wealth. Not all reservation businesses succeed, let alone produce overflowing revenue streams. For the majority of Native American communities, poverty and welfare dependence are the norm, as they have been for decades. Many enduring issues of Native Americans in American politics are occasioned by widespread, endemic economic depression. In the face of such circumstances, Native Americans have retained their identity as separate peoples and persisted in asserting rights as organized societies separate from the American mainstream. Despite centuries of overt and covert aggression against them as peoples, despite every attempt to convert Native American political conflicts from sovereignty struggles to civil rights issues, Native Americans endure as independent societies with the goal, if not the guarantee, of independent political existence.

The "Discovery" of Native Americans

Native Americans entered American politics well before the American Revolution. One might fairly say that Native Americans were part of American politics during the entire period from initial colonial settlements to the present. One might stretch the matter only a little to say that the real beginning was in 1492, since the entire hemisphere is in some sense "America," and not only that portion of territory between present-day Mexico and Canada. Current usage refers to "the Americas," and the Organization of American States (OAS) is an important political institution in hemispheric relations among contemporary nation-states as well as between those states and indigenous peoples who still exist (and in some cases are still a majority of the population) inside boundaries claimed by the states.

This larger context is more than an academic issue. The basic and continuing issues of Native Americans in American politics are identical to the issues of indigenous peoples in all the Americas. A full understanding of Native Americans in American politics depends on a grasp of the big picture of hemispheric American colonialism. This is not the place to provide the whole of that picture, but at least its outlines may be shown.

The (in)famous story of Christopher Columbus is known around the world: his adventure and daring as he set sail into uncharted waters, his great mistake in thinking he had reached the Indies, his lust for gold, his passion for the spread of Christianity—all these are part of the public imagination. What is less known is that his adventure was not sponsored by Spain, but by the kingdoms of Castile and Leon, which were only in the process of becoming "Spain"—a process that included the conquest of the Iberian peninsula from the Moors, and which would be fueled by, if not dependent upon, wealth extracted from the New World.

The significance of this point is that it contradicts a conventional view of American civilization as something transplanted more or less whole from across the Atlantic—"the providential history" of the United States. What moved across the ocean was not European civilization, but something much more fragmentary and undefined, something in the making, and the making that followed was intertwined with events unfolding on the new side of the Atlantic. In other words, the colonization of America was an integral part of the creation of Europe. In this sense, Native Americans are not just part of American politics, rather American politics has centered around Native Americans—their existence, their lands, their ways of life so radically different from the Christian nationalists who "discovered" them.

Furthermore, though the United States emerged dominant from the colonial era, its dominance was acquired not only through warfare, but through cooperation with Native Americans. Their prior rights to land, as well as their prior ability to organize workable economies, were factors that worked toward the perpetuation of some form of Native American independence, circumscribed as it may have become.

> Thus, in examining the American past, an ethnohistorian finds, not the triumph of civilization over savagery, but an acculturation of Europeans and Indians that was marked by the interchange or diffusion of cultural traits and the emergence of social and cultural dominance by the Europeans in a large society marked by a submerged Indian subculture. (Jennings, 1976, 13)

Felix Cohen, the architect of federal legal policy toward Native Americans in the important years of the "New Deal," went even further, declaring that "what is distinctive about America is Indian, through and through" (Cohen, 1970, 316).

It is crucial to understand that the New World was not new, but already ancient when it was "discovered" by Columbus. Multiform civilizations existed across the length and breadth of the land, literally from the Arctic to Amazonia. As Francis Jennings put it, America was not "virgin" when the colonists arrived, but became "widowed" by disease and genocide. In the process, something new was created from the interactions of what was already present and what was imported. That something is what became America. The colonizers and natives made use of each other's economies and social structures. Even after the colonizers felt strong enough to attempt to ignore or remove the natives, something of the original inhabitants remained, either separate from the colonizing society or incorporated within it, as a determining factor in the shape and extent of what was possible in America.

The proper naming of the indigenous peoples of America is a recurring issue. Most people know the story that the inhabitants of the New World came to be called "Indians" because Columbus thought he had arrived in India. The "American" part came later, after everyone but Columbus had admitted his error, and the land had been named for another Italian navigator, Amerigo Vespucci. "American Indians" is therefore not the real name of anyone.

It became fashionable with the rise of a self-conscious multi-cultural perspective in late twentieth century American society to refer to the peoples who were here before Columbus as "Native Americans," rather than "American Indians." Ironically, perhaps, the latter phrase remains more common among native peoples themselves. John Trudell, an early American Indian Movement (there it is again) activist and contemporary performing artist, observed at the time, "They changed our name and treated us the same." "American Indian" also continued to predominate in United States statutes and court decisions.

"Native American" has its own semantic problems. The word "native" has a generic meaning, referring to anyone or anything that is in its place of origin. "Native" also has a pejorative meaning in English colonization, as in "The natives are restless tonight." "Native" carries the connotation of "primitive," which itself has both a generic definition, meaning "first" or "primary," and a pejorative use, meaning "backward" or "ignorant."

"Native American" came into use as an effort to recognize ethnic diversity in the United States while insisting on an over-arching American unity. Groups became identified as hyphen-American—African-American, Irish-American, Italian-American, and so on. For the original inhabitants of the land, the correct term became Native-American. It seemed that the only full, un-hyphenated Americans were those who made no claim of ethnicity at all. Many of them asserted they were in fact the real "native" Americans.

There are no American Indians or Native Americans. There are many different peoples, hundreds in fact, bearing such names as Wampanoag, Cherokee, Seminole, Shawnee, Hopi. These are the traditional, real names of people.

But the conundrum of names doesn't end there. Some of the apparently traditional or "real" names are not actually derived from the people themselves, but from their neighbors or even enemies. Mohawk is a Narraganset name, meaning "flesh eaters." Sioux is a French corruption of an Ojibwa word for "enemy." Similarly, "Apache" is a Spanish corruption of a Zuni word for "enemy," while Navajo is from the Spanish version of a Tewa word. To be fully authentic is to inquire into the language of each people to find the name they call themselves. It may not be surprising to find that the deepest real names are often a word for "people" or the homeland or some differentiating characteristic of the people as seen through their own eyes.

The problem of naming the indigenous peoples in American history is one consequence of the fact that self-definitions of the prior inhabitants of the land—their "names" in the largest sense—were generally subsumed within the colonists' own histories. Christian colonizers saw themselves as carrying out a divine mandate in all its aspects. The Bible tells a story of God giving Adam the power to name the animals and other parts of creation, as an aspect of the power to "subdue . . . and have dominion over . . . every living thing" (Genesis 1:28). William Cronon has discussed the difference between native and colonial naming of the landscape, showing how the names reflected entirely different cosmologies.

Detailed qualification and reassessment of the early history may seem unnecessary to a present understanding of Native Americans in American politics. Some may think it enough to acknowledge the fallaciousness of the notion of "discovery," with all it implies in the way of colonial arrogance. The fact that colonial arrogance became part of the institutional structure of American politics and has never been repudiated means it is impossible to leave all this behind with a simple backward glance. The position of Native Americans in American politics consists of a continual reaffirmation of core colonial concepts. One cannot appreciate the content or persistence of the issues in the absence of an understanding of these concepts.

Christian Colonization and "Plenary Power"

The sixteenth-century "discovery of non-Christian forms of life in the Americas posed (a) . . . threat to the stability of Christian values."

> (T)he discovery of the American Indians . . . (t)he confrontation with something radically different from the Christian way of life raised the question of what kind of relations it is possible to entertain with this Other. First, to what extent is it possible to know the Indian except as something inferior? . . . Second, . . . to what extent is it possible to bring him into the framework of universal law by giving him the status of a legal subject? (Bartelson, 1995, 128, 131)

The Western response to this discovery was "an effort to . . . (make) everything speak . . . with one voice" (Bartelson, 1995, 108). In this effort, Native American societies were given a "choice": to assimilate to the colonial system and give up their independent self-definition, or to maintain their self-definition and be denied a place in the world's legal and political order. The underlying assumption was that there is only one reality and it is Western. But "Indigenous is nearly synonymous with diversity" (Barrerio, 1997, 2).

It is best to be specific about the conceptual core of Christian colonization, and to emphasize that it was "Christian" as opposed to "European" colonization that reached the shores of the New World. Columbus's voyage was the occasion for Pope Alexander VI to issue a bull dividing the world between Spain and Portugal, laying down the doctrine of Christian discovery and conquest:

> INTER CAETERA, MAY 3, 1493—Among other works well pleasing to the Divine Majesty and cherished of our heart, this assuredly ranks highest, that in our times especially the Catholic faith and the Christian religion be exalted and everywhere increased and spread, that the health of souls be cared for and that barbarous nations be overthrown and brought to the faith itself. . . . (O)ur beloved son Christopher Columbus, . . . sailing . . . toward the Indians, discovered certain very remote islands and even mainlands . . . . (W)e, . . . by the authority of Almighty God . . . do . . . give, grant, and assign forever to you and your heirs and successors, kings of Castille and Leon, all and singular the aforesaid countries and islands. . . .

An earlier papal bull issued by Nicholas V had already declared the legitimacy of Christian domination over "pagans," sanctifying their enslavement and expropriation of their property:

> ROMANUS PONTIFEX, JANUARY 8, 1455— (W)e bestow suitable favors and special graces on those Catholic kings and princes, . . . athletes and intrepid champions of the Christian faith . . . to invade, search out, capture, vanquish, and subdue all Saracens and pagans whatsoever, and other enemies of Christ wheresoever placed, and . . . to reduce their persons to perpetual slavery, and to apply and appropriate . . . possessions, and goods, and to convert them to . . . their use and profit. . . .

Leaping four centuries ahead, we find that Chief Justice John Marshall, one of the greatest figures in the pantheon of the United States Supreme Court, borrowed from these papal bulls the essential legalisms he needed to affirm American power over indigenous peoples. He encased Christian religious premises within the rhetoric of European expansion.

> On the discovery of this immense continent, the great nations of Europe were eager to appropriate to themselves so much of it as they could respectively acquire. Its vast extent offered an ample field to the ambition and enterprise of all; and the character and religion of its inhabitants afforded an apology for considering them as a people over whom the superior genius of Europe might claim an ascendancy. The potentates of the old world found no difficulty in convincing themselves that they made ample compensation to the inhabitants of the new, by bestowing on them civilization and Christianity. (*Johnson v. McIntosh*, 8 Wheat, 572–73 [1823])

Henry Wheaton, reporter for the *Johnson* Court, later elaborated the concept of Christian nationalism.

> (T)he heathen nations of the other quarters of the globe were the lawful spoil and prey of their civilized conquerors, and as between the Christian powers themselves, the Sovereign Pontiff was the supreme arbiter of conflicting claims. . . . It thus became a maxim of policy and of law, that the right of the native Indians was subordinate to that of the first Christian discoverer. (Wheaton, 1855, 220)

Justice Joseph Story also independently discussed the laws of Christendom as the basis for the Court's opinion in *Johnson*.

> (I)nfidels, heathens, and savages . . . were not allowed to possess the prerogatives belonging to absolute, sovereign and independent nations. (Story, 1833, 134)

Later cases tended to omit explicit reference to Christian doctrines, in keeping with a general understanding that the government of the United States was separate from any establishment of religion. Some explicit references and acknowledgments did occur. For example, regarding federal interference with "occupancy of the Indians."

> (I)t is to be presumed that in this matter the United States would be governed by such considerations of justice as would control a Christian people in their treatment of an ignorant and dependent race." (*Beecher v. Weatherby*, 95 U.S. 525 [1877])

As recently as 1946, Supreme Court Justice Stanley Reed argued against monetary compensation for a federal taking of Native American lands on the ground that

> (D)iscovery by Christian nations gave them sovereignty over and title to the lands discovered. (*United States v. Alcea Band of Tillamooks*, 329 U.S. 58 [1946])

The fact that papal authority is at the legal core of American politics affecting Native Americans is not generally understood, even by lawyers who work with the arcanum of federal Indian law. The essential jurisprudential point has been summarized succinctly by Steve Newcomb.

> Indian nations have been denied their most basic rights . . . simply because, at the time of Christendom's arrival in the Americas, they did not believe in the God of the Bible, and did not believe that Jesus Christ was the true Messiah. This basis for the denial of Indian rights in federal Indian law remains as true today as it was in 1823. (Newcomb, 1993, 309)

The Supreme Court's decision in *Johnson v. McIntosh*, 8 Wheat, 543 (1823), has never been overruled. "Christian discovery" remains the legal foundation for United States sovereignty over Native Americans and their lands. But it is concealed, as most foundations are, because *Johnson v. McIntosh* acts as a laundromat for religious concepts. After Marshall's opinion, no lawyer or court would need to acknowledge that land title in United States law is based on a doctrine of Christian supremacy. From that time on, in law and history books, "European" would be substituted for "Christian," so that schoolchild and lawyer alike could speak of the "age of discovery" as the age of "European expansion."

Marshall knew what he was doing. After writing that "Christian princes" could take lands "unknown to all Christian peoples," he admitted that the doctrine was an "extravagant . . . pretension" that "may be opposed to natural right" and may only "perhaps, be supported by reason." Nonetheless, he concluded that it "cannot be rejected by courts of justice."

The discovery doctrine was not self-effectuating. It required force. As Marshall wrote, "These claims have been maintained and established . . . by the sword." The (in)famous "Spanish Requirement" of 1513 is perhaps the most straightforward example. It was called the requirement because royal law required it to be read before hostilities could be undertaken against a native people. In Latin or Spanish, witnessed by a notary, the conquistadors read the following:

> On the part of the king, Don Fernando, and of Doña Juana, his daughter, queen of Castile and Leon, subduers of the barbarous nations, we their servants notify and make known to you, as best we can, that the Lord our God, living and eternal, created the heaven and the earth, and one man and one woman, of whom you and we, and all the men of the world, were and are descendants, and all those who come after us. . . . Of all these nations God our Lord gave charge to one man, called St. Peter, that he should be lord and superior of all the men in the world, that all should obey him, and that he should be the head of the whole human race, wherever men should live, and under whatever law, sect, or belief they should be; and he gave him the world for his kingdom and jurisdiction. . . . One of these pontiffs, who succeeded that St. Peter as lord of the world in the dignity and seat which I have before mentioned, made donation of these isles and Terra-firma to the aforesaid king and queen and to their successors, our lords, with all that there are in these territories. . . . Wherefore, as best we can, we ask and require you that you consider what we have said to you, and that you take the time that shall be necessary to understand and deliberate upon it, and that you acknowledge the Church as the ruler and superior of the whole world. . . . But if you do not do this, and maliciously make delay in it, I certify to you that, with the help of God, we shall powerfully enter into your country, and shall make war against you in all ways and manners that we can, and shall subject you to the yoke and obedience of the Church and of their highnesses; we shall take you, and your wives, and your children, and shall make slaves of them, and as such shall sell and dispose of them as their highnesses may command; and we shall take away your goods, and shall do you all the mischief and damage that we can, as to vassals who do not obey, and refuse to

receive their lord, and resist and contradict him: and we protest that the deaths and losses which shall accrue from this are
your fault, and not that of their highnesses, or ours, nor of
these cavaliers who come with us. (Washburn, 1964, 306-09)

These documents and the precision of their jurispruden-
tially ordained violence are generally not part of current legal
education. In the wider public arena, it is now fashionable,
especially around Columbus Day, to speak about the "encounter" of the Old and New Worlds, as a way of trying to forget
exactly how bloody this event was. Michael Shapiro countered this soft terminology with the comment, "National
societies that . . . have thought of themselves as a fulfillment
of a historical destiny, could not be open to encounters"
(Shapiro, 1996, 56).

The Puritans are the best example of a bloody Christianity as the *modus operandi* of American colonization. Skillful
Puritan propaganda has secured them an historical niche as
champions of religious freedom. Their self-proclaimed mission to "save the souls of the natives" was a formula for success
in garnering financial support from English churches. The
image of Puritan godliness survives as one of the great American myths. Nevertheless, these "lords" of New England were
ruthless in their attacks on "heathen" natives whose economic
and military aid they outgrew.

The American holiday of Thanksgiving, historically understood, is a day of mourning for the Native Americans who
met Pilgrim thievery with generosity. One of the first things
the Pilgrims did was to rob Wampanoag storehouses for food
and graves for tools. The Wampanoag, seeing all this and realizing how unfortunate these boat people were, extended the
hand of friendship and offered help instead of retribution. Probably also the Wampanoag realized that it is better to feed your
neighbors than to have them desperate with hunger at your
door.

The Wampanoag understood that these newcomers from
across the water must have been fleeing terrible conditions to
endure the hardship and privation of such a journey. Who
would willingly leave the land of their birth, the home of their
ancestors? The colonists claimed to be seeking freedom for
their faith, and told stories of corruption and oppression in
the lands they left behind. When the Wampanoag showed themselves open to spiritual teachings, but not necessarily to
conversion, the Puritans reacted with anger.

Massacres of Pequot (1637) and Narraganset (1675) communities are the most horrific large-scale incidents of Puritan
violence against Native Americans. Lesser-known incidents
include the establishment of groups of "praying Indians," the
first Indian reservations—or, as they were called well into the
nineteenth century, "concentrations"—where native people
were forcibly subjected to the missionary work of such icons
of Puritan purity as John Eliot. The only path for natives to
relative security from Puritan violence was to move to villages established under Puritan command and to attend to
missionary preaching. "Freedom" in Puritan terms was the

freedom to impose an orthodoxy of Bible worship, to eradicate the diversity of indigenous spiritual practices that were
seen as ignorance, "devil-worship," and idolatry.

Christianity as an essential part of the process for "civilizing" native peoples under British colonial policy was
reaffirmed well into the nineteenth century by a House of
Commons Select Committee on Aborigines (1837): "True civilization and Christianity are inseparable: the former has never
been found, but as a fruit of the latter" (Armitage, 1995, 76).

As Michael Dorris wrote, encompassing the whole history of American politics, from colonial era to the present,

> The pre-existent variety of Native American societies . . . has
> been consistently obscured and disallowed. Every effort has
> been made to almost existentially enclose the non-Western
> world into a European schema, and then to blame unwilling
> elements for being backward, ignorant, or without vision. . . .
> Federal Indian policy was . . . shaped from the beginning at
> least as much toward deculturation as acculturation. (Dorris,
> 1979, 75, 76)

It has often been noted that the work of missionaries was
intertwined with the work of soldiers. For their part, Native
Americans frequently point out that their original forms of
self-government are spiritually based, given to them as part
of their "original instructions" from the Creator. The eradication of Native American spirituality—through forcible
induction of individuals into missionary churches and through
political subversion of the power and respect accorded to traditional spiritual leaders—was a key element in colonial policy
that continued well into twentieth-century United States policy.

Formal renunciation of Bureau of Indian Affairs prohibi-
tions affecting Native American spiritual practices occurred
in conjunction with the Indian Reorganization Act (1934).
Explicit recognition was withheld until 1978, when Congress
passed the American Indian Religious Freedom Act (AIRFA).
As to the latter, the Supreme Court ruled in 1988, "Nowhere
in the law is there so much as a hint of any intent to create a
cause of action or any judicially enforceable individual rights"
(*Lyng v. Northwest Indian Cemetery Protective Association*,
485 U.S. 452 [1988]). AIRFA survives as a general statement
of unenforceable federal policy. In 1990, Congress passed the
Native American Graves Protection and Repatriation Act to
require federally funded museums and other institutions to
return skeletons and burial goods to Native American communities that can prove ancestral connections to these items.
Disturbance of Native American graves continues to be an
issue, however, because many state laws protecting graves have
been held inapplicable to traditional native burials where there
is no headstone or other conventional cemetery parapherna-
lia.

Tribal Councils and Trusteeship

The colonies and later the United States did not have sufficient resources to maintain martial rule over peoples and
territories they wanted to control. They resorted to indirect

rule by puppet governments through the mechanism of appointed (and often bribed) chiefs. But they found that despite every attempt to make indigenous social structures disappear—including allotment of communal lands and prohibition of spiritual practices—Native Americans survived as peoples. By the twentieth century, the condition of their survival was an embarrassment to the United States. Franklin D. Roosevelt's New Deal administration set out to reorganize Native American societies into elected corporate political structures—a formalized system of tribal councils. The concept of American Indian sovereignty was used to justify sufficient authority in the tribal councils to maintain order within the tribe while denying these councils any authority beyond the territory that was reserved for them.

The 1934 Wheeler Howard Act, commonly known as the Indian Reorganization Act (IRA), was presented as the restoration of Native American self-government. The act was not the result of a treaty process (treaty-making had been formally ended by Congress in 1871), but the fact that it halted some of the most destructive of prior government policies—especially forced land cessions authorized by the 1887 General Allotment Act (Dawes Act)—made it acceptable to many Native Americans. Although the Reorganization Act was intended to stabilize the land base and social conditions of Native Americans, it was also intended—as its title states—to reorganize the Indians, overthrowing traditional organizations and promoting a "democratic" tribal council system structured along the lines of a corporate business. Not all Native American peoples formally adopted the IRA system, but its major features became the typical form of tribal self-government.

In 1971, the Alaska Native Claims Settlement Act—a major piece of legislation designed to make a final settlement of all Native American land rights (as well as hunting and fishing rights) in Alaska—took the corporate model approach much further. The Settlement Act, displacing traditional political structures, created regional and village for-profit corporations to manage land and business activities for stockholders who were the native peoples themselves. The resulting struggles of Alaska natives to maintain coherent societies and exercise political authority over their lands are far from over.

The complexities of Native American self-government under the federally sponsored tribal council system can be illustrated by the case of the Western Shoshone. In 1863, the Western Shoshone and the United States signed a Treaty of Peace and Friendship at Ruby Valley in the heart of Western Shoshone country. The treaty acknowledged Western Shoshone control over their homelands and provided for easements across their land and some mining and related activities. One hundred years later, massive strip-mines had begun to tear up Western Shoshone lands and pollute and destroy the waters. The United States added to this destruction by designating Yucca Mountain in Shoshone territory as a site for disposal of high-level radioactive waste.

Although Western Shoshone land title has never been proven to have been ceded or lost, the Supreme Court has ruled that the Western Shoshone are precluded from litigating their title. Western Shoshone people who oppose the destruction of their lands as violations of their title and treaty are depicted as outlaws. This came about through denial of traditional Western Shoshone self-determination and by affirmation of the kind of sovereignty that the Western Shoshone have under federal law.

In accordance with Reorganization Act principles, the federal government recognized various Western Shoshone tribal councils as the agents of Western Shoshone sovereignty. The Temoak Band, one of the councils empowered to govern the Western Shoshone people and to represent them in dealing with the outside world, filed a claim in 1951 under the Indian Claims Commission Act (1946). That act was passed ostensibly to right past wrongs by compensating for land-takings that had violated Native American ownership. More fundamentally, the act was intended to wipe out all Native American title for non-reservation lands by providing money compensation for such lands. The act did not require that a claim represent all or even a majority of the Native Americans in whose name it was filed. As a result of the Temoak claim—which the traditional, non-recognized Western Shoshone opposed (1974) and the Temoak council subsequently tried to withdraw (1976)—the Indian Claims Commission held (1979) that Western Shoshone lands had been taken and that the Western Shoshone would receive compensation.

The Western Shoshone refused to accept the compensation. One family (the Danns), charged by the United States with trespassing on public lands, defended themselves by asserting Western Shoshone title to the lands. In 1983, the Ninth Circuit Court of Appeals ruled that Western Shoshone title had never actually been litigated, that none of the claims made against it were sufficient to take it away, and that since the Western Shoshone had refused the Claims Commission compensation, they still held title. The United States Supreme Court reversed the Ninth Circuit in 1985, declaring that the Western Shoshone could not argue about their title because the compensation had been accepted on their behalf by the United States, acting as their trustee!

As Milner Ball pointed out in criticizing the Supreme Court ruling,

> (T)he Court held a "payment" had been effected, although the Indians received no money and opposed the conversion of their land. The trust doctrine was the device the Court struck upon for executing this maneuver. The United States was not only the judgment debtor to Indians, the Court said, but was also trustee to the Indians. Therefore the United States as debtor can pay itself as trustee, say this change in bookkeeping constitutes payment to Indians, and the Court will certify the fiction as a reality. (Ball, 1987, 65)

The Western Shoshone case is not atypical. Similar events have unfolded for many other Native Americans under United States law. The point is that in federal law Native American sovereignty—defined as the powers of federally sponsored tribal councils—is a tool for separating Native American lands from state and local control and for subordinating the original powers of indigenous self-determination to United States jurisdiction. Native American sovereignty operates in conjunction with so-called "trust" and "wardship" doctrines—concepts proclaimed unilaterally by the United States Supreme Court in the Cherokee Nation case to legitimize federal power over Native Americans and to determine the scope and structure of Native American self-government. The Western Shoshone case demonstrates that the United States is intent on maintaining powers it has asserted for almost two centuries on the basis of fifteenth-century theological decrees.

> To argue that the Indian people may not challenge the theoretical framework set forth by Marshall in the *Johnson* ruling is to say that they must simply acquiesce in a 170-year-old precedent predicated on the belief that the first Christian discoverer (or its legal successor) has a divine right to subjugate the heathens who were discovered. It is to contend that Indian nations ought to learn to accept a judicial pretention based on religious and cultural prejudice that asserts that their rights to complete sovereignty and to territorial integrity may be impaired, diminished, denied, or displaced simply because they were not Christian people at the time of European arrival to the Americas. It is to accept the preposterous idea that federal Indian law will forever rest on the foundation of a subjugating Christian ideology. (Newcomb, 1993, 336)

The legal position of Native Americans in American politics appears as a crazy-quilt pattern in decisions of the Supreme Court. In 1831, the Cherokee Nation sued the state of Georgia in the Supreme Court to protect Cherokee lands. The Court denied the Cherokee suit on the ground that an Indian nation is not a foreign nation entitled to sue a state in the Supreme Court. That decision has never been overruled and is cited frequently today. In 1997, the Supreme Court decided that the Coeur d'Alene Tribe could litigate its land claims against the state of Idaho only in Idaho's courts. The Coeur d'Alene were claiming "aboriginal title," a subsidiary title subject to the trusteeship of the United States. They were trying to work within the limited concept of Native American sovereignty. In throwing the Coeur d'Alene suit out of federal court, the Supreme Court stated that the basis of its decision is that "Indian tribes . . . should be accorded the same status as foreign sovereigns, against whom States enjoy Eleventh Amendment immunity" (*Idaho v. Coeur d'Alene Tribe*, No. 94-1474, June 23, 1997). The Cherokee were barred from suing in the Supreme Court because an Indian nation is not a foreign nation. The Coeur d'Alene were barred from suing in district court because an Indian nation is a foreign nation! The shell game continues into the twenty-first century.

Termination and Self-Determination

Native Americans continue to assert forms of self-government carried forward from their original independence, however modified in the course of dealings with colonial, state, and federal governments. Resistance to these forms also persists.

In the 1950s, as political support for New Deal programs waned, a concerted effort was mounted in Congress to terminate all federal relations with Native Americans as separate peoples. In 1953, House Concurrent Resolution 108 declared the "policy of Congress . . . to make the Indians within the United States subject to the same laws and entitled to the same privileges . . . as are applicable to other citizens." Two weeks later, Public Law 280 was passed, authorizing state governments to exercise civil and criminal jurisdiction on Indian reservations without Native American consent.

The premise of the termination policy was that elimination of federal trusteeship over Native American wards would result in assimilation of individual Native Americans into the general population and the divesting of Native Americans of all reservation lands. It is one of the great anomalies of federal Indian law that termination of the trust would result in the assets of the trust going to the former trustee rather than the former beneficiary. Such a result is contrary to the ordinary law of trusts.

Termination remained official federal policy through the 1960s, although it was pursued with less vigor as its economic unworkability and moral and political unpalatability became clear. In 1968, President Lyndon Johnson declared that Native American self-determination should be the basis of federal policy, and Congress passed an Indian Bill of Rights that limited the application of P.L. 280, but also subjected Native American governments to federally defined civil rights standards.

In 1970, President Richard Nixon formally recommended that Congress "renounce, repudiate and repeal the termination policy," because it is "morally and legally unacceptable. . . (and) produces bad practical results" (Wunder, 1999, 160–61). The 1975 Indian Self-Determination and Education Act was Congress's response, and continues to be official policy. Under this act, tribal councils may subcontract to perform services previously provided by federal agencies. But it has been noted that this policy is not real self-determination.

> Indian-controlled education was not actually self-determination because Indians did not determine what kind of education their children would receive; they only replaced non-Indian bureaucrats and educators in institutions that changed very little with the shifting of personnel. Nevertheless, Indians believed that they were directing their own fortunes because they were at least visibly in charge. (Deloria and Lytle, 1984, 223)

In an overall sense, the latest federal policies for Native American self-determination put tribal councils on the same footing as state and municipal governments with regard to acquiring federal funds, thus undermining the unique treaty-based position of Native Americans in American politics.

Official federal policy has not eradicated the political viability of termination concepts. In 1997, the United States Senate appropriations bill for the Department of Interior became the focus of an attempt to eliminate Native American sovereignty as a condition for receipt of federal funds. Although the provision was rejected after substantial outcry, the very attempt shows several important things. First, the struggle over Native American sovereignty—however it is defined and limited—is far from over and is indeed a hot topic in American politics. Second, even the congressional defenders of Native American sovereignty argued that the United States could eliminate it if Congress wished to do so. Third, the notion that federal funding to Native American governments is rooted in treaty obligations, not in discretionary programs, was almost wholly suppressed in favor of a welfare definition of the status of Native Americans. Fourth, the attack on Native American sovereignty was packaged in a rhetoric of "helping the poor Indians." The Puritan argument survives in the U.S. Senate.

> Termination has always been implicit in federal native policy, or at least since the period when the government saw fit to deny the native groups self-government and substituted instead the wardship system. (Forbes, 1964, 122)

Author Tony Hillerman, noted for his contemporary novels about a Navajo detective, commented on the furor over the attempt in the Senate to strip Native Americans of their sovereignty. He wrote that his friend, Navajo elder Hastiin Alexander Etcitty, "would say that the notion that any human, or group thereof, has sovereignty over any part of Mother Earth is a myth based upon the white man's Origin Story." He concluded that the problem of Native American sovereignty "involves more than how to save what they have from the whites who yearn for it. It can become an internal fight over values." (Hillerman, 1997)

Native Americans as Indigenous Peoples

In the face of ongoing threats to real self-determination, Native Americans are increasingly turning toward a global and international perspective. In light of the history of treaty-making and with an eye toward restoring the sense of equality between nations that justified the treaty process to begin with, Native Americans—in concert with indigenous peoples worldwide—are asserting a sense of their own sovereignty. The United Nations Draft Declaration of the Rights of Indigenous Peoples is at the center of this global struggle for self-determination. The Declaration is the product of 20 years of negotiating among indigenous peoples and U.N. bodies.

"Peoples" in international law implies rights of self-determination, which the United States took the lead to challenge as not applicable to indigenous peoples. The U.S. argued against the Draft Declaration, asserting that self-determination exists only through states, and that people not organized in nation-state form are merely groups of individuals with shared cultural, linguistic, and social features, without any legal status as "peoples." This argument contradicted the U.S. claim that it deals with Native Americans on a government-to-government basis, a fact that was noticed by Native Americans whose critique of limited sovereignty under federal law has been increasingly strongly articulated.

The classical attributes of nation-state sovereignty foreshadow the problem of applying this concept to Native Americans: absolute, unlimited power held permanently in a single person or source, inalienable, indivisible, and original (not derivative or dependent). These are characteristics of power associated with divine right monarchy and the papacy. They were the brainchild of Western political theorists of the sixteenth and seventeenth centuries (especially Jean Bodin and Thomas Hobbes) as a solution to the problem of religious civil wars. They are not the characteristics of power in traditional Native American and other indigenous societies.

Contemporary Native American political theory confronts the question of whether conventional sovereignty can become an instrument of liberation from government policies and practices rooted in colonialism. If "state" and "sovereignty" refer to a framework of "supreme coercive power," and such power is absent in "tribes," is this a justification for "domestic dependent nation," or is it rather a sign of the inadequacy of state sovereignty as the organizing principle of world politics? Is the resurgence of Native American self-determination—defined by Native Americans themselves in conjunction with a global indigenous peoples' movement—the threshold of a new way of organizing politics that will, like the state before it, rearrange everything from villages to the world?

As one observer noted, the Native American challenge to federal power raises questions about the nature of that power in general.

> (W)e hold our government to be limited and to have no unlimited power. If the federal government nevertheless exercises unrestrained power over Indian nations, then what we say is not true, and we have a different kind of government than we think we have. And if our government is different in fact in relation to Native Americans, perhaps it is not what we believe it is in relation to other Americans, including ourselves. The Court is regarded as the institution of restraint and a protector of rights. If the Court restrains neither Congress nor itself in taking away tribal rights, then we are confronted by a fundamental contradiction between our political rhetoric and our political realities. (Ball, 1987, 61)

Nation-state sovereignty—the notion of "absolute, unlimited power held permanently in a single person or source, inalienable, indivisible, and original"—is today a theory under siege. Indigenous peoples are only one of the besiegers, but their presence is felt worldwide. Who would have thought that Canada would enter the twenty-first century in deep conflict with indigenous peoples within its borders, or that the Australian high court would find it necessary in 1992 to abandon the doctrine of *terra nullius*—the legal fiction that the land was empty before colonization, by which the rights and interests of indigenous inhabitants in land were treated as nonexistent?

Colonial powers have achieved worldwide hegemony, but have not been able to end their conflicts with those they regard as aboriginal, as being here before the beginning. The prior inhabitants of colonized lands have survived and continue to assert prior ownership of lands in domestic and international proceedings. Unabashed colonialism continues internationally in the guise of multinational corporatism, but has been transformed domestically into welfare-state social service programs. The twin political problems of domination and resistance persist. The world is not yet "safe" for the juggernaut of Western (Christian) "civilization." Neither is it comfortable for humans whose societies persist around ancient and sustainable relations with the earth.

From an indigenous perspective, state sovereignty is a claim that violates the pre-existing self-determination of indigenous peoples. Western jurisprudence has done a great deal to exclude "non-state societies" from the domain of law because they lack hierarchical authority structures. This Western thinking itself is grounded in theological-political concepts of Christian nationalism. The notion of "absolute, unlimited power held permanently in a single person or source, inalienable, indivisible, and original" is a definition of the Judeo-Christian-Islamic God. This "God died around the time of Machiavelli. . . . Sovereignty was . . . His earthly replacement" (Walker, 1996, 22).

> All significant concepts of the modern theory of the state are secularized theological concepts, not only because of their historical development . . . but also because of their systematic structure (Bartelson, 1995, 88).

State sovereignty "is a 'religion' and a faith."

> The skillfully drawn borders that cartographers have provided for us are . . . spiritual and philosophical abstractions representative of a form of quasi-belief. They are . . . not detached maps of reality as proponents would have us believe. These geographies reflect an ardent desire to make (or impose) sovereignty as a physical reality as natural as the mountains, rivers and lakes. (Lombardi, 1996, 154)

What does this mean for Native Americans, with a multitude of non-sovereign Creators and an entire Creation of sovereign beings? Native Americans at the close of the twentieth century are reassessing political discourse, working toward a terminology and perspective that will link post-modern world politics and pre-modern roots of their own societies.

The most pressing problem for indigenous self-determination is the problem of "the people." Indigenous peoples who have been subjected to centuries of state violence in the name of state sovereignty face "a profound crisis of the meaning of community, a crisis of political identity" (Ruiz, 1990, 86). This crisis is an echo of the problem of names: "Who is an Indian?"

Ultimately, it is land—and a people's relationship to land—that is at issue in Native American political struggles. To understand sovereignty as a legal-theological concept is to view these struggles as spiritual projects involving questions about what it means to be a people. Sovereignty arises from within a people as their unique expression of themselves among other peoples. It is not produced by court decrees or government grants or even by international declarations, but by the actual ability of a people to sustain themselves in a place. This is self-determination.

It has been said that Native American self-determination will be attained "through means other than those provided by a conqueror's rule of law and its discourses of conquest" (Williams, 1990 327). The anachronistic premises of the current system of international law—discovery and state sovereignty—are being challenged by Native Americans to understand self-determination clearly and see a way to manifest it. This is the struggle: "to redefine radically the conceptions of their rights and status. . . . to articulat(e) and defin(e) (their) own vision within the global community" (Williams, 1990, 328).

The uniqueness of Native Americans in American politics is not so much that Native Americans have self-determination where other minorities do not, but that they have the historical right and once again the political will to struggle for self-determination. Native Americans, whose colonization is officially denied or presented in the past tense, are among the world's indigenous peoples struggling for self-determination against various guises of colonialism as the twentieth century closes.

Bibliography

Armitage, Andrew. *Comparing the Policy of Aboriginal Assimilation: Australia, Canada, and New Zealand.* Vancouver: University of British Columbia Press, 1995.

Ball, Milner S. "Constitution, Court, Indian Tribes." *Am. B. Found. Res. J.* (1987): 1.

Barrerio, Jose. "First Words." *Native Americas.* Ithaca: Akwe:kon Press (Cornell University) xiv, 2 (Summer, 1997): 2.

Bartelson, Jens. *A Genealogy of Sovereignty.* Cambridge: Cambridge University Press, 1995.

Beecher v. Weatherby, 95 U.S. 517 (1877).

Cherokee Nation v. Georgia, 5 Pet. 1 (1831).

Cohen, Felix. "Americanizing the White Man." In *The Legal Conscience.* Archon Books, 1970.

Deloria, Vine, Jr., and Lytle, Clifford. *The Nations Within.* Pantheon Books, 1984.

Dorris, Michael. "Twentieth Century Indians: The Return of the Natives." In Raymond L. Hall, ed. *Ethnic Autonomy— Comparative Dynamics.* New York: Pergamon Press, 1979, pp. 66–84.

Forbes, Jack D., ed. *The Indian in America's Past.* Prentice-Hall, 1964.

Hillerman, Tony. "Who Has Sovereignty Over Mother Earth? *New York Times,* 18 September 1997.

Idaho v. Cour d'Alene Tribe, No. 94-1474 (June 23, 1997).

Jennings, Francis. *The Invasion of America.* W.W. Norton & Co., 1976.

Johnson v. McIntosh, 8 Wheat. 543 (1823).

Lombardi, Mark Owen. "Third-World Problem-Solving and the 'Religion' of Sovereignty: Trends and Prospects." In Mark E. Denham and Mark Owen Lombardi, eds. *Perspectives on Third-World Sovereignty.* Macmillan Press, Ltd., 1996.

Lyng v. Northwest Indian Cemetery Protective Association, 485 U.S. 439 (1988).

Newcomb, Steve. "The Evidence of Christian Nationalism in Federal Indian Law: The Doctrine of Discovery, *Johnson v. McIntosh*, and Plenary Power." *New York University Review of Law & Social Change* xx, 2 (1993): 303–41.

O'Connell, Barry. *On Our Own Ground*. Amherst: University of Massachusetts Press, 1992.

Ruiz, Lester Edwin J. "Sovereignty as Transformative Practice." In R.B.J. Walker and Saul H. Mendlovitz, eds. *Contending Sovereignties*. Lynne Rienner Publishers, 1990, pp. 79–96.

Rusco, Elmer R. "Historic Change in Western Shoshone Country: The Establishment of the Western Shoshone National Council and the Traditionalist Land Claims." *American Indian Quarterly* 16 (1992): 337–60.

Shapiro, Michael. "Moral Geographies and the Ethics of Post-Sovereignty." In Mark E. Denham and Mark Owen Lombardi, eds. *Perspectives on Third-World Sovereignty*. Macmillan Press, Ltd., 1996.

Story, Joseph. *Commentaries on the Constitution of the United States*. Boston: Hilliard, Gray, & Co., 1833.

United States v. Alcea Band of Tillamooks, 329 U.S. 40 (1946).

United States v. Blackfeet Tribe, 364 F.Supp. 192 (1973).

United States v. Dann, 470 U.S. 39 (1985).

United States v. Dann, 873 F.2d 1189 (9th Cir., 1989), cert. den., 493 U.S. 890 (1989).

Walker, R.B.J. "Space/Time/Sovereignty." In Mark E. Denham and Mark Owen Lombardi, eds. *Perspectives on Third-World Sovereignty*. Macmillan Press, Ltd., 1996.

Washburn, Wilcomb E. *Red Man's Land, White Man's Law*. 2nd ed. University of Oklahoma, 1995.

——, ed. *The Indian and the White Man*. New York: New York University Press, 1964.

Western Shoshone Legal Defense and Education Association v. United States, 531 F.2d 495 (1976).

Wheaton, Henry. *Elements of International Law*. Boston: Little, Brown & Co., 1855.

Williams, Robert A., Jr. *The American Indian in Western Legal Thought*. Oxford University Press, 1990.

Wunder, John R. *Retained by the People*. Oxford University Press, 1994.

ABC: Americans Before Columbus

As a result of the civil rights movement during the 1960s, there was much related activity in the Native American communities. *ABC: Americans Before Columbus* was one of several newspapers and periodicals that began publication during this time. It was published by the **National Indian Youth Council** beginning in October 1963. **See also** Culture and Identity; Indian Identity. (MRC)

BIBLIOGRAPHY

"ABC, Americans Before Columbus." *OCLC Online Union Catalog*. Dublin, OH: OCLC, 1998.

Bloom, Alexander and Wini Breines, eds. *Takin' It To the Streets*. New York: Oxford University Press, 1995.

Acoma, Battle of. *See* Battle of Acoma

Hank Adams (1943–)

Assiniboine/Dakota activist Hank Adams played an important role in the Northwest Indian fishing rights controversy. During the 1960s and 1970s, he organized fish-ins and demonstrations to protest Washington State's violation of Indian treaty rights. His efforts helped bring about *United States v. Washington* (1974), and Adams has since become a leading advocate of cooperative management and tribal fishery programs. (AHF)

BIBLIOGRAPHY

Cohen, Fay G. *Treaties on Trial: The Continuing Controversy over Northwest Indian Fishing Rights*. Seattle: University of Washington Press, 1986.

Josephy, Alvin, Jr. *Now That the Buffalo's Gone: A Study of Today's American Indians*. Norman: University of Oklahoma Press, 1984.

Akwesasne Notes

Akwesasne Notes, established in 1968, is the official publication of the Mohawk Nation Council and has come to be known as "the voice of Indigenous people." Since its inception, it has documented most of the activist, resistance, and political struggles of Native America, beginning with the 1968 Bridge Blockade by the Mohawk people of Akwesasne at the Canada–United States border that straddles their territory. *Akwesasne Notes* has covered countless land claim struggles and prece-dent-setting court cases involving native people, as well as providing a forum for critical discussion of political issues, expressions of creative writing, and the concerns of international indigenous peoples' movements. **See also** John Mohawk. (HHB)

BIBLIOGRAPHY

Akwesasne Notes. Buffalo, NY: Progress in American Studies of the State University of New York at Buffalo, 1969.

Alaska Allotment Act of 1906

The Alaska Allotment Act permitted Alaska natives to acquire individual lands in the manner available to other Native Americans under the General Allotment Act of 1887 (the **Dawes Act**). The act was an attempt by the Congress to protect native lands from encroachment and reflected its belief in the unsuitability of reservation policies. Natives could gain 160 acres of nonmineral land as an "inalienable and non-taxable" homestead, thus defining land titles as belonging to individual natives and not to tribal groups. The courts interpreted these land rights as subject to specific federal trust responsibility. Although repealed by Congress in ANCSA (1971), a savings clause for pending applications has kept the act's provisions alive in Alaska land rights cases and has continued federal

Native Alaskans have posed special circumstances for U.S. policy toward Native Americans. *Library of Congress.*

oversight of native land rights. **See also** Allotment. **See** Dawes Act (1887) in Appendix 1. (GAM)

BIBLIOGRAPHY

Case, Davis S. *Alaska Natives and American Laws*. Fairbanks: University of Alaska Press, 1984.

Alaska Federation of Natives (AFN)

The Alaska Federation of Natives (AFN) was formed in 1966 to lead all Alaska natives in the land claims battle with the state and federal governments. Instrumental in the development of the **Alaska Native Claims Settlement Act** (ANCSA) of 1971, AFN has remained the most powerful representative of Alaska natives' interests—political, legal, economic, and social. The AFN is governed by a 12-member board representing each of the regional for-profit corporations established under ANCSA; associations have influence as well. In the 1980s, AFN led the effort to amend ANCSA to provide shares in the corporations for natives born after 1971 and to protect lands from being lost. In the 1990s, AFN has concentrated on protecting native subsistence rights to fish and game species. The AFN convention meets every October in Anchorage. (GAM)

BIBLIOGRAPHY

Arnold, Robert D. *Alaska Native Land Claims*. 2nd ed. Anchorage: Alaska Native Foundation, 1978.

McBeath, Gerald A. and Thomas A. Morehouse. *Alaska Politics and Government*. Lincoln: University of Nebraska Press, 1994.

———. *The Dynamics of Alaska Native Self-Government*. Lanham, MD: University Press of America, 1980.

Alaska Native Brotherhood (ANB)

The Alaska Native Brotherhood (ANB), organized by 12 Tlingit Indians (and one Tsmishian) from southeast Alaska in 1912, is the oldest native organization in Alaska. From its inception, ANB has sought to advance native rights (e.g., to citizenship and voting), secure economic and educational opportunities, and gain social welfare benefits for natives. ANB permitted the extension of the **Indian Reorganization Act** to Alaska; it was instrumental in winning passage of the Tlingit–Haida Claims Act in 1935, which brought about recognition of Tlingit–Haida aboriginal claims to much of southeast Alaska. The ANB also played an early role in the Alaska native land claims movement, but it was soon eclipsed in influence by the **Alaska Federation of Natives (AFN)**. The ANB is supported by the Alaska Native Sisterhood (ANS), a separate but organizationally related institution. (GAM)

BIBLIOGRAPHY

Case, David S. *Alaska Natives and American Laws*. Fairbanks: University of Alaska Press, 1984.

Drucker, Philip. "The Native Brotherhoods: Modern Intertribal Organizations on the Pacific Coast." *Bureau of American Ethnology Bulletin* (1958).

Hope, Andrew, III. "Founders of the Alaska Native Brotherhood." Sitka, AK: privately published, 1975.

Alaska Native Claims Settlement Act of 1971

Passed by Congress to forestall the extension of the reservation system to Alaska, the Alaska Native Claims Settlement Act (ANCSA) extinguished aboriginal title to that state's 365 million acres of land. It also abolished aboriginal rights to hunt and fish on that land, thereby making Alaska natives subject to state and federal conservation laws. As compensation, the natives received $962.5 million and 44 million acres of land, to be divided among 12 regional corporations and 200 village corporations. The corporations, in turn, made a single issue of shares to some 80,000 village and at-large shareholders. Heralded at the time as the most generous settlement ever reached with Native Americans, ANCSA contained several unforeseen flaws and failed to respect indigenous cultures and uses of their land.

ANCSA imposed an artificial corporate structure that was ill-suited to communal life in the Alaskan wilderness. Although the regional corporations have fared better than their village counterparts, the act has produced only limited economic development. Lawsuits over land and resources sapped several native corporations, and many of ANCSA's economic benefits fell to nonnatives. Meanwhile, native lands remained vulnerable to alienation through sale or taxation when the ban on the sale of shares ended in 1991.

Unprepared to have 44 million acres of land suddenly thrown onto the market, Congress amended ANCSA in 1988. Under the so-called "1991 amendments," the ban on share sales will continue unless the shareholders vote to eliminate it, and undeveloped village lands will remain exempt from taxation unless borrowed against. Congress and the State of Alaska continue to resist fundamental changes in ANCSA, but native demands for the "retribalization" of their lands has produced a greater role for traditional native government. In 1993 the United States extended federal recognition to 226 Alaskan tribes, and in 1994 the Clinton administration reaffirmed the government-to-government relationship. (AHF)

BIBLIOGRAPHY

Berger, Thomas R. *Village Journey: The Report of the Alaska Native Review Commission*. New York: Hill and Wang, 1995.

Lazarus, A. and W.R. West. "The Alaska Native Claims Settlement Act: A Flawed Victory." *Law and Contemporary Problems* 40 (1976): 132–65.

McNabb, Steven Leslie and Lynn A. Robbins. "Native Institutional Responses to the Alaska Native Claims Settlement Act: Room for Optimism." *Journal of Ethnic Studies* 13, no. 1 (1985): 13–27.

Walsh, John F. "Settling with the Alaska Native Claims Settlement Act." *Stanford Law Review* 38 (1985): 227–63.

Alaska Native Reorganization Act of 1936

The Alaska Native Reorganization Act extended to Alaska the provisions of the **Indian Reorganization Act** (IRA) of 1934. Congress drafted the IRA in a major change of federal Indian policy, to reverse the allotment act (the **Dawes Act of 1887**) that had destroyed the effectiveness of **tribal governments.**

The first section of the legislation resembled sections of the IRA. It allowed groups of natives living in neighborhoods, communities, or rural districts (or sharing a common bond of occupation or association) to organize on the same basis as Indian bands or tribes in the 48 contiguous states. These groups could adopt a constitution and bylaws and receive federal recognition. They could apply for federal loans, operate federal programs for natives, and organize cooperatives. This section of the act, as interpreted by the Department of the Interior, gives Alaska Native communities all the powers of inherent **sovereignty** (such as the power to determine their own membership)

The Alaska Native Reorganization Act of 1936 brought Alaska natives, such as this mother and her child, under the same governance arrangements that applied to the Native people of the 48 contiguous states. *National Archives.*

available to Indian tribes; it confirms the self-governing status of native villages and permits them to enforce local ordinances. By the 1980s, more than 80 IRA governments had formed in Alaska.

The second section of the Act (repealed in 1976) allowed the secretary of the interior to designate reservations in Alaska based on traditional native use or occupancy. Under this authority, six IRA reserves were created in Alaska, with the largest (1.4 million acres) in Venetie. The effect of the Alaska Native Reorganization Act was to erase most of the remaining differences between Alaska Natives and Indians of the 48 contiguous states. It is the essential foundation for native sovereignty in Alaska today. (GAM)

BIBLIOGRAPHY
Case, David S. *Alaska Natives and American Laws*. Fairbanks: University of Alaska Press, 1984.
Morehouse, Thomas A., Gerald A. McBeath, and Linda Leask. *Alaska's Urban and Rural Governments*. Lanham, MD: University Press of America, 1984.
Naske, Claus-M. and Herman E. Slotnick. *Alaska: A History of the Forty-ninth State*. Norman: University of Oklahoma Press, 1987.
Price, Robert. *Native Rights: A Report to the Alaska Statehood Commission*. Juneau: Alaska Department of Law, 1982.

Albany Plan

The Albany Plan was part of a conference held in New York City in 1754 as an attempt to secure the support and cooperation of the Iroquois Confederation in the **French and Indian War.** Benjamin Franklin proposed the plan as a cooperative measure among the seven British colonies to regulate Indian affairs and monitor the westward expansion. The 150 Indian representatives who attended the conference accepted the gifts and hospitality granted them, but left the conference without committing their people to the British. Although the Albany Plan was not adopted, it was the first step toward union and the independence of the American colonies. (AMM)

BIBLIOGRAPHY
Graymont, Barbara. *The Iroquois in the American Revolution*. Syracuse, NY: Syracuse University Press, 1972.

Alcatraz Island Occupation

Alcatraz Island is the site of a former federal prison in San Francisco Bay. In March 1964, the prison buildings were occupied by four Indians for three hours, and then again for 19 hours on November 9, 1969. A few weeks later, a group called **United Indians of All Tribes** was joined by the **American Indian Movement** (AIM) for a 19-month occupation of the island, from November 20, 1969, until June 11, 1971. In 1982, **Dennis Banks** held an "unthanksgiving ceremony" on the island. **See also** Richard Oakes; Reoccupation of Fort Lawton (1970); John Trudell. (RAC)

BIBLIOGRAPHY
Blue Cloud, Peter. *Alcatraz Is Not an Island*. Berkeley, CA: Wingbow Press, 1972.
Fortunate Eagle, Adam. "Invading Alcatraz." In Peter Nabakov, ed. *Native American Testimony*. New York: Penguin, 1991.

Alcoholism and Other Social Problems on Reservations

Reservations for American Indians were initially set up as homelands for Indians during their transition toward assimilation into the Euro-American world. To many non-Indians today, reservations have become an embarrassment representing the American version of apartheid. But, to the Natives living on the reservations, it is a testimony to their survival and to their ability to hang on to their land, their homes. However, problems remain prevalent on reservations, among them alcoholism and its dysfunctional social imparts.

The European settlers first introduced alcohol to Native Americans, and even during the colonial period there were attempts to prohibit the sale or trade of alcohol to the natives. Native Americans were conscious of the ill effects that alcohol was having on their culture. They asked President Thomas Jefferson to stop the sale of liquor to native peoples. Jefferson responded, and territorial governors were warned that people would be penalized if caught trafficking alcohol to the natives; however, no matter how much legislation was passed, the bootleggers were always able to supply the native people with plenty of liquor.

During the mid- to late-nineteenth century, there was a large movement to reform "the Indian." Many of the reformers approached Indian affairs with sincerity in wanting to help the native peoples retain their land. At the same time, the reformers wanted the natives to learn how to become acceptable to Euro-Americans. Civilization programs were started in hopes that many natives would learn to farm. But greed stopped much of the civilization process. Although reformers wanted natives to keep their land, they could not hold off the westward advances of whites. As settlers continued pushing westward, the government sought more ways to control Indians, and one of the ways they controlled them was by enacting liquor laws. Despite the good intentions of missionaries and reformers, liquor laws were part of the civilization process.

The government forced the Indian populations onto smaller and smaller reservations, decreasing their chances of economic stability, and they justified the segregation of the reservation system on the plague of drunkenness among the Indians.

Prucha reports that the secretary of the Board of Indian Commissioners called liquor "the greatest obstacle to Indian civilization." Under the guise of helping the poor Indians, governments were able to forcefully regulate the trade and living conditions of Indian peoples. Missionaries were well meaning in their efforts, but their attempts to bring sobriety to the Indian communities only supported the continuation of the ill effects of "worship." The **Indian Liquor Act of 1897** was well received among the reformers and the missionaries as a way of removing the stumbling block of alcoholism from the path of the Indians. However, this bill also included a provision that made the sale or trade of any foodstuff or medicine with an alcohol base to an Indian illegal. Again, the government took control of what Indian peoples were allowed to have and have not.

Reformers preached an accelerated acculturation. Prucha asserts that the Indians were unable to deal with the whirlwind of changes: "the nomadic life of a buffalo hunter to the sedentary life of a small farmer, from communal patterns to fiercely individualistic ones, from native religious ceremonials to Christian practices, from Indian languages and oral tradition to spoken and written English." The reformers became disenchanted with the reservation process of civilization and the reservations became an embarrassment. The reformers eventually supported the Dawes Allotment Acts to destroy reservations and promote individualism.

Alcoholism, for natives and nonnatives, offers a form of escape, yet alcoholism has been a prevalent problem for the Native-American communities. According to Christine Bolt, there is still a certain amount of racism that is attached to Native Americans and alcohol. Since the reformers and government officials, whites have thought erroneously that Indians did not have the ability to drink alcohol in moderation. She contends that "modern research has demonstrated that neither Indians nor any other ethnic group have a physiological incapacity to cope with alcohol." The racist assertion, that Indian peoples are prone to alcoholism because of their genetic make-up, infiltrates mainstream American beliefs about Native Americans. However this does not mean that a problem does not exist among Native American communities. According to Bolt, alcohol contributes to an Indian arrest rate that is higher than the national average of alcohol-related crimes and the "Indian death rate of cirrhosis of the liver is about three times that of the population as a whole and appears to be a factor in dismissal from jobs and the large number of suicides among Indian groups." Michael L. Lobb and Thomas D. Watts report that alcoholism is attributed to high numbers of accidental deaths, suicides, and crimes.

In the 1990s, there has certainly been a push for tribal sovereignty, which means that individual native communities want to assume a role of autonomy when dealing with their own governments, their own people, their own moneys and resources, and their own problems. Within native communities, there have been more programs developed that are suited to native needs in terms of counseling that look closely at Indian attitudes about drinking. Michael Everett in the introduction to *Drinking Behavior Among Southwestern Indians* calls for Native Americans to be employed as staff in treatment centers for alcoholism, because they are closely related to the Native-American communities and may be better able to serve the needs of the patients. In Fernando Escalante's essay "Group Pressure and Excessive Drinking Among Indians," he contends that the issue of drinking problems among Native Americans is more complex than that their condition is the result of social pressures, but that it is dependent on the dynamics of the community in which the Native Americans are involved.

In 1953, Congress lifted the ban on off-reservation liquor sales to Indians and authorized tribal governments to decide whether to allow liquor sales on the reservation. This act was a move toward tribal governments' establishment of authority. (MKJ)

BIBLIOGRAPHY

Amber, Marjane. *Breaking the Iron Bonds: Indian Control of Energy Development*. Lawrence: University of Kansas Press, 1990.

Bolt, Christine. *American Indian Policy and American Reform Case Studies of the Campaign to Assimilate the American Indians*. London: Allen and Unwin, 1987.

Escalante, Fernando. "Group Pressure and Excessive Drinking Among Indians." In Jack O. Waddell and Michael W. Everett, eds. *Drinking Behavior among Southwestern Indians: An Anthropological Perspective*. Tucson: University of Arizona Press, 1980.

Everett, Michael W. "General Introduction." In Jack O. Waddell and Michael W. Everett, eds. *Drinking Behavior among Southwestern Indians: An Anthropological Perspective*. Tucson: University of Arizona Press, 1980.

Lobb, Michael L. and Thomas D. Watts, eds. *Native American Youth and Alcohol*. New York: Greenwood Press, 1989.

Prucha, Francis Paul. *American Indian Policy in Crisis: Christian Reformers and the Indian 1865–1900*. Norman: University of Oklahoma Press, 1976.

———. *American Indian Policy in the Formative Years: The Indian Trade and Intercourse Acts 1790–1834*. Cambridge, MA: Harvard University Press, 1962.

Elise Allen (1899–1990)

Elise Allen worked with the Native American Advisory Council from 1979 to 1981 on Sonoma State University's Warm Springs Cultural Resources Study, during which time she fought for the rights of her fellow Native Americans. Allen also associated herself with various cultural and historical studies and efforts concerning Native-American tribes, including the Warm Springs Dam-Lake Sonoma Project. Allen spent most of her time focusing on the native art of basketweaving; not only did she teach weaving at the California Mendocino Art Center, but she made Pomo baskets that were displayed across the world. In 1972, she published her autobiography, which focused on her ancestral art.

BIBLIOGRAPHY

Allen, Elise. *Pomo Basketweaving: A Supreme Art for the Weaver.* Healdsburg: Maturegraph Publishers, 1972.

Allotment

Allotment was an effort of the United States government to assimilate American Indian nations by assigning some of their lands individually to their members and opening the remaining ones to white settlement. The process began as early as the eighteenth century but reached its zenith on February 8, 1887, when the General Allotment Act **(Dawes Act)** was passed. Indian lands shrank from 104,314,349 acres in 1889 to 12,071,380 in 1891; nearly a 90 percent decrease. The law had two main purposes: to open Indian-owned lands to white settlers and to dispossess American Indians not only from most of their lands but also from their tribal ownership and sovereignty over them. The Dawes Act disregarded treaties and failed to take into account cultural differences that made allotment unreasonable to most American Indians.

On the contrary, the Dawes Act aimed at recreating Indians as white American citizens with a value system of private ownership. The standard share was 160 acres to each male head of a family. After Indians expressed opposition to the alien "head of a family" concept, the act was amended in 1891 to provide equal shares to all men, women, and children — 80 acres of agricultural land, 160 acres of grazing land. Indian nations tried to unite against the Dawes Act but were effectively countered when the commissioner of Indian Affairs confined all American Indians to their reservations for six days prior to the passage of the law. Indian protest against allotment, mainly unrecorded, was made by Indians throughout the United States as their tribal holdings and their native groupings were broken up by enforcement of the Dawes Act. All allottees became citizens of the United States but lost the protection they had from their tribes; standing alone before the white man's law and courts, they were mostly helpless. A few reservations escaped the Dawes Act, such as the Navajo Reservations, mainly because their lands were unattractive to homesteaders. In 1928 the Brookings Institute published a report that described the deplorable conditions of poverty, disease, lack of social and economic adjustment, suffering, and discontent among American Indians; the allotment policy was cited as the main cause for these conditions. (MS)

BIBLIOGRAPHY

Debo, Angie. *A History of the Indians of the United States.* Norman: University of Oklahoma Press, 1970.

McDonnell, Janet A. *The Dispossession of the American Indian 1887–1934.* Bloomington: Indiana University Press, 1991.

American Horse (ca. 1840–1908)

After resisting United States expansion in the 1860s, American Horse (Wasicu Tasunka), an Oglala Lakota, favored peaceful relations. He advocated Indians taking land in severalty and Indian children attending government boarding schools. His diplomatic trips to Washington, D.C., supporting "progressive" policies, earned the enmity of conservative Lakotas. (TMK)

BIBLIOGRAPHY

Hyde, George E. *Red Cloud's Folk: A History of the Oglala Sioux Indians.* Norman: University of Oklahoma Press, 1971.

Olson, James C. *Red Cloud and the Sioux Problem.* Lincoln: University of Nebraska Press, 1965.

American Horse fought in Red Cloud's War for the Bozeman Trail, but he eventually resigned himself to reservation life. Here he is photographed receiving his allotment from government agents at Pine Ridge. *Library of Congress.*

American Indian Affairs Association Education Conference

The American Indian Affairs Association Conference was held in 1966 to examine the problems of education confronting American Indian students. This two-day conference was attended by more than 35 specialists and the chief of education for the **Bureau of Indian Affairs** (BIA). These and other participants examined statistics concerning poor educational performances by Indian children while also looking at the practices of the 81 boarding schools maintained by the BIA. It was concluded that these boarding schools, which were sometimes up to 600 miles away from the Indian children's homes, caused homesickness and other related problems. Furthermore, it was found that the 91,000 Indian students attending boarding schools often faced serious adjustments and discrimination problems. These difficulties contributed to a 50 percent dropout rate among Native American adolescents. As a result of the conference and these findings, a number of educational reforms were formulated, including the creation of better, closer schools and the initiation of support programs.

BIBLIOGRAPHY

Szasz, Margaret C. *Education and the American Indian.* Albuquerque: University of New Mexico Press, 1974.

American Indian Chicago Conference (AICC)

The largest multi-tribal gathering in decades, the American Indian Chicago Conference (AICC) brought together 460 Indians from 90 separate tribes during the week of June 13–20, 1961. Sol Tax, an anthropologist at the University of Chicago, and his assistant Nancy Lurie organized the convocation for the voicing of concerns on various topics ranging from education and health care to the protection of water rights and the abolition of certain Bureau of Indian Affairs area offices. At the end of the conference, the group issued the "Declaration of Indian Purpose." The AICC indicated to the nation that a Pan-Indian movement was imminent. This information led to increased activism among Indians, including the youth who established the National Indian Youth Council later that summer. After the AICC it was clear that a unified effort was more productive than individual efforts. (MRC)

BIBLIOGRAPHY

Cornell, Stephen. *The Return of the Native.* New York: Oxford, 1988.

Lurie, Nancy O. "The Voice of the American Indian: Report on the American Indian Chicago Conference." *Current Anthropology* 2 (December 1961): 478–500.

Prucha, Francis Paul. *Documents of United States Indian Policy.* Lincoln: University of Nebraska Press, 1990.

American Indian Defense Association (AIDA)

The American Indian Defense Association (AIDA) heralded the onset of reform in Indian policy during the 1920s. In 1923 **John Collier** and other friends of the Pueblo Indians formed the association to fight the Bursum bill, which threatened the Pueblos' Spanish land grants in New Mexico. After helping to defeat that legislation and secure the passage of the Pueblo Lands Act of 1924, the AIDA moved into the vanguard of the reform movement and served as the chief promoter of Collier's agenda until he became commissioner of Indian Affairs in 1933. (AHF)

BIBLIOGRAPHY

Kelly, Lawrence C. *The Assault on Assimilation: John Collier and the Origins of Indian Policy Reform.* Albuquerque: University of New Mexico Press, 1983.

Philip, Kenneth R. *John Collier's Crusade for Indian Reform, 1920–1954.* Tucson: University of Arizona Press.

American Indian Movement (AIM)

The American Indian Movement (AIM) was founded in Minneapolis on July 28, 1968, by **Dennis Banks, Clyde Bellecourt,** and George Mitchell, all Ojibwe of Minnesota.

The movement led the Native-American activism of the 1970s and gathered a massive following from all parts of the Indian population, including some participation and support of traditional elders. The American Indian Movement's confrontational politics provided the movement with exposure and influence but also made it a target of government intervention. The most widely known actions of AIM, which gave the movement international attention, were the Trail of Broken Treaties and the BIA building takeover in 1972; the confrontation with armed federal authorities at **Wounded Knee** in 1973; and the Longest Walk in 1978. In 1977 the movement founded the International Indian Treaty Council in the United Nations. This sort of action gave way to more local events. Today the movement includes a number of chapters across the country and a national board that oversees their activities. Initially, AIM developed the AIM Patrols in response to police brutality against American Indians in Minneapolis, which dramatically reduced violence and undue arrests. The leaders of the movement established a host of organizations to assist American Indians in the city with legal advice, jobs, housing, and education. The American Indian Movement's main concerns are treaty rights of Indian nations with emphasis on the issue of sovereignty; the movement encourages returning to Native-American traditions and strengthening communities. **See also** Russell Means.(MS)

BIBLIOGRAPHY

Dewing, Rolland. *Wounded Knee: The Meaning and Significance of the Second Incident.* New York: Irvington Publishers, 1985.

Means, Russell and Marvin J. Wolf. *Where White Men Fear to Tread.* New York: St. Martin's Press, 1995.

American Indian Policy Review Commission

The American Indian Policy Review Commission was established by an act of Congress in January 1975 (under Public Law 93-580). It was first proposed by Senator James Abourezk (D-SD) in the wake of increased violence and activism on behalf of Native Americans in the early 1970s. Abourezk and his supporters hoped that the commission could explain the problems plaguing federal–Indian relations and make recommendations for improving the relationship.

The Commission was composed of 11 individuals. Abourezk was the chairman, Representative Lloyd Meeds (D-WA) was vice-chairman, and Ernest Stevens (Oneida) was the executive director. Also on the commission were two more congressmen, another representative, and four additional Native Americans. Of the five Indians on the commission, three were from **reservations**, one was an urban Indian, and another came from a federally unrecognized tribal group.

The commission formed 11 task forces with a total of 33 members, 31 of whom were Native American. The task forces investigated and reported on issues of **trustee responsibility** and the federal–Indian relationship; **tribal government**; federal administration; federal, state, and tribal jurisdiction; Indian higher education; Indian health; natural resource development and protection; urban and rural nonreservation Indians; Indian law; terminated and unrecognized tribal groups; and alcohol and drug abuse. In addition, two special task forces issued reports, one on Alaska native issues and another on the management of the **Bureau of Indian Affairs**. The Commission issued its Final Report in 1977. (RAC)

BIBLIOGRAPHY

Prucha, Francis Paul. *The Great Father.* vol. 2. Lincoln: University of Nebraska Press, 1984.

American Indian Policy Review Commission.' *Final Report.* Washington, DC: U.S. Government Printing Office, 1977.

American Indian Policy Review Commission Report

The Final Report of the **American Indian Policy Review Commission** (Abourezk Commission), presented to Congress on May 17, 1977, endorsed the philosophy behind the **Indian Self-Determination and Education Act of 1975** and stressed the special nature of the trust relationship established between the federal government and Indian tribes. It criticized the complexity of federal–Indian relations, as well as the lack of bureaucratic cooperation among the federal agencies that dealt with native populations. In addition, the report detailed the damaging effects forced removal and isolation had on Indian economics and culture. Finally, it recommended the development of a uniform, accurate database that could be used to track government programs and expenditures, and to monitor their effects.

The Commission was doomed from the beginning because of splits within the national Indian community. Both the radical younger Indians and the traditional Indians felt excluded from it. The Commission did not hold field hearings, but organized eleven task forces to collect data from around the country. The effort was haphazard and the recommendations were so varied and so hastily crafted as to be ineffectual at the time. The Final Report contained 206 different recommendations, so diverse that Congress was unable to view the document as a working paper. In all, the Commission was mainly symbolic, and had the effect of muffling the voices of Indian dissent. (RAC; AMM)

BIBLIOGRAPHY

American Indian Policy Review Commission. *Final Report.* Washington, DC: U.S. Government Printing Office, 1977.

New Directions in Federal Indian Policy: A Review of the American Indian Policy Review Commission. Los Angeles: UCLA American Indian Studies Center, 1979.

Philp, Kenneth R. *John Collier's Crusade for Indian Reform, 1920–1954.* Tucson: University of Arizona Press, 1977.

Prucha, Francis Paul. *The Great Father: The United States Government and the American Indians.* Lincoln: University of Nebraska Press, 1984.

American Indian Religious Freedom Act (1978)

The American Indian Religious Freedom Act, 92 Stat. 469 (1978) (also called AIRFA), was passed as a joint resolution of Congress in response to widespread allegations of disruption of traditional native spiritual practices by state and federal laws and government agencies. Congressional investigations substantiated these allegations, showing both intentional and unintentional governmental actions that prevented access to sacred sites and prohibited or restricted sacred ceremonies.

The House of Representatives issued a report of findings in support of Congressional action to redress the situation. The joint resolution subsequently passed stated that ". . . [I]t shall be the policy of the United States to protect and preserve for Native Americans their inherent right of freedom of belief, expression, and exercise of traditional religions of the American Indian. . . ." The resolution further stated that the rights protected includes "access to sacred sites, use and possession of sacred objects, and the freedom to worship through ceremonials and traditional rites."

The Religious Freedom Act has had largely symbolic impact, because—as a joint resolution of policy—the act has no enforcement or penalty provisions. The stated policy can be and is violated with impunity. The courts have interpreted the act to require that government officials "consider" native spiritual concerns but need not actually respect or refrain from impeding them. In *Lyng v. Northwest Indian Cemetery Protective Association* **(1988),** the U.S. Supreme Court ruled that "Nowhere in the law is there so much as a hint of any intent to create a cause of action or any judicially enforceable individual rights." AIRFA therefore exists as a general statement of unenforceable federal policy. **See also** American Indian Religious Freedom Act of 1978; *Oregon v. Smith* (1990); *People v. Woody* (1964); Religious Freedom Restoration Act of 1993. (PPE)

BIBLIOGRAPHY

Pevar, Stephen L. *The Rights of Indians and Tribes.* Carbondale: Southern Illinois University Press, 1992.

American Revolution

Native Americans were key actors during the American Revolution. While the French held the balance of power between the British and the young United States in the more well-known battles of the coastal areas, native nations held the balance in the interior. Large confederacies, such as the Iroquois (the **Six Nations** Confederacy) in the North, the Shawnee in the West, and the Cherokee in the South, sided with the British. Smaller tribes such as the Catawba in South Carolina supported the colonists. For the Indians, war had been nearly continuous on the eastern part of the continent in the late 1700s, but the Revolution unleashed new levels of violence in native North America. Leadership within some native nations changed due to the tumult of the period. There was widespread loss of life and destruction of towns, and many Indians became refugees.

Despite their key role in Revolutionary battles, Native Americans were not mentioned in the 1783 Treaty of Paris between Britain and the newly independent United States. For native nations, the end of the Revolutionary War meant fewer opportunities for diplomacy, because the British abandoned their native allies; Indians therefore lost the ability to play a balancing role. There was not, however, an end to warfare. The struggle in the interior continued into the 1800s, as Native Americans faced a new flood of settlers. These settlers no longer needed to flout British laws to move west; they were encouraged by the United States to claim Indian lands for themselves. **See also** Molly Brant; Cornplanter; Five Nations Neutrality Policy; Red Jacket. **See** "Brother, the Great Spirit Has Made Us All" by Red Jacket (1805) in Appendix 1. (LCJ)

BIBLIOGRAPHY

Calloway, Colin G. *The American Revolution in Indian Country.* New York: Cambridge University Press, 1995.

Graymount, Barbara. *The Iroquois in the American Revolution.* Syracuse, NY: Syracuse University Press, 1972.

Owanah Anderson (1926–)

Anderson, born in Choctaw County, Oklahoma, is probably best known for her efforts in progressing the status of Native American women. She founded the Ohoyo Resource Center for the United States Department of Education in 1979. The resource center helps Native American women accomplish their career goals. Anderson served on the U.S. Department of Health, Education, and Welfare Committee on Rights and Responsibilities from 1977 to 1980. She then served as a member of President Jimmy Carter's Advisory Committee on Women for three years. Anderson was the only American Indian representative on the Commission on Security and Cooperation in Europe, held in Madrid, Spain, in 1980. She has also been involved with Native American Ministries of the Episcopal Church since 1984.

BIBLIOGRAPHY

Bataille, Gretchen M., ed. *Native American Women.* New York: Garland Publishing, 1993.

William Apess (1798–1839)

Despite his mixed heritage of Pequot Indian, African-American, and white lineages, William Apess ascended the social scale to become a Methodist minister in 1830. He published five books, the most important of which was *A Son of the Forest* in 1829. He alienated himself by championing Mashpee self-determination in Massachusetts. Apess died destitute and disillusioned with white society. (GO)

BIBLIOGRAPHY

O'Connell, Barry, ed. *On Our Ground: The Complete Writings of William Apess, a Pequot.* Amherst: University of Massachusetts Press, 1992.

Appropriation Act of 1799

This act, which actually was two separate pieces of legislation, provided $35,000 for the payment of expenses to negotiate treaties with Native Americans. The first piece of legislation authorized no more than $25,000 and the second authorized $10,000 to defray the cost of treaties negotiated with the Six Nations, Creek, Cherokee, and Chickasaw. **See also** Federal Indian Policy; Indian Appropriations Act of 1871.

BIBLIOGRAPHY

Cohen, Felix S. *Felix Cohen's Handbook of Federal Indian Law.* Charlottesville, VA: Mitchie, Bobbs-Merrill, 1982; Ft. Lauderdale, FL: Five Rings Press, 1986.

Anna Mae Pictou Aquash (1945–1976)

Anna Mae Aquash, a Micmac, was an **American Indian Movement** activist involved in numerous political and cultural activities in the 1970s. Active on the Pine Ridge Reservation at a time of great turmoil, including Wounded Knee II, Aquash was murdered and her body was found near Wanblee, South Dakota. The case remains open. (RAC)

BIBLIOGRAPHY

Crow Dog, Mary. *Lakota Woman.* New York: HarperPerenniel, 1991.

Matthiessen, Peter. *In the Spirit of Crazy Horse.* New York: Penguin Books, 1991.

Archaeological Resources Protection Act of 1979

The Archaeological Resources Protection Act of 1979 (ARPA) was passed as Public Law 96-95 (and codified as 16 U.S.C. 470) to provide protections for archaeological resources on public lands or Indian lands, declaring them to be part of the country's heritage. Archaeological resources means any material remains of past human life or activities which are of archaeological interest. Additionally, ARPA prohibits acts and provides criminal penalties. ARPA prohibits the attempt or removal, damage, alteration, or defacement of archeological resources without a permit. ARPA expressly prohibits the trafficking of wrongfully obtained archaeological resources in interstate or foreign commerce. Notification to Indian tribes is required if the site has religious or cultural importance. Tribal law can regulate an Indian tribe or tribal member getting a permit to excavate or remove on their own lands. Finally, ARPA recognizes the Native Americans' right to maintain possession and control of culturally important objects. **See also** Native American Graves and Repatriation Act of 1990; Repatriation of Remains. (PAP)

BIBLIOGRAPHY

Platzman, Steven. "Comment: Objects of Controversy: The Native American Right to Repatriation." *The American University Law Review* 41, no. 1 (Winter 1992): 517.

Arizona v. California (1963)

Arizona v. California, 373 U.S. 546 (1963), which is one of the landmark rulings regarding Indian water rights, ironically involves no Indians as parties. The question the U.S. Supreme Court sought to answer was how much water from the Colorado River each of the arid lower-basin states (Arizona, California, Nevada, New Mexico, and Utah) was legally entitled to. Because of the substantial presence of tribes in these states (Arizona, for example, is home to 19 tribes), the calculation over water rights necessarily included consideration of tribal rights to the water. A special master, appointed by the Court, found that as a matter of fact and law when the reservations were created the tribes were guaranteed not only the land, but also enough water from the Colorado River to irrigate the land. Thus, the Court said that each reservation in the lower-basin states had a right to water for all "practicably irrigable acreage," a standard that is still good law today—

although there are continuing problems in quantification of "practicably irrigable acreage." **See also** Land and Water Rights; *Winters v. United States* (1908). (GTH)

BIBLIOGRAPHY

Burton, Lloyd. *American Indian Water Rights and the Limits of Law.* Lawrence: University Press of Kansas, 1991.

Getches, David H., Charles Wilkinson, and Robert A. Williams Jr. *Federal Indian Law: Cases and Materials.* St. Paul, MN: West Publishing, 1993.

Claudeen Bates Arthur (1942–)

Claudeen Bates Arthur, a Navajo attorney, worked in social services and as a high school science teacher before graduating from Arizona State University Law School in 1974. She served with the Interior Solicitor's Office in Washington, D.C. (1977); was Navajo Nation attorney general (1983–1987); and was general counsel, White Mountain Apache Tribe (1988–1990), before becoming legislative counsel for Navajo Nation Council (1990–1995) where she oversaw the updating of the Navajo Nation Code. (JN)

BIBLIOGRAPHY

Arthur, Claudeen Bates. Telephone interview. November 17, 1997.

Articles of Confederation

The Articles of Confederation comprised the national constitution of the United States from 1781 to 1788. During these years federal officials and congressmen viewed and treated Native Americans as "conquered peoples," whom the United States had defeated in the Revolutionary War and whose property, like that of white Loyalists, was forfeit. Accordingly, at a series of treaty conferences between 1784 and 1786, federal commissioners obliged the Iroquois, Ohio Valley, and southeastern Indian nations to acknowledge American sovereignty over them and commanded the Iroquois and Ohio Valley nations to cede several million acres of Ohio land to Congress. However, the government's "conquest theory" did not conform with reality, for the Indians who had fought with Britain did not consider themselves to have been defeated by the United States. Few were willing to accept a punitive settlement without a fight. Since the Articles gave Congress no independent authority to levy taxes or raise troops, the federal government was unable to muster an army large enough to force its policy on the Indians. Therefore, the result of the postwar treaties was not peace but a protracted war (1786–1794) between the Northwest Confederacy and Anglo-American settlers and soldiers in Ohio and Kentucky. Moreover, the Ninth Article of Confederation limited Congress's authority over Indian affairs to "Indians not members of any of the states," allowing individual states to devise their own policies toward the Indians within their borders. North Carolina and Georgia, in particular, extracted punitive land cessions from the Cherokee and Creek nations, thereby igniting another war in the Southeast and at the same time violating the federal Treaty of Hopewell. **See also** Six Na-

tions (Haudenosaunee) Confederacy/Iroquois Confederacy. (DAN)

BIBLIOGRAPHY

Horsman, Reginald. *Expansion and American Indian Policy, 1783–1812.* East Lansing: Michigan State University Press, 1967.

Merrell, James. "Declarations of Independence: Indian–White Relations in the New Nation." In Jack Greene, ed. *The American Revolution: Its Character and Limits.* New York: New York University Press, 1987.

Mohr, Walter H. *Federal Indian Relations, 1774–1788.* Philadelphia: University of Pennsylvania Press, 1933.

Assimilationist Policy

Assimilationist policy was intended to "civilize" the native inhabitants so they could eventually join the dominant society. Successful assimilation meant the dissolution of Indian culture and the total absorption of Indians into mainstream North American life. This highly paternalistic policy focused on developing three specific traits: self-reliant individualism, capitalism, and Christianity.

Boarding school was a key ingredient in assimilationist policy. Indian children were taken from their families and sent to boarding schools, where the children were forced to cut their hair and relinquish their Indian names, clothing, language, and culture. They were expected to learn a trade and join the workforce in areas off the **reservations.**

Assimilationists also attempted to replace communal tribal economics with capitalism. Potlatches and gift-giving ceremonies were outlawed. Many Native Americans were forced to adopt an agricultural lifestyle, farming smallholdings with implements provided to them by the Indian Office. Land that was not used according to regulations was sold to white homesteaders. Under the **Dawes Act of 1887,** to facilitate agricultural progress, annuities were often given to the Indians in the form of tools and seed, rather than cash (which might not be spent as the Indian agents desired). Strict laws governed commerce with the tribes, but such commerce was encouraged as a "civilizing" tool.

In an effort to bring Christianity to the Indians, missionaries were given special permission to live and work on reservation lands. In addition, most of the cultural and spiritual practices of the Native Americans were outlawed, in the hope that they would adopt Christian rituals and beliefs. The majority of schools operated on the reservation were run by missionaries, and the curriculum included religious instruction.

Assimilationism lost popularity in the mid-1930s; however, it remains an important foundation of federal Indian policy. **See also** Conservatism and Liberalism; Forced Assimilation; Indian Civilization Act of 1819; Kidnapping of Navajo Children; White Man's Burden. **See** Dawes Act (1887) in Appendix 1. (RAC)

BIBLIOGRAPHY

Prucha, Francis Paul. *The Great Father.* vol. 1. Lincoln: University of Nebraska Press, 1984.

B

Bacon's Rebellion

In 1675–1676, Native Americans found themselves caught in a power struggle between Virginia governor William Berkeley and frontier planter Nathaniel Bacon. Discontented over the lack of protection and support for frontier settlements, Bacon and his followers indiscriminately led expeditions against any tribal group in the immediate area. The Susquehannocks felt the brunt of the attacks. The friendly Occaneechees and Pamunkeys also felt Bacon's wrath. Eventually Bacon and his followers turned their attentions on the governor, rebelled against the established Virginia governing body, and burned Jamestown to the ground. The rebellion came to an end when Bacon died and his men deserted their posts.
See also Queen Anne of Pamunkey (KJB)

BIBLIOGRAPHY

Washburn, Wilcomb. *The Governor and the Rebel.* Chapel Hill, NC: University of North Carolina Press, 1957.
Webb, Stephen. *1676: The End of American Independence.* Cambridge, MA: Harvard University Press, 1984.

Dennis J. Banks (1937–)

Banks, also known as Nowacumig, is one of the founders (and currently a field director of) the **American Indian Movement** (AIM). Banks, an Anishinabe, was born on Leech Lake Reservation in northern Minnesota. He entered the United States Air Force in 1953 and served in Japan. After his time with the Air Force, he spent two and a half years in jail for a grocery store robbery. He formed AIM in 1968 after getting out of jail; the organization's purpose was to improve Indian conditions and help exercise Indian rights. He was elected leader of AIM in 1973 after AIM's 71-day takeover of **Wounded Knee**, site of the 1890 massacre. This takeover is perhaps the most notable feat of AIM, for they had to fight off tanks, helicopters, and heavy artillery. In 1975, Banks fled to California after a South Dakota court found him guilty of his actions in a riot. He escaped by receiving amnesty from California governor Jerry Brown, until Brown's term expired in 1983. Banks surrendered himself in 1985 and was placed in a South Dakota penitentiary for 18 months. In 1987, Banks went to Kentucky to organize reburial ceremonies for the uncovered remains of American Indians whose grave sites had been desecrated by artifact hunters. Banks was instrumental in achieving the later enactment by Kentucky and Indiana of strict legislation against grave desecration. In 1988, Banks' autobiography, *Sacred Soul,* was published in Japan and won the 1988 Non-fiction Book of the Year Award. In 1978, Banks used the traditional concept of sacred running to begin the Sacred Run, which is now a multi-cultural, international event with participants from around the world joining Native American runners in carrying the message of the sacredness of all life and of humanity's relationship to the earth. By 1996, Banks had led runners over 58,000 miles through the United States, Alaska, Europe, Japan, Canada, Australia, and New Zealand. In 1994, Banks led the four-month **Walk for Justice (WFJ)** from Alcatraz Island in San Francisco Bay to Washington, D.C. The purpose of the WFJ was to bring public awareness to current Native-American issues. Banks agreed to head the "Bring Peltier Home" Campaign in 1996; the campaign brought Native Americans and other supporters together in an international drive for executive clemency for political prisoner **Leonard Peltier**.

Banks has had roles in the movies *War Party, The Last of the Mohicans,* and *Thunderheart.* He completed *Still Strong,* a musical cassette featuring Banks' original work and traditional Native American songs, in 1993 and a musical video with the same name in 1995.
See also Wounded Knee II.

BIBLIOGRAPHY

Matthiessen, Peter. *In the Spirit of Crazy Horse.* New York: Viking, 1983.
Printup, Wade. "Run for Land and Life: Japan." *Turtle Quarterly* (Winter–Spring 1989): 4–14.
Trahant, LeNora B. "Walk for Justice Supporters Move through Utah." *News from Indian Country* (April 1994): 1–2.

Bannock War

From 1850 through the 1870s, tensions grew between the Bannock Indians and the United States government resulting from native land rights disputes and Indian raiding parties. In 1878, these issues came to a head after hogs owned by white settlers began eating roots located on the Camas Prairie, which overstepped the boundaries established in previous treaties. As a result, a Bannock Indian, upset over the matter, wounded two settlers in May of 1878. This action became cause for the creation of a 200-member war party under the leadership of

Buffalo Horn, which culminated in the offical beginning of the Bannock War. In June of 1878, Buffalo Horn was killed in a conflict with Idaho volunteers. Seeking leadership, his war party joined with the Paiute under the command of Chiefs Egan and Oyte to provide an even more formidable front. General Oliver Howard soon mobilized troops from Fort Boise, and the conflict between the Bannock and the U.S. Army erupted throughout Idaho and Oregon. On July 8, 1878, most of the Indians were captured at Birch Creek, Oregon, with others being held later at the Umatilla Agency in Pendleton, Oregon. In September of 1870, the last of the warriors were captured near Yellowstone Park.

As a result of the Bannock War, the entire Malheur Reservation, where many of the Indians had dwelled, was made public domain land. Residents of this Oregon reservation were interned for five years during the 1880s at the Yakima Reservation before eventually being separated and moved to a variety of other locations, including Pyramid Lake in Nevada, the Miller Creek section of the Duck Valley Reservation in Idaho, Fort McDermitt in Nevada, the Warm Springs Reservation in Oregon, and Fort Bidwell Reservation in California. Many consider this to be one of the most drastic Native-American land cessions.

BIBLIOGRAPHY
Numa: A Northern Paiute History. Reno: Inter-Tribal Council of Nevada, 1976.

Barboncito or Hastiin Dagha (ca. 1820–1871)

Barboncito was a Navajo peace chief and blessingway chanter. He was a leader in the 1860 attacks on Fort Defiance, as well as a signatory of the 1858 and 1861 treaties. As "Head Chief" of the Navajo he was spokesman for negotiating the Bosque Redondo Treaty and was instrumental in keeping the peace and returning captives and stolen livestock. (JN)

BIBLIOGRAPHY
Johnson, Broderick H. and Virginia Hoffman. *Navajo Biographies*. Rough Rock, AZ: Navajo Curriculum Center, Rough Rock Demonstration School, 1978.

Battle of Acoma

The Battle of Acoma took place between December 1598 and February 1599 in the Acoma Pueblo plateau region of New Mexico. In May 1598, Don Juan de Onate, governor and captain general of New Mexico, arrived in the Rio Grande Valley, where he made local Indians swear allegiance to Spain or forced them out of their homes. In October of that year, Juan de Zaldivar and 30 other men following Onate's path arrived in Acoma Pueblo, where Zaldivar demanded Indian alliance and the generous supplying of food, blankets, and other provisions. As a result of these demands, the Acoma killed Zaldivar and 12 others. In response, Onate declared war on the Acoma, and on January 21, 1599, he sent forces under the command of Vincente de Zaldivar to overcome the Indians. In two days of fighting, over 800 Acoma were killed, and the remaining 500 Indians were captured.

On February 12, 1599, Onate passed judgment on the surviving Acoma. He declared that all men over 25 had to have a foot cut off and then serve 20 years as slaves; all men between 12 and 25 and all women over 12 had to serve 20 years as slaves; and all elderly natives had to serve as slaves for the Querechos Plains Apache. Onate also stated that all native children under 12 would be given to Father Fray Alonso Martinez and Vincente de Zaldivar. Two Hopi men who were at Acoma when the conflict began had their right hands cut off and were sent back to their people as a warning.

BIBLIOGRAPHY
Harrigan, Lana M. *Acoma*. New York: Forge, 1997.
Simmons, Marc. *The Last Conquistador*. Norman: University of Oklahoma Press, 1991.

Battle of the Little Bighorn

Also known as Custer's Last Stand, the Battle of the Little Bighorn was a military encounter on June 25, 1876, in which General George Armstrong Custer and about 210 U.S. soldiers were killed by Cheyenne and Sioux Indians. Custer and his regiment had separated from an army force in the Montana Territory that was organized to gather Native Americans and place them in **reservations**. Custer discovered a Cheyenne and Sioux village and was under the belief that it had about 1,000 warriors. He split his regiment of 650 into three groups, which attacked the village from three different directions. The Indian village, whose leaders at the time included **Crazy Horse** and **Sitting Bull**, actually contained over 2,000 warriors. Two of the U.S. groups retreated, while Custer's was destroyed. **See also** Gall; Rain-in-the-Face (Ite-O-Magajo).

BIBLIOGRAPHY
Graham, W.A. *The Story of the Little Bighorn, Custer's Last Fight*. New York: Bonanza Books, 1959.
Hofling, Charles K. *Custer and the Little Bighorn: A Psychobiographical Inquiry*. Detroit, MI: Wayne State University Press, 1981.

Battle of Saybrook

The Battle of Saybrook is officially documented as having occurred from September of 1636 to May of 1637 in Saybrook, Connecticut, although hostilities can be traced to earlier events. Difficulties first surfaced in 1634 when a treaty was established between the Pequots and the people of Massachusetts Bay, in which the Pequots were allowed free trade with Massachusetts and peaceful relations with the Narragansetts in return for wampum (beads made from the shells of quahaug clams and the beaded belts made from this). When the amount of wampum did not meet the expectations of Massachusetts officials, governor John Winthrope Sr. declared in 1936 that the Pequots had violated treaty agreements, thereby relinquishing their Connecticut land rights. As a result, Fort Saybrook was created at the mouth of the Connecticut River, and John Winthrope Jr. was made the fort's governor.

In August of 1636, colonial militiamen sailed to Block Island, where they avenged the murder of Captain John

Oldman, perpetrated earlier that year by the Narragansetts. These troops then traveled back to the mainland, where they used the Block Island incident as an excuse to take Pequot lands. In November of 1636, the oppressed and angry Pequot cut Fort Saybrook off from other colonial contact, isolating it for nine months. Pequot forces were finally defeated in Mystic, Connecticut, in May 1637. As a result of the war, which saw the deaths of over 700 Native Americans, the Treaty of Hartford was signed, dissolving the Pequot Nation.

BIBLIOGRAPHY

Selesky, Harold E. *War and Society in Colonial Connecticut.* New Haven, CT: Yale University Press, 1990.

Clyde Bellecourt (1936–)

Clyde Bellecourt (aka Nee-Gaw-Nway-Wee-Dun or Thunder before the Storm) is a member of the Anishinabe-Ojibwe Nation of Minnesota. Bellecourt was a cofounder and director of the **American Indian Movement (AIM),** and was a major figure in the occupation of **Wounded Knee** in 1973. He has also been actively involved with the Legal Rights Center and the **International Indian Treaty Council**. Bellecourt is also director of the Peacemaker Center for Indian youth and of the AIM Patrol, which provides security for the Minneapolis Indian community. He is an organizer of the National Coalition on Racism in Sports and the Media and is founder and current chairman of the board of the American Indian Opportunities Industrialization Centers, an innovative job program that has moved over 14,000 people from welfare to full-time employment. **See also** Wounded Knee II.

BIBLIOGRAPHY

Means, Russell and Marvin J. Wolf. *Where White Man Fear to Tread.* St. Martin's Press, 1995.
Smith, Paul Chatt and Robert Allen Warrior. *Like a Hurricane: The Indian Movement from Alcatraz to Wounded Knee.* The New Press, 1996.

Ramona Bennet (1938–)

Born in Seattle, Washington, Bennet is probably best known as chairperson of the Puyallup tribe from 1971 through 1978, and as a Puyallup tribal administrator for 11 years. She has actively spoken on many topics concerning Native Americans, such as **education**, fishing rights, and health issues. She was a founder of the American Indian Defense Association in 1964, and also one of its first officers. Many of her efforts were rewarded in the final outcome of **United States v. Washington (1974),** which supported Native American fishing rights and clarified boundaries on **reservations. See also** Fishing and Hunting Treaty Rights; *Puyallup Tribe v. Department of Game.*

BIBLIOGRAPHY

Josephy, Alvin M., Jr. *Now that the Buffalo's Gone: A Study of Today's American Indians.* New York: Alfred A. Knopf, 1982.

Robert LaFollette Bennett (1912–)

Robert LaFollette Bennett (Wisconsin Band Oneida) served as commissioner of Indian Affairs between 1966 and 1969. A career **Bureau of Indian Affairs (BIA)** employee (1933–1969), Mr. Bennett was only the second Indian appointed commissioner. He enacted the 31-year "Bennett Freeze" on housing and development in the western Navajo Reservation, which continues to this day. He was forced to resign by Secretary of Interior Walter Hickel, a longtime enemy. After leaving the Department of the Interior, he became the founding director of the University of New Mexico Native American Law Center, organized the Haskell Indian National University Board of Regents, and helped found Southwestern Indian Polytechnic Institute. (JN)

BIBLIOGRAPHY

Bennett, Robert L. Telephone interview, November 6, 1997, and subsequent correspondence, November 12, 1997.
Nelson, Mary Caroll. *Robert Bennett: The Story of an American Indian.* Minneapolis, MN: Dillon Press, 1976.

BIA Office Takeovers

In the fall of 1972, a group of Indians from both reservation and urban areas embarked upon what they called the **Trail of Broken Treaties**, a caravan destined for Washington, D.C. The four-mile-long trail of cars and buses arrived on November 3, and Indian leaders asked for an audience with policy makers. They proposed a 20-point plan that would have dramatically increased tribal sovereignty through renegotiation of existing treaties, restoration of the eroded Indian land base, and tribal exemption from state laws. Faced with a reticent bureaucracy, the protesters staged a sit-in at the **Bureau of Indian Affairs (BIA)** office, which developed into a full-fledged occupation lasting five days. In the course of the occupation, much damage was done to the offices of the Department of the Interior. There was no bloodshed, and the government eventually offered to pay travel expenses for all protesters to return to their homes. The staff of the BIA was subsequently fired, and the BIA was moved to a more secure location. (RAC)

BIBLIOGRAPHY

Jackson, Curtis E. *A History of the Bureau of Indian Affairs.* San Francisco: R and E Research, 1977.
Porter, Frank W. *The Bureau of Indian Affairs.* New York: Chelsea, 1988.

Big Foot (ca. 1825–1890)

Big Foot (Si Tanka), a principal Mnikowoju Lakota leader, earned his people's reverence by engineering compromises to end disputes within his and other Lakota bands. He embraced the **Ghost Dance Movement** in 1890 for its conservative, pro-Indian message. That, along with his reputation for resisting Americanization policies, made him a target for arrest. On December 29, 1890, the U.S. Army killed Big Foot and at least 145 of his followers at **Wounded Knee** Creek, South Dakota. (TMK)

BIBLIOGRAPHY

Utley, Robert M. *The Last Days of the Sioux Nation.* New Haven, CT: Yale University Press, 1963.

Black Hills

The Black Hills, Paha Sapa, is sacred to the Lakota people, who are waging a sustained struggle to hold on to it. The United States government formally recognized Lakota sovereignty and national ownership over the region through treaties in 1851 and 1868 but later expropriated the lands. The Lakota Nation sued the government in an effort to regain their lands; they were offered large sums of money instead, which they refused. The outcome of this dispute should have a significant impact on native rights to land and self-determination throughout the United States. (MS)

BIBLIOGRAPHY

Churchill, Ward. "The Black Hills Are Not For Sale: The Lakota Struggle for the 1868 Treaty Territory." *Ward Chruchill, Struggle for Land.* Common Courage Press, 1993.

Lazarus, Arthur. *Black Hills, White Justice: The Sioux Nation versus the United States, 1775 to the Present.* New York: HarperCollins Publishers, 1991.

Black Kettle (Motavato) (c. 1815–1868)

Black Kettle was a Southern Cheyenne leader who worked for peace through years of conflict between the United States and Indians of the Plains. His village was attacked in 1864 and 1868, both times after being promised protection. Black Kettle died in the latter massacre. (LCJ)

BIBLIOGRAPHY

Brown, Dee. *Bury My Heart at Wounded Knee: An Indian History of the American West.* New York: Holt, Rinehart & Winston, 1970.

Roberta Blackgoat (1917/18–)

Roberta Blackgoat, a Navajo, was born in either late 1917 or early 1918. For nearly 30 years, Blackgoat has resisted along with fellow Dine (Navajo) the United States government's attempts to forcibly relocate thousands of their people who continue to reside on the west side of Big Mountain in northern Arizona. (KJB)

BIBLIOGRAPHY

Website: www.earthlegacy.com

Board of Indian Commissioners

The Board of Indian Commissioners was created in 1869 by President Ulysses S. Grant as part of his plan of peace in working with Native Americans. The agency was made up of private citizens appointed by the president who presided over the federal administration of Indian affairs in the Department of the Interior. The board concentrated mainly on the physical conditions of Native Americans, for their philosophy was that they could assimilate into the American culture if they were in good physical health. The board lost a large amount of control after their initial reluctance to criticize the Bursum Bill. This bill, proposed in 1922, sought to grant immediate title to purchasers of reservation land from 1848 to 1913. The land was designated as Pueblo Indian land by the U.S. government. The board was disbanded in 1933. **See also** Bureau of Indian Affairs; Federal Indian Policy; Office of Indian Affairs.

BIBLIOGRAPHY

Fritz, Henry. *The Movement for Indian Assimilation, 1860–1890.* Philadelphia: University of Pennsylvania, 1963.

Mardock, Robert W. *The Reformers and the American Indian.* Columbia: University of Missouri Press, 1971.

Gertrude Simmons Bonnin (1876–1938)

Reformer Gertrude Simmons Bonnin was born at Yankton Sioux Agency in South Dakota on February 22, 1876. Beginning in her mid-30s, Bonnin became active in Indian affairs. She lobbied for citizenship rights for Native-American peoples and focused on reform measures to improve health and education programs on reservations. (KJB)

BIBLIOGRAPHY

Young, "Gertrude Simmons Bonnin." In Edward T. James, Janet Wilson James, and Paul S. Boyer, eds. *Notable American Women 1607–1950.* Cambridge, MA: The Belknap Press of Harvard University Press, 1971.

Boarding Schools. *See* Education

Elias Boudinot (1804–1839)

Elias Boudinot (Galagina Watie) founded and edited the first bilingual Native-American newspaper, the *Cherokee Phoenix.* As editor (1828–1832), Boudinot used the *Phoenix* to report the Cherokees' acculturational "progress"—national laws, school events, revivals, temperance society meetings—to eastern philanthropists and editors, to build political support for the Cherokees during their legal battle with Georgia over land. The Cherokee National Council forced Boudinot to resign in 1832 for supporting removal. He later signed the controversial Treaty of New Echota and, in June 1839, antitreaty partisans assassinated him in Oklahoma. **See also** *Cherokee Nation v. Georgia* (DAN)

BIBLIOGRAPHY

Perdue, Theda, ed. *Cherokee Editor: The Writings of Elias Boudinot.* Knoxville: University of Tennessee Press, 1983.

——. "Rising from the Ashes: The Cherokee Phoenix as an Ethnohistorical Source." *Ethnohstory* 24, no. 3 (fall 1977): 207–18.

Molly Brant (1736–1796)

Molly Brant, also known as Gonwatsijayenni, is considered to be the most influential Mohawk woman in the New World during the eighteenth century. She married William Johnson, an Irishman who was superintendent of Indian affairs and who maintained relations with Native Americans in the colonies. Johnson died in 1774, and Brant sided with the British by taking a Loyalist stance during the **American Revolution.** During the revolution, she fled with loyalist colonists and Iroquois to Canada where she resumed her loyalist activities.

She was considered unique, for she defended the Iroquois and the British.

BIBLIOGRAPHY

Gundy, H. Pearson, "Molly Brant—Loyalist," *Ontario History* 14 (1953): 97–108.
Bataille, Gretchen M., ed. *Native American Women*. New York: Garland Publishing, 1993.

Brendale v. Confederated Tribes and Bands of the Yakima Indians (1989)

Brendale v. Confederated Tribes and Bands of the Yakima Indians, 492 U.S. 408 (1989), involved the right of tribes to zone land on the reservation owned by non-Indians. The Supreme Court held that tribal government did not have jurisdictional authority over non-Indians on the reservation and therefore could not issue zoning regulations on land that was substantially owned by non-Indians. However, tribes did have authority over lands that were tribal or owned by Indians. This ruling put into question the extent of civil jurisdiction that tribes have on reservations. (AMM)

BIBLIOGRAPHY

Goeppele, Craighton. "Solutions for Uneasy Neighbors: Regulating the Reservation Environment." (Case Note) *Washington Law Review* G5, no. 2 (April 1990): 417–36.
Singer, Joseph William. "Sovereignty and Property." *Northwestern University Law Review* 86, no. 1 (fall 1991): 1–56.

Louis R. Bruce, Jr. (1906–1989)

Louis Bruce, Jr. (Mohawk/Sioux) served as commissioner of Indian Affairs (1969–1972) under President Richard M. Nixon. Having previously served as executive director of the **National Congress of American Indians,** he was noted for filling the upper echelon of the **Bureau of Indian Affairs (BIA)** with native employees. He left office after his superiors accused him of sympathizing with the **American Indian Movement** in the 1972 occupation of BIA headquarters. (SRC)

BIBLIOGRAPHY

Forbes, Jack. *Native Americans and Nixon: Presidential Politics and Minority Self-Determination, 1969–1972*. Los Angeles: University of California American Indian Studies Center, 1981.
Gross, Emma. *Contemporary Federal Policy Toward American Indians*. Westport, CT: Greenwood Press, 1989.

Bryan v. Itasca County (1976)

In *Bryan v. Itasca County*, 426 U.S. 373, the U.S. Supreme Court interpreted Public Law 280 to grant to states jurisdiction over criminal law and private civil litigation involving reservation Indians, but not general civil regulatory authority, so Minnesota could not apply its personal property tax on a reservation. "Criminal/prohibitory" laws prohibiting certain conduct fall within Public Law 280 jurisdiction, but not "civil/regulatory" laws that permit but regulate the conduct at issue. This distinction became crucial in *Seminole Tribe v. Butterworth* (1981) and *California v. Cabazon Band of Mission Indians* (1987), which permitted reservation gaming. (RS)

BIBLIOGRAPHY

Jolly, Brad. "The Indian Gaming Regulatory Act: The Unwavering Policy of Termination Continues." *Arizona State Law Journal* 29 (spring 1997): 273–311.

Bureau of Indian Affairs (BIA)

The Bureau of Indian Affairs was founded as the Indian Office (or, more formally, the **Office of Indian Affairs**) in 1824 within the Department of War; the bureau then became part of the new Department of the Interior in 1849. The mission of the bureau has been to exercise the United States government's "trust" relationship over Native Americans and, since 1970, to assist **tribal governments** in achieving increased self-government.

President Jimmy Carter visits with employees of the Bureau of Indian Affairs (BIA) in January 1977. *National Archives*.

Later renamed the Bureau of Indian Affairs (BIA), the agency holds power over virtually every aspect of Native Americans' lives, particularly those who live on **reservations.** The agency decides which native governments will be "recognized" by the United States, controls the creation of reservations, and has the final say over tribal legislation and land-use decisions.

The BIA has a history of problems. It is widely seen as the most poorly managed agency of the U.S. government, with repeated abuses of funds, gross mismanagement, and policy failures. However, it sometimes also acts as a buffer between Native Americans and non-Indian interests, making many hesitant to abolish it entirely. **See also** BIA Office Takeovers; John Collier; Department of the Interior Act of 1849; Federal Acknowledgment of Indian Tribes; Federal Indian Policy; Indian Department of the United States Government; Benjamin Reifel; Snyder Act of 1921; Trusteeship Responsibility; White Man's Burden. (LCJ)

BIBLIOGRAPHY

Deloria, Vine, Jr., ed. *American Indian Policy in the Twentieth Century*. Norman: University of Oklahoma Press, 1985.

McCool, Daniel. *Command of the Waters: Iron Triangles, Federal Water Development, and Indian Water*. Berkeley, CA: University of California Press, 1987.

Burke Act of 1906

The Burke Act of 1906 modified the General Allotment Act of 1887 (**Dawes Act**), by providing that the Native Americans who are allotted land would not become citizens of the United States until they were deemed legally competent to manage their own affairs. It also provided that the trust period could be extended beyond 25 years, as originally intended; however, an individual could be declared competent before the end of the 25-year period and thus be allowed to sell his land and pay taxes on it. This act extended indefinitely the time limit on trust land. **See also** General Citizenship Act of 1924; Federal Indian Policy. **See** Dawes Act (1887) in Appendix 1. (AMM)

BIBLIOGRAPHY

Kvasnicka, Robert M. and Herman J. Viola, eds. *The Commissioners of Indian Affairs, 1824–1977*. Lincoln: University of Nebraska Press, 1979.

C

California Indian Treaties

The discovery of gold in California signalled the end of federal removal policy. A group of Indian commissioners visiting California expressed the dilemma as follows: "As there is no further West to which they can be removed, the General Government and the people of California appear to have left but one alternative . . . extermination or domestication." Both policies were employed. Between 1851 and 1852, 18 California bands signed treaties creating model reservations for "domesticating" the Indian; however, the U.S. Senate refused to ratify the treaties. (AMM)

BIBLIOGRAPHY

Bleyhl, Norris A. *Indian-White Relationships in Northern California, 1849–1920, in Congressional Set of U.S. Public Documents*. Chico, CA: Association for Northern California Records and Research, 1979.

Heizer, Robert F. *Languages, Territories and Names of California Indian Tribes*. Berkeley: University of California Press, 1966.

California v. Cabazon Band of Mission Indians (1987)

California v. Cabazon Band of Mission Indians et al., 480 U.S. 202 (1987), tested whether Public Law 280, which gave several states large grants of civil and criminal jurisdiction over Indian tribes within their borders, restricted tribal bingo enterprises. The U.S. Supreme Court ruled that bingo operations by tribal governments were not subject to state regulation under either Public Law 280 or the Organized Crime Control Act of 1970. The Supreme Court ruled that because California permits bingo games by organizations under certain limited conditions, bingo fell under the definition encompassed by "civil/regulatory" statute, not "criminal/prohibitory." The effect of this ruling was to make tribal gaming legal, if the state in which the tribe was located permitted the games, even in extremely limited form. (AMM)

BIBLIOGRAPHY

Haslam, Connie K. "Indian Sovereignty: Confusion Prevails." *Washington Law Review* 63, no. 1 (January 1988): 169–93.

Monette, Richard. "Indian Country Jurisdiction and the Assimilative Crimes Act." *Oregon Law Review* 60, no. 2 (spring 1990): 269–94.

Ben Nighthorse Campbell (1933–)

Ben Nighthorse Campbell, the only Native American currently serving in the United States Senate, was born to Mary Vierra, a Portuguese immigrant and Albert Campbell, a northern Cheyenne Indian. Campbell, who stated in his 1998 reelection campaign, "My goal is for our children and grandchildren to have a future that is better than my past," came through a rough childhood (a mother with tuberculosis, alcoholism in the family, and some time in an orphanage). Leaving high school to join the U.S. Air Force (where he received his GED), he served in Korea (1951–1953) as an Airman second class. Returning to civilian life he went to college and graduated with a B.A. in physical

Colorado Republican Senator Ben Nighthorse Campbell switched parties (from the Democrats) because he believed the Republicans better addressed the issues important to him and Native Americans. *Courtesy of U.S. Senate.*

education and fine arts from San Jose State University in 1957. In 1960 he left for Japan to attend Meiji University (Tokyo) as a special research student. As a young man, Campbell competed in judo; he was an All American, a three-time U.S. champion, gold medal winner in the 1963 Pan-American Games, and captained the U.S. Olympic judo team at the Tokyo games in 1964. In 1966 he married Linda Price, and they have two adult children: Colin and Shanan. He has received the honor of being inducted into the Council of 44 Chiefs, Northern Cheyenne Tribe, Lame Deer, Montana.

Campbell, a self-employed jewelry designer (award winning), rancher, and former trainer of champion quarter horses, won the Democratic primary in 1982 and then defeated a Republican opponent for a seat in the Colorado State Legislature. His service in the legislature from 1983 to 1986 received recognition both from the Colorado Bankers Association which named him "1984 Outstanding Legislator" and from his colleagues in the legislature who voted him one of the "Ten Best Legislators" in 1984. In 1986 he was elected to the U.S. House of Representatives, where he served until he was elected to the U.S. Senate in 1992. In 1995 he chose to leave the Democratic party (but not the Senate). He won reelection to the Senate in 1998 as a Republican.

Campbell succeeded in 1991 in getting the Custer Battlefield Monument in Montana renamed the Little Bighorn Battlefield National Monument to acknowledge all those who died there in battle. He initiated and saw legislation pass that established the National Museum of the American Indian within the Smithsonian Institution. He has worked at developing preventive programs for the treatment of fetal alcohol syndrome. He serves on the following Senate committees: Agriculture, Nutrition and Forestry; Energy and Natural Resources; Indian Affairs; and Veteran's Affairs. **See also** Battle of the Little Bighorn; Federal Indian Policy; National Museum of the American Indian Act of 1989. (TJH)

BIBLIOGRAPHY
Salant, Jonathan D. "Colorado's Campbell Switches to Republican Party." *Congressional Quarterly Weekly Report* 53 (March 4, 1995): 664.
Viola, Herman J. *Ben Nighthorse Campbell: An American Warrior.* New York: Orion Books, 1993.

Harold Cardinal (1945–)

In 1968, Harold Cardinal became a board member of the National Indian Brotherhood. Cardinal went on to combat discrimination and oppression against Native Americans by writing *The Unjust Society: The Tragedy of Canada's Indians, Citizens Plus, and The Rebirth of Canada's Indians.* In 1977, Cardinal became regional director general in Alberta, helping coordinate Indian affairs. Cardinal went on to become elected chief of the Sucker Creek Band in 1982, as well as vice chief of the prairie region of Canada by the Assembly of First Nations.

BIBLIOGRAPHY
Cardinal, Harold. *The Rebirth of Canada's Indians.* Toronto: New Press Publishers, 1977.
———. *The Unjust Society: The Tragedy of Canada's Indians.* Edmonton: New Press Publishers, 1977.

George Catlin (1796–1872)

George Catlin, a Pennsylvania-born, self-taught artist, spent eight years (1832–1839) traveling among the Plains Indians, recording their lives through art and letters. Supported by William Clark (**Lewis and Clark Expedition**), superintendent of Indians for the western tribes, he became the historian of the Plains Indians by chronicling their costumes, customs, and likenesses. His paintings are still considered the best account of the dress of the native peoples. Displayed in New York and Europe, his works found a home with the Smithsonian Institution in 1879. (AMM)

BIBLIOGRAPHY
Catlin, George. *North American Indians: Being Letter and Notes on Their Manners, Customs, and Conditions, Written During Eight Years' Travel Amongst the Wildest Tribes of Indians in North America, 1832–1839.* Philadelphia: Leary, Stuart & Co., 1913.
McCracken, Harold. *George Catlin and the Old Frontier.* New York: Bonanza Books, 1984.

Alfred Chato (Chatto) (1860–1934)

Alfred Chato, Chiricahua Apache, was a major leader in the Apache Wars of 1881–1884 with Geronimo. He surrendered to the U.S. Army in 1884. As a scout for the army, he tracked down Geronimo in 1885. He was part of an Apache delegation to Washington, D.C., to plead on behalf of prisoners sent to Florida with Geronimo. He lost land and family; eventually he was allowed to return to New Mexico. (EW)

BIBLIOGRAPHY
Cole, D.C. *The Chiricahua Apache, 1846–1876: From War to Reservation.* Albuquerque: University of New Mexico Press, 1936.
Debo, Angie. *Geronimo: The Man, His Times, His Place.* Norman: University of Oklahoma Press, 1976.

Cherokee Nation v. Georgia (1831)

Cherokee Nation v. Georgia, 5 Pet. 1 (1831), was second in the so-called "Marshall trilogy" of cases that form the foundation of federal Indian law, together with *Johnson v. McIntosh* **(1823)** and *Worcester v. Georgia* **(1832).** In *Cherokee Nation,* the United States Supreme Court, under Chief Justice John Marshall, suggested the now-famous (or infamous) concept that the relation between indigenous nations and the United States "resembles that of a ward to his guardian." This description, although stated as metaphor and dictum, became a dogmatic axiom in federal Indian law.

The case arose when the Cherokee Nation sued Georgia in the Supreme Court to prevent the state from violating Cherokee self-government. Georgia had passed laws abolishing Cherokee government and asserting jurisdiction over Cherokee lands within boundaries established in an 1802 agreement with the federal government. The legal question the Court focused on was whether it had jurisdiction to hear the case. The decision was negative, on the ground that only a "state" or a "foreign nation" may sue in the Supreme Court, and that the "framers of our Constitution had not the Indian tribes in view" when they defined the judicial power. Justices Smith Thompson and Joseph Story dissented, stating that "the Cherokee Indians form a sovereign state according to the doctrine of the law of nations." The Cherokee were subsequently forced by the federal **Indian Removal Act of 1830** to move to a "reservation" west of the Mississippi River.

The ward–guardian concept in *Cherokee Nation* underlies the federal government's self-declared "**trusteeship responsibility**" toward native nations. This "trusteeship" provides a rationale for the entire range of federal programs directed at Indians, including the **Bureau of Indian Affairs** and the Indian Health Service. **See also** Federal Indian Policy;

Guardianship; Land and Water Rights; Sovereignty; Trail of Tears; Treaty of New Echota (1835). (PPE)

BIBLIOGRAPHY

Filler, Louis and Guttmann, Allen. *The Removal of the Cherokee Nation*. Boston: D.C. Heath, 1962.

Norgren, Jill. *The Cherokee Cases: The Confrontation of Law and Politics*. New York: McGraw-Hill, 1996.

Cherokee Phoenix

In the early nineteenth century, Cherokees faced difficult choices. Either they adopted Euro-American cultural values such as Christianity, patriarchy, and cash-crop agriculture or they retained their traditional belief systems and risked losing their land. While some Cherokees favored assimilation and some rejected any accommodation to white society, a growing number of Cherokees sought to travel both roads at once. The *Cherokee Phoenix* resulted from this attempt to be both "civilized" in the manner of white Americans while also fostering a Cherokee national identity.

First published in 1827, the *Cherokee Phoenix* published news and editorials in the Cherokee syllabary, developed by **Sequoyah,** and in English. The paper's first editor, Cherokee Christian convert **Elias Boudinot,** envisioned the paper as a forum to publish the laws of the Cherokee National Council and to document the progress of Cherokees towards education, Christianity, and other "arts of civilized life." Newspapers throughout eastern America often reprinted Boudinot's editorials against Cherokee removal in the West. (GO)

BIBLIOGRAPHY

Perdue, Theda. *Cherokee Editor: The Writings of Elias Boudinot*. Athens: University of Georgia Press, 1996.

Cherokee Republic

In 1820 the Cherokee, attempting to forestall western removal, adopted a republican form of government modeled after the United States. The nation was divided into eight districts, each entitled to send four representatives to the Cherokee national legislature at New Echota, the capital. The legislature consisted of two houses: National Committee (upper) and National Council (lower). The chief executive was the president of the National Council. The government included a judicial branch and had the power to lay and collect taxes. A national constitution was adopted by a general convention at New Echota on July 27, 1827. (AMM)

BIBLIOGRAPHY

Parris, John. *The Cherokee Story*. Asheville, NC: The Stephens Press, 1950.

Starkey, Marion L. *The Cherokee Nation*. New York: Russell and Russell, 1972.

Wendell Chino (1923–)

Born on the Mescalero Apache reservation, Chino is a descendant of the followers of **Geronimo**. He became president of the Mescalero Apache Nation in 1962. Chino led Native Americans in court as they fought the constitutionality of the **Indian Gaming Regulatory Act of 1988.**

BIBLIOGRAPHY

Thompson, William N. *Native American Issues*. Santa Barbara, CA: ABC-CLIO, 1996.

Chippewa Treaty of 1836

The Chippewa Treaty of 1836 was an expression of the federal removal policy. It replaced earlier treaties (1785, 1789, 1795, and 1807) and provided that the Chippewa cede all of their lands to Michigan. They were allowed to reside on certain tracts for five years, but no longer. The treaty promised $200,000 to the tribe when the Chippewa vacated the land and an annual interest payment until that time. Since the Chippewa did not surrender their lands, the annual interest payment continued for years. After petition by the Chippewa chiefs and Indian agents, the 1836 treaty was amended by the treaty of 1855, which provided that the allotted Indian lands were to be held in trust by the United States. (AMM)

BIBLIOGRAPHY

Zapffe, Carl A. *Minnesota's Chippewa Treaty of 1837*. Brainerd, MN: Historic Heartland Association, 1994.

_____. *Chippewa Off-Reservation Treaty Rights: Origins and Issues*. Madison: State of Wisconsin, Legislative Reference Bureau, 1991.

Chrytos (1946–)

Chrytos, a lesbian Native American poet, is an influential activist in both gay and Indian rights causes. She gained national attention when Senator Jesse Helms (R-NC) became angered after an anthology of her work, which contained poems on lesbian love, was supported by the National Endowment for the Arts. A number of anthologies containing Chrytos's poems have seen widespread publication, including *Not Vanishing* and *Dream On.*

BIBLIOGRAPHY

Chrytos. *Dream On.* Vancouver: Press Gang Publishers, 1991.

Chrytos. *Not Vanishing.* Vancouver: Press Gang Publishers, 1985.

Civil War (1861–1865)

Indians, like other Americans, had divided loyalties during the Civil War. The **Five Civilized Tribes** (the Cherokee, the Creek, the Choctaw, the Chickasaw, and the Seminole) in **Indian Territory** generally supported the Confederacy because of their adoption of the southern, slave-holding culture, and because of a long-standing animosity toward the federal government. However, a sizable number of Creeks, Cherokee, and Seminoles preferred neutrality and rallied under the leadership of Creek chief Opothleyaholo. Confederate generals, equating Indian neutrality with hostile opposition, ringed Opothleyaholo's camp on December 26, 1861, and massacred the inhabitants. This was the first battle of the Civil War in Indian Territory. After several battles in 1862 and 1863, Union troops captured Fort Smith (in modern-day Arkansas) on September 1, 1863, ending the war in the Indian Territory, although minor guerrilla skirmishes by Indian raiders continued for the next two years.

Outside of the Indian Territory, the Civil War had little direct effect on Indian tribes; however, the war did affect Indian–white relations in the West. Because of the war, there were few troops left to police the frontier, leading to numerous engagements between Indians and settlers. The Battle of Bear River (1863) and the Navajo removal to Bosque Redondo (1864) (following the **Navajo War**) were examples of the secondary war being waged in the west.

Part Native American, Union General William Tecumseh Sherman was an effective military officer during the Civil War and in many conflicts with Native Americans in the years after. *National Archives.*

After the Civil War, a Reconstruction plan was proposed for the Five Civilized Tribes of the Indian Territory, which included permanent peace treaties, abolishing slavery among the tribes, recognition of slaves as tribal members, and the surrendering of land for colonization by other tribes. Not only was the United States trying to punish the tribes for secession, but it was also using the treaty as a way of opening more farm land in Kansas to settlement. The Reconstruction treaties spelled the beginning of the end for the Indian Territory, which in 1907 became the State of Oklahoma.(AMM)

BIBLIOGRAPHY

Abel, Annie Heloise. *American Indian as Participant in the Civil War. The American Indian in the Civil War, 1862–1865.* Lincoln: University of Nebraska Press, 1992.

Hauptman, Laurence M. *Between Two Fires: American Indians in the Civil War.* New York: Free Press, 1995.

Henry Roe Cloud (1884–1950)

Born in Nebraska, Henry Roe Cloud was a member of the Winnebago tribe. In 1910, he was the first Native American to graduate from Yale University, and he earned a masters in 1914. In 1915, he established the Roe Indian Institute (renamed American Indian Institute) in Wichita, Kansas, that provided college preparatory education to Native American boys. The institute was the first to offer a college prep curriculum for Native Americans, encouraging its students to go to college. In 1926, Roe became a member of the Institute for Government Research (the Brookings Institute), working as a coauthor of the **Meriam Report** in 1928. From 1933 until 1935, he was the head of the Haskell Institute in Lawrence, Kansas. From 1935 until 1947, Roe held several posts within the **Bureau of Indian Affairs** where he focused largely on issues of education. He also served on a number of special government committees investigating the status of Native Americans. In 1947 he left Washington, D.C. when he was named the superintendent of the Umatalla Reservation Agency in Oregon. **See also** National Council of American Indians.

BIBLIOGRAPHY

Cloud, Henry Roe. "From Wigwam to Pulpit." *Southern Workingman* (July 1916): 400–06.

Gridley, Marion. *Indians of Today.* Chicago: Millar, 1947.

Tyler, S. Lyman. *A History of Indian Policy.* Washington, DC: Bureau of Indian Affairs, 1973.

Cochise (d. 1874)

Goci (Cochise) was a leader of the Chokonen band of the Apache (N'de) during the critical years of the mid-1800s. Cochise allied himself with **Mangas Coloradas** through marriage and gained leadership through personal integrity and skills as a negotiator, planner, and war leader. The Apache were long-term enemies of Mexico, but Cochise negotiated peace with the United States upon its entry into his band's territory. Betrayed by an army officer when members of his family were killed in 1861, he turned into an adversary in what became the most costly war between a Native nation and the United States. In 1872, through negotiations with General Oliver Otis Howard and mail agent Thomas Jeffords, Cochise made peace and, with his band, began the difficult transition to reservation life. For Cochise, this transition was cut short by his death in 1874. (LCJ)

BIBLIOGRAPHY

Cole, D.C. *The Chiricahua Apache: 1846–1876: From War to Reservation.* Albuquerque: University of New Mexico Press, 1988.

Sweeney, Edwin R. *Cochise: Chiricahua Apache Chief.* Norman: University of Oklahoma Press, 1991.

Coeur d'Alene War (1855–1858)

Between 1855 and 1858, the Coeur d'Alene, Palouse, Cayuse, and Spokane, led by Chief Kamiakin, alternately fought and negotiated with the United States for rights to their land. Gold miners swarmed over the land of the Indians and demanded that the government ensure their safe passage. The United States tried to convince the Indians to move onto reservations where they would be forced to live with traditional enemies, often far removed from their native lands. The Indians, distrustful of the U.S. Army, refused to accede to the terms. Kamiakin continued to stir up the Indians to fight. On September 5, 1858, Colonel George Wright defeated the tribes in the Battle of Spokane Plains. Father Pierre de Smet acted as intermediary, and the war was officially ended in November 1858. (AMM)

BIBLIOGRAPHY

Deloria, Vine, Jr. *Indians of the Pacific Northwest: From the Coming of the White Man to the Present Day.* New York: Doubleday, 1977.

Glassley, Ray Hoard. *Pacific Northwest Indian Wars.* Portland, OR: Binfords and Mort, 1953.

John Collier

John Collier was known to most as a radical reformer for Native Americans. He was a social worker from New York City, but he came to admire the Pueblo culture on a visit to New Mexico in 1921. He started writing articles as a field representative for the General Federation of Women's Clubs. Collier created the **American Indian Defense Association** to defeat the Bursum bill in New Mexico. Collier authored almost all of the association's publications, was the chief fund-raiser, and was their spokesperson in Washington, D.C. Collier was appointed commissioner of Indian Affairs in 1933, at which point he attacked the state of the schools run by the **Bureau of Indian Affairs (BIA)**. He was committed to cultural pluralism, so he challenged BIA, for he felt the bureau was keeping Native American children isolated. Because he wanted the parents to be closer to their children, he helped cut a dramatic number of boarding schools, and in turn, opened many day schools on reservations. **See also** Education; Federal Indian Policy.

BIBLIOGRAPHY

Kelly, Lawrence C. *The Assault on Assimilation: John Collier and the Origins of Indian Policy Reform.* Albuquerque: University of New Mexico Press, 1983.

Philip, Kenneth R. *John Collier's Crusade for Indian Reform, 1920–1954.* Tucson: University of Arizona Press, 1984.

Mangas Coloradas (ca. 1790–1863)

Mangas Coloradas was born sometime between 1790 and 1795 in what is now southern New Mexico. At the time, the land was part of New Spain and relations between the Apaches and Mexicans were generally peaceful. However, relations deteriorated in 1831 when the Mexican government no longer provided rations for the Apaches. The result was increased conflicts between the Indians and Mexican villagers leading to a declaration of war. In April 1837, a scalp hunter named John Johnson massacred a relative of Mangas Coloradas, Juan Jose, and his band of Apaches. Mangas retaliated by killing American miners. In 1851, after being whipped by a number of miners near Santa Rita, Mangas's attacks upon whites became increasingly brutal. A peace treaty negotiated in 1852 between the United States and Mangas was not ratified by the Senate and the conflict continued. In January 1863, Mangas was captured and taken to Fort McLean in Arizona where he was killed by his guards. Mangas's body was mutilated by the guards, including scalping him, which only further incited the Apaches. **See also** Cochise.

BIBLIOGRAPHY

Griffen, William B. *Apaches at War & Peace.* Albuquerque: University of New Mexico Press, 1988.

Worchester, Donald E. *The Apaches.* Norman: University of Oklahoma Press, 1979.

Columbus Day Celebrations

The celebration of October 12 as "Columbus Day" has long been controversial to Native Americans, who point out that Christopher Columbus did not "discover" anything. His actual historical role was to open the Americas to European economic interests and to begin the centuries-long genocide of Native American peoples. The celebration was particularly controversial during the 1992 quincentennial of Columbus's first voyage, when Native American objections led to the scrapping or scaling back of many planned activities. (LCJ)

BIBLIOGRAPHY

Churchill, Ward. *Since Predator Came: Notes from the Struggle for American Indian Liberation.* Littleton, CO: Aegis Publications, 1995.

Rawls, James J. *Chief Red Fox is Dead: A History of Native Americans since 1945.* New York: Harcourt Brace, 1996.

Colorado River Compact

The Colorado River Compact provided for the equal division of water between the Upper Basin states: Colorado, Utah, and Wyoming; and the Lower Basin states: Arizona, California, and Nevada. The Upper Basin states reached an agreement on appropriation of water but the Supreme Court had to determine those for the Lower Basin in *Arizona v. California* (1963). The federal government, acting on behalf of the Chemehuevi, Cocopah, Yuma, Colorado River, and Fort Mohave tribes, argued for Indian reserve water rights under the Winters Doctrine. Arizona answered that these were not "treaty tribes" and therefore the state did not have to reserve water rights. The Supreme Court ruled that both treaty and executive order reservations were entitled to reserve water rights. (AMM)

BIBLIOGRAPHY

Hundley, Norris, Jr. *Water and the West: The Colorado River Compact and the Politics of Water in the American West.* Berkeley: University of California Press, 1975.

Commissioner of Indian Affairs

In 1832, Congress authorized the president to appoint, with consent of the Senate, a commissioner of Indian Affairs to "prescribe, have the direction and management of all Indian affairs, and of all matters arising out of Indian relations." Prior to creation of the position of commissioner, Indian affairs were handled by the secretary of war and his assistants. The commissioner of Indian Affairs was given supervision over Indian agents, whose responsibilities included negotiating treaties, trading with Indians, and attempting to resolve disputes between U.S. citizens and tribal members. The commissioner was also to direct the removal of Indians to **reservation** lands starting in the 1830s. For better or for worse, the commissioner has had, over the decades, a profound impact on **federal Indian policy,** particularly in the early years of the position, and again in the 1930s under the dynamic leadership of commissioner **John Collier.** Since 1973, the commissioner of Indian Affairs reports directly to the secretary of the interior. Prior to this, the commissioner reported to an Interior Department assistant secretary. **See also** Bureau of Indian Affairs; Indian Removal; Office of Indian Affairs. (GTH)

BIBLIOGRAPHY

Prucha, Francis Paul. *The Great Father: The United States Government and the American Indians.* Lincoln: University of Nebraska Press, 1984.

Schmeckebier, Laurence F. *The Office of Indian Affairs: Its History, Activities and Organization.* Baltimore: The Johns Hopkins Press, 1927.

Committee of 100

The Committee of 100 was created in 1923 as a result of pressure by reformers on the United States government to improve Indian living conditions and rising discontent among American-Indian tribes. The organization included such noted Native-American leaders as Henry Roe Cloud, Arthur C. Parker, Charles Eastman, and Thomas L. Sloan, along with other prominent figures such as General John J. Pershing, Bernard M. Baruch, William Jennings Bryan, Frederick W. Hodge, and Alfred L. Kroeber.

The group was appointed by Secretary of the Interior Hubert Work to survey all American-Indian policies and make needed recommendations. Some of the recommendations included increased funding for health care, public education, and scholarship allotments, as well as improvements in the claims courts system and scientific investigation into the effects of peyote usage by Native Americans. In spite of these suggestions, neither President Warren Harding nor President Calvin Coolidge did much to follow up on the committee's recommendations. The group did, however, help to influence the creation of the **Meriam Report** of 1928.

BIBLIOGRAPHY

Mardock, Robert W. *The Reformers and the American Indian.* Columbia: University of Missouri Press, 1971.

Competency

When the General Allotment Act (Dawes) was passed in 1887, Congress intended that it would be the method of assimilating Indians from their communal traditions into an economic and social system based on individualism and free enterprise. It was recognized, at the time, that there would have to be a period of transition. During this period, the United States would act as the trustee over the affairs of the Indians until they were sufficiently acclimated to the new culture, so they would not be swindled out of their properties. The initial period was for 25 years, though that period was later extended. Nevertheless, it was not intended that the period of trusteeship be indefinite. In 1908, Secretary of the Interior James R. Garfield directed all Indian agents to urge all "competent persons" to apply to have the restrictions of the trust removed. Certificates of competency were issued to those Indians who would leave their tribal affiliation. These certificates not only eliminated any BIA control but also bestowed upon the individual U.S. citizenship. In 1910, competency commissions were created to examine individual Indians throughout the United States to determine who was ready for the full rights of citizenship. (AMM)

BIBLIOGRAPHY

Bureau of Indian Affairs. *Emancipated Citizenship for American Indians.* Washington, DC: U.S. Government Printing Office, 1931.

Confederated Bands and Tribes of the Yakima Indian Nation v. Washington (1979)

Part of the larger controversy surrounding **Public Law 280** (P.L. 280), *Confederated Bands and Tribes of the Yakima Indian Nation v Washington,* 439 U.S. 463 (1979), disputed the state of Washington's assumption of civil and criminal jurisdiction over Indian lands. When the state moved to implement P.L. 280 without tribal consent, the Yakima Nation sued in federal district court, arguing that the state had not complied with the procedural requirements of P.L. 280; that P.L. 280 did not allow the state to assert partial jurisdiction over an Indian reservation; and that the state's action violated the equal protection and due process guarantees of the **Fourteenth Amendment.** After extensive litigation, the U.S. Supreme Court ruled against the tribe and affirmed the state's assumption of partial jurisdiction on the reservations of nonconsenting tribes. (AHF)

BIBLIOGRAPHY

Baris, Allan. "Washington's Public Law 280 Jurisdiction on Indian Reservations." *Washington Law Review* 53 (1977/1978): 701–27.

Goldberg, Carol E. *Public Law 280: State Jurisdiction Over Reservation Indians.* Los Angeles: UCLA American Indian Studies Center, 1975.

Confederated Tribes of Colville Reservation et al. v. Washington (1980)

In *Confederated Tribes of the Colville Indian Reservation et al. v. Washington* 447 U.S. 134 (1980), the Colville, Lummi, and Makah tribes challenged the application of state taxes and other state laws to on-reservation business activities. The central question concerned the state of Washington's power to levy excise and sales taxes on cigarettes sold to nonmembers of a tribe at reservation smoke shops. The federal district court ruled that state taxation contradicted the Indian Commerce Clause of the U.S. Constitution and impeded tribal economic development and self-government. But the U.S. Supreme Court also held that tribal **sovereignty** did not bar the state from taxing the on-reservation tobacco purchases of nonmembers. (AHF)

BIBLIOGRAPHY

Chen, Bess Lee. "What about *Colville?*" *American Indian Law Review* 8 (1980): 161–73.

Mundell, Thomas C. "The Tribal Sovereignty Limitation on State Taxation of Indians: From *Worcester* to *Confederated Tribes* and Beyond." *Loyola of Los Angeles Law Review* 15 (1982): 195–225.

Conference on the Future of the American Indian

Held at the Museum of Modern Art, New York City, from March 4 to 7, 1941, in connection with an exhibition of Indian art, the Conference on the Future of the American Indian was sponsored by the American Association on Indian Affairs (which changed its name to the Association on American Indian Affairs in 1946). The purpose of the conference was to discuss the current status of Native Americans especially issues of health, **education,** and economic participation. **See also** Indian Confederation of American Indians.

BIBLIOGRAPHY

"Dr. F. Lorimer Reports on the Future to the Institute on the Future of the American Indian." *New York Times* (March 23, 1941): II-5.

Conservatism and Liberalism

The political ideologies of conservatism and liberalism, in their varied interpretations, have played key roles in shaping federal Indian policy. The historical impact is complex, because both ideologies have included and continue to include ideas in which both sanction cultural pluralism and tribal self-government as well as forced assimilation.

Although, as early as colonial times, some Euro-Americans advocated assimilation, it was not until the late 1880s that assimilation became the predominant goal of federal Indian policy. Such a goal was consistent with nineteenth-century "laissez-faire liberalism" (later termed "conservatism" or "libertarianism") and the "reform liberalism" or "aggressivism" of the early decades of the twentieth century.

Admittedly, laissez-faire and reform liberalism differed in important ways. While all forms of liberalism favor (at least ostensibly) individual liberty and human progress, laissez-faire liberals sought to achieve these goals through limiting government power and promoting economic freedom. Reform liberals often advocated scientific management, efficiency, moral reform, and at least a limited form of state intervention in the economy to ensure individual political and economic liberty. Nevertheless, liberals from both camps advocated Indian assimilation. Euro-American advocates of both laissez-faire and progressivism tended to view the world in terms of a racial and cultural hierarchy in which Anglo-Saxon Protestants and their civilization occupied the highest rungs. Hence, "progress" required that "inferior" races and cultures be remade. It was also thought that assimilation would allow the government to abolish the Bureau of Indian Affairs (BIA), which appealed to laissez-faire proponents of limited government and to progressive advocates of efficiency. Assimilation also allowed for the conversion of tribal reservation lands into individually owned plots through the 1887 General Allotment Act or **Dawes Act**. "Surplus" lands were made available to non-Indians, thus enhancing economic freedom and ending the "wasteful" use of lands by Indians.

By the late 1920s, many policy makers had recognized the failure of the assimilation policy. Investigations into In-

dian affairs (including the 1928 **Meriam Report**) showed many American Indians remained unassimilated and suffered from poverty and dependency. The Great Depression and the election of Franklin Roosevelt in 1932 led to the development of new forms of liberalism, which resulted in new Indian policies within the administration's "New Deal" reform programs. For Indian policy during the 1930s and World War II, the most important of these new forms could be called the "community New Deal" or "community liberalism." Like reform liberalism, community liberals believed in progress and freedom and the use of federal power to accomplish their goals. Liberals of this school generally lamented the tendency of industrialization to break up communities and to promote atomization and excessive materialism. Hence, they advocated using federal power to foster a sense of community among people based upon shared values and economic cooperation at the local level.

The champion of community liberalism in the BIA was Commissioner of Indian Affairs **John Collier**. Collier had long opposed assimilation and advocated bolstering Indian tribes and cultures because they "offered a model of communal living for an individualistic-oriented American society." The 1934 **Indian Reorganization Act (IRA)** reflected the community liberalism philosophy. The measure ended allotment (thus protecting the land base Collier felt was necessary to build Indian communities), provided funds for economic development, and increased opportunities for tribal self-government. Collier also oversaw the creation of an Indian arts and crafts board, protection for native religions, and the promotion of Indian cultures in schools.

Admittedly, Native Americans did not achieve complete political and cultural autonomy through the Indian New Deal. The IRA allowed the secretary of interior to "review" certain decisions of the tribal governments. Collier also forced the Navajos to comply with a livestock reduction program that devastated their economy. Nevertheless, the programs that grew out of community liberalism provided many Native Americans with the chance to improve their economic status, to preserve their tribes, and to maintain a sense of cultural distinctiveness.

By the mid- to late-1940s, however, the New Deal community liberalism had lost much of its influence because the Second World War and the Cold War had altered liberal views. The struggles against fascism, Nazism, and communism prompted many in the United States to favor individualism over community, and national unity over pluralism. The Indian New Deal's emphasis on preserving the tribal cultures and societies seemed, at least to some critics, subversive. Nazi racism, which culminated in the Holocaust, convinced many liberals that racial distinction should be eliminated and that all minorities should be integrated into mainstream society. The full employment achieved during the Second World War because of federal spending convinced many liberals that progress could best be achieved through the stimulation of economic growth, thereby ensuring jobs and prosperity for all. Beyond protecting individual rights ("rights-based liberalism") and promoting prosperity ("commercial Keynesian liberalism"), it was widely believed that additional federal intervention in the economy and society would be largely unnecessary. Such views, which predominated throughout the administrations of Harry Truman and Dwight Eisenhower, led to the Indian policy of "termination."

Termination advocates sought to achieve assimilation and self-sufficiency by encouraging Indians to relocate to urban areas, by abolishing special federal services for Indians, and by removing the federal trust status of reservations. The last meant that Indian lands would be subject to taxation, state laws, and acquisition by non-Indians. Termination, as embodied in such measures as House Concurrent Resolution 108 and Public Law 280, did not endure as an official policy much past the early 1960s. Most Native Americans strongly opposed the policy, making its implementation difficult. In addition, the abolition of federal services tended not to promote self-reliance but rather to increase poverty, since most of the terminated tribes were relatively small and powerless.

While termination became increasingly discredited, community liberalism experienced a resurgence during the John Kennedy and Lyndon Johnson administrations. The 1960s community liberals (like their New Deal predecessors) advocated using federal power to promote human progress. This meant satisfying what President Johnson called "the hunger for community," a hunger that material prosperity had failed to satisfy. As a result, federal anti-poverty initiatives (known as the "War on Poverty") strengthened communities by allowing local people to develop and run their own programs utilizing federal funds.

As during the Depression, community liberalism provided for enhanced tribal self-rule and the maintenance of native cultures. Under what became known as the "self-determination" policy, tribes had the chance to create and administer their own programs of economic development (including tribal businesses), housing, and health care. Indians also altered their educational system by creating Native American-run schools (such as Navajo Community College) and getting non-Indian-controlled schools to address Indian cultures in their curricula.

Frustration and disillusionment with the Vietnam War, the inability of the War on Poverty to quickly eradicate privation, the "white backlash" against minority rights, and other events caused liberalism to lose its position as the dominant political ideology in the United States by the end of the 1960s. A new conservative ideology began to fill the vacuum.

This conservatism included a range of different ideas. Libertarians, like laissez-faire liberals, believed (at least officially) in constraining centralized government power as a way to promote and protect political and economic liberty. Traditionalists and fundamentalists argued that the good society must be based less upon individual freedom and more upon adherence to certain traditions and (supposedly) universal values. For fundamentalists, such traditions and values derived from their interpretation of Christianity.

The rise of conservatism presented both opportunities and threats to Native American self-determination in the 1970s, 1980s, and 1990s. The libertarian desire for political decentralization facilitated the process whereby tribal governments took over functions previously performed by federal agencies. All of the presidents since 1969, including self-described conservatives, have endorsed self-determination. Richard Nixon formally repudiated termination in 1970 and endorsed several self-determination measures; Gerald Ford signed the 1975 Indian Self-Determination Act, allowing the BIA to contract with tribes to provide services; Ronald Reagan asserted that tribes enjoyed "government to government" relations with the United States; George Bush signed the Self-Governance Demonstration Act (1991), allowing tribes greater say over the allocation of federal funds.

Other elements of the conservative philosophy have proven less hospitable to Indian self-determination. Calls by traditionalists and fundamentalists for adherence to "universal Western values" would seem to be at odds with the vision of a pluralistic society in which distinctive Native-American cultural values survive and flourish. In *Lyng v. Northwest Indian Cemetery Protective Association* (1988), a majority of the conservatives on the Supreme Court refused to block the construction of a road through a site sacred to certain California Indians. Conservative efforts to cut funding for tribal governments, social services, and federal enforcement of treaty rights threaten to destroy self-government and promote de facto assimilation. As Standing Rock Sioux Vine Deloria Jr. put it, without a secure economic base, "Self-government is probably a farce."

Over the course of American history, both liberalism and conservatism have included a wide range of ideas and impulses. Some of these ideas and impulses have promoted policies sympathetic to the maintenance of tribal societies, governments, and cultures, while others have given philosophical justification for assimilation. Given the fact that both liberalism and conservatism have tended to emphasize, at least in theory, individual rights rather than group rights, it is remarkable that Native-American tribes and cultures have endured as long as they have. (CKR)

BIBLIOGRAPHY

Deloria, Vine, Jr. and Clifford M. Lytle. *The Nations Within: The Past and Future of American Indian Sovereignty.* New York: Pantheon Books, 1984.

Fixico, Donald L. *Termination and Relocation: Federal Indian Policy, 1945–1960.* Albuquerque: University of New Mexico, 1986.

Hoxie, Frederick E. *A Final Promise: The Campaign to Assimilate the Indians, 1880–1920.* Lincoln: University of Nebraska Press, 1984.

Koppes, Clayton R. "From New Deal to Termination: Liberalism and Indian Policy, 1933–1953." *Pacific Historical Review* XLVI, no. 4 (November 1977): 543–66.

Philp, Kenneth R., ed. *Indian Self-Rule: First-Hand Accounts of Indian-White Relations from Roosevelt to Reagan.* Logan, UT: Utah State University Press, 1995.

Philp, Kenneth R. *John Collier's Crusade for Indian Reform, 1920–1954.* Tucson: University of Arizona Press, 1977.

Riggs, Christopher. "Indians, Liberalism, and Lyndon Johnson's Great Society, 1963–1969." Ph.D. diss., University of Colorado, 1997.

Cornplanter (ca. 1735–1836)

Cornplanter (John O'Bail) was the chief of the Allegheny Senecas and the war leader of the Iroquois Confederacy in the early national era. A veteran of the **French and Indian War** and the **American Revolution**, Cornplanter later became an American ally and served as an intermediary between the United States and the Northwest Indian Confederacy in the 1780s and 1790s. He firmly supported the federal government's "civilization" program, which he believed would repair the Senecas' war-damaged economy and strengthen their legal claim to their land. He alternated between support of and rivalry with his brother, the prophet **Handsome Lake**. (DAN)

BIBLIOGRAPHY

Carfield, William. *Legends of the Iroquois*. New York: A. Wessels Co., 1904.
Wallace, Anthony F.C. *The Death and Rebirth of the Seneca*. New York: Knopf, 1970.

Council of Energy Resource Tribes (CERT)

The Council of Energy Resource Tribes (CERT) was founded by the governments of 25 Native American tribes in 1975, a time when the "energy crisis" in the United States had turned attention to increased use of coal, uranium, and other resources that are abundant on western reservations. The council was envisioned as a way for Native Americans to control their energy resources and gain fair prices from corporations wishing to extract resources from reservation lands.

The council's focus on developing tribal energy resources and its financial links to energy corporations made it controversial on reservations where there was opposition to mining, power plants, coal gasification, and similar projects. Through the 1980s, the organization increasingly focused on pollution problems, non-energy economic development, and technical education for Native American students. In 1995, the council's membership included 53 federally recognized U.S. tribes and four Canadian Indian nations. **See also** Land and Water Rights. (LCJ)

BIBLIOGRAPHY

Ambler, Marjane. *Breaking the Iron Bonds: Indian Control of Energy Development*. Lawrence: University of Kansas Press, 1990.
Churchill, Ward. *Struggle for the Land: Indigenous Resistance to Ecocide, Genocide, and Expropriation in Contemporary North America*. Monroe, ME: Common Courage Press, 1993.
Jorgensen, Joseph G., ed. *Native Americans and Energy Development II*. Boston: Anthropology Resource Center, 1984.

Courts for Indian Justice

The Courts for Indian Justice was originally the Coordinating Committee on Indian Affairs. It was formed in 1947 to help with providing assistance to the Navajo Indians with irrigation and health issues, among other things. It now consists of the American Civil Liberties Union and the **Indian Rights Association**, among other groups. The organization's name officially changed when the **National Congress of American Indians** joined the group in the 1950s. The majority of the group's focus is on **education**, but it also focuses on other topics, such as health, housing, and employment. It held the American Indian Capital Conference on Poverty in 1964, which influenced the Johnson administration.

BIBLIOGRAPHY

Washburn, Wilcomb E. ed. *History of Indian–White Relations*. Washington, DC: Smithsonian Institute, 1988.

Crazy Horse

Crazy Horse, Tesunke Witko, was a famous Oglala warrior in the mid-eighteenth century. He grew to be a legendary figure as an able warrior and leader who never gave up his principles or loyalty to his people. Crazy Horse was born probably in 1842. He was known in his youth as Curly and later as the Strange Man. As Crazy Horse, in the 1860s, he led fighting against the encroachment of the white presence in the Black Hills. He never signed any treaty with the U.S. government. Crazy Horse was one of the major leaders of the **Battle of Little Big Horn** in June 1876, which was a key Indian victory over American forces and in which General George Custer met his death.

Crazy Horse's formal and informal fame as a warrior and as a gifted tactician won him an enthusiastic following among his people; but rapid success and familial matters also made him some enemies. Shortly after the battle of Greasy Grass, with the growing American power in the Black Hills area, Crazy Horse and his people were forced to join **Red Cloud** and other warriors who had surrendered. He was brought to Fort Robinson in Nebraska where he was killed in September 1877 by American soldiers and fellow Indians. He is remembered as an uncompromising warrior and as a role model of a leader totally committed to his people. A monument of Crazy Horse is being carved out of the Black Hills not far from Mt. Rushmore. (MS)

BIBLIOGRAPHY

Ambrose, Stephen E. *Crazy Horse and Custer: The Parallel Lives of Two American Warriors*. New York: Doubleday and Company, 1975.
Sandoz, Mari. *Crazy Horse: The Strange Man of the Oglala*. Lincoln: University of Nebraska Press, 1961.

Crow Dog (ca. 1834–ca. 1911)

Born in the Montana Territory, Crow Dog became a central figure in many events that shaped the relationship between the government and the Lakotas in the late nineteenth century. In 1877, when **Crazy Horse** surrendered to federal authorities, Crow Dog went with him to Fort Robinson. Crow Dog's influence grew after the murder of Crazy Horse in the fort's jail, when he convinced the Lakotas not to retaliate. Impressed with what he had done at Fort Robinson, the government appointed Crow Dog chief of the Rosebud Indian police. However, his appointment only lasted until 1879 when he was removed because of conflict with the Indian agent Cicero Newell over land claims.

On August 5, 1881, Crow Dog shot and killed Spotted Tail, the chief of the Lakotas. Crow Dog was angered by Spotted Tail's dealing with the federal government and his selling of Lakota land to railroads. Spotted Tail had been taking the proceeds of the sale of a railroad rights-of-way for himself. Following Lakota custom, Crow Dog gave Spotted Tail's family horses, blankets, and $600 for having killed Spotted Tail. While this satisfied the Lakotas, the federal government decided to charge Crow Dog with murder.

Convicted of murder by an all-white jury in Deadwood, South Dakota, Crow Dog was sentenced to hang. His conviction was appealed to the United States Supreme Court who heard the appeal as *Ex Parte Crow Dog* (1883). Crow Dog's attorneys successfully argued that the federal government did not have jurisdiction of the case, because the murder had taken place on Indian territory.

Returning to the Rosebud Reservation, Crow Dog was largely ostracized from his tribe. In 1889, he became one of the leaders of the Lakota **Ghost Dance Movement**. In 1890 he and other Lakotas fled the reservation and went to the Badlands. Tensions between the group and federal authorities were high and fighting broke out. After the hostilities ended, Crow Dog lived the remainder of his life on the Pine Ridge Reservation.

BIBLIOGRAPHY

Dyck, Paul. *Brule: The Sioux People of Rosebud*. Flagstaff, AZ: Northland Press, 1971.

Hyde, George E. *Spotted Tail's Folk: A History of the Brule Sioux*. Norman: University of Oklahoma Press, 1961.

Mooney, James. *The Ghost-Dance Religion and the Sioux Outbreak of 1890*. Chicago: University of Chicago Press, 1965.

Mary Crow Dog (1953–)

Mary Crow Dog, born Mary Brave Bird, is a Brule Sioux. She has been an **American Indian Movement (AIM)** activist, and was the wife of Leonard Crow Dog, a Sioux medicine man. She was a participant in the 1972 occupation of the **Bureau of Indian Affairs (BIA)**, as well as the **Wounded Knee** takeover.

BIBLIOGRAPHY

Crow Dog, Mary. *Lakota Woman*. New York: HarperPerennial, 1990.

——. *Ohitika Woman*. New York: Grove Press, 1993.

Culture and Identity

Native-American culture and identity have played a definitive role in political relations between native and nonnative peoples since early contact. These issues have been paramount in the development of government policies designed to eliminate, assimilate, manage, and control native peoples; in the types and content of native resistance to European incursions; and in the agreements made between native and nonnative nations.

From their first encounters with Europeans, Native North Americans were seen as independent, autonomous, self-sufficient peoples with extensive cultural, political, and knowledge systems. During the 1600s, the French and British recorded a great diversity of native cultural and linguistic groups; a wide spectrum of subsistence practices, including agricultural village settlements; and far-ranging hunting, gathering, and fishing complexes. They also noted multiple forms of government, great confederacies, and extensive trade relations between aboriginal nations, which led them to establish their own diplomatic and trade alliances with various native groups.

The 1700s marked an era of much conflict and treaty making between native and nonnative nations as the United States established itself as a nation, and as the British and French vied for the territory to the north. Settlers took over native lands, displacing native peoples, competing with them for resources, and undermining their ways of life. In many treaties the continuity of native culture and identity was part of the agreements, with emphasis on natives' rights to use traditional ceremonial or hunting and fishing grounds, even when those lands fell within areas used by settlers.

It has been suggested that cultural differences, particularly in regard to different notions of land ownership, are what have led to much of the conflict between native and nonnative peoples surrounding treaties. This claim suggests that native leaders were either tricked or did not understand European ideas about private ownership and exploitation of land, which contrasted with native notions of communal and conservationist land use. In counterpoint, while treaty negotiation was not uniform, treaties were made on a nation-to-nation basis, and although there may have been some misunderstanding and some trickery, native leaders negotiated in good faith and knew what they expected of these agreements. Later conflict generally involved demands that the United States abide by treaty terms.

At times, the culture of Native Americans has come into conflict with other political issues, such as whaling. Whaling is an important economic and cultural aspect to life for many tribes, such as these native Alaskans. *Library of Congress.*

Native culture is very relevant to the treaty-making process in that treaties made between nations have sacred significance. Treaties and politics are not separated from the cultural and spiritual realms of life; the nations making the agreements are expected to honor them. Spiritual and political practices are integrated in the agreement process, as exemplified by using sacred wampum, smoking the sacred pipe, or performing specific songs and ceremonies to demonstrate respect for and commitment to the agreements made between nations.

The criteria for identity or membership in native societies continued to be defined by native peoples themselves throughout most of the period of early nonnative contact and settlement. Racial or "blood-quantum" measurements of native identity was not officially introduced until the mid-nineteenth century when the government enacted assimilationist policies, which included the elimination of entire groups of people by not according them tribal acknowledgment. Blood quantum was used in the Dawes Act (1887) as a requirement for land allotment. It was further entrenched in federal Indian law by the **Indian Reorganization Act of 1934**.

In the post-World War II period, the United States enacted a relocation program for native peoples willing to leave the reservations and move to large cities. For a time, many native peoples in cities felt ashamed of their native heritage, and denied their identity if it was physically possible. However, they soon began organizing their own cultural centers and social service agencies, and it was in the cities where many identity movements began in the 1960s. Urban native communities now constitute approximately 70 percent of all native peoples who live off-reservation.

With exposure to civil rights and other social movements, a diversity of native resistance movements emerged, drawing public attention to the plight of native communities and stressing a general pride in native identity. The **American Indian Movement (AIM)** rose directly from the urban experience, gaining notoriety for its vocalization of empowerment based on native identity and its militant approaches to bringing native issues to the forefront of American politics. The **National Congress of American Indians**, formed in 1944, was a significant force, as was the **National Indian Youth Council**, founded in 1961, made up mostly of native college students. The younger generation of native activists promoted both the assertion of tribal and national native identities and the formation of the ideology of "Red Power." They began to break away from a lobbying approach to adopt protest and direct action methods. Whether people agreed with, or opposed, their tactics, the actions of these Native-American activists inspired some of the most wide-sweeping and lasting effects on Native-American consciousness. The resultant reaffirmation of Native-American identity and culture has formed a generation with strong leadership at the local, national, and international levels.

The issues of cultural appropriation and perpetuation of negative or romanticized stereotypes of native peoples have been critically taken to task by many articulate voices in native politics today. Native cultural materials, including the bones of their dead, were robbed for centuries by both professional and amateur nonnative collectors. These materials have served to legitimize the scientific racism professed by early anthropologists who interpreted them as evidence of "primitive" cultures, and have been inappropriately displayed like trophies. While some legislation has been enacted since the early twentieth century to protect artifacts, the perspectives of Native Americans were considered only marginally until passage of the 1990 **Native American Graves Protection and Repatriation Act**. The stereotypical representation of native culture and identity in the media and sports teams, as well as by anthropologists, has also been highly criticized, particularly in terms of how it perpetuates negative images of native people.

In the 1980s and 1990s, the struggles relating to Native-American culture and identity were taken to international forums. Native Americans joined with indigenous peoples from all over the world in encouraging such organizations as the United Nations to acknowledge the inherent rights of aboriginal peoples. Indigenous peoples also emerged as critical interest groups in the international environmental movement. (HHB)

BIBLIOGRAPHY

Churchill, Ward. *Indians Are Us? Culture and Genocide in Native North America*. Monroe, ME: Common Courage Press, 1994.

Deloria, Vine, Jr. *Behind the Trail of Broken Treaties: An Indian Declaration of Independence*. Austin: University of Texas Press, 1985.

Green, Michael K., ed. *Issues in Native American Cultural Identity*. New York: Peter Lang Publishing, 1995.

Hertzberg, Hazel W. *The Search for American Indian Identity: Modern Pan-Indian Movements*. Syracuse: Syracuse University Press, 1971.

Nagel, Joane. *American Indian Ethnic Renewal: Red Power and the Resurgence of Identity and Culture*. New York: Oxford University Press, 1996.

Royal Commission on Aboriginal Peoples. Report of the Royal Commission on Aboriginal Peoples. Vol. 1–5. Ottawa: Supply and Services Canada, 1996.

Smith, Paul Chaat and Robert Allen Warrior. *Like a Hurricane: The Indian Movement from Alcatraz to Wounded Knee*. New York: The New Press, 1996.

Wright, Ronald. *Stolen Continents: The "New World" Through Indian Eyes*. Toronto: Penguin, 1993.

Charles Brent Curtis (1860–1936)

Charles Curtis was inaugurated as the thirty-first vice president of the United States after Herbert Hoover won the presidency in 1928. Born on land later to become part of North Topeka, Kansas, Curtis was the son of a white father and a mixed-blood mother. In 1885 he was elected as county attorney for Shawnee County, Kansas. He continued his political life by being elected to the U.S. House of Representatives as a Republican from the 4th District of Kansas in 1892. He remained in the position for 14 years. He was the author of the **Curtis Act of 1898,** which extended the General Allotment Act (the **Dawes Act of 1887**) to the **Five Civilized Tribes** of Oklahoma. Many remember this legislation as one that destroyed much tribal **sovereignty**. Curtis was designated to fill an unexpired term in the U.S. Senate in 1907 and was then elected in the same year. After losing the office the following election, he was reelected to it in 1914. He remained in the position until 1926. During that time he was designated party whip in 1915, and the majority leader in 1924. Hoover and Curtis lost their reelection attempt in 1932.

BIBLIOGRAPHY

Moses, L.G. and Raymond Wilson, ed. "Charles Curtis: The Politics of Allotment." In *Indian Lives: Essays on Nineteen Twentieth Century Native American Leaders*. Albuquerque: University of New Mexico Press, 1985, pp. 113–38.

Seitz, Don C. *From Kaw Teepee to Capitol: The Life Story of Charles Curtis, Indian, Who Has Risen to High Estate*. New York: Frederick A. Stokes, 1928.

Curtis Act of 1898

The Curtis Act of 1898, named for its sponsor, **Charles Brent Curtis** (R-KS), became the transition mechanism that changed the **Indian Territory** into the state of Oklahoma, by eliminating tribal holdings and substituting individual land ownership. It also provided that if 200 residents of a town wanted to incorporate, they could do so under the laws of Arkansas. This law was an outgrowth of the Oklahoma land rush of 1889, which had violated the promise of the United States that the Indian Territory would remain Indian land in perpetuity. **See also** Five Civilized Tribes. (AMM)

BIBLIOGRAPHY

Moses, L.G. and Raymond Wilson, eds. *Indian Lives*. Albuquerque: University of New Mexico Press, 1985.

Seitz, Don C. *From Kaw Tepee to Capitol*. New York: Frederick A. Stoker, 1928.

D

Dartmouth College

Dartmouth College, Hanover, New Hampshire, was established December 13, 1769, through a charter from King George III. The college had its antecedents in Moor's Indian Charity School of Lebanon, Connecticut, founded by the Reverend Eleazar Wheelock. Lack of support from Connecticut led Wheelock to open Dartmouth College in 1770 in a log cabin in the New Hampshire wilderness. It was named after the second Earl of Dartmouth, benefactor and trustee of the original endowment. Disputes between John Wheelock, second president, and the legislature of New Hampshire led to *Dartmouth College v. Woodward* (1797), which prohibited states from altering the obligations of contracts. The college is regarded as a premier liberal arts college in New England. (AMM)

BIBLIOGRAPHY

Graham, Robert B. *The Dartmouth Story*. Hanover, NH: Dartmouth, 1990.
McCallum, James Dow. *Eleazar Wheelock*. New York: Arno Press, 1969.

Dawes Act of 1887

The Dawes Act, also known as the General Allotment Act, was part of the late-1800s United States policy of assimilating Native Americans into the non-Indian mainstream. Named after Republican Senator Henry Dawes of Massachusetts, the act was designed to encourage Indians to farm by "allotting" each head of household 160 acres of land, with smaller amounts to other family members. The land was to be held as private property. The Dawes Act was designed to break up the collective land tenure that was common among native nations; the act often served to disrupt traditional governments as well. Reservation lands that were "surplus" after each individual received his or her tract were sold, generally to non-Indians.

Allotment was supported by a broad coalition of interests. Some people simply wanted native lands. Others believed they were doing Native Americans a favor by creating private ownership, which they thought would protect native lands from mineral prospectors.

Between 1887 and 1934, when the **Indian Reorganization Act** ended the allotment policy, Native Americans lost control of about 100 million acres of land—representing two-thirds of the land base they had held in 1887. Often, the lands that left native control were the most prosperous reservation lands—good for agriculture or timbering—while the lands that were left were unsuitable for economically viable activities. In the western United States, where most reservation lands were located, 160 acres of land were not nearly enough for ranching, which was the main economic activity.

Over the years, ownership of allotted lands has become split among many heirs to the original allottees. It is not unusual for 100 people to have an ownership interest in one parcel of land. This makes it difficult for Native Americans to make a living—or even build housing—on many reservations. Allotment also increased the number of non-Indians living on reservations, making tribal governance and legal jurisdiction problematic. Some native nations rejected or avoided the Allotment Act and have relatively intact reservations, such as the Red Lake Anishinabe within northern Minnesota and the Hopi in the Southwest. **See also** Burke Act of 1906; Competency; Forced Assimilation; Friends of the Indian; Indian Land Consolidation Act of 1893; Land and Water Rights. **See** Dawes Act (1887) in the Appendix 1. (LCJ)

BIBLIOGRAPHY

Ambler, Marjane. *Breaking the Iron Bonds: Indian Control of Energy Development*. Lawrence: University of Kansas Press, 1990.
Otis, D.S. *The Dawes Act and the Allotment of Indian Lands*. Norman: University of Oklahoma Press, 1973.
Prucha, Francis Paul. *Indian Policy in the United States: Historical Essays*. Lincoln: University of Nebraska Press, 1981.

Declaration of Allegiance to the Government of the United States by the North American Indian

While many tribal leaders believed that the declaration that they signed and attested to was a treaty with the United States, it was actually only a publicity stunt headed by Rodman Wanamaker who convinced President William Howard Taft to participate in a signing ceremony at Fort Wadsworth in New York City. At the event, newly coined Buffalo nickels were distributed.

The Declaration stated, "With our right hands extended in brotherly love and our left hands extended holding the Pipe of Peace, we hereby bury all past ill feelings and proclaim abroad to all the nations of the world our firm allegiance to this Nation and to the Stars and Stripes."

When Woodrow Wilson entered the White House, he had the document taken to every Indian reservation in the country. By December 1913, the document was signed by more than 900 Indians from 189 tribes.

BIBLIOGRAPHY

Reynolds, Charles R. *American Indian Portraits from the Wanamaker Expedition of 1913*. Brattleboro, VT: Greene Press, 1971.

Declaration of Policy Statement

The Declaration of Policy Statement was issued in 1917 by Franklin Land, Secretary of the Department of the Interior, and Cato Sells, Commissioner of the Office of Indian Affairs. This legislative document stated that competent Indians did not need **guardianship** and, as a result, should not be treated under "half ward, half citizen" status. The statement also declared that needy Native Americans should be the focus of governmental assistance instead of having legislation continuously dictate the actions of all Indians. While supporters saw the Declaration of Policy Statement as a safeguard against governmental interference in traditional Indian life and as a departure from the Indians' often discriminatory status, critics saw it as a way to take away needed benefits allotted to the Native American people.

BIBLIOGRAPHY

Deloria, Vine. *American Indian Policy in the Twentieth Century*. Norman: University of Oklahoma Press, 1985.

Angel Decora Dietz (1871–1919)

Angel Decora Dietz was a Winnebago illustrator, lecturer, and writer whose art education included studies at Smith College, the Drexel Institute, and the Boston Museum of Fine Arts. She established a reputation as an illustrator in Boston and New York. She was instrumental in promoting the use of Indian art motifs, practices that were later incorporated in the Indian New Deal policy and in the creation of the Indian Arts and Crafts Department in 1935. (EW)

BIBLIOGRAPHY

Decora Dietz, Angel. "Angel Decora: An Autobiography." In *The Red Man*, by Red Man. Carlisle, PA: Carlisle Indian Press, 1911.
Dockstader, Frederick J. *Great North American Indians*. New York: Van Nostrand Reinhold, 1977.

DeCoteau v. District County Court (1975)

DeCoteau v. District County Court, 420 U.S. 425 (1975), involved the 1889 (ratified by Congress in 1891) absolute cession of all unallotted lands "within the [Lake Traverse] Reservation" of South Dakota. The issue in this case was whether or not that cession amounted to termination of the reservation. Despite favorable construction for the Indians, the Supreme Court ruled that it did. Justices William Douglas, William Brennan, and Thurgood Marshall dissented, arguing that "within the reservation" was a clear statement of Congress' intent to maintain the 1889 size. **See also** Allotment; Termination Resolution. (AMM)

BIBLIOGRAPHY

Wunder, John R., ed. *Recent Legal Issues for American Indians, 1968 to the Present*. New York: Garland Publishing, 1996.

Ada E. Deer (1935–)

Ada Deer was assistant secretary for Indian Affairs. Appointed by President Bill Clinton in 1993, Deer was the first female head of the **Bureau of Indian Affairs (BIA)**. Born in 1935 on the Menominee Indian Reservation in Wisconsin, Deer was the first member of her tribe to graduate from college. She went on to become the first Native American to receive a master's of social work degree from Columbia University. Deer led the successful struggle to restore the Menominee tribe after its termination in 1959, which resulted in the passage of the Menominee Restoration Act, signed into law by President Nixon in December of 1973. Shortly after that victory, Ms. Deer was elected tribal chairperson. She became involved in Democratic Party politics, and was a delegate to the 1984 Democratic Convention. Deer has served on the boards of numerous organizations, including the **Native American Rights Fund**, and is a member of the President's Inter-Agency Council on Women. (RAC)

BIBLIOGRAPHY

Deer, Ada, with R.E. Simon Jr. *Speaking Out*. Chicago: Children's Press, 1970.

Deganawida

Deganawida designed the Great Law of Peace that formed the foundation of the Haudenosaunee (Iroquois) Confederacy between A.D. 1000 and 1450. Known as The Peacemaker, Deganawida is believed to have been Huron. Dismayed at the constant warfare among Native Americans living near the eastern Great Lakes, Deganawida was inspired with a plan for peace, which he called the Great Law. However, he was not a good speaker—he stuttered—so he enlisted Ayonwatha (**Hiawatha**), an Onondaga, to help him spread his plan. This took many decades.

The government Deganawida designed consisted of a 50-chief Grand Council divided into two parts. The chiefs were chosen by clanmothers and ratified by the whole population and by the council itself. The council operated on a consensus basis and was symbolized by the white pine tree. The resulting Haudenosaunee confederacy was a model for the Articles of Confederation. (LCJ)

BIBLIOGRAPHY

Barreiro, Jose. *Indian Roots of American Democracy*. Ithaca, NY: Akwekon Press, Cornell University, 1992.
Great Law of Peace (Kaianerekowa) of the Longhouse People (Hotinonsionne). Rooseveltown, NY: White Roots of Peace, 1971.

Delaware Treaty of 1818

The Delaware Treaty of 1818 superseded all earlier treaties and again provided for the relocation of the Delaware Indians. This time the move was from Indiana to land west of the

Mississippi. In addition, the federal government promised the tribe a perpetual annuity of $4,000. Removal was provided for in the Treaty of 1829, which granted the Delaware a tract of land between the Kansas and Missouri Rivers. Although the Delaware eventually settled in **Indian Territory** (Oklahoma), their land claim was not settled until 1970. (AMM)

BIBLIOGRAPHY
Prucha, Frances P. *American Indian Treaties.* Berkeley: University of California Press, 1997.

Delaware Walking Purchase

In 1737, Pennsylvania officials convinced a number of Delaware chiefs to abide by a 1686 deed that stated that the Delawares were to cede all the land "as far as a man can go in a day and a half," and from there to the Delaware River and down its course. Deceitfully, a team of three runners covered about 65 miles in the allotted time. This "Walking Purchase" deprived Delawares of the last of their lands in the upper Delaware and Lehigh Valleys in Pennsylvania. (GO)

BIBLIOGRAPHY
Calloway, Colin. *The World Turned Upside Down: Indian Voices from Early America.* Boston: Bedford Books of St. Martin's Press, 1994.
Weslager, C.A. *The Delaware Indians: A History.* New Brunswick, NJ: Rutgers University Press, 1972.

Vine Deloria, Jr. (1933–)

Vine Deloria, Jr. (Standing Rock Sioux) is a lawyer, activist, professor, and writer. He cofounded the **National Indian Youth Council**, and he was a defense witness at the **Wounded Knee** trials of 1974. He called for increased scholarship and writing on contemporary Indian history and issues. (RAC)

BIBLIOGRAPHY
Deloria, Vine, Jr. *Custer Died for Your Sins.* New York: MacMillan, 1969.
Deloria, Vine, Jr. and Clifford Lytle. *The Nations Within: The Past and Future of American Indian Sovereignty.* New York: Pantheon Press, 1984.

William G. Demmert, Jr. (1934–)

From 1968 to 1970, William Demmert Jr. served as the chief administrator of the public school system of Klawock, Alaska. In 1969, Demmert attended the First Convocation of American Indian Scholars, where he helped found and became director for the **National Indian Education Association**. Demmert went on to become a consultant to the United States Senate in the development of the Indian Education Act of 1972 and eventually joined the Department of Education, where he acted from 1972 to 1975 as an official for Indian education. Demmert next worked from 1975 to 1976 as deputy commissioner of education in the United States Office of Education, moving on to serve from 1976 to 1978 as director of Indian Education for the **Bureau of Indian Affairs (BIA)**. During the 1980s, he functioned as Alaska's commissioner of education. In 1991 he became co-chair of the Indian Nations at Risk Force.

BIBLIOGRAPHY
Demmert, William G., Jr. "Native Education: The Alaskan Perspective." *Indigenous Peoples and Education in the Circumpolar North.* In William G. Demmert Jr., ed. Gouthab, Greenland: Gronlands Seminarium, 1986.

Department of the Interior Act of 1849

In 1849, the Department of the Interior was created to manage both natural resources and Indian affairs. Administration of Indian affairs had previously been conducted by the Office of Indian Affairs in the Department of War. The Office of Indian Affairs had begun in 1824 as a diplomatic corps to handle negotiations with the tribes. It was transferred in 1849 to the Department of the Interior and was renamed the **Bureau of Indian Affairs (BIA)** in 1947. (AMM)

BIBLIOGRAPHY
Clement, Fred. *The Department of the Interior.* New York: Chelsea House, 1989.
Utley, Robert and Barry MacKintosh. *The Department of Everything Else: Highlights of Interior History.* Washington, DC: U.S. Department of the Interior, 1988.

"Destroy the Indian and Save the Individual" Educational Policy

This so-called educational policy was the most explicit among forced assimilation policies, which were aimed at destroying Native-American nations and assimilating Indian individuals into the dominant culture. To "destroy the Indian," children who were taken to boarding schools were stripped of their traditional clothes, which were burned, and their hair was cut short. They were not allowed to speak their languages or practice any of their traditional ways. To "save the individual," or to create indistinguishable American individuals, they were dressed with white children's clothes, given English names, and taught that their traditional ways were evil. In a variety of forms this policy continued until the 1970s when, under President Nixon, the United States government reversed its policy through such acts as the **Indian Self-Determination and Educational Assistance Act** and **The Indian Child Welfare Act**. **See also** Education. (MS)

BIBLIOGRAPHY
Duran, Eduardo and Bonnie Duran. *Native American Postcolonial Psychology.* New York: State University of New York, 1995.
Pratt, Richard Henry. *Battlefield and Classroom: Four Decades and the American Indian 1867–1904.* New Haven: Yale University Press, 1964.

Doctrine of Discovery

The "doctrine of "discovery" was enunciated by the United States Supreme Court in ***Johnson v. McIntosh,*** 8 Wheat. 543 (1823), to decide that land title received from an indigenous nation was not valid against a competing title granted by the United States, on grounds that colonial "discovery" took away indigenous **sovereignty.** The Court acknowledged the doctrine's theological foundation that "Christian princes" could take lands "unknown to all Christian peoples." Chief

Justice Marshall admitted the doctrine is an "extravagant . . . pretension" that may be "opposed to natural right" and may only "perhaps, be supported by reason." Nonetheless, he concluded that it "cannot be rejected by courts of justice."

Theological grants were the legal foundation for claims of sovereignty by all colonial powers in America. Adoption of these claims by the United States flew in the face of theories of religious freedom and separation of state and church. *Johnson v. McIntosh* has never been overruled, and "discovery" remains the legal foundation for federal sovereignty over indigenous peoples' lands. (PPE)

BIBLIOGRAPHY

Newcomb, Steve. "The Evidence of Christian Nationalism in Federal Indian Law: The Doctrine of Discovery, *Johnson v. McIntosh*, and Plenary Power." *NYU Review of Law & Social Change* 20, no. 2 (1993): 303–41.

Henry Chee Dodge (ca. 1857–1947)

Henry Chee Dodge was the first chairman of the Navajo Tribal Council. He envisioned a unified Navajo nation under a centralized tribal government. As chairman, he fought to strengthen the nation by increasing land holdings and controlling tribal resources. (MR)

BIBLIOGRAPHY

Hoffman, Virginia. *Navajo Biographies*. Rough Rock, AZ: Dine, 1970.

Parman, Donald L. *The Navajos and the New Deal*. New Haven: Yale University Press, 1976.

Edward P. Dozier (1916–1971)

Edward Dozier was an anthropologist at the University of Oregon (1951–1952) and Northwestern University. After living with the Kaling tribe of northern Luzon in the Philippines from 1959 to 1960, Dozier went on to publish the account of his stay with the Kaling and other relevant research in his 1966 book *Mountain Arbiters: The Changing Life of a Philippine Hill People.* From 1961 into the 1970s, Dozier worked as a professor of anthropology and linguistics at the University of Arizona, where he helped develop programs designed to meet the needs of Native-American students; he also served at this time with the Association on American Indian Affairs. Before his death, Dozier published *The Pueblo Indians of North America*, which contained facts compiled from a lifetime of research.

BIBLIOGRAPHY

Dozier, Edward. *Mountain Arbiters: The Changing Life of a Philippine Hill People*. Tucson: University of Arizona Press, 1966.

———. *The Pueblo Indians of North America*. New York: Holt, 1970.

Dull Knife (Tahmelapashme) (c. 1810–1883)

Dull Knife was a northern Cheyenne and ally of the Lakota during the **Plains Wars.** After surrendering to the United States in 1877, the northern Cheyenne were moved south to **Indian Territory**, where they found conditions unbearable. Dull Knife

and Little Wolf led 300 Cheyennes back north. Pursued by soldiers and hampered by cold, most of the Cheyennes died on the journey. After escaping from Fort Robinson in Nebraska, Dull Knife reached the Pine Ridge Reservation. He died in the same year that the northern Cheyenne established a reservation in their home territory in Montana. (LCJ)

A chief of the Northern Cheyenne, Dull Knife resisted the movement of his people to Indian Country. *National Archives.*

BIBLIOGRAPHY

Brown, Dee. *Bury My Heart at Wounded Knee: An Indian History of the American West*. New York: Holt, Rinehart & Winston, 1970.

Dummer's War of 1722

The first steps toward Dummer's War were made in the Treaty of Utrecht, which ended **Queen Anne's War** in 1713. Under the terms of the treaty, France gave to England the territory of Acadia (in modern-day Nova Scotia). With the support of French Jesuits, including Father Rasles, the Abenaki went to war to defend Acadia, for it was mostly theirs. Dummer's War continued for three years, until most of the eastern band of Abenaki, named the Pigwacket, were killed. Even though the eastern band of Abenaki signed a treaty, the western band continued fighting under Chief Grey Lock until 1727.

BIBLIOGRAPHY

Calloway, Colin G. *The Abenaki*. New York: Chelsea House Publishers, 1989.

Duro v. Reina (1990)

The 1990 Supreme Court ruling in *Duro v. Reina* forbade any Indian tribe from exercising criminal jurisdiction over an Indian from another tribe, even if that Indian lives on the tribe's reservation. Albert Duro, a California Indian, murdered a 14-year-old boy on the Pima Reservation in Arizona. The Pima courts convicted him on misdemeanor firearms charges. After appeals, the Supreme Court overturned this decision, thus creating a jurisdictional void because neither state, tribe, nor federal government had jurisdiction in such cases. Congress overturned this decision in 1991. (SRC)

BIBLIOGRAPHY

Newton, Nell Jessup. "Commentary: Permanent Legislation to Correct *Duro v. Reina*." *American Indian Law Review* 17 (1991): 89–97.

Quinn, William W., Jr. "Intertribal Integration: The Ethnological Argument in *Duro v. Reina*." *Ethnohistory* 40, no. 1 (1993): 38–57.

E

John Echohawk (1945–)

John Echohawk (Pawnee), a founding member of the Native American Rights Fund (NARF), has served as its executive director since 1977. Born in Albuquerque, New Mexico, August 11, 1945, he received the B.A. (1967) and J.D. (1970) from the University of New Mexico, where he was the first graduate of its special program to train Indian lawyers. He is recognized as one of the 100 most influential lawyers in America by the *National Law Journal*. (AMM)

BIBLIOGRAPHY

Chambers, Reid Peyton and John E. Echohawk. "Implementing the Winters Doctrine of Indian Reserved Water Rights: Producing Indian Water and Economic Development without Injuring non-Indian Water Users?" *Gonzaga Law Review* 27, no. 3 (spring 1992): 447–70.

Larry EchoHawk (1948–)

Larry EchoHawk (Pawnee) received a B.A. from Brigham Young University and a J.D. from the University of Utah. After serving in the military he worked as a lawyer for the California Indian Legal Service. Later he served as chief counsel for the Shoshone-Bannock tribes of the Fort Hall Reservation, Idaho. While working for the Shoshone-Bannock, EchoHawk served in the Idaho State House of Representatives from 1983 to 1986. He left to become Bannock County prosecutor. In 1990, EchoHawk was elected as Idaho's attorney general, the first Native American to be elected to a statewide office. He ran for governor in 1994, but was defeated. He is presently a professor of law at Brigham Young University. His older brother, John Echohawk, is director of the Native American Rights Fund. (AMM)

BIBLIOGRAPHY

EchoHawk, Larry. "Idaho May be Ready for a Full-Scale ADR Program." *Advocate* (Idaho) 37, no. 8 (August 1994): 7(1).

Walter R. Echo-Hawk, Jr. (1948–)

Walter R. Echo-Hawk, Jr. (Pawnee) graduated from Oklahoma State University (B.A., 1970), then attended the University of New Mexico where he earned the J.D. in 1973. He is a staff attorney with the Native American Rights Fund (NARF) in Boulder, Colorado, where he has served as codirector of NARF's American Indian Religious Freedom Project and director of the Indian Corrections Project. (AMM)

BIBLIOGRAPHY

Echo-Hawk, Walter R. "Museum Rights vs. Indian Rights: Guidelines for Assessing Competing Legal Interests in Native Cultural Resources." *New York University Review of Law and Social Change* 14, no. 2 (spring 1986): 437–53.
Quade, Vicki. "Who Owns the Past; How Native American Indian Lawyers Fight for their Ancestors' Remains and Memories." *Human Rights* 16, no. 3 (winter 1989): 24(9).

Charles Edenshaw (1839–1920)

Edenshaw, a Haida airtist also known as Tahayren ("Noise in the House"), and Nungkwigetklahls ("They Gave Ten Potlatches for Him"), is best known for his art work and his position as a tribal leader. He was elected chief of the Sta Stas Eagle clan when his uncle Eda' nsa, the famous former chief, passed away. His work as an artist was mostly seen though his carvings, which were later collected by art patrons and museums.

BIBLIOGRAPHY

Boas, Franz. *Primitive Art*. New York: Dover Publications, 1955.
Appleton, F.M., "Life and Art of Charles Edenshaw." *Canadian Geographical Journal* (July 1970): 20–25.

Education

Boarding schools for Indian children were established by missionaries as early as the 1600s. The Christian mission played a decisive role in the process of forced assimilation of American Indians in the United States. The American government worked closely with the mission in what was later called the "alliance of the gun and the bible." Reservations were allocated by the government to the different churches, which forced assimilation through the powerful tool of the school system on and off the reservations. Initially boarding schools were formed only far from Indian homelands. These schools removed children from their families, changed their appearances, taught them that their religions and everyday ways of being were not only incorrect but evil, and forbade them from speaking their native languages. The experiences of students in boarding schools in Carlisle, Pennsylvania; Albuquerque, New Mexico; Sherman, California; and a host of other places have been documented as being unsafe, oppressive, and hostile.

Although boarding schools were planned as total systems with full domination over the activities and behavior of their residents in every waking hour, the children managed to create underground networks out of the controlling gaze of the teachers in which they spoke their languages and practiced their traditions. Moreover, thrown together into these alien, frightening environments with only each other for emotional support, youth from contrasting cultures discovered that they had attitudes and experiences in common by virtue of simply being American Indians. This created a sense of camaraderie that later was conducive to the creation of political alliances and Pan Indianism.

After the **Meriam Report** of 1928 and some educational reforms, there was a change in the emphasis on where children would be educated. The government, through the **Bureau of Indian Affairs (BIA)**, established new Indian schools closer to the students' homes. The main goal, however, remained the same: to re-create the students in the form of "good" Americans. Soon after the turn of the century American-Indian children were also allowed to attend schools with nonnative students. Strategies of survival took a different turn in the 1960s when American-Indian activism, especially the influential **American Indian Movement (AIM)**, rekindled a sense of pride in Indian cultures.

American Indians also started to build their own educational institutions as alternatives to what was offered by the American system; most important among these are urban survival schools and tribal colleges. Survival schools were first established as a Native-American solution to high numbers of Indian dropouts from the American public education system. The schools, which today are present in several cities in the United States and Canada, emphasize placing control of education back into native hands. Indian self-determination in education was further developed by establishing tribal community colleges that are planned and managed by Indians. These colleges provide vocation and liberal arts education, preserve the various tribal cultures, and serve the chartering tribes. The legacy of the past, however, still haunts Indian education. Indian youth are still often caught between becoming educated in "the white man's ways" or dropping out of school to retain one's "Indianness." Nevertheless, there is a growing number of Indians who are graduating college and going on to professional schools. **See also** "Destroy the Indian and Save the Individual" Educational Policy; Indian Self-Determination and Education Assistance Act of 1975. (MS; BB)

BIBLIOGRAPHY

Deyle, D. and K. Swisher. "Research in American Indian and Alaska Native Education: From Assimilation to Self-determination." *Review of Research in Education* 22 (1997):113–94.

Duran, Eduardo and Bonnie Duran. *Native American Postcolonial Psychology*. State University of New York, 1995.

Haig-Brown, Celia. *Taking Control: Power and Contradiction in First Nations Adult Education*. Vancouver: UBC Press, 1995.

Jippenconnick, J.W., III and K. Swisher. "American Indian Education." In M.C. Alkin, ed. *Encyclopedia of Educational Research*. New York: Macmillan, 1992.

Lipka, J. and K. Stairs. "Negotiating the Culture of Indigenous Schools" [Special Issue]. *Peabody Journal of Education* 69 (1994).

Oppelt, Norman T. *The Tribally Controlled Indian Colleges: The Beginnings of Self Determination in American Indian Education*. Tsaile, AZ: Navajo Community College Press, 1990.

Pavel, M., K. Swisher, and M. Ward. "Special Focus: American Indian and Alaska Native Demographics and Educational Trends." *Minorities in Higher Education*, 13th Annual Status Report. (1995): 33–60.

Pratt, Richard Henry. *Battlefield and Classroom: Four Decades and the American Indian 1867–1904*. New Haven: Yale University Press, 1964.

Education Appropriation Act of 1897

In 1897, the Congress passed the Education Appropriation Act to accomplish two goals. The first was to bar the use of federal funds earmarked for Native American education from being used at sectarian schools. The second was to encourage the attendance of Native Americans at Indian day and industrial schools. Many of the earliest schools available to Native Americans were established by religious missionaries who had come to Christianize Indians. However, by the 1880s the **Bureau of Indian Affairs** had developed a large network of off-reservation boarding schools to help assimilate Indian children. Since Indian territory could not be taxed by state officials, Congress was left to fund these schools through appropriation acts such as this one in 1897. **See also** Assimilationist Policy; Education; Federal Indian Policy; Indian School Act of 1891.

BIBLIOGRAPHY

Deloria, Vine, Jr. and Clifford M. Lyttle. *American Indians, American Justice*. Austin: University of Texas Press, 1983.

Much of the education offered to Native Americans, such as that given to these students at the Indian Service School in Taos, New Mexico, in 1936, has been vocational in nature. *Library of Congress.*

Elk v. Wilkins (1884)

Elk v. Wilkins, 112 U.S. 94 (1884), addressed the citizenship status of American Indians. John Elk had voluntarily left his tribe (his tribal affiliation is never listed) and moved to Omaha, Nebraska. After a time, Elk registered to vote, claiming that the **Fourteenth** and Fifteenth **Amendments** gave him U.S. citizenship. His registration application was rejected by Charles Wilkins, the city registrar, on the grounds that Elk, as an Indian, was not a citizen of the United States.

The Supreme Court rejected Elk's constitutional claims, holding that Indians belonged to "alien nations." The majority decision maintained that even if individual Indians met basic citizenship requirements they still could not be enfranchised unless Congress passed a law authorizing such a change in their legal standing. Indians were awarded citizenship by Congress in the Citizenship Act of 1924. (DEW)

BIBLIOGRAPHY

Deloria, Vine, Jr. *Behind the Trail of Broken Treaties: An Indian Declaration of Independence.* Austin: University of Texas Press, 1985.

Employment Assistance Program

The Employment Assistance Program—a renamed and modified version of the Voluntary Relocation Program of the 1950s—provided job training and placement assistance to Native Americans from 1961 to 1972. The policy stemmed from Indian demands for expanded vocational training, the lack of on-reservation job opportunities, and the desire to promote greater Indian self-reliance. Although efforts were made to train and place Indians on or near reservations, Employment Assistance Program participants often had to relocate to urban areas.

The program had mixed results. Some Native Americans completed their training and secured gainful employment. Others finished training and found jobs, but their wages proved inadequate—this was particularly true in the case of single mothers. Some who relocated had difficulty adjusting to city life and suffered unemployment, poor living conditions, physical abuse, and alcoholism. Many simply returned to their home communities to unemployment or underemployment. The Employment Assistance Program ended in 1972, and elements of the program were incorporated into the 1973 Comprehensive Employment and Training Act (CETA), a consolidation of several federal job training programs. (CKR)

BIBLIOGRAPHY

MacKay, Kathryn L. "Warrior into Welder: A History of Federal Employment Programs for American Indians, 1878–1972." Ph.D. diss., University of Utah, 1987.

Sorkin, Alan L. *American Indians and Federal Aid.* Washington, DC: The Brookings Institute, 1971.

Ex Parte Crow Dog (1883)

Ex Parte Crow Dog, 109 U.S. 556 (1883), was an appeal by **Crow Dog** of a federal murder conviction for killing Spotted Tail. The men's families had already come to agreement to resolve the killing in accordance with their nation's customs (Brule Sioux). The federal attorney for Dakota Territory nevertheless prosecuted Crow Dog under U.S. law and secured a conviction in territorial court. Crow Dog's appeal was facilitated by federal money, although it is not clear why, because Spotted Tail had been a chief who favored accommodation with the United States. The Supreme Court reversed the conviction on grounds that the 1868 Sioux Treaty reserved exclusive Sioux jurisdiction over crimes among the Sioux in their own country. The Court stated that the jurisdiction provision was designed to help the Sioux "advanc[e] from the condition of a savage tribe" to become "self-governed." Congressional reaction to the case resulted in passage of the **Major Crimes Act,** 23 Stat. 362 (1885), extending exclusive federal jurisdiction over murder and six other crimes in **Indian country** generally. **See also** Guardianship. (PPE)

BIBLIOGRAPHY

Cohen, Felix S. *Handbook of Federal Indian Law.* Washington, DC: U.S. Government Printing Office, 1942.

Federal Acknowledgment of Indian Tribes

In order to be a party to the trust relationship between the federal government and Indian tribes, and thus have access to programs run by the **Bureau of Indian Affairs**, a tribe must be federally recognized. For a variety of reasons, many tribal groups either have never had federal recognition or have had that recognition removed through termination.

In 1978, the director of the Bureau of Indian Affairs, John Shappard, in consultation with numerous Indian groups, nonrecognized tribes, legislators, historians, sociologists, and legal scholars, developed guidelines for federal acknowledgment. These guidelines are used by the Federal Acknowledgment Project (FAP), a branch of the BIA, in adjudicating the claims of groups that assert they are Indian tribes but do not have federal recognition of their tribal status, for purposes of incorporating them into the federal system of Indian administration.

The criteria for acknowledgment include long-term political cohesion and self-identification as a tribe, which is mirrored by members of the dominant society. In addition, the tribe must demonstrate its Indian ancestry and provide the FAP with tribal rolls and an explanation of membership criteria.

Between 1978 and 1997, 185 petitions for recognition were filed with the FAP. Fifteen petitions were denied during this period, and 14 groups were acknowledged through the administrative process (eight have been recognized congressionally).

In 1992 and 1993, the retired BIA director Shappard testified to congressional committees that the FAP's process was costly, slow, and complicated, and that its decisions were highly subjective. In response, Congress enacted an expedited process that allowed terminated tribes to have quicker access to acknowledgment proceedings. The criteria for acknowledgment, however, were little changed. **See also** House Concurrent Resolution 108; Termination Resolution. (RAC)

BIBLIOGRAPHY

Deloria, Vine, Jr. *American Indian Policy in the Twentieth Century.* Norman, OK: University of Oklahoma Press 1985.

Federal Indian Policy

Federal Indian law and policy is a vast, complex body of statutes, court decisions, and administrative regulations pertaining to relations between the indigenous peoples of this land and the governments of the United States and the individual states. The laws and customs of the different nations that preexisted the formation of the United States are not part of federal Indian law, except insofar as a statute, court decision, or agency rule may have taken notice of them. Within federal Indian law, the existence of native nations is legally defined by the federal government, not by the native nations themselves. Thus, a given nation (referred to as a "tribe") is said to be "recognized" or "unrecognized" by the federal government.

The foundation of federal Indian law is colonialism. Prior to the formation of the United States, the crowns of various colonial powers laid claim through the "doctrine of discovery" to the lands of the American continent. The colonial powers developed from this the doctrine of "discovery," which stated that any Christian prince who discovered lands unknown to any other Christian prince could claim sovereignty over these lands. This doctrine was adhered to by all colonial powers of the region, and was adopted for the United States by the Supreme Court in 1823, in *Johnson v. McIntosh*, 8 Wheat 543.

The framework of federal Indian law is loosely based on the United States Constitution, which mentions Indians twice: once, in Art. 1, sec. 2, cl. 3, to exclude "Indians not taxed" from the population base for apportioning representatives and taxes; and once more, in Art. 1, sec. 8, cl. 3, to give Congress power to "regulate Commerce . . . with the Indian tribes." There is no constitutional provision for general federal or state power over indigenous nations. The indigenous nations were not part of the formation of the Constitution and in this sense were not part of the federal system at all.

The initial phase of federal Indian law dealt primarily with relations between native peoples and colonists: federal law provided for treaties about land and trade and established agencies for ongoing negotiations. Overall authority for these federal activities was in the secretary of war. The first Congress passed a **"trade and intercourse act,"** 1 Stat. 137 (1790), to license traders and restrict transactions between settlers and native peoples. In 1831, the Supreme Court declared in *Chero-*

kee Nation v. Georgia, 5 Pet. 1, that native nations were not "foreign states," and suggested they were "domestic dependent nations." As such, the Court said, they had a right to "occupy" their lands, but the United States "assert a title independent of their will." The next year, in *Worcester v. Georgia*, 6 Pet. 515 (1832), the Court decided that relations with native nations were "exclusively" the province of the federal government, and outside the power of the states.

The first forms of federal intervention into internal affairs of native nations began during this early period. In 1819, Congress appropriated a "civilization fund," 3 Stat. 516, for education to "introduc[e] among them the habits and arts of civilization." With this act, and with the creation of the **Bureau of Indian Affairs (BIA)** in the War Department in 1824 (transferred to the Interior in 1849), began the tortuous history of federal programs designed to transform native societies into an ideal of Christian civilization.

Even as federal programs to "civilize" Indians were promulgated, other policies were aimed at forcible removal. President Andrew Jackson pushed an **Indian Removal Act,** 4 Stat. 411 (**1830**), through Congress, forcing the Cherokee and other indigenous nations to choose between giving up their own society and dispersing within the states or moving to a "reservation" west of the Mississippi River. Some remained, most marched west.

By the middle of the nineteenth century, federal policies of internal transformation and external removal were in full swing. Though contradictory on the surface, the combined purpose of the two aspects of federal Indian law was to eradicate the basic features of native nations as they existed prior to colonialism. Federal policies especially targeted land. Land cessions were a key piece of every treaty; often the offer of "education" was in exchange for land, to provide a means of training Indians to live individually on small parcels instead of communally on large terrain. "**Reservations**" were intended as an intermediary form of landholding that would give way to individual property; meanwhile rations and education would be provided.

Dominant forces in Congress during this period became increasingly impatient with the reservation system. A coalition of expansionists, eager to gain control of remaining communal land in native hands, and "humanitarians," eager to see Indians "progress" toward civilization, united to "break the tribal mass" by means of land allotment. The General Allotment Act of 1887, 24 Stat. 388 (**Dawes Act**) expanded earlier sporadic practices of individualizing land ownership among Indians into a full-blown national scheme to divide all Indian lands into individual and family-sized holdings, opening the remainder to non-Indian settlement. Indian citizenship was enacted in 1924, 43 Stat. 253.

Allotment was the "backbone of federal Indian law" well into the twentieth century. By 1934, however, it was clear to most people that the allotment system was not going to result in disappearance of the "Indian problem." True enough, Indian land had disappeared: nearly 100 million acres were gone;

and of the remaining Indian land, about half was desert or semi-desert. The New Deal for Indians culminated in 1934 with the Indian Reorganization Act (IRA), 48 Stat. 984. This law formally ended the allotment era, provided that land could be added to remaining reservations, established educational and finance programs, and instituted an overall policy of Indian "self-government" within federal Indian law. The general response to the act was favorable, especially since the 1928 report of the Institute for Government Research (known as the **Meriam Report**) had chronicled the statistics of despair in Indian country and failure in federal Indian administration.

A central part of Indian "reorganization" was the creation of incorporated tribal councils as the vehicle for "self-government." While these were a step away from direct federal administration of all aspects of Indian life, they were not a step toward restoration of indigenous nations in their own right. The denial of sovereignty to native nations that began with colonialism continued under federal Indian law even into Indian "self-government." **The Indian Reorganization Act** built on the foundation of "domestic dependent nation" a structure of "tribal government." The "Indian" in federal Indian law continued to be defined by federal standards and policies. The Indian Reorganization Act tribal councils represented a more subtle and sophisticated system of federal Indian law than had existed previously. As the Senate report of the act declared, a central purpose was "To stabilize the tribal organization of Indian tribes by vesting such tribal organizations with real, though limited, authority, and by prescribing conditions which must be met by such tribal organizations."

In 1946, an **Indian Claims Commission**, 60 Stat. 1049, was created to award compensation for stolen lands and broken treaties. In the process, however, the commission also foreclosed the possibility of restoring land or recognizing native title to land. Once again, "humanitarian" and expansionist faces appeared together in federal Indian law. In the 1950s, Congress entered another forceful expansionist phase, encouraging a BIA "relocation program" to entice Indians to move from reservations to cities, permitting a number of states to assert civil and criminal jurisdiction over Indian land (P.L. 280, 67 Stat. 588); and, in House Concurrent Resolution 108, 76 Stat. B132, the **Termination Resolution**, calling for "termination" of Indian reservations. By 1962, "termination," presented as "freedom from federal supervision," had been imposed on 61 communities. Some of these were later re-"recognized."

Federal Indian law continues to teeter back and forth between policy modes, though still on the same foundation of ultimate federal control of Indian land. Since 1970, when President Richard Nixon formally renounced "termination" and called for a policy of "**self-determination**," federal Indian law has been aimed at maximizing local participation in "tribal management." In 1975, Congress established a mechanism for **tribal governments** to contract for federal services otherwise channeled through the Bureau of Indian Affairs (P.L. 93–638, 88 Stat. 2203). Philip Deloria's assessment in "The

Era of Indian Self-Determination: An Overview," in *Indian Self Rule*, edited by Kenneth R. Philp, may serve as a general summary of the concept of "self-government" in federal Indian law and policy: "The transition of recent federal policy from termination to self-determination reflects only a tactical shift in the fundamental commitment of the society to bring Indians into the mainstream, not a movement toward a true recognition of a permanent tribal right to exist." (PPE)

BIBLIOGRAPHY
Ball, Milner S. "Constitution, Court, Indian Tribes." *Am. Bar Foundation Research J.* 59, no. 1 (winter, 1987): 1–140.
Cohen, Felix S. *Handbook of Federal Indian Law*. Washington, DC: U.S. Government Printing Office, 1942.
Deloria, Vine, Jr. and Clifford Lytle. *The Nations Within*. New York: Pantheon, 1984.
Forbes, Jack D., ed. *The Indian in America's Past*. Englewood Cliffs, NJ: Prentice-Hall, 1964.
National Lawyers Guild. *Rethinking Indian Law*. New York: National Lawyers Guild, Committee on Native American Struggles, 1982.
Newcomb, Steven T. "The Evidence of Christian Nationalism in Federal Indian Law: The Doctrine of Discovery, *Johnson v. McIntosh*, and Plenary Power." *NYU Rev. of Law and Social Change* XX, no. 2 (1993): 303–41.
Philp, Kenneth R., ed. *Indian Self-Rule*. Salt Lake City: Howe Brothers, 1986.
Purcha, Francis Paul, ed. *Documents of United States Indian Policy*. Lincoln: University of Nebraska Press, 1990.
Savage, Mark. "Native Americans and the Constitution: The Original Understanding." *American Indian Law Rev.* 16 (1991): 57–118.
Washburn, Wilcomb E. *Red Man's Land, White Man's Law*, 2nd ed. Norman: University of Oklahoma Press, 1995.

Felix Cohen's *Handbook of Federal Indian Law*

More than half a century after its initial appearance, Felix Cohen's *Handbook of Federal Indian Law* remains one of the most influential works in the field of federal Indian law, not only in terms of theoretical constructs, but in terms of real-world application. First published in 1942 by the Department of the Interior and reissued twice, the *Handbook* was intended as a practical guide for lawyers, judges, and other specialists dealing with the complex, confusing, and often contradictory facts and ideas comprising federal Indian law.

Cohen's treatise was the first attempt to organize and gather in one place the principles of Indian law that had evolved over time in court decisions, treaties, and acts of the executive and of Congress. The *Handbook* gave judges and government officials a resource that helped them make sense of the overwhelming amount of complex and difficult material relating to federal Indian law. The theoretical impact of the volume has been immeasurable. Whether scholars agree or disagree with Cohen's interpretations, almost all make reference to his work and use it as a starting point. The *Handbook* is required reading for any serious student of federal Indian law.

The practical influence of the book has also been immense. The Handbook has been cited in well over 100 opinions issued by state and federal courts, and an untold number of government officials have used it as a reference when making policy decisions. Although the list of titles relating to federal Indian law has grown substantially in the last two decades, none have come close to Cohen's masterpiece in terms of visibility or impact. **See also** Federal Indian Policy. (GTH)

BIBLIOGRAPHY
Cohen, Felix S. *Handbook of Federal Indian Law*. Washington, DC: U.S. Government Printing Office, 1942; Charlottesville, VA: Merrill, 1982.
Deloria, Vine, Jr. and Clifford M. Lytle. *American Indians, American Justice*. Austin: University of Texas Press, 1983.
Wilkinson, Charles F. *American Indians, Time, and the Law: Native Societies in a Modern Constitutional Democracy*. New Haven, CT: Yale University Press, 1987.

Final Disposition of Affairs of Five Civilized Tribes Act of 1906

On April 28, 1906, Congress authorized the sale at public auction of all unallotted surplus land in Oklahoma previously held in trust for the Cherokee, Choctaw, Chickasaw, Creek, and Seminole tribes (known as the **Five Civilized Tribes**). Monies collected by the federal government for the sale of this surplus land was to be held in interest-bearing accounts for the civilized tribes. The tribal governments of these nations were to be disbanded and the land to come under the jurisdiction of the State of Oklahoma. **See also** Citizenship Act of 1901; Five Civilized Tribes Heirship Act of 1918. (AMM)

BIBLIOGRAPHY
Report of Commissioner of Indian Affairs Cato Sells, September 21, 1914. *The American Indian and the United States: A Documentary History*. Wilcomb E. Washburn Smithsonian Institution (Westport Covert Grenwood Press): 843–44.

First Seminole War

Spain regained control of Florida from the British as a result of the Treaty of Paris (1783). When the British withdrew, they encouraged the Seminoles living in the area to attack Americans in southeast Georgia. They also encouraged black slaves to run away from their white masters and find safe haven with the Indians. The United States wanted to acquire Florida, hoping to control the runaway slaves and Indians, but did not want to find themselves fighting the British (War of 1812) on one side and Spain on the other.

Nothing was done to control these problems, and the raids continued. The response to the Indians came on November 21, 1817. Major General Andrew Jackson was sent to handle the Indians "in a manner he may judge best." Jackson, with the support of the Creeks, moved east, destroying any Indian resistance in his way. The lands that were taken by Jackson were quickly returned to Spain by President Monroe. The Spanish government realized that the wise move would be to transfer Florida to the United States. This was completed by the treaty in 1819. The Seminoles and other Indians still remained in Florida, much to the white man's displeasure. (MRC)

BIBLIOGRAPHY

Buckmaster, Henrietta. *The Seminole Wars*. New York: Crowell-Collier, 1966.

Miller, David H., ed. *Treaties and Other International Acts of the United States of America*. 8 vols. Buffalo: W. S. Hein, 1977.

Patrick, Rembert W. *Florida Fiasco: Rampant Rebels on the Georgia-Florida Border, 1810–1815*. Athens: University of Georgia Press, 1954.

Fishing and Hunting Treaty Rights

Fishing and hunting have been central to most Native-American cultures. In addition to providing food, clothing, shelter, and tools for Indian peoples, these activities occupied an important place in the economic, social, and spiritual lives of many native groups.

Accordingly, many of the treaties made between the federal government and Native-American nations included provisions securing traditional Indian rights to hunt and fish both on and off their reservations. Although the federal government believed that Indians would ultimately assimilate into mainstream American society, treaty commissioners generally recognized that tribes would not sign agreements that failed to protect their access to traditional subsistence resources. Thus, to soften the shock of land cessions and ease the expected transition to Euro-American "civilization," many treaties explicitly reserved Indian rights to hunt, fish, and gather on ceded lands. The 1789 Wyandot Treaty, for example, stated that "individuals of the said nation shall be at liberty to hunt within the territory ceded to the United States, without hindrance or molestation, so long as they demean themselves peaceably, and offer no injury or annoyance to any of the subjects or citizens of the said United States." The 1837, 1842, and 1857 treaties with the Lake Superior Chippewas (Ojibways) guaranteed "The privilege of hunting, fishing, and gathering the wild rice, upon the lands, the rivers and the lakes included in the territory ceded . . . during the pleasure of the United States." Treaties with other tribes had similar provisions. After Congress ended formal treaty making in 1871, executive orders, federal statutes, and congressionally approved agreements occasionally secured tribal hunting and fishing rights on ceded lands.

Controversies over fishing and hunting rights have revolved around the differing Indian-white expectations for and interpretations of the treaties themselves. Whereas the federal government foresaw an eventual end to off-reservation hunting and fishing as "civilization" took root, most Native Americans believed that the treaties protected their rights perpetually. As Yakama fisherman David Sohappy Sr. explained in 1978, his ancestors had been told that their 1855 treaty would endure "as long as that mountain [Mt. Adams] stood there, as long as the sun rose in the east and long as the grass grows green in the spring and rivers flow. To me, that meant forever, not to be abrogated or changed or done away with any other way."

The canons of construction established by the Supreme Court dictate that treaties must be interpreted as the Indians would have understood them; that all doubtful or ambiguous terms must be resolved in favor of the Indians; and that treaties in general must be liberally construed to the benefit of the Indians. In practice, however, the courts have only considered express treaty or statutory language reserving off-reservation hunting and fishing rights. Since much of this language is ambiguous, the existence and scope of these rights remains a subject of contention between state and tribal governments.

The central issue in most state-tribal disputes has been the extent to which the states can regulate Indian hunting and fishing rights. Faced with declining stocks of fish and game, as well as growing pressure from sport and commercial interests, state governments began implementing regulatory programs that generally favored sportsmen in the name of conservation. Native-American hunters and fishers, in turn, found their off-reservation subsistence activities increasingly restricted by a web of state laws governing illegal gear, trespassing, licensing, closed seasons, prohibited areas, catch limits, and the sale of game or fish. When Indians hunted or fished in violation of these laws—either knowingly or unknowingly—state authorities often arrested and jailed them for poaching.

Many Native Americans also had their guns or gear confiscated, adding to the economic and cultural hardships posed by the inability to take traditional resources for subsistence, ceremony, and sale. In their defense, the Indians argued that federal treaties protected their rights to hunt and fish without interference from the states. State courts typically dismissed native assertions of treaty rights, and the federal government rarely intervened on behalf of Indian defendants. In *Ward v. Race Horse* (1896), the Supreme Court held that Wyoming's game laws superseded Shoshone-Bannock treaty rights because of the Constitution's "equal footing" doctrine. In the Pacific Northwest, state courts also used the treaty language "in common with the citizens of the Territory" to contend that Indians had only the same rights as non-Indians and were thus equally subject to state laws. Treaty tribes in Washington and Oregon repeatedly challenged this interpretation in the federal courts, and fishing rights cases reached the Supreme Court seven times during the twentieth century. On each occasion, the Court affirmed the existence of Indian treaty rights but failed to foreclose fully the states' power to regulate them. Decades of litigation over fishing and hunting rights climaxed in the 1970s and 1980s.

Following a series of Indian "fish-ins" and increasingly violent confrontations with state authorities, the United States filed suit on behalf of 14 Northwest treaty tribes. In *United States v. Washington* (1974), better known as the "Boldt decision," federal district court Judge George Boldt held that the phrase "in common" gave the tribes the right to harvest 50 percent of the allowable salmon catch and to participate in management of the resource. Five years later, the Ojibways and Ottawas of northern Michigan won recognition of their treaty rights in *United States v. Michigan* (1979). And in 1983 the U.S. Court of Appeals' ruling in *Lac Courte Oreilles Band v. Voigt* affirmed the off-reservation rights of the Lake Superior Chippewas. Although each of these decisions triggered a vicious anti-Indian backlash and strong state efforts to obstruct or overturn them, the various state and tribal governments involved have gradually moved away from litigation as a solution to the controversy. The resurgence of states' rights sentiments in the Supreme Court has again raised the specter of abrogation, but the present political climate emphasizes the negotiation of differences and the cooperative management of wildlife resources.

The current criteria for state regulation of Indian treaty rights depend on the particular treaty or statute and the various federal, state, and tribal interests involved. Generally speaking, tribes may regulate on-reservation hunting and fishing free from state interference. In some cases, however, tribal governments lack the authority to prevent non-Indians from hunting or fishing on reservation lands that are not owned by Indians or by the tribe itself. Furthermore, some federal conservation laws (e.g., the Eagle Protection Act) supersede both on- and off-reservation treaty rights. State governments may only regulate off-reservation hunting and fishing when they present a sufficient conservation or safety risk. To justify such regulation, the state must demonstrate that a significant hazard exists, that the state cannot meet its objectives by regulating non-Indians alone, and that the regulation represents the least restrictive alternative available. Poor environmental quality and dwindling stocks of fish and game pose the most serious threats to Indian hunting and fishing rights. In the Pacific Northwest, for example, salmon runs have declined precipitously because of decades of overfishing, logging, irrigation, industrial pollution, and hydroelectric development. All of the great aboriginal fishing sites on the Columbia River have been inundated by dams, and intertribal disputes over allocation of the Indians' shrinking 50 percent share have triggered a fresh wave of litigation on Puget Sound. Although Phase II of the Boldt decision affirmed the treaty tribes' rights to protection of the resource, powerful political and economic interests have slowed the implementation of effective salmon recovery plans. Meanwhile, in the Great Lakes region, mercury contamination endangers the health of Indian and non-Indian fishermen alike.

Whatever the future holds, it seems certain that Native Americans will continue to fight. To many Indians, the right to fish and hunt represents the right to remain Indian, becoming an issue of **cultural identity** and tribal sovereignty. (AHF)

BIBLIOGRAPHY

American Friends Service Committee. *Uncommon Controversy: Fishing Rights of the Muckleshoot, Puyallup, and Nisqually Indians*. Seattle: University of Washington Press, 1970.

Cohen, Fay G. *Treaties on Trial: The Continuing Controversy over Northwest Indian Fishing Rights*. Seattle: University of Washington Press, 1986.

Doherty, Robert. *Disputed Waters: Native Americans and the Great Lakes Fishery*. Lexington: The University of Kentucky Press, 1990.

Hornstein, Donald T. "Indian Fishing Rights Return to Spawn: Toward Environmental Protection of Treaty Fisheries." *Oregon Law Review* 61 (winter 1982): 93–122.

Institute for Natural Progress. "In Usual and Accustomed Places: Contemporary American Indian Fishing Rights Struggles." In M. Annette Jaimes, ed. *The State of Native America: Colonization, Genocide, and Resistance*. Boston: South End Press, 1992.

Landau, Jack L. "Empty Victories: Indian Treaty Fishing Rights in the Pacific Northwest." *Environmental Law* 10 (1980): 413–56.

Reynolds, Laurie. "Indian Hunting and Fishing Rights: The Role of Tribal Sovereignty and Prevention." *North Carolina Law Review* 62 (1984): 743–93.

Satz, Ronald M. *Chippewa Treaty Rights: The Reserved Rights of Wisconsin's Chippewa Indians in Historical Perspective*. Eau Claire: Wisconsin Academy of Sciences, Arts, and Letters, 1991.

Senior, Jeanie. "Indian Activist Sohappy Dies." *The (Portland) Oregonian* (May 9, 1941): A1.

Wilkins, David E. "Indian Treaty Rights: Sacred Entitlements or 'Temporary Privileges?'" *American Indian Culture and Research Journal* 20, no. 1. (1996): 87–129.

Fish-Ins

Starting in the mid-1950s, Native Americans in the Pacific Northwest staged "fish-ins" to challenge and protest state regulation of their treaty fishing rights. Modeled after the "sit-ins" of the black civil rights movement, these demonstrations involved the deliberate violation of state laws and often entailed violent confrontations with game wardens, police, and hostile white fishermen. Indian participants risked losing their boats, nets, and fish, and many faced criminal prosecution and imprisonment. But the fish-ins ultimately achieved their objective of securing test cases and seizing national attention. **See also** Adams, Hank; Fishing and Hunting Treaty Rights; Frank, Billy, Jr. (AHF)

BIBLIOGRAPHY

Cohen, Fay G. *Treaties on Trial: The Continuing Controversy over Northwest Indian Fishing Rights*. Seattle: University of Washington Press, 1986.

Josephy, Alvin, Jr. *Now That the Buffalo's Gone: A Study of Today's American Indians*. Norman: University of Oklahoma Press, 1984.

Five Civilized Tribes

The Cherokee, Chickasaw, Creek, Choctaw, and Seminole became known as the "Five Civilized Tribes" because of their early adoption of European social and political norms. The first contact the tribes had with Europeans was in 1540 when Hernando de Soto left a trail of death and destruction across the Southeast. During the 1600s these tribes began trading with the British and French. The **American Revolution** saw the tribes allied with the British. In the Treaty of Paris, which ended the Revolution, the British made no provisions for their Indian allies.

Euro-American emigrants moving into the Southeast in the 1800s found the region occupied by the Five Civilized Tribes. The tribes were agrarian, living in permanent settlements; they worked large farms, lived in European-style houses, sent their children to school, had adopted European dress, owned black slaves, and had become Christians.

Removal of the southeastern tribes became an official national policy under President Andrew Jackson with the passage of the **Indian Removal Act of 1830**. The Five Civilized Tribes had largely assimilated into the Euro-American world; they were quite aware of their treaty rights and stubbornly resisted removal. The state of Georgia attempted to take Cherokee lands beginning in 1828. The Cherokee took Georgia to the U.S. Supreme Court in two landmark cases, *Cherokee Nation v Georgia*, 30 U.S. 1 (1831), **and** *Worcester v. State of Georgia*. 31 U.S. 515 (1832). The Court ruled that tribes were domestic dependent nations and tribal lands could only be ceded to the United States. The Court also ruled that tribes were distinct political entities with territorial boundaries within which their authority was exclusive.

President Jackson disregarded the Court's decision and began removing tribes west of the Mississippi. The Five Civilized Tribes had a choice—they could stay in the South and submit to state law or they could move west. Eventually more than 60,000 members of these five tribes were removed to what is now Oklahoma, Arkansas, and Kansas. Part of this relocation was the forced march of 18,000 Cherokees on the **Trail of Tears** during the winter of 1838–1839, when 4,000 members of the tribe died of disease, exposure, and starvation.

The Five Civilized Tribes have grown and prospered. In the 1990s, Oklahoma had the largest Native American population in the country. Three of the largest tribes in the United States are the Cherokee, Choctaw, and Creek. The original tribes, still identified as the Five Civilized Tribes, continue to be perceived by many to have close ties to Euro-American culture. **See also** *Cherokee Phoenix*; *Cherokee Republic*; Civil War; Final Disposition of Affairs of Five Civilized Tribes Act of 1906; Indian Territory; Sequoyah; Treaty of New Echota (1835). (MM)

BIBLIOGRAPHY

Josephy, Alvin M. *The Indian Heritage of America*. Boston: Houghton Mifflin, 1991.

Sturtevant, William C., ed. *History of Indian-White Relations*. Handbook of North American Indians, vol. 4. Washington, DC: Smithsonian Institution, 1988.

Viola, Herman J. *After Columbus: The Smithsonian Chronicle of the North American Indians*. Washington, DC: Smithsonian Institution, 1990.

Five Civilized Tribes Citizenship Act of 1901

In 1901, Congress passed the Five Civilized Tribes Citizenship Act, which made every Native American in the **Indian Territory** (now Oklahoma) a United States citizen. This measure ended the campaign to destroy the Indian exclusiveness of the territory by instead destroying Indian national identity and tribal **sovereignty**. The **tribal governments** and national councils were allowed to continue until the lands were liquidated, subject to the approval of the U.S. government. (MR)

BIBLIOGRAPHY

Debo, Angie. *And Still the Waters Run: The Betrayal of the Five Civilized Tribes*. Princeton, NJ: Princeton University Press, 1940.

Prucha, Francis Paul. *The Great Father: The United States Government and the American Indian*. abridged ed. Lincoln: University of Nebraska Press, 1984.

Five Civilized Tribes Heirship Act of 1918

This act gave jurisdiction to the probate court of the state of Oklahoma to settle the estates of members of the **Five Civilized Tribes** (Cherokee, Creek, Seminole, Chickasaw, and Choctaw). Specifically, the act called for the disbursement of lands only to full-blooded heirs of deceased allottees. Generally, the decision of who would inherit allotted lands was a function of the federal government or the individual tribe. The Five Civilized Tribes Heirship Act of 1918 was the first in a series of acts to specifically give an exception to those general rules. **See also** Allotment.

BIBLIOGRAPHY

Cohen, Felix S. *Felix Cohen's Handbook of Federal Indian Law*. Charlottesville, VA: Mitchie, Bobbs-Merrill, 1982; Ft. Lauderdale, FL: Five Rings Press, 1986.

Five Nations Neutrality Policy

On August 2, 1775, the Iroquois League adopted an official position of neutrality toward the belligerents in the **American Revolution**. The neutrality policy was both controversial and contentious for the Five Nations. On May 20, 1776, the agreement was shattered when a combined force of British and Mohawk warriors defeated an American force at the Battle of the Cedars. Shortly thereafter, members of the Oneida, Tuscarora, and Stockbridge Christian tribes formed an Indian company under American command. A new council meeting was held to discuss the neutrality policy, but the Oneida and Tuscarora boycotted the meeting. The Seneca, who had favored neutrality reluctantly, agreed to join the Mohawks in supporting the British. The split in ranks of the confederacy and the decision of two nations to join Britain resulted in General George Washington announcing at the end of the war that the Iroquois were a "conquered province." (AMM)

BIBLIOGRAPHY

Jennings, Francis, ed. *The History and Culture of Iroquois Diplomacy: An Interdisciplinary Guide to the Treaties of the Six Nations and Their Leagues*. Syracuse, NY: Syracuse University Press, 1985.

O'Brien, Sharon. *American Indian Tribal Governments*. Norman: University of Oklahoma, 1989.

Forced Assimilation

Forced assimilation was a set of policies used by the American government to destroy Native-American traditions and societies by recreating the individuals as indistinguishable Americans to achieve control over the continental lands. Treaties that were signed with Indian nations recognized their status as sovereign entities. Later, when the United States wished to practice continuous sovereignty across the continent, native sovereignty came to be known as "the Indian problem" and policies of forced assimilation were imposed. It was hoped that by destroying tribal cultures and nations' ties to their traditional lands, native identities would disappear and the individuals would be assimilated into the American melting pot.

A host of policies were developed to achieve assimilation. Children were taken to boarding schools far away from home and were taught in words and acts that their traditions were not only wrong but evil. Bureaucrats estimated that within five or six years American-Indian cultures would be erased and children would be easily assimilated into the white society. The General Allotment Act of 1887 liquidated many Indian nations and their ties with traditional lands. At the close of the nineteenth century a range of indigenous spiritual practices were banned, including the Lakota Sun Dance and the Potlatch ceremonies of the nations of the Pacific Northwest. In 1924 American citizenship was imposed on Native Americans, and in the 1950s the Relocation policy moved American Indians from reservations to American cities. Although the policies of forced assimilation caused tremendous damage to individuals, families, and tribes, many of the traditions were kept alive, sometimes secretly. Since the 1960s, increasing efforts have been made to bring back ceremonies, traditions, and cultures and to rebuild communities. (MS)

BIBLIOGRAPHY

Jaimes, M. Annette, ed. *The State of Native America: Genocide, Colonization and Resistance*. South End Press, 1992.
Nabokov, Peter. *Native American Testimony, 1492–1992*. Penguin Books, 1992.

Fourteenth Amendment

Adopted in 1868, the Fourteenth Amendment to the Constitution of the United States defined American citizenship for the first time as "all persons born or naturalized in the United States, and subject to the jurisdiction thereof." It specifically excluded "Indians not taxed" as persons to be counted in determining representation in the House of Representatives. It also guaranteed constitutional "privileges or immunities," "due process of law," and "equal protection of the law" to all citizens of the United States. Since Native Americans were members of "domestic, dependent nations," they were not considered to be citizens unless they left their tribes and took on the habits of "civilization."

Since the mid-nineteenth century, federal officials had conferred token citizenship on Native Americans as a concession for complying with removal and **allotment** legislation. By 1906, Native Americans in the former **Indian Territory** received constitutional protection and privileges, at least in theory. *United States v. Nice* (1916) and World War I forced the federal government to extend citizenship to more Native Americans. Finally, in the **General Citizenship Act of 1924**, Congress proclaimed that all noncitizen Indians would be granted citizenship. However, it was not until 1968, in the

Indian Civil Rights Act, that the rights and privileges promised in the Fourteenth Amendment were applied to Indians within Indian tribes. (KJB)

BIBLIOGRAPHY

Lee, R. Alton. "Indian Citizenship and the Fourteenth Amendment." *South Dakota History* 4 (Spring 1974): 196–221.
Stein, Gary. "The Indian Citizenship Act of 1924." *New Mexico Historical Review* 47 (July 1972): 257–74.

Billy Frank, Jr. (1931–)

Nisqually activist Billy Frank Jr. has been a prominent figure in the Northwest Indian fishing rights controversy since the 1950s. His involvement in fish-ins and test cases helped set the stage for *United States v. Washington*. He now works through the Northwest Indian Fisheries Commission to foster cooperative management and to reconcile tribal-state differences without litigation. (AHF)

BIBLIOGRAPHY

American Friends Service Committee. *Uncommon Controversy: Fishing Rights of the Muckleshoot, Puyallup, and Niqually Indians*. Seattle: University of Washington Press, 1970.
Cohen, Fay G. *Treaties on Trial: The Continuing Controversy over Northwest Indian Fishing Rights*. Seattle: University of Washington Press, 1986.

French and Indian War (1754–1763)

The last of four conflicts between France and Great Britain for commercial and territorial control of North America (the other clashes were **King William's War,** 1689–1697; **Queen Anne's War,** 1702–1713; and **King George's War,** 1744–1748), the French and Indian War began when a group of Virginia militia upset the shaky balance of power between the two colonial powers and the Iroquois (**Six Nations**) Confederacy. The confederacy, a defensive alliance among the Mohawk, Seneca, Cayuga, Onondaga, and Oneida, had established an uneasy trading relationship with French and British colonists and had managed for more than 100 years to coexist with the colonial powers by diplomatically playing the one against the other.

Iroquois neutrality during past imperial wars had forced other Native American nations to choose sides based on their own needs and goals. The defeat in 1754 of a Virginian militia unit (which had tried to force French troops out of a fort on the Ohio River) appeared to the Indians a sign of British weakness, and many Indians decided to ally themselves with the French. In the North, French allies included the Chippewas, Ottawas, Miamis, Abenakis, Caughnawagas (Mission Iroquois), Wyandots, Shawnees, and Western Delawares. In the South, French colonial officials believed they could count on the support of the Creek and Choctaw and perhaps a Cherokee faction. During the first few years of the conflict, British colonists, unable to convince the Iroquois to join them (with the exception of the Mohawks), relied on their own resources with the help of the Chickasaws and approximately 600 Cherokee warriors in the South.

Unsuccessful in defending themselves against raids by French and Indians, many English settlers withdrew east of the Allegheny Mountains. The future of Anglo-America looked dim. By 1758, however, British colonists received much needed assistance with the arrival of British troops from England. Their blockade of French ports in North America seriously affected France and her Native American allies. Quickly realizing the futility of continuing the conflict without adequate supplies, French Indian allies returned to their villages. By 1760, British military success over the French strongholds of Quebec and Montreal concluded the war in North America. The peace treaty, which went into effect in 1763, gave Great Britain the imperial victory, enlarging territorial holdings at the expense of Native Americans, and causing British and colonial officials to formulate a centralized Indian policy. **See also** Cornplanter; Five Nations Neutrality Policy. (KJB)

Bibliography

Jacobs, Wilbur R. *Dispossessing the American Indian: Indians and Whites on the Colonial Frontier.* New York, 1972.

Nammack, Georgiana C. *Fraud, Politics, and the Dispossession of the Indians.* Norman: University of Oklahoma Press, 1969.

Peck, Howard H. *The Colonial Wars, 1689–1762.* Chicago: University of Chicago Press, 1964.

Philbrick, Francis S. *The Rise of the West, 1754–1830.* New York, Harper & Row 1965.

Friends of the Indian

The Friends of the Indian was created in 1879 as a Pan-Indian organization consisting primarily of Euro-Americans. In a series of conferences held in the mid- to late-1800s at Lake Mohawk, New York, the group drafted several alternative strategies for government involvement with Native Americans.

In 1882, the group created the **Indian Rights Association**, an organization dedicated to lobbying the United States government for better Native-American rights. This organization also made several recommendations upon its formation, including asking for the total assimilation of native peoples into the whole of American society. Both the Friends of the Indian and the Indian Rights Association believed that Native Americans would be better off if they replaced their traditional lifestyle with American ideals of individualism, democracy, and Christianity. While their intentions were pure, both organizations gained opposition in these plans by native groups seeking to maintain their heritage.

By pursuing their goals, the Friends of the Indian helped usher in a number of legislative acts. The group supported the Major Crimes Act of 1885, which brought Native Americans under the jurisdiction of American law; the General Allotment Act of 1887, which replaced traditional collective land ownership practices of Indians with the concept of individualized land ownership; as well as the 1924 Indian Citizens Act, which incorporated all Native Americans into U.S. citizenship. The group also supported boarding schools as a means of providing a standard education for Native Americans and denounced Indian spiritual rituals.

Bibliography

Cornell, Steven. *The Return of the Native: American Indian Political Resurgence.* London: Oxford University Press, 1988.

Gadsden Purchase (1853)

The Gadsden Purchase was created on December 30, 1853, as a land agreement between the United States and Mexico. Negotiations took place between Mexican delegates and U.S. diplomat James Gadsden, a former South Carolina railroad promoter in the service of President James Buchanan. The document, which was ratified on June 29, 1854, gave the United States a number of territorial holdings formerly controlled by Mexico, including parts of present-day Arizona, New Mexico, and California. In all, 45,535 square miles were purchased by the United States for only $10 million. Provisions also created the present boundary line between the two nations, thereby ending boundary disputes caused by the **Treaty of Guadalupe Hidalgo** and the Mexican War. Indian nations existing within the land holdings, such as the Tohono O'odhams and the Chiricahua Apaches, were placed under the jurisdiction of the American government without much regard to their own desires. As a result, most of these Native Americans ignored the borders established by the Gadsden Purchase.

BIBLIOGRAPHY
Faulk, Odie B. *Too Far North*. Los Angeles: Westernlore Press, 1967.

Gall (1840–1894)

Gall, a talented Hunk-papa Sioux war chief and lieutenant of **Sitting Bull**, defeated Major Marcus Reno and then led a frontal attack against General George Armstrong Custer at the **Battle of the Little Bighorn** (1876). He fled with Sitting Bull to Canada but returned to the United States in 1881. He settled on the Standing Rock reservation and was instru-

Once his people were confined to the reservation, Gall, a Sioux war chief who fought with Sitting Bull, advocated assimilation. *Library of Congress.*

mental in the agreement between the Sioux and the United States in 1889 that subdivided the large Sioux reservation into several smaller ones, ceding the remaining land to the United States. **See** "You Are Living in a New Path" by Sitting Bull (1880) in Appendix 1. (AMM)

BIBLIOGRAPHY
Bleeker, Sonia. *The Sioux Indians.* New York: William Morrow, 1962.
Utley, Robert M. *The Lance and the Shield.* New York: Henry Holt, 1995.

Gaming

Gaming is a part of every Indian culture, but in today's parlance gaming is a euphemism for gambling, particularly casino gambling. Wagering on games of luck or skill is also an old Indian practice, but the neon-and-glass casino has been a white-person's game. When Indians adopted gaming in the Las Vegas and Atlantic City sense, they crossed the political radar screen of the dominant culture.

Indian gaming as a national political issue began when two California Indian tribes found a novel solution to the poverty and unemployment that characterize most reservation life in the United States. The Cabazon and Morongo Bands of Mission Indians opened bingo parlors on their land which offered jackpots in excess of the $250 allowed under California statutes regulating bingo. In addition, the Cabazon Band opened a card club that collected a "house cut" from the proceeds of poker and other card games. It was undisputed that even though the gaming took place on Indian land, most of the players were non-Indian individuals who presumably came to the reservations for the purpose of playing for higher stakes than would be allowed off the reservations. These gambling enterprises produced all of the tribes' income and most of their employment.

When the county government adjoining the reservations sought to enforce California gambling laws against the tribes, the case found its way to the United States Supreme Court. In *California v. Cabazon Band of Mission Indians* (**1987**), the Court upheld the traditional distinction between "criminal/prohibitory" statutes, which may be enforced on Indian reservations within a state, and "civil/regulatory" statutes, which may not. Because gambling was legal in California, the state could not enforce its rules regarding the conduct of games against Indian tribes on Indian land. The Court made it clear that if California had banned gambling completely, that ban could have extended to Indian land.

The *Cabazon* case set off two stampedes: Indian tribes to casinos and state officials to Congress, since most states allowed gambling in some form. Even states without government-run lotteries often permitted low-stakes gambling for charitable purposes and were therefore possibly vulnerable to the Court's holding in *Cabazon*.

Ten years after *Cabazon*, almost half of the federally recognized Indian tribes were attempting to participate in high stakes gaming. Because of high start-up costs and the necessity of hiring outside management firms, only about one-fifth of the federally recognized tribes are realizing substantial revenue gains. No other tribe has approached the success of the Mashantucket Pequots of Connecticut, an almost extinct tribe that had the good fortune to own land within easy commuting distance of New York City. The Pequots' Foxwoods Casino has employed every member of the tribe and guaranteed the education of every Pequot child from preschool through a doctorate.

The stampede of state officials seeking congressional relief proceeded with more alacrity, resulting in a federal statute a mere one year after *Cabazon*. Congress had failed to enact any of the Indian gaming regulations introduced every session since 1983, while the issues were being litigated in several federal circuits, but as soon as the Supreme Court spoke favorably to the Indian position, Congress found its voice. The **Indian Gaming Regulatory Act** (IGRA) of 1988 diminished the Indian sovereignty recognized by the *Cabazon* court.

IGRA created three classes of gaming. Only Class I—social games for prizes of minimal value or games conducted by tribal members as a part of traditional ceremonies—remained entirely within tribal control. Class II includes traditional and instant bingo as well as certain non-banking card games. Class III includes all other games and most usual casino offerings: banking card games (blackjack, baccarat, chemin de fer), slot machines, craps and pari-mutuel betting. Class II and Class III gaming are regulated by a National Indian Gaming Commission within the Department of the Interior and, of course, cannot be conducted at all unless state law allows the same class of gaming off reservations. Class III gaming cannot be conducted without a tribal-state compact governing the terms of the gaming, and the states are directed by IGRA to negotiate in good faith to achieve a tribal-state compact. "Good faith" may appear to be an uncertain standard, but there is a substantial body of labor law concerning the duty to bargain in good faith that has been accumulating in the federal courts for over 50 years. Tribes are specifically granted a right to sue in federal court a state that fails to negotiate in good faith.

While tribal-state negotiations might include such matters as wager limits, hours of operation, or location of a casino, a primary subject of negotiations in these cases is what amount of the gaming proceeds the state will take in lieu of taxes.

While these "contributions" to state government might appear at first blush to be extortion, tribes have in fact raised little concern about making payments in gaming compacts, understanding that the payments often secure an effective monopoly that the state could take away by simply legalizing all casino gambling. In addition, the payments typically come from profits, which are determined without including the wages paid out to tribal members employed in gaming. For some tribes, the gain in employment is a greater motivation than casino profits.

While most tribes have substantial motivators driving them to the bargaining table, the same is not true of states. Many states do not wish to allow casino gambling but still do not wish to criminalize it. The Mashantucket Pequots were able to enter Class III gaming because of a statute allowing certain types of organizations to raise funds by games of chance on "Las Vegas Nights." Connecticut took the position that an occasional "Las Vegas Night" does not cross the line between "criminal/prohibitory" and "civil/regulatory," but the federal courts disagreed. Other states still cling to what they consider trivial amounts of legal gambling and still seek to keep the door closed to Indian gaming.

One of the cases where a tribe and a state could not see eye to eye reached the Supreme Court in *Seminole Tribe of Florida v. Florida* (1996), where the Court held that Congress lacks the authority abrogate the states' sovereign immunity. The state of Florida, like any other sovereign, could not be sued without its permission. Therefore, the provision in IGRA allowing a tribe to sue a state in federal court for failure to negotiate in good faith over a gaming compact is unconstitutional.

Commentators are divided on the long range impact of *Seminole Tribe*. Some believe that tribes in nominally anti-gambling states, having lost the power to bring states into federal court, will never have a chance at the "new buffalo" of casino wealth. Others believe that the Department of the Interior has the authority to impose a gaming compact upon a state under the provision of IGRA that remain in force. There is even a seldom-advanced argument that *Seminole Tribe*, by destroying IGRA's principal enforcement mechanism, returned the law to the situation after *Cabazon* and before IGRA—that is, states that allow gambling may not regulate it on Indian land.

Parsing out what remains of IGRA presents the difficulty of hitting a moving target. Each session of Congress considers numerous amendments, most calculated to diminish tribal authority and supported not only by states but by gaming interests from Nevada and New Jersey. Both established gaming interests and Indian tribes have contributed generously to politicians in the hope of gaining legislative ground.

In 1998, California voters adopted Proposition 5, essentially legalizing existing Indian casinos in that state in spite of court decisions finding the casinos in violation of IGRA and a "No on 5" television campaign bankrolled by Nevada casinos. The battle over Proposition 5 in California cost approximately $100 million dollars, an indicator that both sides of the high stakes gambling issue perceive the high stakes involved.

The only thing that is certain in all of the policy confusion around Indian gaming is that the "new buffalo" will eventually go the way of the old buffalo. If it is not killed by Congress, the herd will certainly be thinned out by competition as more states legalize non-Indian casinos and more states enter the field in their own right with lotteries and pari-mutual betting. Tribes currently control about 3 percent of the legal gaming revenues in the United States, with states controlling 36 percent and the balance in the hands of individuals. Those tribes that make the wisest use of casino dollars while those dollars are flowing will be best positioned to maintain their employment gains when casino gambling becomes, once more, the white man's game. **See also** Reservation Economics; Reservations; Tribal-State Affairs. (SR)

BIBLIOGRAPHY

Eadington, William, ed. *Indian Gaming and the Law*. Reno, NV: Institute for the Study of Gambling and Commercial Gaming, 1990.

Grant, Michael. "*Seminole Tribe v. Florida*—Extinction of the 'New Buffalo?'" *American Indian Law Review* 22, no. 1 (Spring 1997): 171–89.

Haslam, Connie K. "Indian Sovereignty: Confusion Prevails—*California v. Cabazon Band of Mission Indians*. *Washington Law Review* 63, no. 1 (January 1988): 169–93.

Lane, Ambrose I. *Return of the Buffalo: The Story Behind America's Indian Gaming Explosion*. Westport, CT: Bergin & Garvey, 1995.

Levin, Stephanie. "Betting on the Land: Indian Gambling and Sovereignty." *Stanford Law and Policy Review* 8, no. 1 (Winter 1997): 125–39.

Mezey, Naomi. "The Distribution of Wealth, Sovereignty, and Culture through Indian Gaming." *Stanford Law Review* 48, no. 3 (February 1996): 711–37.

Moore, Christopher J. "What is Good for the Goose is Good for the Gambler: How the Indian Gaming Regulatory Act Fails to Abrogate State Immunity and Protects Tribal Immunity." *Ohio Northern University Law Review* 21, no. 4 (Fall 1995): 1203–26.

Santoni, Roland. "The Indian Gaming Regulatory Act: How Did We Get Here? Where are We Going?" *Creighton Law Review* 26, no. 2 (February 1993): 387–447.

Wolf, Sidney M. "Killing the New Buffalo: State Eleventh Amendment Defense to Enforcement of IGRA Indian Gaming Compacts." *Washington University Journal of Urban and Contemporary Law* 47, no. 1 (Winter 1995): 51–119.

General Allotment Act. *See* Dawes Act

General Citizenship Act of 1924

In recognition of the quasi-sovereign status of Indian tribes, tribal members were not included in that part of the **Fourteenth Amendment** which defines citizens as those "born or naturalized within the United States." Through a variety of statutes and treaties, most notably the General Allotment Act (**Dawes Act of 1887**), many tribes or Indian individuals had been granted citizenship on a piecemeal basis. During the final stages of the assimilation era, Congress passed the General Citizenship Act in 1924, conferring United States citizenship on all Indians born within the United States. Indians therefore have multiple status as U.S. citizens, citizens of the states in which they reside, and citizens of their tribes, and they are entitled to the rights and privileges of each. Their status as U.S. citizens does not deny tribal members of any property rights or other tribal rights, nor does it abrogate the **trusteeship responsibility** of the federal government vis-à-vis tribes. **See also** Burke Act of 1906; Federal Indian Policy; Indian Rights Association; U.S. Citizenship for Indian Veterans of World War I Act of 1919.

BIBLIOGRAPHY

Cohen, Felix S. *Felix Cohen's Handbook of Federal Indian Law*. Charlottesville, VA: Mitchie, Bobbs-Merrill, 1982; Ft. Lauderdale, FL: Five Rings Press, 1986.

Geronimo (ca. 1829–1909)

Goyathlay (Geronimo), a Bedonkohe Apache (N'de) who lived with the Chokonen band, was one of the most intractable foes ever faced by the United States Army. Leading with a combination of charisma and military prowess, Geronimo first fought alongside other Chiricahua chiefs in the mid-1800s, then walked away when Cochise made peace with the United States in 1872. With his followers, he raided back and forth across the Mexico-United States border for the following 14 years.

Perhaps more than any other individual, Geronimo became a symbol of Native-American resistance to the United States and of Indian—particularly Apache—ferocity. He was vilified in the press, and his capture became the key military goal of the United States. After his capture, his band was shuttled among several prisons, where the poor conditions again brought him to public attention. He became a subject of public fascination, attending both the St. Louis World Fair and Theodore Roosevelt's inauguration parade. He died a prisoner of war at Fort Sill, Oklahoma. (LCJ)

BIBLIOGRAPHY

Cole, D.C. *The Chiricahua Apache: 1846–1876: From War to Reservation*. Albuquerque: University of New Mexico Press, 1988.

Debo, Angie. *Geronimo: the Man, His Time, His Place*. Norman: University of Oklahoma Press, 1976.

Sonnichsen, C.L., ed. *Geronimo and the End of the Apache Wars*. Lincoln: University of Nebraska Press, 1986.

Ghost Dance Movement

The Ghost Dance Movement, a messianic Indian religion, originated in Nevada around 1870; it then faded, only to re-emerge in its best-known form in 1889. Most white scholars view it as a response to deprivation resulting from American conquest. Tävibo, a Nevada Paiute and first Ghost Dance prophet, preached that white people would disappear from the earth and dead Indians would return to enjoy a utopian life. The movement spread through Nevada and to parts of California and Oregon but subsided after the prophecies failed to materialize. Another Nevada Paiute prophet, **Wovoka**, revived the movement in 1889. Wovoka preached peaceful co-existence and taught songs and dances to resurrect dead Indians and eliminate whites from the earth. The second Ghost Dance enjoyed greatest acceptance among Plains tribes, particularly Lakotas. Lakota practitioners added militant elements to the Ghost Dance, which provoked hysteria among neighboring whites and culminated in the massacre at **Wounded Knee (1890).** That disaster hastened the movement's demise, although some Plains tribes practiced the ceremonies into the twentieth century. **See also** Big Foot; Crow Dog; Red Cloud; Smohalla. (TMK)

BIBLIOGRAPHY

Mooney, James. *The Ghost Dance Religion and the Sioux Outbreak of 1890.* Washington, DC: Government Printing Office, 1896.

Utley, Robert M. *The Last Days of the Sioux Nation.* New Haven, CT: Yale University Press, 1963.

Tim Giago (1934–)

Tim Giago, an Oglala Sioux, was the founder, editor, and publisher of the largest independently owned American Indian weekly newspaper, *Indian Country Today.* Born on a reservation in South Dakota, Giago is known for protesting trends in U.S. society that show a lack of respect for Native Americans. Giago was injured while serving with the Navy in the Korean War. He was the first Native American to be accepted into the Nieman Fellowship program at Harvard University. He won the Harvard University Award for contributions to American Journalism. He has also been inducted into the South Dakota Hall of Fame. Giago sold the newspaper to the Oneida Nation in 1998, but continues in an advisory capacity. **See also** Culture and Identity; Indian Identity.

BIBLIOGRAPHY

Giago, Tim. *The Aboriginal Sin: Reflections on the Holy Rosary Indian Mission School.* San Francisco: Indian Historian Press, 1978,

———. "I Hope the Redskins Lose." *Newsweek* (January 27, 1992).

Gold Rush

The California gold rush, which started in 1848, had a huge impact on Native Americans of the West. John Sutter, a federal Indian subagent, was credited with the discovery of gold.

The gold discovery occurred in the same year as the **Treaty of Guadalupe Hidalgo**, which ended the Mexican War with the United States and upheld Native-American control of large portions of California under Hispanic customs. But as gold-fevered whites streamed into the California territory (which became a state in 1850), entire tribes were wiped out. The rapid population influx overran what had been a Native American majority; massacres were common, and federal authorities were unable to maintain order. Meanwhile, the new state's government set out to extinguish Indians' civil rights and their land titles.

In 1851, President Millard Fillmore and the new Department of the Interior sent a treaty commission into the state, which offered Indians "extermination or domestication." A number of treaties were negotiated, but they did not protect California's Native Americans from miners, militias, and the state government. By 1880, the native population had sunk to 23,000, about 15 percent of the 1848 population.

The gold rush's impacts were not limited to California. They stretched across the Great Plains, as thousands of Euro-Americans streamed along the Santa Fe and Oregon trails heading for the gold fields. These migrants invaded Indian lands, killed the game, built railroads, and eventually demanded that the Native Americans of the Plains and Southwest be confined on reservations. The population shifts caused by the gold rush were, in turn, a cause of the **Plains Wars. See also** Rogue River War. (LCJ)

BIBLIOGRAPHY

Brown, Dee. *Bury My Heart at Wounded Knee: An Indian History of the American West.* New York: Holt, Rinehart & Winston, 1970.

Garner, Van H. *The Broken Ring: The Destruction of the California Indians.* Tucson, AZ: Westernlore Press, 1982.

Hurtado, Albert L. *Indian Survival on the California Frontier.* New Haven, CT: Yale University Press, 1988.

Gradual Civilization Act of 1857

The Gradual Civilization Act of 1857 inaugurated the Canadian government's campaign to assimilate its Indian subjects. Based on recommendations by Methodist missionaries and the Bagot Commission of 1842–1844, the act enfranchised individual Indians who met the legislature's standards of "civilized" behavior: literacy in English or French, freedom from debt, and good "moral character." However, Indian leaders opposed it as an encroachment on band **sovereignty**, and only one man, Elias Hill, ever met the law's strict prerequisites for enfranchisement. **See also** Conservatism and Liberalism. (DAN)

BIBLIOGRAPHY

Milloy, John. "The Early Indian Acts." In Ian Getty and Antoine Lussier, eds. *As Long As the Sun Shines and Water Flows.* Vancouver: University of British Columbia Press, 1983.

Tobias, John. "Protection, Civilization, Assimilation: An Outline History of Canada's Indian Policy." In Ian Getty and Antoine Lussier, eds. *As Long As the Sun Shines and Water Flows.* Vancouver: University of British Columbia Press, 1983.

Grant's Peace Policy (1869–1882)

Grant's Peace Policy was an assimilation plan that centered on removing the Indians to reservations where they were to be turned into Christian farmers. The burden of preparing the Indians for citizenship was transferred from government agents to the Christian churches. However, due to internal corruption and a constant lack of funds, the government was unable to accomplish its goals of providing for the Indians or maintaining peace on the frontier, and the program was abandoned by 1882. (MR)

BIBLIOGRAPHY

Fritz, Henry E. *The Movement for Indian Assimilation, 1860–1890.* Philadelphia: University of Pennsylvania Press, 1963.

Prucha, Francis Paul. *American Indian Policy in Crisis: Christian Reformers and the Indian, 1865–1900.* Norman: University of Oklahoma Press, 1976.

Guardianship

The guardianship concept in federal Indian law was first suggested in *Cherokee Nation v. Georgia* (1831). The Cherokee had sued to enforce their treaty with the United States after Georgia threatened Cherokee government. The suit was dismissed on the ground that only a "foreign nation" may sue a state in the Supreme Court. The Court acknowledged the Cherokee Nation "as a State . . . capable of managing its own affairs and governing itself," but continued, "They may, more correctly, perhaps, be denominated domestic dependent nations. . . . [W]e assert a title independent of their will. . . . [T]hey are in a state of pupilage. Their relation to the United States resembles that of a ward to his guardian." This dictum was soon treated as a basic principle of federal Indian law.

Guardianship cuts two ways. In *Ex Parte Crow Dog* (1883), the court upheld Sioux Nation jurisdiction over its members, saying the Sioux were "subject to the laws of the United States, not in the sense of citizens, but, as they had always been as wards subject to a guardian." Three years later, in *United States v. Kagama* (**1886**), the Court upheld a federal law taking away such jurisdiction, saying, "These Indian tribes are the wards of the nation. They are communities dependent on the United States."

Guardianship remains an ambiguous principle of federal Indian law, used sometimes to defend indigenous self-government and used other times to undercut it. **See also** Trusteeship Responsibility; White Man's Burden. (PPE)

BIBLIOGRAPHY

Ball, Milner S. "Constitution, Court, Indian Tribes." *American Bar Foundation Research Journal* 59, 1(Winter 1987): 1–140.

Cohen, Felix S. *Handbook of Federal Indian Law.* Washington, DC: U.S. Government Printing Office, 1942.

Deloria, Vine, Jr. and Clifford Lytle. *American Indians, American Justice.* Austin: University of Texas Press, 1983.

Prucha, Francis Paul. *The Indians in American Society.* Berkeley: University of California, 1985.

Handbook of Federal Indian Law. See Felix Cohen's *Handbook of Federal Indian Law*

Handsome Lake (ca. 1735–1815)

Handsome Lake, a Seneca spiritual leader, was born near Avon, New York. In 1799, after a long period of illness due to alcohol abuse, Handsome Lake claimed to have had a series of visions that were warnings about the moral decay of his people. His teachings included what became known as the Handsome Code, which outlawed drunkenness, witchcraft, sexual promiscuity, wife beating, and gambling. Passionate in his pursuit of witches, his standing declined as many began to consider him overzealous. However, his teaching again came into favor during the **War of 1812**. **See also** Handsome Lake Movement.

BIBLIOGRAPHY

Dockstader, Frederick J. *Great North American Indians*. New York: Van Nostrand Reinhold, 1977.

Handsome Lake Movement

Handsome Lake (1735–1815) was an Iroquois (Seneca) religious leader. In the aftermath of the **American Revolution**, the Iroquois people suffered severe social disruption; the United States confiscated nearly all of their land base, and the Iroquois experienced poverty, indebtedness, and alcohol abuse. Suffering from too much drink and on the brink of death in 1799, Handsome Lake awakened and recounted visions he saw while unconscious.

In the visions, the Creator told Handsome Lake to promote abstinence, the importance of family ties, and the rejuvenation of traditional ceremonies, songs, and dances of Thanksgiving. Handsome Lake encouraged his growing group of followers to learn the language of the white man by sending some of their children to schools, preached against vanity, and warned against the Evil One who embodied sin. Despite borrowing from Christianity, Handsome Lake's religion remained grounded in traditional Iroquois culture, while offering the Iroquois a way out of cultural despair. **See** The Constitution of the Iroquois Nations in Appendix 1. (GO)

BIBLIOGRAPHY

Fenton, William N. ed. *Parker on the Iroquois*. Syracuse, NY: Syracuse University Press, 1968.

Wallace, Anthony F.C. *The Death and Rebirth of the Seneca*. New York: Knopf, 1969.

Suzan Shown Harjo (1945)

Suzan Shown Harjo, a Cheyenne and Hodulgee Muscogee, is a writer, lecturer, policy analyst; and serves as the executive director of The Morning Star Institute. Her work calls attention to native causes such as religious freedom, repatriation of artifacts, and environmental protection. (MKJ)

BIBLIOGRAPHY

"Harjo, Suzan Shown." *Native American Indian Values for a New Millennium*."

http://www-dept.usm.edu/~philrel/indian/harjo.html

LaDonna Crawford Harris (1931–)

LaDonna Crawford Harris (Comanche) is a consultant and nationally known speaker on Indian issues. Born to William and Lily Tabbytite Crawford in Temple, Oklahoma, she attended Oklahoma public schools and married Fred Harris (later U.S. senator from Oklahoma) in 1949. In 1970, she founded Americans for Indian Opportunity, which she continues to lead. (AMM)

BIBLIOGRAPHY

Schwartz, Michael. *LaDonna Harris*. Austin, TX: Raintree Steck-Vaughn, 1997.

Harrison v. Laveen (1948)

Harrison v. Laveen, 67 Ariz. 334 (1948), overruled an earlier case, *Porter v. Hall* (1928), in which the Arizona Supreme Court had ruled that Indians were "persons under **guardianship**" and therefore ineligible to vote. In *Harrison*, the court held that the term "persons under guardianship" in the Arizona constitution did not apply to the trust relationship between the United States and the Indian tribes. (AMM)

BIBLIOGRAPHY

Wilkins, David E. *American Indian Sovereignty and the U.S. Supreme Court*. Austin: University of Texas Press, 1997.

William L. Hensley (1941–)

William Hensley was a member of the Alaska house of representatives from 1966 to 1970, after which he moved on to serve in the Alaska state senate. Beginning in 1966, he functioned as a member, organizer, and eventual president of the Alaska Federation of Natives. Hensley also acted as chairman of the Land Claims Task Force in 1968, as well as a member of the Rural Affairs Commission from 1968 to 1972 and a board director of the Northwest Regional Educational Laboratory from 1968 to 1969. During his career, Hensley served on the board of directors for the Northwest Alaska Native Association Regional Corporation and, from 1968 to 1970, as a member of the **National Council on Indian Opportunity.**

BIBLIOGRAPHY
Jackson, Robert. "William Hensley." *Rocky Mountain News* (November 23, 1996): 54A.

Hiawatha (Ayonwatha)

Ayonwatha (Hiawatha) was an Onondaga who worked with **Deganawida** (The Peacemaker) to end the long tradition of bloodshed among Native Americans living near the eastern Great Lakes between A.D. 1000 and 1450. Ayonwatha was a great orator and, over a period of decades, convinced the Mohawk, Seneca, Oneida, Onondaga, and Cayuga to join under the form of government that Deganawida called the Great Law of Peace. Thus, the Haudenosaunee (Iroquois) Confederacy, a model for the United States Constitution, was formed. (LCJ)

BIBLIOGRAPHY
Barreiro, Jose. *Indian Roots of American Democracy.* Ithaca, NY: Akwekon Press, Cornell University, 1992.
Great Law of Peace (Kaianerekowa) of the Longhouse People (Hoinonsionne). Rooseveltown, NY: White Roots of Peace, 1971.

Hinmatoya'latk'it. *See* Joseph

Linda Hogan (1947–)

Linda Hogan is a Chickasaw poet, essayist, and novelist. She was the winner of the American Book Award for *Seeing Through the Sun*, and a Pulitzer prize finalist for *Mean Spirit*. Hogan's writing is explicitly political, expressing the pain of native colonial experiences and natives' sacred relationship with the land. She currently teaches at the University of Colorado. (SRC)

BIBLIOGRAPHY
Hogan, Linda. *Solar Storms.* New York: Simon and Schuster, 1995.
Owens, Louis. *Other Destinies: Understanding the American Indian Novel.* Norman: University of Oklahoma Press, 1992.

Hoover Commission

Reorganization of the government was one of the proposed ways to cut down federal expenses after World War II. Former president Herbert Hoover led a commission that looked into this matter in 1949. One of its proposals was that American Indians should be integrated by transferring all federal programs from the **Bureau of Indian Affairs** to state or local governments. The commission also recommended the termination of tax exemptions for Indian lands, relocation of Indians to cities after jobs, and forming of tribal enterprises on a corporate or cooperative basis. This report had a significant influence on the termination legislation of the 1950s. **See also** Self-Determination; Sovereignty. (JP)

BIBLIOGRAPHY
The Hoover Commission Report on Organization of the Executive Branch of the Government. Westport, CT: Greenwood Press, 1970.

Hopewell Treaty (1785)

The Hopewell (Georgia) Treaty was signed in 1785 between the United States and the Cherokees. It stated that anyone (U.S. citizen or not) who had attempted to settle on Cherokee lands in the previous six months had to remove their settlement. If they did not, then they were no longer under the protection of the U.S. government, and were subject to Cherokee punishment. **See also** Five Civilized Tribes.

BIBLIOGRAPHY
Deloria, Vine, Jr. and Clifford M. Lytle. *American Indians, American Justice.* Austin: University of Texas Press, 1983.

House Concurrent Resolution 108

House Concurrent Resolution 108 (HCR 108) was passed in 1954 by a new Republican Congress under the new Republican President, Dwight D. Eisenhower, in order to terminate the federal trust relationship with the Indian tribes and to "make the Indians within the territorial limits of the United States subject to the same laws and entitled to the same privileges and responsibilities as are applicable to other citizens of the Untied States." The effect of the resolution was to transfer ownership of tribal lands to individuals (often non-Indians), impose state legislative and judicial jurisdiction over former reservation lands, and impose state taxation on Indians. Federal programs to tribes and individuals were to be discontinued, and tribal **sovereignty** was to be ended. The intention of HCR 108 was to "put Uncle Sam out of the Indian business." The resolution sought to "terminate" all tribes, but only about 3 percent were actually affected. Initially, the largest, most economically independent tribes were slated for termination, but most of the 109 tribes and bands terminated were small and weak. Since HCR 108 required legislation to implement it, the larger tribes were able to raise sufficient funds to lobby members of Congress to save their lands and government. The Kennedy administration did not initiate any new terminations but signed off on those already begun. The Johnson administration recognized the permanency of the Indian tribes, and the Nixon administration established the era of **self-determination.** The 1960s civil rights movement led to the founding of the **American Indian Movement** (AIM) and other political action groups demanding restoration of treaty rights, which in turn led to tribes such as the Klamath, Menominee, and Catawba ultimately receiving federal status. **See also** Federal Acknowledgment of Indian Tribes; Indian Self-Determination and Education Assistant Act of 1975; *Menominee Tribe of Indians v. United States* (1968); Public Law 280; Termination Resolution; Trusteeship Responsibility. (AMM)

BIBLIOGRAPHY

Prucha, Francis Paul, ed. *Documents of United States Indian Policy.* Lincoln: University of Nebraska Press, 1990.

Hump (1848–1908)

Hump, chief of the Minniconjou (Lakota), fought alongside **Red Cloud** from 1866 to 1868 to protect land rights along the Bozeman Trail. In 1866, he also participated in the ambush of Fort Phil Kearny in Wyoming and in the denial of the Treaty of Fort Laramie. Hump was an active contributor from 1876 to 1877 in the Sioux War for the Black Hills, and in 1877 he served as a scout in the **Nez Perce War**. From 1877 to 1890, Hump worked with the Cheyenne River Agency's Indian police force, even though he was a vocal denouncer of the 1888 Sioux Act. In 1890, Hump joined the **Ghost Dance Movement** because of his growing dissatisfaction with the government and the treatment of his people, yet he eventually abandoned this stand to return to the Cheyenne River Police.

BIBLIOGRAPHY

Utley, Robert M. *The Last Days of the Sioux Nation.* New Haven: Yale University Press, 1963.

Indian Act of 1876

The Indian Act of 1876 contained three provisions. The first provision provided for the removal of all eastern Indians to lands west of the Mississippi. The second provision allowed for the allotment of Indian lands in severalty, with any surplus land being sold to white settlers. The final provision called for the U.S. government to extend its judicial jurisdiction over the Indians. (MW)

BIBLIOGRAPHY

Prucha, Francis Paul. *Documents of United States Indian Policy*. Lincoln: University of Nebraska Press, 1990.

Indian Act of 1951

The Indian Act of 1951 gave widespread control of Indian activities and issues to the Department of Indian Affairs and Northern Development, including providing it with jurisdiction over land and resource development. The act reaffirmed previous legislation that denied Indian status to those who married out of their tribe. The act also amended the **Indian Act of 1876** by allowing Indian religious ceremonies, political fund-raising, and alcohol consumption off reservation lands, along with renewed enforcement of previous reservation income and land taxation exemptions. The Indian Act of 1951 led to Native American voting rights being established in 1960.

BIBLIOGRAPHY

Cohen, Felix. *Felix Cohen's Handbook of Federal Indian Law*. Charlottesville, VA: Michie/Bobbs-Merrill, 1982; Ft. Lauderdale, FL: Five Rings Press, 1986.

Indian Agent Act of 1892

The Indian Agent Act of 1892 allowed for the use of military officers as Indians' agents. These Indian agents would be under orders and the direction of the secretary of the interior. Exceptions could be made if the president thought that a civilian could better render the needed public service. The appointment of army officers had a generally negative impact on the delivery of services to the Indians. **See also** Federal Indian Policy. (MW)

BIBLIOGRAPHY

Cohen, Felix. *Felix Cohen's Handbook of Federal Indian Law*. Charlottesville, VA: Michie/Bobbs-Merrill, 1982; Ft. Lauderdale, FL: Five Rings Press, 1986.

Indian Appropriations Act of 1871

In 1871, a rider was attached to the Indian Appropriations Act stipulating that the United States government would no longer negotiate treaties with any Indian nation. The members of the U.S. House of Representatives had for many years been angered about the appropriations they were forced to make to the tribes as a result of the treaty-making process of which they had no part. The rider was their way of becoming part of the process. The act expressly stated that no existing treaty would be invalidated or impaired as a result of the statute. Agreements after this time were created through executive orders, and Congress continued to establish reservations. However, this act ushered in the beginning of the **assimilationist policy** period which that include the **Dawes Act.** In *Antoine v. Washington* (1975), the U.S. Supreme Court ruled that since Congress had plenary power to legislate on Indian matters, the Appropriations Act of 1871 had no significant effect, because both congressional statutes and treaties were "the supreme law of the land." **See** Dawes Act (1887) in Appendix 1. (AMM)

BIBLIOGRAPHY

Cohen, Felix. *Felix Cohen's Handbook of Federal Indian Law*. Charlottesville, VA: Michie/Bobbs-Merrill, 1982; Ft. Lauderdale, FL: Five Rings Press, 1986.

Indian Arts and Crafts Board Act of 1935

This legislation composed one program in what became known as the Indian New Deal. President Franklin Roosevelt's Commissioner of Indian Affairs, **John Collier**, aggressively pursued policies intended to grant Indian people more autonomy over their domestic affairs. Key components of the act included the preservation of traditional native craftsmanship, procurement of a wider market for the sale of art, and the institution of direct marketing from reservation to customer, in order to avoid unscrupulous middlemen. **See also** Conservatism and Liberalism; Meriam Report. (GO)

BIBLIOGRAPHY

Philp, Kenneth R. *John Collier's Crusade for Indian Reform, 1920–1954*. Tucson: University of Arizona Press, 1977.

Schrader, Robert Fay. *The Indian Arts & Crafts Board: An Aspect of New Deal Indian Policy*. Albuquerque: University of New Mexico Press, 1983.

Indian Child Welfare Act of 1978

The Indian Child Welfare Act of 1978 was promoted to protect the interests of Indian children and to provide stability to American Indian families. Prior to this Act, Indian children were often taken from homes deemed unsuitable by the **Bureau of Indian Affairs** (BIA) and placed with non-Indian families, in much the same way that Indian children were once forcibly sent to boarding schools. By 1958, BIA facilitated the adoption of Indian children by non-Indian parents by establishing the Indian Adoption Project in concert with the Child Welfare League of America. Concerned that these actions were less an action taken for the child's welfare and more a destructive force against tribal **sovereignty**, Indian rights groups such as the North American Indian Women's Association pushed for tribal jurisdiction over custody cases. In 1978, with the separation of Indian children from their families and tribes growing at a rate of 25 percent to 35 percent, Congress agreed to place the responsibility for custody proceedings with Indian tribal, rather than state, courts. The Indian Child Welfare Act provided for the right of the tribes or families to intervene in custody proceedings and to grant preference to the child's extended family or tribe in adoption. Special efforts were made to place the child in an appropriate cultural setting by establishing grants that encouraged Indian tribes and organizations to maintain family service programs. However, the act's attitude toward **self-determination** was not clearly defined. Ultimate supervision remained with the federal government and the funds for the family programs still remained with the BIA. The act has been an important step toward the elimination of assimilationist tendencies, but it has also reaffirmed the traditional government–Indian relationship. Despite critics' warnings that the interests of the tribe would be put above those of the child, the tribal family court and foster care systems have been greatly improved since the act's passage. **See also** Kidnapping of Navajo Children. (MR)

BIBLIOGRAPHY

Hurtado, Albert L. and Peter Iverson. *Major Problems in American Indian History.* Lexington, MA: D.C. Heath, 1994.

Prucha, Francis Paul. *The Great Father: The United States Government and the American Indian.* abridged ed. Lincoln: University of Nebraska Press, 1984.

Indian Civil Rights Act of 1968

In 1968, President Lyndon Johnson signed Public Law 90-284, the Indian Civil Rights Act (ICRA). The act sought (1) to protect individual American Indians by requiring that **tribal governments** abide by certain provisions of the Bill of Rights, and (2) to protect tribal **sovereignty** by limiting states' ability to assume civil and criminal jurisdiction over reservations. Both Indian attitudes toward and effects of the measure proved mixed.

The act grew out of Native American opposition to **Public Law 280** (which allowed states to assume civil and criminal jurisdiction over Indian lands) and complaints that some tribal governments were abusing their power. The bill's author, Sena-

tor Sam Ervin, Jr. (D-NC), sponsored the ICRA as part of a political maneuver to defeat the 1968 Open Housing Act. The scheme failed, and Congress instead passed the ICRA.

The ICRA protected individual Indian rights by mandating that tribal governments abide by most of the provisions of the First, Fourth, Fifth, Sixth, Seventh, Eighth, and **Fourteenth Amendments** to the Constitution. Hence, the legislation guaranteed such rights as equal protection, due process, and free speech. Also, the bill prohibited states from assuming legal jurisdiction over reservations without tribal consent.

While most Indians applauded the repeal of P.L. 280, many feared applying the Bill of Rights to tribal governments would erode Indian sovereignty and cultures. Admittedly, the ICRA replaced traditional, informal mechanisms for problem-solving with formal tribal court proceedings. In *Santa Clara Pueblo v. Martinez* (1977), however, the Supreme Court ruled that only tribal mechanisms could be used to enforce the ICRA. This ruling limited the federal government's ability to enforce the 1968 act and thereby limited its ability to encroach upon tribal sovereignty and cultures. (CKR)

BIBLIOGRAPHY

Deloria, Vine, Jr. and Clifford M. Lytle. *American Indians, American Justice.* Austin: University of Texas Press, 1983.

Wilkinson, Charles F. *American Indians, Time, and the Law.* Native Societies in a Modern Constitutional Democracy. New Haven, CT: Yale University Press, 1987.

Winfrey, Robert Hill, Jr. "Civil Rights and the American Indian: Through the 1960s." Ph.D. dissertation, University of Oklahoma, 1986.

Indian Civilization Act of 1819

The Indian Civilization Act began nearly two centuries of direct federal aid to Indian education. It created a $10,000 annual fund for the establishment of primary and secondary schools among the Indians, with the goal of more swiftly "civilizing" them. Superintendent of Indian Trade Thomas McKenney and Secretary of War John Calhoun solicited the aid of Protestant mission societies in both sponsoring and implementing the act, and by 1826 these organizations had, with the government's assistance, founded 30 new schools in **Indian country**. (DAN)

BIBLIOGRAPHY

Beaver, R. Pierce. *Church, State, and the American Indian.* St. Louis: Concordia, 1966.

Berkhofer, Robert, Jr. *Salvation and the Savage.* Lexington: University of Kentucky Press, 1965.

Indian Claims Commission

In 1946 Congress created the Indian Claims Commission (ICC) to settle all outstanding tribal claims against the United States. Intended as a first step toward termination of the federal trust relationship with Indian tribes, the commission had the authority to award monetary compensation for unconscionable seizing of aboriginal land. The tribes could not recover any territory, and their awards would theoretically end the need for further federal assistance. Although many Indians questioned its purpose and provisions, ICC considered more than 600 separate claims. When it finally expired in 1978, after four extensions, the commission had completed 342 dockets and awarded some $818 million in compensation. **See also** House Concurrent Resolution 108; Termination Resolution. (AHF)

BIBLIOGRAPHY

Fixico, Donald. *Termination and Relocation: Federal Indian Policy, 1945–1960*. Albuquerque: University of New Mexico Press, 1986.

Rosenthal, H.D. *Their Day in Court: A History of the Indian Claims Commission*. New York: Garland Publishing, 1990.

Indian Claims Commission Act of 1946

The Indian Claims Commission Act of 1946, 60 Stat. 1049, was enacted, in the words of the House report, "to right a continuing wrong to our Indian citizens for which no possible justification can be asserted." The "wrong" was stolen lands and broken treaties that had taken millions of acres from indigenous nations. The commission would adjudicate claims and award money for the value of lands assessed as of the time of their taking. The drafters of the act intended that resolving land claims would prepare for termination of federal obligations to Indians, while clearing land titles of Indian claims.

The **Indian Claims Commission** was not authorized to recognize Indian title; a finding of no taking (the confiscation of land by a government authority) resulted in no compensation, rather than in the confirming of Indian title. The act permitted claims to be filed by "any member of an Indian tribe . . . or identifiable group of Indians." This resulted in situations in which claims were brought in the name of a tribe or group without full consent or participation of the entire tribe or group. An award in such cases terminated the interests of all members of the group.

The commission continued until 1978, when it was disbanded by Congress. The "termination" of federal obligations toward Indians, which was a purpose of the act, was partially implemented during the 1950s, then revoked in 1970. **See also** House Concurrent Resolution 108; Termination Resolution. (PPE)

BIBLIOGRAPHY

Sutton, Imre, ed. *Irredeemable America: The Indians' Estate and Land Claims*. Albuquerque: University of New Mexico Press, 1985.

Indian Confederation of American Indians

Held on February 18, 1944, in New York City, the Indian Confederation of American Indians was a pow-wow of 15 Native American tribes. In addition to conducting tribal business and celebrating their heritage, the event was organized with the explicit purpose of exposing the people of New York City to American Indian culture. The program also raised money for impoverished Native Americans in the New York area. **See also** Conference on the Future of the American Indian.

BIBLIOGRAPHY

"Indian Confederation of American Indians Sponsors Annual Pow-wow." *New York Times* (March 23, 1941): 38.

Indian Country

"Indian country" is a legal term used to identify lands set aside primarily for use by Native Americans, under the supervision of the United States government. The term is defined in Title 18 of the United States Code.

Indian country includes: (1) all lands within reservation boundaries, including those not owned by Indians and those not held in trust by the federal government; (2) "dependent Indian communities," such as the Pueblos within New Mexico; and (3) tribally or individually held lands that were allotted or that are held in trust. These lands are under tribal and federal laws, not under state laws.

United States courts often deal with cases attempting to differentiate "Indian country" from other lands. In the 1990s, cases have addressed the existence of "Indian country" within Alaska, and whether state land can be redesignated as "Indian country" for purposes of economic development, particularly gaming operations. (LCJ)

BIBLIOGRAPHY

Pevar, Stephen L. *The Rights of Indians and Tribes*. Carbondale: Southern Illinois University Press, 1992.

Indian Defense League

The Indian Defense League was founded in 1925 by Clinton Rickard, a Tuscarora chief, in order to help further the fight for Native American rights. The group protested against the flooding of Indian lands by the New York Power Company, which desired to establish hydroelectric dams in the area. It also strove for free passage rights for Indians across the American–Canadian border, a freedom originally granted in **Jay's Treaty** of 1795. In the 1920s the group protested this cause by refusing to comply with U.S.–Canadian border restrictions like passports and duties, while also staging reenactments of the Jay Treaty signing. Later on, the Indian Defense League protested the governmental noncompliance of the **Treaty of Ghent** (1814), which mandated that peaceful relations be established with the former Indian allies of the British during the **War of 1812.** In 1949, a chapter of the group established an annual theatrical pageant at the Six Nation Reserve (Ontario, Canada), which included an outdoor stage depiction of the history of the Six Nations of the Iroquois. **See also** Six Nations (Haudenosaunee) Confederacy/Iroquois Confederacy; Tuscarora Protest.

BIBLIOGRAPHY

Empsak, Jesse. "Indians Cross Spar to Assert Treaty Rights." *Buffalo News* (July 17, 1994): 6.

Indian Department of the United States Government

Recognizing the need to address the question of relations with Native Americans in a more centralized manner, Congress authorized the creation of the Indian Department in 1786. The department was created to deal with the growing number of concerns about Native Americans and also to remove authority from state officials. Furthermore, the department was given greater control over both traders and settlers in Indian lands. The Indian Department was a precursor to the **Office of Indian Affairs** (which later became the **Bureau of Indian Affairs**). **See also** Federal Indian Policy.

BIBLIOGRAPHY

Horsman, Reginald. *Expansion and American Indian Policy, 1783–1812*. East Lansing: Michigan State University Press, 1967.

Prucha, Francis Paul. *American Indian Policy in the Formative Years*. Lincoln: University of Nebraska Press, 1970.

Indian Departments of the First Continental Congress

At the beginning of the **American Revolution,** the Continental Congress adopted a policy of neutrality or noninvolvement toward the Indian tribes. However, when tribes of the Iroquois (**Six Nations**) Confederacy joined the British in attacking American forces, the Congress changed the policy. On the recommendation of the standing committee on Indian affairs, the Continental Congress established three departments to conduct Indian relations, one each for the northwest, southwest, and Fort Pitt tribes. Each department had commissioners charged with maintaining good relations with the tribes and countering British influence. Later these three departments were reduced to two: one for tribes above the Ohio, the other for those below. Generally the British were more successful in winning Indian allies during the war because they had more resources to give. (AMM)

BIBLIOGRAPHY

Burnett, Edmund C. *The Continental Congress*. New York: Macmillan, 1941.

Sanders, Jennings Bryan. *Evolution of Executive Departments of the Continental Congress, 1774–1789*. Glouester, MA: Peter Smith, 1971.

Indian Depredation Act of 1891

Also known as the Judicial Act of 1891, the Indian Depredation Act provided the jurisdiction by which a claim against an Indian or white for loss of property could be adjudicated. The act was one of a series enacted between 1796 and 1920 that established a depredation system. The purpose of the system was to prevent interracial violence from erupting between Indians and settlers. The need for a special tribunal was necessary because of the sovereign nature of Indian reservations, which lay largely outside of the jurisdiction of local and state courts. The 1891 act made the court of claims the proper venue for final adjudication of suits.

BIBLIOGRAPHY

Skogen, Larry C. *Indian Depredation Claims, 1796–1920*. Norman: The University of Oklahoma Press, 1996.

Indian Economic Report (1962)

In 1962, Dr. Leona Baumgartner, as assistant secretary of state, concluded a report on the state of Native Americans in terms of economic prosperity. In her report, Baumgartner found that the average native American had an income of $1,500. This figure was half of the national average of $3,000, the level that marked the poverty line. The unmistakable conclusion of the report was that most Native Americans were living in conditions of immense poverty largely created by the **reservation** system that prevented them from earning a decent living. **See also** Reservation Economies.

BIBLIOGRAPHY

Moore, John H., ed. *The Political Economy of North American Indians*. Norman: University of Oklahoma Press, 1993.

Indian Financing Act of 1974

The Indian Financing Act of 1974 was passed on April 12, 1974, by the United States Congress. The act provided $250 million in credit, as well as up to $50,000 in grants, for the economic development of the Indian people and of Native-American organizations. On October 4, 1984, amendments were passed to reauthorize the funding provisions detailed under the original act.

BIBLIOGRAPHY

Case, David S. *Alaska Natives and American Laws*. Fairbanks: University of Alaska Press, 1984.

Indian Gaming Regulatory Act of 1988

Congress passed the Indian Gaming Regulatory Act in 1988 (25 USC 2702) as a response to demands by state government to regulate Indian gaming. The intent of the act was to promote tribal economies, protect Indian gaming from organized crime, and establish the National Indian Gaming Commission. The act defined three classes of gambling and gaming. Class I games, to be regulated by the tribes, were traditional Indian games or games played solely for social reasons. Class II games, which included bingo and pull tabs, were allowed for gambling purposes if the state within which the tribe was located allowed them under any conditions. Class III gaming, casino games, required a tribe/state compact, approved by the secretary of the Interior. The act resulted in the proliferation of gambling establishments on Indian trust land. (AMM)

BIBLIOGRAPHY

Jackson, Vicki C. "Seminole Tribe, the Eleventh Amendment, and the Potential Evisceration of Ex Parte Young." *New York University Law Review* 72, no. 3 (June 1997): 495–546.

Monaghan, Henry Paul. "The Sovereign Immunity 'Exception'." *Harvard Law Review* 110, no. 1 (November 1996): 102–33.

Indian Health Care Improvement Act of 1976

The Indian Health Care Improvement Act of 1976 was intended to improve the health of urban Indians as well as residents of the reservations. The act was a result of the refusal of the Indian Health Service to render care to urban Indians. This Act provided funding for urban Indians by funneling more funds into the Indian Health Service and by providing "outreach and referral services." Despite the intention of the act, Indian health status remains far below that of the general population of the United States. (AMM)

BIBLIOGRAPHY

Cohen, Felix. *Felix Cohen's Handbook of Federal Indian Law.* Charlottesville, VA: Michie/Bobbs- Merrill, 1982; Ft Lauderdale, FL: Five Rings Press, 1986.

In July 1970, the Department of Health, Education and Welfare sponsored a television show, "You and Your Heritage," which addressed the health concerns of Native Americans. *Library of Congress.*

Indian Historian

One of several newspapers and periodicals that began publication as a result of increased activism in American Indian communities in the 1960s was *The Indian Historian.* Published by the American Indian Historical Society, *The Indian Historian* was dedicated to research and teaching about Native Americans from an Indian perspective. Publication began in 1964 and continued until 1979 when it merged with **Wasaja, the Indian Historian.** (MRC)

BIBLIOGRAPHY

The Indian Historian. San Francisco: American Indian Historical Society, 1964–1979.

The Indian Historian Press

The Indian Historian Press had its beginnings in 1967 when Rupert and Jeannette Costo, along with a group of Indian scholars and elders, came together to review the treatment of Native Americans in public school textbooks in California. The findings of this group led to the founding of the Indian Historian Press in 1973. The first work published was *Text-*

books and the American Indian by Rupert Costo and Jeannette Henry. Since its publication, the Press has published numerous other works relating to the treatment of Indians, particularly within the state of California. (AMM)

BIBLIOGRAPHY

American Indian Historical Society. *Indian Voices.* San Francisco: Indian Historian Press, 1970.

Costo, Rupert and Jeannette Henry. *Textbooks and the American Indian.* San Francisco: Indian Historian Press, 1970.

Indian Identity

Native American identity was first grounded in social relations and the circumstances of everyday practice. Marriage and adoption between members of different native cultural groups were common, and cultural mechanisms existed to absorb or integrate immigrant members. Often, one's identity as a member of a given native group depended on the individual's capacity to demonstrate understanding of, and commitment to, the cultural practices and norms of the group. Later, many Europeans were also absorbed into native groups through these cultural mechanisms.

In the nineteenth century, the federal government took charge of defining native identity, and newly formulated assimilation policies started the implementation of a "blood-quantum" measurement for native identity (such measurements are still in use today.) By the 1880s the popularization of bio-evolutionary concepts of race were the main factors in defining Indian identity. Over time, Indian identity based on "blood" has become internalized, creating divisions in native communities, and literally excluding millions of native people who do not meet the blood-quantum criteria. Even those tribes whose enrollment is not based on "blood quantum," such as the Cherokee, still require proof of "descendency."

By the 1960s, native people sought to repossess control of their identity, as wide-scale movements emerged promoting general pride in native identity as a means of generating solidarity and addressing political issues. Activists recognized how their adverse social conditions and the injustices they felt were intimately tied to who they were, and they sought empowerment from this common identification and the strengths of the diversity of native cultures. Issues were expressed through protest and direct action; a number of manifestos articulated the primacy of self-government and urged the reestablishment of nation-to-nation relations among nonnative governments. Building on the ideology of "**Red Power,**" the period was dubbed a time of "awakening" of native consciousness. This affirmation of Indian identity has had generally positive effects on the native population and remains a central issue in native politics today. **See also** Assimilationist Policy; Culture and Identity; Self-Determination. (HHB)

BIBLIOGRAPHY

Jaimes, M. Annette, ed. *The States of Native America: Genocide, Colonization, and Resistance.* Boston: South End Press, 1992.

Nagel, Joane. *American Indian Ethnic Renewal: Red Power and the Resurgence of Identity and Culture.* New York: Oxford University Press, 1996.

Indian Land Consolidation Act of 1983

The Indian Land Consolidation Act was an attempt to solve problems that resulted when small parcels of land provided to individuals under the General Allotment Act (the **Dawes Act of 1887**) were inherited by increasing numbers of people over several generations. The act passed the ownership of small parcels of land with little current value from individuals to **tribal governments**. The act has been controversial, because individuals have lost control of land. A key part of it was declared unconstitutional in *Hodel v. Irving,* 481 US 704 (1987). **See also** Allotment. **See** Dawes Act (1887) in Appendix 1. (LCJ)

BIBLIOGRAPHY

Ambler, Marjane. *Breaking the Iron Bonds: Indian Control of Energy Development.* Lawrence: University of Kansas Press, 1990.

Indian Liquor Act of 1897

During the nineteenth century, there were several reform movements undertaken to Christianize Native Americans. The federal government and nonnative sympathizers took the role of guardians of native peoples. One of the movements that attempted to reform and protect natives was the Indian Liquor Act of 1897. This bill sought to prohibit the selling or giving liquor to Indians or supplying them with food or medicine that contained any alcoholic content or base. According to Francis Prucha, this bill was highly acclaimed by the Indian Rights Association and the Commissioner of Indian Affairs. As Prucha notes, although the creators of this bill had good intentions, they were still more interested in "civilizing" the Indians and not "in providing for the basic human needs of the Indians in the process." This bill also helped the United States secure more control over Indians when many natives were having lands taken away under the **Dawes Act of 1887**. **See also** Alcoholism and Other Social Problems on Reservations. **See** Dawes Act (1887) in Appendix 1. (MKJ)

BIBLIOGRAPHY

Prucha, Francis Paul. *American Indian Policy in Crisis: Christian Reformers and the Indian 1865–1900.* Norman: University of Oklahoma Press.

Indian Property Protection Act of 1862

The Indian Property Protection Act of 1862 was part of a trend begun in the 1850s to allot land reserved for Indians in severalty—meaning that the government gave land that had been set aside by treaty for specific tribes to individual Indians rather than having the land remain in communal trust for the entire tribe. The theory behind severalty of allotment was that it would enable easier assimilation of Indians into settler communities. This practice continued until the passage of the General Allotment Act of 1887, also known as the **Dawes Act.** The Indian Property Protection Act of 1862 was designed to protect the property of Indians whose tribe had signed a treaty with the United States, and who individually had adopted the "civilized life." **See also** Allotment; Assimilationist Policy.

BIBLIOGRAPHY

Cohen, Felix S. *Felix Cohen's Handbook of Federal Indian Law.* Charlottesville, VA: Mitchie, Bobbs-Merrill, 1982; Ft. Lauderdale, FL: Five Rings Press, 1986.

Indian Removal

During the 1820s government officials argued for assimilation of Indians into Euro-American society and for the removal of the eastern tribes to west of the Mississippi. The first U.S. Supreme Court decision to formulate a position on tribal legal rights to tribal lands was *Johnson v. McIntosh,* 8 Wheat. 543 (1823). It established that tribes occupied their lands only at the sufferance of the U.S. government. President Andrew Jackson helped pass the **Indian Removal Act of 1830** and was the first president to use military force to remove the tribes.

Demands to remove the tribes reached a peak in the early 1830s. The state of Georgia demanded it be given jurisdiction over tribal lands before it ceded its western territories to the United States The federal government refused and Georgia acted unilaterally to take over Cherokee lands. The Cherokee went to the U.S. Supreme Court twice in *Cherokee Nation v. Georgia,* 5 Pet. 1 (1831) and *Worcester v. State of Georgia,* 6 Pet. 515 (1832). The Court ruled that tribes were "domestic, dependent nations" and tribal lands could only be ceded to the United States. It also ruled that tribes were distinct political entities with territorial boundaries within which their authority was exclusive.

Jackson disregarded the Court's decisions and began removing tribes to the west. This was the era of "manifest destiny," and the tribes stood in the way of expansion and progress. From 1840 to 1850 the Euro-American population increased by one-third but the land occupied by them increased by 70 percent.

The federal government began negotiating removal treaties with tribes located from the Great Lakes to the Gulf of Mexico. Ceded lands were put up for sale. Some tribes fought removal but were, for the most part, unsuccessful. In the Great Lakes area 50 tribes (such as the Delaware, Miami, Sac, and Fox) were removed. In the Southeast the major tribes removed were the Cherokee, Chickasaw, Choctaw, Creek, and Seminole (the **Five Civilized Tribes**). The tribes had a choice—stay and submit to state law or move west. By 1840 more than 100,000 Indians were removed to "**Indian Territory**" (now Oklahoma, Arkansas, and Kansas). **See also** Federal Indian Policy. (MM)

BIBLIOGRAPHY

Foreman, Grant. *Indian Removal.* Norman: University of Oklahoma Press, 1982.

O'Brien, Sharon. *American Indian Tribal Governments.* Norman: University of Oklahoma Press, 1989.

Sturtevant, William E., ed. *History of Indian-White Relations,* Handbook of North American Indians. vol. 4. Washington, DC: Smithsonian Institution, 1988.

Indian Removal Act of 1830

On May 28, 1830, President Andrew Jackson signed the Indian Removal Act, which allowed for the "voluntary" exchange of eastern Indian lands for territory west of the Mississippi. The act was part of a settlement made with Georgia to eliminate Indian title to lands within the state in exchange for the state's western lands claim. Jackson had argued in his first address to Congress (December 8, 1829) that the U.S. Constitution forbade the establishment of a "foreign and independent government" within the boundaries of a state. The discovery of gold hastened Georgia's claim to the Cherokee lands in 1829, when the state legislature extended its legal authority over the lands, to take effect June 1, 1830. Meanwhile, the Cherokee were suing for their rights in the U.S. Supreme Court, in the cases *Johnson v. McIntosh* **(1823)**, *Cherokee Nation v. Georgia* **(1831)**, and *Worcester v. Georgia* **(1832)**. Chief Justice John Marshall argued that the Indians were "domestic, dependent nations" and that treaties were the "supreme law of the land," thus upholding the Cherokees' right to their land. President Jackson ignored the Court's rulings and sent the army to enforce the terms of removal. In 1838, 18,000 Cherokee were force marched on the Trail of Tears to the Oklahoma Territory; at least a quarter of them died on the march, from exposure, starvation, and other privations on the trail. The Creek and the Choctaw tribes were also eventually relocated, along with most of the tribes of the southeastern United States. **See also** Federal Indian Policy; John Ross. (AMM)

BIBLIOGRAPHY

Jahoda, Gloria. *The Trail of Tears*. New York: Holt, Rinehart and Winston, 1975.
Perdue, Theda and Michael Green. *The Cherokee Removal: A Brief History with Documents*. Boston: Bedford Books of St. Martin's Press, 1995.

Indian Removal Policy

Removal was historically the alternative to extermination in the dealings of the United States with Native Americans. Even before independence, British officials encouraged native peoples to move beyond the boundary of colonial settlement established by the **Royal Proclamation of 1763**. By 1803, Congress had authorized the president to negotiate the resettlement of eastern tribes on lands west of the Mississippi. For the next 30 years, the goal of federal treaty-making with eastern Indian Nations was "voluntary" removal west.

As American settlements increasingly impinged on native lands, federal protection of native communities became a political issue. With the **Indian Removal Act of 1830**, Congress gave President Andrew Jackson authority to remove Indian nations from their lands by force.

Five southeastern nations—the Cherokee, Choctaw, Chickasaw, Creek, and Seminole (also called the **Five Civilized Tribes**)—were adopting a "Europeanized" way of life, growing wealthy and blocking settlers who wanted the lands they occupied in the southeastern states. Between 1830 and 1850, more than 60,000 members of these nations were re-

moved, including the 18,000 Cherokees taken on the "**Trail of Tears**" over the winter of 1838–1839.

After the **Civil War,** the Navajo, Jicarilla and White Mountain Apache, and Cheyenne nations, among others, were removed from their homelands, often at great expense to the tribe. In the twentieth century, relocation of individuals, families, and communities continues. The San Lucy District Tohono O'odham and the entire Mandan-Arikara Hidatsa community at Fort Berthold in North Dakota were removed from their lands to make way for reservoirs. The most egregious current example of removal is the ongoing "voluntary" relocation of thousands of Navajo families from lands awarded the Hopi tribe by the federal government. By the end of the 1990s, the United Nations Human Rights Commission was studying involuntary removal of indigenous peoples to determine whether it is a violation of human rights. **See also** California Indian Treaties; Indian Peace Commission. (JN)

BIBLIOGRAPHY

Foreman, Grant. *Indian Removal: The Emigration of the Five Civilized Tribes*. Norman: University of Oklahoma Press, 1932; reprint: 1972.
Scudder, Thayer. *No Place to Go: The Effects of Compulsory Relocation on Navajos*. Philadelphia, PA: Institute for the Study of Human Issues, 1982.
Tyler, Lyman S. *A History of Indian Policy*. Washington, DC: U.S. Department of Interior, Bureau of Indian Affairs, 1973.

Indian Reorganization Act of 1934

The Indian Reorganization Act (IRA), 48 Stat. 984 (1934), was a major piece of "New Deal" legislation in President Franklin D. Roosevelt's administration. A central purpose of the act was to end the federal "**allotment**" process that had decimated indigenous landholdings and to provide for acquisition of lands to add to what remained of Indian reservations. The act established a framework "to stabilize . . . tribal organization" and permit Indian tribes to form themselves into business corporations. It also encouraged local education, health, and housing programs; instituted an Indian preference in **Bureau of Indian Affairs** hiring; and authorized an economic development revolving credit fund for **tribal councils**, among other efforts intended to "revitalize" indigenous nations in the United States.

The IRA's explicit rejection of allotment and the new encouragement to developing reservation economies became political liabilities in the subsequent "cold war" period of the 1950s, when "communalism" looked suspiciously like communism and "reorganization" gave way to "termination."

The IRA was vastly significant in federal Indian law. The "tribal council" system it established as a vehicle for "self-government," and the financial incentives it promised (but did not always deliver) to such councils, interjected a whole new structure and organizing principle into the lives of indigenous nations. The act literally set about to "reorganize" the internal dynamics of native societies, overriding their original forms of organization with entities similar to corporate organizations with elected boards of directors. Traditional-minded

Indians across the country were typically strongly opposed to "reorganization." The **tribal council** system, now entrenched in federal Indian law, is a continuing subject of controversy in **Indian country. See also** Conservatism and Liberalism; House Concurrent Resolution 108; National Council of American Indians; Longest Walk; Meriam Report; Reservation Economics; Self-Determination; Termination Resolution. (PPE)

BIBLIOGRAPHY

Cohen, Felix S. *Handbook of Federal Indian Law*. Washington, DC: U.S. Government Printing Office, 1942.

Philp, Kenneth R. ed. *Indian Self-Rule*. Salt Lake City, UT: Howe Brothers, 1986.

Tullberg, Steven M. "The Creation and Decline of the Hopi Tribal Council." In National Lawyers Guild, ed. *Rethinking Indian Law*. New York: National Lawyers Guild, Committee on Native American Struggles, 1982.

Indian Rights Association (IRA)

Now inactive, the Indian Rights Association (IRA) entered the twentieth century as the most effective organization for securing Native American rights. It was founded by Herbert Welsh in 1882 and was composed of interdenominational philanthropists. It reflected the views of most reformers in the late nineteenth century, as they attempted to protect Indian rights until complete assimilation into American culture. They drafted legislation for the **General Citizenship Act of 1924**. They also pushed the legislation through Congress that guaranteed 22 million acres of executive order reservations (reservations established by presidential order rather than legislature) to Native Americans in 1927. The IRA grew increasingly inactive and had its last annual election of officers in 1987. **See also** Courts for Indian Justice.

BIBLIOGRAPHY

Hagan, William T. *The Indian Rights Association: The Herbert Welsh Years, 1882–1904*. Tucson: University of Arizona Press, 1985.

Indian Rights Association. *Papers, 1882–1965: Indian Rights Association*. Glen Rock, NJ: Microfilming Corporation of America, 1975.

Indian School Act of 1891

The Indian School Act of 1891 provided funds to build industrial schools for Indians, primarily in the states of Wisconsin, Michigan, and Minnesota; the schools were modeled on the Indian Training and Industrial School at Carlisle, Pennsylvania. The Carlisle school was an off-reservation boarding school that offered Indians vocational training and attempted to foster assimilation. The act provided that these schools were not to cost more than $30,000 each. **See also** Assimilationist Policy; Destroy the Indian and Save the Individual Educational Policy; Education; Education Appropriation Act of 1897.

BIBLIOGRAPHY

Blauch, L. *Educational Services for Indians*. Washington, DC: U.S. Government Printing Office, 1939.

The Indian School Act of 1891 established boarding schools like this one in Leupp, Arizona. *National Archives*.

Indian Self-Determination and Education Assistance Act of 1975

One of the most important reforms of U.S. policy toward Native Americans enacted in response to the Indian political movement of the 1960s, the Indian Self-Determination and Education Assistance Act of 1975, P.L. 93-638, 88 Stat. 2203 (1975), required the Bureau of Indian Affairs and Indian Health Service to honor requests by **tribal governments** to contract for the operation of federal programs for the benefit of Indians.

The Indian Self-Determination Act was a key element of President Richard Nixon's proposed reforms of U.S. Indian policy in 1970. Citing the Indian Community Action Programs of the War on Poverty as evidence that tribes were ready for greater autonomy, Nixon suggested that tribes automatically take over requested programs, with the tribes having the right to retrocede control of programs to the federal government. However, Congress supported the contract method, which many Indian leaders believed would provide greater assurance of continued federal support

Intended by Congress to bring about "an orderly transition from federal domination" to "effective and meaningful participation by the Indian people" in program planning and implementation, the act has facilitated tribal administration of hundreds of millions of federal program dollars annually and, supporters say, promoted the movement of real decision-making power to Indian-controlled organizations.

On the other hand, critics assert that the law has fallen short of its avowed aims because of: (1) lack of responsiveness by the **Bureau of Indian Affairs** and the Indian Health Service to tribal contracting requests; (2) inadequate funding of tribal overhead costs and of the federal programs that tribes operate; and (3) limitations of the act itself, which defined self-determination as tribal government administration of existing federal programs.

Since the late 1970s Congress has attempted to rectify flaws in the contracting process, including passage of major amendments to the self-determination act in 1988. Among those amendments was an experimental program of block grants to selected tribal governments, an approach designed to give tribes greater control of federal funds; if successful, this approach may replace contracts as the principal federal strategy of promoting tribal autonomy. **See also** Conservatism and Liberalism; "Destroy the Indian and Save the Individual" Education Policy; Nixon's Special Message to Congress (1970); Self-Determination. (EFM)

BIBLIOGRAPHY

Bee, Robert L. *The Politics of American Indian Policy.* Cambridge, MA: Schenkman, 1982.

Cornell, Stephen. *The Return of the Native.* New York: Oxford University Press, 1988.

Prucha, Francis Paul. *The Great Father: The United States Government and the American Indians.* vol. 2. Lincoln: University of Nebraska Press, 1984.

Stuart, Paul H. "Financing Self-Determination: Federal Indian Expenditures, 1975–1988." *American Indian Culture and Research Journal* 14, no. 2 (1990): 1–18.

Indian Territory

Indian Territory refers to the Indian-occupied central region of the United States that encompasses present-day Oklahoma. After the **Louisiana Purchase**, the idea for an Indian territory on the western side of the Mississippi developed as a refuge for eastern tribes, where they could live undisturbed by white settlement and slowly accept the Euro-American way of life. During the first phase of this western settlement, eastern tribes were voluntarily removed to the territory, but the **Indian Removal Act of 1830** forcibly removed the remainder of the "**Five Civilized Tribes**" (Cherokee, Choctaw, Chickasaw, Creek, and Seminole) west along "the Trail of Tears." Their new home, which was not part of any state or organized territory, remained an unorganized territory with ambiguous boundaries for its entire existence, being governed entirely by the resident tribes, who established complex judicial and legislative systems. When the tribes supported the Confederacy during the **Civil War**, the federal government forced them to sign Reconstruction treaties that ceded their western territories. **The Dawes Act** (1887) divided tribal lands into individual plots and sold the excess to white settlers, and thus tribal landholdings were further decreased and tribal sovereignty undermined. White settlement increased until 1890, when the territory was divided into the separate Indian and Oklahoma Territories. In 1905, with the admittance of the state of Oklahoma looming on the horizon, the tribes organized a constitutional convention to establish a separate Indian state of Sequoyah, but Congress rejected the idea. When Oklahoma became a state in 1907, the whole of Indian Territory laid within its borders. **See also** Curtis Act of 1898. (MR)

BIBLIOGRAPHY

Debo, Angie. *And Still the Waters Run: The Betrayal of the Five Civilized Tribes.* Princeton, NJ: Princeton University Press, 1940.

Goble, Danney. *Progressive Oklahoma: The Making of a New Kind of State.* Norman: University of Oklahoma Press, 1980.

Institute for the Development of Indian Law

The Institute for the Development of Indian Law is a nonprofit, legal research organization. The institute was founded in 1977 by three Native American attorneys, **Vine Deloria, Jr.,** Franklin D. Ducheneaux, and **Kirke Kickingbird.** The goal of the institute is to strengthen Native American rights so that the people can govern themselves effectively and securely through tribal **sovereignty**. The institute conducts research and publishes the findings about Native American rights. The group also helped implement the Indian Education Act by winning *Red Man v. Ottina*, which funded $18 million dollars to Native Americans. The institute was also vital in the creation of the Coalition of Eastern Native American Organizations.

BIBLIOGRAPHY

Building from Yesterday to Tomorrow: The Continuing Federal Role in Indian Education. 15th Annual Report to the United States Congress, 1988.

U.S. Department of Education. The Indian at Risk Task Force. *Indians at Risk: An Educational Strategy for Action.* Washington, DC: DOE, 1991.

Institute of North American Indian Arts

The Institute of North American Indian Arts was founded in 1962 in Santa Fe, New Mexico, to provide artistic instruction to Native American students between the ages of 15 and 22. The institute was created through the efforts of Hildegard Thompson, director of Indian education for the **Bureau of Indian Affairs (BIA)**, and superintendent George Boyce of the BIA. The school was sponsored by the Southwest Indian Arts Project, the Rockefeller Foundation, the John F. Kennedy administration, the **Indian Arts and Crafts Board,** and writer–poet **John Collier**. The institute went on to become a chartered organization in 1986, allowing it to participate in nonprofit fund-raising, and it opened a museum in Santa Fe in 1992.

BIBLIOGRAPHY

Walsh, Larry. *Surviving Columbus.* West Los Angeles, CA: PBS Home Video, 1992.

International Indian Treaty Council

The International Indian Treaty Council is an important representative of the indigenous peoples of North, Central, and South America and the Pacific. It works in a variety of international forums, including the United Nations, where since 1977 it has been a nongovernmental organization with consultative status at the Economic and Social Council (ECOSOC). The council was the first indigenous entity to achieve such status.

The council was formed as a result of a 1974 conference sponsored by the **American Indian Movement**, hosted by the Standing Rock Sioux Tribe, and attended by 4,000 representatives from 97 tribes. The council focuses on promotion of indigenous **sovereignty** and **self-determination.** It has contributed to public and governmental forums on treaty rights, environmental contamination, human rights, genocide, sacred lands, and colonialism. The group played a key role in the 1982 formation of the United Nations Working Group on Indigenous Populations and in the drafting of the Universal Declaration on the Rights of Indigenous Peoples. **See also** Russell Tribunal. (LCJ)

BIBLIOGRAPHY

Jaimes, M. Annette, ed. *The State of Native America: Genocide, Colonization, and Resistance*. Boston: South End Press, 1992.

Intoxication in Indian Country Act of 1892

Since colonial times, the trafficking of alcohol to Indians had been forbidden. The first federal law addressing it, enacted in 1802, was passed during the administration of Thomas Jefferson, who had been personally lobbied by an Indian chief. The Intoxication in Indian Country Act of 1892, therefore, is one in a series of laws designed to curb the introduction of liquor into **Indian country**. Violations of the act carried with them the possible punishment of up to two years in prison. **See also** Alcoholism and Other Social Problems on Reservations; Federal Indian Policy.

BIBLIOGRAPHY

Cohen, Felix S. *Felix Cohen's Handbook of Federal Indian Law*. Charlottesville, VA: Mitchie, Bobbs-Merrill, 1982; Ft. Lauderdale, FL: Five Rings Press, 1986.

Ite-O-Magajo. *See* Rain-in-the-Face

Jay's Treaty (1795)

During the spring and summer of 1795, more than 20,000 Indian warriors battled American forces for control of the Northwest frontier of the country. Faced with the loss of support from their previous ally, the British, Native Americans suffered severe losses. While the fighting continued between British troops and Americans along the disputed U.S–Canadian border, U.S. diplomat John Jay secured agreements with Great Britain regarding their continued presence along the western American frontier. The signed treaty proclaimed that all British forces would withdraw from their posts on American soil no later than June 1, 1796, giving the United States undisputed sovereignty over the entire territory.

Although Jay's Treaty resulted in nearly a decade of peace on the frontier (and the eventual removal of Spain from their American posts), it left the Indians as the sole obstacle in the continuing American drive for control of the continent and the land itself. (KJB)

BIBLIOGRAPHY

Prucha, Francis Paul. *American Indian Policy in the Formative Years.* Cambridge, MA: HECes University Press, 1962.

Alice Mae Lee Jemison (1901–1964)

An Indian activist, Alice Mae Lee Jemison was born October 9, 1901, in Silver Creek, New York, one of three children of a Cherokee father and Seneca mother. Nine years after marrying LeVerne Leonard Jemison, a Seneca, she was divorced and became the sole support of her two children and her mother. Her experiences trying to provide for her family and the deplorable conditions of her people led Jemison to become active in the Indian rights movement. She served the Seneca Nation as secretary and president and later became a lobbyist in Washington, D.C., for the Seneca as well as for the American Indian Federation. Two beliefs that guided Jemison throughout her life were the sanctity of Indian treaty rights and the idea that the **Bureau of Indian Affairs** should be abolished. She urged repeal of the **Indian Reorganization Act of 1934** and opposed construction of the Blue Ridge Parkway through the Cherokee reservation in North Carolina. (MRC)

BIBLIOGRAPHY

Malinowski, Sharon, ed. *Notable Native Americans.* Detroit: Gale 1995.

Johnson-O'Malley Act of 1934

This act was one of the many pieces of New Deal legislation directed toward Native Americans. Commissioner of Indian Affairs, **John Collier**, intended the act to provide federal money for local assistance in the areas of Indian health, education, agriculture, and social welfare. The educational component was the most crucial, as well as the most contested.

The act proposed that money allotted proportionally to the number of Indian students be used by public schools to establish programs specifically for these children. School officials balked at federal intrusion and displayed a pervasive bias against Indian students. They and church groups throughout the country voiced their strong opposition to a facet of the act calling for an end to compulsory church attendance or other religious instruction for the pupils. In the end, despite good intentions, the Johnson-O'Malley Act's impact on native communities proved minimal. (GO)

BIBLIOGRAPHY

Philp, Kenneth R. *John Collier's Crusade for Indian Reform, 1920–1954.* Tucson: University of Arizona Press, 1977.
Prucha, Francis Paul. *The Great Father: The United States Government and the American Indians.* Lincoln: University of Nebraska Press, 1984.

Johnson v. McIntosh (1823)

Johnson v. McIntosh, 8 Wheat. 543 (1823), was the first of the so-called "Marshall trilogy" of cases that laid the foundation for federal Indian law (the other two cases were ***Cherokee Nation v. Georgia* (1831)** and ***Worcester v. Georgia* (1832).** In this decision, the United States Supreme Court, under Chief Justice John Marshall, established the rule in this case that indigenous nations do not have **sovereignty** over their lands. The basis for the decision was the famous (or infamous) "**doctrine of discovery**."

"Discovery" is the principle that a colonial power acquires sovereignty over lands it finds that are "unknown to all Christian peoples." The Court acknowledged the theological basis of its decision, but Justice Marshall reformulated the principle so that the reference to Christianity could be ignored in subsequent cases.

Johnson v. McIntosh involved a land conflict between two white men, one of whom claimed title from a deed given by Piankeshaw Indians and the other from a grant by the United States. The Court decided the Piankeshaw deed was invalid because power over land, taken by the discovering power, had been transferred to the federal government after the Revolution. **See also** Federal Indian Policy. (PPE)

BIBLIOGRAPHY

Newcomb, Steven T. "The Evidence of Christian Nationalism in Federal Indian Law: The Doctrine of Discovery, *Johnson v. McIntosh*, and Plenary Power." *NYU Review of Law & Social Change* 20, no. 2 (1993): 303–41.

Johnson's Special Message to Congress

President Lyndon Johnson's special message to Congress on Indian affairs (delivered March 6, 1968)—the first special presidential message dealing with Native Americans—officially articulated the new federal Indian policy of "**self-determination.**" This meant that "Indians must have a voice" in creating and implementing policy while maintaining a distinct identity if they wished. To accomplish this, Johnson announced the creation of a **National Council on Indian Opportunity** and called for increased federal assistance for Indian economic development, education, and social welfare programs. The message spelled out the premises that have, at least ostensibly, governed Indian policy ever since. (CKR)

BIBLIOGRAPHY

Johnson, Lyndon B. *Public Papers of the Presidents of the United States: Lyndon Baines Johnson, 1963–1969.* vol. 1 (January 1–June 30, 1968). Washington, DC: U.S. Government Printing Office, 1970.

Joseph (Hinmatoya'latk'it) (1840–1904)

Born in April 1840 and christened Joseph by the Reverend Henry Spalding of the Lapwai Mission, Chief Joseph, who was also called "Young Joseph" to distinguish him from his father, was a pacifist chief of the Nez Perce people, who lived in an area comprising the future northwestern states of the United States. In 1863, disputes between the Indians of the region and white gold miners led the United States government to renegotiate its treaty with the Nez Perce in an effort to reduce the Nez Perce reservation from 10,000 to 1,000 square miles. The Nez Perce resisted this effort and the dispute dragged on until 1877, when the government sent General O.O. Howard, with 400 soldiers and several Indian scouts, to crush Joseph and his people. For 108 days, Joseph led a band of 700 Nez Perce (only 150 of whom were warriors) on a 1,700-mile trek through the mountains of Idaho, across the Continental Divide, and then northward toward the safety of Canada. During this trek, which was avidly followed by the American media, Joseph several times outmaneuvered the army

generals and slipped through their traps. Finally, on October 4, recognizing that he was surrounded, hopelessly outgunned, and outmanned, Joseph stopped a few miles short of the border and surrendered, saying, "From where the sun now stands, I will fight no more forever." His people were too hungry, cold, and tired to go on. Joseph died on the Colville Reservation in Washington State in 1904. **See also** Hump; Looking Glass; Nez Perce War; Thief Treaty. **See** "I Will Fight No More Forever" by Chief Joseph (1877) in the Appendix 1. (LCJ; AMM)

Converted to Christianity, Chief Joseph of the Nez Perce eventually accepted reservation life rather than risk the destruction of his people. *National Archives.*

BIBLIOGRAPHY

Brown, Dee. *Bury My Heart at Wounded Knee: An Indian History of the American West.* New York: Holt, Rinehart & Winston, 1970.

Howard, Helen Addison. *Saga of Chief Joseph.* Caldwell, ID: Caxton Printers, 1965.

Joseph. *Chief Joseph's Own Story.* Billings: Montana Indian Publications, 1972.

Alvin M. Josephy, Jr. (1915–)

After serving in the United States Marine Corps from 1943 to 1945, Alvin Josephy, Jr. worked as an associate editor for *Time* magazine from 1951 to 1960. Josephy went on to become editor-in-chief of the American Heritage Publishing Company, working in this capacity from 1960 to 1979. In 1963 Josephy also functioned as a consultant for the Secretary of the Interior, then becoming commissioner and vice-chairman of the Indian Arts and Crafts Board for the Department of the Interior in Washington, D.C., from 1966 to 1970. Josephy holds ranking membership with the Association of American Indian Affairs and the Museum of the American Indian and has written many award-winning books about American Indians. **See also** Josephy Report.

BIBLIOGRAPHY

Josephy, Alvin M., Jr. *The Indian Heritage of America.* New York: Knopf, 1968.

Josephy Report

In 1969, Alvin Josephy Jr., historian and editor, conducted a study of federal Indian policy at the direction of President Richard M. Nixon. Josephy recommended presidential action to end termination policy and allay tribal fears. He also recommended that the **Bureau of Indian Affairs (BIA)** be transferred from the Department of the Interior to the Executive Office of the President. President Nixon, following the Josephy Report, recommended legislation rescinding termination in his speech to Congress in July 1970. (AMM)

BIBLIOGRAPHY

Josephy, Alvin, Jr. *The Indian Heritage of America*. New York: Knopf, 1968.

_____. *Now That the Buffalo's Gone: A Study of Today's American Indians*. New York: Knopf, 1982.

Betty Mae Tiger Jumper (1923–)

Betty Jumper was born in Indiantown near Lake Okeechobee in southern Florida. In 1967 she was elected as the first woman to serve as chairman of the Seminole Tribal Council. She worked toward making the Seminoles more economically self-sufficient. In 1970 she was named one of the "Top Indian Women" of the year. (LL)

BIBLIOGRAPHY

Jumper, Betty Mae. *. . . and with the Wagon Came God's Word*. Hollywood, FL: Seminole Tribe, 1980.

Wickman, P. R. "State Awards Highest Folklife Honor to Tribune Editor, Tribal Leader, Betty Mae Jumper." *Seminole Tribune* (June 10, 1994): 1.

Kanien'kehaka. *See* Mohawk Nation

Kansas Indians

The Kansas Indians were a Siouan tribe who were living on the Kansas River when the United States signed a treaty of peace with them on October 28, 1815. Two treaties (1825, 1846) reduced their lands in Kansas and Nebraska until, in 1873, the tribe sold the remaining land and purchased a reservation in the Oklahoma Territory. (AMM)

BIBLIOGRAPHY

Vandergriff, James H. *The Indians of Kansas*. Emporia, KS: Teachers College Press, 1973.

William Wayne Keeler (1908–1987)

W.W. Keeler, who was born in Dalhart, Texas, served as the principal chief of the Cherokee Nation of Oklahoma. At the same time, he served in the highest levels of Phillips Petroleum Company of Oklahoma. He also served with the Department of the Interior to represent and study Native American affairs. There were numerous accusations about the possibilities of Keeler misusing tribal and company funds in the late 1960s and early 1970s. Yet he stabilized the Cherokee tribe financially and won national attention for Native American issues.

BIBLIOGRAPHY

"Cherokees Mourn Former Chief W.W. Keeler." *Cherokee Advocate* 11, no. 9 (September 1987): 2.
"Tribal Complex Named for W.W. Keeler." *Cherokee Advocate* 11, no. 4 (April 1987): Section A1.

Kenekuk of the Kickapoo (1785–1852)

Kenekuk was leader of the Kickapoo tribe living by the Osage River in Illinois, and in this role he encouraged his people to maintain themselves through farming and to keep good relations with the white settlers. In 1819 the Treaty of Edwardsville forced the Kickapoo off their land while granting them lands in Missouri, which were occupied by their traditional enemy, the Osages. Some Kickapoos reacted to this by migrating to Texas or Mexico, while others destroyed or stole white property; meanwhile, Kenekuk managed to stall relocation proceedings for a number of years. In 1832, after the volatile Black Hawk War, Kenekuk was forced to sign the Treaty of Castor Hill and moved his people the following year to Kansas. Kenekuk continued to be a diplomatic and spiritual leader for his people until his death.

BIBLIOGRAPHY

Herring, Joseph B. *Kenekuk, the Kickapoo Prophet*. Lawrence: University of Kansas, 1988.

Kennedy Special Subcommittee on Indian Education

The Special Subcommittee on Indian Education was chaired by Senator Edward M. Kennedy (D-MA). The committee was charged with the study of the state of Indian **education** on and off **reservations**. Reporting its findings in 1969, the committee concluded that the educational system established for Native Americans was in terrible shape and in need of immediate reforms. The committee concluded that underperformance and the lack of assimilation was due to inferior schools. The committee recommended more than 60 changes, including that Native Americans be given greater control over educating their children. However, many critics of the sympathetic report noted that the findings failed to address the real cultural differences between Native Americans and the white majority. Education had been used as a tool to force assimilation, often pitting one generation against another. The report did not bring about much change after its release. However, it was used as the basis for the Indian Education Act of 1972, although many of the specific situations addressed by that bill no longer existed. **See also** Indian Self-Determination and Education Assistance Act of 1975.

BIBLIOGRAPHY

Deloria, Vine, Jr. and Clifford M. Lyttle. *American Indians, American Justice*. Austin: University of Texas Press, 1983.

Keokuk (ca. 1785–1848)

Keokuk was a leader of the Sauk nation in what is now Illinois, Iowa, and Wisconsin. He is best known as the rival of Black Hawk, who led one faction of the Sauk against the United States in 1832. Keokuk, meanwhile, remained pro-United States. **See** "Farewell to Black Hawk" by Black Hawk in the Documents section. (LCJ)

BIBLIOGRAPHY

Josephy, Alvin M., Jr. *The Patriot Chiefs: A Chronicle of American Indian Resistance.* New York: Penguin Books, 1993.

Kicking Bird (ca. 1835–1875)

Kicking Bird (Tene-angpote), became an influential Kiowa leader based upon his battlefield exploits. By 1865, Kicking Bird advocated peace with the United States and agreed to accept a reservation. He signed the Medicine Lodge Treaty of 1867, which placed the Kiowas on a reservation in present Oklahoma. Kicking Bird's staunch peace policy, support for American-style education for his people, and conversion to Christianity led Americans to recognize him as the Kiowas' head chief. However, some Kiowas followed leaders who retained Kiowa religion and advocated continued resistance to U.S. Indian policy. (TMK)

BIBLIOGRAPHY

Mayhall, Mildred P. *The Kiowas.* Norman: University of Oklahoma Press, 1962.

Wunder, John R. *The Kiowa.* New York: Chelsea House, 1989.

Kirke Kickingbird (1944–)

Kirke Kickingbird is a prominent lawyer and a defender of legal rights for Native Americans. He has served as a director of the Native American Legal Resource Center at the Oklahoma City University School of Law since 1988. He cofounded and serves as executive director of the **Institute for the Development of Indian Law** in Washington, D.C. He has taught American Indian law and has served as vice-chairman of the board of commissioners for the Oklahoma Indian Affairs Commission. He has also held positions with the **American Indian Policy Review Commission** of the U.S. Congress and the Legal Services Corporation.

BIBLIOGRAPHY

Kickingbird, Kirke. *Economic Perspectives of American Indian History.* Washington, DC: Institute for the Development of Indian Law, 1979.

Kickingbird, Kirke and Karen Ducheneaux. *100 Million Acres.* New York: Macmillan, 1973.

Kidnapping of Navajo Children

The Navajo long suffered large-scale kidnapping and removal of their children, usually as the result of government policy. New Mexico church records indicate that the great majority of captives taken in organized slave raids were children. By 1868, 25 percent of all Navajos were enslaved.

In the 1880s, boarding schools were established in and near Navajo country, with the goal of assimilating Indian children. Every year Navajo children were hunted down and taken from their families by soldiers, Indian police, or officials from the Indian Office (later to be called the **Bureau of Indian Affairs**). Once caught, children were not allowed to return home for years at a time. It was policy to lodge them with white families during summers and holidays.

Religious organizations, such as the Church of Jesus Christ of Latter-day Saints, gave thousands of children attending mission schools the "opportunity" to live with non-Indian families, in the hopes that the Navajo children would be raised as white children.

Social service and adoption agencies practice a modern form of official kidnapping. Welfare agencies take Navajo children from their parents, placing them in foster care or an institution. Agencies refused to return children to their extended families, whose homes, incomes, or family situations usually did not meet dominant-society standards. Many such children were adopted, lost to their families and the Navajo Nation. Navajo women giving birth in hospitals were routinely pressured to give up their children for adoption. The infants, their records sealed, were usually never seen again by their families.

There are hundreds of stories of lost and stolen Navajo children, but no reliable statistics. Figures as high as 25 percent to 35 percent and as low as 3 percent have been given. Since passage of the **Indian Child Welfare Act of 1978**, it has become far more difficult for social service and adoption agencies to take Navajo or other Indian children. The Navajo Nation now tracks all such actions, intervening when necessary. Unfortunately, children are still lost when welfare agencies unknowingly take the Navajo child of a non-Indian single parent, and when children are lured away to the white world by church and missionary organizations. **See also** Assimilationist Policy; Forced Assimilation. (JN)

BIBLIOGRAPHY

Brugge, David M. *Navajos in the Catholic Church Records of New Mexico 1694–1875.* Tsaile, AZ: Navajo Community College Press, 1985

Coolidge, Dane. "Kid Catching on the Navajo Reservation: 1930." In Richard Unger, ed. *The Destruction of American Indian Families.* New York: Association on American Indian Affairs, 1977.

Mannes, Marc. "Factors and Events Leading to the Passage of the Indian Child Welfare Act." *Child Welfare* 74, no. 1 (January–February 1995): 264–82.

United States Senate, Subcommittee on Indian Affairs of the Committee on Interior and Insular Affairs. *Problems that American Indian Families Face in Raising their Children, and How These Problems Are Affected by Federal Action or Inaction.* Record of hearings held in Washington D.C., 1974

King George's War (1744–1748)

Like the previous imperial wars between Great Britain and France fought in North America, no true victor emerged at the conclusion of King George's War. (The other conflicts were **King William's War,** 1689–1697; **Queen Anne's War,** 1702–1713; and the **French and Indian War,** 1754–1763.) Tensions increased after Britain erected defensive posts in Iroquois territory (upstate and western New York) at the request of the Iroquois themselves, who feared their neutral stance would not protect them from French and Indian forces that were attacking British settlements along the Hudson River. As relations between Great Britain and France deteriorated, British colonists continued to pressure the Iroquois to join them against the French colonists and the Indian nations that were allied with France. In 1744, British colonial and Iroquois leaders met in Lancaster, Pennsylvania. The Iroquois refused to shift from their neutral stance, although a few Mohawks joined British forces in the North.

In the South, Cherokees warred against French-backed Choctaw and Creek factions. In the lower Mississippi Valley, Chicasaws were able to close the Mississippi River to French shipping and sever communication between Canada and Louisiana. In 1748 the fighting ended, at least for a short time, until the final imperial conflict, the French and Indian War, erupted six years later. **See also** Six Nations (Haudenosaunee) Confederacy/Iroquois Confederacy. (KJB)

BIBLIOGRAPHY

Peckham, Howard H. *The Colonial Wars, 1689–1762*. Chicago: University of Chicago Press 1964.

King Philip's War (1675)

King Philip's War, an Indian revolt in Massachusetts, began in 1675 when well-armed Indians, protesting Puritan demands and intrusions on native lifestyles, began raiding English settlements. The Wampanoags, led by their chief Metacomet (whom the English called King Philip), made a bid to regain cultural and political autonomy. Subjected to English law and forced to obey the Puritans' civil and religious practices, King Philip and his followers were joined by Nipmuck, Narragansett, and Abenaki warriors. Most reservation, or Christian, Indians refused to support the insurgents. Despite their removal to smaller reservations, and restrictions that prohibited a return to tribal villages, several Christian Indians agreed to serve with colonial troops and to act as scouts for the English. After the defeat and death of King Philip, colonial victors sold the surviving insurgents into slavery, or exchanged them for Indian slaves from the Carolinas, and claimed the now-vacant land in western Massachusetts as war reparations. **See also** Massasoit. (KJB)

BIBLIOGRAPHY

Vaughn, Alden T. *New England Frontier: Puritans and Indians, 1620–1675*. Boston: Little Brown, 1965.

King William's War (1689–1697)

Fought mainly in New England, northern New York State, and the St. Lawrence Valley, King William's War was the first of four European and intercolonial wars that occurred between 1689 and 1763 in which Britain and France fought for imperial supremacy (the other conflicts were **Queen Anne's War,** 1702–1713; **King George's War,** 1744–1748; and the **French and Indian War,** 1754–1763). Threatened by an Iroquois–British expansion into their territory and suffering from trade disadvantages, French leaders realized the necessity of eliminating the Iroquois Confederation's protection of English colonial settlements and the Iroquois' support of British commercial ventures. In an attempt to neutralize the Iroquois–British alliance, French colonial troops and their Indian allies raided English settlements in New England and New York State, but they concentrated on Iroquois Confederation villages. Indians allied with the French weakened the opposing forces and destroyed food sources for all Native American tribes in the affected territory. The Iroquois, despite British objections, met several times with French officials, eventually committing themselves to a stance of neutrality. (KJB)

BIBLIOGRAPHY

Peckham, Howard H. *The Colonial Wars, 1689–1762*. Chicago: University of Chicago Press 1964.

Kinzua Dam Protests

Approved in 1956, the construction of Kinzua Dam on the Allegheny River proceeded despite determined resistance from the Seneca Nation of Iroquois (the dam was completed in 1965). The U.S. Army Corps of Engineers designed the project to control floods, improve navigation, dilute industrial pollution, and enhance recreation. But the same reservoir that provided these benefits would also inundate over 10,000 acres of the Senecas' Allegheny reservation in western New York and the entire Cornplanter Tract in Pennsylvania. Arguing that the dam violated the Canandaigua Treaty of 1794, which guaranteed their right to the land, the Senecas lobbied aggressively and sought a court injunction to stop construction and force the adoption of an alternative plan. They lost their case before the U.S. Court of Appeals, and Congress continued to appropriate funds for the project, thereby unilaterally breaking the treaty. Although Congress awarded the Seneca Nation $15 million in compensation, the dam left the Indians with only 2,300 acres of habitable land and required the relocation of 134 families and 3,000 Seneca graves, including that of the Seneca chief **Cornplanter**. Iroquois anger at the loss contributed to the rise of the **Red Power** movement in the late 1960s. **See also** St. Lawrence Seaway Challenges; Tuscarora Protest. (AHF)

BIBLIOGRAPHY

Bilharz, Joy Ann. *The Allegany Senecas and Kinzua Dam: Forced Relocation Through Two Generations*. Lincoln: University of Nebraska Press, 1998.

Hauptman, Laurence. *The Iroquois Struggle for Survival: World War II to Red Power*. Syracuse, NY: Syracuse University Press, 1986.

Ethel C. Krepps (1937–1996)

A registered nurse, attorney, author, and member of the Kiowa tribe, Krepps provided legal services to Indian tribes and individuals. Her particular focus involved family counseling and helping Indian parents obtain custody of Indian children. She served on a number of commissions and committees, including the board of directors for the North American Council on Adoption of Children. She became a spokeswoman for the importance of **education** for Indian people as well. Active throughout her life, she served on a number of prominent Native American law and nursing organizations. (KJB)

BIBLIOGRAPHY

Burke, Ronald K. *American Public Discourse*. Lanham, MD: University Press of America, 1992.

Winona LaDuke (1959–)

Winona LaDuke (Chippewa), an environmentalist and indigenous rights activist, founded the White Earth Land Recovery Project and has served on the board of numerous prominent organizations. LaDuke ran for vice president of the United States on the Green Party ticket in 1992. (LCJ)

BIBLIOGRAPHY

Jaimes, M. Annette, ed. *The State of Native North America: Genocide, Colonization, and Resistance.* Boston: South End Press, 1992.

Rosalie LaFlesche Farley (1861–1900)

Rosalie LaFlesche Farley was a daughter of Omaha Indian Chief Joseph LaFlesche. This female Indian reformer fought for new legislation that would improve the living and economic conditions of her people through active participation in the Society of American Indians (SAI) in Washington, DC, which lobbied "for Indian self-determination." (LL)

BIBLIOGRAPHY

Green, Rayna. *Women in American Indian Society.* New York: Chelsea House Publishers, 1992.

Susette LaFlesche Tibbles (1854–1902)

Omaha Indian Susette LaFlesche Tibbles spoke before crowds, particularly in the East, about the plight of the Poncas Indians and their chief, Standing Bear, who was placed under arrest for leaving the reservation to bury his son in their homeland. Her eloquent speeches inspired reformers such as Senator Henry L. Dawes and writer Helen Hunt Jackson. (KJB)

An effective orator, Susette LaFlesche Tibbles traveled and lectured on the plight of Native Americans. *Library of Congress.*

BIBLIOGRAPHY

Wilson, Dorothy Clarke. *Bright Eyes: The Story of Susette LaFlesche, An Omaha Indian.* New York: McGraw-Hill Book Co., 1974.

Lake Mohonk Conference

Albert A. Smiley, a wealthy Quaker philanthropist and member of the Board of Indian Commissioners, began a series of biennial conferences in 1883. The participants included Henry Dawes, Lyman Abbott, Herbert Welsh, and Merrill E. Gates, all of whom championed assimilationist policies and the eradication of the reservations through the allotment of reservation lands to members of the tribe or nation. Although these men considered themselves "friends of the Indians," their policies and recommendations were all aimed at destroying tribalism. The General Allotment Act (**Dawes Act of 1887**) was a direct outcome of these conferences. **See also** Allotment; Assimilationism. **See** Dawes Act (1887) in the Appendix 1. (AMM)

BIBLIOGRAPHY

Utley, Robert M. *The Indian Frontier of the American West, 1846–1890.* Albuquerque: University of New Mexico Press, 1984.

Lame Deer (ca. 1900–1976)

John (Fire) Lame Deer considered himself a medicine man. During the late 1960s and early 1970s, he participated in several political struggles involving the **Black Hills** and the gunnery lands, attending the 1974 First International Indian Treaty Conference organized by the **American Indian Movement (AIM)** in South Dakota. (KJB)

BIBLIOGRAPHY

Lame Deer, John and Richard Erdoes. *Lame Deer, Seeker of Visions: The Life of a Sioux Medicine Man.* New York: Simon and Schuster, 1972.

Land and Water Rights

The control of land, water, and other natural resources has always been at the center of the political relationships between Native-American nations and the United States. These relationships have varied from the early period of diplomacy and treaty making, through United States usurpation of native lands and the resulting periods of open warfare, to the modern focus on legislation and negotiation. Common political arenas for these issues include Congress, federal agency proceedings, the media, and federal courts.

When Europeans first colonized North America, they repeatedly recorded the generosity of the continent's indigenous peoples. Generally, Europeans were welcomed and were provided a place to build their towns. The cultures of Europe and North America, however, had—and have—very different understandings about land and its control. Most native nations have always had some way to determine who could use various lands and resources. However, they did not share the European idea that a person could have the right to control land to the extent of using up whatever resources it contained. Native-American resource use was designed to be sustainable over the long term.

Native North Americans conceived themselves and the land to be part of a living and sacred system. This system was based on reciprocity, meaning people who occupy the land are supposed to give something back to it in exchange for the use of its resources. When the United States was formed, it continued the practice begun by the European colonial nations of making treaties with native nations. The treaties usually "reserved" certain lands, "reservations," for Native-American use. The battles fought for control of the continent were generally of two types: Native-American attempts to protect their remaining resources, which resulted in pitched battles, and efforts by non-Indians to exterminate entire villages, which took the form of one-sided massacres.

While modern conflicts over land and resources seldom break into violence, there is still constant conflict among Indians and non-Indians surrounding these issues. Most reservations are embroiled in some form of boundary dispute. These disputes include treaty-based conflicts with long historical roots, attempts by adjoining states to assert jurisdiction, conflicts over control of burial grounds and sacred sites, and efforts to consolidate or expand tribally held lands.

These problems have been intensified by a series of Congress-led policies that split up tribal land holdings, opened some reservation lands to non-Indian ownership, attempted to end treaty and reservation status, and extended federal—and sometimes state—criminal jurisdiction over Native-American lands. These policies have included the General Allotment Act (**Dawes Act**) of 1887, the establishment of the Indian Claims Commission (1946), the Termination Act (1953), and Public Law 280 (1954).

Federal courts have complicated the situation. The Supreme Court's first decisions offered some respect for Native-American nations' sovereignty (***Cherokee Nation v. Georgia***, 20 U.S. [5 Pet.] 1, 1831, and ***Worcester v. Georgia***, 31 U.S. [5 Pet.] 551, 1832). Later Court decisions gave Congress plenary, or complete, control over Indians' lives and lands (***Lone Wolf v. Hitchcock***, 187 U.S. 553, 1903). In general, the Court has tended to erode native land rights, but the decisions often conflict with each other on particulars. Among the most hotly contested natural resource issues have been water rights, energy resources, and Native-American sacred sites. In each

of these arenas, Indians face unique legal situations and great difficulty asserting their rights in United States forums.

Water rights became an issue as soon as reservations were formed. Most treaties reserved not only land, but also Native-American water rights. The right to use water is generally hotly contested in the arid and semiarid West, where most reservations are located.

From the beginning, most reservations were pockets of poverty; thus, while Native Americans retained the legal right to use water (sometimes called "paper water"), they were unable to build dams, pipelines, irrigation structures, and the other infrastructures needed to harness and use water resources. This meant that non-Indians diverted and began using surface water resources before Indians could meet their basic needs for human, livestock, and agricultural water.

The United States Supreme Court entered the fray in the 1908 case, ***Winters v. United States***, 207 U.S. 564. In that precedent-setting case, the Court said that reservation residents have the right to enough water to put their lands to good use. This means Native Americans often have the legal right to large amounts of water, but most still face the problem of getting enough money to build the structures needed to harness and use the water.

Continual conflict exists between the precedent set in *Winters* and the water laws of western states. State laws give water rights to whoever first puts water to "beneficial use." So state laws favor the descendants of those who first used water for irrigation or municipalities—usually non-Indian—while federal law supports Native-American water rights.

Energy resources have been another area of conflict between Native Americans and the United States. When **reservations** were created, Indians were often left with lands that were considered "worthless" because they were not appropriate for agriculture. However, as the twentieth century advanced, those same lands were discovered to hold a high percentage of the coal, uranium, oil, and gas that existed within the boundaries of the United States.

A few tribes managed to turn these resources into wealth for their members. Most, however, were victimized by a federal government leasing system that took advantage of Native Americans' lack of information about their resources' values, modern mineral leasing procedures, and environmental protection practices. Federal policy also encouraged companies to build polluting power plants and processing facilities on reservations.

This meant that tribal governments sold resources to companies at a small fraction of their actual worth, and tribal members suffered the consequences of massive air and water pollution. In addition, Native Americans who got jobs working for energy companies often performed the most dangerous jobs under substandard conditions, such as uranium mining in the Southwest.

In the 1970s, tribal governments began to attempt to get better prices for their resources, gaining changes in federal law and working through organizations like the **Council of**

Energy Resource Tribes. In addition, Native Americans formed groups on many reservations, including chapters of the **American Indian Movement**, to call attention to health impacts from energy activities and to demand local control or cessation of energy development.

Through the mid-1990s, a series of investigations found that the **Bureau of Indian Affairs** had massively mishandled the revenues from energy transactions, leaving many Native Americans without any accounting for their mineral income. Mining and processing of coal, oil, and gas are still major economic activities on some reservations and on lands that are not under Indian control, but are claimed under treaties. So energy issues are a continuing source of political activity.

Native-American sacred sites have been another key point of conflict in the land and resources arena. Because Native-American spiritual practices are inextricably intertwined with the land, sacred sites have been an issue across the continent. United States law forbade the practice of Indian religions during the late 1800s and early 1900s, and some native spiritual practices are still not protected by the First Amendment's guarantee of free exercise of religion. These factors have led many native nations to hide the locations of their sacred sites.

As non-Indian activities expand onto more lands—and into more remote areas—Native Americans have increasingly had to take action to protect sacred sites. Some sites were preserved, and Native Americans have negotiated for at least minimal use of others. Still, many locations have been mined, flooded, or otherwise destroyed. In 1988, the Supreme Court found that a road could be built through a Native-American sacred site for economic reasons. This decision, ***Lyng v. Northwest Indian Cemetery Protective Association***, 485 U.S. 439, has had a chilling effect on efforts to protect sacred sites, despite the fact that the road was never built.

Ironically, some of the recent threats to sacred sites have come from non-Indian admirers of native cultures. Adherents of the "New Age" movement have often trampled sacred sites or ignored Native-American requests to respect their practices. There has also been increasing destruction of historical and sacred sites by people looking for artifacts. While federal law protects historical sites, the law is not well enforced.

The political activities surrounding Native-American land and water rights have always been central to native nations' interactions with the United States and its citizens. (LCJ)

BIBLIOGRAPHY

Ambler, Marjane. *Breaking the Iron Bonds: Indian Control of Energy Development.* Lawrence: University of Kansas Press, 1990.
Churchill, Ward. *Struggle for the Land: Indigenous Resistance to Genocide, Ecocide and Expropriation in Contemporary North America.* Monroe, ME: Common Courage Press, 1993.
Deloria, Vine, Jr., ed. *American Indian Policy in the 20th Century.* Norman: University of Oklahoma Press, 1985.
Gedicks, Al. *The New Resource Wars: Native and Environmental Struggles Against Multinational Corporations.* Boston: South End Press, 1993.
Grinde, Donald A. and Bruce E. Johansen. *Ecocide of Native America: Environmental Destruction of Indian Lands and Peoples.* Santa Fe: Clear Light Publishers, 1995.
Jaimes, M. Annette, ed. *The State of Native North America: Genocide, Colonization, and Resistance.* Boston: South End Press, 1992.
Jorgensen, Joseph, ed. *Native Americans and Energy Development II.* Boston: Anthropology Resource Center and Seventh Generation Fund, 1984.
McCool, Daniel. *Command of the Waters: Iron Triangles, Federal Water Development, and Indian Water.* Berkeley: University of California Press, 1987.
Pevar, Stephen L. *The Rights of Indians and Tribes*, 2nd ed. Carbondale: Southern Illinois University Press, 1992.

League of North American Indians

Founded in 1957 with the aid of the **Indian Defense League**, the League of North American Indians (LONAI) was an early Indian civil rights organization. Using traditional methods of resisting government policy, LONAI has been a major influence on later Indian rights organizations and movements.

BIBLIOGRAPHY

Means, Russell and Marvin J. Wolf. *Where White Men Fear to Tread.* New York: St. Martin's Press, 1995.
Wunder, John R. *"Retained by the People": A History of American Indians and the Bill of Rights.* New York: Oxford University Press, 1994.

Leavitt Act of 1932

Representative Scott Leavitt of Montana, chairman of the House Committee on Indian Affairs, introduced this act on July 1, 1932, which came to carry his name. The act authorized the cancellation of debts against Indian land and postponed the due date on irrigation construction charges as long as land remained under Indian ownership. These charges were often incurred without Indian consent. The act thus guarded Indian lands against seizure. It was an effort to develop tribal self-government, and one of the first acts in the reform era in **federal Indian policy. See also** Reservation Economics. (JP)

BIBLIOGRAPHY

McNickle, D'Arcy and Harold Fey. *Indians and Other Americans: Two Ways of Life Meet.* New York: Harper Perennial, 1970.

Lewis and Clark Expedition (1804–1806)

In 1803 after the purchase of Louisiana from Napoleon, President Thomas Jefferson sent Meriwether Lewis, his private secretary, and Lieutenant William Clark to head an expedition to explore the newly acquired territory and find the fabled Northwest Passage to the Pacific Ocean. The expedition left St. Louis, Missouri, on May 14, 1804, traveling up the Missouri River. By November they reached present-day North Dakota, where they built a fort and spent the winter with the Mandan Indians. During the winter they became acquainted with a French-Canadian trapper, Toussaint Charbonneau, whom they employed as scout and interpreter, along with his wife, **Sacajawea**, and infant son. Sacajawea's presence was especially beneficial when the expedition fortuitously encountered her brother (chief of the Shoshones), who sold them horses and provided guides over the Bitteroot Mountains. At the Clearwater River, the party traded horses for canoes and then paddled down the Clearwater, Snake, and Columbia Rivers. On November 15, 1805, the expedition reached the mouth of the Columbia where they built Fort Clatsop and spent the winter. The following year, the explorers retraced their steps, returning to St. Louis, amid much fanfare, on September 23, 1806. Both Lewis and Clark were given land and significant political appointments. Lewis became governor of the Louisiana Territory, and Clark of the Missouri Territory. The Lewis and Clark expedition provided invaluable information on the interior of the North American continent and finally dispelled the myth of the Northwest Passage. (AMM)

Spurred by the Louisiana Purchase in 1803, the federal government supported the expedition of Meriwether Lewis (top) and William Clark from St. Louis, Missouri, to the Pacific Ocean. *Library of Congress.*

BIBLIOGRAPHY

Ambrose, Stephen. *Undaunted Courage: Meriwether Lewis, Thomas Jefferson, and the Opening of the American West.* New York: Simon & Schuster, 1996.

Lewis, Meriwether. *History of the Expedition under the Command of Captains Lewis & Clark to the Sources of the Missouri, Then across the Rocky Mountains and down the River Columbia to the Pacific Ocean.* London: D. Nutt, 1905.

Liberalism. *See* Conservatism and Liberalism

Little Bighorn, Battle of. *See* Battle of Little Bighorn

Little Turtle's War

As Ohio Valley Indians and Kentucky settlers waged border warfare in the late 1780s, the federal government dispatched army troops to the area to quell Indian resistance. The Miami war chief Little Turtle (c. 1752–1812) led a force of Miamis, Delawares, and Shawnees that defeated General Josiah Harmar's forces in 1790 and then dealt the American army its worst defeat ever at the hands of Native Americans by crushing General Arthur St. Clair's army on the upper Wabash River in 1791. The Indian confederation under Little Turtle eventually lost at the Battle of Fallen Timbers in August 1794. **See** Treaty of Greenville (1795) in Appendix 1. (GO)

BIBLIOGRAPHY

Carter, Harvey Lewis. *The Life and Times of Little Turtle.* Urbana: University of Illinois Press, 1987.

Sword, Wiley. *President Washington's Indian War: The Struggle for the Old Northwest, 1790–1795.* Norman: University of Oklahoma Press, 1985.

Arlinda Faye Locklear (1951–)

As an attorney for the **Native American Rights Fund**, Locklear successfully defended the right of the Cheyenne River Reservation Sioux to retain criminal jurisdiction in their territory. With this case, *Solem v. Bartlett,* 465 U.S. 463 (1984), she became the first Indian woman to argue before the United States Supreme Court. (KJB)

BIBLIOGRAPHY

Malinowski, Sharon, ed. *Notable Native Americans.* Detroit: Gale 1995.

Lone Wolf v. Hitchcock (1903)

Lone Wolf, a Kiowa, brought a suit to block the sale of surplus land on **reservations** without tribal consent. The courts ruled that the government did not need the consent of the tribes to sell the land. In *Lone Wolf v. Hitchcock* (1903), the U.S. Supreme Court ruled that the treaties could be breached in times of federal necessity. This demonstrated to Congress that Native American treaties had a political vulnerability.

BIBLIOGRAPHY

Cohen, Felix S. *Felix Cohen's Handbook of Federal Indian Law.* Charlottesville, VA: Mitchie, Bobbs-Merrill, 1982; Ft. Lauderdale, FL: Five Rings Press, 1986.

Getches, David, Charles F. Wilkinson, and Robert A. Williams, Jr. *Cases and Materials of Federal Indian Law.* 3rd ed. St. Paul, MN: West Publishing, 1993.

Long Walk

In an effort to achieve territorial continuity, control over resources, and full **sovereignty**, the U.S. government made removal of Indians from their lands a formal policy in the 1830s. By the 1860s American expansion into New Mexico was increasing rapidly partly as a result of the **Civil War**. Brigadier General James H. Carleton launched an active campaign against the Indians, using Kit Carson, a colonel in territorial militia, to lead the attack against the Mescalero Apaches and the Navajos. In the winter of 1863 the U.S. Army, led by Carson, rounded up thousands of Navajos and forced them to march over 400 miles to the Bosque Redondo Reservation, which was established for their exile.

Approximately 11,000 Navajos survived the "Long Walk" and, together with about 450 Mescalero Apaches, were kept in the reservation, which more resembled a concentration camp. The Bosque Redondo experiment was described as a "nightmarish catastrophe" because of a combination of corrupt and ill-planned government administration, natural disasters, and a smallpox epidemic that killed more than a fourth of all people detained there. The Mescalero Apaches escaped one night in November 1865, and the Navajos were allowed to return to a fraction of their lands in Arizona on June 18, 1868. The Long Walk and the years at Bosque Redondo remain as vivid in the minds of the Navajos and Mescalero Apaches as does the **Trail of Tears** in the minds of the Cherokee. (MS)

BIBLIOGRAPHY

Gordon-McCutchan, R.C. *Kit Carson: Indian Fighter or Indian Killer?* Boulder: University Press of Colorado, 1996.

Trafzer, Clifford E. *The Kit Carson Campaign: The Last Great Navajo War.* Norman: University of Oklahoma Press, 1982.

Longest Walk

The Longest Walk started in February 1978 in San Francisco and ended in July of the same year in Washington, D.C. The march was led by the **American Indian Movement (AIM)**, and its goal was to expose and challenge the backlash movement against Indian treaty rights, which was gaining strength. The number of participants who walked across the country varied along the way and reached the assessed number of 80,000 upon arrival to Washington, D.C. On July 25, 1978, at the mass rally held at the Washington Monument, AIM members delivered a manifesto challenging the forces advocating resumption of the termination policy, the federal definition of self-determination, and the entire structure of the **Indian Reorganization Act**. The American Indian Movement also demanded the acknowledgment of the right of sovereignty for all indigenous nations. It is hard to assess the impact of the Longest Walk, but most of the threatening congressional bills were not passed, while the American Indian Freedom of Religion Act was passed, in the same year. (MS)

BIBLIOGRAPHY

Robbins, Rebecca L. "American Indian Self-Determination: Comparative Analysis and Rhetorical Criticism." *Issues in Radical Therapy/New Studies on the Left* XIII, nos. 3 and 4 (summer-fall 1988): 48–58.

Looking Glass (ca. 1823–1877)

Looking Glass was one of the principal chiefs of the nontreaty Nez Perces. He opposed the 1863 "**Thief Treaty**," but he pursued a policy of passive resistance until federal troops attacked his village during the 1877 **Nez Perce War**. After joining Chief Joseph's people in their flight to Canada, Looking Glass died at the Battle of the Bear Paw Mountains. (AHF)

BIBLIOGRAPHY

Josephy, Alvin M., Jr. *The Nez Percé Indians and the Opening of the Northwest.* Lincoln: University of Nebraska Press, 1979.

Lavender, David. *Let Me Be Free: The Nez Perce Tragedy.* New York: HarperCollins, 1992.

Lord Dunmore's War (1773–1774)

In 1773, Lord Dunmore, governor of Virginia, sent surveyors across the Ohio River. Conflict broke out between the Shawnee, who did not want the surveyors on their land, and the English. Despite attempts at peace by the Shawnee principal chief, Cornstalk, the conflict continued and on June 10, 1774, Lord Dunmore declared war. Both the English and Shawnee suffered from inept planning and execution, so they signed a truce on October 26, 1774. (AMM)

BIBLIOGRAPHY

Voris, Michael J. *The Colonial Trilogy: Lord Dunmore's War.* Cincinnati: Society of Colonial Wars in the State of Ohio, 1972.

Louisiana Purchase

The Louisiana Purchase (1803) was probably the most important event of President Thomas Jefferson's first term of office. The United States government was concerned because the new nation was surrounded on all sides by land controlled by other countries. An allegiance with Britain seemed necessary. France offered to sell the Louisiana land for about $15 million dollars, which the United States accepted. In return they received 827,487 square miles of land. The territory stretched from the Mississippi River to the Rocky Mountains, and from the Gulf of Mexico to the Canadian border. The acquisition stretched the guidelines of the Constitution, for the document did not authorize new purchases of land.

The purchase was not positive news for the Plains Indians. Land-hungry Americans raced across the territory, claiming land for themselves. The Caddo tribe seemed to be the only enthusiastic Indian tribe, because Americans paid far more for furs than the French or the Spanish did. There was a provision in the Louisiana Territory stating that the Indian land claims were to be respected, but this provision was ignored. **See also** Indian Territory; Plains Wars.

BIBLIOGRAPHY

Keats, John. *Eminent Domain: the Louisiana Purchase and the Making of America.* New York: Charter House, 1973.

Sprague, Marshall. *So Vast, so Beautiful a Land: Louisiana and the Purchase.* Boston: Little, Brown, 1974.

Lyng v. Northwest Indian Cemetery Protective Association (1988)

The U.S. Supreme Court's decision in *Lyng v. Northwest Indian Cemetery Protective Association,* 485 U.S. (1988), eroded the First Amendment rights of Native Americans and eviscerated the **American Indian Religious Freedom Act.** For over a decade prior to the ruling, the Yurok, Karok, and Tolowa Indians fought to stop the U.S. Forest Service from paving a road and harvesting timber in a culturally sensitive portion of the Six Rivers National Forest in northern California. The federal district and appellate courts upheld the Indians' argument that the proposed development would threaten an area central to their religious beliefs and burden the free exercise of their religion. But the Supreme Court overruled these decisions and subjected Indian religious freedom to a stricter test. Since *Lyng*, Indians must prove that they have either been penalized for practicing their beliefs or coerced into violating them. If neither condition is met, then no infringement has occurred. (AHF)

BIBLIOGRAPHY

McAndrew, Stephen. "*Lyng v. Northwest Indian Cemetery Protective Ass'n*: Closing the Door to Indian Religious Sites." *Southwestern University Law Review* 18 (1989): 603–29.

Wunder, John R. *"Retained by the People": A History of American Indians and the Bill of Rights*. New York: Oxford University Press, 1994.

M

Peter MacDonald (1928–)

Peter MacDonald was born on the Navajo Reservation. He served in the Marines in the Pacific campaign as a Navajo code talker. After the war he worked as a migrant worker. However, military service changed his life by exposing him to the mainstream of American culture. Utilizing the G.I. Bill, he attended Bacone College in Oklahoma and finished an electrical engineering degree at the University of Oklahoma in 1957. He worked for Hughes Aircraft in Los Angeles, participating in the Polaris missile program. MacDonald returned to the reservation to work for the Navajo Nation in 1963. He had a kind of education the nation needed and knew how to move within both worlds. He worked for the tribe during a period of enormous change, when the Navajos struggled to ward off the exploitation of their mineral deposits. Mining companies' long-term cheap leases made with the **Bureau of Indian Affairs (BIA)** pitted them against tribal interests. The odds were against the tribe at the time of enormous boom in the West.

MacDonald was elected tribal chairman four times, serving in 1970–1983 and 1987–1991. In 1975 he cofounded the **Council of Energy Resource Tribes** (CERT), a group of 25 Indian tribes with valuable resources. CERT advocated utilization of these resources to create jobs and self-sufficiency financially. By the mid-1970s, tribal resources had been exploited to little benefit for the tribes themselves and with serious environmental consequences. CERT worked to change this. The development of resources caused divisions within the tribe. MacDonald's tribal government was accused of corruption, and in 1991 he was convicted of fraud and embezzlement and sentenced to federal penitentiary. (JP)

BIBLIOGRAPHY

Iverson, Peter. *The Navajo Nation*. Albuquerque: University of New Mexico Press, 1983.

MacDonald, Peter with Ted Schwarz. *The Last Warrior: Peter MacDonald and the Navajo Nation*. New York: Orion Books, 1993.

Major Crimes Act (1885)

The Major Crimes Act, 23 Stat. 362 (1885), was enacted by Congress to eliminate Indian jurisdiction over seven crimes—murder, manslaughter, rape, burglary, larceny, assault with intent to kill, and arson. It has since been amended piecemeal to include kidnapping, incest, and several other crimes.

The act was a response to the decision of the U.S. Supreme Court in **Ex Parte Crow Dog** (1883), upholding exclusive Sioux jurisdiction over wrongful acts among the Sioux in their own country. Sioux customs permitted the families of offenders and victims to resolve wrongs by compensation and agreement; this tradition stirred up hostility in Congress and generated support for asserting United States jurisdiction over Indians for wrongs committed among themselves.

The act overrode a substantial area of indigenous self-government, bringing specified crimes within the power of federal law-enforcement agencies to be prosecuted in federal courts, notwithstanding that the alleged perpetrator(s) and victim(s) might be members of the same native nation. Subsequent aggressive intervention by federal law-enforcement officials greatly undercut the cohesion of indigenous nations, as their own social processes were increasingly denied and their members subjected to federal criminal law for "major" offenses. **See also** Friends of the Indian; *United States v. Kagama* (1886). (PPE)

BIBLIOGRAPHY

Cohen, Felix S. *Handbook of Federal Indian Law*. Washington, DC: U.S. Government Printing Office, 1942.

Wilma Mankiller (1945–)

Born in Tahlequah, Oklahoma, on November 18, 1945, to a full-blooded Cherokee and his Euro-American wife, Wilma Mankiller served one term as deputy principal chief and two as principal chief of the Cherokee Nation. Due to health considerations, she refused to seek reelection in 1995.

The first woman to serve as chief of any major Native-American tribe, she became active in supporting Native-American protesters during the takeover of Alcatraz Island in 1969. In 1981, she founded the Cherokee Nation's Community Development Department, which developed and activated projects that modernized homes on the reservation. As chief she signed an agreement with the United States in 1990 that allowed the Cherokee Nation to manage its federal funds; also, under her direction, Cherokees saw an improvement of their tribal police force and courts. In 1992, President Bill Clinton asked Mankiller to serve as representative for all Native Americans at a national economic summit in Little Rock, Arkansas. (KJB)

BIBLIOGRAPHY

Mankiller, Wilma and Michael Wallis. *Mankiller: A Chief and Her People*. New York: St. Martin's Press, 1993.

Swartz, Melissa. *Wilma Mankiller: Principal Chief of the Cherokees*. New York: Chelsea House, 1994.

George Manuel (1921–1989)

In 1958, George Manuel helped form the Aboriginal Native Rights Committee of the Interior Tribes to organize a united Indian front against Canadian government policies on alcohol prohibition, voting rights, land claims, and educational reform. Manuel also acted in the 1950s as chief of the Shusway. Manuel was president of the National Indian Brotherhood from 1970 to 1976, president of the Union of British Columbian Indian Chiefs from 1977 to 1981, and president of the World Council of Indigenous Peoples from 1975 to 1981. In 1974, Manuel published *The Fourth World: An Indian Reality*, a work that outlined his philosophical and spiritual beliefs.

BIBLIOGRAPHY

Manuel, George. *The Fourth World: An Indian Reality*. New York: Free Press, 1974.

Manuelito (1818–1893)

Manuelito (Hastiin Chilhaajinii, also known as Holy Boy and Pistol Bullet) was a Navajo war chief and son-in-law of Narbona. He broke with Narbona on the issue of accommodation with the Americans, and advocated war after Narbona was murdered. The Navajo headmen selected him as spokesman at the signing of the treaty of Laguna Negra (1855). He led a siege of Fort Defiance (1860) with **Barboncito**. He was the last Navajo leader to surrender in the Navajo War, and was a signatory to the **Treaty of Bosque Redondo** (1868). As leader of the Navajo Council (1883), he requested U.S. compliance with treaty terms. An implacable and deadly enemy, Manuelito was known as an enforcer of customary law who could kill without mercy or hesitation. In later years he advocated education for his people and supported compliance with terms of treaty. (JN)

BIBLIOGRAPHY

Johnson, Broderick H. and Virginia Hoffman. *Navajo Biographies*. Rough Rock, AZ: Navajo Curriculum Center, Rough Rock Demonstration School, 1978.

Roman Bitsuie, personal communications, November, 1997.

Mungo Martin (ca. 1880–1962)

Kwakwaka'wakw (Kwakiutl) chief and carver Mungo Martin facilitated a modern revitalization of Northwest Coast art and culture. Known for his superlative totem posts, Martin helped preserve traditional ceremonies, stories, and artistic techniques during a long period of government repression. He defied the Canadian Indian Act's ban on potlatches, and he lived to see it lifted in 1951. The year after his death, Martin became the first Native American to receive the Canada Council Medal. (AHF)

BIBLIOGRAPHY

DeLaguna, Frederica. "Mungo Martin, 1879–1962." *American Antrhopologist* 65 (August 1963): 894–96.

Nuytten, Phil. *The Totem Carvers: Charlie James, Ellen Neel, and Mungo Martin*. Vancouver, BC: Panorama Publications, Ltd., 1982.

Massasoit (d. 1661)

Massasoit led a confederation of Wampanoag Indians at the time Plymouth settlers established the first permanent English colony in the area in 1620. He encouraged close ties with the English that resulted in demands for Wampanoag land. His successor, Metacomet (**King Philip**), led a revolt against the English in 1675. (GO)

BIBLIOGRAPHY

Bourne, Russell. *The Red King's Rebellion: Racial Politics in New England, 1675–1678*. New York: Oxford University Press, 1990.

Salisbury, Neal. *Manitou and Providence: Indians, Europeans, and the Making of New England, 1500–1643*. New York: Oxford University Press, 1982.

McClanahan v. Arizona State Tax Commission (1973)

The decision in *McLanahan v. Arizona State Tax Commission* 411 US 164 (1973) eroded tribal **sovereignty**. The courts said that the question was not about sovereignty, but instead whether treaties and tribal laws had given rise to a "preemption" in the area under consideration, which would allow state intrusions into **Indian country**. The state had been warned that it could not tax on a Navajo reservation without the Indians waving their treaty rights, but the Navajo reservation was not an allotted reservation. Therefore, state taxation was allowed. **See also** Reservation Economics; Taxation; Tribal–State Affairs.

BIBLIOGRAPHY

Deloria, Vine, Jr. and Clifford M. Lytle. *American Indians, American Justice*. Austin: University of Texas Press, 1983.

Janet McCloud (1934–)

Janet McCloud (Tulalip) has been active in women's causes, Indian education, cultural preservation, and native fishing rights. McCloud is the cofounder of several organizations, including the Northwest Indian Women's Circle and the Indigenous Women's Network. (MR)

BIBLIOGRAPHY

Katz, Jane. *Messenger of the Wind: Native American Women Tell Their Life Stories*. New York: Ballantine Books, 1995.

McKay v. Campbell (1871)

In *McKay v. Campbell*, 16 Fed. 161 (1871), William C. McKay, a "nine-sixteenths" blood Indian (part English and part Chinook), charged that he had been denied the right to vote under the laws of Oregon. The voting registrar, James A. Campbell, based his denial on the fact that McKay was "an alien and not a citizen of the United States." Federal district judge Deady said the case centered around a single point of law: "Was the plaintiff born subject to the jurisdiction of the United States—under its allegiance?"

Upon review, Judge Deady ruled that McKay was not a citizen and could not vote. McKay had relied on the **Fourteenth** and Fifteeenth **Amendments** which, he argued, applied to half-breed Indians who were born in the geographical limits of the United States.

But Deady stated that regardless of whether McKay adopted his mother's status as a Chinook Indian (which made him an "alien"), or his father's status (as a British National), the only way McKay could become a U.S. citizen was by "complying with the laws for the naturalization of aliens." (DEW)

BIBLIOGRAPHY

Wunder, John R. *Native American Law and Colonialism, Before 1776 to 1903*. New York: Garland, 1996.

D'Arcy McNickle (1904–1977)

D'Arcy McNickle, a scholar, activist, writer, and one of the most important Native American figures in the twentieth century, was born on the Flathead Reservation in western Montana. He was an enrolled member of the Confederated Salish and Kootenai Tribes. He attended boarding schools on the reservation and in Chemawa, Oregon, the University of Montana, and Oxford University in England, and decided to pursue a literary career. His novels *The Surrounded* (1936), *Runner in the Sun* (1954) and *Wind from an Enemy Sky* (1978) combine fiction and Native American history. In 1936, he joined **John Collier's** staff at the **Bureau of Indian Affairs**. He resigned in 1952 because of the U.S. government's termination policy. He then started a career in applied anthropology publishing several scholarly works, such as *Indians and Other Americans* (1959) with Harold Fey. He was a founding member of the **National Congress of American Indians** in 1944, and an organizer of the **American Indian Chicago Conference** in 1961. In 1966 the University of Saskatchewan at Regina invited him to develop its new anthropology department. In 1971 McNickle helped found the Center for the History of the American Indian at the Newberry Library in Chicago. McNickle died in Albuquerque in 1977. (JP)

BIBLIOGRAPHY

Parker, Dorothy. *Singing an Indian Song: A Biography of D'Arcy McNickle*. Lincoln: University of Nebraska Press, 1992.

Russell C. Means (1939–)

Russell Means was born an Oglala Dakota in 1939 on the Pine Ridge Indian Reservation near the Black Hills of South Dakota. Means is a radical political leader and **American Indian Movement (AIM)** organizer. He took part in the **Trail of Broken Treaties**, the siege of **Wounded Knee**, and other protests in the 1970s. Means continues to be an influential activist, as well as a recording artist, actor, and writer. He has written on the incongruence of Marxism and indigenism, and spoken out against the cultural appropriation of Indian ways by New Age spiritualists. For over 12 years, Means has traveled throughout the world working with the United Nations. In 1991, Means began a career in Hollywood. He has starred in numerous feature films, written his autobiography, recorded two albums, and started his own production company. (RAC)

BIBLIOGRAPHY

Means, Russell. "The Same Old Song." In Ward Churchill, ed. *Marxism and Native Americans*. Boston: South End Press, 1983.

Menominee Tribe of Indians v. United States (1968)

Menominee Tribe of Indians v. United States, 391 U.S. 404 (1968), concerned the method by which the federal government could terminate its treaty obligations to tribes. In 1954 the Menominee Tribe was legally terminated by federal law and the tribe came under state jurisdiction. The state gradually imposed its hunting and fishing regulations over the Menominee people, operating from the jurisdictional posture that the Menominee Termination Act had abrogated the Indians' hunting and fishing rights that had been implicitly reserved under the 1854 Treaty of Wolf River.

The tribe brought suit against the United States to recover just compensation for the loss of these rights. The question before the Supreme Court was whether the tribe's rights to hunt and fish were extinguished by the 1954 Termination Act. The Court held that these valuable property rights had survived the termination legislation because the act had made no mention of hunting and fishing rights. The Court decision stated, "The intention to abrogate or modify a treaty is not to be lightly imputed to the Congress." **See also** Deer, Ada; Fishing and Hunting Treaty Rights; House Concurrent Resolution 108; Termination Resolution. (DEW)

BIBLIOGRAPHY

Foerster, Arthur F. "Divisions and Delusion." *UCLA Law Review* 46 (1999) 1333–74.

Meriam Report of 1928

This exhaustive study of **federal Indian policy,** ranging from the passage of the General Allotment Act of 1887 (the **Dawes Act)** to the 1920s, was conducted by the Brookings Institute under a special grant from John D. Rockefeller. The findings were published as *The Problem of Indian Administration*, but the document is commonly referred to as the Meriam Report after the study's principal author, Lewis Meriam. The report discusses issues of health, economics, **education,** and federal administration.

The Meriam Report was largely critical of the services provided by the federal government and of its overall management of Indian affairs. The report cited specific cases of malnutrition, inadequate education, and high rates of tuberculosis and infant mortality. Finding the condition of most Native Americans "deplorable," the report recommended many changes in the administration of programs, including increased autonomy for native peoples. It also urged Congress to allot the necessary funds to meet all outstanding treaty obligations.

Highly influential, the report was used as the basis of many reforms that occurred during the Hoover and Roosevelt administrations. Its impact can be best seen in the adoption of various "Indian New Deal" measures under Franklin Roosevelt, including the **Indian Reorganization Act of 1934** (which increased Native American self-government and protected cultural events). **See also** Henry Roe Cloud; Indian Arts and Crafts Board Act of 1935

BIBLIOGRAPHY

Brookings Institution. *The Problem of Indian Administration.* New York: Johnson Reprint Corp., 1971.

Holm, Tom. *Indians and Progressives: From Vanishing Policy to the Indian New Deal.* Ann Arbor, MI: University Microfilms International, 1979.

Mesa Verde

Mesa Verde National Park in Colorado, established by Congress on June 29, 1906, was the first cultural park set aside in the National Park System. Mesa Verde, Spanish for "Green Table," is famous for the cliff dwellings and numerous mesa-top villages built by ancestral Pueblo people between 600 and 1300 A.D. The United States negotiated with Weminuche Ute Chief Ignacio for the ruins, in exchange for $300 per year and grazing rights. However, the land specified in the 1906 act left out many of the major ruins, so Congress added an amendment to it to include any ruins within five miles of the proposed park. In 1908, the Utes contested the "five mile" designation. After further negotiations an agreement was submitted to Congress in 1913 which gave the park an additional 24,500 acres in exchange for 30,240 acres added to the Ute Mountain reservation. UNESCO designated Mesa Verde as a World Cultural Heritage Site on September 8, 1978. (AMM)

BIBLIOGRAPHY

Lister, Robert H. and Florence C. Lister. *Mesa Verde National Park: Preserving the Past.* Mancos, CO: ARA Mesa Verde Co., 1987.

Hazel Mary Martell. *Native Americans and Mesa Verde.* New York : Dillon Press, 1993.

Mescalero Apache Tribe v. Jones (1973)

Mescalero Apache Tribe v. Jones, 411 U.S. 145 (1973), resulted from the tribe's construction of the Sierra Blanca Ski Resort on land owned by the tribe and bordering, but not on, the reservation. New Mexico levied a sales tax on the gross receipts of the ski resort and a use tax on the materials used to build the ski lifts. The tribe argued that it was exempt from state taxes. The U.S. Supreme Court ruled that while income derived from trust lands is exempt from state taxation, income earned by the tribe acting as a business on lands not in trust was taxable. This case is contrasted with *McClanahan v. Arizona State Tax Commission* (1973), issued the same day, which invalidated the imposition of a state tax on income earned on the reservation by an Indian. (AMM)

BIBLIOGRAPHY

Wunder, John R., ed. *Recent Legal Issues for American Indians, 1968 to the Present.* Garland Publishing, 1996.

Mexican War (1846–1848)

Since virtually no one believes the war with Mexico was necessary in terms of national defense, there is lively debate about the causes. Some historians see a cabal of slaveholding interests seeking to expand the United States in an area contiguous to the slave states as a counterbalance to the ongoing expansion in the **Louisiana Purchase** territories, most of which were contiguous to free states.

Another school of thought blames mercantile interests of the North seeking to profit from war and the plunder of war. The extent of President James K. Polk's personal responsibility, and therefore his motivations, is open to question.

This debate illustrates that many segments of U.S. society had something to gain by a war with a militarily inferior power, while few had anything to lose. Add to this the romantic ideal of "manifest destiny," and it becomes almost as useful to speculate upon why the Mexican War stopped with the annexation of an area from West Texas to California.

Part of the answer is that the acquisition of what is now the southwestern United States from Mexico carried with it a dark-skinned population of Spanish and American Indian ancestry for whom English was often a third language when it was spoken at all. The territory ceded to the United States by Mexico included Indian pueblos along the Rio Grande (Rio Bravo) drainage that predated the Spanish Conquest, as well as ancestral homes of the Diné (Navajo), Indé (Apache), Hopi, Ute, Tohono O'odham (Papago), Akimel O'odham (Pima), and other tribes. Some of these tribes had never bent their knees to the Spaniards or the Mexicans, and they would continue to offer violent resistance to the Americans until near the end of the nineteenth century.

The new border created by the Mexican War was porous and remains so to this day, with many extended families settled on both sides of the border and border crossings made in isolated parts of the Chihuahuan and Sonoran Deserts without formality. **See also** Treaty of Guadalupe-Hidalgo (1848) and see the text of the treaty in Appendix 1. (SR)

BIBLIOGRAPHY

Bauer, K. Jack and Robert W. Johannsen. *The Mexican War, 1846–1848.* Lincoln: University of Nebraska Press, 1992.

Eisenhower, John S. D. *So Far from God: The U.S. War with Mexico, 1846–1848.* New York: Random House, 1989.

Mahin, Dean B. *Olive Branch and Sword: The United States and Mexico, 1845–1848.* Jefferson, NC: McFarland and Co., 1997.

Ruiz, Ramon Eduardo. *The Mexican War—Was It Manifest Destiny?* New York: Holt, Rinehart and Winston, 1963.

Missionaries

An integral part of the colonizing effort of major European powers, missionaries became the vanguard of the commercial and territorial invasion of America. Those converted by the

Europeans often went on to serve as missionaries to other Native Americans. Christian Indians lived in "praying towns," segregated from their more so-called savage native neighbors. These towns became the first reservations.

On reservations and sometimes in remote areas, missionaries established schools. For some tribes, particularly in the South, missionaries became a necessary component in tribal survival strategy. Cherokee, Creek, Choctaw, and Chickasaw leaders encouraged missionaries to enter the communities and establish schools, so that their children could compete in the emerging Anglo-American society. Congregationalists, Presbyterian (American Board), and Moravian missionaries answered the call to educate the southern Indian nations, shaping an educated elite of future Native American leaders among the nations that became known as the **Five Civilized Tribes**.

As Euro-Americans continued to push into the interior of the continent, representatives of various denominations joined them. Moravian, Quaker, Baptist, Episcopal, Methodist, Congregational, Presbyterian, and Dutch Reformed churches sent representatives west as the American frontier moved across the continent. While conversion remained a primary goal, several missionaries attempted to protect Native American rights, although their reform efforts often did more harm than good. In several instances, missionary influence caused nations to divide in Christian versus non-Christian factions or caused confusion when two or more denominations competed for converts. By the mid-nineteenth century, missionaries were being used by the United States government as "peace policy" agents in an attempt to end corruption on the reservations and, eventually, as agents of indoctrination in the Americanization process. Not until the 1930s would Native Americans find bans on tribal religions, dances, festivals, and other cultural manifestations less restrictive. (KJB)

BIBLIOGRAPHY

Axtell, James. *The Invasion Within: The Contest of Cultures in Colonial North America.* New York: Oxford University Press, 1985.

McNickle, D'Arcy. *Native American Tribalism: Indian Survivals and Renewals.* New York: 1973.

Prucha, Francis Paul. *American Indian Policy in Crisis: Christian Reformers and the Indian, 1865-1900.* Norman, OK: University of Oklahoma Press, 1976.

Tinker, George E. *Missionary Conquest: The Gospel and Native American Cultural Genocide.* Minneapolis: Fortress Press, 1993.

Mississippi Choctaw Band v. Holyfield (1989)

Problems occurred when the Mississippi Choctaw Band tried to stop an adoption agreement signed by the parents of two Indian children. According to the Indian Child Welfare Act of 1978, which dealt with problems originating from the large numbers of Indian children separated from their families, the tribal courts had jurisdiction to control such adoption agreements. The family, however, disagreed, stating that the children were not born on and had never lived on the reservation and, as a result, were not legal reservation citizens.

The Supreme Court of Mississippi found the adoption contract binding, agreeing that the children had never dwelled on the reservation and were therefore exempt from its jurisdiction. The United States Supreme Court, however, disagreed; in a decision made on April 3, 1989, in *Mississippi Choctaw Band v. Holyfield*, 490 U.S. 30, the Court stated that the children were legal residents of the reservation because their parents were. The ruling moved this custody issue under the review of the tribal courts.

BIBLIOGRAPHY

Beane, Syd. "Indian Child Welfare Social Policy History Module." *In Collaboration: The Key to Defining Entry Level Competencies for Public Child Welfare Workers Serving Indian Communities.* Tempe, AZ: State University, School of Social Work, 1989.

Moe v. Confederated Salish and Kootenai Tribes (1976)

In *Moe v. Confederated Salish and Kootenai Tribes*, 425 U.S. 463 (1976), Justice Rehnquist argued that the sales tax imposed by Montana could not lawfully be collected when items were sold on the reservation to Indians. However, the tax should lawfully be collected from non-Indians, even when purchases were made from Indian sellers on the reservation. In this case, Rehnquist held that the doctrine of federal preemption is not a barrier to otherwise lawful state taxation. (AMM)

BIBLIOGRAPHY

Minnis, Michael. "Judicially Suggested Harassment of Indian Tribes: the Potawatomis Revisit Moe and Colville." *American Indian Law Review* 16, no. 2 (Summer 1991): 289–318.

John Mohawk (1945–)

John Mohawk worked as editor for *Akwesasne Notes* from 1976 to 1983, eventually becoming in 1985 president of Associated Indigenous Communications. During his career, Mohawk has served as a lecturer in the American Studies program of the State University of New York, Buffalo, while also acting as chairman of the board for the Seventh Generation Fund and as a board member of the Indian Law Resource Center.

BIBLIOGRAPHY

Mohawk, John C. "Indian Economic Development: An Evolving Concept of Sovereignty." *Buffalo Law Review* 39, no. 2 (Spring 1991): 495–506.

Mohawk Nation (Kanien'kehaka)

The Mohawks were one of the founding nations of the Iroquois Confederacy, also called the **Six Nations (Haudenosaunee) Confederacy,** which provided one model for the form of government adopted by the United States. The Mohawks, as strong warriors and "true Americans," were symbolically adopted by colonists in the protest against British rule known as the Boston Tea Party. Ironically, the Mohawk sided with the British during the **American Revolution** and have maintained their claim to independence from the United States ever since. **See** The Constitution of the Iroquois Nation in Appendix 1. (LCJ)

BIBLIOGRAPHY

Alfred, Gerald R. *Heeding the Voices of Our Ancestors: Kahnawake Mohawk Politics and the Rise of Native Nationalism*. New York: Oxford University Press, 1995.
Lyons, Oren, et al. *Exiled in the Land of the Free: Democracy, Indian Nations, and the U.S. Constitution*. Santa Fe, NM: Clear Light Publishers, 1992.

Montana v. United States (1981)

The Supreme Court's decision in *Montana v. United States,* 450 U.S. 544 (1981), held that a Native American government generally has no authority over those who are not members of the tribe, even if they own land within reservation boundaries. The case involved the jurisdiction of the Crow Tribe (in eastern Montana) over hunting and fishing by non-Indians who had purchased land within its reservation.

The decision followed the Court's negation of tribal control over nonmembers in ***Oliphant v. Suquamish Indian Tribe***, 435 U.S. 191 (1978). However, ***Montana v. United States*** had a broader impact: the Court stated that the only times **tribal governments** could assert authority over nonmembers were when nonmembers entered into agreements with tribes or their members, or when major interests of the tribe or its government were at stake. One result of the decision was that many tribal governments had to turn to state or federal governments for any enforcement of environmental laws on reservations. **See also** Tribal–State Affairs. (LCJ)

BIBLIOGRAPHY

Meredith, Howard. *Modern American Indian Tribal Government and Politics*. Tsaile, AZ: Navajo Community College Press, 1993.
O'Brien, Sharon. *American Indian Tribal Governments*. Norman: University of Oklahoma Press, 1989.

Carlos Montezuma (1865–1923)

Carlos Montezuma (Yavapai) was revered as a physician and as a Native-American rights activist. Montezuma attended the University of Illinois and Northwestern University and worked as a doctor through the Office of Indian Affairs. From 1916 until his death in 1923, Montezuma became a political activist for

From 1889 to 1896, Carlos Montezuma, a Yavapai Indian, worked for the Office of Indian Affairs as a physician. *Library of Congress.*

American-Indian causes and published a controversial newspaper called *Wassaja*, which constantly challenged governmental policies concerning native affairs and brought attention to native rights. His work often accused the United States government of imprisoning Indian peoples. (MKJ)

BIBLIOGRAPHY

Iverson, Peter. *Carlos Montezuma and the Changing World of American Indians*. Albuquerque: University of New Mexico Press, 1982.

Morton v. Mancari (1974)

The U.S. Supreme Court decided *Morton v. Mancari,* 417 U.S. 535, on June 17, 1974. With its decision, the Court reversed a finding of the U.S. district court, New Mexico District, which held that the BIA's preferential hiring practices violated the Fifth Amendment. The Supreme Court held that the **Bureau of Indian Affairs'** practice of giving preference to Indians when hiring was not a "racial" preference at all, but a condition of employment designed to make the BIA more responsive to its constituents. In addition, the decision reaffirmed the special trust status of Indians with the federal government. (RAC)

BIBLIOGRAPHY

Farnsworth, Wayne R. "Bureau of Indian Affairs Hiring Practices." (Case note). *Brigham Young University Law Review* no. 2 (spring 1996): 503–30.
Newton, Nell Jessup. "Federal Power Over Indians: Its Sources, Scope, and Limitations." *University of Pennsylvania Law Review* 132, no. 2 (January 1984): 195–288.

Moss Lake Occupation

A dissident group of Mohawks occupied state-owned land at Moss Lake (Herkimer County, New York) from 1974 to 1979, claiming that the 1797 treaty by which the state of New York acquired title to this land was invalid. In return for withdrawing from Moss Lake, the Mohawks received land in Clinton County, New York. **See also** Land and Water Rights. (MRC)

BIBLIOGRAPHY

"Moss Lake Indian Negotiations Files, 1974–1979." *Guide to Records Relating to Native Americans*. Albany: New York State Archives and Records Administration.
Pertusati, Linda. *In Defense of Mohawk Land*. Albany: State University of New York Press, 1997.

Motavato. *See* Black Kettle

Mourning Dove (1884–1936)

Mourning Dove, or Christine Quintasket, was the first Native-American woman to publish a novel, *Co-Ge-We-A,* in 1927, and the first woman to be elected to her tribal council, the Colville Federated Tribes of eastern Washington State, in 1935. She was particularly outspoken as an advocate for native women's issues and worked to generate understanding between native and nonnative peoples. (HHB)

BIBLIOGRAPHY

Miller, Jay, ed. *Mourning Dove: A Salishan Autobiography*. Lincoln and London: University of Nebraska Press, 1990.

Mourning Dove. *Co-Ge-We-A, the Half-Blood: A Depiction of the Great Montana Cattle Range*. Boston: Four Seas, 1927.

Mary Musgrove (1700–1765)

Beginning in 1733 Mary Musgrove worked as interpreter for James Oglethorpe, founder of the colony of Georgia, to help in negotiations with the Creeks (Muscogee). In the late 1740s she declared herself empress of the Muscogee Nation, claiming land in Georgia and three offshore islands: St. Catherine's, Ossabaw, and Sapelo. After demanding payment for past services, Musgrove, her husband Reverend Thomas Bosomworth, and a group of Muscogee Indians marched on Savannah, Georgia, in 1749. In 1759 settlements were made.

BIBLIOGRAPHY

Todd, Helen. *Mary Musgrove: Georgia Indian Princess*. Savannah, GA: Seven Oaks, 1981.

Raymond Nakai (1921–)

Raymond Nakai was Navajo Tribal Chairman between 1962 and 1970. A World War II veteran and radio personality, Chairman Nakai advocated education and economic development. His administration saw the adoption of the Navajo Bill of Rights and the founding of Navajo Community College in Tsaile, Arizona, in 1969. He worked with Interior Secretary Stewart Udall to negotiate deals beneficial for the tribe with energy firms interested in exploiting mineral and other resources on tribal lands. (JN)

BIBLIOGRAPHY

Johnson, Broderick H. and Virginia Hoffman. *Navajo Biographies.* Rough Rock, AZ: Navajo Curriculum Center, Rough Rock Demonstration School, 1978.

Natchez Revolt (1729)

In 1713, French traders began building trading posts along the Natchez region of the Mississippi River. Because the construction angered many the local Indians, the French erected Fort Rosalie in 1716 to protect whites in these areas from Native American attacks. In 1728, Fort Rosalie Commandant De Chepart announced plans to create a plantation on lands near the Natchez White Apple Village. Any Indian who was unwilling to leave these lands would be relocated by armed force. On November 28, 1729, the Natchez, fearing the seizure of their lands, began attacking French settlements. The Natchez killed 200 colonists and captured 50 other whites and about 300 slaves. On January 27, 1730, Sieur Jean-Paul Le Seur led an army of 500 Choctaw Indians against the Natchez in a campaign that freed about 100 slaves and rescued the majority of the captured women and children. A week later, more troops arrived, and on February 25, 1730, the Natchez surrendered. As a result of their defeat, over 400 Natchez Indians were sent to the West Indies as slaves and many others were scattered across the area. The defeat led to the eventual destruction of the Natchez culture.

BIBLIOGRAPHY

Campbell, Janet and Archie Sam. "The Primal Fire Lingers." *Chronicles of Oklahoma* 53, no. 4 (1976): 463–75.

Van Tuyl, Charles D. *The Natchez: Annotated Translations from Antoine Simon le Page du Pratz's Histore de la Louisiane.* Oklahoma Historical Society Series in Anthropology, No. 4. Oklahoma City: The Oklahoma Historical Society, 1979.

National Congress of American Indians (NCAI)

The National Congress of American Indians (NCAI), founded in 1944, is the oldest and largest national Indian organization. Its purpose is to protect the rights of Indian nations, to enhance the quality of life of Indian and native people, and to promote a better understanding among non-Indian people of Indian and native government, people, and rights. The NCAI serves as a forum for information-sharing between **tribal governments** and federal, state, and industry representatives. It also participates in numerous coalitions with national and regional organizations, businesses, and environmental and civil rights groups. It has a cooperative agreement with the U.S. Department of Energy to disseminate information to tribal governments and act as an intermediary on nuclear waste issues. (AMM)

BIBLIOGRAPHY

Hurtado, Albert L. and Peter Iverson, eds. *Major Problems in American Indian History: Documents and Essays. 1994.* Lexington, MA: D.C. Health.

National Council of American Indians

The National Council of American Indians was founded in 1926 as part of the "red progressive" movement. The council sought Indian voting rights and New Deal legislation in order to help assimilate Native Americans into the general U.S. culture. Founded by **Gertrude Simmons Bonnin** (Zitkala-Sa), a Sioux writer and musician, the group also included **Henry Roe Cloud** and Thomas L. Sloan among its leadership. First organized under the name Society of American Indians, the group worked from the motto "Help the Indians Help Themselves in Protecting their Rights and Properties." The organization was an important part of the lobbying efforts that secured the passage of the **Indian Reorganization Act of 1934**. The council went out of existence after World War II.

BIBLIOGRAPHY

Krupat, Arnold. *Native American Autobiography.* Madison: University of Wisconsin Press, 1994.

Rappaport, Doreen. *The Flight of the Red Bird.* New York: Dial, 1957.

National Council on Indian Opportunity

The National Council on Indian Opportunity was established by President Lyndon Johnson on March 6, 1968, to oversee and coordinate U.S. government efforts for Native Americans. The council was designated part of the Office of the Vice President; its membership included the vice president as chair, the principal cabinet officers in Indian affairs, and six Indian leaders appointed by the president. The council operated only until June 30, 1974, but it played an important role in developing President Richard Nixon's "**self-determination** without termination" policy and legislative program. **See also** Nixon's Special Message to Congress (1970). (EFM)

BIBLIOGRAPHY
Josephy, Alvin, Jr. *Red Power*. New York: McGraw-Hill, 1971.

National Indian Education Association (NIEA)

The National Indian Education Association (NIEA) was founded in 1969 to improve educational opportunities for American Indians and Alaska natives. NIEA is the largest and oldest Indian education organization in the nation; its headquarters is in Alexandria, Virginia. Its goal is to put Indian people in control of Indian education. A governing board of 12 members represents tribes across the country in lobbying Congress on issues relating to education in **Indian country**. NIEA holds an annual convention each year for all persons involved in Indian education. (MRC)

BIBLIOGRAPHY
"Indian Convention Tacoma's Largest." *Seattle Times* (October 27, 1997): B2.
Valencia, Carmen. "Indians Search for Answers on Education." *San Diego Union-Tribune* (October 19, 1990): B3.

National Indian Youth Council (NIYC)

The National Indian Youth Council (NIYC) was created in August 1961 in Gallup, New Mexico, by a group of 10 Native American college students who had met previously at a conference of the National Congress of American Indians at the University of Chicago. Founding members of the NIYC included Director Herbert Blatchford, Chairperson Mel Thom, President Clyde Warrior, and Vice President Shirley Witt. In the 1960s, the NIYC began focusing on the educational problems and discrimination faced by American Indians; members spoke across the nation on these and other relevant topics. In 1963, the NIYC began publishing their own activist newspaper, *ABC: Americans Before Columbus*. In 1964, the NIYC participated in "fish-ins" in Washington State. The group fished in waters that were restricted by state law but that, according to long-standing treaties, should have been open to Native American fishers. By the 1970s, the NIYC had opened chapters on a number of reservations and college campuses, and had expanded its activities by taking legal action against mining companies, creating Circle Films, and fighting for the preservation and protection of native rituals and sacred lands. By 1994, the group had grown to over 47,000 members.

BIBLIOGRAPHY
Steiner, Stan. *The New Indians*. New York: Dell Publishing Co., 1968.

National Museum of American Indian Act of 1989

The National Museum of American Indian Act was passed by Congress in 1989 with the intention of providing a place for the preservation, study, and exhibition of the life, language, literature, history, and arts of Native Americans. In October 1994, the museum was opened at The George Gustav Heye Center in Manhattan. Presently, the Heye Center contains both permanent and temporary exhibits that explore the diversity of the native people of the Americas. In 1998, the Cultural Resources Center will replace the museum's research branch in the Bronx, New York. The Cultural Resources Center will serve as home to the museum's collections, library and archives. The National Museum of the American Indian is scheduled to open on the Mall in Washington, D.C., in 2002, between the National Air and Space Museum and the Capitol. The museum will be a center for ceremonies and performances, as well as exhibits. (AMM)

BIBLIOGRAPHY
Cohen, Felix. *Felix Cohen's Handbook of Federal Indian Law.* Charlottesville, VA: Michie/Bobbs-Merrill, 1982; Ft. Lauderdale, FL: Five Rings Press, 1986.

National Office for the Rights of the Indigent

In 1974 the National Office for the Rights of the Indigent was absorbed by the National Association for the Advancement of Colored People (NAACP) Legal Defense and Educational Fund. One of the leaders in the association was **Vine Deloria Jr.,** a member of the Sioux family. (MRC)

BIBLIOGRAPHY
Wiget, Andrew. *Handbook of Native American Literature*. New York: Garland, 1996.

National Tribal Chairman's Association (NTCA)

The National Tribal Chairman's Association (NTCA) was an outgrowth of the **National Congress of American Indians** (NCAI). The group was formed in 1971 to focus on specific concerns of **tribal government** on the reservation, whereas NCAI was largely interested in the concerns of urban Indians. Over the years, NTCA has had an ambivalent relationship with NCAI, sometimes supportive, sometimes antagonistic, as each organization has attempted to speak for Native peoples. (AMM)

BIBLIOGRAPHY
Balz, Dan. "Indians See Dire Budget-Cut Consequences." *Washington Post* (March 14, 1981): A4.

Native American Graves Protection and Repatriation Act of 1990 (NAGPRA)

The Native American Graves Protection and Repatriation Act (NAGPRA) governs the relationships between federally recognized Native American tribal groups and federal or federally funded institutions, relating to archaeological excavations on federal or tribal lands. NAGPRA requires that Native Americans be consulted about the excavation of burial sites. The act also requires museums and other collection managers to produce inventories of the human remains, funerary objects, and sacred objects in their possession, and disclose this information to tribal groups. The tribal groups may then make repatriation claims on the materials. The goal of the NAGPRA is to ensure that Native American remains and funerary objects are treated in the same manner as Euro-American remains are, by giving Native Americans a legal say in defining ownership and control of cultural material. In many instances, NAGPRA has facilitated new positive relationships between Native Americans and museums. However, the legislation has been criticized from both sides. Some opponents claim that NAGPRA interferes with scientific investigation; others feel it does not go far enough to protect burial sites and enforce repatriation, or it is too general and difficult to apply in diverse, local circumstances. **See also** Repatriation of Remains. (HHB)

BIBLIOGRAPHY

Swidler, Nina, Kurt E. Dongoske, Roger Anyon, and Alan S. Downer, eds. *Native Americans and Archaeologists: Stepping Stones to Common Ground*. Walnut Creek, CA: Altamira Press, 1997.

Native American Programs Act of 1974

The Native American Programs Act of 1974 expanded guidelines in the Indian Education Act of 1972, which had provided financial assistance to districts, institutions, and agencies that had Native American students within their community schools. The 1974 amendments allowed Native Hawaiian groups to be included under these guidelines, thereby also providing them with financial benefits.

BIBLIOGRAPHY

Gros, Emma R. *Contemporary Federal Policy Toward American Indians*. Westport, CT: Greenwood Press, 1989.

Taylor, Theodore W. *American Indian Policy*. Mt. Airy, MD: Lomond Publications, 1983.

The Native American Rights Fund (NARF)

The Native American Rights Fund (NARF) is a nonprofit law firm that provides legal services to American Indians. NARF began in 1970 as an outgrowth of the federal government's Legal Services program and a Ford Foundation grant. The organization has played—and continues to play—a crucial role in defending Indian rights.

Based in Boulder, Colorado, NARF has assisted more than 190 tribes through litigating and lobbying on behalf of such issues as natural resources, tribal **sovereignty**, and human rights. In 1974, NARF convinced a federal court to uphold the fishing rights of Washington Indians. Through NARF's arguments in *Solem v. Bartlett* (1984), the Supreme Court barred South Dakota from exercising criminal jurisdiction over **Indian lands**. NARF helped convince Congress to pass the

Native American Graves Protection and Repatriation Act of 1990 (NAGPRA), which provided for the return of Indian remains and cultural artifacts held by federal agencies and museums. According to Executive Director **John Echohawk** (Pawnee), such victories are "building a better America for everyone—Indian and non-Indian." **See also** Arlinda Faye Locklear. (CKR)

BIBLIOGRAPHY

Wunder, John R. *"Retained by the People": A History of American Indians and the Bill of Rights*. New York: Oxford University Press, 1994.

Navajo Tribe of Indians v. United States (1966)

The Navajo Tribe had leased a portion of its lands to a private corporation so that the corporation could exploit oil and natural gas reserves. When the company began its drilling operations, it discovered large quantities of helium gas; the company then informed the Bureau of Mines about the helium reserves on the leased property. The federal government was interested in helium production, as part of its military needs during World War II, and assumed the lease of the corporation. In *Navajo Tribe of Indians v. United States*, 364 F. 2d 320 (1966), the federal court ruled that the federal government was liable for usurpation of Indian resources by the Bureau of Mines, because the tribe might have profited from the exploitation of the helium gas if it had known about the opportunity. *Navajo Tribe of Indians v. United States* illustrates the potential conflict of interest between the government's desire to further a national interest and its fiduciary responsibilities to the Indians. **See also** Trusteeship Responsibility.

BIBLIOGRAPHY

Price, Monroe E. and Robert N. Clinton. *Law and the American Indian*. Charlottesville, VA: Michie, 1973.

Navajo War

The Navajo War began with the United States takeover of Nuevo Mexico (New Mexico) in 1846. Previous to the American entry, the history of the Southwest had been one of conflict and shifting alliances among the Spanish New Mexicans, the Pueblo peoples, and the various bands and groups of Navajos, Apaches, and Utes. The wealthy and populous Navajos had held the New Mexicans to a boundary about 50 miles west of the Rio Grande, preserving their independence and that of the Hopi and other tribes west. The wars with the Americans ended that world.

American military and civil authorities initiated contacts with the Navajos in an attempt to settle the ongoing conflict between that tribe and the New Mexicans. From the start Americans viewed the "wild tribes"—the Navajos, Apaches, and Utes—as a problem to be resolved so that the settled peoples—New Mexican and Pueblo Indian—could have peace. The desire of New Mexicans to expand their grazing operations into Navajo lands, the Americans' belief that the Navajo country held deposits of gold and other minerals, the anti-American intrigues of agents of the Mormon Nation of Deseret, and the Navajo reaction to the murder of Narbona, a prominent member of the tribe, at an 1849 parley were all added incentives to war.

The six separate treaties Navajo leaders signed with the Americans between 1846 and 1861 never led to more than temporary peace. American military campaigns in 1846, 1849, 1851, and 1860 punished Navajo raiding, while New Mexican, Ute, and Pueblo raids against the Navajos were unabated.

A Naachid—a lengthy winter ceremony involving war chiefs and peace chiefs which was a feature of traditional Navajo government—was held in 1859–1860. At this Naachid the Navajos determined to drive the Americans out. An attack on and siege of Fort Defiance that spring and summer forced the abandonment of the post, but joint American–New Mexican campaigns that fall and winter forced the Navajos to accept harsh peace terms in 1861.

For the next year and a half, American forces were diverted by a Confederate offensive into New Mexico. In 1862 the Army opened its internment camp for Indians at Fort Sumner. In 1863 field commander Christopher "Kit" Carson reoccupied Fort Defiance and issued an ultimatum to the Navajos to surrender or be removed. Carson's strategy relied on a "scorched earth" campaign by regulars and Ute mercenaries, supported by independent New Mexican and Pueblo Indians raiding for livestock and slaves. By Navajo estimates, about half of the Nation—9,000 people—had surrendered by 1866; their relocation on foot to internment at Fort Sumner is remembered by Navajos as the "**Long Walk**."

At the ill-sited Fort Sumner, or Bosque Redondo, camp the Navajos were sickened by bad water, weakened by overcrowding, and exposed to attack by Comanches, and they quickly exhausted firewood supplies. Efforts to raise irrigated crops were a failure, and the federal government had to feed and clothe the Navajos at a cost of millions of dollars a year. In 1868 the United States and the Navajo leadership negotiated the **Treaty of Bosque Redondo**, allowing the Navajo to return to their homes. **See also** Barboncito; Manuelito; Indian Peace Commission. (JN)

BIBLIOGRAPHY

Bailey, Lynn R. *The Long Walk: A History of the Navajo Wars, 1846–68.* Los Angeles: Westernlore Press, 1964.

Corell, Lee J. *Through White Men's Eyes: A Contribution to Navajo History.* 6 vols. Window Rock, AZ: Navajo Heritage Center, 1979.

McNitt, Frank. *Navajo Wars: Military Campaigns, Slave Raids, and Reprisals.* Albuquerque: University of New Mexico Press, 1976.

Thompson, Gerald. *The Army and the Navajo: The Bosque Redondo Reservation Experiment, 1863–68.* Tucson: University of Arizona Press, 1976.

Sadie Brower Neakok (1916–)

For two decades in Barrow, Alaska, Sadie Brower Neakok served as the magistrate of a region the size of California, successfully blending Eskimo law and custom and the U.S. legal code. Born to an Inupiaq woman and a Caucasian whaler named Charles Brower, Sadie Brower Neakok was educated outside Alaska, returning to work as a teacher, health aide, and welfare worker, before becoming the community's sole legal officer in the 1960s and 1970s. Known for her compassion and common sense approach, she brought a human touch to the administration of justice and legitimized it for her people. (GAM)

BIBLIOGRAPHY

Blackman, Margaret B. *Sadie Brower Neakok: An Inupiaq Woman.* Seattle: University of Washington Press, 1989.

Nevada v. United States (1983)

The U.S. Supreme Court's decision in *Nevada v. United States*, 103 S.Ct. 2906 (1983), was a result of many attempts by the Pyramid Lake Paiutes to protect their resources. The Paiutes brought the suit because a 1944 agreement negotiated by the federal government had minimized their water rights. As a result, the tribe's livelihood, its fisheries, were dying out. The Court decided not to reopen the 1944 agreement for renegotiation, stating that it was not desirable to disturb past settlements, even if the federal government had done a poor job of protecting Indian rights. See also *Pyramid Lake Paiute Tribe v. Morton* (1973). (LCJ)

BIBLIOGRAPHY

Burton, Lloyd. *American Indian Water Rights and the Limits of Law.* Lawrence: University Press of Kansas, 1991.

McCool, Daniel. *Command of the Waters: Iron Triangles, Federal Water Development, and Indian Water.* Berkeley: University of California Press, 1987.

Nez Perce War

The Nez Perce tribe, unlike many of its neighbors in the Pacific Northwest, maintained friendly relations with the Euro-American immigrants, and many members of the tribe converted to Christianity. However, in 1860, gold was discovered on the Nez Perce reservation on Orofino Creek, which led to miners moving into the area. Rather than preventing miners from entering the reservation, the federal government appropriated part of the reservation for non-Indians. In 1863, the government met with the Nez Perce chiefs to negotiate a treaty (the so-called **Thief Treaty**). The head chief Lawyer lived within the reduced reservation and was willing to agree, but Big Thunder led a band who lived in the area being appropriated. The result was a split in the tribe. In 1867, Lawyer and his followers, about one-third of the tribe, signed the treaty. The other Nez Perce refused to acknowledge the reduced reservation and tried to keep their homes. The dispute continued until 1877, when the Commissioner of Indian Affairs asked **William Tecumseh Sherman**, commander of the U.S. Army, to move the nontreaty bands to the reservation. On June 16, 1877, 103 cavalry troops and 10 volunteers under Captain David Perry descended upon the camp of nontreaty Nez Perces led by the chief **Joseph (Hinmatoya'latk'it)**. In the resultant fighting, 34 soldiers were killed, but the Indians escaped without casualties. On June 22, General O.O. Howard led 400 soldiers, 100 supply workers, and several Indian scouts to defeat Joseph and his band. For the next 108 days, Joseph led his band of 700 Nez Perces (only 150 were warriors) on a 1,700-mile trek, through the mountains of Idaho, across the Continental Divide, and then northward to Canada and safety. Finally, on September 30, General Nelson Miles intercepted the caravan encamped on Snake Creek, near the Bear Paw Mountains, only 40 miles from the Canadian border. Recognizing that he was surrounded, hopelessly outgunned and outmanned, Joseph surrendered on October 4, 1877, saying, "From where the sun now stands, I will fight no more forever." Seventy-nine men, 78 women, and 174 children were taken to Fort Levenworth, Kansas, and from there they were sent to **Indian Territory**. Eight years later, 92 adults and 12 children returned to the Nez Perce Reservation. **See also** Hump; Looking Glass; Yakima War. **See** "I Will Fight No More Forever" by Chief Joseph (1877) in Appendix 1. (AMM)

BIBLIOGRAPHY
Ruby, Robert H. and John A. Brown. *Indians of the Pacific Northwest*. Norman: University of Oklahoma Press, 1981.

Nixon's Special Message to Congress (1970)

President Richard Nixon's special message to Congress on Indian affairs, issued July 8, 1970, proclaimed a policy of "**self-determination** without termination" of U.S. government protection and support for Native American tribes. The president's message contained seven legislative proposals, several of which became lasting features of federal policy: formal Congressional repudiation of the termination policy of the 1950s; the **Indian Self-Determination and Education Assistance Act of 1975**, which encouraged tribes to take over from federal agencies the control of programs that were for the benefit of Indians; and the creation of an Assistant Secretary of the Interior for Indian Affairs. Also endorsed by Nixon and enacted by Congress were increased federal aid for tribal economic development and the return of land near Blue Lake, New Mexico, to Taos Pueblo. A proposed independent Indian Trust Counsel Authority, intended to strengthen federal protection of Indian natural resource rights, was not established.

Preparation of the special Indian message took about six months and involved domestic policy staff in the White House, Vice President Spiro Agnew's office, and the **National Council of Indian Opportunity**. Although not all Native Americans supported the President's Indian policies, as evidenced by numerous incidents of Indian militancy during his presidency, many Indian leaders and policy scholars credited Nixon's Indian initiatives as the most progressive from a U.S. President

since the Indian New Deal of Franklin Roosevelt. **See also** Return of Blue Lake Lands Act of 1970. (EFM)

BIBLIOGRAPHY
Hoff, Joan. *Nixon Reconsidered*. New York: Basic Books, 1994.
Josephy, Alvin, Jr. *Red Power*. New York: McGraw-Hill, 1971.

Northwest Ordinance (1787)

Although the Northwest Ordinance of 1787 anticipated settlement and eventual statehood of western territories, the territory that the United States government proposed to subdivide and offer for sale was claimed by Native Americans who lived in the region. While the language of the ordinance committed the U.S. government to treat Native Americans with "utmost good faith," in actuality Native Americans found themselves unable to secure fair treatment toward their person, land, or property. The measure gave further authority to the federal government by stating "they [Indians] shall never be invaded or disturbed, unless in just and lawful wars authorized by Congress." Such open-ended statements gave U.S. citizens and their elected officials authority to claim land as they saw fit. Although the ordinance exhibited just and humanitarian goals in treatment afforded Native Americans, land-hungry American settlers used the statute to further their own goals, the acquisition of land which belonged to Native Americans. (KJB)

BIBLIOGRAPHY
Horsman, Reginald. *Expansion and Indian Policy*. Ann Arbor: University of Michigan Press, 1967.

Bonita Wa-Wa-Chaw Nunez (1888–1972)

Bonita Wa-Wa-Chaw Nunez was an activist for feminist and Native American causes. Nunez began her career as a teenager by lecturing at the Astor Hotel under the sponsorship of Carrie Chapman Catt, a noted activist for woman suffrage. Nunez went on to speak at conferences and meetings across the nation on both Indian Rights and women's safety. As a celebrated painter, Nunez often illustrated through her art the social problems that were plaguing her, making these paintings as much a vehicle for reform as her speeches. Nunez later worked with Dr. Carlos Montezuma in fund-raising programs for the Wassaja Project, a healthcare project, and also planned Indian rights campaigns with him. During her life, Nunez became intellectual companions with such noted figures as Sir Arthur Conan Doyle, Arthur C. Parker, General Richard H. Pratt, and Sir Oliver Lodge.

BIBLIOGRAPHY
Nunez, Bonita. *Spirit Woman*. San Francisco: Harper & Row, 1986.

Richard Oakes (1942–1972)

Richard Oakes, a Mohawk Indian, was an important leader of the **Alcatraz Island occupation** that unleashed the **Red Power** era. Oakes was shot and killed by a YMCA guard in northern California in 1972. His death accelerated the decision to move forward with the **Trail of Broken Treaties**. (MS)

BIBLIOGRAPHY

Johnson, Troy R. *The Occupation of Alcatraz Island: Indian Self Determination and the Rise of Indian Activism.* Urbana: University of Illinois Press, 1996.

Smith, Paul Chatt and Robert Allen Warrior. *Like a Hurricane: The Indian Movement from Alcatraz to Wounded Knee.* New York: The New Press, 1996.

Office of Indian Affairs

The Office of Indian Affairs was the precursor to the **Bureau of Indian Affairs.** Without approval from Congress, in 1842 then-Secretary of War John C. Calhoun established what he called the Bureau of Indian Affairs within the War Department. Congress condoned the action by creating the Office of Indian Affairs (also sometimes called the Indian Office or the Indian Service). The Office of Indian Affairs was responsible for "the direction and management of all Indian affairs, and of all matters arising out of Indian relations." The office continued in this capacity, under the auspices of the War Department, until 1849 when Congress, recognizing the changing nature of the federal/Indian relationship, transferred responsibility for Indian affairs from military to civilian control, housing the office within the newly created Department of the Interior. Although throughout its existence the Office of Indian Affairs was often called the Indian Bureau, it did not become officially known as the Bureau of Indian Affairs until 1947. **See also** Department of the Interior Act of 1849. (GTH)

BIBLIOGRAPHY

Prucha, Francis Paul. *The Great Father: The United States Government and the American Indians.* Lincoln: University of Nebraska Press, 1984.

Schmeckebier, Laurence F. *The Office of Indian Affairs: Its History, Activities and Organization.* Baltimore: The Johns Hopkins University Press, 1927.

Office of the Superintendent of Indian Trade

Established in 1806, this office supervised the network of public Indian trading factories which the United States maintained from 1795 to 1822. Superintendents John Shee (1806–1807), John Mason (1807–1816), and Thomas McKenney (1816–1822) bore overall responsibility for hiring and firing public traders, constructing new trading posts, purchasing and shipping trade goods, and marketing furs for their Indian customers. Congress closed the office and the factories in 1822 after several senators leveled charges of corruption, waste, and lack of a legitimate public function. (DAN)

BIBLIOGRAPHY

Peake, Ora. *A History of the United States Indian Factory System.* Denver: Sage Books, 1954.

Way, Royal B. "The United States Factory System for Trading with the Indians." *Mississippi Valley Historical Review* 6, no. 2 (September 1919): 220–35.

Oklahoma Indian Welfare Act of 1936

The Oklahoma Indian Welfare Act of 1936 was an attempt by Commissioner of Indian Affairs **John Collier** to administer the **Indian Reorganization Act of 1934** to the Oklahoma tribes. The congressional representatives from Oklahoma were able to block the inclusion of the tribes into the 1934 act because they did not want to discontinue taxation of reservation mineral deposits and stop selling Indian lands, as the act required. Collier, committed to extending the legislation to include the Oklahoma tribes, toured the state soliciting Indian opinion, which was mostly favorable. The 1936 act resembled the Reorganization Act, but it was designed specifically to address the problems of the Oklahoma tribes. Although it left matters of Indian property and probate in the hands of state courts and allowed continued taxation, it attacked the assimilationist movement by encouraging Indian self-government. The act provided for the establishment of tribal constitutions and corporations, the extension of credit, and land purchase provisions. Most important, it enabled Indians within a close proximity of each other to receive a charter of incorporation and draw upon a revolving credit fund. (MR)

BIBLIOGRAPHY

Debo, Angie. *And Still the Waters Run: The Betrayal of the Five Civilized Tribes*. Princeton, NJ: Princeton University Press, 1940.

Prucha, Francis Paul. *The Great Father: The United States Government and the American Indian*. Abridged ed. Lincoln: University of Nebraska Press, 1984.

Barney Old Coyote (1923–)

Since 1970, Barney Old Coyote has been the director of the American Indian Studies program at Montana State University, where he is a professor. For his promotion of Native American affairs, he received the honorary Doctor of Humane Letters from Montana State University. Old Coyote completed more than 50 missions for the United States Air Force in World War II. He went on to spend 21 years with the **Bureau of Indian Affairs.** He was the first president of the American Indian National Bank. This also made him the first Native American bank president. Old Coyote also served as the special assistant to the secretary of the U.S. Department of the Interior from 1964 to 1969. There he received a Distinguished Service Award.

BIBLIOGRAPHY

"Barney Old Coyote and the American Indian National Bank." *Banker's* 157 (Autumn 1974): 17–18.

Earl Old Person (1929–)

In 1954, Earl Old Person became the youngest member of the Blackfeet Tribal Business Council, the ruling body of the Montana-based tribe. In 1964, Old Person was elected tribal council chairman, and from 1969 to 1971 he acted as president of the National Congress of the American Indians. He was re-elected vice president of the group in 1990. In 1975, Old Person helped organize the Council of Energy Resources Tribes (CERT), and in July 1978 was given the honorary lifetime appointment of chief of the Blackfeet Nation. While in service with the Blackfeet tribe, Old Person has helped sustain the community on a rich economy of timber, fuel, and agriculture while assisting in the establishment of a reservation community college, an industrial park, a housing development, tourism facilities, and other community-based centers.

BIBLIOGRAPHY

Johnson, Bryan R. *The Blackfeet: An Annotated Bibliography*. New York: Garland Publishing, 1988.

Oliphant v. Suquamish (1978)

In *Oliphant v. Suquamish*, 435 U.S. 191 (1978), two non-Indians who had violated Suquamish tribal law within the reservation's boundaries were arrested and arraigned in tribal court. The two subsequently challenged the tribe's authority to extend its jurisdiction over them. The issue before the Supreme Court was whether tribes have inherent criminal jurisdiction over non-Indians who commit offenses on Indian lands. In a problematic 6 to 2 ruling, the Court held that tribes lacked such jurisdiction over non-Indians because the tribes' purported dependent status was inconsistent with such authority and because Congress, in the Court's opinion, had never expressly delegated this power to tribes in treaties or statutes. (DEW)

BIBLIOGRAPHY

Maxfield, Peter C. "Oliphant v Suquamish Tribe: The Whole Is Greater than the Sum of the Parts." *Journal of Contemporary Law* 19, no. 2 (Fall 1993): 391–443.

Volk, Paul S. "The Legal Trail of Tears: Supreme Court Removal of Tribal Court Jurisdiction over Crimes by and against Reservation Indians." *New England Law Review* 20, no. 2 (Spring 1985): 247–83.

Opechancanough (1545–1644)

Opechancanough, a brother of the powerful **Powhatan** (head chief of the Virginian Algonquian confederacy), captured John Smith but was later captured by him, resulting in Opechancanough's undying hatred of Englishmen. He became the leader of the confederacy after Powhatan's death in 1618. In 1622, he orchestrated the massacre of the Jamestown settlement. In the last year of his life, he led another massacre of English settlements in which 300 settlers were killed. He was caught, taken prisoner, and shot by a guard in Jamestown. He later died from his wound. **See also** Powhatan Confederacy; Second Virginia War. (AMM)

BIBLIOGRAPHY

Bridenbaugh, Carl. *Jamestown, 1544 to 1699*. New York: Oxford University Press, 1980.

Open Housing Act of 1968

The Open Housing Act of the Civil Rights Act of 1968, the first open housing law in the United States, prohibits discrimination based on race, sex, national origin, color, religion, handicap, and familial status and also in the sale, rental, financing and advertising of housing. The act further provides stiff penalties for violators, grants authority to the Department of Housing and Urban Development to initiate complaints, and gives litigation authority to the Department of Justice. (VDD)

BIBLIOGRAPHY

Bartley, Numan V. and Hugh D. Graham. *Southern Politics and the Second Reconstruction*. Baltimore: Johns Hopkins University Press, 1975.

Oregon Boundary Treaty

Signed in 1846 between the United States and Great Britain, the Treaty of Oregon established the boundary between the United States and Canada at the forty-ninth parallel. During the latter part of the eighteenth century, Europeans had explored the Pacific Northwest territory in search of the Northwest Passage to China. In 1789 a fort at Nootka Sound on Vancouver Island was established by the Spanish to secure trade in sea otter pelts, which brought exorbitant prices in China. Soon the Americans, British, and Russians were all involved. The area was divided into three basic regions. The Spanish retained lands below the forty-second latitude (1795), the Russians were southeast of Alaska, and by 1818 the Americans and British jointly occupied the area in between but continued to dispute the border between the United States and Canada. Native peoples benefited materially from the traders and continued to increase their economic well-being. The American Fur Company's post at the mouth of the Columbia River was lost during the **War of 1812** and eventually it was taken over by the Hudson Bay Company. For the next 30-plus years, the Hudson Bay Company controlled the Northwest Coast; the company's control ended when the overland migration of Americans along the Oregon Trail tilted possessory rights in favor of the United States. (MRC)

BIBLIOGRAPHY

Barrows, William. *Oregon: The Struggle for Possession.* New York, AMS Press, 1973.

Oregon v. Smith (1990)

The U.S. Supreme Court's decision in *Employment Division, Department of Human Resources of Oregon, et al. v. Smith et al.,* 494 U.S. 872 (1990), represented a major setback for American Indian religious freedom. The case arose when two Oregon Indians, Alfred Smith and Galen Black, lost their jobs with a private drug-treatment organization after using peyote in a Native American Church ceremony. They applied for unemployment benefits, but the state employment division denied their request on the grounds that they had been fired for work-related misconduct. The Oregon Court of Appeals reversed this judgment, holding that it violated the applicants' First Amendment rights, and the Oregon Supreme Court affirmed. Nevertheless, in a five-to-four opinion, the U.S. Supreme Court ruled that peyote use could be prohibited under a state criminal statute. Dismissing established precedent and the sacramental significance of peyote, the majority held that Oregon's law violated neither the Free Exercise clause of the Constitution nor the American Indian Religious Freedom Act. In his dissent, however, Justice Harry Blackmun argued that the decision would render those protections "merely an unfulfilled and hollow promise" for Native Americans. **See also** *People v. Woody* (1964); Religious Freedom Restoration Act of 1993. (AHF)

BIBLIOGRAPHY

Lawson, Paul E. and Patrick Morris. "The Native American Church and the New Court: The Smith Case and Indian Religious Freedoms." *American Indian Culture and Research Journal* 15, no. 1 (1991): 79–91.

Wunder, John R. *"Retained by The People": A History of American Indians and the Bill of Rights.* New York: Oxford University Press, 1994.

Osceola (ca. 1804–1838)

Osceola, or Ussa Yaholo (a.k.a. Billy Powell), was one of the principal war leaders of the Seminoles during the Second Seminole War in the 1830s. In 1835, after executing pro-removal chief Charley Amathla, Osceola led the assault on Fort King, which began the war. American officials captured Osceola under a flag of truce in 1837 and imprisoned him in Fort Moultrie, South Carolina, where he became a tourist attraction and a symbol of the defeat of the "wild Indian." He died in prison and was buried there in January 1838. (DAN)

Osceola was one of the leaders of the Seminole resistance to removal. He was imprisoned for his activities and died in confinement. *Library of Congress.*

BIBLIOGRAPHY

Perdue, Theda. "Osceola: The White Man's Indian." *Florida Historical Quarterly* 70, no. 4 (April 1992): 475–88.

Wickman, Patricia. *Osceola's Legacy.* Tuscaloosa: University of Alabama Press, 1991.

Oshkosh (Os'koss) (1795–1858)

Oshkosh led the Menominee Nation's bargaining with neighboring native nations and with the invading United States in the mid-1800s, including securing the right of his people to stay in Wisconsin until 1948. Originally reaching leadership due to his bravery in war and his grandfather's own leadership position, Oshkosh was a master negotiator. (LCJ)

BIBLIOGRAPHY

Ourada, Patricia K. *The Menominee Indians: A History.* Norman: University of Oklahoma Press, 1979.

Shames, Deborah, ed. *Freedom with Reservation: The Menominee Struggle to Save Their Land and People.* Madison: Wisconsin Indian Legal Services, 1972.

Ouray (ca. 1825–1881)

Ouray, leader of the Uncomphagre Utes, in Colorado and Utah, was lead negotiator for his nation during the mid-1800s. He helped maintain Ute control over some of their traditional land, despite the influx of non-Indians into the mountains of Colorado. He alienated many of his people by living lavishly on a United States salary. **See also** Ute War. (LCJ)

BIBLIOGRAPHY

Brown, Dee. *Bury My Heart at Wounded Knee: An Indian History of the American West.* New York: Holt, Rinehart & Winston, 1970.

Marsh, Charles S. *People of the Shining Mountains: The Utes of Colorado.* Boulder, CO: Pruett Publishing, 1982.

P

Paiute War (Pyramid Lake War)

The Paiute (Pyramid Lake) War began in 1860 when traders at Williams Station on the California Trail abducted and raped two Indian girls. The Southern Paiutes burned the station and killed five whites. Retaliating, a force of 105 whites ambushed and attacked the Pyramid Lake settlement, killing half the Indians. The devastation of that attack ended the Paiute War. (AMM)

BIBLIOGRAPHY

Bunte, Pamela A. *The Paiute.* New York: Chelsea House, 1990.

Parent Consent for Education Act of 1894

In 1894, Congress passed the Parent Consent for Education Act in order to end the practice of sending Indian children to boarding schools in order to more quickly assimilate Native American youth into the broader American culture. Specifically, the act did two things. First, it served as a general appropriations act for the supervision of education issues. Second, the act prohibited the sending of children to schools outside the state or territory without the specific consent of their parents or guardians. **See also** Education; Forced Assimilation.

BIBLIOGRAPHY

Cohen, Felix S. *Felix Cohen's Handbook of Federal Indian Law.* Charlottesville, VA: Mitchie, Bobbs-Merrill, 1982; Ft. Lauderdale, FL: Five Rings Press, 1986.

Arthur C. Parker (1881–1955)

Arthur C. Parker, also known as Gawasowanah ("Big Snowsnake"), was one of the prominent intellectuals of the early twentieth century. He made major contributions to the fields of anthropology, social activism, and museology. Born on a reservation in New York State, he believed in the melting pot theory in accordance with the future of the American Indian race. Parker was director of the Rochester (NY) Museum. He founded and edited the *Quarterly Journal,* the official publication of the Society of American Indians. In 1920 he became president of the New York Welfare Society. He was elected chairman of the first meeting of the Committee of One Hundred, the National Advisory Committee of the Secretary of the Interior. This committee pushed the Pueblo Land Act into effect in 1924. He also founded the Philosophical Society of Albany and the New York State Archaeological Association.

BIBLIOGRAPHY

Hauptman, Lawrence. "The Iroquois School of Art: Arthur C. Parker and the Seneca Arts Project, 1935–1941." *New York History* 60 (July 1979): 283–312.
Hertzberg, Hazel W. *The Secret for an American Indian Identity: Modern Pan-Indian Movements.* Syracuse, NY: Syracuse University Press, 1971.

Ely Samuel Parker (1828–1895)

Ely Parker (Seneca) was the first Native American to become the commissioner of Indian Affairs. As Ulysses S. Grant's commissioner, Parker supported assimilation but sought major reform within the **Bureau of Indian Affairs (BIA)** and supported the just treatment of the western tribes through the implementation of previous treaty provisions. Appointed by Grant, Parker favored a policy of assimilation. A controversial figure, he resigned after being cleared of charges of fraud. Prior to his service in the BIA, Parker distinguished himself in the service of the Union during the **Civil War.** In 1863, he became Grant's staff officer. (MR)

BIBLIOGRAPHY

Armstrong, William H. *Warrior in Two Camps: Ely S. Parker, Union General and Seneca Chief.* Syracuse: Syracuse University Press, 1978.

Quanah Parker (1845–1911)

Quanah Parker, son of Chief Peta Nocona and Cynthia Ann Parker, a white woman captured as a child, was a daring Comanche chief and raider. Left an orphan in 1860, when his father was killed and his mother was recaptured by her uncle, Isaac Parker, Quanah left the Nocona band and joined the Kwahadies who refused to make peace when the Comanche, Kiowa Apache, Cheyenne, and Arapahoe signed the Treaty of Medicine Lodge (1867). For years he led raids against the army, buffalo hunters, and settlers, finally surrendering in 1875. He spent the rest of his life bettering the lives of the Comanche through successful business ventures. (AMM)

BIBLIOGRAPHY

Hagan, William T. *Quanah Parker.* Norman: University of Oklahoma Press, 1993.
Wilson, Claire. *Quanah Parker.* New York: Chelsea House, 1992.

Passamaquoddy

The Passamaquoddy ("Pollock-Spearing Place") tribe has two reservations located in Maine's easternmost county, which happens to be one of the country's poorest counties. Sipayik is the main village of the Pleasant Point Reservation in Passamaquoddy Bay. Motahkokmikuk is on the Schoodic Lakes chain. Each reservation has a biennially elected government. The highest governing body is the 16-member joint **tribal council.** In 1972 the Native American Rights Fund filed suit for the tribe against the Department of the Interior for its sale and lease of 6,000 acres of reservation land (*Passamaquoddy v. Morton*). The courts ruled in their favor, which led to the 1980 Maine Indian Claims Settlement Act. **See also** Land and Water Rights.

BIBLIOGRAPHY

Brodeur, Paul. *Restitution: The Land Claims of the Mashpee, Passamaquoddy, and Penobscot Indians of New England.* Boston: Northeastern University Press, 1985.

Stevens, Susan M. "Passamaquoddy Economic Development in Cultural and Historical Perspective." In Susan Stanley, ed. *American Indian Economic Development.* Paris: Mouton, 1978.

Pawnee Treaty (1857)

The Pawnee Treaty was ratified by Congress in 1857 after the Kansas Nebraska Act of 1854. The Pawnees had been driven south of the Platte River from 1842 to 1846 by the Great Sioux. The treaty had them return north to resettle Loupfork as a Pawnee reservation. They also received government aid. They were moved again in 1874 by policy makers to the undeveloped **Indian territory**, now part of Oklahoma. The Pawnee still receive an annual annuity of $30,000 from the treaty.

BIBLIOGRAPHY

Blaine, Martha Royce. *The Pawnees: A Critical Bibliography.* Bloomington: Indiana University Press, 1980.

Hyde, George E. *The Pawnee Indians.* New ed. Civilization of the American Indian, vol. 128. Norman: University of Oklahoma Press, 1974.

Paxton Boys' Massacre

In December 1763, the men of Paxton, Pennsylvania, massacred eight peaceful Conestoga Indians. The 14 remaining members of the Native American group were gathered by the sheriff and placed in the Lancaster city jail for protection. Despite Governor William Penn's proclamation against the earlier slaughter, the Paxton men raided the jail and killed the remaining Conestogas.

The colony's pacifist Quaker leaders were horrified. The governor's attempts to bring the Paxton men to justice became a struggle between the central state government and the Irish and Scottish Presbyterians of the frontier. The Paxton men, planning to kill Indians who were under protection in Philadelphia, led an invasion of that city in January 1764. This forced the Quakers to arm themselves and then (led by Benjamin Franklin) to defend the city. This time, things were resolved without bloodshed, but the massacre of the

Conestogas fed Native American anger and encouraged eastern Indians to join **Pontiac's War.** (LCJ)

BIBLIOGRAPHY

Parkman, Francis. *The Conspiracy of Pontiac and the Indian War after the Conquest of Canada.* Boston: Little, Brown and Company, 1933.

Waters, Frank. *Brave Are My People: Indian Heroes Not Forgotten.* Sante Fe, NM: Clear Light Publishers, 1993.

Peace Commission Act of 1867

Congress authorized the president of the United States to appoint a special commission to negotiate a peace settlement with hostile native groups, including the Kiowa, Comanche, Cheyenne, Arapaho, and Nez Perce. The commission hoped to adopt the plan of converting the tribes into agricultural groups, similar to the experiment conducted by California's superintendent of Indian Affairs, Edward F. Beale.

BIBLIOGRAPHY

Cohen, Felix S. *Felix Cohen's Handbook of Federal Indian Law.* Charlottesville, VA: Mitchie, Bobbs-Merrill, 1982; Ft. Lauderdale, FL: Five Rings Press, 1986.

Jeanine Pease-Windy Boy (1949–)

Jeanine Pease-Windy Boy began serving Native Americans in 1970 when she counseled Indian students at Navajo Community College in Arizona while also developing the Upward Bound Program at Big Bend Community College. In 1981 Pease-Windy Boy began working for Eastern Montana College, assisting Native American students to enter the school and find employment after graduation. In 1982 she went on to become president of Big Horn College. Later, she pointed out voting discrimination practices in the landmark case of *Windy Boy v. Bighorn County.* Pease-Windy Boy continues to lobby for Native American rights and also serves as a trustee for the National Museum of the American Indian and as an appointee by President Bill Clinton to the NACIE. **See also** National Museum of the American Indian Act of 1989.

BIBLIOGRAPHY

Mooney, Carolyn J. "Head of Blossoming Tribal College: A Product of My Community." *Chronicle of Higher Education* (November 29, 1989): A3.

Leonard Peltier (1944–)

Leonard Peltier is a Chippewa-Lakota activist and a leader of **American Indian Movement** (AIM). Committed to a national movement of Indians striving to restore their traditional culture and reclaim the rights guaranteed them by treaties, he participated in demonstrations, such as the **Trail of Broken Treaties** in 1972 and the 1973 face-off at **Wounded Knee II,** which lasted 71 days. The continued FBI and AIM presence on the Pine Ridge Reservation resulted in a shoot-out on June 26, 1975, in which two FBI officers were killed. On June 1, 1977, Leonard Peltier was sentenced to two consecutive life sentences for the murders of the two officers. Despite highly suspect circumstantial evidence and alleged FBI repression of witnesses, Peltier's appeals have failed and he continues to serve in Fort Leavenworth, Kansas. AIM considers him a political prisoner, and active efforts to free him continue; see, for instance, the "Free Peltier" Web site at <freepeltier/index.html>. **See also** Walk for Justice. (JP)

BIBLIOGRAPHY

Matthiessen, Peter. *In the Spirit of Crazy Horse.* New York: Penguin, 1995.

Messerschmidt, Jim. *The Trial of Leonard Peltier.* Boston: South End Press, 1983.

Pennsylvania Colony and the Delaware Treaty

The first Indian treaty negotiated by the fledgling United States after its declaration of independence from Great Britain was with the Delaware Indians of Pennsylvania, signed in 1778. Three years after the beginning of the **American Revolution,** the United States desperately needed allies—and found them in the Delaware Indians. In the treaty, the Delawares agreed to help the new nation by allowing passage of U.S. troops through its territory, allowing individual Delawares to enlist in the colonial armies, and by the sale of supplies to the army. The treaty, which promised "perpetual peace and friendship," also said that the Delawares, along with other tribes, could apply for admission as a state. The treaty was important because it signaled that the United States intended to pursue the legal relationship between two sovereigns, which had been started by Great Britain. (GTH)

BIBLIOGRAPHY

Deloria, Vine, Jr. and Clifford M. Lytle. *American Indians, American Justice.* Austin: University of Texas Press, 1983.

O'Brien, Sharon. *American Indian Tribal Governments.* Norman: University of Oklahoma Press, 1989.

People v. Woody (1964)

People v. Woody (1964) was a California state case involving religious freedom. John Woody and a Navajo group met on April 28, 1962, near Needles, California, to participate in a peyote ceremony. The police discovered the ceremony and arrested the group, charging them with possession of a controlled substance. The group was convicted of drug charges in the San Bernardino County Court. Woody appealed and the California supreme court found in his favor. They said that the state could not outlaw religious sacraments (such as the peyote ceremony). **See also** American Indian Religious Freedom Act of 1978; *Oregon v. Smith* (1990); Religious Freedom Restoration Act of 1993.

BIBLIOGRAPHY

Olson, James S. and Raymond Wilson. *Native Americans in the Twentieth Century,* 1984.

Pequot War (1637)

The Pequot were a feared Algonquian tribe who occupied southern Connecticut from the Niantic River to the Rhode Island border. By 1634, the great Chief Sassacus had extended his control over 26 other tribes or bands. The deaths of two English traders, Captains Stone and Oldham, by these related tribes resulted in English retaliation against the Pequots. The Pequots tried to ally with the neighboring Narragansetts, but the latter, traditional enemies of the Pequot, joined the British colonists. In 1638, the British and Narragansett sailed up the Mystic river to a Pequot fort, where on May 25 they set the fort ablaze, trapping 800 men, women, and children in the inferno. Those who managed to escape were shot by the soldiers who surrounded the fort. After this event, the surviving Pequots were scattered among the tribes of the northeast. The Pequot survivors were treated so harshly by the other Indians that in 1655 they were gathered into two villages on a reserve near Ledyard, Connecticut, by the colonial government. (AMM)

BIBLIOGRAPHY

Cave, Alfred A. *The Pequot War.* Amherst: University of Massachusetts Press, 1996.

Petalesharo (ca. 1797–ca. 1832)

Petalesharo, "Chief of Men," son of Lachelesharo, was a principal chief of the Pawnee. One of his best-known accomplishments was abolishing the Morning Star Ceremony in which a young girl of another tribe was sacrificed at the summer solstice. The tribe respected this challenge to the priestly clan and its power, and Petalesharo's reputation grew as a result. In the political arena, he headed a delegation of Pawnee to Washington, D.C., in 1821–1822. In 1825, he and his father signed the Pawnee Treaty to cease raids along the Santa Fe Trail. His portrait in the Indian Portrait Gallery was among the first to be commissioned by Thomas McKenney. (EW)

BIBLIOGRAPHY

Dockstader, Frederick. *Great North American Indians.* New York: Van Nostrand Reinhold, 1977.

Hyde, George E. *The Pawnee Indians,* 2nd Edition. Norman: University of Oklahoma Press, 1974.

Helen White Peterson (1915–)

Helen White Peterson has been most well known as a lecturer and negotiator in Indian and Hispanic affairs. She has been a writer and editor of American Indian and Hispanic publications. She was director of the Rocky Mountain Council of Inter-American Affairs at the University of Denver Social Science Foundation, while serving in Nelson Rockefeller's National Office of Inter-American Affairs. Peterson founded the Colorado Field Service Program, which consists of community service clubs. She presented a resolution on Indian education, which she authored at the second Inter-American Indian Conference in Cuzco, Peru. The resolution was ratified. She also held the position of executive director of the **National Congress of American Indians.** Peterson established the first **Bureau of Indian Affairs** intergovernmental relations office, in Denver in 1972. Another notable accomplishment was her involvement for 14 years in summer leadership training workshops where Native Americans could receive college credit.

BIBLIOGRAPHY
Bataille, Gretchen M., ed. *Native American Women*. New York: Garland Publishing, 1993.

Archie Phinney (1903–1949)

In 1934, Archie Phinney published *Nez Perce Texts*, an anthology of translated traditional Nez Perce Indian stories, myths, and folklore. Phinney went on to work for the Bureau of Indian Affairs as superintendent of the northern Idaho Agency, as well as for the National Congress of American Indians. During his career, Phinney also lobbied for Native American rights while acting as a Nez Perce anthropologist and activist.

BIBLIOGRAPHY
Phinney, Archie. *Nez Perce Texts*. New York: Columbia University Press, 1934.

Connie Redbird Pinkerman-Uri

A Choctaw-Cherokee physician, Connie Redbird Uri was subjected to U.S. government harassment (and assassination attempts, according to her supporters) after she exposed the overuse and abuse of sterilization procedures on Native women of childbearing age. This procedure was systematically practiced in **Bureau of Indian Affairs** (BIA) Indian Health Service clinics during the 1970s. (KJB)

BIBLIOGRAPHY
Dillingham, Brint. "American Indian Women and I.H.S. Sterilization Practices." *American Indian Journal* (January 1997).

Plains Wars

The wars between Native American nations of the Great Plains region and the expanding United States in the latter half of the 1800s determined control of a large portion of what is now the Untied States. Most of these vast lands, rich with bison and river basins, were claimed by the United States under the **Louisiana Purchase.** While the streams of immigrant wagon trains that began in the 1840s disrupted life for the native peoples of the Plains, conflict was sporadic until the 1860s.

The largest concentrations of warfare were in the Powder River basin of what is now Wyoming and in the southern plains of what are now Oklahoma and Texas. In the north, the Lakota (Sioux), Cheyenne, and Arapaho won a series of battles that led the United States to abandon the forts along the Bozeman Trail (in present-day eastern Wyoming) in 1868. Eight years later, many of the same warriors defeated General George Custer at the **Battle of the Little Bighorn** on the eve of what he expected to be his nomination for president. In the south, the extermination of millions of bison and the privations of reservation life led the Kiowas and Comanches to war in the 1870s.

The last military action of the Plains Wars occurred on December 29, 1890, when Lakota followers of the **Ghost Dance** religion were surrounded, disarmed, and attacked at **Wounded Knee.**

The Plains Wars were important not only for their direct political impacts but also as the source of a number of stereotypes of "Indians." These stereotypes have been perpetuated by the media and still disguise the diversity of Native American cultures, governments, and economies. **See also** War for the Bozeman Trail. **See** "You Are Living in a New Path" by Sitting Bull (1880) in Appendix 1. (LCJ)

BIBLIOGRAPHY
Brown, Dee. *Bury My Heart at Wounded Knee*. Chicago: Holt, Rinehart & Winston, 1970.
Greene, Jerome A., ed. *Lakota and Cheyenne: Indian Views of the Great Sioux War: 1876–1877*. Norman: University of Oklahoma Press, 1994.
Neeley, Bill. *The Last Comanche Chief: The Life and Times of Quanah Parker*. New York: John Wiley & Sons, Inc., 1995.

Plenty Coups (ca. 1848–1932)

A Crow Indian warrior and leader, Plenty Coups led the Crows in their transition to a **reservation** existence. He made several trips to Washington, D.C., from his Montana homeland between 1880 and 1921, lobbying the government to retain Crow autonomy. He strongly advocated formal **education** among his people as an avenue to better integrate with whites. Plenty Coups was a successful rancher and farmer. Upon his death, he willed some of his alotted lands for a state park as a symbol of the friendship between the Crow and whites. (GO)

BIBLIOGRAPHY
Hoxie, Frederick E. *Parading through History: The Making of the Crow Nation in America, 1805–1935*. New York: Cambridge University Press, 1995.

In October 1974, Crow delegates presented Interior Secretary Morton with the Plenty Coups Award for his efforts on behalf of Native Americans. *U.S. Department of the Interior/BIA.*

Pocahontas (ca. 1595–1617)

Pocahontas (Matoaka), daughter of **Powhatan,** chief of the **Powhatan Confederacy,** was instrumental in saving the life of Captain John Smith of England who had been taken prisoner by her father and sentenced to be executed. Her actions

Perhaps the best known of all Native Americans, Pocahontas aided English settlers in seventeenth-century Virginia. *Library of Congress.*

improved relations between the two peoples, and Pocahontas often visited Jamestown. After Smith left Jamestown (1610), relations between the colony and the confederation deteriorated. Captain Samuel Argall took Pocahontas hostage and held her for ransom. While held prisoner, she was taught European customs, baptized, and given a Christian name, Rebecca. In 1612, Pocahontas married John Rolfe, and two years later returned with him to England, where she was hailed as a "princess." She died in 1617 of smallpox or pneumonia while aboard ship waiting to sail for America. (AMM)

BIBLIOGRAPHY

Mossiker, Frances. *Pocahontas: The Life and the Legend.* New York: Knopf, 1976.

Rountree, Helen C. *Pocahontas' People:The Powhatan Indians of Virginia Through Four Centuries.* Norman, Oklahoma: University of Oklahoma Press, 1990.

Political Participation and Political Representation

According to Aristotle, man is by nature a political animal. The two basic approaches to political participation are direct democracy, in which individuals participate in decision making, and representative democracy, where the "many" elect the "few" to make decisions on their behalf. American Indians traditionally have tended toward direct democracy based on consensus whereas contemporary U.S. politics involves "representative" democracy.

Traditional Indian Participation

June Helm quoted a young Indian leader's understanding of traditional Indian decision making:

> See the way people make decisions when a group goes hunting. They sit around in the evening and drink tea and talk about everything. They talk about the weather, they talk about where the moose might be, they talk about times they've hunted in the past. Everybody talks, everybody listens to everybody else. . . People realize what they need and everybody talks about it. It comes out through conversation. There's no formal decisions. Nobody makes any motions. People just talk until there's a general agreement, nobody gives orders to anybody else.

Conventional Participation and Representation of Indians in National Government

American Indians, like other Americans, participate in the major political parties and pay attention to political issues. On a national level their party identification and political orientations have been remarkably stable (i.e., statistically no significant changes have occurred over the 20-year period from 1974 to 1994). As table 1 indicates, 42.5 percent of Indians see themselves as Democrats, almost 20 percent as Republicans, and 38 percent as Independents. Further, almost 75 percent are likely to identify themselves as either moderate or conservative in political orientation. One should take care with these national figures, because one may find that members of certain tribes may be more likely to be Republican, and other tribes may be much more liberal than these national averages would indicate.

Alternative delegate Chief William Spotted Crow from South Dakota attended the 1948 Republican National Convention. *ACME.*

Table 1: Party Identification and Political Orientation among American Indians (1974–1994)	
Party Identification	
Democrat	42.5%
Independent	38.0%
Republican	19.6%
Political Orientation	
Liberal	25.4%
Moderate	44.6%
Conservative	30.0%
Source: National Opinion Research Center, General Social Survey	

Indians today do participate in electoral politics. They pay attention to politics, vote, and participate in other ways. Table 2 indicates that a majority of eligible Indians participate in some way in presidential elections. An examination of that table will show, that they (like other citizens) participate at lower levels in nonpresidential years.

Table 2: American Indian Participation in Electoral Politics by Year

Year	P=Pres. Election, C=Cong. Election	Participant (Vote and/or some other campaign activity)
1972	P	67.7%
1974	C	45.5%
1976	P	69.5%
1980	P	65.5%
1982	C	57.9%
1984	P	55.2%
1986	C	39.3%
1988	P	51.6%
1990	C	39.7%
1992	P	65.5%
1994	C	45.5%

Source: National Election Studies (NES)

In presidential elections from 1972 to 1992 (see table 3), Indians have variously supported Republicans and Democrats. Some presidential candidates have apparently learned that some issues hold an appeal across tribes. In 1980, a substantial majority of the Indians polled here voted for the Democratic candidate for president. After President Ronald Reagan's speech in January of 1983 in which he stated, "Our policy is to reaffirm dealing with Indian tribes on a government-to-government basis and to pursue the policy of self-government for Indian tribes without threatening termination," there was a large shift to the Republican candidate in 1984, giving Ronald Reagan a majority of the Indian vote.

Table 3: American Indian Participation in Presidential Elections and Candidate Choice

Year	Percent Eligible Who Voted	Vote for Democratic Nominee	Vote for Republican Nominee	Vote for Other Candidate
1972	45.2%	49.3%	50.7%	
1976	53.6%	69.3%	30.7%	
1980	62.2%	65.1%	30.2%	4.7%
1984	58.4%	46.9%	53.1%	
1988	57.7%	46.2%	53.8%	
1992	60.9%	49.4%	28.1%	22.5%

Source: National Opinion Research Center, General Social Survey

Since the nineteenth century, eight American Indians have served as members of the House of Representatives and five have been members of the U.S. Senate. (See Appendix 3 for a listing.) Currently Ben Nighthorse Campbell is one of the two senators representing the state of Colorado. Overall, the record of Indian participation in national politics has been mixed. On the one hand, Indians have been sorely underrepresented in the U.S. House of Representatives, even though Indians are a little less than one percent of the American population. On the other hand, because self-interested, competitive politics are not consistent with Native traditions of cooperation and seeking the benefit of the whole community and because Indians have also had long periods where portions of their population were denied the franchise to vote, their success in electoral politics over the years is remarkable.

Other Forms of Political Participation

Francis Paul Prucha states that "Indian tribes are composed of United States citizens, who nevertheless have a governmental power that antedates the United States and is in a sense separate from and independent of the sovereignty of the general government." As part of this sovereignty, tribal members participate in the decision making within their tribes. It may be that here is where one would find more evidence of the survival of direct democracy.

Litigation through the courts is another front on which tribes participate to maintain their political rights. An example is the suit the ACLU and Indian Law Center filed under the federal Voting Rights Act challenging that Montana's legislative districts were drawn to dilute Indian voting power. Tribal members from seven different reservations in Montana are plaintiffs in the case.

Lobbying in Washington is another political activity in which Indians participate. Today the focus of lobbying efforts are primarily on the activities of the House Committee on Resources and the Senate Committee on Indian Affairs.

Indians also have been involved in direct action politics, i.e., protest participation and aggressive political participation. The **American Indian Movement** (AIM) has drawn attention to the situation of American Indians over the years through various means, including protests. American Indians and the general population have varying levels of support for protest and aggressive political participation. (See table 4.) A majority of American Indians support the right of people to involve themselves in protest participation. Less than a third of those responding, Indians and non-Indians alike, supported the right of people to participate in aggressive political participation.

BIBLIOGRAPHY

Deloria, Vine, Jr. *Custer Died for Your Sins.* New York: Avon Books, 1969.

Helm, June. "Indian Dependency and Indian Self-Determination: Problems and Paradoxes in Canada's Northwest Territories." In Ernest L. Schusky, ed. *Political Organization of Native North Americans.* Washington, DC: University Press of American, Inc., 1980.

Holm, Tom. "Indian Lobbyists: Cherokee Opposition to the Allotment of Tribal Lands." *American Indian Quarterly* 5, no. 2 (May 1979): 115–34.

Table 4: Support for the Right to Participate in Various Unconventional Political Activities

Type of Activity	General Population	American Indians
Organize protests of government	76.8%	75.0%
Publish protest pamphlets	69.5%	64.3%
Organize demonstrations	69.6%	60.8%
Publish books advocating overthrow of government	62.7%	57.7%
Public meetings of those who want to overthrow government	57.8%	51.4%
Organize nationwide strike of all workers against government	24.0%	29.0%
Allow revolutionaries to teach 15-year-olds in school	20.5%	21.4%
Occupy government offices and stop their work	11.1%	11.6%
Damage government buildings	3.8%	5.6%

Source: National Opinion Research Center, General Social Survey

Melody, Michael E. "Lakota Myth and Government: The Cosmos as The State." *American Indian Culture and Research Journal* 4, no. 3 (1980): 1–19.

Muller, Edward N. *Aggressive Political Participation.* Princeton: Princeton University Press, 1979.

Prucha, Francis Paul. *The Indians in American Society.* Berkeley, CA: University of California Press, 1988.

Schusky, Ernest L. *Political Organization of Native North Americans.* Washington, DC: University Press of America, Inc., 1980.

Tyler, S. Lyman. *A History of Indian Policy.* Washington, DC: U.S. Department of the Interior, 1973.

Pontiac (1720–1769)

Pontiac, an Ottawa chief, was a daring strategic planner who led a loose confederacy of the Ottawa, Potawatomi, and Ojibwa. Worried about the survival of his people, he planned a brilliant strategy to wrest control away from the British. He led tribes from Lake Superior to the lower Mississippi in coordinated surprise attacks on British forts on May 7, 1763. The plan was to attack the nearest fort, massacre the garrison, and wipe out surrounding settlements. Pontiac led the attack on Detroit, but his surprise was spoiled when news of the plan was leaked to the garrison commander. After three years of war (**Pontiac's War**), a peace treaty was signed in July 1766. Three years later while attending a drinking party in Illinois, he was stabbed and killed by a Peoria tribesman. (AMM)

BIBLIOGRAPHY

Ellis, Edward Sylvester. *The Life of Pontiac, the Conspirator, Chief of the Ottawas.* New York: Hurst & Company, 1910.

Peckham, Howard H. *Pontiac and the Indian Uprising.* Detroit: Wayne State University Press, 1994.

Pontiac's War

Pontiac was an Ottawa chief who sided with the French in their wars against the English for control of North America. Angered by English refusal after the French surrender to continue the French practice of providing supplies in exchange for Indian friendship and assistance, and by the generally imperious English attitude toward Indians and Indian land, Pontiac led an uprising against the English in 1763. Pontiac's forces won many battles, but they were not sufficiently supplied to maintain sieges of the key strongholds of Fort Pitt and Fort Detroit. Sporadic resistance continued into the next year, but the general uprising was not sustained.

The most infamous aspect of Pontiac's War was the British use of smallpox-infected blankets to spread disease among Indians besieging the forts. This early form of germ warfare was explicitly discussed and approved by English Commander-in-Chief Lord Jeffrey Amherst in an exchange of letters with Colonel Henry Bouquet during the summer of 1763. (PPE)

BIBLIOGRAPHY

Parkman, Francis. *The Conspiracy of Pontiac and the Indian War after the Conquest of Canada.* Boston: Little, Brown, 1886.

Alexander Lawrence Posey (1873–1901)

Alexander Lawrence Posey was active in Creek politics. He became the first Native-American owner of a daily newspaper, in which he argued the case of the Indian against the federal government. He is often best remembered for the writing of his "Fus Fixico" letters. These letters were high political satire in which he criticized the policies of the federal government toward **allotment** and Creek independence.

BIBLIOGRAPHY

Kosmider, Alexia M. *Tricky Tribal Discourse.* Moscow: University of Idaho Press, 1998.

Littlefield, Daniel F. *Alexander Posey.* Lincoln: University of Nebraska Press, 1992.

Poundmaker (ca. 1842–1886/7)

In 1879 Poundmaker (Pitikwahanapiwiyin), as chief of the River People bands, accepted a reserve in Saskatchewan on which to settle with 182 followers, where he began acting as a representative for the Cree and spokesman with the government. Although he attempted to maintain peace, in 1885 he was tried on a treason-felony charge, found guilty, and sentenced to three years in the Stony Mountain Penitentiary in Manitoba. He was released early due to ill health, and he died shortly afterward. (KJB)

BIBLIOGRAPHY

Shuman, Norma. *Poundmaker.* New York: McGraw-Hill, 1967.

Powhatan (ca. 1580–1618)

Powhatan was the chief of the **Powhatan Confederacy,** which stretched along the coastal area of Virginia. The father of **Pocahontas,** Powhatan pursued a policy of accommodation of the early British settlers, including the initial group led by

Captain John Smith. Powhatan believed that the two groups could peacefully coexist. However, by 1609, he had changed his mind and his confederacy was openly hostile to settlers. The conflicts ended around 1614, the time his daughter married John Rolfe.

BIBLIOGRAPHY

Rountree, Helen C. *Pocahontas's People: The Powhatan Indians of Virginia through Four Centuries.* Norman: University of Oklahoma Press, 1990.

Powhatan Confederacy

The Powhatan Confederacy consisted of some 200 Virginian Algonquian tribes led by the powerful chief **Powhatan.** Its territory included the Tidewater section of Virginia from the Potomac River to the James River and inland to the fall line from Fredericksburg to Richmond. At its height during the settlement of Jamestown, the confederacy consisted of about 200 towns and perhaps as many as 8,000 people. After Powhatan died in 1618, his brother **Opehanacanough** took control of the tribe and led it in war from 1622 to 1636. War broke out again in 1641; Opehanacanough was killed, and the confederacy disbanded. War with the Iroquois between 1676 and 1722 decimated the Powhatan tribes and led to their extinction. **See also** Second Virginia War; Six Nations (Haudenosaunee) Confederacy/Iroquois Confederacy. (AMM)

BIBLIOGRAPHY

Nee, Kay Bonner. *Powhatan.* Minneapolis, MN: Dillon Press, 1977.

Project Own

In 1968 the Small Business Administration (SBA) and the Service Corps of Retired Executives created Project Own. The purpose of Project Own is to aid Native Americans in opening service businesses including laundromats, gas stations, convenience stores, etc. The two groups, working through the **Bureau of Indian Affairs,** have attempted to change the lending practices of banks in regard to Indians. As part of the initiative, the SBA would guarantee loans up to 90 percent of $350,000. In special economic areas, the SBA has guaranteed 100 percent of loans up to $25,000.

BIBLIOGRAPHY

Parris, Addion W. *The Small Business Administration.* New York: Praeger, 1968.

Public Law 280

From the late 1940s to the early 1960s, Congress made "termination" the basis of federal Indian policy. Termination involved abolishing federal responsibility and services for Indians as a way to eradicate **reservations** and thereby assimilate Native Americans into white society. Public Law 280 (P.L. 280) was designed to facilitate these goals by allowing states to assume civil and criminal jurisdiction over selected Indian reservations. The law generated problems both for tribes and states, and it provoked widespread opposition among Native Americans. The concerns about the law were so severe that P.L. 280 was ultimately modified.

Passed by Congress and signed by President Dwight Eisenhower in 1953, P.L. 280 allowed California, Minnesota, Nebraska, Oregon, and Wisconsin to assume civil and criminal jurisdiction over most or all Indian lands within their borders. It permitted other states to assume authority over Indian lands if they amended their constitutions or passed relevant statutes. The law did not permit states to tax land held in trust for Native Americans by the federal government or to modify hunting and fishing rights. Nevertheless, states were expected to provide Indians with services previously provided by the federal government.

P.L. 280 often proved problematic. It eroded tribal **sovereignty** because state authority supplanted tribal courts and law enforcement functions on affected reservations. In many cases, state officials failed to provide meaningful services because the reservations were not subject to state taxation. In other instances, states violated the provisions of P.L. 280 and tried to regulate hunting and fishing on Indian lands. As Cheyenne River Sioux Tribal Chairman Frank Ducheneaux put it, P.L. 280 threatened to "wipe out our tribal laws and **tribal government** without giving us a voice in the matter."

As a result, P.L. 280 provoked widespread Indian opposition and led to a number of lawsuits between tribes and state governments. In some cases—such as *Application of Andy* (1956) and *In Re Colwash* (1960)—the courts limited states' jurisdiction over reservations. Ultimately, Native American opposition led to a modification of P.L. 280. The **Indian Civil Rights Act of 1968** stipulated that states could not exercise civil or criminal jurisdiction over reservations without the Indians' permission. The effective repudiation of P.L. 280 reflected the growing rejection of termination by the late 1960s and the growing acceptance of **self-determination** as the basis for Indian policy. **See also** *Bryan v. Istasca County* (1976); *California v. Cabazon Band of Mission Indians* (1987); Land and Water Rights; *Seminole Tribe of Florida v. Butterworth* (1981); Termination Resolution. (CKR)

BIBLIOGRAPHY

Burt, Larry W. *Tribalism in Crisis: Federal Indian Policy, 1953–1961.* Albuquerque: University of New Mexico, 1982.
Deloria, Vine, Jr. and Clifford M. Lytle. *American Indians, American Justice.* Austin: University of Texas Press, 1983.
Fixico, Donald L. *Termination and Relocation: Federal Indian Policy, 1945–1960.* Albuquerque: University of New Mexico Press, 1986.
Wilkinson, Charles F. *American Indians, Time, and the Law.* New Haven: Yale University Press, 1987.

Pushmataha (ca. 1764–1824)

A Choctaw leader and warrior, Pushmataha commanded a Choctaw war party that assisted Andrew Jackson in battle against the Red Stick Creeks in 1813–1814. He considered the U.S. government friendly to his people and worked for better relations. Pushmataha staunchly opposed Christian missionary efforts, while simultaneously encouraging education. He used portions of an annuity he received from his military service to fund a school and blacksmith shop that used white methods. While in Washington, D.C., for treaty negotiations in 1824, he died of the croup and was buried in the Congressional Cemetery. **See also** Red Stick War. (GO)

BIBLIOGRAPHY

DeRosier, Arthur H., Jr. *The Removal of the Choctaw Indians.* Knoxville: University of Tennessee Press, 1970.

Lincecum, Gideon. "Life of Apushimataha." *Mississippi Historical Society Publications* 9 (1906): 415–85.

Puyallup Tribe v. Department of Game: I (1968), *II* (1973), *III* (1977)

Dubbed the "Puyallup Trilogy" because it reached the U.S. Supreme Court on three separate occasions, *Puyallup Tribe v. Department of Game* affirmed the treaty fishing rights of Northwest Indians. In *Puyallup I*, 391 U.S. (1968), the Court upheld the tribe's right to catch both salmon and steelhead in the Puyallup River. When the Washington State Department of Game subsequently prohibited Indians from netting steelhead, the Supreme Court struck down the ban in *Puyallup II*, 414 U.S. 44 (1973). In the final round, *Puyallup III*, 433 U.S. 165 (1977), the Court affirmed the state's authority to allocate 45 percent of the river's wild steelhead to the tribe. Although the Puyallup Trilogy failed to address the hatchery issue and allowed state regulation for conservation purposes, it secured significant victories for Northwest Indian fishing rights. **See also** Fishing and Hunting Treaty Rights. (AHF)

BIBLIOGRAPHY

Cohen, Fay G. *Treaties on Trial: The Continuing Controversy over Northwest Indian Fishing Rights.* Seattle: University of Washington Press, 1986.

Galligan, Thomas C., Jr. and Michael T. Reynvaan. "Comments: Pacific Northwest Indian Treaty Fishing Rights." *University of Puget Sound Law Review* 5 (1981): 99–129.

Pyramid Lake Paiute Tribe v. Morton (1973)

In *Pyramid Lake Paiute Tribe v. Morton*, 354 F. Supp. (1973), Judge Gesell ruled that "takings" by the federal government with Indians are "to be liberally construed to the benefit of the Indians." The secretary of the interior had issued regulations concerning water rights on the Truckee River, which the Pyramid Lake Paiute Tribe argued would threaten the level of the lake, and hence their livelihood which was dependent on fishing. Gesell ruled that the secretary had violated his fiduciary trust responsibility to the tribe. As a result of the decision, the secretary of the interior issued new regulations that limited the amount of water that could be diverted from the Truckee River for irrigation. In a later case, *Nevada v. United States* **(1983),** the Supreme Court ruled that the secretary was barred from abrogating or modifying previous water rights. **See also** Land and Water Rights. (AMM)

BIBLIOGRAPHY

Wunder, John R., ed. *Recent Legal Issues for American Indians, 1968 to the Present.* New York: Garland Publishing, 1996.

Queen Anne of Pamunkey (1650–1725)

Queen Anne assumed leadership of the Pamunkey Indians in the 1670s after her husband, Totopatomoi, died fighting with colonists against inland tribes. In 1675 Virginia governor William Berkeley asked Queen Anne for help against Nathaniel Bacon and his band of rebels. Anne rejected the plea, citing numerous injustices against her people, but eventually relented after Berkeley promised appropriate compensation. As a result, Pamunkey warriors assisted in overcoming the 1676 **Bacon's Rebellion**, even though the only compensation they received was a silver badge inscribed to the "Queen of Pamunkey." Queen Anne came before government officials again in 1715, asking for assistance and an end to discrimination, yet her pleas went unheard.

BIBLIOGRAPHY

Rountree, Helen C. *Pocahontas's People: The Powhatan Indians of Virginia through Four Centuries.* Norman: University of Oklahoma Press, 1990.

Queen Anne's War (1702–1713)

Queen Anne's War was one of four conflicts that resulted from the rivalry of European powers for control of North America (together with **King William's War,** 1689–1697; **King George's War,** 1744–1748; and the **French and Indian War,** 1754–1763). Threatened by British commercial and territorial expansion into the trans-Appalachian West, French colonists and their Indian allies began raiding British colonial settlements in New Hampshire, Massachusetts, and Maine. Britain responded by raising its own Indian–colonial forces and attempted to persuade the Iroquois to join the British in the conflict. The Iroquois, however, refused to take sides. In the south along the Gulf coast, the French sought to gain the support of the Creeks, Cherokees, Choctaws, and Chicasaws. Although the Cherokees refused to align themselves against Great Britain, Creek and Choctaw factions joined French colonists in disrupting British trade between Charleston and the lower Mississippi Valley. Great Britain's most important ally in the South was the Chickasaw nation, who neutralized the threat posed by the Creek and Choctaw groups. No true victor emerged on the North American continent; only an uncertain truce developed. **See also** Dummer's War of 1722; Six Nations (Haudenosaunee) Confederacy/Iroquois Confederacy. (KJB)

BIBLIOGRAPHY

Peckham, Howard H. *The Colonial Wars, 1689–1762.* Chicago: University of Chicago Press, 1964.

Quinnipiac Reservation

In 1638, the Puritans created the first-ever Indian reservation, one established for the Quinnipiac Nation living near what is present-day New Haven, Connecticut. In guidelines provided for the enactment of the reservation, the Quinnipiac were allowed to keep only 1,200 acres of their original lands, which previously encompassed a large amount of Connecticut. Provisions were also made stating that remaining "free" Indian lands would fall under the jurisdiction of an English magistrate or agent; furthermore, the Quinnipiac were not allowed to sell or leave their lands, nor were they to receive any Indian visitors from other areas. Besides these restrictions, the Quinnipiac Indians had to relinquish their traditional beliefs, which the Puritans felt to be Satanic, in order to accept the practices of Christianity. Most of the involved Native Americans agreed reluctantly to these provisions, fearing retaliation if they did not comply.

BIBLIOGRAPHY

Townsend, Charles H. *The Quinnipiac Indians and Their Reservation.* New Haven, CT: Tuttle, Morehouse & Taylor, 1900.

R

Rain-in-the-Face (Ite-O-Magajo) (1840–1905)

Rain-in-the-Face was a Hunkpapa Lakota (Sioux) leader during the **Plains Wars.** Rain-in-the-Face was a strong warrior; he fought at the **Battle of the Little Bighorn** and then went to Canada with **Sitting Bull.** He lived on Standing Rock Reservation in his later years. **See** "You Are Living in a New Path" by Sitting Bull (1880) in Appendix 1. (LCJ)

BIBLIOGRAPHY

Walstrom, Veryl. *My Search for the Burial Sites of Sioux Nation Chiefs.* Lincoln, NE: Dageforde Publishing, 1995.

Red Cloud (1821–1909)

Red Cloud (Mahpiya Luta), an Oglala Lakota, excelled both as a military and political leader. Red Cloud built his reputation by leading successful military campaigns, including the Fetterman Massacre along the Bozeman Trail in 1866. That

Red Cloud (center, seated) served as an effective negotiator between the Lakota and the U.S. government. *National Archives.*

victory, coupled with his role in negotiating and signing the **Treaty of Fort Laramie** of 1868, led many Americans to regard him as the spokesman for all Lakotas. In 1871, Red Cloud settled at the agency that bore his name and spent the remainder of his life mediating between his people and the United States. His compromise positions on pivotal events such as ceding the **Black Hills** in 1876, reducing the reservation in 1889, and the **Ghost Dance Movement** in 1890 proved unpopular, but he retained his powerful reputation and remained a staunch defender of Lakota culture. (TMK)

BIBLIOGRAPHY

Larson, Robert W. *Red Cloud: Warrior-Statesman of the Lakota Sioux.* Norman: University of Oklahoma Press, 1997.
Paul, R. Eli, ed. *Autobiography of Red Cloud: War Leader of the Oglalas.* Helena: Montana Historical Society Press, 1997.

Red Fox v. Red Fox (1975)

Red Fox v. Red Fox, Or. App. 393, 542 P.2d. 918 (1975), raised the issue of the validity of a divorce decree given by the tribal court for the Confederated Tribes of the Warm Springs Reservation in Oregon. According to the judge's ruling, the tribal court decisions were deserving of the "same deference shown decisions of foreign nations as a matter of comity." This decision set precedence in determining the legitimacy of tribal courts. (MKJ)

BIBLIOGRAPHY

"Red Fox v. Red Fox Or. App. 393, 542 P.2d. 918 (1975)." *Pacific Reporter* 2nd Series, vol. 42, P. 2d, nos. 1–5. St. Paul, MN: West Publishing, 1976.

Red Jacket (ca. 1750–1830)

Red Jacket (Sagoyewatha) was an influential civil chief of the Senecas during the early national period. A veteran of the Revolutionary War (on the British side) and the **War of 1812** (on the American side), Red Jacket served as a diplomat for the Iroquois from 1784 to 1826, and he acquired a reputation as a gifted and powerful orator. After 1800, he became the leader of the Senecas' "Pagan party" and an opponent of the federal government's "civilization" program, white missionaries, **Handsome Lake's** revival movement, and negotiations with the Ogden Land Company. (DAN)

BIBLIOGRAPHY

Hubbard, J. Niles. *An Account of Sagoyewatha.* New York: Burt Franklin, 1886.
Manley, Henry. "Red Jacket's Last Campaign." *New York History* 31, no. 2 (April 1950): 149–68.

Red Power

Red Power is a general name for all American Indian activist groups formed and actions taken in the late 1960s and in the 1970s. The **American Indian Movement** (AIM) has been the most powerful, influential, and lasting among them, acting in the name of all Native American people. The context of Red Power was the era of the Civil Rights Movement, which openly challenged American society and government. The Red Power era started with the occupation of **Alcatraz Island** in 1968, and ended roughly with the **Longest Walk** in 1978. It included many occasions of open confrontation over issues such as U.S./Indian relations, American Indian **self-determination**, the status of treaties, and land, water, and fishing rights. Red Power brought tremendous attention to Indian issues in the United States, a sense of shared community among American Indians, and changes in federal Indian policy. **See also** Trail of Broken Treaties; Wounded Knee II; Land and Water Rights. (MS)

BIBLIOGRAPHY

Deloria, Vine Jr. *Behind the Trail of Broken Treaties: An Indian Declaration of Independence.* University of Texas Press, 1974.
Johnson, Troy R. *The Occupation of Alcatraz Island: Indian Self Determination and the Rise of Indian Activism.* Urbana: University of Illinois Press, 1996.

Red River War (1874–1875)

The Red River War started when a group of settlers entered the Comanche and Kiowa territory without the permission of the tribes. The tribes attacked because they feared that the group was intending to settle on tribal land. The army was called to settle the affair once and for all. The war ended Indian resistance on the Southern Plains and marked the end of President Ulysses Grant's peace policies toward the Indians. The signing of the Treaty of Medicine Lodge in 1867 gave the Comanche and Kiowas reservations in the Western Indian Territory. It was also believed by the tribes that this treaty would give them exclusive rights to use the panhandle in Texas as their hunting grounds, but that was not to be the case. (MW)

BIBLIOGRAPHY

Haley, James L. *The Buffalo War.* Norman: University of Oklahoma Press, 1985.

Red Stick War

A Muskogee faction called Red Sticks was hostile to the United States because of its invasion of their territory. These young warriors joined Tecumseh's confederacy in 1812, inspired both by his political allegiance and religious devotion to help their people in the struggle against the whites. Promises of Spanish and British help and raids by white frontiersmen provoked the Red Sticks to attack Fort Mims at Mobile Bay, Alabama, in August 1813. The resulting deaths of whites gave the United States an excuse to crush the Muskogees. U.S. Army forces, led by Andrew Jackson, defeated the Muskogee warriors in the Battle of Horseshoe Bend on the Tallapoosa River on March 27, 1814. The Treaty of Fort Jackson concluded the Red Stick War, ceding 14 million acres of Muskogee lands to the United States. **See also** Pushmataha; War of 1812. (JP)

BIBLIOGRAPHY

Martin, Joel. *Sacred Revolt: The Muskogees' Struggle for a New World.* Boston: Beacon Press, 1991.

Benjamin Reifel (1906–1990)

Benjamin Reifel, a Native American and World War II veteran, served as an administrator in the Department of the Interior and the **Bureau of Indian Affairs** beginning in 1933 until he was elected to the United States Congress in 1961 as a Republican from South Dakota. He remained there until 1971.

BIBLIOGRAPHY

Fielder, Mildred. *Sioux Indian Leaders.* Seattle: Superior Publishing, 1975.

Religious Freedom Restoration Act of 1993

The Religious Freedom Restoration Act of 1993 represented a broadly bipartisan response to the U.S. Supreme Court's decision in *Oregon v. Smith* **(1990)**, in which the Court ruled that the Free Exercise clause of the First Amendment did not protect Native Americans using peyote in religious rituals. The act declared government at any level "shall not substantially burden a person's exercise of religion" except as the least restrictive means of furthering a compelling government interest. Rastafarians used the act to protect ritual marijuana use and Sikhs used it to protect the carrying of ceremonial knives by Sikh schoolchildren. Other groups used the act to protect various practices considered more mainstream. The Court overturned the act in *City of Boerne v. Flores* (1997), ruling that it unconstitutionally usurped powers belonging to federal courts and the states. Meanwhile, the more narrowly focused American Indian Religious Freedom Act of 1994 protects ritual peyote use from federal and state prosecutions. **See also** American Indian Religious Freedom Act of 1978; *People v. Woody* (1964). (TMK)

BIBLIOGRAPHY

"Court Strikes Down RFRA." *The Christian Century* 114, no. 20 (July 2, 1997): 619.
Rosen, Jeffrey. "Anti-antidisestablishmentarianism: Too Much Religious Freedom." *The New Republic* 216, no. 8 (February 24, 1997): 10.

Reoccupation of Fort Lawton (1970)

The federal government was in the process of closing unneeded forts and declaring them federal surplus so that they could be sold or donated to others at inexpensive prices. Senator Henry Jackson (D-WA) arranged for Fort Lawton, located 50 miles south of Seattle, to be donated to the city of Seattle so it could be converted into a park. **United Indians of All Tribes**, an Indian rights group modeled on Indians of All Tribes, occupied the fort in protest and called on the federal government to give the fort to Native Americans. Seventy-seven protesters, including actress Jane Fonda, were removed from the property on March 8, 1970. One week later, 78 protesters re-entered the fort and were arrested. The Native Americans repeated their demands that the land be given to them to use as a cultural center. On April 2, 1970, the day when those arrested on March 15 were arraigned, the fort was once again occupied. Fifteen additional protesters were arrested, but the charges were dropped. In 1971, the federal government awarded Fort Lawton to the Indians, who built the Daybreak Star Cultural Center on the site. **See also** Alcatraz Island Occupation.

BIBLIOGRAPHY

Hedgepath, W. "Alcatraz: The Indian Uprising that Worked." *Look* (June 2, 1970): 44–45.

Smith, Paul Chaat. *Like a Hurricane: The Indian Movement from Alcatraz to Wounded Knee*. New York: New Press, 1996.

Repatriation of Remains

Indian peoples in the United States have sought for decades to have the remains of their ancestors returned to them for traditional burial. The human remains or burial offerings of more than 2 million Native Americans are possessed by such nontribal entities as museums, state historical societies, universities, the National Park Service, and curio shops. The 1906 Antiquities Act was the first federal attempt to protect gravesites, but the law—which was largely ignored—included nothing about return of previously obtained remains or artifacts. Organized efforts by Native Americans to encourage repatriation came in the late 1970s, most notably the "**Longest Walk**," in which hundreds of Native Americans marched across the country, finding museum after museum in which the bones of Indians were kept in display cases or in storage. In 1986, during a trip to Washington, D.C., a group of northern Cheyenne chiefs went to the Smithsonian to view the collection of Cheyenne artifacts. As the group was leaving, they saw a warehouse with row upon row of Indian skeletal remains. That the Smithsonian casually held the remains of more than 18,000 indigenous peoples enraged tribal groups and led to negotiations between the Smithsonian and two Native American groups for return of a small part of its vast collection of skeletal remains. The first federal law to deal substantially with repatriation of remains came in the **Native American Graves and Repatriation Act of 1990.** Among other things, the act directs federal agencies and museums receiving federal assistance to identify the tribal origins of human remains in their collections; it also requires repatriation to the appropriate tribe upon request. The bill also establishes federal funds to assist museums in their inventories and to assist tribal groups in petitioning museums for repatriation of remains. Implementation of the act has been slow and problematic, most notably because of the difficulty in linking the remains to the appropriate tribe. **See also** Archaeological Resources Protection Act of 1979. (GTH)

BIBLIOGRAPHY

Boyd, Thomas H. "Disputes Regarding the Possession of Native American Religious and Cultural Objects and Human Remains: A Discussion of the Applicable Law and proposed Legislation." *Missouri Law Review* 55 (1990): 883–936.

Deloria, Vine, Jr. "A Simple Question of Humanity: The Moral Dimensions of the Reburial Issue." *Native American Rights Foundation Legal Review* 14, no. 4 (1989): 1–12.

Reservation Economics

With few notable exceptions, Indian reservation economies rank among the most deprived in the nation. While mainstream economists have tended in the past to attribute this condition to the failure of reservations to be fully integrated into the capitalist system, the problem is best viewed as a matter of how tribes have been integrated into the national political economy.

Among the numerous factors that account for reservation underdevelopment, four interrelated factors stand out: (1) marginal lands; (2) isolation from metropolitan areas; (3) lack of capital; and (4) excessive federal interference in reservation affairs.

As a result of the mass liquidation of millions of acres of tribal land over the centuries, much of the land left in Indian control is submarginal, arid, and lacking in fecundity. This poor-quality land complicates the possibility of pursuing economic development through agricultural endeavors, or even the exploitation of natural resources. This situation is confounded by a lack of renewable natural resources and the confining boundaries of reservations, which can sustain only a limited population. Added to those conditions are the problems of trust and allotted land. Trust land cannot be alienated without the permission of the **Bureau of Indian Affairs (BIA)** and allotted land is often so limited as to have only rental value when combined with other allotments. Lacking either adequate natural resources and capital, many tribes are forced to rely on federal largess.

The remoteness of many reservations also creates formidable obstacles to balanced development. Some western reservations are situated hundreds of miles from markets and commercial centers. Because of the high costs of transportation of certain goods and services, it is difficult for tribes to pursue certain forms of development contingent upon the shipment of goods. Moreover, this remoteness discourages outside investments in reservation initiatives, and it also contributes to the high costs of goods and services on the reservation. For those tribes with abundant cultural and natural resources, tourism constitutes one development strategy to counter the barriers imposed by isolation. However, since many reservations lie within the "snowbelt," tourism is usually a seasonal enterprise at best. Tourism can also be problematic in that it facilitates an intrusion upon tribal cultural values and the privacy of tribal members. Until recently, for example, it was not uncommon for tourists at some of the New Mexico Pueblos to walk uninvited into the homes of tribal members, assuming the homes to be museum pieces.

The lack of capital on reservations can be attributed first to the fact that most Indian tribes never had capital in the first place. Native Americans are relatively new arrivals in the world capitalist system, and their first introduction to a cash economy came in the form of modest and irregular treaty annuities. Access to the amount of capital required to develop reservation economic endeavors is severely restricted not only by distance from commercial centers, but also by the reluctance of outside brokers to invest in Indians. This is racially motivated in some instances; in others, it is derived from culturally biased stereotypes. Many potential investors believe that the communal values espoused by Native Americans are incompatible with the individualistic, aggressive values of capitalism. Moreover, potential investors are reluctant to engage in negotiations with tribal governments, which they perceive as being unstable, localized forms of banana republics.

The initial conduit to capital investment on reservations was the federal government. Ironically, it has also posed perhaps the greatest obstacle to balanced development. Since the inception of the reservation system, the BIA has dominated many aspects of the lives of reservation Indians. Federal annuities and grants are almost always regulated by the BIA and are frequently mismanaged. A 1987 investigation, for instance, revealed that tribes received only 10 cents for every federal dollar that is allocated for Indian affairs after it passes through the bureaucracy. BIA oversight in tribal governmental affairs frequently exceeds ethical limits. For years, businesses wishing to engage in development activities on reservations bypassed the tribal government altogether and negotiated with BIA agents and Interior Department officials. As a result, billions of dollars worth of minerals and other resources have been removed from Indian lands while tribes have received few, if any, financial or other benefits. In recent years, a number of tribes have confronted this problem with some success. Through litigation and intertribal political alliances (such as the **Council of Energy Resource Tribes**) many tribes have convinced extractive industries and other corporations to negotiate directly with tribal governments. Smaller tribes, however, lack the economic and political clout to prompt such bargaining.

While the federal government often manipulates and limits the parameters of tribal **sovereignty**, it rarely addresses the real issues, most notably the lack of tribal control. Moreover, federal policy rarely considers the impact of development strategies on tribal culture. The **Indian Arts and Crafts Board Act of 1935**, for example, sanctioned the marketing of Native culture, while not considering how this appropriation might clash with Native values.

In the meantime, the federal courts have placed severe restrictions on tribal capacity to regulate or gain access to the resources necessary for equitable economic development. Although the 1908 case of *Winters v. United States* acknowledged the supremacy of tribal water rights as inherent, subsequent renderings have placed states' rights in superior positions. Tribes such as the Tohono O'Odham of Arizona

have been forced to compromise their original water allocations while their reservation aquifer is depleted by neighboring non-Indian agribusinesses and cities. Most recently, in the case of *Seminole Tribe v. Florida* (1996), the Court has ruled that states may prohibit gaming on reservations. For many tribes, gaming is a last resort when resources are deficient.

The economic situation is fortunately not bleak for all tribes. The **Passamaquoddy** Tribe of Maine received millions of dollars and a significant amount of land through a 1980 claims settlement. Rather than opting for per-capita payments, tribal members voted to invest the money in projects that benefit the tribe as a whole. As a result, the Passamaquoddy tribe invested in a lucrative blueberry industry, started a successful construction company, and now manages thousands of acres of sustainable forest land. After gaining federal recognition in the 1980s, the Mashantucket Pequots of Connecticut, a tribe of only 800 members, channeled their efforts into the opening of a large casino. Strategically located between Boston and New York, the casino now grosses over $1 million per day, and every tribal member is guaranteed an annual income of at least $30,000. The Ak-Chin O'Odham tribe of Arizona, who two decades ago faced the near loss of their reservation aquifer while battling with hostile farmers, successfully negotiated a water compact that brought water from the Colorado River into their valley, benefitting both the tribe and non-Indians. They now operate a highly successful agribusiness with sophisticated machinery, and a casino, and are beginning to use their irrigation canals to develop a potentially profitable aquaculture industry.

These success stories have two things in common. In each of these tribes, development endeavors were locally controlled, and in each case, these initiatives relied heavily on the impetus of grassroots community members. The latter condition has been a frequent problem on reservations, as tribal leaders sometimes make economic decisions without the approval of their constituents, and open the door for extractive industries that may put money into the tribal coffer, but the money rarely diffuses to community members. Most of the aforementioned success stories also involved tribes that made concerted efforts to rely on federal aid as little as possible. Through the provisions of the Tribal Self-Governance Project Act of 1994, which allows tribes the option of receiving block grants directly from Congress for tribally controlled and designed programs, the frequency of local control and grassroots impetus may increase significantly in **Indian country**, provided that **federal Indian policy** remains consistent. (SRC)

BIBLIOGRAPHY

Ambler, Marjane. *Breaking the Iron Bonds: Indian Control of Energy Development.* Lawrence: University Press of Kansas, 1990

Cornell, Stephen and Joseph P. Kalt, eds. *What Can Tribes Do? Strategies and Institutions in American Indian Economic Development.* Los Angeles: University of California American Indian Studies Center, 1992.

Jorgensen, Joseph G. "Indians and the Metropolis." In Jack O. Waddell and O. Michael Watson, eds. *The American Indian in Urban Society.* Boston: Little, Brown, and Co., 1971.

Ortiz, Roxanne Dunbar, ed. *Economic Development in American Indian Reservations.* Albuquerque: University of New Mexico Native American Studies Center, 1979.

Pratt, Raymond B. "Tribal Sovereignty and Resource Exploitation." *Southwest Economy and Society* 4, no. 3 (1979): 38–74.

White, Robert H. *Tribal Assets: The Rebirth of Native America.* New York: Henry Holt and Co., 1990.

Wilkins, David E. "Modernization, Colonialism, and Dependency: How Appropriate are These Models for Providing an Explanation of North American Indian Underdevelopment?" *Ethnic and Racial Studies* 16, no. 3 (1993): 390–419.

Reservations

A reservation is a tribally governed, in most cases federally administered, land base set aside for Indian use and habitation.

The reservation policy of the United States government began in the late 1800s, and it quickly became the centerpiece of United States/Indian relations. Under President Andrew Jackson, a policy of forced removal was instituted. Tribes were forced from their land, moved west of the Mississippi, and relocated on reservations. Proponents of removal cited numerous advantages to the policy: reservations were seen as enclaves, protecting the unsophisticated Indians from disingenuous whites; they were touted as havens for the assimilation process, where Native Americans could be controlled and schooled in the ways of the dominant society. Finally, many proponents argued that reservations were the only alternative to extinction for the Native American. However, as many critics argue, much of the removal and relocation was in reality a cynical attempt to clear native land for white settlement and exploitation.

Numerous pieces of legislation have affected reservation life and governance. The General Allotment (Dawes) Act of 1887 ordered the subdivision of reservations; lands not allotted were sold to white settlers. The Indian landbase, already greatly reduced, dropped from 138 million to 48 million acres at this time.

In 1934, **John Collier** introduced the **Indian Reorganization Act** (IRA), which promoted tribal reorganization, incorporation, and constitution making. The IRA gave a stronger role to tribal governments and helped to bolster reservation economies. This prosperity was temporarily reversed by termination (a policy that sought to end the reservation system), legislated in the 1950s. Although it was supposed to be consensual, many tribes found themselves unwillingly cut off from the federal relationship, and few could survive economically. President Nixon officially reversed termination in 1970; he declared a policy of **self-determination** and pledged governmental aid. Many **reservations** became the recipients of much needed Great Society programs, which gave money directly to tribal governments for food, **education**, and infrastructure. Later legislation clarified the relationship between the **Bureau of Indian Affairs (BIA)** and tribal governments, giving the former more power on the reservation.

Currently, more than 220 federally operated reservations are in existence, as well as 15 state-operated reservations in the 48 contiguous United States. These reservations are incredibly diverse in terms of population, size, resources, development, and government. States have little jurisdiction over federal reservations; they may not alienate, tax, or probate tribal trust properties, nor may they interfere with hunting, fishing, or trapping rights. **See also** Dawes Act; Nixon's Special Message to Congress (1970). (RAC)

BIBLIOGRAPHY

Castile, George Pierre and Robert L. Bee, eds. *State and Reservation: New Perspectives on Federal Indian Policy.* Tucson: University of Arizona Press, 1992.

Matthiessen, Peter. *Indian Country.* New York: Viking, 1984.

Return of Blue Lake Lands Act of 1970 (PL 91–550)

Signed by President Richard Nixon on December 15, 1970, the Return of Blue Lake Lands Act required that the federal government give back to the Taos Pueblo 48,000 of the 50,000 acres that were taken away in 1906 by President Theodore Roosevelt in order to establish a public recreation park. This case set an important precedent for other Indian tribes attempting to reclaim sacred lands. **See also** Nixon's Special Message to Congress (1970). (MKJ)

BIBLIOGRAPHY

Keegan, Marcia. *The Taos Pueblo and Its Sacred Blue Lake.* Santa Fe, NM: Clear Light Publishers, 1991.

Everett Ronald Rhoades (1931–)

Everett Rhoades, also known as Dau-ahlm-gya-toyah ("One Who Makes a Quest for Healing Power"), was the first person from the Kiowa tribe of Oklahoma to receive a medical degree. His most notable position was as director of the Indian Health Service (IHS), where he oversaw the health care for nearly 1.5 million Native Americans and Alaska natives. Rhoades joined the U.S. Air Force in 1952 and served as chief of the infectious disease section at Wilford Hall USAF Hospital at Lackland Air Force Base (Texas) from 1961 to 1966. While there, he was promoted to major. After leaving the air force, Rhoades returned to the University of Oklahoma to teach. There he held the position as chief of infectious disease at the Veterans Administration Medical Center in Oklahoma City until 1982. Rhoades was commissioned rear admiral for the U.S. Public Health Service in 1982, just before becoming director of the IHS.

BIBLIOGRAPHY

Jackson, Robert, "Rhoades 1st Kiowa to Become Doctor." *The Denver Rocky Mountain News* (November 25, 1997): 53A.

Rhode Island Indian Claims Settlement Act (1978)

Congress passed the Rhode Island Indian Claims Settlement Act in response to lawsuits filed by the Narragansett Indians. It restored 1,800 acres of formal tribal land to the Indians. Half of the land was to be given by the state. The land was transferred to a state-chartered, Indian-controlled corporation. **See also** Land and Water Rights.

BIBLIOGRAPHY

Washburn, Wilcomb E., ed. *History of Indian–White Relations.* Washington, DC: Smithsonian Institution, 1988.

Rice v. Rehner (1983)

Rice v. Rehner, 463 U.S. 713 (1983), challenged whether California could regulate liquor distribution on the Pala Indian Reservation. The U.S. Supreme Court ruled that California could regulate liquor sales because liquor was not a traditional factor in tribal **sovereignty** and because the federal government had explicitly authorized state regulation of liquor on Indian reservations. (AMM)

BIBLIOGRAPHY

Mikkanen, Arvo Q. "Rice v. Rehner: A Limitation on the Exercise of Tribal Governmental Powers Based on Historical Factors?" *American Indian Journal* 9, no. 2 (Summer 1986): 2–15.

Ryan, Anne M. "Confusion in the Land of Indian Sovereignty: The Supreme Court Takes a Detour." *Arizona Law Review* 25, no. 4 (Fall 1983): 1059–68.

Rogue River War

The Rogue River War of 1855–1856 was the climax in a long series of mutual depredations and skirmishes between American settlers and the Indian groups of the Rogue River Valley in southern Oregon. Known collectively as "Rogues," these tribes resented the large numbers of whites who moved into their territory following the discovery of gold during the late 1840s and early 1850s. Rising hostility exploded into war after a group of miners massacred 24 Indians near the Table Rock reservation in the Rogue River Valley. The Rogues defeated mixed forces of volunteers and regulars at three battles in the autumn of 1855, and coastal Indians laid siege to Port Orford the following spring. Indian resistance soon collapsed, however, and by summer the territorial government had removed most of the Rogues and their allies to the Grand Ronde and Siletz reservations in northwestern Oregon. (AHF)

BIBLIOGRAPHY

Beckham, Stephen Dow. *Requiem for a People: The Rogue Indians and the Frontiersmen.* Norman: University of Oklahoma Press, 1971.

O'Donnell, Terence. *An Arrow in the Earth: General Joel Palmer and the Indians of Oregon.* Portland: Oregon Historical Society, 1991.

Roman Nose (Sauts) (ca. 1830–1868)

Roman Nose, leader of the Cheyenne Dog Soldier Society during the **Plains Wars**, was a powerful fighter and astute strategist. He was killed at the Battle of the Arikaree (Beecher Island fight) after eating from pointed metal utensils, in violation of the power (a magical war bonnet) that protected him in battle. (LCJ)

BIBLIOGRAPHY

Brown, Dee. *Bury My Heart at Wounded Knee: An Indian History of the American West.* New York: Holt, Rinehart & Winston, 1970.

John Ross

John Ross was the principal chief of the Cherokees. He argued successfully to the U.S. Supreme Court that the **Indian Removal Act of 1830** was unconstitutional in *Cherokee Nation v. Georgia* (1833). The act required the Indians to trade their home property for property in Oklahoma. President Andrew Jackson ignored the Supreme Court's decision. As the **Civil War** started, Ross tried to remain neutral. Yet he tolerated slavery and aligned the Cherokee nation with the Confederacy. Many Cherokees, especially the Keetoowah, split with the tribe to side with the Union. **See also** Five Civilized Tribes; Indian Territory.

BIBLIOGRAPHY

Mails, Thomas E. *The Cherokee People: The Story of the Cherokees from Earliest Origins to Contemporary Times.* Tulsa, OK: Council Oak Books, 1992.

Norman, Geoffrey. "The Cherokee: Two Nations, One People." *National Geographic* (May 1995): 72–97.

Royal Proclamation of 1763

The Royal Proclamation of 1763 was issued on October 7 of that year by the British to create boundaries between American Indian lands and colonial settlements. The Proclamation was drafted primarily by John Pownall, the undersecretary of the Board of Trade.

The Royal Proclamation of 1763 set out three major guidelines. First, no colonial governments could survey or patent lands beyond the headwaters of any river connected to the Atlantic Ocean, thereby slowing all westward expansion. Second, the proclamation stopped colonists from purchasing Indian lands, which would both prevent potential disagreements between settlers and Native Americans and hinder any overabundance of colonial growth. Third, the document declared that Quebec, Grenada, East Florida, and West Florida were new British colonies, thereby causing all settlers in these regions to fall under Royal jurisdiction. The proclamation did not stop westward expansion and became a burning issue between colonists and the British. The proclamation ceased to have any legal effect on the American colonies with the outbreak of the American Revolution.

BIBLIOGRAPHY

Boivin, Richard. "The Cote Decision: Laying to Rest the Royal Proclamation." *Canadian Native Law Reporter.* no. 1 (Winter 1995): 1–22.

Markowitz, Harvey, ed. *Ready Reference American Indians.* Englewood Cliffs: Salem Press, 1995.

Russell Tribunal

The Fourth Russell Tribunal on the Rights of the Indians of North and Latin America was held in November 1980. At the tribunal, representatives of Native American nations testified about the challenges they faced and their attempts to survive. The tribunal led to the creation of the United Nations Working Group on Indigenous Populations in 1982. The working group drafted the Declaration for Rights of Indigenous Peoples, and it monitors and reports on the situations faced by indigenous peoples within nation-states. **See also** International Indian Treaty Council. (LCJ)

BIBLIOGRAPHY

Jaimes, M. Annette. *The State of Native America: Genocide, Colonization, and Resistance*. Boston: South End Press, 1992.

Russell Tribunal. *The Rights of the Indians of the Americas*. Rotterdam, The Netherlands: Fourth Russell Tribunal, 1980.

Sacajawea (ca. 1786–ca. 1812/1884)

Sacajawea (Sacagawea, Sakakawea) was born about 1786 in present-day central Idaho. A member of the Lemhi band of the Shoshoni Indians, she was captured and enslaved by the Hidatsa (or Minnetaree) tribe about 1800. In 1804, her husband, Toussaint Charbonneau, a French Canadian trapper; Sacajawea; and their son, Jean Baptiste Charbonneau, born during the journey, joined the **Lewis and Clark expedition** on its journey westward. A happenstance meeting with Sacajawea's brother, Cameahwait, chief of the Lemhi Shoshone, provided the expedition with horses and guides over the continental divide. After the expedition returned to St. Louis, Sacajawea fell into obscurity. Unverified reports of her death place it as early as 1812 at Fort Manuel, where trader John Luttig wrote in his diary that the "snake wife of Toussaint Charbonneau" died, and as late as 1884 on the Wind River Resrevation in Wyoming, when a Shoshoni woman called Sacajawea, who had a son named Jean Baptiste, died and was buried. (AMM)

BIBLIOGRAPHY

Kessler, Donna J. *The Making of Sacagawea: a Euro-American Legend.* Tuscaloosa, AL: University of Alabama Press, 1996.

Madsen, Brigham. *The Lemhi: Sacajawea's People.* Caldwell, ID: Caxton Printers, 1979.

St. Lawrence Seaway Challenges

During the late 1950s, the St. Regis (Akwesasne) and Caughnawaga Mohawks vigorously opposed the expropriation of Iroquois land for the St. Lawrence Seaway. Built to improve inland navigation and generate hydroelectricity, the seaway entailed the condemnation of property on two reservations in the United States and Canada and the relocation of numerous Indian families. The Mohawks filed lawsuits to stop the seizure of land, arguing that it violated treaties with the British crown and the United States government, and the tribe petitioned the United Nations for a hearing in the World Court. When their legal challenges failed, several Caughnawaga Mohawk families simply refused to move until construction crews forced them out. Some Akwesasne Mohawks threatened to blockade the Cornwall-Massena International Bridge, while another group claimed an area in upstate New York as an Iroquois homeland and remained there until evicted by court order. These protests, along with resistance to the Kinzua and Tuscarora dam projects, strengthened Iroquois solidarity and fueled the **Red Power** movement of the late 1960s. **See also** Kinzua Dam Protests; Land and Water Rights; Tuscarora Protest. (AHF)

BIBLIOGRAPHY

Ghobashy, Omar Z. *The Caughnawaga Indians and the St. Lawrence Seaway.* New York: The Devin-Adair Company, 1961.

Hauptman, Laurence. *The Iroquois Struggle for Survival: World War II to Red Power.* Syracuse, NY: Syracuse University Press, 1986.

Buffy Sainte-Marie (1942–)

Buffy Sainte-Marie (Cree) is a singer, composer, and activist well known for her lyrics about the oppression of Native peoples and for her presence in Native political movements since the 1960s. Her songs have contributed considerably to the raising of Native political awareness, and her "Now That the Buffalo Are Gone" is often cited as the first Native protest song. She remains active in Native political affairs, often performing in support of Native organizations. She is the founder of the Native North American Women's Association, and the Nihewan fund to support Native students pursuing degrees in law. (HHB)

BIBLIOGRAPHY

Wilson, Art. *Heartbeat of the Earth: A First Nation's Artist Records of Injustice and Resistance.* Gabriola, BC: New Society Publishers, 1996.

Salt River Reservation

The Salt River Reservation, near Phoenix, Arizona, is home to the second largest concentration of the Pipatsji Indians. The Pipatsji (part of the Maricopa tribe) live in an area near the Salt River called Lehi, where they had relocated in the nineteenth century in response to increasing encroachments by white settlers. The Salt River reservation is just east of the Gila River reservation, home to the Pima tribe. In 1879 President Rutherford B. Hayes issued an executive order that enlarged the Gila River reservation by adding additional land by the Salt River, thus creating the Salt River Reservation.

BIBLIOGRAPHY

Dobyns, Henry F. *The Pima-Maricopa.* New York: Chelsea House Publishers, 1989.

Spier, Leslie. *Yuman Tribes of the Gila River.* New York: Cooper Square, 1970.

Samoset (1590–1653)

In March of 1621, Samoset, chief of the Abenaki, welcomed the English to Massachusetts, making him one of the first Native Americans that colonists encountered. Samoset became the first chief to negotiate treaties and land sales with the white settlers, while also acting as a diplomat between the people. Samoset helped create the 55-year mutual defense pact between the English and the Wampanoug. Samoset also helped Christopher Levett in establishing fur trades with the Natives and selling land to English colonists.

BIBLIOGRAPHY

Bakeless, John. *America as Seen by Its First Explorers: The Eyes of Discovery.* New York: Dover, 1950.

Bonfanti, John. *Biographies and Legends of the New England Indians.* Wakefield, MA: Pride Publications, 1968.

Calloway, Colin, ed. *Dawnland Encounters: Indians and Europeans in Northern New England.* Hanover, NH: University Press of New England, 1991.

Russell, Howard S. *Indian New England before the Mayflower.* Hanover: University Press of New England, 1980.

Sand Creek Massacre

The massacre at Sand Creek occurred on November 29, 1864, in what is today southeastern Colorado. In the early 1860s, American expansion into the area, partly due to the **Civil War**, was aggressive and massive, and there were ongoing conflicts between American forces and local Native Americans. Two months prior to the massacre, 600 Southern Cheyenne and Arapaho people, two-thirds of whom were women and children, surrendered and came to live by Fort Lyons under a white flag. One of the main leaders, **Black Kettle**, explicitly expressed their peaceful intentions to Colonel John Chivington and the local governor, so they would not be mistaken for hostile enemies. Despite this effort, the Native American camp was attacked. About 200 Arapahos and Cheyennes, mostly women, children, and old men, were killed in the massacre by Chivington and his Colorado Volunteers of 700 men. Bodies were mutilated and human parts were cut out and used by the soldiers as ornaments and trophies. About a year after the massacre, representatives of the American authorities apologized to the survivors of the massacre and made some arrangements for financial compensation. (MS)

BIBLIOGRAPHY

Cutler, Bruce. *The Massacre at Sand Creek: Narrative Voices.* Norman: University of Oklahoma, 1995.

Hoig, Stan. *The Sand Creek Massacre.* Norman: University of Oklahoma, 1961.

Santa Clara Pueblo v. Martinez (1978)

The central question in *Santa Clara Pueblo v. Martinez,* 436 U.S. 49 (1978), was whether the federal courts could rule on the validity of a tribal law. In 1939, the Santa Clara Pueblo passed an ordinance that allowed the children of men who marry outside the tribe to become tribal members, but not the children of women who marry outside the tribe. Julia Martinez, who had children by a non-tribal member, challenged the law in federal court, saying that it violated the **Indian Civil Rights Act of 1968** which, among other things, has an equal protection clause. Recognizing the preconstitutional and extraconstitutional status of tribes, the U.S. Supreme Court found that even though ICRA had been imposed on tribes by Congress, the tribes have the final say over noncriminal enforcement of ICRA. As such, the case represents a reaffirmation of tribal **sovereignty**. **See also** Tribal Legal System. (GTH)

BIBLIOGRAPHY

Wilkins, David E. *American Indian Sovereignty and the U.S. Supreme Court: The Masking of Justice.* Austin: University of Texas Press, 1997.

Wilkinson, Charles F. *American Indians, Time, and the Law.* New Haven: Yale University Press, 1987.

Satanta (1820–1878)

Satanta, a Kiowa chief, was considered hostile by the federal government because he fought to maintain Kiowa lands. Eventually, Satanta urged his tribe to make peace with the military. Dissatisfied with **reservation** life, he and over 100 other Kiowa left the reservation and attacked supply wagons. He was arrested and sentenced in 1871 to prison but refused parole from President Ulysses Grant, which would have required him to remain on the reservation. Leaving the reservation to hunt in 1874, Satanta was captured and sent to federal prison in Huntsville, Texas, where he served time until his death. (MKJ)

BIBLIOGRAPHY

Worcester, David. "Satanta." In David Edmunds, ed. *American Indian Leaders: Study in Diversity.* R. Lincoln: University of Nebraska Press, 1980. 107–31.

Katherine Siva Saubel (1920–)

A reservation-born member of the Cahuilla tribe, Saubel grew up determined to preserve her people's heritage. Her resolve resulted in the founding of the Malki Museum at the Morongo Reservation in California. A trained ethnoanthropologist, Saubel has been recognized for her efforts to preserve her tribe's culture by being named American Indian Woman of the Year in 1995 and by her inclusion in the National Women's Hall of Fame. (KJB)

BIBLIOGRAPHY

http://www.greatwomen.org/saubel.htm

Saybrook, Battle of. *See* Battle of Saybrook

Seattle (ca. 1786–1866)

During the early period of Euro-American settlement on Puget Sound, Seattle (Si'al) rose to prominence as the leader of a Duwamish, Suquamish, and Lushootseed confederacy. Because of his status as a warrior and member of the tribal nobility, the federal government appointed him a regional "head chief" for the purpose of treaty negotiations. Seattle stayed at peace with the whites, and in 1854, he warned his namesake settlement of an impending Indian attack. However, most Americans remember Seattle for his famous "web of life" speech. Although scholars continue to debate its authenticity, the passage remains a favorite of modern environmentalists. (AHF)

BIBLIOGRAPHY
Anderson, Eva Greenslit. *Chief Seattle.* Caldwell, ID: Caxton Printers, 1943.
Hilbert, Vi. "When Chief Seattle (Si'al) Spoke." In Robin K. Wright, ed. *A Time of Gathering: Native Heritage in Washington State.* Seattle: University of Washington Press, 1991.

Second Seminole War

White settlers in Florida continued to agitate for the removal of the Seminoles to lands west of the Mississippi, as provided in the **Indian Removal Act of 1830.** The Indians agreed to move; the tribe was destitute and offers of food and clothing in a treaty of 1832 appeased them. However, they refused to emigrate until they had an opportunity to view the new lands in Creek country. Another agreement, the Treaty of Fort Gibson, was signed on March 28, 1833, in which the Seminoles agreed to leave their lands for ones further west. The Seminoles, however, ignored the treaty; they denied having made the agreement and retreated into the Everglades to avoid removal. This sparked the Second Seminole War, also called the Florida War, which lasted from 1835 to 1842. The Seminoles fought bravely but unsuccessfully, and the remnants of the tribe was forcibly removed. It was during this war that the Seminole leader **Osceola** was captured; he later died in prison. **See also** First Seminole War. (MRC)

BIBLIOGRAPHY
Prucha, Francis Paul. *American Indian Treaties: The History of a Political Anomaly.* Berkeley: University of California Press, 1994.
Weeks, Philip. *Farewell, My Nation: The American Indian and the United States 1820–1890.* Arlington Heights, IL: Harlan Davidson, 1990

Second Trade and Intercourse Act

Continuing in the manner of the Ordinance of 1786 and earlier colonial legislation, the Trade and Intercourse Acts provided the U.S. government with tools to enforce its authority over citizens in interactions with Native peoples. Responsibility for governing and punishing in matters not concerning the whites was left up to the Indians. The Second Trade and Intercourse Act, signed on March 1, 1793, was stronger and more inclusive than the first. It expanded the 1790 Act from 7 sections to 15. Added were sections authorizing the president to give goods and money to the tribes to promote civilization and secure their friendship and to stop horse stealing. The bulk of the increase, however, was aimed at protecting the Indians from the outrages committed by the white man. Six additional acts were issued between 1790 and 1834 (1790, 1793, 1796, 1799, 1802, and 1834). (MRC)

BIBLIOGRAPHY
Prucha, Francis Paul. *American Indian Policy in the Formative Years: The Indian Trade and Intercourse Acts, 1790–1834.* Cambridge, MA : Harvard University Press, 1962.

Second Virginia War

The Second Virginia War, waged against the Virginia colony by the **Powhatan Confederacy**, lasted from 1644 to 1646. Constant expansion into Indian lands by the English settlers caused the Powhatans and their allies, the Rappahannock, to retaliate. The war ended with a treaty that prohibited further English expansion. The Indians, however, retained only a portion of their former holdings, became subject to Virginia courts, and were forced to pay an annual tribute of beaver pelts. **See also** Opehanacanough; Powhatan. (MRC)

BIBLIOGRAPHY
Nee, Kay Bonner. *Powhatan.* Minneapolis, MN: Dillon Press, 1971.

Self-Determination

The federal Indian policy of self-determination has sought to provide American Indians greater control over their own lives. This policy has enhanced tribal **sovereignty**, improved access to federal funds, and provided American Indians greater opportunities to maintain their cultural distinctiveness.

By the late 1950s, widespread Native American opposition to termination made it clear that an alternative to federal termination was necessary. Then in the early 1960s, the Kennedy administration launched a series of initiatives to reduce poverty, and the Johnson administration expanded on these initiatives with its War on Poverty. These initiatives, especially the 1964 Economic Opportunity Act (EOA), allowed local communities—including Indian tribes—to receive federal dollars to develop and run their own anti-poverty projects. This greatly enhanced tribal self-government because Indians gained a greater opportunity to use federal funds in ways they desired. Consequently, Indian communities sponsored economic development programs, social service programs, and projects to revitalize Indian cultures.

Key pieces of legislation since EOA have further bolstered self-determination. The 1972 Indian Education Act provided grants for Indian education programs and mandated consultation with Native Americans regarding such programs. Through the **Indian Self-Determination and Education Act of 1975,** tribes were permitted to administer programs previously controlled by the **Bureau of Indian Affairs** (BIA). The 1991 Self-Governance Demonstration Project Act allowed tribes greater say over the allocation of federal funds.

Eroding political support for social welfare spending in the 1990s, however, threatened the substance of self-determination. Among other actions, Congress advocated cutting funds for tribal programs and refused to enforce Native Alaskans' hunting and fishing rights. Whether self-determination can endure such declining federal financial backing remains to be seen. **See also** Conservatism and Liberalism; House Concurrent Resolution 108; Indian Reorganization Act of 1934; Reservation Economics; Termination Resolution. (CKR)

BIBLIOGRAPHY

Philp, Kenneth R., ed. *Indian Self-Rule: First Hand Accounts of Indian–White Relations from Roosevelt to Reagan.* Logan: Utah State University Press, 1995.

Nagel, Joane. *American Indian Ethnic Renewal: Red Power and the Resurgence of Identity and Culture.* New York: Oxford University Press, 1996.

Washburn, Wilcomb E. "The Native American Renaissance, 1960–1995." In *The Cambridge History of the Native Peoples of the Americas.* vol. 1, *North America.* Cambridge: Cambridge University Press, 1996.

Seminole Nation of Indians v. United States (1942)

In *Seminole Nation of Indians v. United States* 316 US 286 (1942), the leaders of the Seminole tribe sued the United States government for the mishandling of its trust fund that was established in accordance with an 1856 treaty. The tribal leaders alleged that the federal government had made payments to previous Seminole tribal governments knowing that the Seminole government was corrupt and would not administer the funds properly. While the U.S. Supreme Court remanded the case to lower federal courts for a determination of the case, it did state that the government of the United States had to be judged by the "most exacting fiduciary standards." **See also** Trusteeship Responsibility.

BIBLIOGRAPHY

Deloria, Vine, Jr. and Clifford M. Lytle. *American Indians, American Justice.* Austin: University of Texas Press, 1983.

Seminole Tribe of Florida v. Butterworth (1981)

In *Seminole Tribe of Florida v. Butterworth*, 658 F. 2d 310 (1981), the U.S. Fifth Circuit Court of Appeals granted the Seminole Tribe a declaratory judgment that the Florida bingo statute did not apply to its operation of a bingo hall on its reservation. Relying on the distinction between state "criminal/prohibitory" laws and "civil/regulatory" laws established in *Bryan v. Itasca County* (1976), the court of appeals held that Florida's bingo statute was regulatory rather than prohibitory, so tribes retained the power to regulate reservation bingo on their own terms. The U.S. Supreme Court adopted this reasoning and expanded it to casino gaming in ***California v. Cabazon Band of Mission Indians*** (1987), and it was also reflected in the **Indian Gaming Regulatory Act of 1988**. (RS)

BIBLIOGRAPHY

Duthu, N. Bruce. "Crow Dog and Oliphant Fistfight at the Tribal Casino: Political Power, Storytelling, and Games of Chance." *Arizona State Law Journal* 29 (Spring 1997): 171–25.

Getches, David H. "Conquering the Cultural Frontier: The New Subjectivism of the Supreme Court in Indian Law." *California Law Review* 84, no. 6 (December 1996): 1573–1655.

Senate Report on Corruption and Mismanagement of American Indian Land and Money

On November 17, 1989, a special subcommittee of the United States Senate issued its finding after two years of study and investigation into corruption in the management of Indian land and money. Among the reports findings were that the **Bureau of Indian Affairs** (BIA) had given money to **tribal governments** knowing that the tribes were misusing the funds. It also concluded that the BIA had allowed major corporations to defraud the Native Americans in oil leases and other natural resources. Perhaps most disturbing were the revelations of widespread abuse and sexual molestation at BIA boarding schools. In the end, the report recommended that Native Americans be given greater control over their own lands and money. The report favored the creation of a block grant program in which tribes would decide how to spend its funds. **See also** Reservation Economics; Trusteeship Responsibility.

BIBLIOGRAPHY

Bureau of Indian Affairs. *Management Action Plan for the Bureau of Indian Affairs.* Washington, DC: The Bureau, 1991.

Seneca Nation v. United States (1964)

In *Seneca Nation v. United States,* 338 F.2d 55 (1964), Cert. denied 380 U.S. 952 (1965), the Seneca Nation challenged the taking of land by the United States to reroute a highway as part of the Allegheny Reservoir Project. The Seneca argued that the land was protected under the terms of the Treaty of November 11, 1794 (F Stat. 44), the oldest active Indian treaty, which promised the land in perpetuity. The federal court disagreed, citing the power of Congress to take land without regard to treaties. The U.S. Supreme Court denied *certiorari* in the case, thus letting the appeals court decision stand. **See also** Land and Water Rights. (AMM)

BIBLIOGRAPHY

Wunder, John R., ed. *Recent Legal Issues for American Indians, 1968 to the Present.* New York: Garland Publishing, 1996.

Sequoyah (1770–1843)

Sequoyah, also known as George Guess or Guest, was a Cherokee linguist who created a syllabary of his language in the early 1820s. Born in present day Tennessee, Sequoyah moved to Georgia to avoid the growth of white settlements. The syllabary, made up of 86 sounds, was easy to memorize and led to rapid widespread literacy among the Cherokee. During the 1830s, this literacy played an important role in Cherokee resistance to removal to the West. Sequoyah was an advocate for the reunification of the Cherokee Nation. The syllabary permitted correspondence between distanced Cherokee members, and a weekly newspaper, ***Cherokee Phoenix***, existed from 1828 until 1835 when its printing press was confiscated. He left Oklahoma in 1839 and settled in present day Texas where he found a band of Cherokees that had migrated to Texas (then part of Mexico) during the 1838 Georgia Removal. (HHB)

BIBLIOGRAPHY

Foreman, Grant. *Sequoyah.* Norman: University of Oklahoma Press, 1987 [1939].

Shawnee Prophet. *See* Tenskwatawa

William Tecumseh Sherman (1820–1891)

William T. Sherman is best known for his actions as a general in the **Civil War** and as the commanding general of the United States Army for 14 years. He took over the direction of what became known as the "Indian Wars," following a policy of constant, steady attack on Indian villages and their resources. He was called the first modern general, for he not only fought the enemy, but destroyed their economic sources as well. **See also** Nez Perce War; Plains Wars; Treaty of Bosque Redondo (1868).

BIBLIOGRAPHY

Sherman, William T. *Memoirs of General W.T. Sherman.* New York: Library of America, 1990.
Utley, Robert M. and Wilcomb E. Washburn. *Indian Wars.* Boston: Houghton Mifflin, 1977.

Sioux Ghost Dance

The Lakota Sioux bands who adopted the Ghost Dance took the peaceful original message and ceremonies and added militant elements that provoked concern among U.S. government officials and white neighbors; the eventual results included the death of **Sitting Bull** (Tatanka Yotanka) and the massacre at **Wounded Knee** (1890). Early in 1890, Lakota emissaries to the Ghost Dance prophet, **Wovoka**, reported his message that performing Ghost Dance ceremonies and songs would bring back dead Indians, return plentiful buffalo herds, and induce a natural disaster that would sweep away whites, thus restoring the way of life Indians had enjoyed prior to European contact. The Ghost Dance provided a hopeful message to all Indians, but it proved particularly enticing to Lakotas suffering poor conditions on reservations and to Lakota leaders such as Sitting Bull, who had resisted U.S. Indian policy. Lakota participants learned the ceremonies and songs brought by the emissaries, and then they added white muslin shirts known as "ghost shirts." The Lakotas believed that these shirts, decorated with a variety of symbols, protected them from danger, including bullets. The Lakotas' white neighbors and reservation officials believed the Ghost Dance ceremonies and ghost shirts indicated that the Lakotas intended to start a war, and they called on the U.S. government to stop the ceremonies. The government dispatched the U.S. Army and called for the arrest of key leaders such as Sitting Bull and **Big Foot** (Si Tanka). Indian police killed Sitting Bull while arresting him, and the Seventh Cavalry killed Big Foot and at least 145 of his followers at the Wounded Knee massacre, thus eliminating the key leaders most opposed to the United States and its Indian policy. **See also** Crow Dog; Ghost Dance Movement; Red Cloud; Smohalla. **See** "You Are Living in a New Path" by Sitting Bull (1880) in Appendix 1. (TMK)

BIBLIOGRAPHY

Mooney, James. *The Ghost Dance Religion and the Sioux Outbreak of 1890.* Washington, DC: U.S. Government Printing Office, 1896.

Utley, Robert M. *The Last Days of the Sioux Nation.* New Haven, CT: Yale University Press, 1963.

Sioux Indian Act of 1891

In the 1890s the federal government began to develop legislation aimed at dividing the large Sioux reservation of the Dakotas into several individual reservations in which members would be allotted specific lands. **The Sioux Indian Act of 1891** was enacted to bring about these changes. The act allowed for the purchase of any unallotted lands by the federal government, which in many cases was trying to create a right-of-way for the railroads. In return for lands and the acceptance of divided reservations, the Sioux were given increased support for schools and foodstuffs.

BIBLIOGRAPHY

Cohen, Felix S. *Felix Cohen's Handbook of Federal Indian Law.* Charlottesville, VA: Mitchie, Bobbs-Merrill, 1982; Ft. Lauderdale, FL: Five Rings Press, 1986.

Sitting Bull (1831–1890)

Sitting Bull (Tatanka Yotanka), a Hunkpapa Lakota leader, is today a legendary figure. He was the last of the Sioux leaders to succumb to **reservation** life and relentlessly resisted American expansion and assimilation efforts. Sitting Bull was an outstanding war leader from early on. In the early 1860s, he led battles against whites in response to land expropriation and the systematic killing of the buffaloes, which were vital to his people's economy and social order. He refused to sign the **Treaty of Fort Laramie** of 1868, which reduced the tribe's lands to give miners access to Montana's gold and

Sitting Bull was the last of the Sioux leaders to surrender to U.S. authority. *Library of Congress.*

was among the leaders of the nontreaty Sioux who were attacked by the American military in 1876. Together with **Crazy Horse**, he was responsible for the victories in the battles on Rosebud Creek and the Greasy Grass (**Battle of the Little Big Horn**) in June 1876. Chased by the army, Sitting Bull and his band went into exile in Canada in 1877, returning in 1881. Sitting Bull became a military prisoner, but traveled in the U.S. and Canada in 1884 and 1885, partly with Bill Cody's Wild West Show. Sitting Bull was killed on December 15, 1890, by an Indian Police force that came to arrest him because of his support of the Ghost Dance, which was perceived as a threat by the American authorities. Sitting Bull is revered for his resistance, leadership, and concern for subsequent generations. (MS)

BIBLIOGRAPHY

Anderson, Gary C. *Sitting Bull and the Paradox of the Lakota Nationhood*. New York: HarperCollins College Publisher, 1996.

Utley, Robert M. *The Lance and the Shield: The Life and Times of Sitting Bull*. New York: Henry Holt, 1993.

Six Nations (Haudenosaunee) Confederacy/ Iroquois Confederacy

The Six Nations, or Haudenosaunee, Confederacy (also called the Iroquois Confederacy) was formed between 1000 and 1450 A.D. among Native American nations who lived around the eastern Great Lakes. Originally consisting of five nations—the Onondaga, Cayuga, Oneida, Mohawk, and Seneca—the confederacy was formed because its members were tired of constant warfare. They embraced a form of government known as the Great Law of Peace. The confederacy's bicameral, representative government, which was joined by the Tuscaroras in the early 1700s, was a model for the government structure designed in the United States Constitution.

During the American colonial period, the Haudenosaunee controlled the critical lands between those claimed by the French and the British—and later the new United States and the British. In addition to their location, the confederacy produced substantial food and much-respected warriors and was thus a powerful ally. The confederacy fought with the British during the Seven Years' War, and most fought with the British during the **American Revolution.** The largest military campaign launched by George Washington's colonists was directed at the confederacy, earning the first U.S. president the permanent title of "Town Destroyer" among the Haudenosaunee.

After the revolution, one of the new nation's first treaties, the **Treaty of Fort Stanwix,** was signed with the confederacy in 1784. The treaty was controversial from the start, and the Haudenosaunee have remained in conflict with the United States and the State of New York over land and jurisdiction. The confederacy has been active in the United Nations and other international bodies throughout the twentieth century, promoting its own interests and those of other Native American nations. Today, the Haudenosaunee Confederacy is one of the oldest continuous governments in the world. (LCJ)

BIBLIOGRAPHY

Barreiro, Jose. *Indian Roots of American Democracy*. Ithaca, NY: Akwekon Press, Cornell University, 1991.

The Great Law of Peace (Kaianerekowa) of the Longhouse People (Hotinonsione). Rooseveltown, NY: White Roots of Peace, 1971.

Lyons, Oren, et al. *Exiled in the Land of the Free: Democracy, Indian Nations, and the U.S. Constitution*. Santa Fe, NM: Clear Light Publishers, 1992.

Smohalla (ca .1815–1895)

Like **Wovoka**, the Paiute messiah of the Ghost Dance, the Wanapam prophet Smohalla inspired a powerful religious revitalization movement in the nineteenth century. By urging Plateau Indians to reject white culture and refuse land cessions, his Washani Creed (Dreamer faith) inspired strong resistance to federal policies. Smohalla's beliefs continue to influence Plateau life though the derivative Washat (Seven Drums) religion. **See also** Ghost Dance Movement. (AHF)

BIBLIOGRAPHY

Relander, Click. *Drummers and Dreamers: The Story of Smowhala and his Nephew Puck Hyah Toot, the Last Prophet of the Nearly Extinct River People, the Last Wanapums*. 1953; reprint, Seattle: Pacific Northwest National Parks and Forest Association, 1986.

Ruby, Robert H. and John A. Brown. *Dreamer-Prophets of the Columbia Plateau: Smohalla and Skolaskin*. Norman: University of Oklahoma Press, 1989.

Reuben Snake, Jr. (1937–1993)

Reuben Snake, Jr. (Winnebago) became a leading voice in the **Trail of Broken Treaties**, a caravan of Native Americans traveling across America to highlight the abuses of the Bureau of Indian Affairs against native people. He became national chairman of the **American Indian Movement** in 1972, where he fought for Native American rights. In 1975, Snake became chairman of the Winnebago tribe and served with the Native American Church. Snake headed the **National Congress of American Indians** from 1985 to 1987 before moving on to serve as a consultant for the Americans for Indian Opportunity and as a cultural instructor at the Institute of American Indian Arts in Santa Fe.

BIBLIOGRAPHY

Fikes, Jay C. *Reuben Snake*. Santa Fe, NM: Clear Lights Publishers, 1996.

Snyder Act of 1921

Prior to passage of the Snyder Act in 1921, no uniform Indian policy existed. The responsibilities of the federal government toward Indians and Indian tribes were scattered throughout scores of laws and treaties, stated in confusing and often contradictory terms. Adding to the chaos, each agency on each **reservation** received its appropriations separately, directly from the federal government, and most authorizations for funding had to be renewed yearly. The Snyder Act consolidated the disparate Indian programs and directives by giving the Department of the Interior general spending authority for Indian Services. The law stated that the **Bureau of Indian Affairs (BIA)** would dispense funds for the "benefit, care, and assistance of the Indians," including providing such services as education, health, property management, social services, building maintenance, law enforcement and general administrative duties. The BIA no longer had to make yearly requests for appropriations, which gave Indian services some insulation from the whims of Congress.

BIBLIOGRAPHY

Cohen, Felix S. *Felix Cohen's Handbook of Federal Indian Law.* Charlottesville, VA: Mitchie, Bobbs-Merrill, 1982; Ft. Lauderdale, FL: Five Rings Press, 1986.

David Sohappy, Sr. (1925–1991)

Yakima fisherman David Sohappy, a descendant of **Smohalla**, devoted much of his life to defending Northwest Indian treaty fishing rights. His victory in *Sohappy v. Smith* (1968) established the precedent for **United States v. Washington** which limited the restrictions that states could place on fishing rights. And, in the 1980s, Sohappy's imprisonment following the federal "Salmonscam" sting operation attracted national attention to the issue of Indian treaty rights. (AHF)

BIBLIOGRAPHY

Clark, Robert. *River of the West: Stories from the Columbia.* New York: HarperCollins West, 1995.
Cohen, Ray G. *Treaties on Trial: The Continuing Controversy over Northwest Indian Fishing Rights.* Seattle: University of Washington Press, 1986.

A Son of the Forest

A Son of the Forest is the earliest known autobiography of a Native American written in English. Published in 1829, it tells the story of abuses the author **William Apess** (also Apes, 1798–c. 1836) suffered at the hands of his grandmother. Apess, a Pequot, spent many years living with foster families. He fought for the Americans in the **War of 1812** and championed the rights of the Cape Cod Indians. Apess converted to Methodism and became an ordained preacher. He believed Christianity offered hope to the Native Americans. In 1836 Apess disappeared after giving a eulogy in Boston for his ancestor Metacom, a Wampanoag war chief who had been drawn and quartered some 160 years previously. (MRC)

BIBLIOGRAPHY

Apess, William. *A Son of the Forest and Other Writings.* Amherst: University of Massachusetts Press, 1997.

South Carolina v. Catawba Indian Tribe, Inc. (1986)

In *South Carolina v. Catawba Indian Tribe, Inc.*, 476 U.S. 498 (1986), the U.S. Supreme Court ruled that the 1959 Catawba Indian Tribe Division of Assets Act, which terminated the tribe and divided its assets among its members, subjected the tribe's land claim to the state statute of limitations of adverse possession. South Carolina law limits the time of adverse possession to 20 years, which in the Catawba case began in 1963. The statute of limitations had been frozen during the appeal, but after the Court's decision, the clock started running again. Only when the Catawba Indian Tribe threatened to sue nearly 63,000 residents of their former reservation, were South Carolina and the federal government willing to settle. The settlement act was passed by Congress and signed by Republican governor Carroll Campbell in 1993. The act provided for the reinstatement of the Catawba as a federally recognized tribe, the provision for $50,000,000 to settle a land claim dating back to 1840, and the opportunity to expand the size of their reservation. (AMM)

BIBLIOGRAPHY

Verhoeven, Charles K. "Terminating Federal Protection with 'Plain' Statements." (Case note). *Iowa Law Review* 72, no. 4 (May 1987): 1117–46.
Winder, Samuel. "A State's Statute of Limitations Found Applicable to an Eastern Tribe's Land Claim." (Case note). *Natural Resources Journal* 27, no. 4 (Fall 1987): 913–30.

Southern Indian Slave Trade

Long dubbed the "peculiar institution," perhaps more peculiar still was that slavery found its way into **Indian country**. Members of the **Five Civilized Tribes** (Cherokee, Chickasaw, Choctaw, Creek, and Seminole) were often lauded by whites for their use and adoption of such European practices as farming and newspaper publication. And, like their white neighbors in the South, the members of the Five Civilized Tribes took on the practice of owning, purchasing, and selling black slaves. In the 1830s, when the Five Tribes were removed from their ancestral homes in the South and force-marched to Oklahoma (on the **Trail of Tears**), they brought their slaves with them. The practice of chattel slavery by Indian tribes closely resembled that of slavery generally in the South, with the exception that there were very few large plantations in Indian country. Typically, slaves owned by Indians worked on small farms, side by side with their owners. By 1865, estimates showed there were 10,000 black slaves owned by Indians. Reconstruction policies of the tribes toward their former slaves were outlined in four treaties signed in 1866. These treaties forced the tribes to extend a greater array of rights and protections to the freedmen than freedmen generally experienced in the South. Many freedmen were adopted by the tribes that had previously owned them, and some were given small plots of land. (GTH)

BIBLIOGRAPHY

Debo, Angie. *And Still the Waters Run: The Betrayal of the Five Civilized Tribes.* Princeton: Princeton University Press. 1972.
Foreman, Grant. *The Five Civilized Tribes.* Norman: The University of Oklahoma Press. 1934.

Sovereignty

Sovereignty is classically defined as supreme legal authority. The concept was formulated by sixteenth-century legal philosopher Jean Bodin and has been elaborated by many theorists since then. One basic controversy has been whether to trace supreme authority to the people or to a "divine right" of rulers. Another controversy concerns the relation between legal authority and political-economic power. An ambiguous concept from the start, surrounded by disagreement, sovereignty is perhaps most cryptic when it comes to federal Indian law.

The legal history of tribal sovereignty starts with colonialism. From their earliest contacts with the "new world," colonizing powers asserted sovereignty over indigenous peoples, based on a theological-legal theory built on "divine right." Spain, Portugal, and France, and other colonial regimes explicitly based their sovereignty claims on religious doctrines by the Pope, who was regarded as having power to grant titles to portions of the earth for purposes of Christian civilization.

The result of colonial assertions of sovereignty was that indigenous nations were legally stripped of their independent status. Their existence was in some instances not recognized at all, and their lands were treated as legally vacant (*terra nullius*). In other instances, indigenous peoples were declared to have a right of occupancy, *Johnson v. McIntosh*, 8 Wheat 543 (1823), but not ownership of their lands. In either instance, the fundamental principle was that supreme legal authority lay outside the indigenous nations.

The debate about legal authority versus political and economic power also informs the definition of sovereignty in federal Indian law. In the earliest treaties, statutes, and cases, indigenous nations were regarded as having a subordinate sovereignty related to their right of occupancy. Denied full sovereignty as independent nations, they were nevertheless regarded as having authority over their own relations amongst themselves—an "internal" or "tribal" sovereignty." In *Worcester v. Georgia*, 6 Pet. 515 (1832), the Supreme Court declared that the Cherokee Nation possessed "its right to self-government," even though it was dependent on the United States. Justice McLean concurred, saying, "At no time has the sovereignty of the country been recognized as existing in the Indians, but they have been always admitted to possess many of the attributes of sovereignty." McLean went on to question whether there could be any end to this peculiar relation: "If a tribe of Indians shall become so degraded or reduced in numbers as to lose the power of self-government, the protection of the local law, of necessity, must be extended over them."

The Court picked up Justice McLean's suggestion in 1886, in *United States v. Kagama*, 118 U.S. 375, when it reduced indigenous sovereignty almost to a nullity, declaring, "Indians are within the geographical limits of the United States. The soil and the people within these limits are under the political control of the Government of the United States, or of the States of the Union. There exist within the broad domain of sovereignty but these two." The Court did not base its assertion of a broad federal power over Indians on any clause of the Constitution, but on the "right of exclusive sovereignty which must exist in the National Government."

But the Kagama case was not the end of tribal sovereignty. The concept rose again during Franklin Roosevelt's New Deal in the 1930s. Felix Cohen resurrected "tribal sovereignty" as an organizing principle of the Indian Reorganization Act of 1934, 48 Stat. 984. He wrote, in his *Handbook of Federal Indian Law*,"... [T]hose powers which are lawfully vested in an Indian tribe are not, in general, delegated powers granted by express acts of Congress, but rather inherent powers of a limited sovereignty which has never been extinguished." Cohen did not suggest that Congress could not extinguish all Indian sovereignty; he merely argued that until extinguished by federal authority, it remained part of federal Indian law.

The **Indian Reorganization Act** provided for the formation of tribal governments under federal authority as vehicles for Indian self-government. The Act provided a model of government based on democratic and corporate structures often at odds with the original forms of organization among indigenous nations. The fact that the New Deal abandoned some of the grosser exercises of federal authority typical of the allotment era that preceded it made it appear attractive to native peoples, but the contradictions embodied in a concept of "dependent sovereignty" would continue to produce conflict and confusion in federal Indian law.

In 1973, in *McClanahan v. Arizona State Tax Commission*, 411 U.S. 164, the Supreme Court referred to "platonic notions of Indian sovereignty" and referred to Indian sovereignty as "a backdrop" for analyzing treaties and federal statues. Subsequent to McClanahan, the Court swung back and forth repeatedly. In 1978 alone, the Court went from almost completely subordinating indigenous sovereignty under federal law in *Oliphant v. Suquamish Indian Tribe*, 435 U.S. 191, to an affirmation of it as a third kind of sovereignty in *United States v. Wheeler*, 435 U.S. 313. The latter decision was a complete contradiction of the analysis in Kagama. In 1997, in *Idaho v. Coeur d'Alene Tribe*, No. 94-1474, the Supreme Court held that "Indian tribes . . . should be accorded the same status as foreign sovereigns, against whom States enjoy 11th Amendment immunity." This was a startling contrast to the foundational federal Indian law decision in *Cherokee Nation v. Georgia*, 5 Pet. 1 (1831), that the Cherokee were not sovereign as a "foreign nation."

The concept of sovereignty, however convoluted and contradictory, remains an important part of federal Indian law. Tribal councils act as governments and not just as corporations; Indian hunting and fishing rights have been protected against state and local regulations; and Indian nations are regarded as immune from suit without their consent. In short, the idea that indigenous nations have at their roots some aspect of their original, pre-colonial status as independent nations operates—sometimes directly and sometimes by implication—throughout federal Indian law today.

The idea of indigenous sovereignty surfaced internationally and with intensity in the Draft United Nations Declaration on the Rights of Indigenous Peoples, E/CN.4/Sub.2/1994/56, issued in 1994 as a report to the U.N. Commission on Human Rights. This document, which may eventually become the basis for an international protocol or convention, stirred up the ancient debates. The United States took an official position that the word "peoples" was inappropriate in a statement of rights, because it implied group rights, which would threaten the sovereignty of states. The United States and others argued that rights adhere only to individuals, and that no group may be recognized as having any legal existence independent of a state. Indigenous nations, on the other hand, asserted that the Draft Declaration was meant to embody just such group rights, that these were essential for the survival of indigenous peoples worldwide. Struggles about indigenous sovereignty continue into the twenty-first century, on as grand a scale as in any other era. (PPE)

BIBLIOGRAPHY

Cohen, Felix S. *Handbook of Federal Indian Law.* Washington, DC: U.S. Government Printing Office, 1942.

Deloria, Vine, Jr. *Of Utmost Good Faith.* New York: Bantam, 1971.

Deloria, Vine, Jr. and Clifford M. Lytle. *American Indians, American Justice.* Austin: University of Texas Press, 1983.

Fried, Morton H. *The Notion of Tribe.* Menlo Park: Cummings Pub. Co., 1975.

Jennings, Francis. *The Invasion of America.* New York: W.W. Norton & Co., 1976.

Newcomb, Steven T. "The Evidence of Christian Nationalism in Federal Indian Law: The Doctrine of Discovery, *Johnson v McIntosh,* and Plenary Power." *N.Y.U. Rev. of Law & Social Change* XX, no. 2 (1993): 303–41.

Salmond, Sir John. *Jurisprudence.* 8th edition, by C.A.W. Manning. London: Sweet & Maxwell, 1930.

Savage, Mark. "Native Americans and the Constitution: The Original Understanding." *American Indian Law Review* 16 (1991): 57–118.

Scott, Craig. "Indigenous Self-Determination and Decolonization of the International Imagination: A Plea." *Human Rights Quarterly* 18 (November 1996): 814–20.

Williams, Robert A., Jr. *The American Indian in Western Legal Thought.* New York: Oxford University Press, 1990.

Spokane Garry (ca. 1811–1892)

One of the first Plateau Indians to learn English and adopt Christianity, Spokane Garry proselytized nearby Native groups and encouraged the establishment of Protestant missions in the inland Northwest. As principal chief of the Spokanes, Garry advocated peace with the whites and worked to secure a reservation for his people. In 1887, he signed a treaty ceding the tribe's land, but he died without receiving the promised compensation. (AHF)

BIBLIOGRAPHY

Lewis, William S. *The Case of Spokane Garry.* Fairfield, WA: Ye Galleon Press, 1987.

Ruby, Robert H. and John A. Brown. *The Spokane Indians: Children of the Sun.* Norman: University of Oklahoma Press, 1970.

Standing Bear (1819–1908)

Standing Bear was a leader of the Ponca Indians, a tribe whose homelands were located in what is now Nebraska. He won an 1879 Supreme Court case declaring that Native Americans were "persons" in the eyes of United States law and could not be deprived of their civil liberties in *Standing Bear v. Crook* (1879). (LCJ)

BIBLIOGRAPHY

Brown, Dee. *Bury My Heart at Wounded Knee: An Indian History of the American West.* New York: Holt, Rinehart & Winston, 1970.

Standing Bear v. Crook (1879)

Standing Bear v. Crook (1879) was the first court case in U.S. history to recognize the civil rights of Indians. In 1868 the federal government awarded 96,000 acres of Ponca land in the Dakota Territory to the Sioux people. When the Sioux began occupying the territory in 1877, the **Bureau of Indian Affairs (BIA)** relocated the Poncas to **Indian Territory** to prevent a hostile confrontation. The heat, poverty, and malaria devastated the Poncas in their new territory. In 1879, **Standing Bear**, the Ponca chief, left with 30 other Poncas to return to their land in the Dakota Territory, ignoring BIA orders. A number of prominent Americans, such as Senator Henry Dawes of Massachusetts and abolitionist Wendell Phillips, all came to the defense of Standing Bear and filed suit on his behalf. The federal district judge ruled in favor of Standing Bear, stating that an Indian is a person within the laws of the United States. Therefore he was entitled to the same freedom and legal protection. In 1881, the BIA returned the land to the Poncas.

BIBLIOGRAPHY

Murdock, Robert M. *The Reformers and the American Indian.* Columbia: University of Missouri Press, 1971.

Dorothy Amora Stanley (1924–1990)

Dorothy Amora Stanley (Miwok) was born in Los Angeles and educated at the Indian Boarding School in Stewart, Nevada. She spent a lifetime in public service in a variety of roles, from chairperson of seasonal festivals to **tribal council** chair and member of the federal advisory board of Indian affairs, public health and education committees. She also fought to preserve her people's cultural past at archeological sites. (EW)

BIBLIOGRAPHY

Who's Who of American Women. Chicago: Marquis Who's Who, 1973.

Stephens v. Cherokee Nation (1899)

In *Stephens v. Cherokee Nation,* 174 U.S. 445 (1899), a case involving the allotment and security of funds in the Cherokee Nation, the U.S. Supreme Court held that the Congress has "plenary power of legislation" over Indian tribes that is "subject only to the Constitution of the United States." The Court's decision removed any doubt that may have existed about Indian autonomy. **Reservations,** Indian governments, etc. were now subject to Congress's discretion. **See also** Tribal Government.

BIBLIOGRAPHY

Deloria, Vine, Jr. and Clifford M. Little. *American Indians, American Justice.* Austin: University of Texas Press, 1983.

William Grady Stigler (1891–1952)

William Stigler, born in **Indian country,** served as a second lieutenant in the United States Infantry during World War I. After this, he was city attorney for Stigler, Oklahoma, from 1920 to 1924, and then he served in the State Senate from 1925 to 1932. From 1925 to 1938, Stigler also served as a lieutenant colonel in the Oklahoma National Guard. Stigler, a Democrat, was elected to the United States House of Representatives to fill the vacancy caused by the resignation of Jack Nichols; Stigler remained in Congress until his death in 1952.

BIBLIOGRAPHY

U.S. Congress. House. "The Late Honorable William G. Stigler, A Representative from the State of Oklahoma." Comments by Representative Carl Albert. *Congressional Proceedings and Debates of the 83rd Congress, First Session.* Washington, DC: U.S. Government Publishing Office, 1953.

"[Obituary:] William G. Stigler, Representative, 61." *New York Times* (August 22, 1952): 21.

Ross Owen Swimmer (1943–)

Ross Owen Swimmer (Cherokee) was counsel to the Cherokee Nation from 1972 to 1974. He was named Principal Chief of the Nation in 1976 and remained in this position until 1985, when he was appointed Assistant Secretary for Indian Affairs during the Reagan administration. He served in this capacity from 1985 until 1993. Swimmer was born in Oklahoma City, October 26, 1943, to Robert Otis and Virginia Marie Pounder Swimmer. He married Margaret Ann McConnell, June 30, 1965, and they have two children. He received his B.A. (1965) and J.D. (1967) from the University of Oklahoma. (AMM)

BIBLIOGRAPHY

Hurtado, Albert L. and Peter Iverson, eds. *Major Problems in American Indian History: Documents and Essays.* Lexington, MA: D.C. Health, 1994.

Tahmelapashme. *See* Dull Knife

Talton v. Mayes (1896)

Talton v. Mayes, 163 U.S. 376 (1896), was an intra-tribal criminal law case centering on the Cherokee Nation's sovereign authority to administer justice free of outside constraints. The case originated in the Supreme Court of the Cherokee Nation, where Bob Talton had been convicted in the murder of another Cherokee.

The specific question before the Court was whether the U.S. Constitution's Fifth Amendment grand jury provision applied to the decisions of tribal courts. Justice Edward White, speaking for a unanimous court, ruled that "as the powers of local self-government enjoyed by the Cherokee nation existed prior to the Constitution, they are not operated upon by the Fifth Amendment."

Since the Constitution and its amendments only demarcate the actions of the federal and state governments, the U.S. Constitution is not applicable to tribal nations who derive their **sovereignty** from their aboriginal status. (DEW)

BIBLIOGRAPHY

Cohen, Felix S. *Felix S. Cohen's Handbook of Federal Indian Law.* Rennard Strickland, ed. Charlottesville, VA: Mitchie/Bobbs-Merrill, 1982; Ft. Lauderdale, FL: Five Rings Press, 1986.

Pevar, Stephen L. *The Rights of Indians and Tribes.* Carbondale and Edwardsville: Southern Illinois University Press, 1992.

Tashunkopipape. *See* Young Man Afraid of His Horses

Taxation

With the exception of income earned from individual allotments, all Indians pay federal income tax. Each state's power to tax tribes or tribal members, however, is quite limited. States cannot tax federally allotted Indian properties. Nor may a state tax any land within a reservation, even if the land is owned by a non-Indian. Additionally, states are barred from taxing individual income of Indians (if that income is earned from reservation sources), or from taxing corporations if they are Indian-owned and within the reservation. The immunity of Indian properties and revenues from state taxation comes from several sources. Most important, tribes are sovereigns, and the imposition of state taxes interferes with tribal **sovereignty**. The courts have also ruled that because tribes have a strong relationship with the federal government, the doctrine of federal preemption and intergovernmental tax immunity sometimes disallows state taxation. The federal **trusteeship responsibility** toward tribes also works to limit state taxation powers within **Indian country**. Recent battles between states and tribes over taxation revolve around the sale of cigarettes on the reservation. Currently, a state may impose a sales tax on cigarettes sold on the reservation to non-Indians, although sales to Indians are not taxed by the state. Tribes themselves have the authority to tax, although historically they have rarely used that power on their own members. An increasing number of tribes do, however, impose taxes on businesses within the reservation, particularly when those businesses are owned by non-Indians. **See also** *McLanahan v. Arizona State Tax Commission* (1973); Reservation Economies; Tribal–State Affairs. (GTH)

BIBLIOGRAPHY

Canby, William C., Jr. *American Indian Law.* St. Paul, MN: West Publishing, 1988.

O'Brien, Sharon. *American Indian Tribal Governments.* Norman: University of Oklahoma Press, 1989.

Tecumseh (1768–1813)

Tecumseh, also known as "The Panther Passing Across," "Moves from One Place to Another," and "Shooting Star," was a Shawnee war chief and one of the most influential Indians of all time. He was greatly disturbed by the increasing amount of white settlers claiming land for themselves. He envisioned a unified Indian people who would bring a stop to the white expansion. Tecumseh recruited hundreds of warriors to stand with him. William Henry Harrison, governor of the Indiana Territory, held him as the true power of the Tippecanoe community. Tecumseh offered his people as support to the British efforts against the Americans in the early 1800s. He was put in charge of all the Indian forces that joined with the British in the conquest of Detroit. Tecumseh met his death in the Battle of Thames when U.S. forces proved too large to overcome. **See also** Tippecanoe, Battle of (1811); War of 1812.

BIBLIOGRAPHY

Eckert, Allan W. *A Sorrow in Our Heart*. New York: Bantam, 1992.

Edmunds, R. David. *Tecumseh and the Quest for Indian Leadership*. Boston: Little Brown, 1984.

Sugden, John. *Tecumseh's Last Stand*. Norman: University of Oklahoma Press, 1985.

Tee-Hit-Ton Indians v. United States (1955)

Tee-Hit-Ton Indians v. United States, 348 U.S. 273 (1955), addressed the aboriginal land rights of indigenous peoples. In this case, the Tee-Hit-Ton, a clan of the Tlingit Nation in Alaska, sued the United States for just compensation for harvesting timber without their permission from land the clan claimed under aboriginal title. The question before the Court was whether the taking of aboriginal title was compensable under the Fifth Amendment's just compensation clause.

The Court held that such a taking was not compensable because Congress had complete authority under the twin doctrines of discovery and conquest to manage all aboriginal title. In a stunning ruling, the Court held that aboriginal title was "not a property right," but was merely a right of occupancy which the United States could terminate at any time. To qualify for compensation under the Fifth Amendment, an indigenous group's land rights must have been expressly recognized by treaty or statutory law. (DEW)

BIBLIOGRAPHY

Bloxham, Steven John. "Aboriginal Title, Alaskan Native Property Rights, and the Case of the Tee-Hit-Ton Indians." *American Indian Law Review* 8, no. 2 (Spring 1981): 299–331.

Newton, Nell Jessup. "At the Whim of the Sovereign: Aboriginal Title Reconsidered." *Hastings Law Journal* 31, no. 6 (July 1980): 1215–85.

Tenskwatawa (Shawnee Prophet) (1778–1837)

In 1805, Tenskwatawa of the Shawnee tribe awoke from a deep trance claiming to be a prophet, having visited the spirit world and communed with the Master of Life. As a result, he began preaching in favor of traditional Indian ways, denouncing interracial marriage and white customs involving religion, clothing, and alcohol. His followers increased in number on June 16, 1806, after he correctly predicted an eclipse of the sun. In 1808, Tenskwatwa established the Miami village of Tippecanoe to provide a haven for Native Americans away from white society. Tenshwatawa's influence decreased after he inaccurately promised that his magic would help defeat the troops of Governor William Henry Harrison. With the Indian defeat at Tippecanoe on November 7, 1811, Tenshwatawa moved to Canada, where he stayed until 1826.

BIBLIOGRAPHY

Edmunds, R. David. *The Shawnee Prophet*. Lincoln: University of Nebraska Press, 1983.

Termination Resolution

The passage of **House Concurrent Resolution 108** in 1953 marked the formal adoption of the policy known as termination, which advocated ending the special trust relationship between Indian tribes and the federal government. The shift toward termination began during the 1940s and drew strength from growing opposition to the "Indian New Deal" of Commissioner of Indian Affairs John Collier. Citing Native Americans' patriotic service in World War II as evidence of their desire to assimilate, policy makers opposed to Collier's cultural pluralism began pushing to "get the government out of the Indian business." Fiscal conservatives also saw termination as a way to trim the federal budget, while many Western legislators hoped that it would open reservation lands for development. The **Indian Claims Commission Act of 1946** started the process by creating a judicial body to settle all outstanding tribal claims against the federal government. The following year, the **Bureau of Indian Affairs** began to identify Indian groups that it believed could manage without federal services or trust protection. This "hit list" of over 100 tribes provided the blueprint for specific termination bills following the passage of HCR 108.

Despite substantial Indian opposition, Republican Senator Arthur Watkins of Utah and his supporters initially overrode weak congressional resistance to individual termination acts. Between 1954 and 1964, Congress terminated numerous groups, including the California rancherias; the Klamaths and 61 other tribes and bands in Oregon; the Southern Paiutes and the Uintah and Ouray Utes of Utah; the Poncas of Nebraska; the Peorias, Ottawas, and Wyandots in Oklahoma; the Alabama-Couchattas in Texas; the Catwabas of South Carolina; and the Menominees of Wisconsin. Other groups faced the threat but managed to avoid it.

Each termination act ended most aspects of the trust relationship between the federal government and the tribes. Although termination did not expressly extinguish tribal **sovereignty**, it removed federal recognition and subjected the tribes to state legislative authority, legal jurisdiction, and taxation. Most groups lost their reservation lands through sale or alienation, and many found it impossible to exercise their governmental powers after relinquishing their territory. In addition, the terminated tribes lost access to federal programs of education, health, housing, and welfare assistance. The resulting poverty and cultural distress fueled rising political opposition to termination, and by the late 1960s Congress had largely repudiated it as a failure. Some groups have since had their federal recognition and reservations restored, but others remain landless, scattered, and unable to exercise their sovereign powers or to receive government benefits. **See also** Federal Acknowledgment of Indian Tribes; Federal Indian Policy; *Menominee Tribe of Indians v. United States* (1968); Trusteeship Responsibility. (AHF)

BIBLIOGRAPHY

Fixico, Donald L. *Termination and Relocation: Federal Indian Policy, 1945–1960.* Albuquerque: University of New Mexico Press, 1986.

Peroff, Nicholas C. *Menominee Drums: Tribal Termination and Restoration, 1954–1974.* Norman: University of Oklahoma Press, 1982.

Philp, Kenneth R. "Termination: A Legacy of the Indian New Deal." *Western Historical Quarterly* 14 (1983): 165–80.

Walch, Michael C. "Terminating the Indian Termination Policy." *Stanford Law Review* 35 (1983): 1181–1215.

Thief Treaty (1863)

In 1855 the Nez Perce Indians signed a peace treaty with the United States that created boundary lines for their reservation and secured hunting and fishing rights to the tribe. In 1860, however, whites discovered gold on the Nez Perce reservation in Idaho, and prospectors began moving into the area. Nez Perce leaders complained to the federal government that these actions violated the 1855 treaty, but the United States was already occupied with the **Civil War**, and the government refused to provide military assistance to protect the reservation lands.

In 1863, the U.S. government created a new treaty—later called "the Thief Treaty" by the Nez Perces—that reduced the Nez Perce reservation to allow for more "legal" gold prospecting. All the Nez Perce chiefs refused to sign this treaty, with the sole exception of the head chief Lawyer, who agreed to the treaty. The document was ratified by Congress and signed by the president, even though the treaty was signed by only one chief. Most Nez Perces, including the chief **Joseph (Hinmatoya'latk'it),** refused to follow guidelines of the Thief Treaty, and this noncompliance eventually contributed to the **Nez Perce War** (1877). See "I Will Fight No More Forever" by Chief Joseph (1877) in Appendix 1.

BIBLIOGRAPHY

Prucha, Francis Paul. *American Indian Treaties.* Berkeley: University of California Press, 1994.

Grace F. Thorpe (1921–)

Grace Thorpe is the daughter of the Olympic athlete Jim Thorpe (Fox and Sauk tribes). She has devoted much of her time working toward the reinstatement of her father's Olympic medals. Along with her sister, Thorpe has created the Jim Thorpe Museum located in Yale University. Thorpe is also a former lobbyist for the **National Congress of American Indians**. She is also a part-time Sauk and Fox tribal court judge. Her recent efforts have been directed at keeping nuclear waste out of **Indian country.**

BIBLIOGRAPHY

Hebert, Emily. "Jim Thorpe's Daughter Fights Nuclear Waste." *The Columbus Dispatch* (September 28, 1996): 3C.

Thorpe, Grace F. "The Jim Thorpe Family," *Chronicles of Oklahoma* 59, no. 2 (Summer 1981): 91, 179.

Tippecanoe, Battle of (1811)

The Battle of Tippecanoe dealt a severe blow to the push for Indian unity envisioned by The Shawnee Prophet (**Tenskwatawa**) and his brother **Tecumseh**. While Tecumseh traveled among southern Indian groups to gather support for the anti-American confederacy, the governor of the Indiana Territory, William Henry Harrison, invaded the confederacy's main village at Prophetstown. Numerically, the Americans lost as many people as the Indians, but politically, the confederacy under the Shawnee Prophet scattered and failed to regain the level of power it once held. (GO)

BIBLIOGRAPHY

Edmunds, R. David. *The Shawnee Prophet.* Lincoln: University of Nebraska Press, 1983.

———. *Tecumseh and the Quest for Indian Leadership.* Boston: Little, Brown and Company, 1984.

Trade and Intercourse Act of 1799

This act reiterated and renewed the provisions of the 1796 Trade and Intercourse Act regarding the boundary between white and Indian settlement, the apprehension and punishment of intruders, the prosecution of crimes, the licensing of traders, the appointment of agents, and providing of livestock and agricultural hardware to the Indians. As a concession to white frontiersmen, the 1799 law also limited the U.S. Army's power to detain intruders and smugglers prior to remanding them to civil authorities. **See also** Second Trade and Intercourse Act; Trade and Intercourse Act of 1834. (DAN)

BIBLIOGRAPHY

Prucha, Francis Paul. *American Indian Policy in the Formative Years.* Cambridge, MA: Harvard University Press, 1962.

Trade and Intercourse Act of 1802

This was the fifth Indian and Intercourse Act, and the first without an internal time limit. It renewed the provisions of the **Trade and Intercourse Act of 1799** respecting boundaries, trade licensing, intrusions, criminal proceedings, appointment of agents, and "civilization" annuities. It also empowered the president to "prevent or restrain" the sale of alcohol in **Indian country.** The act remained in force (with a few modifications) until its repeal by the **Trade and Intercourse Act of** 1834. (DAN)

BIBLIOGRAPHY

Prucha, Francis Paul. *American Indian Policy in the Formative Years.* Cambridge, MA: Harvard University Press, 1962.

Trade and Intercourse Act of 1834

The 1834 Trade and Intercourse Act was a milestone in the history of federal Indian legislation, initiating a more "paternalistic" and one-sided relationship between Native Americans and the U.S. government. The act transferred law enforcement from Indian councils to the Indian Department and stiffened the penalties imposed on whites who sold liquor to the Indians or settled, hunted, or grazed their cattle on Indian land. The law also repealed all or part of 14 earlier pieces of Indian legislation. **See also** Trade and Intercourse Act of 1799; Trade and Intercourse Act of 1802. (DAN)

BIBLIOGRAPHY

Prucha, Francis Paul. *American Indian Policy in the Formative Years.* Cambridge, MA: Harvard University Press, 1962.

Satz, Ronald. *American Indian Policy in the Jacksonian Era.* Lincoln: University of Nebraska Press, 1975.

Trail of Broken Treaties

The Trail of Broken Treaties was a caravan led by the **American Indian Movement (AIM)**, which started in San Francisco and Seattle in October 1972. It gathered participants from reservations and cities as it moved east and converged in Minneapolis on the way to Washington, D.C., where it arrived on the eve of the national elections in November 1972. The Trail ended in the occupation of the **Bureau of Indian Affairs (BIA)** building in Washington, D.C., from November 3 to 9, 1972. The thousand American Indians in the caravan represented nearly every tribe, age group, political persuasion, and ideology in Indian country. The Trail of Broken Treaties presented 20 points, which were decided upon by caravan members and which summarized the demands of American Indians from the federal government. The 20 points, which accurately reflected the feelings of Indians around the country, outlined a relationship with the federal government that would have limited its arbitrary exercise of power over the rights of tribes, and that would have raised the status of Indian treaties to that accorded foreign treaties. The occupation of the BIA building ended when the federal administration promised to respond to the 20 points within 60 days. When the response came in January 1973, it dismissed the treaty issue as unimportant, which was a great disappointment to Indians everywhere. The frustration and anger that ensued were significant factors in the second battle of **Wounded Knee**. (MS)

BIBLIOGRAPHY

Deloria, Vine, Jr. *Behind the Trail of Broken Treaties: An Indian Declaration of Independence.* Austin: University of Texas Press, 1974.

Trail of Tears

As a result of the **Indian Removal Act of 1830**, President Andrew Jackson continued to press for the relocation of Indians into areas west of the Mississippi River. In October 1838, the Cherokee began a forced march west, as their homes and possessions were burned. The southeastern states of Georgia, Alabama, and Tennessee had experienced a terrible drought that year, which had dried up streams and vegetation. Carrying limited provisions, this trek by some 18,000 Cherokee people proved to be a deadly one. At least 25 percent of the walkers along the trail died of disease, exposure, or malnutrition. This passage became known as the Trail of Tears.

A second Trail of Tears in the 1850s and 1860s was the result of the Indians being pushed out of Kansas and Nebraska

by both the pro- and anti-slavery factions. Members of the **Five Civilized Tribes** (Cherokee, Choctaw, Chickasaw, Creek and Seminole) were removed because of their participation on the side of the Confederacy during the **Civil War**. **See also** Treaty of New Echota (1835). (MRC)

BIBLIOGRAPHY

Thorton, Russell. "Cherokee Population Losses during the Trail of Tears: A New Perspective and a New Estimate." *Ethnohistory* 31, no. 4 (1984): 289–300.

Worcester, Donald E., ed. *Forked Tongues and Broken Treaties.* Caldwell, ID: Caxton, 1975.

Treaty at Dancing Rabbit Creek (1830)

In 1830, a Choctaw Indian commission negotiated with U.S. officials about the removal of the Choctaws west of the Mississippi River. The Choctaw commission offered little opposition to the idea of removing to the West, but they insisted on a guarantee that the United States would never try to possess the new lands. Despite opposition to the treaty by Choctaw women and other nonparticipants, and concerns about the quality of the new lands among the Choctaw negotiators, the treaty was signed on September 27 at Dancing Rabbit Creek, Choctaw Nation, Mississippi. (GO)

BIBLIOGRAPHY

DeRosier, Arthur H. *The Removal of the Choctaw Indians.* Knoxville: University of Tennessee Press, 1970.

Halbert, Henry S. "The Story of the Treaty of Dancing Rabbit." *Publications of the Mississippi Historical Society* 6 (1902).

Treaty at Doak's Stand (1820)

The Treaty at Doak's Stand established the groundwork for removing Choctaws to west of the Mississippi River. Its stipulations called for Choctaws to cede a large portion of their Mississippi homeland for lands in the Arkansas Territory. Andrew Jackson led the American negotiating team and threatened Choctaws with military intervention if they failed to comply. The Choctaw leader **Pushmataha** eloquently voiced his opposition to the treaty, but he signed the treaty on October 18. The U.S. commissioners promised falsely to seek no more Choctaw territory. (GO)

BIBLIOGRAPHY

DeRosier, Arthur H. *The Removal of the Choctaw Indians.* Knoxville: University of Tennessee Press, 1970.

Lincecum, Gideon. "Life of Apushimataha." *Mississippi Historical Society Publications* 9 (1906): 415–85.

Treaty at Fort Harmar (1789)

The Treaty at Fort Harmar (January 9, 1789) was actually a pair of treaties signed by the Northwest Territorial governor Arthur St. Clair and leaders of the Iroquois (**Six Nations**) and Northwest Indian confederacies. The Indian signatories affirmed the land cessions they had made in the **Treaty of Fort Stanwix** (1784) and the Treaty of Fort McIntosh (1785), placed themselves once again under U.S. protection, and agreed to abide by federal laws regarding land sales and trade. In return, the United States paid the Iroquois and Northwest tribes $9,000 for their cessions (which comprised most of modern-day Ohio) and restored their hunting right thereon. The parties to the treaties signed them during an intensifying frontier war, and none expected the agreement or the peace it created to last. Most of the Northwest Indians held the Fort Harmar treaty to be illegitimate because it did not establish an Ohio River boundary, and because noninfluential chiefs had signed it. For his part, St. Clair mainly hoped that the treaty would divide and weaken the Northwest Confederacy. It did indeed have that effect, although the confederacy remained powerful enough to defeat the United States in battle in 1790 and 1791. (DAN)

BIBLIOGRAPHY

Horsman, Reginald. *Expansion and American Indian Policy, 1783–1812*. East Lansing: Michigan State University Press, 1967.

White, Richard. *The Middle Ground*. Cambridge: Cambridge University Press, 1991.

Treaty of Bosque Redondo (1868)

Signed June 1, 1868, the Treaty of Bosque Redondo formally ended the **Navajo War** and released the Navajo people from their captivity at Fort Sumner (Bosque Redondo). It increased the size of the Navajo Reservation from that delineated in the treaties of 1858 and 1861.

The ill-sited Bosque Redondo internment camp cost the government millions of dollars a year to feed, house, and clothe the 9,000 Navajos who had been relocated there. Eager to end this financial drain, the federal government sent General **William Tecumseh Sherman** to negotiate an end to the Navajo internment. Negotiating for the Navajo were 10 headmen, with **Barboncito** as their elected spokesman. The negotiators forestalled Sherman's attempt to send them to **Indian Territory**, secured a 3.5 million-acre reservation within the Navajo homeland, and received livestock to rebuild their herds. Other treaty terms bound the United States to provide teachers and schools, medical services, and rations.

The Navajos returned to their old homes, rejoining the 50 percent of the tribe who had never surrendered. In the same year, Navajo and Hopi leaders met at First Mesa to renew a previous peace agreement, to set boundaries between the two tribes, and to provide material assurances.

The 1868 treaty's provisions for health, education, and economic development were cited to justify the Navajo–Hopi Rehabilitation Act of 1950 (P.L. 87-431). The Navajo Nation regards the 1868 treaty as the foundation of its government-to-government relationship with the United States. (JN)

BIBLIOGRAPHY

Bitsuie, Roman. Personal communication. October and November 1997.

Corell, Lee J. *Through White Men's Eyes: A Contribution to Navajo History*. 6 vols. Window Rock, AZ: Navajo Heritage Center, 1979.

Thompson, Gerald. *The Army and the Navajo: The Bosque Redondo Reservation Experiment, 1863–68*. Tucson: University of Arizona Press, 1976.

Young, Robert. *A Political History of the Navajo Nation*. Tsaile, AZ: Navajo Community College Press, 1978.

Treaty of Buffalo Creek (1832, 1842)

The Tonawanda Seneca fought to regain title to their reservation, which had been taken from them in the Buffalo Creek Treaty of 1832. This treaty was considered null and void by their chiefs because none of the Tonawanda Seneca had participated in any way. The reservation had still not been restored by the 1842 Treaty of Buffalo Creek. They did not regain a portion of their former reservation until 1870. (MRC)

BIBLIOGRAPHY

Prucha, Francis Paul. *American Indian Treaties*. Berkeley: University of California Press, 1994.

Treaty of Fort Laramie (1868)

The Treaty of Fort Laramie was negotiated between the Lakota (Sioux) and the United States after the war for the Powder River country of what is now Wyoming. It is one of the few treaties that resulted from a U.S. military defeat, and it may be the only one in which the United States agreed to abandon a large tract of territory it had claimed within its exterior boundaries. The treaty excluded non-Indians from that territory and led to the abandonment of the Bozeman Trail and forts associated with it.

The Fort Laramie treaty was violated by the United States in 1874, when General George Custer publicized the presence of gold in the **Black Hills**, an area in the center of the treaty territory that is sacred to the Lakota and other native peoples. Although the treaty contains a provision that it may not be altered except with written permission of three-fourths of the adult male Lakota, parts of the states of South Dakota, Wyoming, Montana, and Nebraska were carved out of the treaty area. In ***United States v. Sioux Nation of Indians* (1980)**, the U.S. Supreme Court agreed that the Black Hills area, where Mount Rushmore is located, was illegally taken from the Lakota.

While the Lakota wanted the Black Hills returned, U.S. law provides only for payment for the land. With interest, the $17.5 million set aside as payment for the Black Hills had grown to $330 million by 1995. The Lakota have consistently refused the money, despite the fact that their home reservations include the poorest areas within the United States. They continue to assert the terms of the Fort Laramie Treaty. **See also** Hump; War for the Bozeman Trail. (LCJ)

BIBLIOGRAPHY

Brown, Dee. *Bury My Heart at Wounded Knee*. New York: Holt, Rinehart & Winston, 1970.

Ortiz, Roxanne Dunbar. *The Great Sioux Nation*. San Francisco/Berkeley: International Indian Treaty Council/Moon Books, 1977.

Treaty of Fort Stanwix (1784)

The Treaty of Fort Stanwix was signed between members of the **Six Nations (Haudenosaunee) Confederacy**, also called the Iroquois Confederacy, and the United States in the unsettled days between the **American Revolution** and the completion of the U.S. Constitution. The Haudenosaunee were a focus of attention immediately after the war, because they were British allies occupying the area between the United States and Canada.

During treaty negotiations, the United States held hostages to encourage Haudenosaunee cooperation. Haudenosaunee leaders did not approve the treaty, because the signers were not representative of the confederacy as a whole. Nevertheless, in exchange for giving up their claims to Ohio Valley land, the Haudenosaunee were promised secure control of northern lands. This angered leaders of New York State, who tried to make a separate treaty. Pennsylvania officials successfully negotiated a separate agreement.

After the Treaty of Fort Stanwix was completed, New York State violated it repeatedly and the new United States government, under the terms of the **Articles of Confederation**, was not able to enforce the treaty or control the actions of any particular state. Despite the Haudenosaunee's rejection of the treaty, the confederacy lost control of most of their land. **See also** Six Nations (Haudenosaunee) Confederacy/ (Iroquois Confederacy). (LCJ)

BIBLIOGRAPHY

Lyons, Oren, John Mohawk, et al. *Exiled in the Land of the Free: Democracy, Indian Nations, and the U.S. Constitution.* Santa Fe, NM: Clear Light Publishers, 1992.

Wallace, Anthony F.C. *The Death and Rebirth of the Seneca.* New York: Vintage Books/Random House, 1972.

Treaty of Ghent (1814)

The Treaty of Ghent was signed by the British and the United States in 1814 to end **the War of 1812**. The treaty returned U.S. posts that had been captured by the British back to the United States. It carried the principles of the Treaty of Amnesty and Commerce of 1794, which was used to maintain trade between Canada and the United States. It also provided that both countries make peace with and provide free passage across their land to the Native Americans of North America. (MW)

BIBLIOGRAPHY

Cohen, Felix S. *Handbook of Federal Indian Law.* Washington, DC: U.S. Government Printing Office, 1942.

Jones, Dorothy V. *License for Empire: Colonialism by Treaty in Early America.* Chicago: University of Chicago Press, 1982.

Treaty of Guadalupe-Hidalgo (1848)

The Treaty of Guadalupe-Hidalgo ended the **Mexican-American War** with cessions of lands, settling the southern boundary of Texas at the Rio Grande (Rio Bravo), and expanding the territories ruled by the United States all the way to the Pacific Ocean. The Treaty also recognized that ". . . a great part of the (ceded) territories . . . (are) now occupied by savage tribes" (Art. XI). Many of these "savage tribes" had never recognized Spanish sovereignty or Mexican sovereignty, and the struggle to force them to recognize U.S. sovereignty would continue almost to the end of the century.

Although the treaty purported to safeguard existing private land holdings, the U.S. legal paradigm did not recognize *ejidos*, commonly held grazing and wood-gathering rights that preexisted European contact in some places and had been protected under the Spanish and the Mexicans. The United States claimed these areas as public domain in the sense that the land could be sold to individuals and fenced for their exclusive use. This changed understanding and sharp business practices by Anglo-Americans caused a massive shift in land ownership away from the Hispano-Indian occupants and led to many years of protests, notably the raid on the courthouse in Tierra Amarilla, New Mexico, led by Reis Lopez Tijerina on June 5, 1967.

As Tijerina and other land grant activists rely on the Treaty of Guadalupe-Hidalgo, some scholars today suggest using the arbitration clause in the treaty to resolve the ongoing dispute between the United States and Mexico over application of the death penalty to Mexicans in the United States.

Another irony for the occupants of land ceded by Mexico under the Treaty of Guadalupe-Hidalgo has been the recent creation of a "Hispanic" census category that lumps together many Indians with their Spanish conquerors even when the blood had not mixed. Until the rise of Mexican-American civil rights organizations in the 1960s and 1970s, children found themselves punished in school for speaking Spanish when their ancestors may have been punished by the Spanish for speaking Indian languages.

It is against this violent backdrop of international conflict that Indian tribes still survive in the southwestern United States, often with more of their language and culture intact than tribes on the East Coast, who actually encountered Europeans later. (SR)

BIBLIOGRAPHY

Boyle, Francis A. and Lee Jeorge Penya. "Open Letter to All Progressive People in Mexico on Executions." *Social Justice* 20, no. 1–2 (Spring–Summer 1993): 163–66.

Cheever, Federico M. "A New Approach to Spanish and Mexican Land Grants and the Public Trust Doctrine: Defining the Property Interest Protected by the Treaty of Guadalupe-Hidalgo." *UCLA Law Review* 33, no. 5 (June 1986): 1364–1409.

Del Castillo, Richard Griswold. *The Treaty of Guadalupe-Hidalgo: A Legacy of Conflict.* Norman: University of Oklahoma Press, 1990.

Klein, Christine A. "Treaties of Conquest: Property Rights, Indian Treaties and the Treaty of Guadalupe-Hidalgo." *New Mexico Law Review* 26, no. 2 (Spring 1996): 201–55.

Nabokov, Peter. *Tijerina and the Courthouse Raid.* 2nd ed. Albuquerque: University of New Mexico Press, 1970.

Toro, Luis Angel. "'A People Distinct from Others': Race and Identity in Federal Indian Law and the Hispanic Classification in OMB Directive No. 15." *Texas Tech Law Review* 26, no. 4 (1995): 1219–74.

Treaty of Holston (1791)

The Treaty of Holston was signed in July 1791, by United States commissioners and 41 principal chiefs of the Cherokee Nation. The treaty was intended to settle the differences left undone by the Treaty of Hopewell (1785). It provided for the first Indian agent, or superintendent, to direct U.S. government policy among the Indians. (AMM)

BIBLIOGRAPHY

Prucha, Francis Paul. *American Indian Treaties*. Berkeley: University of California Press, 1994.

Treaty of New Echota (1835)

Under the terms of the Treaty of New Echota (December 29, 1835), the Cherokee Nation ostensibly ended its legal battle with Georgia and the United States and submitted to the **Indian Removal Act of 1830**. The Cherokee signatories ceded their nation's lands in the southeastern United States to the federal government and agreed that the Cherokees would move to Oklahoma within two years of ratification. In return, the United States promised the Cherokees 13.8 million acres of land in **Indian Territory** and $4.5 million to cover emigration expenses and as compensation for abandoned farms and other improvements. However, the men who signed the agreement represented a minority faction of Cherokees—later known as the "Treaty Party"—who had convened a rump session of the National Council while Principal Chief **John Ross** was in Washington D.C. Ross and other Cherokee leaders denounced the New Echota treaty as illegitimate and asked the Senate to reject it, but to no avail. In 1838–1839 the U.S. Army executed the treaty's terms by forcibly expelling the Cherokees from the Southeast. In June 1839 antitreaty partisans assassinated three of the Treaty Party's leaders—Elias Boudinot, John Ridge, and Major Ridge—in Oklahoma, thereby igniting a seven-year-long civil war. **See also** Five Civilized Tribes; Trail of Tears; Stand Watie. (DAN)

BIBLIOGRAPHY

Perdue, Theda. "The Conflict Within: The Cherokee Power Structure and Removal." *Georgia Historical Quarterly* 73, no. 3 (Fall 1989): 467–91.

Wilkins, Thurman. *Cherokee Tragedy: The Ridge Family and the Decimation of a People*. 2nd ed. Norman: University of Oklahoma Press, 1986.

Treaty of Spring Wells (1815)

Signed on September 8, 1815, at Spring Wells, near Detroit, Michigan, this was one of 20 treaties between the United States and various Indian tribes in which the American government restored the prewar rights and status to those tribes that fought and supported the British in the **War of 1812**. By signing the Treaty of Spring Wells, the United States was complying with the terms of the **Treaty of Ghent**. (MRC)

BIBLIOGRAPHY

Prucha, Francis Paul. *American Indian Treaties*. Berkeley: University of California Press, 1994.

Tribal Councils

Tribal councils vary so much that they are difficult to generalize. However, they can be divided to two basic criteria: their form of government and their relationship to the United States government.

Tribal councils may have a government that is essentially a continuation of traditional Native American organization, or they may have a form that was developed by following certain aspects of the U.S. Constitution. The "traditional" councils take a wide variety of forms and may be selected by clans, through voting, by one or the other gender, or by some other process. The councils that are inspired by the Constitution have a written basis and—at least on paper—a three-branch system of government.

As for relationships with the U.S. government, tribal councils may either be recognized by the United States, or they may be unrecognized. United States "recognition" of **tribal governments**, while different in terms of administration, is otherwise similar to diplomatic recognition of international governments. **See also** Tribal Governance. (LCJ)

BIBLIOGRAPHY

Meredith, Howard. *Modern American Indian Tribal Government and Politics*. Tsaile, AZ: Navajo Community College Press, 1993.

O'Brien, Sharon. *American Indian Tribal Governments*. Norman: University of Oklahoma Press, 1989.

Tribal Government

At the time of first contact, a great variety of forms of government were in place among tribal peoples. Some tribes formed loose confederations of hunting groups who spoke similar languages (such as the Lakota or Shoshone). Other tribes, such as those in the Pacific Northwest, had almost no political organization. Some tribes were theocracies (such as the Hopi of Arizona) where government was organized around religious beliefs. Other tribes, such as the Cheyenne, were governed by civil tribal councils led by priestly chiefs. Some tribes had highly sophisticated forms of government. The Creek Confederacy, in the Southeast, had 50 to 80 separate towns in the Confederacy. The Confederacy separated civil functions of government from war-making functions. White towns were governed by civil councils and enacted the civil laws of the Confederacy. Red towns conducted war on behalf of the Confederacy. The most highly developed tribal government in North America was the Iroquois (Haudenosaunee) League composed of five nations (eventually six) located in the Northeast. The League was ruled by a constitution called the Great Law of Peace. Each nation had its own tribal council to handle internal matters. A Grand Council handled defense of the League and foreign relations and diplomacy.

Early contact with European settlers and the need to deal with Europeans commercially and politically forced tribes to change traditional governance within a few decades of contact. Some tribes, such as the **Five Civilized Tribes** (Cherokee, Choctaw, Creek, Chickasaw, and Seminole) in the Southeast, actually adopted European-style governments. The Chickasaw went so far as to start calling their tribal leader "governor," copying the British title.

During the **American Revolution**, the Continental Congress attempted to influence tribes, through promises, to ally with the Colonies. It promised the Delaware their own state after the Revolution, and the Cherokee a representative in Congress. The Treaty of Paris, ending the Revolution, however, made no mention of these promises. The tribes who supported the colonists or who had remained neutral in the war were treated no better than those who had been British allies.

In 1787, the Continental Congress adopted the **Northwest Ordinance**. The ordinance stated "The utmost good faith shall always be observed toward the Indians; their lands and property shall never be taken from them without their consent; and in their property, rights and liberty they shall never be invaded or disturbed, unless in just and lawful wars authorized by Congress." This document set the

In the 1950s, two Seminole Indians vote on whether to adopt a tribal form of government. *Library of Congress.*

stage for tribal expectations of fair and just treatment from the U.S. Government. Subsequent actions by the United States limited and abolished the rights of tribes and dashed their hopes for fair and equitable treatment. A few years later, when the U.S. Constitution was written, it seemed that the founding fathers perceived of Native Americans as irrelevant. Native Americans are mentioned in the Constitution as an afterthought to the interstate commerce clause, "regulate commerce with foreign nations, among the several states, and with Indian tribes." Upon these five words was eventually hung an elaborate edifice of federal legislation, U.S. Supreme Court decisions, hundreds of federal programs, and the U.S. Bureau of Indian Affairs.

By the early 1800s, theological racism and the "doctrine of discovery" had firmly shaped the U.S. image of the Indian as "uncivilized." This description justified removal of tribes westward. Removal led to reservations as Americans could see destiny manifest in the westward migration of America. The social darwinism of the period was used as justification for government policies toward the Native Americans, which were intended to move Indians from the aboriginal cultural patterns to an agricultural existence.

Once on reservations, Indian governing practices changed again. The Indian agent on the reservation assumed an authoritarian role and became the liaison between tribes and the federal government. For the tribes placed on reservations, traditional tribal government eroded away and was often replaced by tribal councils that worked with the Indian agent whenever he felt some function could be delegated to them. However, many tribes attempted to continue their traditional

ways of governing. Further erosion of traditional tribal governance was caused by the federal government's tendency to create tribes where none existed before. If tribal peoples spoke common or similar languages, the government often put them together and called them a "tribe." Sometimes the federal government would create a "chief" where none existed, so the chief could sign treaties with the federal government. Under the Dawes Act of 1887, many reservations and tribal lands were broken up, allotted in small parcels to individual Native Americans, and surplus lands were sold.

Finally in 1934, Congress admitted the failure of previous policies by passing the **Indian Reorganization Act (IRA)**. This Act strengthened tribal governments, restored tribal lands, funded tribal economic development, and revitalized tribal cultures. The Act gave the tribes an opportunity to organize for the tribe's common welfare and to adopt tribal constitutions. The tribes had two years to accept the provisions of the IRA. One hundred and eighty-one tribes accepted the terms of the Act, and many adopted the model constitution written by the **Bureau of Indian Affairs (BIA)**. Seventy-seven refused, including the Navajo and Pueblos. The U.S. Secretary of Interior, under the IRA, had to approve all tribal constitutions and was given veto power over all tribal government decisions.

In the 1950s under the Eisenhower administration, federal policy once again changed. During this period, the federal government again adopted a policy of tribal termination, the object being assimilation into Euro-American society. By the 1960s and 1970s, federal policy shifted once more. Tribal governments again became viable under the Johnson and Nixon administrations and for many tribes continue today.

In a 1974 study, the Native American Indian Court Judges Association stated that tribal governments today fall into four categories:

1. Representative Government: the tribe elects a governing body that operates under a constitution (such as the Chickasaw).

2. Representative/Traditional: the tribe elects a governing body under a constitution, but some government positions are still held by traditional tribal leaders (such as the Warm Springs Tribes of Oregon).

3. General Council: tribal officials have no substantive authority. When the tribes have to make a decision, a general council of tribal members is called and all tribal members vote on the issue (such as the Crow Tribe of Montana).

4. Theocracy: tribal officials are selected by tribal religious leaders (such as the Pueblo peoples of Arizona and New Mexico). (MM)

BIBLIOGRAPHY

Canby, William C. *American Indian Law.* St. Paul, MN: West Publishing Co., 1988.

Deloria, Vine, Jr. and Clifford M. Lytle. *American Indians, American Justice.* Austin: University of Texas Press, 1983.

O'Brien, Sharon. *American Indian Tribal Governments.* Norman, OK: University of Oklahoma Press, 1989.

Svensson, Francis. *The Ethnics in American Politics: American Indians.* Minneapolis, MN: Burgess Publishing Co., 1973.

Viola, Herman J. *After Columbus. The Smithsonian Chronicle of the North American Indian.* Washington, DC: Smithsonian Books, 1990.

Tribal Legal System

Tribal law is complex, created from a combination of the U.S. Constitution, federal statutes, executive orders, federal regulations, court decisions, state statutes, and tribal laws. As a result, a tribal member may have three sets of rights—federal, state, and tribal. Until 1968, tribal members had no federally protected constitutional rights while on tribal lands. The **Indian Civil Rights Act of 1968** gave Native Americans the constitutional protections given to other Americans.

Historically, disputes among tribal members were handled by elders or chiefs. Contrary to the Western legal tradition of establishing guilt, punishment, or imprisonment, chiefs or elders sought restitution to and compensation for the victim. Few tribes still use these traditional forms of justice. In 1849, with the creation of the U.S. Department of the Interior, tribal justice became the responsibility of Indian agents in cases involving Indians and non-Indians. Domestic issues remained under each tribe's control. During this era, "Courts of Indian Offenses" and the first tribal police forces were formed, both controlled by Indian agents. With passage of the **Indian Reorganization Act of 1934,** tribes assumed control of tribal justice. Most tribes have a trial court and an appeals court.

Tribal courts have civil jurisdiction over tribal members and over non-Indians if the activity affects tribal interests. Regarding criminal law most tribal courts handle minor offenses (misdemeanors) involving tribal members. Federal courts, under the **Major Crimes Act (1885),** handle serious offenses (felonies). Tribes lack criminal jurisdiction over non-Indians unless Congress gives them jurisdiction. States have no jurisdiction over crimes committed on reservations unless given such power by Congress. Many tribal judges are appointed by tribal councils. Some are selected by religious leaders or elected by tribal members. Most serve one- to four-year terms. Most are not trained in the law. **See also** *Santa Clara Pueblo v. Martinez* (1978). (MM)

BIBLIOGRAPHY
Deloria, Vine, Jr. and Clifford M. Lytle. *American Indians, American Justice.* Austin: University of Texas Press, 1983.
Pevar, Stephen L. *The Rights of Indian Tribes.* Carbondale: Southern Illinois University Press, 1992.

Tribal–State Affairs

The political relationship between tribal nations and the federal government is demarcated in the United States Constitution, which declares in article 1, sect. 8 that "the Congress shall have Power . . . to regulate Commerce with foreign Nations, and among the several States, and with the Indian tribes." This relationship is more expressly enunciated in treaties, agreements, executive orders, case law, statutory law, federal regulations, and congressional appropriations.

However, the equally important relationship between Indian nations and the states is not outlined in the federal constitution, is not described in state or tribal constitutions, and suffers from inconsistent directives in federal and statutory case law. It is generally accepted by the tribal nations, the state governments, and the federal government that the primary relationship for most tribes is at the federal level, with tribes and the United States operating in what is popularly known as a nation-to-nation relationship rooted in the doctrines of inherent tribal **sovereignty**, congressional exclusive authority to manage the federal government's affairs with tribes, and the treaty relationship. As a federal appeals court noted in 1959, such historical precedent points to tribes having "a status higher than that of states."

Nevertheless, over the course of history, tribes and states have come to stand as mutual, if different, sovereigns. Today, in the 34 states where there are federally recognized tribes, the two sovereigns share contiguous geographic areas, with every Indian **reservation** or Indian community being surrounded by a state's borders, and they share some common citizens (i.e., tribal citizens who live within reservations are both tribal and state citizens), while non-Indian residents of the reservation enjoy state citizenship but are not tribal citizens.

Although tribal nations and states share citizens and land masses, in their relations as sovereign entities they have each historically jealously guarded their collective rights to political powers, economic and natural resources, and cultural histories. In other words, tribes and states have rarely been friendly neighbors. As the Supreme Court said in *United States v. Kagama* (1886), tribes "owe no allegiance to the States, and receive from them no protection. Because of the local ill-feeling, the people of the States where they are found are often their deadliest enemies."

Tribes resent the states' constant attempts to tax and regulate their lands, wages, and industries, and they are displeased that many states are still reluctant to concede the reality of tribal sovereignty and recognize their competence to handle increasing amounts of regulatory and administrative duties. States resent the fact that while they have jurisdiction over all activities and persons within their borders, this does not generally extend to tribal national affairs or to Indians residing on reservations or trust land that is generally not subject to state jurisdiction or taxation.

The reasons explaining this tension trace back to the colonial period in American history and the debates about whether the national government or the individual colonies/states would manage Indian affairs. At the Constitutional Convention (1787), it was determined that Congress would have exclusive control over trade relations with the sovereign tribes and that the national government would continue the treaty relationship with indigenous nations that other European sovereigns had also negotiated with tribes.

Later, as the United States expanded west, the enabling acts admitting most states to the Union were required to contain disclaimer clauses in which the new states agreed to recognize the federal government's exclusive jurisdiction over the nation's Indian affairs and promised never to tax Indians or Indian trust land. These three factors—congressional plenary power, treaties, and state disclaimer clauses—along with tribal sovereignty, effectively excluded states from any direct involvement in tribal affairs.

The Supreme Court in **Worcester v. Georgia (1832)** provided the first focused analysis of the tribal–state relationship. The court held that state laws could have no force within **Indian country** unless Congress authorized such state action. Chief Justice John Marshall declared that "the treaties and laws of the United States contemplate the Indian territory as completely separated from that of the states; and provide that all intercourse with them shall be carried on exclusively by the government of the Union." Along with federal exclusivity, the doctrine of tribal sovereignty was also relied on by Marshall to bar state intrusion into internal tribal affairs.

The Marshall doctrine, which judicially firmed up the constitutional wall separating tribes from states, gradually deteriorated as non-Indians moved into Indian country. For as whites moved in, so too did various elements of state jurisdiction. There have been six major state intrusions into the historically exclusive tribal–federal relationship. Each of these was precipitated ironically by federal action: (a) **United States v. McBratney (1881)**, which held that states had criminal jurisdiction over non-Indians who commit crimes against other non-Indians within reservations; (b) the General Allotment Act (the **Dawes Act of 1887**), which in individualizing Indian lands gave states jurisdiction over descent and partition and also authorized the state to tax any Indian allotment that leaves trust status; (c) **Public Law 280** (1953), which gave a number of states complete criminal and some civil jurisdiction over Indian reservations located within the state; (d) termination laws (1953–1960s), which legally ended the life of the terminated tribe (such as the Menominee and Klamath nations), placing the tribe's members and their property under state law (except for treaty-based hunting and fishing rights); and (e) the **Indian Gaming Regulatory Act** (1988), which required tribes that want to operate lotteries, slot machines, blackjack, and other casino-type games to negotiate compacts with the states.

Notwithstanding these measures and the special political circumstances of New York State and Oklahoma, which enjoy considerable jurisdiction over the Indians within their borders because of unique historical reasons, the general rule was until recently that state laws had no force within the territory of an Indian tribe in matters affecting Indians, unless Congress had expressly delegated authority to the state, or unless a question involving Indians also involved non-Indians to a significant degree to call state jurisdiction into play.

States for their part have constantly sought ever-greater jurisdiction within Indian country despite the important constitutional and legal barriers precluding it. By 1980 the Supreme Court had shifted away from a reliance on tribal sovereignty as a barrier checking state law. Instead the Court had erected a two-part test to determine which state laws could be applied in Indian country without congressional consent: a

federal preemption test (if a state law is inconsistent with federal law or interferes with overriding federal and tribal interests, it is voided) and an infringement test (if a state's action infringes on the right of reservation Indians to be self-governing, it is nullified).

These tests, however, have been seriously eroded by a series of Supreme Court opinions in the 1980s and 1990s: **Montana v. United States (1980)**, *Cotton Petroleum v. New Mexico* (1989), *Brendale v. Confederated Tribes and Bands of Yakima Indian Nation* (1989), *County of Yakima v. Yakima Nation* (1992), and *South Dakota v. Bourland* (1993). These cases have turned the previous century and a half of federal policy and judicial precedent on its head and they threaten tribal sovereignty's vitality at a time when the doctrine of tribal **self-determination** is evolving into a permanent presence after a century of direct attacks.

The operating presumption of the Supreme Court now is that state law is applicable in Indian country unless the affected tribe can show that the state's action will have significantly adverse impact on the tribe or its resources. As the *Brendale* court held: "The impact must be demonstrably serious and must imperil the political integrity, the economic security, or the health and welfare of the tribe." "This standard," insisted Justice Byron White, "will sufficiently protect Indian tribes while at the same time avoiding undue interference with state sovereignty and providing the certainty needed by property owners."

Even as the Supreme Court is challenging tribal sovereignty's force vis-a-vis states' rights, tribes and states, sometimes supported by federal law and presidential directives and sometimes acting independently of federal involvement, are exercising a greater willingness to engage in constructive dialogue in an effort to avoid frequent and expensive litigation when their rights conflict. In recent years some tribes and their host states have entered into sovereignty accords, have participated in cooperative agreements, have developed comprehensive state and tribal policies on tribal–state relations, have sought to improve the educational process to ameliorate stereotypes and to educate citizens, and have engaged in a number of negotiated settlements in an effort to develop more amicable relations.

But serious fault lines remain between the two sovereigns over issues such as the substance of tribal sovereignty, Indian **gaming**, hunting and fishing rights, water rights, land claims, religious freedom, and civil jurisdiction. Litigation, therefore, remains the most common technique to settle differences, although there is little evidence that it helps to promote a deeper understanding of each other's problems and needs.

The intergovernmental relationship between tribes and states is a dynamic one. It is complicated by the overarching presence of the federal government which, on the one hand, has treaty and trust obligations to tribal nations but, on the other hand, is constitutionally connected to the states. Relations will improve, from a tribal perspective, only if states recognize the fact that tribes are sovereign entities entitled to govern the land and live within their borders. States contend that tribes must in turn be willing to consider the interests of the state if they are embarking on economic development or environmental decisions that may have implications beyond the reservation's borders.

While jurisdictional uncertainties and economic competition will persist, there is growing hope that as the two sovereigns come to recognize the rights of the other to protect the health, safety, and welfare of its own citizens, to engage in economic development that is appropriate for their communities, and to regulate their natural resource endowments and environmental quality, this may lead to more positive tribal–state relations. **See also** Fishing and Hunting Treaty Rights; House Concurrent Resolution 108; *McClanahan v. Arizona State Tax Commission* (1973); *Menominee Tribe of Indians v. United States* (1968); Termination Resolution. (DEW)

Bibliography

Castile, George P. and Robert L. Bee, eds. *State and Reservation.* Tempe: University of Arizona Press, 1992.

Kersey, Harry A. *An Assumption of Sovereignty.* Lincoln: University of Nebraska Press, 1996.

Legters, Lyman H. and Fremont J. Lyden, eds. *American Indian Policy.* Westport, CT: Greenwood, 1993.

Lopach, James J., et al. *Tribal Government Today.* Boulder: University Press of Colorado, 1998.

Sherman, Joseph. *Indian Tribes of North America.* New York: Random House, 1996.

Wilkins, David E. *American Indian Sovereignty and the U.S. Supreme Court.* Austin: University of Texas Press, 1997.

John Trudell (1947–)

John Trudell (Shoshone-Paiuk) became the national spokesman for the **American Indian Movement (AIM)** after his part in the **Alcatraz Island occupation** by the **United Indians of All Tribes** in 1971. He has been involved in many controversial events, including the public defense of the killers of FBI agents at the Jumping Bull Compound at Pine Ridge in 1975. Within 12 hours of his 1979 arrest for burning a U.S. flag, his wife and her family were killed in a blaze that authorities believe was caused by arson. Trudell has released two musical albums on an independent label and has played many benefit concerts for Native American groups.

Bibliography

Matthiessen, Peter. *In the Spirit of Crazy Horse.* New York: Viking, 1983.

Weyler, Rex. *Blood of the Land: The Government and Corporate War against the American Indian Movement.* New York: Everest House, 1982.

Trusteeship Responsibility

"Trusteeship responsibility" in federal Indian law is traced to a suggestion in *Cherokee Nation v. Georgia*, 5 Pet. 1 (1831), that the relation of the "Indian tribes" to the United States "resembles that of a ward to his guardian." For better and for worse, this Supreme Court dictum became a foundation of federal policy.

A trustee is one who holds title to property for the benefit of another. The federal "trusteeship" over Indians is based on an assertion by the United States that it owns Indian lands and that it will use these lands to benefit the original inhabitants, who hold a "right of occupancy." In this sense, "trusteeship"—which is often viewed as a power to help native peoples—is also a remnant of the colonial claim of sovereignty over "discovered" lands. In *United States v. Creek Nation,* 295 U.S. 103 (1935), and ***United States v. Sioux Nation of Indians***, 448 U.S. 371 (1980), the Supreme Court affirmed Congressional power to "control and manage" Indian affairs, "subject to limitations inhering in . . . a guardianship."

The **Bureau of Indian Affairs (BIA)** is the principal agency to administer "trusteeship responsibility," although every federal agency is charged with at least nominal deference to trusteeship in dealing with native nations. In the name of the trust (as well as in the name of treaty obligations) educational, financial, health, and other programs are funded by federal appropriations. Since passage of the **Indian Self-Determination and Education Assistance Act of 1975, tribal councils** have been encouraged to contract for these programs, bringing them under local management. **See also** Doctrine of Discovery; Guardianship; Self-Determination. (PPE)

Bibliography

Ball, Milner S. "Constitution, Court, Indian Tribes." American *Bar Foundation Research* Journal 59, no. 1 (Winter 1987): 1–140.

Cohen, Felix S. *Handbook of Federal Indian Law.* Washington, DC: U.S. Government Printing Office, 1942.

Deloria, Vine, Jr. and Clifford Lytle. *American Indians, American Justice.* Austin: University of Texas, 1983.

Prucha, Francis Paul. *The Indians in American Society.* Berkeley: University of California Press, 1985.

Tuscarora Protest

The Tuscarora Protest began in 1957 in response to a territorial land rights dispute after Robert Moses of the New York State Power Authority attempted to purchase lands owned by the Tuscarora Indians. Moses planned to build a reservoir on Tuscarora land to supply hydroelectric energy for the Niagara Power Project. After the Tuscarora refused the $3 million selling price, officials from the New York State Power Authority tried to invoke legislative powers to have the Native Americans in the valley removed.

Under the leadership of Wallace "Mad Bear" Anderson and William Rickard, a protest committee of Tuscarora natives quickly formed to help preserve their lands. This group engaged in nonviolent stand-in and lay-in tactics, placing themselves in the way of state law enforcement officials and representatives from the New York Power Authority who tried to survey or seize lands. In 1960, the protest ended as the U.S. Supreme Court allowed New York to take Tuscarora lands for the construction of a reservoir. While this ruling was viewed by many Native Americans as a loss in their quest for equal rights, it did help inspire the **Red Power** civil rights movement in the 1960s.

BIBLIOGRAPHY

Hauptman, Lawrence M. *The Iroquois Struggle for Survival: World War II to Red Power.* Syracuse, NY: Syracuse University Press, 1986.

Tuscarora War (1711–1713)

The Tuscarora, an Iroquoian tribe, were living in North Carolina at the time of European settlement. Because of pressure from the immigrants, the Tuscarora petitioned the Shawnee and the Conestoga in 1710 for permission to relocate to Pennsylvania. Because Pennsylvania required a certificate of good behavior before it would allow the move, the move never materialized.

In 1711, the Tuscarora combined with the Coree, Pamlico, Matamuskeet, Bear River, and Machapungo Indians in attacking white settlers. Virginia sent supplies and money, and South Carolina sent men and supplies to support the North Carolinians. The Tuscarora were finally defeated in 1713, and those who were not killed or taken as slaves moved north. They became the sixth, and junior, member of the Iroquois Confederacy. (AMM)

BIBLIOGRAPHY

Milling, Chapman J. *Red Carolinians.* Chapel Hill: University of North Carolina Press, 1940.

United Indians of All Tribes

United Indians of All Tribes, a name reflecting the will to represent all Native Americans, was founded in October 1968 and later incorporated. This organization occupied Alcatraz Island between November 20, 1969 and June 11, 1971. The group reclaimed the island in the name of all American Indians by right of discovery and intended to turn it into a Native American center. The occupation was a turning point in Indian activism and some of its participants became key figures in the events that followed. The organization still seeks to protect nature Awareness Rights as the United Indians of All Tribes Foundation.(MS)

BIBLIOGRAPHY

Fortunate Eagle, *Adam. Alcatraz! Alcatraz! The Indian Occupation 1969–1971*. Berkeley: Heyday Books, 1992.

Johnson, Troy R. *The Occupation of Alcatraz Island: Indian Self Determination and the Rise of Indian Activism*. Urbana: University of Illinois Press, 1996.

United Native Americans

The United Native Americans was founded in 1968 to promote the general welfare of Native Americans. This organization of Native American and European American members dedicated itself to a number of educational and occupational issues. It also provided Indians with legal aid, counseling, housing, food, and other necessities. The group helped establish the Native American Studies program at the University of California at Berkeley, offers a speakers' bureau, sells historic posters to raise funds for a variety of needs, and publishes its own monthly magazine, *Warpath*. The group currently has 12,000 members in 18 local groups.

BIBLIOGRAPHY

Nagel, Joane. *American Indian Ethnic Renewal*. New York: Oxford University Press, 1996.

United Native Americans Conference of 1968

The militant native rights organization **United Native Americans** (UNA) was formed at a conference held during the summer of 1968 in San Francisco, California. The organization selected Lehman Brightman as its first president. UNA sought to unite all Native Americans into a grass-roots organization dedicated to native control of native affairs.

BIBLIOGRAPHY

Means, Russell and Marvin J. Wolf. *Where White Men Fear to Tread*. New York: St. Martin's Press, 1995.

Wunder, John R. *"Retained by the People": A History of American Indians and the Bill of Rights*. New York: Oxford University Press, 1994.

U.S. Citizenship for Indian Veterans of World War I Act

Passed in 1919, the U.S. Citizenship for Indian Veterans of World War I Act granted U.S. citizenship to every Native American who served in the armed forces during World War I and who was honorably discharged. The act further provided that the veterans could, by a court of competent jurisdiction, be granted full individual or tribal rights to property held in trust. This act predated by five years the passage of the **General Citizenship Act**, which provided for the citizenship of all non-citizen Indians born within the United States.

BIBLIOGRAPHY

Cohen, Felix S. *Felix Cohen's Handbook of Federal Indian Law*. Charlottesville, VA: Mitchie, Bobbs-Merrill, 1982; Ft. Lauderdale, FL: Five Rings Press, 1986.

Wunder, John R. *"Retained by the People": A History of American Indians and the Bill of Rights*. New York: Oxford University Press, 1994.

United States Constitution

The United States Constitution mentions American Indians twice. Article 1, sec. 2, cl. 3, excludes "Indians not taxed" from the population base for determining apportionment of representatives and direct taxes among the states. Article 1, sec. 8, cl. 3, states that "Congress shall have Power . . . to regulate Commerce with foreign Nations, and among the several States, and with the Indian Tribes."

There is no constitutional provision for federal "plenary power" over Indians, nor does any part of the Constitution attach any form of "wardship" or "trust" status to the native peoples of the land. Nevertheless, the Supreme Court has repeatedly asserted these various concepts in declaring and upholding a general Congressional power over Indians.

In *United States v. Kagama* (**1886**), without any specific constitutional citation, the Court upheld federal legislation to deprive Indians of criminal jurisdiction in major crimes: "The power of the General Government . . . is necessary to their protection. . . . It must exist in that government, because it has never existed anywhere else. . . ." In *Lone Wolf v. Hitchcock* (1903), the Court stated, "Plenary authority over the tribal relations of the Indians has been exercised from the beginning." In cases where the Court has backed away from such extreme definitions of federal power, for example *United States v. Creek Nation* (1935), and *United States v. Sioux Nation of Indians* (1980), it has still affirmed a basic power of Congress to "control and manage" Indian affairs, "subject to limitations inhering in . . . a guardianship." **See also** Tribal–State Affairs; Trusteeship Responsibility. (PPE)

BIBLIOGRAPHY

Savage, Mark. "Native Americans and the Constitution: The Original Understanding." *American Indian Law Review* 16, no. 1 (Spring 1991): 57–118.

United States v. Dann (1974–1989)

United States v. Dann represents a series of cases beginning in 1974 with a Bureau of Land Management complaint that Mary and Carrie Dann were illegally grazing cattle on public lands. The Danns defended their ranching on the grounds that the Western Shoshone retained title to the lands in question, under the terms of the 1863 Treaty of Ruby Valley. In *United States v. Dann,* 873 F.2d 1189 (9th Cir., 1989), the defense was upheld by the 9th Circuit Court of Appeals, but this decision was reversed by the United States Supreme Court on the grounds that Western Shoshone title had been extinguished by payment of compensation from the **Indian Claims Commission.** Although the Western Shoshone did not accept the payment, the Court held that the United States government accepted it on their behalf, as their "trustee." **See also** Land and Water Rights. (PPE)

BIBLIOGRAPHY

Cohen, Felix S. *Felix Cohen's Handbook of Federal Indian Law.* Charlottesville, VA: Mitchie, Bobbs-Merrill, 1982; Ft. Lauderdale, FL: Five Rings Press, 1986.

Getches, David, Charles F. Wilkinson, and Robert A. Williams, Jr. *Cases and Materials of Federal Indian Law.* 3rd ed. St. Paul, MN: West Publishing, 1993.

United States v. Kagama (1886)

Congress felt the decision of *Ex Parte Crow Dog* **(1883)** was unacceptable, so it passed the **Major Crimes Act** in 1885. This act gave the federal courts jurisdiction in major crimes such as murder on Native American land. In *United States v. Kagama 118 U.S. 375* (1886), two Natives challenged the power of the federal courts after murdering another Native American on a reservation in California. In its decision, the U.S. Supreme Court upheld the Major Crimes Act.

BIBLIOGRAPHY

Cohen, Felix S. *Felix Cohen's Handbook of Federal Indian Law.* Charlottesville, VA: Mitchie, Bobbs-Merrill, 1982; Ft. Lauderdale, FL: Five Rings Press, 1986.

Getches, David, Charles F. Wilkinson, and Robert A. Williams, Jr. *Cases and Materials of Federal Indian Law.* 3rd ed. St. Paul, MN: West Publishing, 1993.

Thompson, William N. *Native American Issues.* Santa Barbara, CA: ABC-CLIO, 1996.

United States v. Mazurie (1975)

Martin and Margaret Mazurie were given a state license to sell alcoholic beverages on private lands within the Wind River Reservation in central Wyoming. The Wind River tribes then passed an ordinance requiring a tribal license to sell alcoholic beverages. The Mazuries were turned down for a tribal license, but they opened up their tavern soon afterward anyway. Lower federal courts overturned the tribal laws, but in *United States v. Mazurie 419 U.S. 544* (1975), the U.S. Supreme Court reversed the lower court's ruling and upheld the tribal ordinance. **See also** Sovereignty; Tribal Government.

BIBLIOGRAPHY

Cohen, Felix S. *Felix Cohen's Handbook of Federal Indian Law.* Charlottesville, VA: Mitchie, Bobbs-Merrill, 1982; Ft. Lauderdale, FL: Five Rings Press, 1986.

Getches, David, Charles F. Wilkinson, and Robert A. Williams, Jr. *Cases and Materials of Federal Indian Law.* 3rd ed. St. Paul, MN: West Publishing, 1993.

Thompson, William N. *Native American Issues.* Santa Barbara, CA: ABC-CLIO, 1996.

United States v. McBratney (1881)

United States v. McBratney, 104 U.S. 621 (1881), is an important criminal law case dealing with the subject of states' rights in **Indian country.** Jack McBratney, a white man, had killed Thomas Casey, another white man, within the boundaries of the Ute Indian Reservation in Southern Colorado. McBratney was indicted and convicted in federal circuit court, which under prevailing law, had jurisdiction over non-Indian or interracial crimes transpiring on a reservation. McBratney appealed his conviction on the grounds that the federal court lacked jurisdiction. The question before the Supreme Court was simple: Did the federal government have jurisdiction over the crime of murder committed by non-Indians inside Indian country?

The Court held, contrary to prior case and statutory law, that when Colorado entered the Union on an "equal footing" with the other states, it implicitly acquired criminal jurisdiction over its own citizens throughout the entire territory even if the crime had taken place within an Indian reservation. **See also** Tribal–State Affairs. (DEW)

BIBLIOGRAPHY

Canby, William. *American Indian Law in a Nutshell.* St. Paul, MN: West Publishing, 1981.

United States v. Nice (1916)

United States v. Nice, 241 U.S. 591 (1916), focused on the citizenship rights of Indian allottees. Fred Nice, a white man, had been indicted for selling whisky to George Cartier, a Rosebud Sioux Indian. Cartier had previously received a land allotment that brought with it federal citizenship. The liquor transaction, nevertheless, was alleged to be a violation of a federal law that prohibited the sale of liquor to Indian allottees whose land was still held in trust by the federal government.

The question before the U.S. Supreme Court was whether Indian allottees remained under "national guardianship" so that Congress could still regulate liquor sales to them despite their U.S. citizenship. The Court held that even with federal citizenship the Indian allottee was still subject to congressional plenary power: "Citizenship is not incompatible with tribal existence or continued guardianship, and so may be conferred without completely emancipating the Indians or placing them beyond the reach of congressional regulations adopted for their protection." This case enshrined in federal Indian law the Indians' contradictory status as citizens and subjects. **See also** Allotment; Dawes Act of 1887; Guardianship; Trusteeship Responsibility. **See** Dawes Act (1887) in Appendix 1. (DEW)

BIBLIOGRAPHY

Wunder, John R., ed. *Recent Legal Issues for American Indians, 1968 to the Present.* New York: Garland Publishing, 1996.

United States v. Sandoval (1913)

The question before the U.S. Supreme Court in United States v. Sandoval, 231 U.S. 28 (1913), involved whether the Pueblo lands, which were owned under a land grant from the Spanish government, constituted "Indian country" over which congressional authority extended. The Court ruled that it was for Congress alone to determine when the guardianship it exercises over the Indians should cease. It further noted that mere possession of citizenship by Indians did not prevent Congress from enacting laws for the benefit and protection of tribal Indians. (AMM)

BIBLIOGRAPHY

Hoxie, Frederick. *A Final Promise: The Campaign to Assimilate the Indians, 1880–1920.* Lincoln: The University of Nebraska Press, 1984.

Meriam, Lewis. *The Problem of Indian Administration.* Baltimore, MD: John Hopkins University Press, 1928.

United States v. Sioux Nation of Indians (1980)

The Supreme Court's decision in *United States v. Sioux Nation of Indians,* 448 U.S. 371 (1980), was the outcome of a 1923 claim (representing the longest-running claim in United States history). The Court stated that the Sioux (Lakota) were improperly deprived of the **Black Hills**, a region they hold sacred, and the tribes was awarded $106 million. The Lakota have refused to accept the award, which (with interest) was worth $300 million by the early 1990s, even though they are among the poorest people in the United States. Instead, they have demanded the return of their land. **See also** Treaty of Fort Laramie (1868); Walk for Justice; Yellow Thunder Camp. (LCJ)

BIBLIOGRAPHY

Jaimes, M. Annette, ed. *The State of Native America: Genocide, Colonization, and Resistance.* Boston: South End Press, 1992.

Lazarus, Edward. *Black Hills, White Justice: The Sioux Nation versus the United States: 1775 to the Present.* New York: HarperCollins, 1991.

Mails, Thomas E. *Fools Crow.* Lincoln: University of Nebraska Press, 1979.

United States v. Washington (1974) and (1980)

Widely known as the "Boldt decision," *United States v. Washington,* 384 F. Supp. 312 (W.D. Wash. 1974), 506 F. Supp. 187 (W.D. Wash. 1980), marked a turning point in the Northwest Indian fishing rights controversy. In Phase I (1974), Judge George Boldt ruled that the treaty tribes' right to fish "in common" guaranteed them 50 percent of the harvestable salmon entering their "usual and accustomed places." Boldt also held that the Indians could regulate their share of the fishery, but anti-Indian hostility and state noncompliance obstructed his decision until the U.S. Supreme Court affirmed it in 1979. In Phase II (1980), Boldt's successor ruled that the treaty tribes had rights to hatchery fish and to protection of the salmon from habitat destruction. Although other problems remain unresolved, *United States v. Washington* set a standard for allocation and revived the Indian fishing economy. **See also** Ramona Bennet; Fishing and Hunting Treaty Rights. (AHF)

BIBLIOGRAPHY

Bentley, Shannon. "Indians' Right to Fish: The Background, Impact, and Legacy of *United States v. Washington.*" *American Indian Law Review* 17 (1992): 1–35.

Cohen, Fay G. *Treaties on Trial: The Continuing Controversy over Northwest Indian Fishing Rights.* Seattle: University of Washington Press, 1986.

United States v. Wheeler (1978)

Anthony Wheeler, a Native American, pleaded guilty in a tribal court to disorderly conduct and contributing to the delinquency of a minor. He was convicted, but federal charges were brought about later for rape. The rape charges stemmed from the same incident Wheeler had already been convicted for. In *United States v. Wheeler,* 435 U.S. 313 (1978), the U.S. Supreme Court ruled that this double jeopardy was not prohibited by the Fifth Amendment of the U.S. Constitution, because tribal courts are not under the same jurisdiction as the federal courts. **See also** Tribal Legal System.

BIBLIOGRAPHY

Cohen, Felix S. *Felix Cohen's Handbook of Federal Indian Law.* Charlottesville, VA: Mitchie, Bobbs-Merrill, 1982; Ft. Lauderdale, FL: Five Rings Press, 1986.

Getches, David, Charles F. Wilkinson, and Robert A. Williams, Jr. *Cases and Materials of Federal Indian Law.* 3rd ed. St. Paul, MN: West Publishing, 1993.

Thompson, William N. *Native American Issues.* Santa Barbara, CA: ABC-CLIO, 1996.

United States v. Winans (1905)

The first of seven fishing rights cases to reach the U.S. Supreme Court, *United States v. Winans,* 198 U.S. 371 (1905), upheld the treaty rights of Northwest Indians to fish at their "usual and accustomed places." Although the decision failed to foreclose state regulation of that right, it did establish two significant principles governing treaty interpretation. The first states that a treaty must be construed as the Indians would have understood it and "as justice and reason demand." The second, known as the reserved rights doctrine, holds that treaties are "not a grant of right to the Indians but a reservation by the Indians of rights already possessed and not granted away by them. (AHF)

BIBLIOGRAPHY

Cohen, Fay G. *Treaties on Trial: The Continuing Controversy over Northwest Indian Fishing Rights.* Seattle: University of Washington Press, 1986.

Cohen, Felix S. *Handbook of Federal Indian Law* [1942]. Reprint: Albuquerque: University of New Mexico Press, 1958.

United States v. Winnebago Tribe of Nebraska (1976)

The Eighth Circuit Federal Appeals Court ruled in *United States v. Winnebago Tribe of Nebraska*, 542 F. 2d 1002 (1976), that Congress had the right to abrogate the terms of a treaty and take land under the right of eminent domain. However, in this case no clear evidence of congressional intent was presented; therefore, the court ruled that the Army Corps of Engineers was without authority when it sought to take tribal lands. (AMM)

BIBLIOGRAPHY

Wunder, John R., ed. *Recent Legal Issues for American Indians, 1968 to the Present.* New York: Garland Publishing, 1996.

Ute War (1879)

The Ute War, also known as the Meeker Massacre, was the result of growing tensions between the Utes and white settlers who had come to Colorado because of silver strikes in the 1870s. Throughout the 1870s, the Utes were convinced and coerced into selling additional land to the settlers who were still flooding into the White River region. With the growing loss of territory and the federal government's Indian agent for the region, Nathan C. Meeker, calling upon the Indians to convert into an agricultural tribe, trust between the two sides deteriorated.

Fearing the possibility of attack, Meeker sent several messages to the U.S. army to send troops to protect settlers. Troops arrived under the command of Major Thomas Thornburg who tried to assure the Utes that the troops were there merely to keep peace. However, when the troops tried to position themselves closer to Ute territory, the Indians attacked. At the battle of Milk Creek Canyon, Thornburg was killed and his troops routed. The Utes went on to attack the Indian agency, killing Meeker and nine other employees. Meeker's wife, children, and another woman were taken captive.

As troops gathered in order to stage a full-scale assault on the Utes, the Ute chief **Ouray** and former Ute Indian agent Charles Adams negotiated a settlement that prevented further violence and obtained the release of the white prisoners.

BIBLIOGRAPHY

Sprague, Marshall. *Massacre: The Tragedy of White River.* Boston: Little Brown, 1957.

Vanishing Americans

The concept of "vanishing Americans" was popularized in Euro-American culture before manifest destiny was championed by the founding fathers. American poet Philip Freneau popularized the image of the dying savage in his book of poems entitled "Death Songs"; the Indian Drama fad of the nineteenth century also added to the notion that Native Americans were simply disappearing with such titles as "Metamora; or, the Last of the Wampanoags"; James Fenimore Cooper's *Last of the Mohicans* again emphasized that Indians were a dying race. This notion was certainly supported and perpetuated by politicians who pushed for **Indian removal** and manifest destiny. In the twentieth century, the theme of the vanishing American persists with films about Indians that portray them as living in the nineteenth century, not the twentieth. As Raymond Steadman contends in *Shadows of the Indian*, the invented Indian models in mainstream politics, literature, and film definitely point to the notion that Native Americans are something of the past. (MKJ)

BIBLIOGRAPHY

Steadman, Raymond William. *Shadows of the Indian: Stereotypes in American Culture*. Norman: University of Oklahoma Press, 1982.

Victorio (d. 1880)

Predecessor of **Geronimo**, the Mimbreno Apache warrior Victorio led a group of no more than 50 disgruntled Apaches in raids, beginning in 1874, against settlements and ranches throughout the Southwest. Respected by his fellow Apaches, he served under **Mangas Coloradas**. Six years later he was killed in northern Mexico by Mexican troops. (KJB)

BIBLIOGRAPHY

Ball, Eve. *In the Days of Victorio: Recollections of a Warm Springs Apache*. Narrated by James Kaywayka. Tucson: University of Arizona Press, 1970.

Walk for Justice

The Walk for Justice was a march led by **Dennis Banks** and Mary Jane Wilson-Medrano of the **American Indian Movement** (AIM). The march began at Alcatraz on February 11, 1994, and ended in Washington, D.C., on July 15, 1994. The group demanded clemency for **Leonard Peltier** (an imprisoned AIM leader), an end to police brutality toward Native Americans, and the return of the **Black Hills** to the Sioux. They also protested the construction of the James Bay Great Whale Project, which threatened the Cree and Ojibway fishing rights, and opposed the government's attempts to settle the Navajo–Hopi land dispute. **See also** *United States v. Sioux Nation of Indians* (1980).

BIBLIOGRAPHY

Champagne, Duane, ed. *Chronology of Native North American History*. Detroit: Gale, 1994.

War for the Bozeman Trail

The Bozeman Trail connected the Oregon Trail to gold fields near Bozeman, Montana. In the War for the Bozeman Trail (1865–1868), the Lakota (Sioux), Cheyenne, and Arapaho forced the United States to abandon its forts in the Powder River country of what is now eastern Wyoming. The war ended with the **Treaty of Fort Laramie**, one of the few treaties that has resulted from a U.S. military defeat. **See also** Plains Wars. (LCJ)

BIBLIOGRAPHY

Brown, Dee. *Bury My Heart at Wounded Knee: An Indian History of the American West*. New York: Holt, Rinehart & Winston, 1970.
Ortiz, Roxanne Dunbar. *The Great Sioux Nation*. San Francisco/Berkeley: International Indian Treaty Council/Moon Books, 1977.

War of 1812

Urged on by Shawnee-Creek brothers **Tecumseh** and the Prophet, who were committed to the expulsion of Anglo-Americans from tribal lands, Native Americans in the Northwest Territory began uniting to reclaim their dignity and their land. Tecumseh spoke with representatives of the Choctaws, Chickasaws, Creeks, and Cherokees, yet only one faction of Creeks joined his movement. Territorial governor William Henry Harrison, determined to destroy the emerging pan-Indian movement, sent troops into the movement's homebase of Prophetstown. In retaliation for this move, the Indians sought revenge and outbreaks of violence erupted over all regions of colonial America. The new United States government believed that Great Britain was instigating and supplying arms for these Native American uprisings and was forced to declare war on Great Britain. Leaders of the Southern tribes (Cherokees, Creeks, Seminoles, Choctaws, Chickasaws) supported the Americans in their fight with Great Britain. When the war ended in 1814, however, their "reward" for loyal service was the expectation by the United States that these tribes would surrender their lands and exile themselves west of the Mississippi River. (KJB)

BIBLIOGRAPHY

Hickey, Donald R. *The War of 1812*. Urbana: University of Illinois Press, 1985.
Nevin, David. *1812*. New York: Forge, 1996.

Nancy Ward (ca. 1738–1824)

A Cherokee "Beloved Woman," Nancy Ward (Nanye'hi) promoted peace between Cherokees and their white neighbors. When white settlers continued to ignore the Royal Proclamation of 1763, she sought to negotiate a settlement that would enable her people to stay in their eastern lands. However, she came to the belief that her people would have to fight to maintain their lands. She nurtured Cherokee orphans and advised the Cherokee Council to avoid land cessions. With her second husband, a trader named Bryant Ward, she had one child, Elizabeth, who married Indian agent Joseph Martin. (GO)

BIBLIOGRAPHY

McClary, Ben Harris. "Nancy Ward: The Last Beloved Woman of the Cherokees." *Tennessee Historical Quarterly* 21(1962): 352–64.
Tucker, Norma. "Nancy Ward, Ghighau of the Cherokees." *Georgia Historical Quarterly* 53 (1969): 192–99.

Warren Trading Post v. Arizona Tax Commission (1965)

Warren owned a store on a Navajo reservation in Arizona, even though he was not a Native American. The state of Arizona levied its 2 percent sales tax on the gross income of the store. The Arizona Supreme Court upheld the levy, but in *Warren Trading Post v. Arizona Tax Commission,* 380 U.S. 685 (1965), the U.S. Supreme Court nullified the tax. The Court argued that Congress had placed itself into a "sole power" position in regulating trade with the Native Americans. **See also** Taxation.

BIBLIOGRAPHY

Cohen, Felix S. *Felix Cohen's Handbook of Federal Indian Law.* Charlottesville, VA: Mitchie, Bobbs-Merrill, 1982; Ft. Lauderdale, FL: Five Rings Press, 1986.

Getches, David, Charles F. Wilkinson, and Robert A. Williams, Jr. *Cases and Materials of Federal Indian Law.* 3rd ed. St. Paul, MN: West Publishing, 1993.

Thompson, William N. *Native American Issues.* Santa Barbara, CA: ABC-CLIO, 1996.

Washakie (ca. 1804–1900)

Washakie, son of a Umatilla father and a Shoshone mother, lived with the Umatilla, the Shoshone, and the Bannock, before settling with the Eastern band (Washakie's band) of the Shoshone. Chief Washakie recognized the benefits—trade goods, protection, and survival—that could be gained by befriending the Oregon, California, and Mormon immigrants. On July 4, 1868, Washakie made his mark on the Fort Bridger Treaty and moved his people to the Wind River Reservation in Wyoming, where he was appointed a scout for the U.S. army. In 1876, President Ulysses S. Grant honored Washakie for his friendship to the travellers of the Oregon Trail. (AMM)

BIBLIOGRAPHY

Hebard, Grace Raymond. *Washakie: Chief of the Shoshones.* Lincoln: University of Nebraska Press, 1996.

Stand Watie (1806–1871)

Stand Watie, born in the state of Georgia, was one of the many Cherokee Indians who were forced to move from the state. A signer of the **Treaty of New Echota** (1835) that acquiesced to removal, he avoided retaliation for his part in the treaty. In the new territory he became one of the leaders of the anti-**John Ross** group. When hostilities broke out between the North and South in the **Civil War**, Stand Watie served the Confederacy and rose to the rank of Brigadier General. He became the last Confederate General to surrender on June 23, 1865. **See also** Five Civilized Tribes.

BIBLIOGRAPHY

Francis, Kenny A. *Stand Watie and the Agony of the Cherokee Nation.* Memphis: Memphis State University Press, 1979.

Annie Dodge Wauneka (1920–1997)

A Navajo advocate for public health, sanitation, and nutrition, Annie Dodge Wauneka, daughter of Chee Dodge, became in 1951 the second woman elected to the Navajo Tribal Council. As chairman of the Council's Health and Welfare Committee, she led a campaign that halved tuberculosis death rates in seven years. Ms. Wauneka was a mentor to a number of prominent Navajo women and received numerous awards and honors including the Presidential Medal of Freedom (1963). (JN)

BIBLIOGRAPHY

Johnson, Broderick H. and Virginia Hoffman. *Navajo Biographies.* Rough Rock, AZ: Navajo Curriculum Center, Rough Rock Demonstration School, 1978.

Nelson, Mary Carroll. *Annie Wauneka: The Story of an American Indian.* Minneapolis, MN: Dillion Press, 1972.

White House Conference on Indian Problems

Over the years, many Native American leaders have traveled to Washington, D.C., to negotiate with White House officials. The largest such event took place in 1994, when President Bill Clinton invited the leaders of all Native American nations within the United States to convene at the White House. Native leaders representing 250 tribes attended. At the conference and follow-up events, Native Americans urged federal officials to recognize Indian treaty rights and deal with tribes on a government-to-government basis. (LCJ)

BIBLIOGRAPHY

Rawls, James J. *Chief Red Fox Is Dead: A History of Native Americans Since 1945.* New York: Harcourt Brace, 1996.

White Man's Burden

The term White Man's Burden was coined by English author Rudyard Kipling in 1899 to refer to the obligation that he felt the more-civilized Western cultures owed to the more barbaric culture of India. The concept has generally been applied to the theory that white men have a duty to manage the affairs of nonwhite people. The concept embraces racial discrimination, imperialistic tendencies, and general prejudice.

While the term can be applied to almost any nonwhite group and has historically been applied to both African Americans and Native Americans, the latter have suffered under its precepts, perhaps more than any other minority group in American politics. Throughout the history of Native-American–white-American relations, the government of the United States had pursued policies such as **guardianship**—which declared Native Americans unfit to manage their own lands, resources, and money—and assimilation—which declared that Native American culture was inferior to white culture and should be driven out of subsequent generations. Even to this day, the **Bureau of Indian Affairs** controls some tribal lands and funds for the "benefit" of the Indian.

In the end, the white man's burden syndrome is simply a form of racism masquerading as good intentions. The result has been the deterioration of Native American culture and a struggle to recapture value in Native American history. **See also** Assimilationist Policy.

BIBLIOGRAPHY

Burgess, Harry E. *God Before the White Man Came.* Chicago: H.E. Burgess, 1916.

Prucha, Francis Paul. *The Great Father.* Lincoln: University of Nebraska Press, 1984.

———. *The Indians in American Society.* Berkeley: University of California, 1985.

White Men and Indian Women Marriage Act (1888)

This federal legislation regulated the rights of both the man and women of an interracial marriage. Specifically, the act prevented the man from obtaining any tribal rights, including rights to protected property, with the exception of the Five Civilized Tribes. The act also allowed the woman to become a U.S. citizen. The act prevented men from marrying Indian women with the sole purpose of obtaining the special status that Indians had under the law. Moreover, it prevented the taking of land by white men under the ruse of marriage. The Indian woman, however, would maintain her rights to property under **allotment**.

BIBLIOGRAPHY

Cohen, Felix S. *Felix Cohen's Handbook of Federal Indian Law.* Charlottesville, VA: Mitchie, Bobbs-Merrill, 1982; Ft. Lauderdale, FL: Five Rings Press, 1986.

Williams v. Lee (1959)

Williams v. Lee, 358 U.S. 217 (1959), signaled the beginning of a new era of tribal sovereignty and self-determination in federal Indian policy. Lee, a non-Indian, brought suit in Arizona courts against a Navajo couple for goods sold on credit at a general store, operated by Lee, on the Navajo reservation. Arizona claimed civil jurisdiction over the matter, because there was no federal law to the contrary. Citing John Marshall's decision in *Worcester v. Georgia* (1832), the U.S. Supreme Court ruled that the tribal courts had exclusive jurisdiction over tribal affairs, including suits by non-Indians against tribal members. The Court enunciated the "infringement doctrine," which provided that states could not infringe upon the right of tribes to govern themselves. (AMM)

BIBLIOGRAPHY

Burke, Joseph C. "The Cherokee Cases: A Study in Law, Politics, and Morality." *Stanford Law Review* 21 (1969): 500–31.
Williams, Robert A. *The American Indian in Western Legal Thought: The Discourses of Conquest.* Oxford, England and New York: Oxford University Press, 1990.

Jack Wilson. *See* Wovoka of the Paiute

Winnebago Treaties

There are several treaties with the Winnebago tribe. The first was the treaty of 1816, which separated the clans living on the Wisconsin River from the remaining Winnebagos. In the treaty of 1837 the tribe signed away the Winnebago's remaining homeland in Wisconsin. Almost immediately the Indians claimed that this particular treaty was unfair to the Winnebago tribe because those who signed the treaty could not read, and they therefore did not know that they were signing away their rights to their land. (MW)

BIBLIOGRAPHY

Prucha, Francis Paul. *American Indian Treaties.* Berkeley: University of California Press, 1994.

Sarah Hopkins Winnemucca (1844–1891)

Sarah Hopkins Winnemucca, a Paiute Indian, was born in present-day Nevada. She lived through the Paiute War of 1860, as well as two forced removals to temporary reservations in Oregon and Washington before her tribe was allowed to return to Nevada. Losing most of her family to violence, she became an outspoken, nationally known critic of the reservation system. Winnemucca published her memoirs, titled *Life among the Paiutes*, in 1883. (RAC)

BIBLIOGRAPHY

Canfield, Gae Whitney. *Sarah Winnemucca of the Northern Paiutes.* Norman: University of Oklahoma Press, 1983.

Winters v. United States (1908)

A landmark decision in the history of Indian water rights, *Winters v. United States,* 207 U.S. 564 (1908), set important precedents that still govern state-tribal litigation. The federal government brought the case against Montana farmers to prevent them from diverting so much water from the Milk River that Indians at the downstream Fort Belknap reservation had insufficient water even for subsistence agriculture. In 1908 the U.S. Supreme Court ruled in favor of the tribe and established the "Winters doctrine" of reserved rights.

This doctrine rests on several principles. First, when the federal government created Indian reservations, it implicitly and perpetually reserved for tribal use enough previously unclaimed water to meet the purposes for which the reservation was established. Second, in accordance with the prior appropriation doctrine, the date of a reservation's creation would be considered the date on which the tribe had implicitly reserved its water. Third, tribes could turn the water to any use that fulfilled the reservation's purposes. Fourth, a tribe's water rights could not be lost through nonuse, as dictated under the prior appropriation system. The Court's decision represented a major victory for the Indians. Although the federal government did not aggressively assert the Winters doctrine during the first half of the twentieth century, the ruling affirmed the tribes' senior water rights in most states and set the stage for future legal disputes over the quantification of tribal water allotments. **See also** *Arizona v. California* (1963); Land and Water Rights. (AHF)

BIBLIOGRAPHY

Burton, Lloyd. *American Indian Water Rights and the Limits of Law.* Lawrence: University of Kansas Press, 1991.
McCool, Daniel. *Command of the Waters: Iron Triangles, Federal Water Development, and Indian Water.* Berkeley: University of California Press, 1987.
McGuire, Thomas R., William B. Lord, and Mary G. Wallace, eds. *Indian Water in the New West.* Tucson: University of Arizona Press, 1993.

Shirley Hill Witt (1934–)

Shirley Hill Witt (Katherine Thundercloud), Mohawk, an anthropologist, author, and Indian activist, was born in Whittier, California. Witt represented the Mohawks at the American Indian Chicago Conference in 1961 and was one of the founding members of the **National Indian Youth Council** (NIYC), serving as one of its first vice-presidents. She received a doctorate in anthropology from the University of New Mexico and taught at the University of North Carolina and Colorado College. In 1981 she became director of the Rocky Mountain Regional office of the U.S. Commission on Civil Rights. In 1983 she was appointed by New Mexico governor Toney Anaya as secretary of natural resources, a post she held less than one year. She returned to academics and her research on anthropological theories to social problems. (MRC)

BIBLIOGRAPHY
W.H. Shirley Hill. *The Tuscanonas*. New York: Crowell Collier, 1972.
Green, Rayna, ed. *That's What She Said*. Bloomington: Indiana University Press, 1983.

Laura Waterman Wittstock (1937–)

Laura Waterman Wittstock (Seneca), a journalist, writer, and political activist for American Indian peoples, has worked on causes such as women's advocacy and alcoholism. She has developed a radio service that presents programs on native peoples, and she has been the director of the American Indian Press Association. (MR)

BIBLIOGRAPHY
Anderson, Owanah, ed. *Ohoyo One Thousand: A Resource Guide to American Indian/Alaska Native Women, 1982*. Wichita Falls, TX: Ohoyo Resource Center, 1982.

Wodziwob

Wodziwob was a shaman of the Paiute tribe. He predicted in the early 1870s that the Indian people across the country would soon experience great upheavals caused by the settlers' destruction of the animals that the Indians had depended on for food and clothing. Wodziwob was correct in his prediction of the great changes that cost his people and other tribes their traditional hunting and gathering grounds. (MW)

BIBLIOGRAPHY
Overholt, Thomas. *Channels of Prophecy*. Minneapolis, MN: Fortress Press, 1989.

Women of All Red Nations

Women of All Red Nations (WARN) was founded by Lorelei Means and Madonna Gilbert on the Pine Ridge Reservation. WARN has documented the effects of environmental contamination on Indian lands; their 1980 report indicated disproportionately high rates of cleft palates, bone cancer, and miscarriage on the reservations. WARN denounced the so-called voluntary sterilization projects of the federal government, in which Indian women were denied full information about the procedure, or the opportunity to consent to or decline the surgery. (RAC)

BIBLIOGRAPHY
Women of All Red Nations. "Radiation: Dangerous to Pine Ridge Women." *Akwesane Notes* (Spring 1980).
Jaimes, M. Annette and Theresa Halsey. "American Indian Women: At the Center of Indigenous Resistance in North America." In M. Annette Jaimes, ed. *The State of Native America: Genocide, Colonization, and Resistance*. Boston: South End Press, 1992.

Women's National Indian Association

The Women's National Indian Association is one of the earliest Native American organizations. It was founded in 1879 by Mary L. Bonney and Amelia S. Quinton. The purpose of this organization, whose membership was largely drawn from Protestant churchwomen, was to foster the keeping of treaties, to promote **education** among the Indians, and to establish missionary and social welfare activities involving the Indians on the **reservations**. The organization also lobbied extensively for the adoption of the **Dawes Act of 1887** (the General Allotment Act). For more than 100 years, the members of this association have campaigned to arouse public opinion in favor of the Indians and to influence congressional decisions on major reforms involving Indians. **See also** National Indian Association. (MW)

BIBLIOGRAPHY
Wanken, Helen M. *Women's Sphere and Indian Reform*. Ann Arbor, MI: University Microfilms, 1997.
Women's National Indian Association. *The Indian's Friend*. Philadelphia: The Association, 1888–1951.

Worcester v. Georgia (1832)

Worcester v. Georgia, 6 Pet. 515 (1832), was third in the so-called "Marshall trilogy" of cases that define the foundation of federal Indian law; the other cases in the trilogy were ***Cherokee Nation v. Georgia* (1831)** and ***Johnson v. McIntosh* (1823)**. The United States Supreme Court, under Chief Justice John Marshall, laid down the rule in *Worcester* that the "whole intercourse" between the indigenous nations and the United States is "vested in the government of the United States," and that state laws "can have no force" in **Indian country.** The principle of federal "plenary power" became a cornerstone of federal Indian law. Exceptions—explained as exercises of federal power—have been created by Congress and courts, but the federal government continues to claim "plenary power" in regard to native peoples.

Samuel Worcester, a Christian missionary from Vermont working among the Cherokee as part of a federally approved effort to "civilize the Indians," was arrested and convicted under a state law excluding non-Cherokee persons from Cherokee territory within the state of Georgia without permission from the state, and sentenced to four years at hard labor.

The Supreme Court reversed Worcester's conviction, on grounds that his presence in Cherokee country was not a matter for state law to determine or interfere in. The Court held that Georgia would have to respect Cherokee self-government until such time as the federal government terminated Cherokee rights, which were protected by federal law in a treaty. President Andrew Jackson, a states' rights supporter, refused to enforce the Court's decision and is reputed to have said, "John Marshall has made his decision. Now let him enforce it." **See also** Federal Indian Policy; Sovereignty; Tribal–State Affairs; Land and Water Rights; *Williams v. Lee* (1959). (PPE)

BIBLIOGRAPHY

Filler, Louis and Allen Guttmann. *The Removal of the Cherokee Nation*. Boston: D.C. Heath, 1962.

Norgren, Jill. *The Cherokee Cases: The Confrontation of Law and Politics*. New York: McGraw-Hill, 1996.

Rosita Worl (1950–)

Rosita Worl is an Alaskan native who has been active in native rights issues on a variety of fronts. In 1977, she chaired the Alaska Native Women's Statewide Caucus and was a delegate to the International Women's Year Conference. During the 1980s, she founded, published, and edited the *Alaska Native News*, and she worked as a special assistant for native affairs for governor Steve Cowper. She has also served as chairperson of the Tlingit and Haida Central Council Business and Economic Development Council.

BIBLIOGRAPHY

Berger, Thomas R. *Village Journey*. New York: Hill and Wang, 1985.

Wounded Knee (1890)

On December 29, 1890, near Wounded Knee Creek on the Pine Ridge Reservation in South Dakota, Mnikowoju Lakotas under **Big Foot** (Si Tanka) who had adopted the Ghost Dance suffered heavy casualties (death toll estimates range from 146 to 300 or more) in a confrontation with the Seventh Cavalry under Colonel James Forsyth, which suffered 25 killed and 39 wounded. The encounter, commonly known as the Wounded Knee Massacre, apparently resulted from a shot fired during a scuffle between cavalrymen and a Mnikowoju who refused to relinquish his rifle as the soldiers disarmed Big Foot's band. The resulting melee lasted several hours and saw

The frozen dead at wounded Knee in 1890. *National Archives.*

the cavalry chase Mnikowojus miles from the scene and kill at least 44 women and 18 children. Wounded Knee marked the tragic climax of the Ghost Dance hysteria that had swept South Dakota during 1890. Reservation officials and white neighbors feared Lakota Ghost Dancers were preparing for war and asked for protection from the U.S. Army. In its effort to stamp out the Ghost Dance, part of the United States' nineteenth-century campaign to eradicate Indian religions and replace them with Christianity, the Army ordered the arrest of Ghost Dance leaders such as **Sitting Bull** (Tatanka Iyotake) and Big Foot, whose bands held large numbers of Ghost Dancers. Indian police killed Sitting Bull while arresting him, which led Big Foot to flee for Pine Ridge, where he intended to surrender. The Seventh Cavalry caught Big Foot's band at Wounded Knee Creek, where the massacre took place. Big Foot was among those killed. Wounded Knee revealed the brutality and weaknesses of U.S. Indian policy; many historians use it to signify the end of the **Plains Wars. See also** Ghost Dance Movement. **See** "You Are Living in a New Path" by Sitting Bull (1880) in Appendix 1. (TMK)

BIBLIOGRAPHY

Brown, Dee. *Bury My Heart at Wounded Knee: An Indian History of the American West*. New York: Henry Holt and Company, 1970.

Jensen, Richard E., Eli R. Paul, and John E. Carter. *Eyewitness at Wounded Knee*. Lincoln: University of Nebraska Press, 1991.

Utley, Robert M. *The Last Days of the Sioux Nation*. New Haven, CT: Yale University Press, 1963.

Wounded Knee II

In 1973 the **American Indian Movement (AIM)** occupied **Wounded Knee**, a small village on the Pine Ridge Reservation, and were encircled by heavily armed federal forces. Gunfire was exchanged between the sides throughout the 71-day siege, which lasted from February 28 to May 10, 1973. The name Wounded Knee II recalls the massacre that took place in the same location during December 1890 when the traditional leader **Big Foot** and his small Lakota band, disarmed and surrounded, were slaughtered by the Seventh Cavalry of the United States Army. Wounded Knee II took place shortly after the **Trail of Broken Treaties** and was partly a response to a governmental refusal to deal seriously with issues concerning treaty rights, including Indian nations' sovereignty. On the Pine Ridge Reservation, the people were divided between supporters of AIM and supporters of the tribal council. Hearings AIM held on the reservation developed into an occupation, which was supported by the presence of revered Indian elders as well as by representatives of the National Council of Churches. The siege in 1973 was the first sustained modern protest by aboriginal peoples against a Western state system and marked a historic watershed in the relations of American Indians and the American government. Wounded Knee II attracted tremendous press attention and gave AIM international recognition. It provided American Indians with a renewed sense of pride and re-introduced an image of the brave Indian warrior. The impasse ended with a negotiated settlement in which both sides withdrew. (MS)

BIBLIOGRAPHY

Deloria, Vine, Jr. *Behind the Trail of Broken Treaties*. University of Texas Press, 1974, 1991.

Dewing, Roland. *Wounded Knee: The Meaning of the Second Incident*. Irvington Publishers, 1985.

Wovoka of the Paiute (Jack Wilson) (ca. 1858–1932)

Founder of the 1890 **Ghost Dance Movement**, the prophet Wovoka, also known as Jack Wilson, received his first vision during a solar eclipse in 1889. Indians throughout the West journeyed to Nevada to hear his message of Indian renewal. Some two hundred Lakotas were massacred by the U.S. Army at **Wounded Knee** on December 29, 1890, for practicing a version of Wovoka's Ghost Dance. (GO)

BIBLIOGRAPHY

Hittman, Michael. *Wovoka and the Ghost Dance: A Sourcebook*. Carson City, NV: Grace Dangberg, 1990.

Mooney, James. *The Ghost Dance Religion and the Sioux Outbreak of 1890*. Chicago: University of Chicago Press, 1965.

Y

Yakima War (1855–1856)

The Yakima War was the result of growing tensions between Native Americans and an influx of gold prospectors into the north central part of what is today Washington State. The territorial governor, Isaac W. Stevens, tried to convince the tribes to move to new lands, but Chief Kamiakin refused to move. When his braves killed Indian Agent Andrew Bolom, widespread fighting erupted. The Second Walla Walla Council was called to end the war and the federal government decided to move the tribes. The Indians were forced by federal troops to give their unconditional surrender. **See also** Nez Perce War; Thief Treaty.

BIBLIOGRAPHY

Stern, Theodore. *Chiefs and Change in the Oregon Country.* Corvallis: Oregon State University Press, 1996.

Yamasee War (1715)

The Yamasee tribe consisted of settlements on the Atlantic coast from Cape Fear, North Carolina, to northern Florida. The Spanish sent missionaries to the Yamasee as early as 1570. In 1687 the Yamasee fled north from the Spanish and settled near Beaufort, South Carolina. They built several towns, the largest being Pocotaligo, where they traded with the English. Dissatisfaction with the traders led them to ally with other tribes in the area. War broke out, and many English and Yamasee were massacred. The Yamasee were finally defeated by South Carolina governor Charles Craven and driven back to Florida, where a small band resided with the Seminole as late as 1812. (AMM)

BIBLIOGRAPHY

Gilbert, William H. *Surviving Indian Groups of the Eastern United States.* Washington, DC: Smithsonian Institution, 1948.

Yellow Thunder Camp

Yellow Thunder Camp was established in April 1981 by **Russell C. Means** and his followers at Victoria Creek Canyon in the Black Hills of South Dakota. The camp was named in honor of Raymond Yellow Thunder, an Oglala Native American who was beaten, killed, and locked in the trunk of a car in Gordon, Nebraska, in 1972. The camp continues as a symbol of the unresolved **Black Hills** land dispute between the Sioux Indians (who refused a monetary settlement to end the dis-

pute) and the United States (which has admitted illegally taking the land of the Black Hills). Prior to establishing the camp, Means had occupied **Wounded Knee**, South Dakota, with 200 members of the **American Indian Movement** as a protest. **See also** *United States v. Sioux Nation of Indians* (1980); Wounded Knee II.

BIBLIOGRAPHY

Smith, Paul Chaat. *Like a Hurricane: The Indian Movement from Alcatraz to Wounded Knee.* New York: New Press, 1996.

Young Man Afraid of His Horses (Tashunkopipape) (ca. 1845–1893)

Young Man Afraid of His Horses was a prominent Oglala Lakota (Sioux) leader in the difficult years of transition from warfare to reservation life. He opposed selling the **Black Hills** to the United States, but worked with reservation agents to restore peace after the massacre at **Wounded Knee (1890)**. **See also** Treaty of Fort Laramie (1868). (LCJ)

BIBLIOGRAPHY

Price, Catherine. *The Oglala People, 1841–1879: A Political History.* Lincoln: University of Nebraska Press, 1996.

Sneve, Virginia Driving Hawk. *They Led a Nation.* Sioux Falls, SD: Brevet Press, 1975.

Young Man Afraid of his Horses (standing, second from right) is pictured with other chiefs and U.S. officials at Pine Ridge, South Dakota in 1891. William F. Cody (Buffalo Bill) is also pictured (standing, fourth from right). *Library of Congress.*

Z

Peterson Zah (1937–)

Peterson Zah (Navajo) served as tribal chairman of the Navajo Nation from 1983 to 1987. In 1989, he founded Native American Consulting Services to gain government assistance in constructing reservation schools, and he served as director of the western regional office of the Save the Children Foundation. In 1990, Zah was elected as the first president of the Navajo Nation, the largest tribe in the United States. Zah served two terms as president before becoming an advisor to the president of Arizona State University. He is still active and influential in tribal politics.

BIBLIOGRAPHY

Matthiessen, Peter. "Four Corners." In *Indian Country*. New York: Penguin, 1984.

Moses, L.G. and Raymond Wilson. *Indian Lives*. Albuquerque: University of New Mexico Press, 1993.

Appendixes

Speeches and Documents

1. The Constitution of the Iroquois Nations: The Great Binding Law, Gayanashagowa (ca. 1500)

(First Section)

1. I am Dekanawidah and with the Five Nations' Confederate Lords I plant the Tree of Great Peace. I plant it in your territory, Adodarhoh, and the Onondaga Nation, in the territory of you who are Firekeepers.

I name the tree the Tree of the Great Long Leaves. Under the shade of this Tree of the Great Peace we spread the soft white feathery down of the globe thistle as seats for you, Adodarhoh, and your cousin Lords.

We place you upon those seats, spread soft with the feathery down of the globe thistle, there beneath the shade of the spreading branches of the Tree of Peace. There shall you sit and watch the Council Fire of the Confederacy of the Five Nations, and all the affairs of the Five Nations shall be transacted at this place before you, Adodarhoh, and your cousin Lords, by the Confederate Lords of the Five Nations.

2. Roots have spread out from the Tree of the Great Peace, one to the north, one to the east, one to the south and one to the west. The name of these roots is The Great White Roots and their nature is Peace and Strength.

If any man or any nation outside the Five Nations shall obey the laws of the Great Peace and make known their disposition to the Lords of the Confederacy, they may trace the Roots to the Tree and if their minds are clean and they are obedient and promise to obey the wishes of the Confederate Council, they shall be welcomed to take shelter beneath the Tree of the Long Leaves.

We place at the top of the Tree of the Long Leaves an Eagle who is able to see afar. If he sees in the distance any evil approaching or any danger threatening he will at once warn the people of the Confederacy.

3. To you Adodarhoh, the Onondaga cousin Lords, I and the other Confederate Lords have entrusted the caretaking and the watching of the Five Nations Council Fire.

When there is any business to be transacted and the Confederate Council is not in session, a messenger shall be dispatched either to Adodarhoh, Hononwirehtonh or Skanawatih, Fire Keepers, or to their War Chiefs with a full statement of the case desired to be considered. Then shall Adodarhoh call his cousin (associate) Lords together and consider whether or not the case is of sufficient importance to demand the attention of the Confederate Council. If so, Adodarhoh shall dispatch messengers to summon all the Confederate Lords to assemble beneath the Tree of the Long Leaves.

When the Lords are assembled the Council Fire shall be kindled, but not with chestnut wood, and Adodarhoh shall formally open the Council.

Then shall Adodarhoh and his cousin Lords, the Fire Keepers, announce the subject for discussion.

The Smoke of the Confederate Council Fire shall ever ascend and pierce the sky so that other nations who may be allies may see the Council Fire of the Great Peace.

Adodarhoh and his cousin Lords are entrusted with the Keeping of the Council Fire.

4. You, Adodarhoh, and your thirteen cousin Lords, shall faithfully keep the space about the Council Fire clean and you shall allow neither dust nor dirt to accumulate. I lay a Long Wing before you as a broom. As a weapon against a crawling creature I lay a staff with you so that you may thrust it away from the Council Fire. If you fail to cast it out then call the rest of the United Lords to your aid.

5. The Council of the Mohawk shall be divided into three parties as follows: Tekarihoken, Ayonhwhathah and Shadekariwade are the first party; Sharenhowaneh, Deyoenhegwenh and Oghrenghrehgowah are the second party, and Dehennakrineh, Aghstawenserenthah and Shoskoharowaneh are the third party. The third party is to listen only to the discussion of the first and second parties and if an error is made or the proceeding is irregular they are to call attention to it, and when the case is right and properly decided by the two parties they shall confirm the decision of the two parties and refer the case to the Seneca Lords for their decision. When the Seneca Lords have decided in accord with the Mohawk Lords, the case or question shall be referred to the Cayuga and Oneida Lords on the opposite side of the house.

6. I, Dekanawidah, appoint the Mohawk Lords the heads and the leaders of the Five Nations Confederacy. The Mohawk Lords are the foundation of the Great Peace and it shall, therefore, be against the Great Binding Law to pass measures in the Confederate Council after the Mohawk Lords have protested against them.

No council of the Confederate Lords shall be legal unless all the Mohawk Lords are present.

7. Whenever the Confederate Lords shall assemble for the purpose of holding a council, the Onondaga Lords shall open it by expressing their gratitude to their cousin Lords and greeting them, and they shall make an address and offer thanks to the earth where men dwell, to the streams of water, the pools, the springs and the lakes, to the maize and the fruits, to the medicinal herbs and trees, to the forest trees for their usefulness, to the animals that serve as food and give their pelts for clothing, to the great winds and the lesser winds, to the Thunderers, to the Sun, the mighty warrior, to the moon, to the messengers of the Creator who reveal his wishes and to the Great Creator who dwells in the heavens above, who

gives all the things useful to men, and who is the source and the ruler of health and life.

Then shall the Onondaga Lords declare the council open.

The council shall not sit after darkness has set in.

8. The Firekeepers shall formally open and close all councils of the Confederate Lords, and they shall pass upon all matters deliberated upon by the two sides and render their decision.

Every Onondaga Lord (or his deputy) must be present at every Confederate Council and must agree with the majority without unwarrantable dissent, so that a unanimous decision may be rendered.

If Adodarhoh or any of his cousin Lords are absent from a Confederate Council, any other Firekeeper may open and close the Council, but the Firekeepers present may not give any decisions, unless the matter is of small importance.

9. All the business of the Five Nations Confederate Council shall be conducted by the two combined bodies of Confederate Lords. First the question shall be passed upon by the Mohawk and Seneca Lords, then it shall be discussed and passed by the Oneida and Cayuga Lords. Their decisions shall then be referred to the Onondaga Lords, (Fire Keepers) for final judgment.

The same process shall obtain when a question is brought before the council by an individual or a War Chief.

10. In all cases the procedure must be as follows: when the Mohawk and Seneca Lords have unanimously agreed upon a question, they shall report their decision to the Cayuga and Oneida Lords who shall deliberate upon the question and report a unanimous decision to the Mohawk Lords. The Mohawk Lords will then report the standing of the case to the Firekeepers, who shall render a decision as they see fit in case of a disagreement by the two bodies, or confirm the decisions of the two bodies if they are identical. The Fire Keepers shall then report their decision to the Mohawk Lords who shall announce it to the open council.

11. If through any misunderstanding or obstinacy on the part of the Fire Keepers, they render a decision at variance with that of the Two Sides, the Two Sides shall reconsider the matter and if their decisions are jointly the same as before they shall report to the Fire Keepers who are then compelled to confirm their joint decision.

12. When a case comes before the Onondaga Lords (Fire Keepers) for discussion and decision, Adodarho shall introduce the matter to his comrade Lords who shall then discuss it in their two bodies. Every Onondaga Lord except Hononwiretonh shall deliberate and he shall listen only. When a unanimous decision shall have been reached by the two bodies of Fire Keepers, Adodarho shall notify Hononwiretonh of the fact when he shall confirm it. He shall refuse to confirm a decision if it is not unanimously agreed upon by both sides of the Fire Keepers.

13. No Lord shall ask a question of the body of Confederate Lords when they are discussing a case, question or proposition. He may only deliberate in a low tone with the separate body of which he is a member.

14. When the Council of the Five Nation Lords shall convene they shall appoint a speaker for the day. He shall be a Lord of either the Mohawk, Onondaga or Seneca Nation.

The next day the Council shall appoint another speaker, but the first speaker may be reappointed if there is no objection, but a speaker's term shall not be regarded more than for the day.

15. No individual or foreign nation interested in a case, question or proposition shall have any voice in the Confederate Council except to answer a question put to him or them by the speaker for the Lords.

16. If the conditions which shall arise at any future time call for an addition to or change of this law, the case shall be carefully considered and if a new beam seems necessary or beneficial, the proposed change shall be voted upon and if adopted it shall be called, "Added to the Rafters."

Although this document was not set in written form until later, the tribal confederacy that it created was in existence before the coming of Europeans in the sixteenth century.

2. Treaty of Greenville (1795)

A treaty of peace between the United States of America, and the tribes of Indians called the Wyandots, Delawares, Shawanees, Ottawas, Chippewas, Pattawatimas, Miamis, Eel Rivers, Weas, Kickapoos, Piankeshaws, and Kaskaskias.

To put an end to a destructive war, to settle all controversies, and to restore harmony and friendly intercourse between the said United States and Indian tribes, Anthony Wayne, major general commanding the army of the United States, and sole commissioner for the good purposes above mentioned, and the said tribes of Indians, by their sachems, chiefs, and warriors, met together at Greenville, the head quarters of the said army, have agreed on the following articles, which, when ratified by the President, with the advice and consent of the Senate of the United States, shall be binding on them and the said Indian tribes.

Art. 1: Henceforth all hostilities shall cease; peace is hereby established, and shall be perpetual; and a friendly intercourse shall take place between the said United States and Indian tribes.

Art. 2: All prisoners shall, on both sides, be restored. The Indians, prisoners to the United States, shall be immediately set at liberty. The people of the United States, still remaining prisoners among the Indians, shall be delivered up in ninety days from the date hereof, to the general or commanding officer at Greenville, fort Wayne, or fort Defiance; and ten chiefs of the said tribes shall remain at Greenville as hostages, until the delivery of the prisoners shall be effected.

Art. 3: The general boundary line between the lands of the United States and the lands of the said Indian tribes, shall begin at the mouth of Cayahoga river, and run thence up the same to the portage, between that and the Tuscarawas branch of the Muskingum, thence down that branch to the crossing place above fort Lawrence, thence westerly to a fork of that branch of the Great Miami river, running into the Ohio, at or near which fork stood Loromie's store, and where commences the portage between the Miami of the Ohio, and St. Mary's river, which is a branch of the Miami which runs into lake Erie; thence a westerly course to fort Recovery, which stands on a branch of the Wabash; thence southwesterly in a direct line to the Ohio, so as to intersect that river opposite the mouth of Kentucke or Cuttawa river. And in consideration of the peace now established; of the goods formerly received from the United States; of those now to be delivered; and of the yearly delivery of goods now stipulated to be made hereafter; and to indemnify the United States for the injuries and expenses they have sustained during the war, the said

Indian tribes do hereby cede and relinquish forever, all their claims to the lands lying eastwardly and southwardly of the general boundary line now described: and these lands, or any part of them, shall never hereafter be made a cause or pretence, on the part of the said tribes, or any of them, of war or injury to the United States, or any of the people thereof.

And for the same considerations, and as an evidence of the returning friendship of the said Indian tribes, of their confidence in the United States, and desire to provide for their accommodations, and for that convenient intercourse which will be beneficial to both parties, the said Indian tribes do also cede to the United States the following pieces of land, to wit:

1) One piece of land six miles square, at or near Loromie's store, before mentioned.

2) One piece two miles square, at the head of the navigable water or landing, on the St. Mary's river, near Girty's town.

3) One piece six miles square, at the head of the navigable water of the Auglaize river.

4) One piece six miles square, at the confluence of the Auglaize and Miami rivers, where fort Defiance now stands.

5) One piece six miles square, at or near the confluence of the rivers St. Mary's and St. Joseph's, where fort Wayne now stands, or near it.

6) One piece two miles square, on the Wabash river, at the end of the portage from the Miami of the lake, and about eight miles westward from fort Wayne.

7) One piece six miles square, at the Ouatanon, or Old Wea towns, on the Wabash river.

8) One piece twelve miles square, at the British fort on the Miami of the lake, at the foot of the rapids.

9) One piece six miles square, at the mouth of the said river, where it empties into the lake.

10) One piece six miles square, upon Sandusky lake, where a fort formerly stood.

11) One piece two miles square, at the lower rapids of Sandusky river.

12) The post of Detroit, and all the land to the north, the west and the south of it, of which the Indian title has been extinguished by gifts or grants to the French or English governments: and so much more land to be annexed to the district of Detroit, as shall be comprehended between the river Rosine, on the south, lake St. Clair on the north, and a line, the general course whereof shall be six miles distant from the west end of lake Erie and Detroit river.

13) The post of Michilimackinac, and all the land on the island on which that post stands, and the main land adjacent, of which the Indian title has been extinguished by gifts or grants to the French or English governments; and a piece of land on the main to the north of the island, to measure six miles, on lake Huron, or the strait between lakes Huron and Michigan, and to extend three miles back from the water of the lake or strait; and also, the Island De Bois Blane, being an extra and voluntary gift of the Chippewa nation.

14) One piece of land six miles square, at the mouth of Chikago river, emptying into the southwest end of lake Michigan, where a fort formerly stood.

15) One piece twelve miles square, at or near the mouth of the Illinois river, emptying into the Mississippi.

16) One piece six miles square, at the old Piorias fort and village near the south end of the Illinois lake, on said Illinois river. And whenever the United States shall think proper to survey and mark the boundaries of the lands hereby ceded to them, they shall give timely notice thereof to the said tribes of Indians, that they may appoint some of their wise chiefs to attend and see that the lines are run according to the terms of this treaty.

And the said Indian tribes will allow to the people of the United States a free passage by land and by water, as one and the other shall be found convenient, through their country, along the chain of posts hereinbefore mentioned; that is to say, from the commencement of the portage aforesaid, at or near Loromie's store, thence along said portage to the St. Mary's, and down the same to fort Wayne, and then down the Miami, to lake Erie; again, from the commencement of the portage at or near Loromie's store along the portage from thence to the river Auglaize, and down the same to its junction with the Miami at fort Defiance; again, from the commencement of the portage aforesaid, to Sandusky river, and down the same to Sandusky bay and lake Erie, and from Sandusky to the post which shall be taken at or near the foot of the Rapids of the Miami of the lake; and from thence to Detroit. Again, from the mouth of Chikago, to the commencement of the portage, between that river and the Illinois, and down the Illinois river to the Mississippi; also, from fort Wayne, along the portage aforesaid, which leads to the Wabash, and then down the Wabash to the Ohio. And the said Indian tribes will also allow to the people of the United States, the free use of the harbors and mouths of rivers along the lakes adjoining the Indian lands, for sheltering vessels and boats, and liberty to land their cargoes where necessary for their safety.

Art. 4: In consideration of the peace now established, and of the cessions and relinquishments of lands made in the preceding article by the said tribes of Indians, and to manifest the liberality of the United States, as the great means of rendering this peace strong and perpetual, the United States relinquish their claims to all other Indian lands northward of the river Ohio, eastward of the Mississippi, and westward and southward of the Great Lakes and the waters, uniting them, according to the boundary line agreed on by the United States and the King of Great Britain, in the treaty of peace made between them in the year 1783. But from this relinquishment by the United States, the following tracts of land are explicitly excepted:

1st. The tract on one hundred and fifty thousand acres near the rapids of the river Ohio, which has been assigned to General Clark, for the use of himself and his warriors.

2nd. The post of St. Vincennes, on the River Wabash, and the lands adjacent, of which the Indian title has been extinguished.

3rd. The lands at all other places in possession of the French people and other white settlers among them, of which the Indian title has been extinguished as mentioned in the 3d article; and

4th. The post of fort Massac towards the mouth of the Ohio. To which several parcels of land so excepted, the said tribes relinquish all the title and claim which they or any of them may have.

And for the same considerations and with the same views as above mentioned, the United States now deliver to the said Indian tribes a quantity of goods to the value of twenty thousand dollars, the receipt whereof they do hereby acknowledge; and henceforward every year, forever, the United States will deliver, at some convenient place northward of the river Ohio, like useful goods, suited to the circumstances of the Indians, of the value of nine thousand five hundred dollars; reckoning that value at the first cost of the goods in the city or place in the United States where they shall be procured.

The tribes to which those goods are to be annually delivered, and the proportions in which they are to be delivered, are the following:

1st. To the Wyandots, the amount of one thousand dollars.

2nd. To the Delawares, the amount of one thousand dollars.

3rd. To the Shawanees, the amount of one thousand dollars.

4th. To the Miamis, the amount of one thousand dollars.

5th. To the Ottawas, the amount of one thousand dollars.

6th. To the Chippewas, the amount of one thousand dollars.

7th. To the Pattawatimas, the amount of one thousand dollars, and

8th. To the Kickapoo, Wea, Eel River, Piankeshaw, and Kaskaskia tribes, the amount of five hundred dollars each.

Provided, that if either of the said tribes shall hereafter, at an annual delivery of their share of the goods aforesaid, desire that a part of their annuity should be furnished in domestic animals, implements of husbandry, and other utensils convenient for them, and in compensation to useful artificers who may reside with or near them, and be employed for their benefit, the same shall, at the subsequent annual deliveries, be furnished accordingly.

Art. 5: To prevent any misunderstanding about the Indian lands relinquished by the United States in the fourth article, it is now explicitly declared, that the meaning of that relinquishment is this: the Indian tribes who have a right to those lands, are quietly to enjoy them, hunting, planting, and dwelling thereon, so long as they please, without any molestation from the United States; but when those tribes, or any of them, shall be disposed to sell their lands, or any part of them, they are to be sold only to the United States; and until such sale, the United States will protect all the said Indian tribes in the quiet enjoyment of their lands against all citizens of the United States, and against all other white persons who intrude upon the same. And the said Indian tribes again acknowledge themselves to be under the protection of the said United States, and no other power whatever.

Art. 6: If any citizen of the United States, or any other white person or persons, shall presume to settle upon the lands now relinquished by the United States, such citizen or other person shall be out of the protection of the United States; and the Indian tribe, on whose land the settlement shall be made, may drive off the settler, or punish him in such manner as they shall think fit; and because such settlements, made without the consent of the United States, will be injurious to them as well as to the Indians, the United States shall be at liberty to break them up, and remove and punish the settlers as they shall think proper, and so effect that protection of the Indian lands herein before stipulated.

Art. 7: The said tribes of Indians, parties to this treaty, shall be at liberty to hunt within the territory and lands which they have now ceded to the United States, without hindrance or molestation, so long as they demean themselves peaceably, and offer no injury to the people of the United States.

Art. 8: Trade shall be opened with the said Indian tribes; and they do hereby respectively engage to afford protection to such persons, with their property, as shall be duly licensed to reside among them for the purpose of trade; and to their agents and servants; but no person shall be permitted to reside among them for the purpose of trade; and to their agents and servants; but no person shall be permitted to reside at any of their towns or hunting camps, as a trader, who is not furnished with a license for that purpose, under the hand and seal of the superintendent of the department northwest of the Ohio, or such other person as the President of the United States shall authorize to grant such licenses; to the end, that the said Indians may not be imposed on in their trade. And if any licensed trader shall abuse his privilege by unfair dealing, upon complaint and proof thereof, his license shall be taken from him, and he shall be further punished according to the laws of the United States. And if any person shall intrude himself as a trader, without such license, the said Indians shall take and bring him before the superintendent, or his deputy, to be dealt with according to law. And to prevent impositions by forged licenses, the said Indians shall, at lease once a year, give information to the superintendent, or his deputies, on the names of the traders residing among them.

Art. 9: Lest the firm peace and friendship now established, should be interrupted by the misconduct of individuals, the United States, and the said Indian tribes agree, that for injuries done by individuals on either side, no private revenge or retaliation shall take place; but instead thereof, complaint shall be made by the party injured, to the other: by the said Indian tribes or any of them, to the President of the United States, or the superintendent by him appointed; and by the superintendent or other person appointed by the President, to the principal chiefs of the said Indian tribes, or of the tribe to which the offender belongs; and such prudent measures shall then be taken as shall be necessary to preserve the said peace and friendship unbroken, until the legislature (or great council) of the United States, shall make other equitable provision in the case, to the satisfaction of both parties. Should any Indian tribes meditate a war against the United States, or either of them, and the same shall come to the knowledge of the before mentioned tribes, or either of them, they do hereby engage to give immediate notice thereof to the general, or officer commanding the troops of the United States, at the nearest post.

And should any tribe, with hostile intentions against the United States, or either of them, attempt to pass through their country, they will endeavor to prevent the same, and in like manner give information of such attempt, to the general, or officer commanding, as soon as possible, that all causes of mistrust and suspicion may be avoided between them and the United States. In like manner, the United States shall give notice to the said Indian tribes of any harm that may be meditated against them, or either of them, that shall come to their knowledge; and do all in their power to hinder and prevent the same, that the friendship between them may be uninterrupted.

Art. 10: All other treaties heretofore made between the United States, and the said Indian tribes, or any of them, since the treaty of 1783, between the United States and Great Britain, that come within the purview of this treaty, shall henceforth cease and become void. In testimony whereof, the said Anthony Wayne, and the sachems and war chiefs of the before mentioned nations and tribes of Indians, have hereunto set their hands and affixed their seals. Done at Greenville, in the territory of the United States northwest of the river Ohio, on the third day of August, one thousand seven hundred and ninety five.

3. "Brother, the Great Spirit Has Made Us All" by Red Jacket (1805)

Friend and Brother! It was the will of the Great Spirit that we should meet together this day. He orders all things, and he has given us a fine day for our council. He has taken his garment from before the sun and has caused the bright orb to shine with brightness upon us. Our eyes are opened so that we see clearly. Our ears are unstopped so that we have been able to distinctly hear the words which you have spoken. For all these favors we thank the Great Spirit and him only.

Brother! This council fire was kindled by you. It was at your request that we came together at this time. We have listened with attention to what you have said. You have requested us to speak our minds freely. This gives us great joy, for we now consider that we stand upright before you, and can speak what we think. All have heard your voice and all speak to you as one man. Our minds are agreed.

Brother! You say that you want an answer to your talk before you leave this place. It is right that you should have one, as you are a great distance from home, and we do not wish to detain you. But we will first look back a little, and tell you what our fathers have told us, and what we have heard from the white people.

Brother! Listen to what we say. There was a time when our forefathers owned this great island (meaning the continent of North America—a common belief among the Indians). Their seats extended from the rising to the setting of the sun. The Great Spirit had made it for the use of Indians. He had created the buffalo, the deer, and other animals for food. He made the bear and the deer, and their skins served us for clothing. He had scattered them over the country, and had taught us how to take them. He had caused the earth to produce corn for bread. All this he had done for his red children because he loved them. If we had any disputes about hunting grounds, they were generally settled without the shedding of much blood. But an evil day came upon us. Your forefathers crossed the great waters and landed on this island. Their numbers were small. They found friends and not enemies. They told us they had fled from their own country for fear of wicked men, and had come here to enjoy their religion. They asked for a small seat. We took pity on them, granted their request and they sat down amongst us. We gave them corn and meat. They gave us poison (spiritous liquor) in return. The white people had now found our country. Tidings were carried back and more came amongst us. Yet we did not fear them. We took them to be friends. They called us brothers. We believed them and gave them a large seat. At length their numbers had greatly increased. They wanted more land. They wanted our country. Our eyes were opened, and our minds became uneasy. Wars took place. Indians were hired to fight against Indians, and many of our people were destroyed. They also brought strong liquors among us. It was strong and powerful and has slain thousands.

Brother! Our seats were once large, and yours were very small. You have now become a great people, and we have scarcely a place left to spread our blankets. You have got our country, but you are not satisfied. You want to force your religion upon us.

Brother! Continue to listen. You say that you are sent to instruct us how to worship the Great Spirit agreeably to his mind; and if we do not take hold of the religion which you white people teach we shall be unhappy hereafter. You say that you are right, and we are lost. How do you know this to be true? We understand that your religion is written in a book. If it was intended for us as well as for you, why has not the Great Spirit given it to us; and not only to us, but why did he not give our forefathers the knowledge of that book, with the means of understanding it rightly? We only know what you tell us about it. How shall we know when to believe, being so often deceived by the white people?

Brother! You say there is but one way to worship and serve the Great Spirit. If there is but one religion, why do you white people differ so much about it? Why not all agree, as you can all read the book?

Brother! We do not understand these things. We are told that your religion was given to your forefathers and has been handed down, father to son. We also have a religion which was given to our forefathers, and has been handed down to us, their children. We worship that way. It teaches us to be thankful for all the favors we received, to love each other, and to be united. We never quarrel about religion.

Brother! The Great Spirit has made us all. But he has made a great difference between his white and red children. He has given us a different complexion and different customs. To you he has given the arts; to these he has not opened our eyes. We know these things to be true. Since he has made so great a difference between us in other things, why may not we conclude that he has given us a different religion, according to our understanding? The Great Spirit does right. He knows what is best for his children. We are satisfied.

Brother! We do not wish to destroy your religion, or to take it from you. We only want to enjoy our own.

Brother! You say you have not come to get our land or our money, but to enlighten our minds. I will now tell you that I have been at your meetings and saw you collecting money from the meeting. I cannot tell what this money was intended for, but suppose it was for your minister; and if we should conform to your way of thinking, perhaps you may want some from us.

Brother! We are told that you have been preaching to the white people in this place. These people are our neighbors. We are acquainted with them. We will wait a little while, and see what effect your preaching has upon them. If we find it does them good and makes them honest and less disposed to cheat Indians, we will then consider again what you have said.

Brother! You have now heard our answer to your talk, and this is all we have to say at present. As we are going to part, we will come and take you by the hand, and hope the Great Spirit will protect you on your journey, and return you safe to your friends.

4. Farewell of Black Hawk (1832)

You have taken me prisoner, with all my warriors. I am much grieved; for I expected, if I did not defeat you, to hold out much longer, and give you more trouble before I surrendered. I tried hard to bring you into ambush, but your last general understood Indian fighting. I determined to rush upon you, and fight you face to face. I fought hard, but your guns were well aimed. The bullets flew like birds in the air, and whizzed by our ears like the wind through the trees in winter.

My warriors fell around me; it began to look dismal. I saw my evil day at hand. The sun rose dim on us in the morning, and at night it sank in a dark cloud, and looked like a ball of fire. That was the last sun that shone on Black Hawk. His heart is dead, and no longer beats quick in his bosom. He is now a prisoner to the white men; they will do with him as they wish. But he can stand torture, and is not afraid of death. He is no coward. Black Hawk is an Indian!

He has done nothing for which an Indian ought to be ashamed. He has fought for his countrymen, against the white men who came, year after year, to cheat them and take away their lands. You know the cause of our making war. It is known to all white men. They ought to be ashamed of it. The white men despise the Indians and drive them back from their homes. But the Indians are not deceitful. The white men speak bad of the Indian, and look at him spitefully. But the Indian does not tell lies. Indians do not steal. An Indian who is as bad as a white man could not live in our nation. He would be put to death and eaten by the wolves.

The white men are bad schoolmasters. They carry false looks and deal in false actions. They smile in the face of the poor Indian, to cheat him; they shake him by the hand to gain his confidence, to make him drunk, and to deceive him. We told them to let us alone, and keep away from us; but they followed on, and beset our paths, and they coiled themselves among us, like the snake. They poisoned us by their touch. We are not safe; we lived in danger. We were becoming like them, hypocrites and liars; all talkers and no workers.

We looked up to the Great Spirit. We went to our Father. We were encouraged. His great council gave us fair words and big promises; but we obtained no satisfaction. Things were growing worse. There were no deer in the forest. The opossum and the beaver were fled. The springs were drying up, and our people were without food to keep them from starving. We called a great council and built a big fire. The spirit of our fathers arose and spoke to us to avenge our wrongs or die. We set up the war whoop and dug up the tomahawk; our knives were ready, and the heart of Black Hawk swelled high in his bosom when he led his warriors to battle. He is satisfied. He will go to the world of spirits contented. He has done his duty. His father will meet him there and commend him. Black Hawk is a true Indian. He feels for his wife, his children, his friends, but he does not care for himself. He cares for the nation and for the Indians. They will suffer. He laments their fate.

The white men do not scalp the head, they do worse—they poison the heart. It is not pure with them. His countrymen will not be scalped, but will in a few years be like the white men, so you cannot trust them; and there must be in the white settlements as many officers as men, to take care of them and keep them in order.

Farewell, my nation! Black Hawk tried to save you, and avenge your wrongs. He drank the blood of some of the whites. He has been taken prisoner, and his plans are stopped. He can do no more! He is near his end. His sun is setting, and he will rise no more. Farewell to Black Hawk!

5. "The Indians' Night Promises to Be Dark" by Seattle (1854)

Yonder sky that has wept tears of compassion upon my people for centuries untold, and which to us appears changeless and eternal, may change. Today is fair. Tomorrow it may be overcast with clouds. My words are like the stars that never change. Whatever Seattle says the great chief at Washington can rely upon with as much certainty as he can upon the return of the sun or the seasons. The White Chief says that Big Chief at Washington sends us greetings of friendship and goodwill. This is kind of him for we know he has little need of our friendship in return. His people are many. They are like the grass that covers vast prairies. My people are few. They resemble the scattering trees of a storm-swept plain. The great—and I presume—good White Chief sends us word that he wishes to buy our lands but is willing to allow us enough to live comfortably. This indeed appears just, even generous, for the Red Man no longer has rights that he need respect, and the offer may be wise also, as we are no longer in need of an extensive country.

There was a time when our people covered the land as the waves of a wind-ruffled sea cover its shell paved floor, but that time long since passed away with the greatness of tribes that are now but a mournful memory. I will not dwell on, nor mourn over, our untimely decay, nor reproach my paleface brothers with hastening it as we too may have been somewhat to blame.

Youth is impulsive. When our young men grow angry at some real or imaginary wrong, and disfigure their faces with black paint, it denotes that their hearts are black, and that they are often cruel and relentless, and our old men and old women are unable to restrain them. Thus it has ever been. Thus it was when the white man first began to push our forefathers westward. But let us hope that the hostilities between us may never return. We would have everything to lose and nothing to gain. Revenge by young men is considered gain, even at the cost of their own lives, but old men who stay at home in times of war, and mothers who have sons to lose, know better.

Our good father at Washington—for I presume he is now our father as well as yours, since King George has moved his boundaries further north—our great and good father, I say, sends us word that if we do as he desires he will protect us. His brave warriors will be to us a bristling wall of strength, and his wonderful ships of war will fill our harbors so that our ancient enemies far to the northward—the Hydas and Tsimpsians—will cease to frighten our women, children and old men. Then in reality will he be our father and we his children. But can that ever be? Your God is not our God! Your God loves your people and hates mine. He folds his strong protecting arms lovingly about the pale face and leads him by the hand as a father leads his infant son—but He has forsaken His red children—if they really are His. Our God, the Great Spirit, seems also to have forsaken us. Your God makes your people wax strong every day. Soon they will fill all the land. Our people are ebbing away like a rapidly receding tide that will never return. The white man's God cannot love our people or He would protect them. They seem to be orphans who can look nowhere for help. How then can we be brothers? How can your God become our God and renew our prosperity and awaken in us dreams of returning greatness? If we have a common heavenly father He must be partial—for He came to His paleface children. We never saw Him. He gave you laws but had no word for his red children whose teeming multitudes once filled this vast continent as stars fill the firmament. No; we are two distinct races with separate origins and separate destinies. There is little in common between us.

To us the ashes of our ancestors are sacred and their resting place is hallowed ground. You wander far from the graves of your ancestors and seemingly without regret. Your religion was written upon tables of stone by the iron finger of your God so that you could not forget. The Red Man could never comprehend nor remember it. Our religion is the traditions of our ancestors—the dreams of our old men, given them in the solemn hours of night by the Great Spirit; and the visions of our sachems, and is written in the hearts of our people.

Your dead cease to love you and the land of their nativity as soon as they pass the portals of the tomb and wander way beyond the stars. They are soon forgotten and never return. Our dead never forget the beautiful world that gave them being. They still love its verdant valleys, its murmuring rivers, its magnificent mountains, sequestered vales and verdant lakes and bays, and ever yearn in tender, fond affection over the lonely hearted living, and often return from the Happy Hunting Ground to visit, guide, console and comfort them.

Day and night cannot dwell together. The Red Man had ever fled the approach of the White Man, as the morning mist flees before the morning sun.

However, your proposition seems fair and I think that my people will accept it and will retire to the reservation you offer them. Then we will dwell in peace, for the words of the Great White Chief seem to be the words of nature speaking to my people out of dense darkness.

It matters little where we pass the remnant of our days. They will not be many. The Indians' night promises to be dark. Not a single star of hope hovers above his horizon. Sad-voiced winds moan in the distance. Grim fate seems to be on the Red Man's trail, and wherever he goes he will hear the approaching footsteps of his fell destroyer and prepare stolidly to meet his doom, as does the wounded doe that hears the approaching footsteps of the hunter.

A few more moons, A few more winters—and not one of the descendants of the mighty hosts that once moved over this broad land or lived in happy homes, protected by the Great Spirit, will remain to mourn over the graves of a people—once more powerful and hopeful than yours. But why should I mourn at the untimely fate of my people? Tribe follows tribe, and nation follows nation, like the waves of the sea. It is the order of nature, and regret is useless. Your time of decay may be distant, but it will surely come, for even the White Man whose God walked and talked with him as friend with friend, cannot be exempt from the common destiny. We may be brothers after all. We will see.

We will ponder your proposition and when we decide we will let you know. But should we accept it, I here and now make this condition that we will not be denied the privilege without molestation of visiting at any time the tombs of our ancestors, friends and children. Every part of this soil is sacred in the estimation of my people. Every hillside, every valley, every plain and grove, has been hallowed by some sad or happy event in days long vanished. Even the rocks, which seem to be dumb and dead as they swelter in the sun along the silent shore, thrill with memories of stirring events connected with the lives of my people, and the very dust upon which you now stand responds more lovingly to their footsteps than to yours, because it is rich with the blood of our ancestors and our bare feet are conscious of the sympathetic touch. Our departed braves, fond mothers, glad, happy-hearted maidens, and even our little children who lived here and rejoiced here for a brief season, will love these somber returning spirits. And when the last Red Man shall have perished, and the memory of my tribe shall have become a myth among the White Men, these shores will swarm with the invisible dead of my tribe, and when your children's children think themselves alone in the field, the store, the shop, upon the highway, or in the silence of the pathless woods, they will not be alone. In all the earth there is no place dedicated to solitude. At night when the streets of your cities and villages are silent and you think them deserted, they will throng with the returning hosts that once filled them and still love this beautiful land. The White Man will never be alone.

Let him be just and deal kindly with my people, for the dead are not powerless, Dead, did I say? There is no death, only a change of worlds.

6. "We Preferred Our Own Way of Living" by Crazy Horse (1876)

My friend, I do not blame you for this. Had I listened to you this trouble would not have happened to me. I was not hostile to the white men. Sometimes my young men would attack the Indians who were their enemies and took their ponies. They did it in return.

We had buffalo for food, and their hides for clothing and for our teepees. We preferred hunting to a life of idleness on the reservation, where we were driven against our will. At times we did not get enough to eat, and we were not allowed to leave the reservation to hunt.

We preferred our own way of living. We were no expense to the government. All we wanted was peace and to be left alone. Soldiers were sent out in the winter, who destroyed our villages.

Then "Long Hair" (Custer) came in the same way. They say we massacred him, but he would have done the same thing to us had we not defended ourselves and fought to the last. Our first impulse was to escape with our squaws and papooses, but we were so hemmed in that we had to fight.

After that I went up on the Tongue River with a few of my people and lived in peace. But the government would not let me alone. Finally, I came back to the Red Cloud Agency. Yet I was not allowed to remain quiet.

I was tired of fighting. I went to the Spotted Tail Agency and asked that chief and his agent to let me live there in peace. I came here with the agent (Lee) to talk with the Big White Chief but was not given a chance. They tried to confine me. I tried to escape, and a soldier ran his bayonet into me.

I have spoken.

7. "I Will Fight No More Forever" by Chief Joseph (1877)

Tell General Howard I know his heart. What he told me before, I have in my heart. I am tired of fighting. Our chiefs are killed. Looking Glass is dead. Too-hool-hool-zote is dead. The old men are all dead. It is the young men who say yes and no. He who led on the young men is dead. It is cold and we have no blankets. The little children are freezing to death. My people, some of them, have run away to the hills and have no blankets, no food; no one knows where they are—perhaps freezing to death. I want to have time to look for my children and see how many of them I can find. Maybe I shall find them among the dead. Hear me, my chiefs! I am tired; my heart is sick and sad. From where the sun now stands I will fight no more forever.

8. "You Are Living in a New Path" by Sitting Bull (1880)

My Dear Grandchildren:

All of your folks are my relatives, because I am a Sioux, and so are they. I was glad to hear that the Black Robe had given you this school where you can learn to read, write, and count the way white people do. You are also being taught a new religion. You are shown how the white men work and make things. You are living in a new path.

When I was your age, things were entirely different. I had no teachers but my parents and relatives. They are dead and gone now, and I am left alone. It will be the same with you. Your parents are aging and will die some day, leaving you alone. So it is for you to make something of yourselves, and this can only be done while you are young.

In my early days I was eager to learn and to do things, and therefore I learned quickly, and that made it easier for my teachers. Now I often pick up papers and books which have all kinds of pictures and marks in them, but I cannot understand them as a white person does. They have a way of communicating by the use of written symbols and figures; but before they could do that, they had to have an understanding among themselves. You are learning that, and I was very much pleased to hear your reading.

In future your business dealings with the whites are going to be very hard, and it behooves you to learn well what you are taught here. But that is not all. We older people need you. In our dealings with the white men, we are just the same as blind men, to help us understand them. We need you to help us understand what the white men are up to. My Grandchildren, be good. Try and make a mark for yourselves. Learn all you can.

With all my heart I thank Black Robe's friends for their goodness and kindness towards me.

9. Dawes Act (1887)

An Act to Provide for the Allotment of Lands in Severalty to Indians on the Various Reservations, and to Extend the Protection of the Laws of the United States and the Territories over the Indians, and for Other Purposes.

Be it enacted by the Senate and House of Representatives of the United States of America in Congress assembled, That in all cases where any tribe or band of Indians has been, or shall hereafter be, located upon any reservation created for their use, either by treaty stipulation or by virtue of an act of Congress or executive order setting apart the same for their use, the President of the United States be, and he hereby is, authorized, whenever in his opinion any reservation or any part thereof of such Indians is advantageous for agricultural and grazing purposes, to cause said reservation, or any part thereof, to be surveyed, or resurveyed if necessary, and to allot the lands in said reservation in severalty to any Indian located thereon in quantities as follows:

To each head of a family, one-quarter of a section;

To each single person over eighteen years of age, one-eighth of a section;

To each orphan child under eighteen years of age, one-eighth of a section; and

To each other single person under eighteen years now living, or who may be born prior to the date of the order of the President directing an allotment of the lands embraced in any reservation, one-sixteenth of a section:

Provided, That in case there is not sufficient land in any of said reservations to allot lands to each individual of the classes above named in quantities as above provided, the lands embraced in such reservation or reservations shall be allotted to each individual of each of said classes pro rata in accordance with the provisions of this act: And provided further, That where the treaty or act of Congress setting apart such reservation provides the allotment of lands in severalty in quantities in excess of those herein provided, the President, in making allotments upon such reservation, shall allot the lands to each individual Indian belonging thereon in quantity as specified in such treaty or act: And provided further, That when the lands allotted are only valuable for grazing purposes, an additional allotment of such grazing lands, in quantities as above provided, shall be made to each individual.

SEC. 2. That all allotments set apart under the provisions of this act shall be selected by the Indians, heads of families selecting for their minor children, and the agents shall select for each orphan child, and in such manner as to embrace the improvements of the Indians making the selection where the improvements of two or more Indians have been made on the same legal subdivision of land, unless they shall otherwise agree, a provisional line may be run dividing said lands between them, and the amount to which each is entitled shall be equalized in the assignment of the remainder of the land to which they are entitled under his act: Provided, That if any one entitled to an allotment shall fail to make a selection within four years after the President shall direct that allotments may be made on a particular reservation, the Secretary of the Interior may direct the agent of such tribe or band, if such there be, and if there be no agent, then a special agent appointed for that purpose, to make a selection for such Indian, which selection shall be allotted as in cases where selections are made by the Indians, and patents shall issue in like manner.

SEC. 3. That the allotments provided for in this act shall be made by special agents appointed by the President for such purpose, and the agents in charge of the respective reservations on which the allotments are directed to be made, under such rules and regulations as the Secretary of the Interior may from time to time prescribe, and shall be certified by such agents to the Commissioner of Indian Affairs, in duplicate, one copy to be retained in the Indian Office and the other to be transmitted to the Secretary of the Interior for his action, and to be deposited in the General Land Office.

SEC. 4. That where any Indian not residing upon a reservation, or for whose tribe no reservation has been provided by treaty, act of Congress, or executive order, shall make settlement upon any surveyed or unsurveyed lands of the United States not otherwise appropriated, he or she shall be entitled, upon application to the local land-office for the district in which the lands are located, to have the same allotted to him or her, and to his or her children, in quantities and manner as provided in this act for Indians residing upon reservations; and when such settlement is made upon unsurveyed lands, the grant to such Indians shall be adjusted upon the survey of the lands so as to conform thereto; and patents shall be issued to them for such lands in the manner and with the restrictions as herein provided. And the fees to which the officers of such local land-office would have been entitled had such lands been entered under the general laws for the disposition of the public lands shall be paid to them, from any moneys in the Treasury of the United States not otherwise appropriated, upon a statement of an account in their behalf for such fees by the Commissioner of the General Land Office, and a certification of such account to the Secretary of the Treasury by the Secretary of the Interior.

SEC. 5. That upon the approval of the allotments provided for in this act by the Secretary of the Interior, he shall cause patents to issue therefor in the name of the allottees, which patents shall be of the legal effect, and declare that the United States does and will hold the land thus allotted, for the period of twenty-five years, in trust for the sole use and benefit of the Indian to whom such allotment shall have been made, or, in case of his decease, of his heirs according to the laws of the State or Territory where such land is located, and that at the expiration of said period the United States will convey the same by patent to said Indian, or his heirs as aforesaid, in fee, discharged of said trust and free of all charge or incumbrance whatsoever: Provided, That the President of the United States may in any case in his discretion extend the period. And if any conveyance shall be made of the lands set apart and allotted as herein provided, or any contract made touching the same, before the expiration of the time above mentioned, such conveyance or contract shall be absolutely null and void: Provided, That the law of descent and partition in force in the State or Territory where such lands are situate shall apply thereto after patents therefor have been executed and delivered, except as herein otherwise provided; and the laws of the State of Kansas regulating the descent and partition of real estate shall, so far as practicable, apply to all lands in the Indian Territory which may be allotted in severalty under the provisions of this act: And provided further, That at any time after lands have been allotted to all the Indians of any tribe as herein provided,

or sooner if in the opinion of the President it shall be for the best interests of said tribe, it shall be lawful for the Secretary of the Interior to negotiate with such Indian tribe for the purchase and release by said tribe, in conformity with the treaty or statute under which such reservation is held, of such portions of its reservation not allotted as such tribe shall, from time to time, consent to sell, on such terms and conditions as shall be considered just and equitable between the United States and said tribe of Indians, which purchase shall not be complete until ratified by Congress, and the form and manner of executing such release prescribed by Congress: Provided however, That all lands adapted to agriculture, with or without irrigation so sold or released to the United States by any Indian tribe shall be held by the United States for the sole purpose of securing homes to actual settlers and shall be disposed of by the United States to actual and bona fide settlers only tracts not exceeding one hundred and sixty acres to any one person, on such terms as Congress shall prescribe, subject to grants which Congress may make in aid of education: And provided further, That no patents shall issue therefor except to the person so taking the same as and homestead, or his heirs, and after the expiration of five years occupancy therefore as such homestead; and any conveyance of said lands taken as a homestead, or any contract touching the same, or lieu thereon, created prior to the date of such patent, shall be null and void. And the sums agreed to be paid by the United States as purchase money for any portion of any such reservation shall be held in the Treasury of the United States for the sole use of the tribe or tribes to whom such reservations belonged; and the same, with interest thereon at three per cent per annum, shall be at all times subject to appropriation by Congress for the education and civilization of such tribe or tribes of Indians or the members thereof. The patents aforesaid shall be recorded in the General Land Office, and afterward delivered, free of charge, to the allottee entitled thereto. And if any religious society or other organization is now occupying any of the public lands to which this act is applicable, for religious or educational work among the Indians, the Secretary of the Interior is hereby authorized to confirm such occupation to such society or organization, in quantity not exceeding one hundred and sixty acres in any one tract, so long as the same shall be so occupied, on such terms as he shall deem just; but nothing herein contained shall change or alter any claim of such society for religious or educational purposes heretofore granted by law. And hereafter in the employment of Indian police, or any other employees in the public service among any of the Indian tribes or bands affected by this act, and where Indians can perform the duties required, those Indians who have availed themselves of the provisions of this act and become citizens of the United States shall be preferred.

SEC. 6. That upon the completion of said allotments and the patenting of the lands to said allottees, each and every member of the respective bands or tribes of Indians to whom allotments have been made shall have the benefit of and be subject to the laws, both civil and criminal, of the State or Territory in which they may reside; and no Territory shall pass or enforce any law denying any such Indian within its jurisdiction the equal protection of the law. And every Indian born within the territorial limits of the United States to whom allotments shall have been made under the provisions of this act, or under any law or treaty, and every Indian born within the territorial limits of the United States who has voluntarily taken up, within said limits, his residence separate and apart from any tribe of Indians therein, and has adopted the habits of civilized life, is hereby declared to be a citizen of the United States, and is entitled to all the rights, privileges, and immunities of such citizens, whether said Indian has been or not, by birth or otherwise, a member of any tribe of Indians within the territorial limits of the United States without in any manner affecting the right of any such Indian to tribal or other property.

SEC. 7. That in cases where the use of water for irrigation is necessary to render the lands within any Indian reservation available for agricultural purposes, the Secretary of the Interior be, and he is hereby, authorized to prescribe such rules and regulations as he may deem necessary to secure a just and equal distribution thereof among the Indians residing upon any such reservation; and no other appropriation or grant of water by any riparian proprietor shall be permitted to the damage of any other riparian proprietor.

SEC. 8. That the provisions of this act shall not extend to the territory occupied by the Cherokees, Creeks, Choctaws, Chickasaws, Seminoles, and Osage, Miamies and Peorias, and Sacs and Foxes, in the Indian Territory, nor to any of the reservations of the Seneca Nation of New York Indians in the State of New York, nor to that strip of territory in the State of Nebraska adjoining the Sioux Nation on the south added by executive order.

SEC. 9. That for the purpose of making the surveys and resurveys mentioned in section two of this act, there be, and hereby is, appropriated, out of any moneys in the Treasury not otherwise appropriated, the sum of one hundred thousand dollars, to be repaid proportionately out of the proceeds of the sales of such land as may be acquired from the Indians under the provisions of this act.

SEC. 10. That nothing in this act contained shall be so construed to affect the right and power of Congress to grant the right of way through any lands granted to an Indian, or a tribe of Indians, for railroads or other highways, or telegraph lines, for the public use, or condemn such lands to public uses, upon making just compensation.

SEC. 11. That nothing in this act shall be so construed as to prevent the removal of the Southern Ute Indians from their present reservation in Southwestern Colorado to a new reservation by and with consent of a majority of the adult male members of said tribe.

Approved, February, 8, 1887

Native American Organizations

Alaska Coalition
408 C Street NE
Washington, DC 20002
(202) 547-1141
(202) 547-6009 Fax
Contact: Melinda Pierce

Founded in 1978. Supports and provides education, research, and legislative pressure in favor of preserving the heritage, natural resources, and culture of Alaska and its natives. Works with the Arctic National Wildlife Refuge to prevent exploitation of gas and oil developing. Supported the Alaska Lands Bill of 1980, which ordered the protection of native Alaskan lands. Also strives to safeguard hunting lands for rural Alaskan Natives.

Alaska Federation of Natives
411 West Fourth Avenue, Ste. 301
Anchorage, AK 99501
(907) 274-3611
President: Julia Kitka

Founded in 1966, the Alaska Federation of Natives advocates and represents Alaska Eskimos, Aleuts, and other Alaskan Indians before Congress, the Alaskan state legislature, and other federal and state organizations.

All Indian Pueblo Council
PO Box 3256
Albuquerque, NM 87190
(505) 881-1992
Chairman: Roy Bernal

Acts as an advocate for 19 Pueblo American Indian tribes on a variety of issues, including health, education, social problems, and economics. Also lobbies state and national government agencies, offers placement services, and provides charity programs. Offers brochures, pamphlets, and other resources.

American Friends Service Committee
1501 Cherry Street
Philadelphia, PA 19102
(215) 241-7000
Web site: http://www.afsc.org
Executive Secretary: Asia A. Bennett

The American Friends Service Committee was founded in 1917. Focuses on housing, employment, legal rights issues, and policymaking as those issues relate to Native Americans and other minority groups. Also seeks to develop refugee relief, peace education, and international understanding.

American Indian Culture Research Center
Box 98
Blue Cloud Abbey
Marvin, SD 57251-0098
(605) 432-5528
(605) 432-4754 Fax
E-mail: Indian@daknet.com
Web site: http://www.daknet.com/~indian.dakota.html
Executive Director: Rev. Stanislaus Maudlin

Founded in 1967 to support Native American leaders, teachers, and citizens in the cultural and philosophical rebuilding of American Indian communities. Assists in funding and managing Indian self-help programs; provides workshops, seminars, and historic collections; and gathers research.

American Indian Graduate Center
4520 Montgomery Blvd. NE, Ste. 1-B
Albuquerque, NM 87104
(505) 881-4584
(505) 884-0427 Fax
Web site: http://www2.aigc.com/aigc/
Executive Director: Reginald Rodriguez

The American Indian Graduate Center was founded in 1969 under the name American Indian Scholarships. Offers scholarship assistance to members of federally recognized tribes, as well as help in obtaining grant money for Native Americans and Alaskan Natives.

American Indian Health Care Association
1550 Larimer Street, No. 225
Denver, CO 80202-1602
Contact: Carol Marquez-Baines

Founded in 1970. Works towards providing quality community education programs, health care delivery management, and other programs to raise Native American health care standards. Provides training, research, and a speakers' bureau.

American Indian Heritage Foundation
6051 Arlington Blvd.
Falls Church, VA 22044
(202) 463-4267
(703) 237-7500
(703) 532-1921 Fax
Web site: http://www.indians.org/aihf
Contact: Dr. Wil Rose

Founded in 1973 to meet the cultural, spiritual, and physical needs of Native Americans. Supports American Indian heritage efforts and strives to inspire and assist Indian youths. Offers a food and clothing distribution program, seminars, cultural concerts for students, and youth awards. Special programs include sponsoring American Heritage Month, the annual National Indian Awards Night, and Miss Indian USA Scholarship Pageant.

American Indian Higher Education Consortium

121 Oronoco Street
Alexandria, VA 22314
(703) 838-0400
(703) 838-0388 Fax
President: Margaret C. Perez

The American Indian Higher Education Consortium was founded in 1972. Promotes post-secondary schooling, tribal colleges, and other higher education facilities. Provides training for administrators, teachers, support staff, and other educators. Promotes the development of Native American and Alaskan Native culture, language, and customs. Monitors relevant education policies and practices. Publishes the quarterly Tribal College: Journal of American Indian Education.

American Indian Institute

University of Oklahoma
555 Constitution Avenue, Ste. 237
Norman, OK 73072-7820
(405) 325-4127
(405) 325-7757 Fax
Director: Anita Chrisholm

Founded in 1951. Supports education, research, career development, and other opportunities beneficial to Native Americans. Strives to assist tribal culture, traditions, history, heritage, and resource development. Focuses on social issues, child welfare, mental health, and education, especially in training needs. Tries to unite tribal leaders, eliminate substance abuse, and develop leadership skills.

American Indian Law Center

PO Box 4456, Sta. A
Albuquerque, NM 87196
(505) 277-5462
Executive Director: Phillip Sam Deloria

Founded in 1967. Funded by government contracts and Native American organizations. Provides research, training, and services in regard to legal issues and the government. Focuses on tribal rights, civil liberties, and prosperity concerns. Coordinates actions by groups such as the Commission on State-Tribal Relations, which promotes intergovernmental relations on Native American reservations.

American Indian Liberation Crusade

4009 South Halldale Avenue
Los Angeles, CA 90062
(213) 299-1810
President: Henry E. Hedrick

Founded in 1952. Provides The American Indian Hour, a national radio broadcast focusing on physical, spiritual, and fund-raising needs of Native Americans. Supports Bible camps and schools, missionary work in American Indian fields, and charity programs. Also provides emergency relief and offers *Indian Crusader*, a quarterly newsletter.

American Indian Movement (AIM)

3145 Geary Blvd., Ste. 517
San Francisco, CA 94118
(415) 386-4373
(415) 386-4547 Fax
Web site: http://www.member.aol.com/nowacumig/aim.html

A politically active group representing Native American rights and working to protect treaties, land rights, spirituality, and other concerns.

American Indian Ritual Object Reparation Foundation

463 East 57th Street
New York, NY 10022-3003
(212) 980-9441
(212) 421-2746 Fax
Web site: http://www.reparationfoundation.org
Coordinator: Polly Nordstrand

Formed in 1992 with the goal of returning sacred ritual items to the Indian Nations. Provides speakers, educational information, research, and publications such as *Mending the Circle: A Native American Repatriation Guide.*

Americans for Indian Opportunity

681 Juniper Hill Road
Bernalillo, NM 87004
(505) 867-0278
(505) 867-0441 Fax
Executive Director: LaDonna Harris

Americans for Indian Opportunity was founded in 1970. The group focuses on supporting self-sufficiency and self-government for American Indians. Focuses on issues concerning politics, culture, and economics. Provides and supports programs in self-help, communication, education, housing, health, leadership, and the environment. Monitors government practices in order to ensure that federal programs benefit Native Americans.

Arrow

1000 Connecticut Avenue NW, Ste. 1206
Washington, DC 20036
(202) 296-0685
Executive Officer: Hazel E. Elbert
Arrow, (Americans for Restitution and Righting of Old Wrongs), was founded in 1941 as the National Congress of American Indian Fund. The group provides programs on substance abuse and child abuse prevention. Focuses on improving educational, cultural, economic, and health care standards for Native Americans, as well as on assisting tribal law and justice. Publications include *Strong Identity Can Protect Native American Youth, Adolescence—A Tough Time for Indian Youth,* and *Americans for the Restitution of Righting Wrongs Annual.*

Assembly of First Nations National Indian Brotherhood

55 Murray Street, 5th Floor
Ottawa, ON, Canada K1N5M3
(613) 236-0673
(617) 238-5780 Fax
Contact: Ovide Mercurdi

Founded in 1969. Represents Canada's First Nations on government issues concerning Native Americans, such as the environment, education, health, housing, and economic development.

Association of American Indian Affairs
PO Box 268
Tekakwitha Complex Agency Road 7
Sisseton, SD 57262
(605) 698-3998
(605) 698-3316 Fax
Executive Director: Jerry Flute

The Association of American Indian Affairs was founded in 1923 as the American Association on Indian Affairs. It focuses on offering legal and technical support to American Indian tribes. Works on a variety of topics, including health, education, family defense, resources use, justice, and economics. Also maintains the American Indian Fund and the Native American Scholarship Fund.

Association of Community Tribal Schools
c/o 4th Avenue W.
Sisseton, SD 57262-1349
(605) 698-3112
(605) 658-7686 Fax
Executive Director: Dr. Roger Bordeaux

Founded in 1982 as the Association of Contract Tribal Schools. Membership consists of American Indian-controlled schools organized under the Indian Self-Determination and Education Assistance Act and the Tribally Controlled Schools Acts, as well as institutions seeking to fall under the guidelines of these two acts. Supports self-determination and Indian-controlled schooling.

Center for Third World Organizing
3861 Martin Luther King Jr. Way
Oakland, CA 94609
(415) 654-9601
Web site: http://www.ctwo.org
Director: Gary Delgado

Founded in 1980. Offers training, research, and political assistance to low-income minority organizations, including welfare, immigrant, and Native American rights groups. Monitors discrimination cases, maintains a speakers' bureau, and provides placement services, publications, and seminars.

Cherokee National Historical Society
PO Box 515
Tahlequah, OK 74465
(918) 456-6007
(918) 456-6165 Fax

Founded in 1963. Seeks to preserve the history, culture, and tradition of the Cherokee Nation. Strives to support, maintain, and establish monuments and grave markers concerning individuals and events important to Cherokee history. Supports educational, charity, and other programs. Maintains museums, historic villages, and other sites.

Committee for Action for Rural Indians
401 Liberty Street
Petoskey, MI 49770
(616) 347-0059
Chairman: Martin J. King

Founded in 1972 as the Native American Recovery Center, the Committee for Action for Rural Indians currently provides a number of services to non-reservation Native Americans, including educational information, referral services, and alcohol and drug abuse rehabilitation programs.

Concerned American Indian Parents
CUHCC Clinic
2001 Bloomington Avenue
Minneapolis, MN 55404
(612) 627-6888
(612) 627-4205 Fax
Contact: Fred Veilleux

Concerned American Indian Parents was formed in 1987 to abolish degrading American Indian symbols, such as the logos for the Washington Redskins and the Cleveland Indians. Also provides educational materials about harmful racial symbols.

Council of Energy Resource Tribes
1999 Broadway, Ste. 2600
Denver, CO 80202
(303) 297-2378
(303) 296-5690 Fax
Executive Director: A. David Lester

Founded in 1975 as a collection of American Indian tribes owning energy resources. Monitors the protection, conservation, control, and management of natural resources. Also focuses on technical assistance, Human resource development and training, and environmental protection. Provides youth education and other programs in order to assist planning and management practices within tribes.

Crazy Horse Memorial Foundation
The Black Hills
Avenue of Chiefs
Crazy Horse, SD 57730-9506
(605) 673-4681
(605) 673-2185 Fax
Web site: http://www.crazyhorse.org
Board Chairman: Ruth Ziolksowski

Founded in 1948 to promote a memorial for Sioux leader Crazy Horse. Offers other historical and artistic items. Seeks public and government support for its actions. Offers a number of publications, such as *Crazy Horse and Korczak*, the quarterly newsletter *Progress, Korczak: Sage of Sitting Bull's Bones,* and *Korczak: Storyteller in Stone.*

Creek Indian Memorial Association
Creek County House Museum
Town Square
Okmulgee, OK 74470
(918) 756-2324

Formed in 1923. Maintains historical and cultural pieces concerning Native Americans. Offers educational programs, fundraising activities, and publications like booklets and brochures.

Dakota Women of All Red Nations
c/o Lorelei DeCoar
PO Box 423
Rosebud, SD 57570
Chairperson: Lorelei DeCora

Founded in 1978 as Women of All Red Nations. Focuses on issues like sterilization abuse, women's health, adoption and foster-care abuse, community education, legal and juvenile justice problems, political imprisonment, and Indian resources development.

First Nations Development Institute

The Stores Building
11917 Main Street
Fredericksburg, VA 22408
(540) 371-5615
(540) 371-3505 Fax
President: Rebecca Adamson

Formed in 1980 as the First Nations Financial Project. Works to assist Native American tribes in becoming politically, economically, and culturally self-sufficient. Supports economic development and commercial enterprises by reservation-based Native-American tribes, as well as provides technical assistance, grants, and loans to these people. Publications include the bimonthly *Business Alert* and the quarterly *Indian Giver.*

For Mother Earth

c/o Community Organizing Center
Old First Presbyterian Church
1101 Bryden Road
Columbus, OH 43205
(614) 252-9255
(614) 291-1984 Fax
E-mail: walk@igc.apc.org

Founded in 1989. Works to assist indigenous peoples, especially Native Americans. Seeks to repeal Public Law 93-531, which forcefully relocated Navajo Indians from tribal lands. Also seeks to end nuclear testing on the homeland of indigenous people, as well as seek inclusion of indigenous nations within UN membership. Conducts educational programs, charity benefits, and research studies. Provides community organizer training and children's services. Publications include *For Mother Earth Newsletter* and *Ohio Peace March for Global Nuclear Disarmament.*

Four Arrows

PO Box 1332
Ottawa, ON, Canada K1P 5R4
(613) 234-5887
(613) 234-5887 Fax
Coordinator: Rarihokwats

Four Arrows was founded in 1968 as the White Roots of Peace. The group seeks to promote and protect the rights of indigenous people. Also supports intercultural exchange and communication, self-sufficiency, and educational and agricultural development. Believes in the strength of culture, tradition, and spiritual strength within Indian communities.

Great Lakes Indian Fish and Wildlife Commission

PO Box 9
Odanah, WI 54861
(715) 682-6619
(715) 682-8847 Fax
Executive Director: James H. Schlender

Founded in 1983 by members of the Chippewa tribes concerned with wildlife conservation in the Great Lakes area. Goals of the organization include the conservation and management of fish, wildlife, and natural resources, promotion of tribal self-government, and protections of the ecosystem. Provides educational and research programs, a speakers' bureau, and a number of reports.

Indian Arts and Crafts Association

122 La Veta Drive NE, Ste. B
Albequerque, NM 87108
(505) 265-9149
(505) 265-8251 Fax
E-mail: iaca@ix.Netcom.com
Web site: http://www.iaca.com
Executive Director: Susan McGuire

The Indian Arts and Crafts Association was founded in 1974. Seeks to promote, preserve, protect, and enhance the understanding of Native American arts and crafts. Conducts seminars and education groups, offers a speakers' bureau, and works with related government organizations. Provides a number of publications.

Indian Educators Federation

PO Box 2020
Farmington, NM 87499
(505) 327-7733
(505) 327-9558 Fax
Web site: http://www.ief-aft.org

Founded in 1967 the National Council of BIA Educators, the Indian Educators Federation consists of educators working in federal schools operated by the Bureau of Indian Affairs. Seeks to promote education opportunities for Native Americans, as well as protects the rights and interests of teachers within American Indian Schools.

Indian Heritage Council

c/o Louis Hooban
Henry Street
Box 2302
Morristown, TN 37816
(423) 581-4448
Contact: Louis Hooban

Founded in 1988, the Indian Heritage Council focuses on cultural, educational, spiritual, and historical preservation and understanding of Native Americans. Provides charity events, research, educational programs, and publications like Indian Drug Usage.

Indian Rights Association

c/o Janney Montgomery
1601 Market Street
Philadelphia, PA 19103
(215) 665-4523
Contact: Janney Montgomery

The Indian Rights Association was founded in 1882. The group protects the welfare, legal rights, and human liberties of Native Americans. Also monitors judicial and legislative situations involving American Indians, as well as maintaining relations with governmental Indian affairs groups. Acts as a clearinghouse for Native American appeals.

Indian Law Resource Center

602 North Ewing Street
Helena, MT 59601
(406) 449-2006
(406) 449-2031 Fax
E-mail: ilrc@mt.net
Executive Director: Robert T. Coulter

Formed in 1978 as a legal, environmental, and human rights organization dedicated to Native Americans. Seeks to overcome discrimination and legal injustice while also preserving American Indian culture. Fights for Human rights, environmental protection, and other issues concerning Native Americans before United States and UN courts.

Indian Youth of America
609 Badgerow Bldg.
PO Box 2786
Sioux City, IA 51106
(712) 252-3230
(712) 252-3712 Fax
Web site: http://www.spc.uchicago.edu/CFP/rsindian.html
Executive Director: Patricia Tradiell Gordon

Founded in 1978 with the purpose of helping Native-American children. Seeks to develop Indian youth in regards to career, education, and cultural awareness. Monitors the Indian Child Welfare Program, which helps broken families, supports rights guaranteed under the Indian Child Welfare Act, and assisting in foster care placement. Also provides various publications and youth social activities.

Indians into Medicine
University of North Dakota
School of Medicine
501 North Columbia Road
Grand Forks, ND 58203
(701) 777-3037
(701) 777-3277 Fax
Director: Eugene DeLorme

Founded in 1973. Strives to place qualified health professionals in Native American communities, help American Indians gain entrance to the health care profession, and coordinate financial needs for Indian health care students. Monitors current trends in agency policy, medicine, and society. Publications include *Serpent, Staff, and Drum*, a quarterly newsletter.

International Indian Treaty Council
54 Mint Street, Ste. 400
San Francisco, CA 94103
(415) 512-1501
(415) 512-1507 Fax
Web site: http://www.treatycouncil.org
Executive Director: Andrea Carmen

Founded in 1974 as an organization of Indian nations seeking to overcome problems and guarantee rights for their people. Holds NGO status with the United Nations, and makes regular presentations to the UN Commission on Human Rights. Cosponsors a conference in Geneva, Switzerland in 1985 in Indigenous People and the Land. Works with human rights groups and publishes the quarterly Treaty Council News.

Institute for the Development of Indian Law
c/o K. Kirke Kickingbird
Oklahoma City University
School of Law
2501 North Blackwelder
Oklahoma City, OK 73106
(405) 521-5188
(405) 521-5017
(405) 521-5185 Fax
Executive Director: K. Kirke Kickingbird

Founded in 1971. Focuses on Indian sovereignty, Naive American self-government, and American Indian rights. Provides legal assistance and research training, technical assistance, seminars, and other educational programs. Also concentrates on federal Indian law, Indian self-confidence, Native American treaties, taxation, Constitutional rights, and curriculum and community development.

Inter-Tribal Indian Ceremonial Association
Box 1
Church Rock, NM 87311
(505) 863-3896
(505) 722-5158 Fax
Executive Director: Lawrence D. Linford

Formed in 1921 as an official agency of the state of New Mexico. Supports the annual Inter-Tribal Indian Ceremonial, specialized education, and children's services. Works in connection with legislation relevant to Native American arts and crafts. Maintains the Red Rock Park.

Leonard Peltier Defense Committee
PO Box 583
Lawrence, KS 66044
Web site: http://freepeltier/index.html
Contact: Lisa Faruolo

Formed in 1976, this organization seeks to gain justice for Leonard Peltier, a Native American who many believe was wrongly convicted of murdering two FBI agents at the Pine Ridge Indian Reservation. The group publishes a bimonthly newsletter, *Spirit of Crazy Horse*, and provides information on social, judicial, and cultural issues.

Maniilaq Association
PO Box 256
Kotzebue, AK 99752
(907) 442-3311
(800) 478-3312
(987) 442-2381 Fax
President: Joseph Ballot

Founded in 1966, the Maniilaq Association was known previously as the Northwest Alaska Native Association and later as the Mauneluk Association. The group currently promotes health and social welfare, the preservation of Eskimo culture, education issues, and social understanding. Maintains a group home, a senior citizen center, a nursing wing, a women's crisis program, and a youth camp, as well as the Maniiaq Medical Center. Other programs include adult education, agriculture, counseling services, a variety of medical and environmental health services, safety education, and substance abuse treatment.

NAIM "North American Indian Ministries"
PO Box 151
Point Roberts, WA 98281
(604) 946-1227
(604) 946-1465 Fax
Web site: http://www.naim.ca/
General Director: Willaim Lottis

Founded in 1949, NAIM Ministries was originally called the North American Mission and later the Marine Medical Mission. Seeks to provide Native American churches in urban areas and on reservations. Offers programs and seminars on cross-cultural communication, economics, education, alcohol treatment and rehabilitation, and social issues. Publications include the monthly *Dear Team*, the quarterly *Infocus*, and the bimonthly *Intercessor*.

National American Indian Court Clerks Association
1000 Connecticut Avenue NW, Ste. 1206
Washington, DC 20036
(202) 296-0685
President: Judge Elbridge Coochise

The National American Indian Court Clerks Association was founded in 1968. The group strives for the improvement of the American Indian court system through education and the achievement of equal protection. Also offers research services, continuing education programs, and training sessions on topics like criminal law, family law, and child welfare.

National American Indian Housing Council
122 C Street NW, Ste. 280
Washington, DC 20001
(202) 783-2667
(202) 347-1785 Fax
Web site: http://www.naihc.indian.com
Executive Director: Virginia E. Spencer

Founded in 1974 as an American Indian tribal housing authority. The group works in conjunction with the U.S. Department of Housing and Urban Development to meet the needs of Native Americans in housing issues.

National Association for Native American Children of Alcoholics
1402 Third Avenue, No. 1110
Seattle, WA 98118
(206) 467-7686
(800) 32205601
(206) 467-7689 Fax
Web site: http://www.nanacoa.org
Executive Director: Anna M. Latimer

Founded in 1988 in order to help and provide awareness of the needs of Native American children of alcoholics. Projects include support programs for American Indian communities, educational activities geared toward local, state, and federal policymakers, and support for social change and community development. Offers a number of resources, including videos such as *The Healing Journey: Hope for Children of Alcoholics,* quarterly publications such as *From Nightmare to Vision: A Training Manual for Native American Adult Children of Alcoholics,* and *Respect Handbook for School Personnel.*

National Center for American Indian and Alaskan Native Health Research
University of Colorado Health Sciences Center
Psychiatry Department
University N. Pavillion AO11-13
4455
East 12th Avenue
Denver, CO 80220
(303) 372-3232
(303) 372-3236
(303) 372-3579 Fax
E-mail: billie.cook@uchsc.edu

Founded in 1987. Conducts, supports, and initiates research on management, prevention, and investigation of Native American and Alaskan Native mental illness. Assists other organizations and agencies with similar goals. Offers numerous publications, including *Behavioral Health Issues Among American Indians and Alaskan Natives: Explorations of the Frontiers of Behavioral Sciences, Call-*

ing From the Rim: Suicidal Behavior Among American Indian and Alaskan Native Adolescents, and *New Directions in Prevention Among American Indian* and *Alaskan Native Communities.*

National Center for American Indian Enterprise Development
953 East Juanita Avenue
Mesa, AZ 85204
(480) 831-7524
(800) 4NCAIED
(480) 491-1332 Fax
Web site: http://www.ncaied.org
President: Steven L.A. Stallings

The National Center for American Indian Enterprise Development, known formerly as the United Indian Development Association, was formed in 1969. It supports business and economic development among Native American tribes. Also focuses on business training services, developing management abilities, assisting with finance proposals and insurance issues, and other similar topics. Publications include the annual *Directory of American Indian Business* and the quarterly *Indian Business and Management.*

National Coalition for Indian Education
8200 Mountain Road NE, No. 203
Albuquerque, NM 87110-7835
(505) 262-2351
President: Dean Chavers

The National Coalition for Indian Education was formed in 1987 as the Coalition for Indian Education. The group seeks to ensure excellence in education, health, and other programs for Native Americans. Conducts research activities, offers information and training services, provides a speakers' bureau, and maintains placement services. Publications include *Tribal Economic Development Directory, Basic Fundraising,* and *Current Issues in Indian Education.*

National Congress of American Indians
2010 Massachusetts Avenue NW, 2nd floor
Washington, DC 20036
(202) 466-7767
(202) 466-7797 Fax
Web site: http://www.ncai.org
Executive Director: JoAnn K. Chase

Founded in 1944, the National Congress of American Indians currently represents 800,000 Native Americans. Goals include protecting and developing Indian natural resources, assisting human resource needs, supporting legislative needs of Native Americans, improving health, economic, and education conditions within the tribes, advocating the needs of American Indians and Alaskan Natives. Also compiles statistics, funds educational programs, and supports charity functions.

National Indian AIDs Hotline
c/o Andrea Green Rush
2100 Lake Shore Avenue, Ste. 1
Oakland, CA 94606
(510) 444-2051
(800) 283 2437
(510) 444-1593 Fax
E-mail: NNAAPC@aol.com
Executive Director: Ron Rowell

Founded in 1987. Seeks to stop the spreading of tuberculosis, HIV, and sexually transmitted diseases among American Indians, Native Hawaiians, and Alaskan Natives, as well as other individuals. Promotes educational programs and information services, especially in the areas of physical, spiritual, and economic health.

National Indian Council on Aging
City Centre, Ste. 510-W
6400 Uptown Blvd. NW
Albuquerque, NM 87110
(505) 888-3302
(505) 888-3276 Fax
Web site: http://www.nicoa.org/index.html
Executive Director: Dave Baldridge

Founded in 1976. Goals include providing improved, comprehensive services to elderly Native Americans and Alaskan Natives, distributing information on Indian aging programs, and assisting in the training and implementation needs of tribal elderly service organizations. Publishes a quarterly newsletter *Elder Voices*.

National Indian Health Board
1385 South Colorado Blvd., Ste. A-708
Denver, CO 80222
(303) 759-3075
(305) 759-3674 Fax
Web site: http://www.nihb.org/home
Executive Director: Levi Mestegh

The National Indian Health Board was founded in 1969. Supports improved health conditions for Native Americans. Provides information, seminars, and workshops on health subjects. Publications include special reports, audiotapes, and *NIHB Health Reporter*, a quarterly newsletter.

National Indian Training and Research Center
2121 South Mill Avenue, ste. 216
Tempe, AZ 85282
(480) 967-9484
(480) 921-1015 Fax
Executive Director: Dr. C. Corbett

The National Indian Training and Research Center was founded in 1969. Provides training and research dedicated to bettering Native Americans in the areas of leadership, economics, and society. Also works in the areas of business, education, and government in order to further its goals.

National Indian Youth Council
318 Elm Street SE
Albuquerque, NM 87102
(505) 247-2251
(505) 247-4251 Fax
Executive Director: Kenneth Tsosie

Founded in 1961. Goals are the protection of American Indian natural resources, protection of religious freedom, supporting civil liberty issues, and striving for treaty rights and federal government support. Also seeks to improve health, education, and employment for Native Americans. Publishes a quarterly newsletter, *Americans Before Columbus*.

National Native American Cooperative
PO Box 1030
San Carlos, AZ 85550-1000
(520) 622-4900
(520) 292-0779 Fax
Executive Officer: Fred Synder

Founded in 1969, the National Native American Cooperative seeks to preserve Native American culture and traditional educa-

tion. Provides services and information on public health, education, career planning, scholarships, and other topics. Publications include *Native American Directory* and *PowWow on the Red Road*.

National Tribal Environmental Council
2221 Rio Grande NW
Albuquerque, NM 87104
(505) 242-2175
(505) 242-2654 Fax
Web site: http://www.ntec.org
Executive Director: Jerry Pardilla

Founded in 1991 by members of native American tribes in order to meet their environmental concerns. Provides information, resources, and speakers on environmental issues; also works toward environmental regulation and reviews pertinent legislative occurrences. Publishes *Tribal Visions*, a quarterly newsletter.

National Urban Indian Council
100068 University Pk. Street
Denver, CO 80250-0168
Chief Executive: Gregory W. Frazier

Formed in 1977, the National Urban Indian Council seeks to connect, network, assist, and support urban-based American Indians and Alaskan natives. Strives for mutual support of all native people. Also focuses on employment, health, housing, and special projects. Publications include *American Indian Review, American Indians, Bulletin Source Document,* and *Urban Indians*.

Nations Ministries
Box 70
Honobia, OK 74549
(918) 755-4570
(918) 755-4577 Fax
Director: Riley Donica

Nations Ministries was formed in 1983. It conducts evangelical Christian ministry on American Indian federal reservations. Also focuses on peace and social justice issues. Maintains a speakers' bureau and offers the bimonthly *Indian Nations News*.

Native American Community
PO Box 572
Lake Andes, SD 57356-0572
(605) 487-7072
(605) 487-7097
(605) 487-7964 Fax
Director: Charon Asetoyer

Founded in 1984 as an organization dedicated to the educational, economic, and social betterment of Native Americans. Maintains and supports the Native American Woman Health Education Resource Center, which provides programs, education, and workshops on issues like AIDS awareness, domestic abuse, reproductive rights, fetal alcohol syndrome, family planning, child development. Also offers adult education programs, employment opportunities, children's services, a placement center, and a speakers' bureau.

Native American (Indian) Chamber of Commerce
PO Box 27626
Tucson, AZ 85726-7626
(520) 622-4900
Director: Fred Synder

Founded in 1990 to support research and education issues involving Native Americans. Issues the group focuses on include health, tribal culture, education, and current events.

Appendix 2: Native American Organizations

Native American Law Students Association
Indian Law Clinic
University of Montana Law School
Missoula, MT 59812
(406) 243-66480
(406) 243-25-76 Fax
President: Dan Belcourt

Founded in 1970 as the American Indian Law Students Association. Supports unity, communication, and cooperation, as well as mutual support among all American Indian, Hawaiian Native, and Native Alaskan law students. Provides financial aid assistance, employment services, educational and research opportunities, and a legal issue discussion forum. Also has a speakers' bureau.

Native American Policy Network
Barry University
11300 2nd Avenue NE
Miami, FL 33161
(305) 899-3473
(305) 899-3279 Fax
Contact: Michael E. Melody

The Native American Policy Network was founded in 1979 by Indian and political leaders, policy makers, and other scholars interested in researching and supporting Native American policy. Also works with the American Political Science Association and the Western Social Science Association.

Native American Public Telecommunications
PO Box 83111
Lincoln, NE 68501
(402) 472-3522
(800) 793-4250
(402) 472-8675 Fax
E-mail: fblythe@unlinfo.unl.edu
Web site: http://www.nativetelecom.org
Executive Director: Frank Blythe

Founded in 1977 as the Native American Public Broadcasting Consortium, the group currently supports tribal sovereignty and history, Native American culture and language, and opportunities for American Indians and Alaskan Natives. Seeks to further its goals through educational and public telecommunications programs on television and radio.

Native American Rights Fund
1506 Broadway
Boulder, CO 80302
(303) 447-8760
(303) 443-7776
Web site: http://www.narf.org

Founded in 1970. Represents Native Americans in legal issues, especially in the categories of tribal existence, human rights, tribal resource protection, and government accountability. Offers library holdings and publications.

Native American Scholarship Fund
8200 Mountain Road NE, No. 203
Albuquerque, NM 87110-7835
(505) 262-2351
(505) 262-0534 Fax
Web site: http://www.nasf.com/index.html
Director: Dean Chavers

Founded in 1986 with the purpose of raising funds and gaining government education money for Native American students. The Native American Scholarship Fund also conducts research, offers educational programs, maintains a speaker's bureau, and provides placement services.

Native Americans for a Clean Environment
PO Box 1671
Tahlequah, OK 74465
(918) 458-4322
(918) 458-0322 Fax
Director: Lance Hughes

Native Americans for a Clean Environment was founded in 1985. The group is dedicated to preventing environmental ruin because of nuclear waste disposal. Also supports research in and the use of renewable and alternative energy resources. Provides information on the nuclear industry, food irradiation, and uranium mining, as well as related topics.

Native Hawaiian Culture and Arts Program
Bishop Museum
1525 Bernice Street
Honolulu, HI 96817-0916
(808) 847-8237
(808) 847-2113 Fax
E-mail: sandi@bishop.hawaii.org
Contact: Dr. Donald Duckworth

Founded in 1986, the Native Hawaiian Culture and Arts Program seeks to support and preserve the culture, beliefs, arts, and values of Native Hawaiians. Provides, conducts, and distributes research, works to instill pride and a sense of heritage among native Hawaiian people, and seeks to educate all people about the values of American Islander culture. Also fights for the psychological, social, economic, and cultural well-being of Native Hawaiians.

North American Indian Association
22720 Plymouth Road
Detroit, MI 48239
(313) 535-2966
(313) 535-8060 Fax
Executive Director: Janis A. Fairman

The North American Indian Association was founded in 1940 as the North American Indian Club. Goals of the organization include the preservation of American Indian culture, meeting Native American educational needs, and bettering all people of Indian ancestry. Offers training programs, employment assistance, adult counseling, and children's services. Publishes *Native Sun*, a quarterly newsletter.

North American Indian Chamber of Commerce
PO Box 27626
Tucson, AZ 85726
(602) 622-4900
(520) 292-0779 Fax
Contact: Fred Synder

The North American Indian Chamber of Commerce was founded in 1983. The organization collects and distributes information at native American events and conferences, as well as sponsoring educational programs.

North American Indian Information and Trade Center
PO Box 1000
San Carlos, AZ 85550-1000

(602) 622-4900
(602) 292-0779 Fax
Director: Fred Synder

The North American Indian Information and Trade Center was formed in 1991 as a division of the National Native American Co-operative. Seeks to provide educational programs, network national events, and provide other services in favor of Native Americans.

Seventh Generation Fund for Indian Development

PO Box 4569
Arcata, CA 95521
(707) 825-7640
(707) 825-7639 Fax
Web site: http://www.honorearth.com/sgf/auditor.html
Executive Director: Chris Peters

The Seventh Generation Fund for Indian Development was formed in 1977 as the Tribal Sovereignty Program. Supports Native American self-reliance, reclamation of tribal land, and protection of American Indian natural resources. Also strives to instill spiritual, cultural, and physical well-being within Native American families. Focuses on Native American rights, family life issues, judicial issues, and self-sufficency through food production, alternate energy use, appropriate technologies, and other factors.

Survival of American Indians Association

7803-A Samurai Drive SE
Olympia, WA 98503
Director: Hank Adams

Founded in 1964, the Survival of American Indians Association offers education on Indian rights, supports independent Indian education institutions, and strives for tribal government reform action. Also maintains a speakers' bureau and offers the publication *The Renegade: A Strategy Journal of Indian Opinion.*

Tiyospaya American Indian Student Organization

405 Central Avenue, Ste. 201
St. Petersburg, FL 33701
(813) 823-3534
(800) 682-7220
(813) 822-3501 Fax
E-mail: fiall@freenet.fsu.edu

Formed in 1986, the Tiyospaya American Indian Student Organization provides programs in substance abuse and prevention and supports American Indian parent/teacher associations. Seeks to improve American Indian education platforms like retention and student support. Believes in Native American treaty rights, sovereignty, and human rights.

United Indians of All Tribes Foundation

Daybreak Star Arts Center
Discovery Park
PO Box 99100
Seattle, WA 98199
(206) 285-4425
(206) 282-3640 Fax
Web site: http://www.unitedindians.com
Executive Director: Bernie Whitebear

Founded in 1970. Provides cultural, social, and educational services to urban Native Americans, as well as maintaining the Daybreak Star Indian Cultural Center. Publishes the monthly magazine *Daybreak Star Press.*

United National Indian Tribal Youth

4010 Lincoln Blvd.
PO Box 25042
Oklahoma City, OK 73125
(405) 424-3010
(405) 424-3018 Fax
Web site: http://www.unityinc.org
Executive Director: J.R. Cook

Founded in 1976. Seeks to provide spiritual, cultural, physical, mental, and social development for young American Indians and Alaskan Natives. Provides leadership training, programs against negative peer pressure and substance abuse, and local youth council assistance. Provides a voice in congressional and Senate hearings. Offers a quarterly newsletter, *Unity News.*

United South and Eastern Tribes

711 Stewarts Ferry Pike S-100
Nashville, TN 37214
(615) 872-7900
(615) 872-7417 Fax
E-mail: 102414.1756@compuserve.com
Web site: http://www.oneida-nation.net/uset
Executive Director: James T. Martin

Founded in 1969 as a collective alliance of 23 Native American tribes. Seeks to assist one another in relevant issues and promote the strength of unity. Operates committees in criminal justice, housing, natural resources, social services, gaming, health, and tribal administration. The United South and Eastern Tribes was previously known as the United Southeastern Tribes.

Women of All Red Nations

4511 North Hermitage
Chicago, IL 60640

Founded in 1990 to help empower Native American women. Offers education services, advocacy programs, and a concerns forum. Publishes the monthly *WARN Newsletter.*

World Emergency Relief

2270 Camino Vida Roble, Suite D
Carlsbad, CA 92009
(760) 930-8001
(760) 930-9085 Fax
Web site: http://www.wer-us.org
President: Rev. Joel MacCollam

Supports economic development and institutional advancement for Native Americans, as well as people in underdeveloped countries. Also provides emergency relief, orphan support services, and a quarterly newsletter, *World Report.*

3
Tables

Native American Members of the U.S. House of Representatives

Name	State	Party	Dates
Charles Curtis	Kansas	Republican	1893-1907
Charles D. Carter	Oklahoma	Democrat	1907-27
W.W. Hastings	Oklahoma	Democrat	1915-21, 1923-35
Will Rogers, Jr.	California	Democrat	1943-44
William G. Stigler	Oklahoma	Democrat	1944-52
Benjamin Reifel	South Dakota	Republican	1961-71
Clem Rogers McSpadden	Oklahoma	Democrat	1972-75
Ben Nighthorse Campbell	Colorado	Democrat*	1987-1993

*Campbell served in the House as a Democrat but switched to the Republican Party in 1995 when he was serving in the U.S. Senate.

Native American Members of the U.S. Senate

Name	State	Party	Dates
Hiram R. Revels	Mississippi	Republican	1870-71
Matthew Stanley Quay	Pennsylvania	Republican	1887-89,1901-04
Charles Curtis	Kansas	Republican	1907-12, 1915-29
Robert L. Owens	Oklahoma	Democrat	1907-25
Ben Nighthorse Campbell	Colorado	Republican*	1993-

*Campbell was elected to the Senate in 1992 as a Democrat but switched to the Republican Party in 1995.

4

Indian Tribal Entities in the United States

This appendix lists all Indian tribal entities within the contiguous 48 states and Alaska that are recognized and eligible to receive services from the United States Bureau of Indian Affairs.

Tribal Entities within the Contiguous 48 States

Absentee-Shawnee Tribe of Indians of Oklahoma
Agua Caliente Band of Cahuilla Indians of the Agua Caliente Indian Reservation, California
Ak Chin Indian Community of the Maricopa (Ak Chin) Indian Reservation, Arizona
Alabama-Coushatta Tribes of Texas
Alabama-Quassarte Tribal Town, Oklahoma
Alturas Indian Rancheria, California
Apache Tribe of Oklahoma
Arapahoe Tribe of the Wind River Reservation, Wyoming
Aroostook Band of Micmac Indians of Maine
Assiniboine and Sioux Tribes of the Fort Peck Indian Reservation, Montana
Augustine Band of Cahuilla Mission Indians of the Augustine Reservation, California
Bad River Band of the Lake Superior Tribe of Chippewa Indians of the Bad River Reservation, Wisconsin
Bay Mills Indian Community of the Sault Ste. Marie Band of Chippewa Indians, Bay Mills Reservation, Michigan
Bear River Band of the Rohnerville Rancheria, California
Berry Creek Rancheria of Maidu Indians of California
Big Lagoon Rancheria, California
Big Pine Band of Owens Valley Paiute Shoshone Indians of the Big Pine Reservation, California
Big Sandy Rancheria of Mono Indians of California
Big Valley Rancheria of Pomo & Pit River Indians of California
Blackfeet Tribe of the Blackfeet Indian Reservation of Montana
Blue Lake Rancheria, California
Bridgeport Paiute Indian Colony of California

Buena Vista Rancheria of Me-Wuk Indians of California
Burns Paiute Tribe of the Burns Paiute Indian Colony of Oregon
Cabazon Band of Cahuilla Mission Indians of the Cabazon Reservation, California
Cachil DeHe Band of Wintun Indians of the Colusa Indian Community of the Colusa Rancheria, California
Caddo Indian Tribe of Oklahoma
Cahuilla Band of Mission Indians of the Cahuilla Reservation, California
Cahto Indian Tribe of the Laytonville Rancheria, California
Campo Band of Diegueno Mission Indians of the Campo Indian Reservation, California
Capitan Grande Band of Diegueno Mission Indians of California: Barona Group of Capitan Grande Band of Mission Indians of the Barona Reservation, California Viejas (Baron Long) Group of Capitan Grande Band of Mission Indians of the Viejas Reservation, California
Catawba Indian Nation (also known as Catawba Tribe of South Carolina)
Cayuga Nation of New York
Cedarville Rancheria, California
Chemehuevi Indian Tribe of the Chemehuevi Reservation, California
Cher-Ae Heights Indian Community of the Trinidad Rancheria, California
Cherokee Nation of Oklahoma
Cheyenne-Arapaho Tribes of Oklahoma
Cheyenne River Sioux Tribe of the Cheyenne River Reservation, South Dakota
Chickasaw Nation, Oklahoma
Chicken Ranch Rancheria of Me-Wuk Indians of California
Chippewa-Cree Indians of the Rocky Boy's Reservation, Montana
Chitimacha Tribe of Louisiana
Choctaw Nation of Oklahoma
Citizen Potawatomi Nation, Oklahoma
Cloverdale Rancheria of Pomo Indians of California
Cocopah Tribe of Arizona
Coeur D'Alene Tribe of the Coeur D'Alene Reservation, Idaho

Cold Springs Rancheria of Mono Indians of California
Colorado River Indian Tribes of the Colorado River Indian
  Reservation, Arizona and California
Comanche Indian Tribe, Oklahoma
Confederated Salish & Kootenai Tribes of the Flathead Reserva-
  tion, Montana
Confederated Tribes of the Chehalis Reservation, Washington
Confederated Tribes of the Colville Reservation, Washington
Confederated Tribes of the Coos, Lower Umpqua and Siuslaw
  Indians of Oregon
Confederated Tribes of the Goshute Reservation, Nevada and
  Utah
Confederated Tribes of the Grand Ronde Community of Oregon
Confederated Tribes of the Siletz Reservation, Oregon
Confederated Tribes of the Umatilla Reservation, Oregon
Confederated Tribes of the Warm Springs Reservation of Oregon
Confederated Tribes and Bands of the Yakama Indian Nation of
  the Yakama Reservation, Washington
Coquille Tribe of Oregon
Cortina Indian Rancheria of Wintun Indians of California
Coushatta Tribe of Louisiana
Cow Creek Band of Umpqua Indians of Oregon
Coyote Valley Band of Pomo Indians of California
Crow Tribe of Montana
Crow Creek Sioux Tribe of the Crow Creek Reservation, South
  Dakota
Cuyapaipe Community of Diegueno Mission Indians of the
  Cuyapaipe Reservation, California
Death Valley Timbi-Sha Shoshone Band of California
Delaware Tribe of Indians, Oklahoma
Delaware Tribe of Western Oklahoma
Dry Creek Rancheria of Pomo Indians of California
Duckwater Shoshone Tribe of the Duckwater Reservation, Nevada
Eastern Band of Cherokee Indians of North Carolina
Eastern Shawnee Tribe of Oklahoma
Elem Indian Colony of Pomo Indians of the Sulphur Bank
  Rancheria, California
Elk Valley Rancheria, California
Ely Shoshone Tribe of Nevada
Enterprise Rancheria of Maidu Indians of California
Flandreau Santee Sioux Tribe of South Dakota
Forest County Potawatomi Community of Wisconsin Potawatomi
  Indians, Wisconsin
Fort Belknap Indian Community of the Fort Belknap Reservation
  of Montana
Fort Bidwell Indian Community of the Fort Bidwell Reservation
  of California
Fort Independence Indian Community of Paiute Indians of the
  Fort Independence Reservation, California
Fort McDermitt Paiute and Shoshone Tribes of the Fort
  McDermitt Indian Reservation, Nevada and Oregon
Fort McDowell Mohave-Apache Community of the Fort
  McDowell Indian Reservation, Arizona
Fort Mojave Indian Tribe of Arizona, California & Nevada
Fort Sill Apache Tribe of Oklahoma
Gila River Indian Community of the Gila River Indian Reserva-
  tion, Arizona
Grand Traverse Band of Ottawa & Chippewa Indians of Michigan
Greenville Rancheria of Maidu Indians of California
Grindstone Indian Rancheria of Wintun-Wailaki Indians of
  California

Guidiville Rancheria of California
Hannahville Indian Community of Wisconsin Potawatomie
  Indians of Michigan
Havasupai Tribe of the Havasupai Reservation, Arizona
Ho-Chunk Nation of Wisconsin (formerly known as the Wiscon-
  sin Winnebago Tribe)
Hoh Indian Tribe of the Hoh Indian Reservation, Washington
Hoopa Valley Tribe, California
Hopi Tribe of Arizona
Hopland Band of Pomo Indians of the Hopland Rancheria,
  California
Houlton Band of Maliseet Indians of Maine
Hualapai Indian Tribe of the Hualapai Indian Reservation,
  Arizona
Huron Potawatomi, Inc., Michigan
Inaja Band of Diegueno Mission Indians of the Inaja and Cosmit
  Reservation, California
Ione Band of Miwok Indians of California
Iowa Tribe of Kansas and Nebraska
Iowa Tribe of Oklahoma
Jackson Rancheria of Me-Wuk Indians of California
Jamestown S'Klallam Tribe of Washington
Jamul Indian Village of California
Jena Band of Choctaw Indians, Louisiana
Jicarilla Apache Tribe of the Jicarilla Apache Indian Reservation,
  New Mexico
Kaibab Band of Paiute Indians of the Kaibab Indian Reservation,
  Arizona
Kalispel Indian Community of the Kalispel Reservation, Washing-
  ton
Karuk Tribe of California
Kashia Band of Pomo Indians of the Stewarts Point Rancheria,
  California
Kaw Nation, Oklahoma
Keweenaw Bay Indian Community of L'Anse and Ontonagon
  Bands of Chippewa Indians of the L'Anse Reservation,
  Michigan
Kialegee Tribal Town, Oklahoma
Kickapoo Tribe of Indians of the Kickapoo Reservation in Kansas
Kickapoo Tribe of Oklahoma
Kickapoo Traditional Tribe of Texas
Kiowa Indian Tribe of Oklahoma
Klamath Indian Tribe of Oregon
Kootenai Tribe of Idaho
La Jolla Band of Luiseno Mission Indians of the La Jolla
  Reservation, California
La Posta Band of Diegueno Mission Indians of the La Posta
  Indian Reservation, California
Lac Courte Oreilles Band of Lake Superior Chippewa Indians of
  the Lac Courte Oreilles Reservation of Wisconsin
Lac du Flambeau Band of Lake Superior Chippewa Indians of the
  Lac du Flambeau Reservation of Wisconsin
Lac Vieux Desert Band of Lake Superior Chippewa Indians of
  Michigan
Las Vegas Tribe of Paiute Indians of the Las Vegas Indian Colony,
  Nevada
Little River Band of Ottawa Indians of Michigan
Little Traverse Bay Bands of Odawa Indians of Michigan
Los Coyotes Band of Cahuilla Mission Indians of the Los Coyotes
  Reservation, California
Lovelock Paiute Tribe of the Lovelock Indian Colony, Nevada

Lower Brule Sioux Tribe of the Lower Brule Reservation, South Dakota

Lower Elwha Tribal Community of the Lower Elwha Reservation, Washington

Lower Sioux Indian Community of Minnesota Mdewakanton Sioux Indians of the Lower Sioux Reservation in Minnesota

Lummi Tribe of the Lummi Reservation, Washington

Lytton Rancheria of California

Makah Indian Tribe of the Makah Indian Reservation, Washington

Manchester Band of Pomo Indians of the Manchester-Point Arena Rancheria, California

Manzanita Band of Diegueno Mission Indians of the Manzanita Reservation, California

Mashantucket Pequot Tribe of Connecticut

Mechoopda Indian Tribe of Chico Rancheria, California

Menominee Indian Tribe of Wisconsin

Mesa Grande Band of Diegueno Mission Indians of the Mesa Grande Reservation, California

Mescalero Apache Tribe of the Mescalero Reservation, New Mexico

Miami Tribe of Oklahoma

Miccosukee Tribe of Indians of Florida

Middletown Rancheria of Pomo Indians of California

Minnesota Chippewa Tribe, Minnesota (six component reservations: Bois Forte Band [Nett Lake]; Fond du Lac Band; Grand Portage Band; Leech Lake Band; Mille Lacs Band; White Earth Band)

Mississippi Band of Choctaw Indians, Mississippi

Moapa Band of Paiute Indians of the Moapa River Indian Reservation, Nevada

Modoc Tribe of Oklahoma

Mohegan Indian Tribe of Connecticut

Mooretown Rancheria of Maidu Indians of California

Morongo Band of Cahuilla Mission Indians of the Morongo Reservation, California

Muckleshoot Indian Tribe of the Muckleshoot Reservation, Washington

Muscogee (Creek) Nation, Oklahoma

Narragansett Indian Tribe of Rhode Island

Navajo Nation of Arizona, New Mexico & Utah

Nez Perce Tribe of Idaho

Nisqually Indian Tribe of the Nisqually Reservation, Washington

Nooksack Indian Tribe of Washington

Northern Cheyenne Tribe of the Northern Cheyenne Indian Reservation, Montana

Northfork Rancheria of Mono Indians of California

Northwestern Band of Shoshoni Nation of Utah (Washakie)

Oglala Sioux Tribe of the Pine Ridge Reservation, South Dakota

Omaha Tribe of Nebraska

Oneida Nation of New York

Oneida Tribe of Wisconsin

Onondaga Nation of New York

Osage Tribe, Oklahoma

Ottawa Tribe of Oklahoma

Otoe-Missouria Tribe of Indians, Oklahoma

Paiute Indian Tribe of Utah

Paiute-Shoshone Indians of the Bishop Community of the Bishop Colony, California

Paiute-Shoshone Tribe of the Fallon Reservation and Colony, Nevada

Paiute-Shoshone Indians of the Lone Pine Community of the Lone Pine Reservation, California

Pala Band of Luiseno Mission Indians of the Pala Reservation, California

Pascua Yaqui Tribe of Arizona

Paskenta Band of Nomlaki Indians of California

Passamaquoddy Tribe of Maine

Pauma Band of Luiseno Mission Indians of the Pauma & Yuima Reservation, California

Pawnee Indian Tribe of Oklahoma

Pechanga Band of Luiseno Mission Indians of the Pechanga Reservation, California

Penobscot Tribe of Maine

Peoria Tribe of Indians of Oklahoma

Picayune Rancheria of Chukchansi Indians of California

Pinoleville Rancheria of Pomo Indians of California

Pit River Tribe, California (includes Big Bend, Lookout, Montgomery Creek & Roaring Creek Rancherias & XL Ranch)

Poarch Band of Creek Indians of Alabama

Pokagon Band of Potawatomi Indians of Michigan

Ponca Tribe of Indians of Oklahoma

Ponca Tribe of Nebraska

Port Gamble Indian Community of the Port Gamble Reservation, Washington

Potter Valley Rancheria of Pomo Indians of California

Prairie Band of Potawatomi Indians, Kansas

Prairie Island Indian Community of Minnesota Mdewakanton Sioux Indians of the Prairie Island Reservation, Minnesota

Pueblo of Acoma, New Mexico

Pueblo of Cochiti, New Mexico

Pueblo of Jemez, New Mexico

Pueblo of Isleta, New Mexico

Pueblo of Laguna, New Mexico

Pueblo of Nambe, New Mexico

Pueblo of Picuris, New Mexico

Pueblo of Pojoaque, New Mexico

Pueblo of San Felipe, New Mexico

Pueblo of San Juan, New Mexico

Pueblo of San Ildefonso, New Mexico

Pueblo of Sandia, New Mexico

Pueblo of Santa Ana, New Mexico

Pueblo of Santa Clara, New Mexico

Pueblo of Santo Domingo, New Mexico

Pueblo of Taos, New Mexico

Pueblo of Tesuque, New Mexico

Pueblo of Zia, New Mexico

Puyallup Tribe of the Puyallup Reservation, Washington

Pyramid Lake Paiute Tribe of the Pyramid Lake Reservation, Nevada

Quapaw Tribe of Indians, Oklahoma

Quartz Valley Indian Community of the Quartz Valley Reservation of California

Quechan Tribe of the Fort Yuma Indian Reservation, California & Arizona

Quileute Tribe of the Quileute Reservation, Washington

Quinault Tribe of the Quinault Reservation, Washington

Ramona Band or Village of Cahuilla Mission Indians of California

Red Cliff Band of Lake Superior Chippewa Indians of Wisconsin

Red Lake Band of Chippewa Indians of the Red Lake Reservation, Minnesota

Redding Rancheria, California

Redwood Valley Rancheria of Pomo Indians of California

Reno-Sparks Indian Colony, Nevada

Resighini Rancheria, California (formerly known as the Coast Indian Community of Yurok Indians of the Resighini Rancheria)

Rincon Band of Luiseno Mission Indians of the Rincon Reservation, California

Robinson Rancheria of Pomo Indians of California

Rosebud Sioux Tribe of the Rosebud Indian Reservation, South Dakota

Round Valley Indian Tribes of the Round Valley Reservation, California (formerly known as the Covelo Indian Community)

Rumsey Indian Rancheria of Wintun Indians of California

Sac & Fox Tribe of the Mississippi in Iowa

Sac & Fox Nation of Missouri in Kansas and Nebraska

Sac & Fox Nation, Oklahoma

Saginaw Chippewa Indian Tribe of Michigan, Isabella Reservation

Salt River Pima-Maricopa Indian Community of the Salt River Reservation, Arizona

Samish Indian Tribe, Washington

San Carlos Apache Tribe of the San Carlos Reservation, Arizona

San Juan Southern Paiute Tribe of Arizona

San Manual Band of Serrano Mission Indians of the San Manual Reservation, California

San Pasqual Band of Diegueno Mission Indians of California

Santa Rosa Indian Community of the Santa Rosa Rancheria, California

Santa Rosa Band of Cahuilla Mission Indians of the Santa Rosa Reservation, California

Santa Ynez Band of Chumash Mission Indians of the Santa Ynez Reservation, California

Santa Ysabel Band of Diegueno Mission Indians of the Santa Ysabel Reservation, California

Santee Sioux Tribe of the Santee Reservation of Nebraska

Sauk-Suiattle Indian Tribe of Washington

Sault Ste. Marie Tribe of Chippewa Indians of Michigan

Scotts Valley Band of Pomo Indians of California

Seminole Nation of Oklahoma

Seminole Tribe of Florida, Dania, Big Cypress, Brighton, Hollywood & Tampa Reservations

Seneca Nation of New York

Seneca-Cayuga Tribe of Oklahoma

Shakopee Mdewakanton Sioux Community of Minnesota (Prior Lake)

Sheep Ranch Rancheria of Me-Wuk Indians of California

Sherwood Valley Rancheria of Pomo Indians of California

Shingle Springs Band of Miwok Indians, Shingle Springs Rancheria (Verona Tract), California

Shoalwater Bay Tribe of the Shoalwater Bay Indian Reservation, Washington

Shoshone Tribe of the Wind River Reservation, Wyoming

Shoshone-Bannock Tribes of the Fort Hall Reservation of Idaho

Shoshone-Paiute Tribes of the Duck Valley Reservation, Nevada

Sisseton-Wahpeton Sioux Tribe of the Lake Traverse Reservation, South Dakota

Skokomish Indian Tribe of the Skokomish Reservation, Washington

Skull Valley Band of Goshute Indians of Utah

Smith River Rancheria, California

Soboba Band of Luiseno Mission Indians of the Soboba Reservation, California

Sokaogon Chippewa Community of the Mole Lake Band of Chippewa Indians, Wisconsin

Southern Ute Indian Tribe of the Southern Ute Reservation, Colorado

Spirit Lake Tribe, North Dakota (formerly known as the Devils Lake Sioux Tribe)

Spokane Tribe of the Spokane Reservation, Washington

Squaxin Island Tribe of the Squaxin Island Reservation, Washington

St. Croix Chippewa Indians of Wisconsin, St. Croix Reservation

St. Regis Band of Mohawk Indians of New York

Standing Rock Sioux Tribe of North & South Dakota

Stockbridge-Munsee Community of Mohican Indians of Wisconsin

Stillaguamish Tribe of Washington

Summit Lake Paiute Tribe of Nevada

Suquamish Indian Tribe of the Port Madison Reservation, Washington

Susanville Indian Rancheria, California

Swinomish Indians of the Swinomish Reservation, Washington

Sycuan Band of Diegueno Mission Indians of California

Table Bluff Reservation—Wiyot Tribe, California

Table Mountain Rancheria of California

Te-Moak Tribes of Western Shoshone Indians of Nevada (four constituent bands: Battle Mountain Band; Elko Band; South Fork Band and Wells Band)

Thlopthlocco Tribal Town, Oklahoma

Three Affiliated Tribes of the Fort Berthold Reservation, North Dakota

Tohono O'odham Nation of Arizona

Tonawanda Band of Seneca Indians of New York

Tonkawa Tribe of Indians of Oklahoma

Tonto Apache Tribe of Arizona

Torres-Martinez Band of Cahuilla Mission Indians of California

Tule River Indian Tribe of the Tule River Reservation, California

Tulalip Tribes of the Tulalip Reservation, Washington

Tunica-Biloxi Indian Tribe of Louisiana

Tuolumne Band of Me-Wuk Indians of the Tuolumne Rancheria of California

Turtle Mountain Band of Chippewa Indians of North Dakota

Tuscarora Nation of New York

Twenty-Nine Palms Band of Luiseno Mission Indians of California

United Auburn Indian Community of the Auburn Rancheria of California

United Keetoowah Band of Cherokee Indians of Oklahoma

Upper Lake Band of Pomo Indians of Upper Lake Rancheria of California

Upper Sioux Indian Community of the Upper Sioux Reservation, Minnesota

Upper Skagit Indian Tribe of Washington

Ute Indian Tribe of the Uintah & Ouray Reservation, Utah

Ute Mountain Tribe of the Ute Mountain Reservation, Colorado, New Mexico & Utah

Utu Utu Gwaitu Paiute Tribe of the Benton Paiute Reservation, California

Walker River Paiute Tribe of the Walker River Reservation, Nevada

Wampanoag Tribe of Gay Head (Aquinnah) of Massachusetts

Washoe Tribe of Nevada & California (Carson Colony, Dresslerville Colony, Woodfords Community, Stewart Community, & Washoe Ranches)

White Mountain Apache Tribe of the Fort Apache Reservation, Arizona

Wichita and Affiliated Tribes (Wichita, Keechi, Waco & Tawakonie), Oklahoma

Winnebago Tribe of Nebraska

Winnemucca Indian Colony of Nevada

Wyandotte Tribe of Oklahoma

Yankton Sioux Tribe of South Dakota

Yavapai-Apache Nation of the Camp Verde Indian Reservation, Arizona

Yavapai-Prescott Tribe of the Yavapai Reservation, Arizona

Yerington Paiute Tribe of the Yerington Colony & Campbell Ranch, Nevada

Yomba Shoshone Tribe of the Yomba Reservation, Nevada

Ysleta Del Sur Pueblo of Texas

Yurok Tribe of the Yurok Reservation, California

Zuni Tribe of the Zuni Reservation, New Mexico

Native Entities within the State of Alaska

Village of Afognak
Native Village of Akhiok
Akiachak Native Community
Akiak Native Community
Native Village of Akutan
Village of Alakanuk
Alatna Village
Native Village of Aleknagik
Algaaciq Native Village (St. Mary's)
Allakaket Village
Native Village of Ambler
Village of Anaktuvuk Pass
Yupiit of Andreafski
Angoon Community Association
Village of Aniak
Anvik Village
Arctic Village (See Native Village of Venetie Tribal Government)
Native Village of Atka
Asa'carsarmiut Tribe (formerly Native Village of Mountain Village)
Atqasuk Village (Atkasook)
Village of Atmautluak
Native Village of Barrow Inupiat Traditional Government (formerly Native Village of Barrow)
Beaver Village
Native Village of Belkofski
Village of Bill Moore's Slough
Birch Creek Village
Native Village of Brevig Mission
Native Village of Buckland
Native Village of Cantwell
Native Village of Chanega (aka Chenega)
Chalkyitsik Village
Village of Chefornak
Chevak Native Village
Chickaloon Native Village
Native Village of Chignik

Native Village of Chignik Lagoon
Chignik Lake Village
Chilkat Indian Village (Kluckwan)
Chilkoot Indian Association (Haines)
Chinik Eskimo Community (Golovin)
Native Village of Chistochina
Native Village of Chitina
Native Village of Chuathbaluk (Russian Mission, Kuskokwim)
Chuloonawick Native Village
Circle Native Community
Village of Clark's Point
Native Village of Council
Craig Community Association
Village of Crooked Creek
Curyung Tribal Council (formerly Native Village of Dillingham)
Native Village of Deering
Native Village of Diomede (aka Inalik)
Village of Dot Lake
Douglas Indian Association
Native Village of Eagle
Native Village of Eek
Egegik Village
Eklutna Native Village
Native Village of Ekuk
Ekwok Village
Native Village of Elim
Emmonak Village
Evansville Village (aka Bettles Field)
Native Village of Eyak (Cordova)
Native Village of False Pass
Native Village of Fort Yukon
Native Village of Gakona
Galena Village (aka Louden Village)
Native Village of Gambell
Native Village of Georgetown
Native Village of Goodnews Bay
Organized Village of Grayling (aka Holikachuk)
Gulkana Village
Native Village of Hamilton
Healy Lake Village
Holy Cross Village
Hoonah Indian Association
Native Village of Hooper Bay
Hughes Village
Huslia Village
Hydaburg Cooperative Association
Igiugig Village
Village of Iliamna
Inupiat Community of the Arctic Slope
Iqurmuit Traditional Council (formerly Native Village of Russian Mission)
Ivanoff Bay Village
Kaguyak Village
Organized Village of Kake
Kaktovik Village (aka Barter Island)
Village of Kalskag
Village of Kaltag
Native Village of Kanatak
Native Village of Karluk
Organized Village of Kasaan
Native Village of Kasigluk

Kenaitze Indian Tribe
Ketchikan Indian Corporation
Native Village of Kiana
Agdaagux Tribe of King Cove
King Island Native Community
Native Village of Kipnuk
Native Village of Kivalina
Klawock Cooperative Association
Native Village of Kluti Kaah (aka Copper Center)
Knik Tribe
Native Village of Kobuk
Kokhanok Village
New Koliganek Village Council (formerly Koliganek Village)
Native Village of Kongiganak
Village of Kotlik
Native Village of Kotzebue
Native Village of Koyuk
Koyukuk Native Village
Organized Village of Kwethluk
Native Village of Kwigillingok
Native Village of Kwinhagak (aka Quinhagak)
Native Village of Larsen Bay
Levelock Village
Lesnoi Village (aka Woody Island)
Lime Village
Village of Lower Kalskag
Manley Hot Springs Village
Manokotak Village
Native Village of Marshall (aka Fortuna Ledge)
Native Village of Mary's Igloo
McGrath Native Village
Native Village of Mekoryuk
Mentasta Traditional Council (formerly Mentasta Lake Village)
Metlakatla Indian Community, Annette Island Reserve
Native Village of Minto
Naknek Native Village
Native Village of Nanwalek (aka English Bay)
Native Village of Napaimute
Native Village of Napakiak
Native Village of Napaskiak
Native Village of Nelson Lagoon
Nenana Native Association
New Stuyahok Village
Newhalen Village
Newtok Village
Native Village of Nightmute
Nikolai Village
Native Village of Nikolski
Ninilchik Village
Native Village of Noatak
Nome Eskimo Community
Nondalton Village
Noorvik Native Community
Northway Village
Native Village of Nuiqsut (aka Nooiksut)
Nulato Village
Native Village of Nunapitchuk
Village of Ohogamiut
Village of Old Harbor
Orutsararmuit Native Village (aka Bethel)
Oscarville Traditional Village

Native Village of Ouzinkie
Native Village of Paimiut
Pauloff Harbor Village
Pedro Bay Village
Native Village of Perryville
Petersburg Indian Association
Native Village of Pilot Point
Pilot Station Traditional Village
Native Village of Pitka's Point
Platinum Traditional Village
Native Village of Point Hope
Native Village of Point Lay
Native Village of Port Graham
Native Village of Port Heiden
Native Village of Port Lions
Portage Creek Village (aka Ohgsenakale)
Pribilof Islands Aleut Communities of St. Paul & St. George Islands
Qagan Toyagungin Tribe of Sand Point Village
Rampart Village
Village of Red Devil
Native Village of Ruby
Village of Salamatoff
Organized Village of Saxman
Native Village of Savoonga
Saint George (See Pribilof Islands Aleut Communities of St. Paul & St. George Islands) Native Village of Saint Michael
Saint Paul (See Pribilof Islands Aleut Communities of St. Paul & St. George Islands)
Native Village of Scammon Bay
Native Village of Selawik
Seldovia Village Tribe
Shageluk Native Village
Native Village of Shaktoolik
Native Village of Sheldon's Point
Native Village of Shishmaref
Native Village of Shungnak
Sitka Tribe of Alaska
Skagway Village
Village of Sleetmute
Village of Solomon
South Naknek Village
Stebbins Community Association
Native Village of Stevens
Village of Stony River
Takotna Village
Native Village of Tanacross
Native Village of Tanana
Native Village of Tatitlek
Native Village of Tazlina
Telida Village
Native Village of Teller
Native Village of Tetlin
Central Council of the Tlingit & Haida Indian Tribes
Traditional Village of Togiak
Native Village of Toksook Bay
Tuluksak Native Community
Native Village of Tuntutuliak
Native Village of Tununak
Twin Hills Village
Native Village of Tyonek

Ugashik Village
Umkumiute Native Village
Native Village of Unalakleet
Qawalangin Tribe of Unalaska
Native Village of Unga
Village of Venetie (*See* Native Village of Venetie Tribal
    Government)
Native Village of Venetie Tribal Government (Arctic Village and
    Village of Venetie)

Village of Wainwright
Native Village of Wales
Native Village of White Mountain
Wrangell Cooperative Association
Yakutat Tlingit Tribe

Timeline

Date	Blacks	Asian Americans	Latinos	Native Americans
1787	The United States Constitution is written; it contains the 3/5ths clause, which states that black slaves will be counted as 3/5ths of a person for purposes of representation and taxation.			The United States Congress passes the Northwest Ordinance, which establishes a mechanism for creating states out of the territories of the Upper Midwest, a region still largely under Native control.
1789	Delaware passes a law forbidding its citizens from participating in the slave trade.			The Indian Department becomes part of the U.S. Department of War.
1790	The U.S. government and the Creek Indians sign a treaty providing for the return of black fugitive slaves.			The first of the Trade and Intercourse Acts is enacted to establish uniform relations with Native tribes.
1791	Vermont enters the Union as a free state.			
1792	Virginia passes a law that punishes whites with six months in prison for marrying a black.			
1793	Congress passes the first Fugitive Slave Act, which calls for the return of runaway slaves.			Federal agents and representatives from 13 tribes meet, but they fail to resolve land disputes.
1794	Richard Allen founds the first AME Church in Philadelphia.			Little Turtle's War begins in the Indiana Territory.

Date	Blacks	Asian Americans	Latinos	Native Americans
1795			The Treaty of San Lorenzo (also known as Pinckney's Treaty) between Spain and the U.S. opens the Mississippi to American navigation.	
1796	Tennessee enters the Union as a slave state.			The Trading Houses Act establishes government-operated trading houses.
1797	Connecticut law emancipates slaves at age 21.		The American Lodge is founded to work for the independence of Spanish colonies in America.	
1798	Georgia abolishes the slave trade.		The Naturalization Act raises the number of years of residence for citizenship from 5 to 14. The Alien Act grants the president authority to expel any alien deemed dangerous.	
1799	Upon his death in December, George Washington frees his slaves.			Handsome Lake's religious movement begins among the Iroquois.
1800	South Carolina bars the entrance of free blacks into the state.			
1802	Governor William H. Harrison of the Indiana Territory seeks suspension of the Northwest Ordinance to allow slavery in the territory.			
1803	Ohio enters the Union as a free state, but disenfranchises blacks.		The United States buys the Louisiana Territory from France for $15 million, bringing areas of Hispanic settlement under U.S. control.	Through the Louisiana Purchase, the United States acquires 800,000 square miles of new territory inhabited by numerous Native tribes.
1804	New Jersey passes a law providing for the gradual emancipation of slaves.			Lewis and Clark begin their expedition of western exploration, making contact with many Native peoples.

Date	Blacks	Asian Americans	Latinos	Native Americans
1806	Virginia requires all freed slaves to leave the state within one year of gaining freedom.			
1807	Two boatloads of Africans in Charleston, South Carolina, starve themselves to death rather than become slaves.			
1808	Congress bars the importation of slaves.			
1809	New York passes a law recognizing marriages between blacks.			By the Treaty of Fort Wayne, the Delaware Tribe to relinquishes approximately 3 million acres. Tecumseh creates a multi-tribal alliance to resist U.S. incursions into Indian lands in the Midwest.
1810	In *Maryland v. Dolly Chapple*, the Court decides that slaves may testify in court when the victims are also slaves.			
1811	Delaware forbids free blacks from entering the state, and those who leave for more than six months lose their residency.		Congress adopts the "no-transfer" resolution to prevent Spanish Florida from passing to another European power.	William Henry Harrison engages Tecumseh's multi-tribal alliance at the Battle of Tippecanoe in the Indiana Territory.
1812	British forces encourage slaves to revolt during the War of 1812.			The British encourage Native Americans to attack American settlements during the War of 1812.
1813	New York State ends slavery.			The Red Stick war begins in the Southeast.
1814	Two black battalions serve at the Battle of New Orleans under the command of General Andrew Jackson.			

Date	Blacks	Asian Americans	Latinos	Native Americans
1815	The Underground Railroad for helping escaped slaves reach safety in the North and Canada is formally established.			To avoid white settlers from the East, Indians begin to migrate to Texas in large numbers.
1816	The American Colonization Society, which advocates resettlement of slaves in Africa, is founded.			
1817	Mississippi enters the Union as a slave state.			The First Seminole War begins in Florida.
1818	Connecticut is the only New England state that still officially disenfranchises blacks.			Delaware Treaty is adopted, in which the Delaware give up Indiana in exchange for land west of the Mississippi River.
1819	Alabama enters the Union as a slave state.		The United States buys Florida from Spain for $5 million as part of the Adams-Onis Treaty.	
1820	Congress adopts the Missouri Compromise, which establishes the boundary between slave and free states.	Arrival of the first Chinese in the United States.		John C. Calhoun argues for Indian guardianship.
1821	Maine outlaws interracial marriages and voids existing ones.			Sequoyah creates the Cherokee syllabary for writing Indian language.
1822	Denmark Vesey and his coconspirators are captured and punished for their planned slave revolt in Charleston, SC.			David Moncock becomes the first Native American to graduate from West Point.
1823	U.S. district court rules that slaves taken to free states become free.		The Monroe Doctrine, which tells European nations to remain out of the Americas, is adopted as U.S. policy.	In *Johnson v. McIntosh*, the U.S. Supreme Court rules that the Native American tribes have land rights. Office of Indian Affairs is created within the War Department.
1824	Dartmouth College opens admissions to blacks.			

Date	Blacks	Asian Americans	Latinos	Native Americans
1825				Tocqueville criticizes U.S. Indian policy and predicts that only the grave will give Indians rest.
1826	Free blacks allowed to own real estate in South Carolina.			The Treaty of Buffalo Creek is signed.
1827	The *Freedman's Journal* begins publication.			Cherokee Nation adopts a constitution.
1828				The *Cherokee Phoenix* begins publication.
1829	South Carolina governor Stephen Miller argues that slavery is a national benefit, not an evil.			William Apess, a Pequot, publishes his book *A Son of the Forest*.
1830	First National Negro Convention is held in Philadelphia.			The Indian Removal Act is passed. The Treaty of Dancing Rabbit Creek cedes to the U.S. more than 10 million acres of Indian land in Alabama and Mississippi.
1831	Nat Turner leads a slave revolt in Virginia.			In *Cherokee Nation v. Georgia*, the U.S. Supreme Court rules that Native American tribes are "domestic dependent nations."
1832	Abolitionist William Lloyd Garrison publishes *Thoughts on African Colonization*.			The Black Hawk War begins in the Midwest. In *Worcester v. Georgia*, the U.S. Supreme Court rules that the federal government has the right to regulate Indian affairs.
1833	The American Anti-Slavery Society, which is open to both blacks and whites, is founded.			
1834	A three-day anti-abolition riot erupts in Philadelphia.			Department of Indian Affairs is reorganized.
1835	President Andrew Jackson forbids the post office from delivering abolitionist literature in the South.			Texas Rangers begin raids against the Comanche. The Second Seminole War begins in Florida.

Date	Blacks	Asian Americans	Latinos	Native Americans
1836	A gag rule is adopted by Congress that forbids the discussion of slavery on the House floor.		The Treaty of Velasco officially marks the establishment of the Republic of Texas.	Creek Indians leave Alabama because of increasing white settlement.
1837	Michigan disenfranchises blacks.			Sioux Treaty calls for the Sioux to cede all lands east of the Mississippi River.
1838	Former President John Quincy Adams defends Africans who took command of the *Amistad* slave ship in American waters.			Forced removal of Cherokees from the Southeast to Indian Territory (Oklahoma) becomes a "Trail of Tears" marked by thousands of deaths.
1839	The Liberty Party, an anti-slavery third party, is founded.			
1840	U.S. House of Representatives votes to refuse abolitionist petitions.			The United States adopts a land policy establishing an Indian Territory in Kansas and Oklahoma.
1841	Frederick Douglass makes his first anti-slavery speech for the Massachusetts Anti-Slavery Society.		Republic of Texas President Mirabeau Lamar sends armed forces to foment revolution in New Mexico; the so-called Santa Fe Expedition is a failure.	
1842	In *Prigg v. Pennsylvania*, an antikidnapping law to prevent the return of slaves to the South is ruled unconstitutional.			
1843	Sojourner Truth begins her abolitionist work.			
1845	Texas enters the Union as a slave state and disenfranchises blacks.		The United States annexes Texas.	
1846	The Odd Fellows, a black fraternal organization, is founded.		Mexican-American War begins.	Navajos resist U.S. settlers in California and New Mexico.
1847	Frederick Douglass begins publication of *Northern Star.*			Last of the Mohicans monument is erected in Norwich, Connecticut.

Date	Blacks	Asian Americans	Latinos	Native Americans
1848	The Free Soil Party, which opposes the extension of slavery, is formed.	Gold rush at Sutter's Creek brings many Chinese to California.	The Treaty of Guadalupe Hildalgo ends the Mexican-American War.	California Gold Rush begins, initiating heavy white settlement.
1849	Harriet Tubman escapes to freedom and begins her work helping others to escape.			The Department of Interior is created and the Bureau of Indian Affairs is put under its jurisdiction.
1850	Congress adopts the Compromise of 1850, which brings California into the union as a free state and creates a stronger Fugitive Slave Act.	A monthly tax, known as the Foreign Miners' License Tax, is enacted in California.		Period of genocide against California Indians begins.
1851	Virginia law requires freed slaves to leave the state within one year or be reinslaved.	Chinese population in California goes from 4,000 to 25,000.	The California Land Act of 1851 is signed, facilitating legalization of land belonging to Californians prior to U.S. takeover.	Treaty of Fort Laramie protects the Mormon Trail against Indian depredations.
1852	Harriet Beecher Stowe's novel *Uncle Tom's Cabin* is published.	First group of Chinese contract laborers land in Hawaii.	Manuel Requema, a Hispanic American, is elected to the first Los Angeles Board of Supervisors.	
1853			With the Gadsden Purchase, the United States acquires 44,000 acres in the Southwest (now parts of Arizona and New Mexico).	California governor John McDougal asks for troops to put down Indian rebellions.
1854	The Kansas-Nebraska Act leaves the question of slavery up to the settlers of the Kansas and Nebraska territories themselves.	In *People v. Hall*, the California Supreme Court rules that Chinese cannot give testimony in court.	The United States offers $130 million to Spain for Cuba and threatens that if Spain does not sell, the United States may support independence for the island (Ostend Manifesto).	The Teton Dakota resist U.S. intrusions into their lands.
1855	Maine, Michigan, and Massachusetts forbid the enforcement of the federal Fugitive Slave Act of 1850.	California passes a law to discourage Chinese from entering the state.	The Anti-Vagrancy Act, known as "the greaser law," prohibits bear-baiting, cockfighting, and bullfights.	The Walla Walla Council negotiates a series of treaties with Native American tribes. The Third Seminole War begins in Florida.

Date	Blacks	Asian Americans	Latinos	Native Americans
1856	Widespread slave insurrections occur in several southern states, including Louisiana, Florida, Arkansas, Georgia, South Carolina, Virginia, Kentucky, and Tennessee.		For eleven days, Manuel Requena serves as mayor of Los Angeles.	When Indian agent Henry L. Dodge goes missing, U.S. troops attack the Apache.
1857	The U.S. Supreme Court rules in *Dred Scott v. Sandford*, denying that slaves can be citizens.			Pawnee Treaty trades Pawnee lands in Nebraska and Dakota for other lands in Dakota.
1858	John Brown leads a raid on a federal arsenal at Harper's Ferry, Virginia.	California legislature passes "An Act to Prevent the Further Immigration of Chinese or Mongolians to This State."		The Navajo War begins over grazing rights.
1859	In *Ableman v. Booth*, the Fugitive Slave Act of 1850 is upheld by the U.S. Supreme Court.	Chinese are excluded from public schools in San Francisco.	Juan Nepomuceno Cortina leads a guerrilla war against settlers in South Texas.	Salt River Reservation is established in Arizona.
1860	Abraham Lincoln is elected as the first Republican president on a platform opposing the extension of slavery in the territories and South Carolina secedes.	Nakahama Manjiro, the first Japanese person in the United States, arrives in San Francisco aboard the *Kanin Maru*.		Choctaw Constitutional Government is established.
1861	Civil War begins.			The Cherokees side with the Confederacy in the Civil War.
1862	Congress authorizes black enlistment.	California passes "An Act to Protect Free White Labor Against Competition with Chinese Coolie Labor and to Discourage the Immigration of the Chinese into the State of California."	Homestead Act is signed, allowing squatters in the West to settle and claim vacant lands.	Little Crow carries out a war of resistance, known as the Minnesota Uprising, against poor treatment by federal authorities.
1863	Emancipation Proclamation takes effect on January 1.	The California Police Tax is ruled unconstitutional by the decision in *Lin Sing v. Washburn*.		The Long Walk of the Navajo occurs.
1864	Fugitive Slave Act is repealed.			The Sand Creek Massacre occurs in Colorado.

Date	Blacks	Asian Americans	Latinos	Native Americans
1865	Thirteenth Amendment, which abolishes slavery, is ratified.	The Central Pacific Railroad recruits Chinese workers for the construction of the transcontinental railroad.		U.S. Army commissions Indian scouts.
1866	Congress overrides President Andrew Johnson's veto of the Civil Rights Act.			The Bozeman Trail wars occur, with Native Americans resisting the building of army forts on their lands.
1867	First Reconstruction Act is passed, which grants blacks voting rights in southern states.			U.S. government purchases Alaska. The Commission Act is signed, for negotiating peace treaties with Native American nations.
1868	Fourteenth Amendment, which guarantees citizenship, is ratified.	The Burlingame Treaty is signed, which allows for the emigration of Chinese to the United States.	U.S. Senate rejects treaty to annex the Dominican Republic.	The Second Treaty of Fort Laramie pledges the protection of Indian lands. U.S. Seventh Cavalry leads the Washita River Massacre.
1869	Ebenezer Don Carlos Bassett becomes the first African-American diplomat when he is appointed minister to Haiti.	The first group of Japanese immigrants comes to mainland United States, settles in Gold Hill (CA), and establishes the Wakamatsu Tea and Silk Farm Colony.	President Ulysses S. Grant announces the building of the Panama Canal.	Board of Indian Commission is formed.
1870	Ratification of the Fifteenth Amendment.	Colorado passes a resolution welcoming Chinese immigrants.		President Ulysses S. Grant adopts a peace policy toward the Indians.
1871	Congress passes the Ku Klux Klan Act to curb the activities of that group.	Anti-Chinese riot breaks out in Los Angeles.		Congress passes an act on March 3 that ends treaty negotiations with Native American nations. In *McKay v. Campbell*, the U.S. Supreme Court holds that Indian people born with "tribal allegiance" are not U.S. citizens.
1872	Black speakers address the Republican National Convention in Philadelphia.	The Chinese Education Mission is organized by Yung Wing.		Modoc War in northern California begins when Modoc Indians led by Captain Jack return from Oregon to reclaim ancestral lands.

Date	Blacks	Asian	Latinos	Native
1873	The Slaughterhouse Cases determine that the Fourteenth Amendment does not guarantee state rights.	The International Workingmen's Association adopts an official anti-coolie policy.		
1874	Joseph H. Rainey (R-SC) becomes the first black to preside over the U.S. House of Representatives.			The Red River War occurs in Texas and the Indian Territory of Oklahoma.
1875	Congress enacts the Civil Rights Act, which guarantees equal rights in public accommodations and jury duty.	U.S. Congress passes an immigration act—the Page Law—that prohibits Chinese, Japanese, and Mongolian convicts and prostitutes from coming to the United States.	The U.S. Supreme Court rules in *Hernandez v. New York* that the federal government has sole authority over immigration.	Camp Verde Reservation is revoked by presidential executive order.
1876	President Ulysses S. Grant sends federal troops into South Carolina to restore peace after race riots.			General Custer and part of his command are wiped out at the Battle of Little Big Horn in Montana.
1877	Reconstruction comes to an end.	Miyama Kanichi organizes the Japanese Gospel Society in San Francisco.	The Salt Wars erupt as Anglos attempt to take control of the salt mines near El Paso (TX).	The Nez Perce tribe is exiled from their homelands in the Northwest; they are then pursued by U.S. forces in an unsuccessful attempt to escape to Canada.
1878	Georgia establishes a poll tax as a method of disenfranchising blacks.	In the case In *re Ah Yup*, the U.S. Supreme Court rules that Chinese are not eligible for naturalized citizenship.		Bancock War erupts in northern Idaho.
1879		California adopts new state constitution that contains many discriminatory measures against Chinese immigrants.		The Carlisle Indian School is founded by Captain Richard H. Pratt.
1880	The U.S. Supreme Court rules in *Stauder v. West Virginia* that the exclusion of blacks from jury duty is unconstitutional.	U.S. government revises the Burlingame Treaty with China.	Immigration to the United States from other parts of the Americas is stimulated by the advent of the railroad.	The ghost dance is banned by the U.S. government.

Date	Blacks	Asian Americans	Latinos	Native Americans
1881	Booker T. Washington founds Tuskegee Institute in Tuskegee, Alabama.	Congress passes an act to suspend Chinese immigration for 20 years, but the act is vetoed by President Chester A. Arthur.		Helen Hunt Jackson publishes *A Century of Dishonor*.
1882		The law known as the Chinese Exclusion Act (Immigration Act of 1882), or "An Act to Execute Certain Treaty Stipulations Relating to Chinese," is signed into law.		The "Act to Civilize Pueblo Indians" is passed.
1883	The Supreme Court rules that the Civil Rights Act of 1875 is unconstitutional.			In *Ex Parte Crow Dog*, the U.S. Supreme Court rules that states have no jurisdiction over crimes committed on Indian reservations.
1884	John R. Lynch is elected as the first black chairman of the Republican National Committee.	Congress passes "An Act to Amend an Act Entitled an Act to Execute Certain Treaty Stipulations Relating to Chinese," which imposes more restrictions.		In *Elk v. Wilkins*, the U.S. Supreme Court rules that Indians who leave the reservations to live among white people are not citizens simply because they were born within the United States.
1885		An Anti-Chinese riot breaks out in Rock Springs, Wyoming.		Congress passes the Indian Major Crimes Act to overturn the impact of *Ex Parte Crow Dog* (1883).
1886	New Mexico Territory repeals its anti-interracial marriage law.	Japan legalizes the emigration of its people abroad. The U.S. Supreme Court rules in the case of *Yick Wo v. Hopkins*, establishing the principle that no state may deny any person of his or her life, liberty, or property without due process of the law.		In *U.S. v. Kagama*, the U.S. Supreme Court upholds the constitutionality of the Indian Major Crimes Act (1885).
1887	Georgia Supreme Court upholds the right of Amanda A. Dickson to inherit her white father's estate.	Japanese replace Chinese as a source of cheap labor after passage of the Exclusion Act.		The General Allotment Act (Dawes Severalty Act) divides reservation lands into individual parcels.

Date	Blacks	Asian Americans	Latinos	Native Americans
1888	Henry P. Cheatham (R-NC) is elected to the U.S. House of Representatives.	Scott Act voids 20,000 Chinese reentry certificates.		Congress passes the White Men and Indian Women Act.
1889	Frederick Douglass is appointed minister to Haiti.	*Chae Chan Ping v. U.S.* upholds the constitutionality of Chinese exclusionary laws.	The International Union of American Republics is founded in Washington, D.C. (forerunner of the Organization of American States).	Oklahoma is opened to white settlers.
1890	Mississippi imposes the understanding test to keep blacks from voting.		Felix Martinez, Jr. founds El Partido del Pueblo Unido, the first Hispanic American third party.	Wounded Knee Massacre occurs on the Pine Ridge Reservation.
1891		First Chinese-English newspaper, *The Chinese World,* begins publication in San Francisco.		The Indian Schools Act is passed.
1892	Ida B. Wells begins her antilynching crusade.	Geary Act prohibits Chinese immigration for another 10 years.		Intoxication in Indian Country Act prohibits the sale of liquor on reservations.
1893	George Murray (R-SC) is elected to the U.S. House of Representatives.	Japanese residents in San Francisco form their first trade association, the Japanese Shoemakers' League.		U.S. troops forcibly gather Hopi children for enforced education.
1894	U.S. Congress repeals the Enforcement Act, making it easier to disenfranchise blacks.	Japanese immigration to Hawaii under the Irwin Convention comes to an end.	Alianza Hispano Americans, a civil rights organization, is founded in Tucson, AZ.	Thomas Edison captures the Sioux Ghost Dance on kinescope.
1895	Booker T. Washington's Atlanta Compromise Address calls for a policy of gradualism and accommodation.	The Native Sons of the Golden State is organized under the leadership of Walter Lum, Joseph Lum, and Ng Gunn.		
1896	In *Plessy v. Ferguson*, the U.S. Supreme Court rules that separate but equal satisfies constitutional requirements.	Chinatown in Honolulu is burned down during a bubonic plague scare.	A revolutionary junta is formed in New York to lead the Puerto Rican independence movement.	
1897		Hawaii's Executive Council on Immigration bans Koreans from being brought into Hawaii as contract laborers.	Miguel A. Otero, Jr. is appointed governor of New Mexico by President William McKinley.	Education Appropriation Act mandates funding for Indian schools. Indian Liquor Act bans sale or distribution of liquor to Native Americans.

Date	Blacks	Asian Americans	Latinos	Native Americans
1898	Louisiana enacts a grandfather clause to prevent freed slaves from voting.	U.S. Supreme Court rules in *U.S. v. Wong Kim Ark* regarding citizenship with relation to parentage.	The USS *Maine* is destroyed in Havana Harbor; this ignites the Spanish-American War. Spain signs the Treaty of Paris transferring Puerto Rico, Guam, and the Philippines to the United States.	The Curtis Act allots the lands of the Cherokee, Choctaw, Chickasaw, Creek, and Seminole as well as abolishes their governments.
1899	Sutton Griggs's *Imperium and Imperio,* the first black power novel, is published.	The Filipino-American War starts. Congress makes Hawaii a territory of the United States.		In *Stephens v. Cherokee Nation*, the U.S. Supreme Court rules that Congress has plenary power over Indian tribes.
1900	W.E.B. Du Bois serves as secretary at the first Pan-African Conference.	Bubonic plague scare in San Francisco leads to quarantine of Chinatown.	The Foraker Act establishes citizenship for Puerto Ricans.	
1901		First Korean immigrant, Peter Ryu, arrives in Hawaii.	The Platt Amendment guarantees U.S. interests in Cuba and is made part of the Cuban Constitution.	Five Civilized Tribe Citizenship Act grants U.S. citizenship to members of the Five Civilized tribes.
1902		Chinese exclusion is extended for another 10 years.	Cuba declares its independence from all foreign countries, including the United States. The Reclamation Act is signed, which dispossesses many Hispanic Americans of their land.	Alex Posey writes his Fus Fixico Letters, which satirizes the Dawes Act.
1903	W.E.B. Du Bois's *The Souls of Black Folk* is published, it rejects the gradualism of Booker T. Washington.	The pensionado program—aimed at giving higher education to Filipino students—begins.	The Hay-Bunau-Virilla Treaty settles the issue of where to build the Panama Canal.	In *Lone Wolf v. Hitchcock*, the U.S. Supreme Court rules that Congress has authority to dispose of Native American lands.
1904	Boley, Oklahoma, an all-black town, is founded.	Japanese contract laborers strike for the first time in Hawaii.	President Theodore Roosevelt issues a corollary to the Monroe Doctrine that states that the United States will exercise police powers in the Western Hemisphere.	

Date	Blacks	Asian Americans	Latinos	Native Americans
1905	The Niagara Movement of African American intellectuals and activists begins under the leadership of W.E.B. Du Bois and William Monroe Trotter.	The Mutual Cooperation Federation is established among Koreans in San Francisco.		In *U.S. v. Winans*, the U.S. Supreme Court rules that treaties may reserve certain hunting and fishing rights off-reservation.
1906	Brownsville (TX) incident occurs in which black soldiers are wrongly court martialed for raiding the town.	San Francisco School Board creates an international incident by ordering children of Japanese and Korean residents to attend the segregated Oriental Public School.		The Burke Act is signed, amending the General Allotment Act. The Alaskan Allotment Act allows Alaska natives to file for 160-acre parcels.
1907	The U.S. Supreme Court determines that railroads may segregate passengers on interstate trains even within states that do not allow segregation.	Theodore Roosevelt signs an executive order banning Japanese immigrants from coming to the mainland from Hawaii, Mexico, or Canada.		Charles Curtis becomes the first Native American to be elected to the U.S. Senate.
1908	In *Berea College v. Kentucky*, the U.S. Supreme Court upholds a segregation requirement in private institutions.	The United States and Japan sign the Gentlemen's Agreement, which limits the number of Japanese laborers emigrating to the United States.		In *Winters v. U.S.*, the U.S. Supreme Court rules that Indians have the right to sufficient water for agricultural purposes.
1909	The National Association for the Advancement of Colored People (NAACP) is formed.	Japanese sugar plantation workers strike in Hawaii.		
1910	The first issue of W.E.B. Du Bois's magazine *Crisis* debuts.	California attempts to stop the immigration of Asian Indians to the state.		The Omnibus Act is signed, establishing procedures to determine Native American heirship of trust lands and other resources.
1911	Marcus Garvey founds the Universal Negro Improvement Association.	President William Howard Taft stops the California legislature from passing anti-Japanese laws.		The Society of the American Indian—a self-sufficiency, self-rule group—is established in Columbus, OH.
1912	James Weldon Johnson's *The Autobiography of an Ex-Colored Man* launches the Harlem Renaissance.			The Classification and Appraisal of Unallotted Indian Lands Act permits the secretary of the interior to reappraise and reclassify unalloted Indian lands.

Date	Blacks	Asian Americans	Latinos	Native Americans
1913	President Woodrow Wilson institutes a policy of government-wide segregation in federal offices, restrooms, and cafeterias.	California passes the alien land law, which prevents aliens ineligible for citizenship from owning or leasing land for more than three years.	Ladislas Lazaro becomes the first Latino congressman from Louisiana.	In *U.S. v. Sandoval,* the Supreme Court upholds the power of Congress to regulate the Pueblo Indians.
1915	In *Guinn and Beal v. U.S.*, the U.S. Supreme Court rules that grandfather clauses are unconstitutional.	The Japanese Chamber of Commerce is formed in southern California.	The Plan de San Diego uprising occurs.	
1916	*The Journal of Negro History* publishes its first volume.			In *U.S. v. Nice*, the U.S. Supreme Court rules that citizenship and guardianship are not incompatible.
1917	The U.S. Supreme Court overturns a Louisville, KY, ordinance that prevents blacks and whites from living in the same neighborhood.	Arizona adopts an alien land law.	The Jones Act is signed, extending U.S. citizenship to Puerto Ricans. The Immigration Act of 1917 passes, imposing a literacy test on all immigrants. Selective Service Act becomes law.	8,000 Native Americans serve in the armed forces.
1918	The African Black Brotherhood, a radical group, is formed.	Servicemen of Asian ancestry who had served in World War I are granted the right of naturalization.		The Native American Church, which uses peyote in its ceremonies, is established in Oklahoma.
1919	Marcus Garvey founds the Black Star Line.	The California Joint Immigration Committee is formed.		U.S. citizenship is granted to Native Americans who served in the armed forces during World War I.
1920		California passes the Alien Land Act to close loopholes in the original law.	The Order of the Sons of America, an early civil rights organization, is founded in Texas.	
1921	George Washington Carver addresses Congress on the peanut tariff.	President Warren Harding signs into law the Quota Immigration Act of 1921.	The Pan American Round Table, a Anglo-Latino organization, is formed to fight discrimination in San Antonio.	The Snyder Act allows for the federal government to make expenditures on behalf of Indians regardless of the amount of their Indian blood.

Date	Blacks	Asian Americans	Latinos	Native Americans
1922	An antilynching bill passes the U.S. House of Representatives but dies in the Senate.	The Cable Act declares that American female citizens who marry an alien ineligible for citizenship lose their citizenship.		
1923	Marcus Garvey is sentenced to five years for mail fraud.	In *U.S. v. Bhagat Singh Thind*, the U.S. Supreme Court rules that Asian Indians are not eligible for naturalized citizenship.	Soledad C. Chacon is the first Hispanic woman elected to state office in New Mexico as secretary of state.	Committee of 100 is appointed to study the condition of Native Americans.
1924		The Immigration Act of 1924 denies entry to almost all Asians.	Fighting breaks out in Argentine, KS, because whites want separate schools from Mexican Americans.	The General Citizenship Act is passed, allowing some Native Americans citizenship.
1925	A. Philip Randolph organizes the Brotherhood of Sleeping Car Porters.	The Filipino Federation of America is founded.	The Border Patrol is created by Congress.	Zane Grey's *The Vanishing Americans* is serialized.
1926	Violette N. Anderson becomes the first black women to argue before the U.S. Supreme Court.		La Sociedad de Madres Mexicanas, the first female civil rights organization, is formed.	The National Council of American Indians is founded by Gertrude Bonnin.
1927	Marcus Garvey's sentence is commuted by President Calvin Coolidge.	The AFL passes a resolution calling on Congress to ban Filipino immigration.		
1928		House Bill 13,900 is introduced to exclude Filipinos from the United States.	New Mexico's Octaviano Larrazolo becomes the first Latino U.S. Senator.	Charles Curtis serves as vice president in the Hoover administration.
1929		The Japanese American Citizens League is formed.	League of United Latin American Citizens (LULAC) is founded in Texas.	
1930	W.D. Fard founds the Temple of Islam.	Anti-Filipino riot in Watsonville, CA, kills Fermin Tober.		U.S. Senate investigates the kidnapping of Navajo children.
1931	Nine African Americans are convicted of raping two white women. These so-called Scottsboro (AL) Boys win a new trial on appeal.	The Cable Act is amended to allow women to retain citizenship even though they are married to aliens ineligible for U.S. citizenship.		

Date	Blacks	Asian Americans	Latinos	Native Americans
1932	Sterling Brown's *Southern Road,* social protest poetry, is published.	Hare-Hawes-Cutting Act makes Filipinos ineligible for citizenship.	The first significant youth civil rights organization, the Mexican American Movement, is formed in Los Angeles.	The Leavitt Act forbids the assessment of Indian lands for construction funds.
1933	President Franklin D. Roosevelt forms an unofficial black cabinet.	The Filipino Labor Union is formed in response to growing anti-Filipino sentiment.	The Roosevelt administration reverses the policy of English as the official language in Puerto Rico. Mexican farm workers strike the Central Valley cotton industry in California.	The Indian New Deal is led by John Collier.
1934	W.D. Fard disappears and Elijah Muhammad takes control of the Nation of Islam.	Tydings-McDuffie Act establishes a plan for Philippine independence and reduces Filipino immigration to 50 persons a year.	Platt Amendment is annulled.	The Indian Reorganization Act is signed. Johnson-O'Malley Act replaces the General Allotment Act.
1935	Mary McLeod Bethune founds the National Council of Negro Women.	The Filipino Repatriation Act provides funds to aid Filipinos to return to the Philippines.	Dennis Chavez is the first Latino elected to the U.S. Senate.	The U.S. government must compensate the Creek Nation for 5,000 acres it took more than 100 years ago, according to the U.S. Supreme Court in *U.S. v. Creek Nation.*
1936	Mary McLeod Bethune is appointed head of the Office of Minority Affairs.	The Cable Act of 1922 is repealed.		The Oklahoma Indian Welfare Act is enacted.
1937	William H. Hastie is appointed the first black federal judge.	A Korean resident, Haan Kil-soo, testifies at a hearing in Hawaii that the Japanese government is trying to organize Asians in Hawaii against whites.		
1938	The decision in the case *Missouri ex rel Gaines* requires equal education facilities.	The first Filipino National Conference is held in California.	Pecan shellers strike in San Antonio.	In *U.S. v. Shoshoni,* the U.S. Supreme Court rules that tribal rights include mineral and natural resources.
1939	Senator Theodore Bilbo (D-MS) introduces a Back to Africa Bill.		El Congresso Nacional del Pueblo de Habla Hispana is founded. The organization seeks to unite all Spanish-speaking ethnic groups.	

Date	Blacks	Asian Americans	Latinos	Native Americans
1940	Benjamin B. Davis, Sr. becomes the first African-American general.	The American Federation of Labor charters the Filipino Federated Agricultural Laborers Association.		Native Americans register for the draft.
1941	Four days of race rioting in East St. Louis, Illinois.	The United States abrogates the treaty of commerce and friendship with Japan and freezes the assets of Japanese nationals in the United States. Japan attacks Pearl Harbor in December.	The Fair Employment Practices Act eliminates discrimination in employment.	Felix Cohen's *Handbook of Federal Indian Law* is published.
1942	Committee on Racial Equality is founded.	President Roosevelt signs Executive Orders 9066 and 9102.		In *Seminole Nation v. U.S.*, the U.S. Supreme Court rules that the U.S. government has the highest responsibility for Indian trust funds.
1943	Blacks riot in Detroit to protest their exclusion from civilian defense jobs; federal troops are used to end the protests.	Tule Lake becomes an internment camp for relocated Japanese Americans.	"Braceros," Mexican agricultural workers, are used during World War II labor shortages. The "Zoot Suit" riots occur in southern California.	
1944	In *Smith v. Allwright*, the U.S. Supreme Court rules that blacks must be permitted to vote in primaries.	U.S. Supreme Court rules in *Korematsu v. U.S.* that the government cannot hold loyal citizens of the United States in detention against their will.	Operation Bootstrap, a program of the Puerto Rican government to meet U.S. labor demands, stimulates migration of workers.	The National Congress of American Indians is founded to guard Native American rights.
1945	Mary McLeod Bethune is sent to San Francisco as part of the U.S. delegation to the United Nations charter meetings.	War Brides Act of 1945 allows U.S. servicemen who marry Chinese women to bring them home as citizens.	In *Mendez et al. v. Westminster School District et al.*, the U.S. Supreme Court rules that the school district may not segregate Mexican Americans.	Iroquois Six Nations seek United Nations membership.
1946	The Committee of Civil Rights is formed by presidential executive order to investigate racial injustice and make recommendations.	Luce-Cellar Act grants naturalization rights to Asian Indians and Filipinos.	Jesus T. Pinero is appointed the first Puerto Rican governor by President Harry Truman.	The Indian Claims Commission Act is signed, providing a legal forum for tribes to sue the federal government for the loss of lands.
1947	Ralph J. Bunche is appointed to the United Nations' Palestine Commission.	President Harry Truman pardons the 267 Japanese Americans who ignore the draft.	The American G.I. Forum is organized by Mexican American veterans.	U.S. Army discontinues its use of Indian scouts.

Date	Blacks	Asian Americans	Latinos	Native Americans
1948	In *Shelley v. Kraemer*, the U.S. Supreme Court rules that segregated housing covenants cannot be enforced.	Displaced Persons Act gives permanent resident status to 3,500 Chinese caught in the United States because of the Chinese Civil War.		Sculptor Korczak Ziolkowski begins work on the Crazy Horse monument in South Dakota.
1949		The United States grants refugee status to 5,000 Chinese after China becomes communist.	Luis Muñoz Marin becomes the first native governor of Puerto Rico.	The Hoover Commission argues that Native Americans need to be integrated into U.S. society.
1950	Ralph Bunche wins Nobel Peace Prize.	Korean War begins.	U.S. Congress upgrades Puerto Rico's political status to commonwealth on July 3.	Dillon S. Meyer, new commissioner of Indian affairs, advocates termination policy.
1951	Douglas MacArthur refuses to desegregate U.S. troops.	Chinese Americans are banned from sending money to relatives in China.	The Bracero Program is revived, bringing an annual average of 350,000 Mexican workers to the United States until 1964.	Public Law 280 is signed, allowing greater state jurisdiction over criminal cases involving Native Americans.
1952		McCarran-Walter Act grants right of naturalization to Japanese.	Congress passes the Immigration and Nationality Act of 1952, known as the McCarran-Walter Act.	
1953	James Baldwin's *Go Tell It on the Mountain* is published.	The Refugee Relief Act allows Chinese political refugees to come to the United States. The armistice ending the Korean War is signed.		The Termination Resolution is initiated by Congress to sever the federal government's relationship with Native American nations.
1954	The U.S. Supreme Court rules in the landmark case *Brown v. Board of Education* that separate but equal is unconstitutional.		Landmark case of *Hernandez v. Texas* acknowledges that Hispanic Americans are not being treated as "whites"; the decision paves the way for legal attacks on discrimination.	Congress enacts numerous termination acts with various tribes.
1955	The Montgomery bus boycott follows the refusal of Rosa Parks to give up her bus seat to a white person.			The Indian Health Service is transferred from the Department of the Interior to the Department of Health, Education, and Welfare.
1956	Southern Manifesto is signed by 101 southern members of Congress calling on states to resist the Brown decision.	California repeals its alien land laws.	Henry B. Gonzalez becomes the first Mexican American elected to the Texas senate.	

Date	Blacks	Asian Americans	Latinos	Native Americans
1957	The Southern Christian Leadership Conference (SCLC) is founded by Martin Luther King, Jr.	The Korean Foundation is organized.	Raymond Telles is elected mayor of El Paso, Texas.	The League of Native American Indians is formed.
1958				In *Williams v. Lee*, the U.S. Supreme Court rules that in some cases tribal governments have exclusive jurisdiction.
1959		Hawaii becomes the 50th state of the Union.	The Mexican American Political Association is founded by Edward Roybal.	Attempts are made to form an organization called United Indian Nations.
1960	Student Nonviolent Coordinating Committee is started.		The Chicano Movement begins.	
1961	Whitney M. Young, Jr. becomes executive director of the National Urban League.		ASPIRA is founded to promote education of Hispanic youth.	W.W. Keeler heads the Task Force on Indian Affairs, which downplays termination.
1962		Daniel K. Inouye is elected a U.S. senator and Spark Matsunaga is elected to Congress.	The United Farm Workers Organizing Committee in California begins as an independent organization, led by Cesar Chavez.	The Indian Economic Report is issued, which finds the average Indian living in abject poverty.
1963	During the March on Washington, Martin Luther King delivers his "I Have a Dream" speech.		In Crystal City, Texas, Mexican Americans oust five white city council members and replace them with Mexican Americans.	The State of Washington rules against Native American fishing rights.
1964	The Twenty-fourth Amendment outlaws poll taxes.	Patsy Takemoto Mink becomes the first Asian American woman to serve in Congress.	Congress enacts the Civil Rights Act of 1964. Title VII establishes the Equal Employment Opportunity Commission (EEOC) to monitor discrimination.	American Indian Historical Society is founded to research and teach about Native Americans.
1965	Malcolm X is assassinated.	President Lyndon Johnson signs into law a new immigration policy to enable large numbers of immigrants from Asian countries to come to the United States.	United Farm Workers organize successful Delano grape strike.	The U.S. Supreme Court rules in *Warren Trading Post v. Arizona Tax Commission* that the state of Arizona cannot tax trading posts on Indian territory because they are regulated by the federal government.

Date	Blacks	Asian Americans	Latinos	Native Americans
1966	Robert Weaver, secretary of Housing and Urban Development, becomes the first black cabinet secretary.	March Fong Eu is elected to the California legislature, becoming the first Asian American woman to serve there.	United Farm Workers become part of the AFL-CIO. Cubans are airlifted to the United States.	Robert LaFollette Bennett becomes only the second Native American to head the BIA.
1967	U.S. Supreme Court unanimously overturns a Virginia law that prohibits interracial marriage.		Hector Perez Garcia is appointed alternative delegate to the United Nations by President Lyndon Johnson.	President Lyndon Johnson, in a special message on Indian affairs, calls for more self-help initiatives.
1968	Martin Luther King, Jr. is assassinated.	Students strike at San Francisco State University demanding the establishment of ethnic studies programs.	La Raza Unida Party is formed in Texas to obtain control of community governments where Chicanos are the majority.	The American Indian Civil Rights Act guarantees reservation residents many civil liberties. The American Indian Movement (AIM) is founded in Minneapolis.
1969	The federal government adopts the Philadelphia Plan, by which contracts valued at more than $500,000 must have a certain number of minority members employed in fulfilling them.	The Japanese American Curriculum Project is founded by Florence M. Hongo.	The First National Chicano Youth Liberation Conference is held in Denver, CO.	Occupation of Alcatraz Island by Native American people begins.
1970	The Congressional Black Caucus is formed.	The Japanese American Citizens League national convention discusses a resolution on redress.	A Chicano Moratorium on the Vietnam War is organized in Los Angeles, where journalist Ruben Salazar is accidentally killed by police.	Native Americans occupy Fort Lawton, hoping to have the federal government donate the closing military base to them for a cultural center.
1971	In *Swann v. Charlotte-Mecklenberg*, the U.S. Supreme Court rules that busing is constitutional.	Herbert Choy, a Korean American, becomes the first Asian American to serve on the federal bench.	La Raza Unida Party wins the city elections in Crystal City, Texas.	Alaska Native Claims Settlement Act is signed.
1972	Angela Davis is acquitted of all charges against her.	The Asian Law Caucus is founded by Dale Minami.	Romana Acosta Banuelos becomes the first Hispanic treasurer of the United States.	The Trail of Broken Treaties Caravan proceeds to Washington, D.C., to protest treaty violations.
1973	Tom Bradley is elected mayor of Los Angeles.		The Labor Council of Latin American Advancement (LCLAA) is formed.	Wounded Knee II seeks to highlight the plight of Native Americans.

Date	Blacks	Asian Americans	Latinos	Native Americans
1974	Maynard Jackson is elected mayor of Atlanta.	The U.S. Supreme Court rules in *Lau v. Nichols* that children who speak little English must be provided with bilingual instruction.	Equal Educational Opportunity Act is enacted.	The Navajo-Hopi Land Settlement Act facilitates negotiations.
1975	William T. Coleman is appointed secretary of the Treasury by President Gerald Ford.	More than 130,000 refugees from Vietnam, Kampuchea, and Laos enter the United States as those countries fall to the communists.	Voting Rights Act Amendments of 1975 ban literacy tests.	Indian Self-Determination and Education Assistance Act expands tribal control over tribal governments and education.
1976	Barbara Jordan is the keynote speaker at the Democratic National Convention.	President Gerald Ford officially rescinds Executive Order 9066.	Vilma Martinez wins the Jefferson Award for public service for her work as director of the Mexican American Legal Defense and Education Fund (MALDEF).	President Gerald Ford announces Native American Awareness Week (October 10).
1977	Clifford Alexander, Jr. becomes the first black secretary of the army.	President Ford pardons Iva D'Aquino, "Tokyo Rose."	Congressional Hispanic Caucus is founded with private funds.	The American Indian Policy Review Commission Report by Congress recommends that Native American nations be considered sovereign political bodies.
1978	Benjamin Hooks becomes head of the NAACP, succeeding Roy Wilkins.	The Japanese American Citizens League adopts resolution calling for redress and reparations for the internment of Japanese Americans during World War II.	United Nations recognizes Puerto Rico as a colony of the United States.	The American Indian Freedom of Religion Act protects the rights of Native Americans to follow traditional religious practices. The Federal Acknowledgment Program is initiated. Indian Child Welfare Act is recognized. The Longest Walk occurs.
1979		John Ta-Chuan Fang starts Asian Week.	Puerto Rican Nationalists accused of shootings in 1954 are released.	2,000 Indian activists protest the mining of uranium in the Black Hills of South Dakota.
1980	The U.S. Supreme Court rules in *City of Mobile v. Bolden* that plaintiffs must show intentional discrimination to have local elections invalidated.	The Orderly Departure Program is established by the UN High Commission on Refugees and the Vietnamese government for the emigration of Vietnamese.	Refugee Act of 1980 removes definition of refugee as one who flees from communist regime.	In *U.S. v. Sioux Nation*, the U.S. Supreme Court upholds a judgment against the federal government's illegal taking of the Black Hills.

Date	Blacks	Asian Americans	Latinos	Native Americans
1981	100,000 march on Washington, D.C., seeking the creation of a federal holiday to honor Martin Luther King, Jr.	Commission on Wartime Relocation and Internment of Civilians concludes that Executive Order 9066 resulted from race prejudice, war hysteria, and a failure of political leadership.	Henry G. Cisneros is elected mayor of San Antonio.	The U.S. Civil Rights Commission issues a report that says U.S. government Indian policies have been marked by inaction and missed opportunities.
1982	Congress extends the provisions of the Voting Rights Act of 1965.	Vincent Chin is beaten to death by two white Americans.	Dorothy Comstock Riley becomes the first Latina to serve on a state supreme court when she is appointed to the Michigan high court.	The Indian Claims Limitations Act limits the time period in which claims can be filed.
1983	Harold Washington becomes first black mayor of Chicago.	The report of the Commission on Wartime Relocation and Internment of Civilians is released.	Federico Pena is elected mayor of Denver.	President Ronald Reagan issues the first Native American policy statement since 1975, in which he commits the U.S. government to dealing with Native American tribes government-to-government.
1984	Wilson Goode is the first black mayor of Philadelphia.	Filipino World War II veterans are denied U.S. citizenship.		Senate Select Committee on Indian Affairs becomes a permanent standing committee.
1985	Reuben V. Anderson becomes the first black to serve on the Mississippi supreme court.	Federal district court overturns Minoru Yasui's conviction for violating curfew orders during World War II.	Xavier Suarez, a Cuban-born citizen, is elected mayor of Miami.	In *Dann v. U.S.*, the U.S. Supreme Court rules that because the Shoshoni tribe kept proceeds from a settlement in an interest-bearing account, the tribe's continued claim on the land was voided.
1986		Federal district court overturns Gordon Hirabayashi's 1942 conviction.	Congress enacts the Immigration Reform and Control Act (IRCA), creating an alien legalization program.	Ben Nighthorse Campbell of Colorado becomes the second Native American to serve in the U.S. House of Representatives.
1987	Kurt Schmoke is elected mayor of Baltimore.	Patricia Saiki becomes the first Republican to represent Hawaii in Congress.	Bob Martinez is the first Hispanic governor of Florida.	

Date	Blacks	Asian Americans	Latinos	Native Americans
1988	Jesse Jackson becomes contender for Democratic presidential nomination.	Civil Liberties Act of 1988 is signed into law by President Ronald Reagan.	President Ronald Reagan appoints the first Hispanic secretary of education, Dr. Lauro F. Cavazos.	Indian Gaming Regulatory Act officially legalizes certain types of gambling on reservations and establishes the National Indian Gaming Commission.
1989	Louis Sullivan is appointed secretary of Health and Human Services by President George Bush.	Elaine L. Chao is appointed deputy secretary of the Department of Transportation.	Ileana Ros-Lehtinen is the first Cuban American elected to Congress.	U.S. Congress approves construction of the National Museum of the American Indian to be part of the Smithsonian Institution. Violence erupts on St. Regis Mohawk Reservation over gambling.
1990	Democrat L. Douglas Wilder becomes the first black governor of Virginia.	President George Bush proclaims May 1990 Asian/Pacific American Heritage Month.	President George Bush appoints the first Hispanic woman surgeon general, Antonia C. Novello.	In *Duro v. Reina*, the U.S. Supreme Court rules that tribes cannot have criminal jurisdiction over non-Indians on reservation lands.
1991	Clarence Thomas is appointed to U.S. Supreme Court.	Patricia Saiki is appointed the head of the Small Business Administration.	The proposed North American Free Trade Agreement expands the maquiladora concept, offering greater tax abatements for U.S. businesses.	Navajo leader Peter MacDonald is convicted of conspiracy, fraud, and extortion; he is sentenced to six years in federal prison and fined $11,000.
1992	The Rodney King riots occur in California.	Korean businesses are looted as a result of the riots in Los Angeles.	Henry Bonilla is elected as the first Republican Hispanic American to serve in Congress from Texas.	Ben Nighthorse Campbell of Colorado is elected as a Democrat to the U.S. Senate.
1993	Democrat Carol Moseley-Braun of Illinois becomes the first black woman senator.		Norma Contu is appointed assistant secretary for civil rights in the Department of Education.	The International Year of Indigenous People is proclaimed. Ada Deer becomes first Native American woman to serve as assistant secretary of Indian affairs.
1994		March Fong Eu is appointed ambassador to Micronesia.	California's Proposition 187 bars undocumented immigrants from receiving public education, welfare, and Medicaid.	The Walk for Justice is staged to draw attention to Native American issues.

Date	Blacks	Asian Americans	Latinos	Native Americans
1995				Wilma Mankiller, chief of the Cherokee Nation of Oklahoma since 1985, resigns her post citing health concerns.
1996	Alexis Herman is nominated as secretary of labor in the second Clinton administration.	The Clinton reelection campaign is tied to illegal Chinese money.	The Hispanic Walk for Justice has 100,000 marchers calling for immigration reform, affirmative action, welfare, and other programs.	
1997	David Satcher is nominated by President Bill Clinton for the post of surgeon general.	Bill Lan Lee is appointed on an acting basis to head the Justice Department's Division of Civil Rights.	Loretta Sanchez becomes the first Mexican American congresswoman from California.	Ada Deer, assistant secretary for Indian affairs, resigns her post.
1998	Anthony Williams is elected mayor of Washington, D.C.	Matt Fong, son of March Fong Eu, is unsuccessful in his bid for the U.S. Senate in California.	Republican Governor George W. Bush of Texas is reelected with widespread support from Hispanic voters.	

Index

by Virgil Diodato

Note: This is the index to both volumes of the *Encyclopedia*. Pages 1–398 are found in Volume 1, and pages 399–774 are found in Volume 2. Boldface page references refer to major entries. Illustrations are indicated by "illus."

Index

Index

Cohen, Felix, 572, 617, 692

Cold War, 230

Colegrove v. Green, 28, 508

Colleges and universities, 26, 67, 467. *See also* Education; School segregation/desegregation, court cases, higher education

Collier, John, 586, **600,** 602, 631, 639, 641, 665, 682, 696

Collins, Barbara-Rose, **47–48**

Collins, Cardiss, **48**

Collins, George W., **48**

Collins, Rose, 76

Colomar O'Brien, Ana, **434–35**

Colombia, 524

Colonization, Christian, 572–75, 579, 610–11, 615, 636, 641–42, 692

"Color blindness," 12, 158, 286

Coloradas, Mangas, 599, **600,** 711

Colorado River Compact, **600**

Colored American (newspaper), 52

Colored Voters League of America, 189

Color-line problem, 3, 8

Columbus, Christopher, 572, 600

Columbus Day celebrations, 575, **600**

Combined Asian-American Resources Project, **260**

Comision Femenil Mexicana Nacional (CFMN), 430, **435,** 457, 490, 513, 559

Commerce clause, **48,** 86, 96, 113

Commerce clause, Indian, 571, 601, 615, 702, 703

Commercial Keynesian liberalism, 603

Commission for Racial Justice, 213

Commission on Asian American Affairs, **261**

Commission on Civil Disorders, 94

Commission on Interracial Cooperation (CIC), 161

Commission on Wartime Relocation and Internment of Civilians (CWRIC), 260, **261,** 288, 314, 329

Commission to Study the Civil Rights of All Races and Faiths, 24

Commissioner of Indian Affairs, **600–01,** 608, 631

Committee against Anti-Asian Violence, 367

Committee for Action for Rural Indians, 735

Committee for Hispanic Arts and Research, 559

Committee for Restoration of Democracy in Burma, 367

Committee of 100, **601**

Committee of Safety, 244, **261,** 303

Committee on Migration and Refugee Affairs, 367

Committee on Women in Asian Studies, 367

"Common Sense" (pamphlet), 7

Communist Party USA (CPUSA), **48,** 56, 165

Community-Action Agencies (CAAs), 180

Community Development Corporations (CDCs), 176

Community liberalism, 602, 603

Community Organization for Public Service (COPS), **435,** 458

Community organizations, **435,** 445, 494

Community organizing model, 417

Community policing strategies, 53

Community Service Organization, 430, 439, 441

Compean, Mario, **435,** 488

Compensation payments, 574, 576, 582, 616, 632–33, 686, 691, 699, 701, 705, 709. *See also* Redress movement; Reparations

Competency, **601,** 608. *See also* Enfranchisement

Comprehensive Employment and Training Act (CETA), 614

Compromise, 8–9, 10. *See also* Compromise of 1850; Compromise of 1877; Hayes-Tilden Compromise; Missouri Compromise

Compromise Address, Atlanta, 27

Compromise of 1850, 8, 9–10, **48**

    African Americans, 20, 46, 148

    Hispanic Americans, 428, **435–36,** 521

Compromise of 1877, 141

Concerned American Indian Parents, 735

Cone, James H., 145

Confederacy, 140–41. *See also* Civil War; Reconstruction

Confederated Bands and Tribes of the Yakima Indian Nation v. Washington, **601**

Confederated Tribes of Colville Reservation et al. v. Washington, **601**

Conference of Prince Hall Grand Masters, 213

Conference on the Future of the American Indian, **602**

Confession Program, **261**

Congreso de Pueblos de Hable Espanola, **436**

Congress. *See* United States House of Representatives; United States Senate; *and specific legislators*

Congress of African People, **48–49**

Congress of National Black Churches, 213

Congress of Racial Equality (CORE), **49,** 72, 90, 107, 108, 213

Congressional Black Associates, 213

Congressional Black Caucus (CBC), **49,** 51, 109, 213. *See also specific legislators*

Congressional Black Caucus Foundation (CBCF), **49**

Congressional Hispanic Caucus (CHC), 410, 411, **436,** 452, 502, 512, 513, 515, 559

Connally, John, 484

Connell, William J., 146

Connerly, Ward, 302

Connor, Eugene "Bull," 30, 44, 98

Conquest theory, and Native Americans, 589

Conservatism

    African Americans, **49–51,** 149, 150, 166, 185

    Asian Americans, **261–63,** 276, 302

    Hispanic Americans, **436–38**

    Native Americans, **602, 603,** 672

Consolidated Benevolent Associations. *See* Chinese Consolidated Benevolent Associations

Constitution. *See* United States Constitution

Constitution (ship), 335

Constitutions

Iroquois Nations, text of, 723–24

Puerto Rico, text of, 554–56

United States. *See* United States Constitution

Contractors Association of Eastern Pennsylvania v. Secretary of Labor, **51**

Contracts, government

    affirmative action, 20, 21, 22, 123, 239, 240, 413–14

    Executive Order 11246, 71

    set-asides, 77, 138, 151, 414

Contributions, political, 234–35, 279, 324

Conyers, John, Jr., **51,** 51 (illus.), 125, 147

Cook, Mercer, **51**

Cookman Institute, 29

Coolidge, Calvin, 601

Coolie bill, **263**

Cooper, Henry, 261

Cooper, James Fenimore, 711

Cooper v. Aaron, **51–52**

Cooper, William G., 51

Cooperative Assistance Fund, 213

Co-optation, **438**

Coordinating Committee on Indian Affairs, 604

COPS. *See* Community Organization for Public Service

Cordova Davila, Felix, **438–39,** 500

Cordova Diaz, Jorge Luis, **438**

CORE. *See* Congress of Racial Equality

Cornish, Samuel Eli, **52**

Cornplanter, **604,** 646

Cornstalk, 651

Corona, Bert, 417, 436, **439,** 488

Coronado, Elaine, **439**

Coronel, Antonio, **439**

Corrada del Rio, Baltasar, **439**

Corruption, Senate report on, **688**

Cose, Ellis Jonathan, **52**

Costa Rica, 524

Costo, Jeannette, 635

Costo, Rupert, 635

Cotera, Martha P., **439–40**

Cotton Kingdom, 160

Cotton Petroleum v. New Mexico, 704

Cotton v. Scotland Neck City Board of Education, **52**

Council for a Black Economic Agenda, 213–14

Council for African American Progress, 213

Council of Energy Resource Tribes (CERT), **604,** 648–49, 653, 666, 681, 735

Council of Federated Organizations (COFO), **52**

County of Yakima v. Yakima Nation, 704

Courts and race, 53. *See also* Crime and punishment

Courts for Indian Justice, **604**

Covenants, restrictive, 28, 37, 70, 88, 158, **330–31**

CPUSA. *See* Communist Party USA

Cracking, of districts, 526

Craig, Barbara Hinkson, 19

Cramer, Anthony, 486

Cranston, Alan, 463

Craven, Charles, 718

Index

Index